Fourth Grade Math
with Confidence
Instructor Guide

Fourth Grade Math with Confidence

Instructor Guide

KATE SNOW

WELL-TRAINED MIND PRESS

Names: Snow, Kate (Teacher), author.

Title: Fourth grade math with confidence. Instructor guide / Kate Snow.

Other titles: Instructor guide

Description: [Charles City, Virginia] : Well-Trained Mind Press, [2024] | Series: Math with confidence | For instructors of fourth grade math students.

Identifiers: ISBN: 978-1-944481-51-3 (paperback) | 978-1-944481-68-1 (eBook/EPUB)

Subjects: LCSH: Mathematics--Study and teaching (Elementary) | LCGFT: Teachers' guides. | BISAC: EDUCATION / Teaching / Subjects / Mathematics.

Classification: LCC: QA107.2 .S664 2024 | DDC: 372.7--dc23

1 2 3 4 5 6 7 8 9   B&B   30 29 28 27 26 25 24

Table of Contents

Welcome to Fourth Grade Math with Confidence!

Fourth Grade Math with Confidence is a complete math curriculum that will give your child a solid foundation in math. It's **hands-on and fun,** with thorough coverage of fourth-grade math skills:

- multiplying and dividing multi-digit numbers
- adding and subtracting fractions and mixed numbers
- equivalent fractions and decimals
- perimeter and area
- lines, angles, quadrilaterals, and triangles
- converting units to solve measurement problems
- line plots and averages
- multi-step word problems

The incremental, confidence-building lessons will help your child develop a strong understanding of math, step by step. Plus, daily review ensures she fully masters what she has learned in previous lessons. With this blend of **deep conceptual understanding** and **traditional skill practice,** you'll give your child a thorough fourth-grade math education.

Fun games like Fraction Three in a Row, Race to 180°, and Decimal War will help your child develop a **positive attitude** toward math. You'll also find optional enrichment lessons at the end of each unit, with suggestions for delightful math picture books and real-world math activities that help your child appreciate the importance of math in everyday life.

Besides this Instructor Guide, *Fourth Grade Math with Confidence* also includes **two colorful, engaging Student Workbooks.** You'll find three workbook pages for each lesson. First, you'll use the Lesson Activities page to teach your child a new topic. Then, your child will complete the Practice and Review pages to practice the new concept and review previously-learned skills. Workbook Part A covers Units 1-8, and Workbook Part B covers Units 9-16.

Many parents worry about their ability to teach math as their children move beyond the primary years. If that's the case for you, don't worry: I promise to guide you every step of the way! *Fourth Grade Math with Confidence* is full of features that will help you teach math with confidence all year long:

- **Scripted, open-and-go lessons** help you clearly explain and teach new math concepts
- **Explanatory notes** help you understand more deeply how children learn math so you feel well-equipped to teach your child
- **Unit Wrap-ups and Checkpoints** at the end of each unit provide assessment and give you guidance on whether your child is ready to move on to the next unit

In the next section, you'll learn how the curriculum is organized and how to get your materials ready. Invest a little time reading this section now (and getting your Math Kit ready), and you'll be ready to teach math like a pro all year long.

Wishing you a joyful year of fourth grade math!
Kate Snow

Introduction

The Goals of *Fourth Grade Math with Confidence*

Fourth Grade Math with Confidence aims to help children become confident and capable math students, with a deep understanding of math concepts, proficiency and fluency with fundamental skills, and a positive attitude toward math.

Deep Conceptual Understanding

You'll focus on one main topic per unit so your child can build deep conceptual knowledge of the new material. (Educators call this a *mastery approach* to new content.) Each new lesson in the unit builds on the previous one so your child gradually develops thorough understanding.

Proficiency with Fundamental Skills

Children need lots of practice to master the basic skills necessary for proficiency in math. *Fourth Grade Math with Confidence* provides continual, ongoing review of these core skills so your child fully grasps them by the end of the year. (Educators call this a *spiral approach* to review, because children periodically revisit topics, just as the curve of a spiral returns to the same point on a circle.)

Positive Attitude

The lessons in *Fourth Grade Math with Confidence* include lots of games and hands-on learning so your child enjoys and even looks forward to math time. Optional enrichment lessons at the end of each unit (with a picture book suggestion and math extension activity) provide a break from the usual routine and help your child appreciate how math is used in everyday life.

Overview

You'll need three books to teach *Fourth Grade Math with Confidence*. All three books are essential for the program.

- This Instructor Guide contains the scripted lesson plans for the entire year.
- Workbook Part A contains the workbook pages for the first half of the year (Units 1-8).
- Workbook Part B contains the workbook pages for the second half of the year (Units 9-16).

Units

Fourth Grade Math with Confidence is organized into 16 units. Each unit focuses on developing thorough understanding of one main concept, such as multi-digit multiplication, long division, or equivalent fractions. Units vary in length from 6 to 12 lessons, and there are a total of 144 lessons. The final lesson in each unit is an optional enrichment lesson.

The preview for each unit includes the following:

- **Overview.** A brief summary of what you'll teach your child.
- **What Your Child Will Learn.** A detailed list of objectives for the unit.
- **Lesson List.** The full list of lessons included in the unit.
- **Extra Materials.** This section gives you a heads-up if you need any extra materials for the unit. You'll sometimes need to supplement your regular math materials with a few everyday household items, such as markers, tape, or scissors. The optional enrichment lessons also usually require some extra materials.
- **Teaching Math with Confidence.** These notes help you understand more deeply how children learn math so that you're well-prepared to teach the new concepts.

Lessons

Each lesson includes several short and varied activities to keep your child engaged and attentive. You'll need both the Instructor Guide and Student Workbook for every lesson. Most pilot families spent an average of 25-35 minutes on each lesson, with 10-15 minutes of parent-led instruction and 15-20 minutes of independent work. However, this will vary depending on your teaching style and your child's learning style—and whether you have any toddlers interrupting you!

This Instructor Guide contains the scripted, open-and-go lesson plans. Within the Instructor Guide:

- **Bold text** indicates what you are to say.
- *Italic text* provides sample answers.
- Gray-highlighted text indicates explanatory notes.

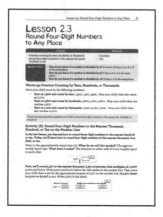

The Student Workbook includes three workbook pages for each lesson. First, you'll use the Lesson Activities page to teach your child the new concept or skill. Then, your child will complete the Practice and Review pages to reinforce what she learned in the lesson and review previously-learned skills.

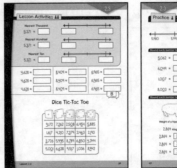 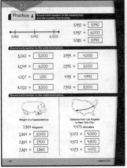 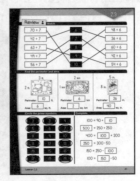

Memory work and warm-up activity with parent

Each lesson begins with a few memory work review questions and a quick warm-up activity. The memory work questions are listed at the top of each lesson. Reviewing a few questions daily helps your child master these important facts and vocabulary words. The warm-up activity eases your child into math time and helps start the lesson on a confident and positive note.

Memory Work →
Warm-up Activity →

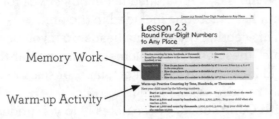

Lesson activities with parent

Next, you'll use the scripted lesson plan and Lesson Activities page to teach your child new concepts and skills. The Instructor Guide and Lesson Activities workbook pages are lettered so that it's easy to see how they align. Some activities are only in the Instructor Guide, without a matching section on the Lesson Activities page.

Instructor Guide   Student Workbook

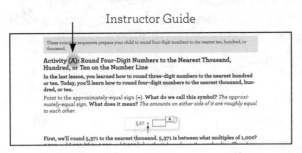 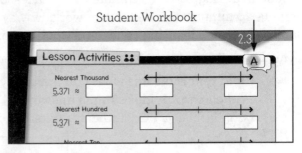

The activity headings and images in the Instructor Guide are lettered
to help you find the matching activity in the Student Workbook.

Instructor Guide

Some activity headings in the Instructor Guide do not have a letter. These activities do not have a matching section in the Student Workbook, and they are completed either orally or with hands-on materials instead.

Independent practice

Last, your child will complete the Practice and Review workbook pages. Most fourth graders will be able to complete these workbook pages independently, but some may need help reading and interpreting the directions.

Try to check the workbook pages as soon as your child finishes them. This immediate feedback shows your child that you value his work, and it helps prevent mistakes from becoming in-grained habits. You'll find answer keys for the Practice and Review pages at the end of each unit.

Enrichment Lessons (Optional)

Optional enrichment lessons are scheduled at the end of each unit. The Instructor Guide provides suggestions for a related picture book and enrichment activity, while the Student Workbook includes a two-page Unit Wrap-Up for your child to complete.

Many parents and children find that the enrichment lessons are their favorite part of the program. (Siblings often enjoy participating in them, too!) However, these lessons are completely optional. You are free to choose the ones that sound the most fun for your family, or skip them entirely if your schedule is too full.

Picture book

Most of the suggested books relate to the math studied in the unit, but some expose your child to other interesting math topics. **The picture books are not required.** You do not need to buy every book or track down every book in your library system. You can also use a book on a similar topic as a substitute.

Enrichment activity

The enrichment activities help your child understand and appreciate how math is used in everyday life. You'll find suggestions for art projects, real-life applications, research activities, and more to make math come alive for your child.

Unit Wrap-up (review and assessment)

The Unit Wrap-Ups provide two pages of additional exercises for the concepts and skills your child learned in the unit. You can use them to casually review the unit, or you can use them as tests to assess your child's progress more formally. Either way, children and parents often find it very satisfying to see this concrete evidence of growth. If you live in a state where you're required to provide evidence of learning, you may want to save them for your child's portfolio.

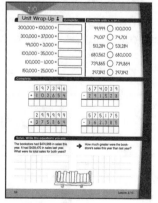

Your child is not expected to fully master every skill from every unit before moving on to the next unit. See below for more on pacing and assessing your child's progress.

Pacing and Checkpoints

Fourth Grade Math with Confidence provides lots of flexibility so your child can learn at his own pace. You know your child best, and you are always welcome to slow down or speed up the pace of the lessons based on your child's needs.

Is My Child Ready to Start *Fourth Grade Math with Confidence*?

Your child is ready to begin this program if he can:

- Read, write, compare, and understand place value in numbers to 10,000.
- Use the traditional process to add and subtract 4-digit numbers written vertically. (You might know these problems as "stack math" or "borrowing and carrying.")
- Name answers to the multiplication and division facts (up to 10×10 and 100÷10). She should be able to recall the answers to most within 3 seconds or so. It's okay if she's still developing fluency with the tricky 7s, 8s, and 9s.
- Use addition, subtraction, multiplication, and division to solve word problems, including two-step word problems.
- Find the area and perimeter of rectangles.
- Read, write, and compare simple fractions.

All of these skills are reviewed in the first few units, so don't worry if your child needs a refresher on a few of them. However, if your child is shaky on many of these skills, *Third Grade Math with Confidence* may be a better fit for her. Math skills build incrementally, and it will be difficult for your child to develop proficiency and confidence with the new fourth-grade skills if she has a weak foundation.

> If your child is not fluent with the multiplication facts but knows the rest of the skills listed above, she is probably ready to begin *Fourth Grade Math with Confidence*. Make sure to add 5 minutes of daily multiplication fact practice to each lesson until your child becomes more fluent with the facts. *Multiplication Facts that Stick* (also available from Well-Trained Mind Press) provide quick games to help your child master these essential skills. The Unit 2 Checkpoint (page 85) also provides more guidance on developing multiplication fact fluency.

How Do I Know Whether to Stick with a Lesson (or Unit) or Move On?

Most children need lots of exposure to a new concept or skill before they fully grasp it. Each lesson in *Fourth Grade Math with Confidence* gently builds on the previous one, but your child doesn't need to completely master every lesson before moving on to the next. The program includes many opportunities for practice and review before your child is expected to achieve full proficiency with a topic.

In general, continue teaching new lessons until you reach the end of a unit. At the end of each unit, you'll find a Checkpoint that provides guidance on whether your child is ready to move on to the next unit.

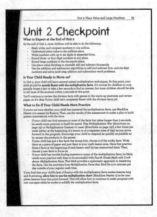

The Checkpoints are divided into three parts:

- **What to Expect at the End of the Unit** This list of skills tells you what fourth graders typically are able to do at the end of each unit.
- **Is Your Child Ready to Move On?** This section tells you what your child needs to have mastered before moving on to the next unit.
- **What to Do if Your Child Needs More Practice** If your child isn't quite ready to move on, this section gives you options for reviewing and practicing the skills your child needs to master before the next unit. (This section is omitted if no specific skills are necessary for the next unit.)

For most units, your child is not expected to fully master all of the material from the current unit before moving on. For example, in Unit 4, your child will learn how to subtract mixed numbers. He'll continue to practice this skill as he studies division in Unit 5, but he does not need to be completely fluent with mixed number subtraction before starting the new unit.

Scheduling

Fourth Grade Math with Confidence includes 144 lessons. 128 are regular lessons, and 16 are optional enrichment lessons. You're welcome to adjust the number of lessons you teach per week to best fit your family's schedule. Some families prefer to teach math 5 days per week, while others prefer to teach math 4 days per week and leave one day open for co-ops, errands, or field trips.

Use the following guidelines to plan your year:

- If you teach 4 lessons per week and teach all the enrichment lessons, *Fourth Grade Math with Confidence* will take you 36 weeks.
- If you teach 4 lessons per week and skip the enrichment lessons, *Fourth Grade Math with Confidence* will take you 32 weeks.
- If you teach 5 lessons per week and teach all the enrichment lessons, *Fourth Grade Math with Confidence* will take you 29 weeks.
- If you teach 5 lessons per week and skip the enrichment lessons, *Fourth Grade Math with Confidence* will take you 26 weeks.

Use this list as a rough guide to planning your year, but don't set it in stone. You'll generally be able to cover one lesson per day, but you may occasionally find that you want to split a lesson over two days.

How Can I Adjust the Lessons to Best Fit My Child and My Schedule?

Children vary tremendously in how quickly they learn new math concepts and skills. Use these suggestions to adjust the lessons to best fit your child's needs and your family's schedule.

- If your student is a fast processor or picks up math skills quickly, you may be able to condense lessons and teach more than one lesson in one day. If so, teach the concepts that are new to your child. Then, have your child complete a selection of exercises on the corresponding Practice and Review pages.
- If your child has a slower processing speed or takes a while to grasp math concepts and skills, some lessons may take longer that you would like (or, longer than your child is able to stay engaged and attentive). If that's the case, set a timer for your desired lesson length, stop when the timer goes off, and continue the next day where you left off. In the elementary years, you are setting a foundation for a lifetime of proficiency and confidence in math. It's okay not to rush through these essential skills.

- If your child doesn't have the stamina to complete the Practice and Review pages at the same time, split the lesson into two parts. Do the Lesson Activities page and Practice page during one part of the day, and then have your child complete the Review page at a different time of the day.
- Adjust your use of manipulatives (like base-ten blocks or play money) to fit your child's learning style. If your child readily understands a skill and doesn't enjoy using manipulatives, allow her to solve the problems without them. If your child learns best with a lot of visual and hands-on reinforcement, allow her to use manipulatives to model problems as much as she needs. Cut out some of the practice problems if the extra manipulative work makes the exercises take too long.
- Games provide a fun way to practice math skills, and they can be a great way to bond with your child. However, if your child doesn't enjoy games, or you don't have time for a game on a particular day, choose a few problems from the game for your child to solve instead. That way, she'll still get the extra practice that the game was meant to provide.
- Don't worry if you have a bad day every once in a while. Extra tiredness, oncoming illness, or just plain grumpiness can make for a less-than-cheerful math lesson. It's perfectly normal for children to occasionally get frustrated, and it doesn't mean that you're a bad math teacher or need to change the way you teach. If emotions rise during math, just cut the lesson short and resume later in the day or the next day. Most of the time, you'll find that the next day goes much better.

What You'll Need

You'll use simple household items to make math hands-on, concrete, and fun in *Fourth Grade Math with Confidence*. Most lessons only require materials from your Math Kit, but you'll also sometimes use everyday objects to enhance the lessons.

How to Create Your Math Kit

You'll use materials from your Math Kit in most lessons. Stick the following materials in a box or basket so they're always ready to go, and keep them handy when you're teaching.

- **40 small counters (20 each of 2 different colors).** Any type of small object (such as plastic tiles, Legos, blocks, or plastic discs) is fine.
- **Play money (20 one-dollar bills, 20 ten-dollar bills, 10 hundred-dollar bills).** Play money from a toy cash register or board game works well, or you can copy and cut out the play money on Blackline Master 11.
- **Pattern blocks.** You will use pattern blocks to teach your child about fractions and mixed numbers, as well as angles. Wood, plastic, or foam pattern blocks are all fine. Real pattern blocks are easiest to use, but you can photocopy and color Blackline Master 9 (page 567) if you don't have access to real pattern blocks.

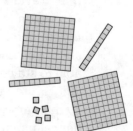

- **Base-ten blocks.** Look for a set with at least 20 unit blocks, 20 rods, and 10 flats. Unlike second and third grade, you'll use base-ten blocks only occasionally this year. So, if you don't already own base-ten blocks, you may want to copy and cut out the paper blocks on Blackline Master 10 (page 569) rather than buying a set.
- **1-foot (or 30-centimeter) ruler.** Make sure your ruler is labeled with both inches and centimeters, as your child will use both units this year.

- **Protractor.** Any clear plastic protractor is fine.
- **2 packs of playing cards and 2 dice.** You'll use playing cards and dice for many of the games. Any standard 52-card decks and regular, six-sided dice will work fine.
- **Blank paper.** Any kind of paper is fine, including plain copy paper. Keep a few pages handy as you'll sometimes need scrap paper.
- **Pencils.** Keep sharp pencils on hand for lessons and workbook pages.

You will also sometimes use Blackline Masters (from the back of this Instructor Guide). Most of the Blackline Masters are used for only a few lessons, but there are a few you may want to put in plastic page protectors for safe-keeping. See page 543 for more information.

 You will occasionally need to save items for future lessons. This symbol will alert you if you need to save anything.

Other Supplies Needed

You'll only need your Math Kit for most lessons, but sometimes you'll also need a few other common household items. You'll find these items listed in three different places in the curriculum to make sure you always know what you need:

- The preview for each unit lists all extra household items needed.
- The top of each lesson lists all supplies you'll need to teach that lesson. These lists include items from your Math Kit as well as extra household items.
- You'll find the complete list of household items needed throughout the year on pages 541-542.

Don't feel you have to gather the extra household items now. Most are common things (like colored pencils or markers, a paper clip, or a tape measure) that you can grab right before you begin the lesson.

Helpful Resources

You'll find an appendix of helpful resources at the back of this book:

- Memory Work
- Complete Picture Book List
- Scope and Sequence
- Materials List
- Blackline Masters

Unit 1
Review Multiplication and Division

Overview

Your child will review several essential skills she learned in third grade:

- multiplication and division facts
- multiplication and division word problems
- how to use long division to solve simple division problems with a remainder

She will also begin to think more abstractly about multiplication and division as she identifies factors and multiples, learns divisibility rules, and tells whether numbers are prime or composite.

Reviewing these skills helps your child start the year on a positive, confident note and refreshes your child's memory if you took a break from math for the summer.

What Your Child Will Learn

In this unit, your child will learn to:

- Find answers for the multiplication and division facts (up to 10 × 10 and 100 ÷ 10)
- Solve multiplication and division word problems
- Use long division to solve simple division problems with a remainder
- Find multiples of a given number
- Tell whether numbers are divisible by 2, 5, or 10
- Find all factors of a given number
- Tell whether a given number is prime or composite

Lesson List

Lesson 1.1	Review Multiplication	Lesson 1.7	Factor Pairs
Lesson 1.2	Review Multiples	Lesson 1.8	Factor Pairs and Area
Lesson 1.3	Review Division	Lesson 1.9	Factor Pairs, Multiples, and Divisibility
Lesson 1.4	Review Fact Families and Word Problems	Lesson 1.10	Prime and Composite Numbers
Lesson 1.5	Divisibility and Remainders	Lesson 1.11	Enrichment (Optional)
Lesson 1.6	Review Simple Long Division		

Extra Materials Needed for Unit 1

- Colored pencils or markers
- For optional Enrichment Lesson:
    - × *I'm Trying to Love Math*, written and illustrated by Bethany Barton. Viking Books for Young Readers, 2019.
    - × 4 sheets of paper
    - × Pan of brownies or sheet cake, optional.

Teaching Math with Confidence: Why Forgetting is Normal

In Unit 1, your child will review multiplication and division. Don't be surprised or worried if your child gives you some blank looks as you review these skills—even though she spent much of last year learning to multiply and divide! While it can be frustrating when children forget what they've learned, it's also perfectly normal.

Brain science shows that our brains don't automatically store every bit of new information. (If that were the case, they'd be stuffed with unimportant details!) Instead, our brains generally decide which information to keep based on how long ago we last recalled the piece of information. After all, if a piece of information hasn't been used in several months, why bother storing it? So, as you review multiplication and division in this unit, keep in mind that all this review teaches your child's brain that these topics are worth remembering for the long term.

Brain science also shows that the harder your brain has to work to remember a piece of information, the better you cement the information in your long-term memory. So, if your child struggles to recall the multiplication and division facts or has trouble remembering the related concepts, resist the urge to immediately jump in with explanations and answers. Instead, ask leading questions, provide hints, and give her plenty of time to think through the problems for herself.

Above all, resist the temptation to get frustrated or blame yourself for not doing enough math over the summer. With a little review, your child will regain her multiplication and division skills within a few weeks. Plus, she'll have cemented them even deeper in her long-term memory.

Lesson 1.1
Review Multiplication

Purpose	Materials
• Set a positive tone for the year and preview what your child will learn • Review the concept of multiplication and multiplication vocabulary • Practice ×2, ×3, ×4, and ×5 multiplication facts	• Counters • Die

Even though you spent many hours on the multiplication facts last year, don't worry if your child is a little rusty after the summer. This lesson is meant to ease your child back into math lessons with the easier multiplication facts. See the Unit 1 **Teaching Math with Confidence** for more on why forgetting is normal (and how best to review forgotten skills).

Some children thrive with a gentle start to the school year, while others want to immediately jump into new skills and concepts. If your child dislikes review and knows the multiplication facts well, briefly review any tricky skills in Lessons 1.1 – 1.4 and then move directly to Lesson 1.5.

Warm-up: Introduce the Workbook

Today, you'll begin your new math book. Let's look at your workbook and see what you'll learn this year. Briefly page through the workbook with your child. **What are you most excited to learn about in math this year?** *Answers will vary.*

Show your child the Lesson 1.1 workbook pages. **Each lesson usually has three pages. The first page is the Lesson Activities page. This page has sample problems for us to complete together, pictures to help you understand math, and game boards and score cards for games.** Point out the icon with two heads at the top of the page. **We'll complete the Lesson Activities pages together.**

Then, you'll complete the Practice and Review pages on your own. Point out the icon with one head at the top of each page. **The Practice page gives you independent practice with the new skills from the lesson. The Review page reviews topics that you've already learned.**

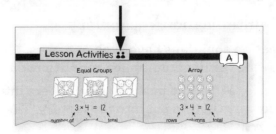

You will complete this page with your child.

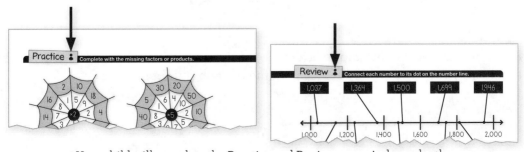

Your child will complete the Practice and Review pages independently.

Many children do not have the writing stamina necessary to complete three full workbook pages. The lesson plans recommend that you write the answers on the Lesson Activities pages yourself, and have your child write the answers on the Practice and Review workbook pages. However, feel free to adjust this based on your child. If your child loves writing in the workbook, she can write all the answers. If she tires easily when writing, scribe some or all of your child's answers on the Practice and Review pages.

Activity (A): Review Multiplication

Today, we'll review multiplication. What are three things you remember about multiplication from last year? *Sample answers: You use it to add up equal groups. You can use it to find area. The ×7 facts were really hard!*

Last year, you learned that we can use multiplication to find the total of equal groups, or the total number of objects in an array. Show your child the first picture in part A. **When we multiply, we put equal groups together. We multiply the number of groups times the size of each group to find the total. In this picture, there are 3 groups, and there are 4 cookies in each group. 3 groups of 4 equals 12, so 3 times 4 equals 12.**

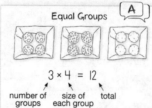

Show your child the second picture in part A. **We can also use multiplication to find the total number of objects in an array. This array has 3 rows and 4 columns. 3 times 4 equals 12, and there are a total of 12 cookies in the array.**

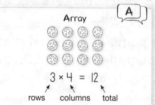

You also learned that we can multiply in any order and still get the same product. We can also multiply the number of columns times the number of rows to find the total number of objects in an array. 3 times 4 equals 12, so what's 4 times 3? *12.*

Activity (B): Review Multiplication Vocabulary

The numbers in multiplication equations have special names. The numbers we multiply are called *factors.* **We call the result of multiplication the** *product.*

One way to remember this is to imagine putting the numbers into a multiplication factory. The factors are the numbers that we put into the factory. The product is the answer that we get out of the factory.

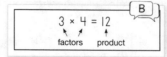

Have your child say each word aloud. Then, cover the words with your hand or a slip of paper and have your child try to recall the name of each number.

Activity (C): Play Climb and Slide

Play Climb and Slide.

Climb and Slide

Materials: 2 different-colored counters to use as game tokens; die

Object of the Game: Be the first player to reach the Finish square.

Each player chooses a counter to use as a game token and places it on the Start Square.

On your turn, roll the die and advance your token the corresponding number of squares. Say the answer to the problem on your landing square.

If you land on a square at the bottom of a ladder, "climb" the ladder and place your game token on the square at the top of the ladder. If you land on a square at the top of a slide, slide down the slide and place your game token on the square at the bottom of the slide.

The first player to reach Finish wins the game.

Independent Practice and Review

Have your child complete the Lesson 1.1 Practice and Review workbook pages.

Many children will need some time to build up the stamina necessary to complete the Practice and Review pages after the summer break. If needed, break up the work and have her complete the Review page at a different time of day than the Practice page.

Lesson 1.2
Review Multiples

Purpose	Materials
• Introduce and practice memory work • Review the term *multiple* • Identify multiples of 6, 7, 8, 9 • Understand how to use the multiplication chart to find answers to multiplication problems	• Memory Work (Blackline Master 1) • Multiplication Chart (Blackline Master 2) • 2 decks of playing cards • Counters

In this lesson, you'll introduce your child to the Memory Work list (Blackline Master 1). Many families find it helpful to post the Memory Work pages near their lesson area to help their children gradually memorize the items over the course of the year.

All Blackline Masters are available at the back of the book. **You can also find all Blackline Masters at welltrainedmind.com/mwc for easy printing.**

The first page of Blackline Master 1 reviews the memory work children learned in *Third Grade Math with Confidence.* If you didn't use *Third Grade Math with Confidence,* you do not need to stop and help your child memorize all these items now. He'll have plenty of opportunities to learn these memory work items over the course of the year. The second page of Blackline Master 1 has new memory work items that will be introduced over the course of this year.

Warm-up: Introduce and Practice Memory Work

Show your child the list of memory work on Blackline Master 1. **You'll memorize these important vocabulary words and facts this year. You already know some of them, and some of them are new. We'll practice them throughout the year so that you learn all of them.** Briefly look over the list with your child and have him point out facts he already knows.

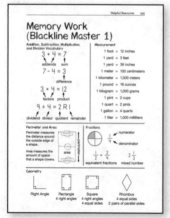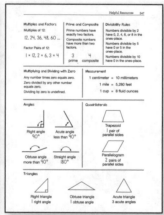

Have your child read aloud the memory work listed under "Addition, Subtraction, Multiplication, and Division Vocabulary." (Or, read it aloud to him.) Then, use the following questions to quiz him on the information. Allow him to peek at the list as needed.

- **What do we call the result when we add numbers together?** *The sum.*
- **What do we call the result when we subtract a number from another number?** *The difference.*
- **What do we call the result when we multiply two numbers?** *The product.*
- **What do we call the numbers in a multiplication equation that we multiply together?** *Factors.*
- **What do we call the number to be divided?** *The dividend.*
- **What do we call the number we divide by?** *The divisor.*
- **What do we call the result when we divide two numbers?** *The quotient.*
- **What do we call an amount that is left over after division?** *The remainder.*

Activity (A): Review Multiples

In the last lesson, we reviewed multiplication. Today, we'll review multiples.

In everyday conversation, *multiple* **just means more than one. I might say that I have** *multiple* **copies of a book or that we have multiple plates in the cabinet. In math, multiples are the numbers you say when you count by a number.** Point to the list of multiples of 6. **These numbers are all multiples of 6.**

You can think of the multiples of 6 as the numbers you say when you count by 6s. Or, you can think of them as the products you can get when you multiply a number by 6. Point to the 24. **What number can you multiply by 6 to get 24?** *4.* If your child's not sure, point out that 24 is the fourth multiple in the list, so 6 times 4 equals 24. Repeat with 42 and 54.

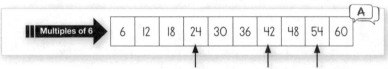

These are only some of the multiples of 6. I could keep counting by 6s forever! Have your child complete the missing numbers in the other lists of multiples.

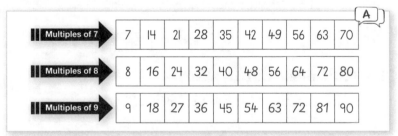

Use the following questions to discuss the lists:

- **Is 63 a multiple of 7?** *Yes.*
- **Is 64 a multiple of 7?** *No.*
- **Is 64 a multiple of 8?** *Yes.*
- **Which multiple of 6 is greater than 50 and less than 60?** *54.*
- **Which multiple of 8 is greater than 40 and less than 50?** *48.*
- **Which lists have only even numbers?** *The multiples of 6 and 8.*
- **Which lists have some odd numbers and some even numbers?** *The multiples of 7 and 9.*
- **Which number is both a multiple of 6 and a multiple of 7?** *42.* **Why do you think it shows up on both lists?** *Sample answer: 6 times 7 equals 42, so 42 is a multiple of both 6 and 7.*

Activity (B): Review the Multiplication Chart

Show your child the multiplication chart (Blackline Master 2). **The multiplication chart shows all the multiplication facts from 1 × 1 up to 10 × 10.**

Point to the row that shows the multiples of 7. *Child points to ×7 row.* **Point to the column that shows the multiples of 8.** *Child points to ×8 column.*

×	1	2	3	4	5	6	7	8	9	10
1	1	2	3	4	5	6	7	8	9	10
2	2	4	6	8	10	12	14	16	18	20
3	3	6	9	12	15	18	21	24	27	30
4	4	8	12	16	20	24	28	32	36	40
5	5	10	15	20	25	30	35	40	45	50
6	6	12	18	24	30	36	42	48	54	60
7	7	14	21	28	35	42	49	56	63	70
8	8	16	24	32	40	48	56	64	72	80
9	9	18	27	36	45	54	63	72	81	90
10	10	20	30	40	50	60	70	80	90	100

Point to 7 × 9. Here's how to use the chart to find 7 times 9. Show your child how to slide one finger across the ×7 row and one finger down the ×9 column until your fingers meet. **What's 7 times 9?** *63.* Write 63 in the blank.

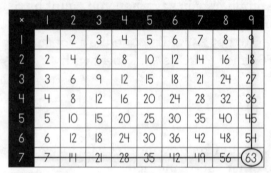

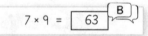

$7 \times 9 =$ [63] **B**

Have your child find 8 × 8 and 6 × 9 in the same way.

$8 \times 8 =$ [64] $6 \times 9 =$ [54] **B**

Activity (C): Play Multiples Four in a Row

Use the game board in part C to play Multiples Four in a Row.

A new game board is included in the Student Workbook every time the Instructor Guide calls for you to play a game. Unlike in earlier levels of *Math with Confidence*, you do not need to save any of the game boards in this book.

Due to space constraints, some of the game boards have small boxes. Your usual counters may be too big for the boxes. If that's the case, here are three options:

1. Unit blocks (from your set of base-ten blocks) work well as counters for this game and other games with small boxes.

2. If you'd prefer to skip using counters, simply X out each box on the game board rather than placing a counter.

3. If you want to be able to reuse the gameboards for extra practice, place the game board in a plastic page protector and mark your turns with a dry erase marker.

Multiples Four in a Row

Materials: 6s, 7s, 8s, 9s from 2 decks of cards (32 cards total); counters of two different colors

Object of the Game: Be the first player to fill 4 boxes in a row, either horizontally, vertically, or diagonally.

On your turn, turn over a card. Use a counter to cover any number on the game board that is a multiple of the number on your card. For example, if your card is a 6, you may cover any multiple of 6.

Sample play. You may choose any number that is a multiple of the number on your card.

Play then passes to the other player. Continue until one player covers 4 boxes in a row, either horizontally, vertically, or diagonally.

You only need to place 4 counters in a row to win, even though there are 5 rows and columns on the gameboard. The extra row and column provide more opportunities to win.

Independent Practice and Review

Have your child complete the Lesson 1.2 Practice and Review workbook pages.

Lesson 1.3
Review Division

Purpose	Materials
• Practice memory work • Review the concept of division and division vocabulary • Practice division facts	• Counters • Die

Warm-up: Practice Memory Work

Have your child read aloud the following memory work listed under "Measurement." (Or, read it aloud to her.) Then, use the following questions to quiz her on the information. Allow her to peek at the list as needed.

- **How many inches equal 1 foot?** *12*.
- **How many feet equal 1 yard?** *3*.
- **How many inches equal 1 yard?** *36*.
- **How many centimeters equal 1 meter?** *100*.
- **How many meters equal 1 kilometer?** *1,000*.

If you did not use *Third Grade Math with Confidence* last year, use a ruler to show her the length of any units that are unfamiliar.

Activity (A): Review Division

Today, we'll review division. What are three things you remember about division from last year? *Sample answers: You use it when you want to split things into equal groups. You can have a remainder. It's the opposite of multiplication.* **Last year, you learned that division is the opposite of multiplication. When we multiply, we put together equal groups to make a total. When we divide, we split a total into equal groups.**

Show your child part A. **Both of these problems involve splitting a total into equal groups. We can use division to answer two different kinds of questions about equal groups.**

Read aloud the first word problem in part A: *12 children split into groups of 4. How many groups do they make?* **What's 12 divided by 4?** *3*. Write 3 in the blank. **The children make 3 groups.**

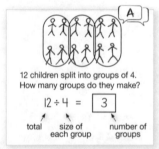

In this problem, we divide the total by the *size* of each group. The answer is the *number* of groups.

Read aloud the second word problem in part A: *12 children split into 4 equal groups. How many children are in each group?* **What's 12 divided by 4?** *3.* Write 3 in the blank. **There are 3 children in each group.**

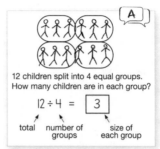

In this problem, we divide the total by the *number* of groups. The answer is the *size* of each group.

Activity (B): Review Division Vocabulary

The first number in a division problem is called the *dividend*, and the second number is called the *divisor*. The dividend is the number to be divided. The divisor is the number we divide by. We call the result of division the *quotient*.

One way to remember these words is that the dividend is on the front *end* of the horizontal equation. Divisor ends in -or like actor, and it *acts* on the dividend when it divides it up.

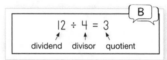

Have your child say each word aloud. Then, cover the words with your hand or a slip of paper and have your child try to recall the name of each number in the equation.

Activity (C): Play Treasure Hunt

Play Treasure Hunt. Encourage your child to use related multiplication facts to find the answers to the division problems on the game board. For example, for 20 ÷ 4: **4 times what equals 20?** *5.* **So, what does 20 divided by 4 equal?** *5.*

Treasure Hunt

Materials: Counters; die

Object of the Game: Win the most counters.

Have each player choose a different-colored counter to use as a game token and place it on one of the Start circles. Place 12 counters in a pile next to the game board. These counters are the treasure chest.

On your turn, roll the die and advance your token the corresponding number of circles clockwise around the path. If you land on a circle with a division problem, say the answer to the problem and take 1 counter from the treasure chest. If you land on a Start circle, roll again. Otherwise, follow the directions on the circle.

Play until all of the counters are gone from the treasure chest. The player who has more counters wins the game.

Independent Practice and Review

Have your child complete the Lesson 1.3 Practice and Review workbook pages.

The Review pages review many of the skills covered in *Third Grade Math with Confidence* so that your child is ready to extend these skills later in the year. If you find that your child has forgotten one of the skills included on the Review pages, briefly explain it to her.

Lesson 1.4
Review Fact Families and Word Problems

Purpose	Materials
• Practice multiplication facts • Review multiplication and division fact families • Review how to use multiplication to solve division problems • Solve multiplication and division word problems	• Playing cards • Multiplication Chart (Blackline Master 2)

Warm-up: Play Multiplication War

Play Multiplication War.

Multiplication War

Materials: Deck of playing cards with jacks, queens, and kings removed (40 cards total)

Object of the Game: Win the most cards.

Shuffle the cards. Deal them face down into two piles.

On your turn, flip over the top two cards in your pile. Find the product of the numbers. For example, if you flip over a 6 and a 7, the product is 42. Then, the other player flips over their top two cards and finds the product of the cards. Whoever has the greater product wins all 4 cards.

The player who flipped over the two 8s wins the cards, since 64 is greater than 42.

If the products are equal, leave the cards face-up on the table and have both players flip over another two cards from their piles. Whoever has the greater product wins all the face-up cards.

Play until the piles run out. Whoever has won more cards wins the game.

Challenge Version: Use only the 5s, 6s, 7s, 8s, and 9s from 2 decks of cards to give your child lots of practice with challenging multiplication facts like 7 × 8 or 9 × 6.

If you'd like another option for practicing the multiplication facts, play Multiplication Greatest to Least. See Lesson 6.1 (page 197) for directions.

Activity (A): Review Multiplication and Division Fact Families

In the last few lessons, we reviewed multiplication and division. Today, we'll review the relationship between multiplication and division with fact families and word problems.

Show your child the array in part A. **How many rows of stickers are in this array?** *3.* **How many columns?** *6.* **What are two multiplication equations we could write to match this array?** *3 times 6 equals 18. 6 times 3 equals 18.* Complete the two division equations as shown.

What are two division equations we could write to match this array? *18 divided by 6 equals 3. 18 divided by 3 equals 6.* If your child's not sure, suggest he divide the total number of stickers by the number of rows or columns. Complete the two division equations as shown.

These four equations are a multiplication and division fact family. They show the multiplication and division relationships between 3, 6, and 18.

Activity (B): Use Multiplication to Solve Division Problems

Since division is the opposite of multiplication, we can use multiplication to help solve division problems.

Point to the first division equation. **To solve 35 divided by 5, we could imagine splitting 35 stickers into 5 equal rows. It's hard to imagine splitting up so many stickers, though! Instead, let's use the matching multiplication fact to find the answer. 5 times what equals 35?** *7.* Write 7 in the multiplication equation. **So, what does 35 divided by 5 equal?** *7.* Write 7 in the division equation.

Point to the next division equation. **To solve 48 divided by 6, we can think "6 times what equals 48?" Let's use the multiplication chart to help find the answer.**

If your child immediately knows the answer, skip the following dialogue. Instead, ask him to "be the teacher" and show you how a student could use the multiplication chart to find the answer if he forgot it.

We want to know 6 times what equals 48, so I look for 48 in the row with the multiples of 6. Point to 48 as shown. **Then, I slide my finger up to find the missing factor.** Slide your finger up until it reaches 8. **6 times 8 equals 48, so 48 divided by 6 equals 8.** Write 8 in both blanks.

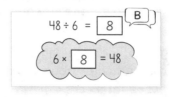

×	1	2	3	4	5	6	7	8
1	1	2	3	4	5	6	7	8
2	2	4	6	8	10	12	14	16
3	3	6	9	12	15	18	21	24
4	4	8	12	16	20	24	28	32
5	5	10	15	20	25	30	35	40
6	6	12	18	24	30	36	42	48

Activity (C): Solve Multiplication and Division Word Problems

Reading math is very different from reading a story. When you read a story, you can enjoy the story even if you don't fully understand every word or detail. But in word problems, every detail matters. You need to fully understand every sentence before you try to solve the problem.

Following these steps will help you understand and solve word problems. Read your child the steps in part A.

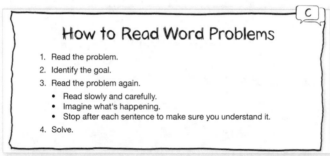

How to Read Word Problems

1. Read the problem.
2. Identify the goal.
3. Read the problem again.
   - Read slowly and carefully.
   - Imagine what's happening.
   - Stop after each sentence to make sure you understand it.
4. Solve.

Read aloud the first word problem: *Sammy is making bows from ribbon. She wants to make 5 bows. She needs 8 inches of ribbon for each bow. How much ribbon does she need?*

What's the goal? *Find how many inches of ribbon she needs.* Then, have your child read the problem again slowly and describe what he imagines. For example: *I imagine a girl cutting pieces of ribbon that are 8 inches long.*

Let's draw a simple sketch to help visualize the problem. She wants to make 5 bows. Draw 5 short horizontal lines as shown. **She needs 8 inches of ribbon for each bow.** Label one of the lines "8 in."

How do we find the total amount of ribbon she needs? *Multiply 5 times 8.* Write "5 × 8 =" in the space below the problem. Have your child complete the equation: 5 × 8 = 40. Have him label the answer with "in." and draw a box around the complete answer.

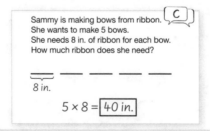

Sammy is making bows from ribbon.
She wants to make 5 bows.
She needs 8 in. of ribbon for each bow.
How much ribbon does she need?

8 in.

$5 \times 8 = \boxed{40 \text{ in.}}$

Labeling the answers reminds your child to make sense of his answers and think about whether they are reasonable. Drawing a box around the answers makes it easier for you to check his work.

Read aloud the second word problem: ***Charlie is making bows from ribbon. He has 36 cm of ribbon. He wants to cut the ribbon into 4 equal parts. How long should he make each piece of ribbon?***

What's the goal? *Find how long each piece of ribbon is.* Then, have your child read the problem again slowly and describe what he imagines. For example: *I imagine a boy cutting a piece of ribbon into 4 equal pieces.*

Let's draw another sketch. He has 36 centimeters of ribbon. Draw 1 long horizontal line as shown and label it "36 cm." **He cuts into 4 equal pieces.** Draw 3 short vertical lines as shown to divide the line into 4 roughly-equal parts.

How do we find the length of each piece of ribbon? *Divide 36 by 4.* Write "36 ÷ 4 =" in the space below the problem. Have your child complete the equation: 36 ÷ 4 = 9. Have him label the answer with "cm" and draw a box around the complete answer.

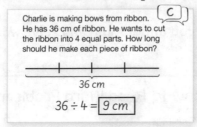

Independent Practice and Review

Have your child complete the Lesson 1.4 Practice and Review workbook pages.

Lesson 1.5
Divisibility and Remainders

Purpose	Materials
• Practice multiplication facts • Review remainders • Introduce divisibility • Learn divisibility rules for 2, 5, and 10	• Playing cards

Warm-up: Play Multiplication War

Play Multiplication War. See Lesson 1.4 (page 23) for directions.

Activity (A): Review Remainders

In the last two lessons, you solved division problems. In all the problems, you were able to divide the quantities evenly, with nothing left over. In real life, division problems don't always work out evenly! Today, we'll review remainders.

Let's pretend that one day you clean your room and find 8 identical socks. How many pairs of socks can you make? *4.* How many socks are left over? *0.* 8 divided by 2 equals 4.

Mathematicians say that a number is *divisible* by another number if the number divides it evenly, without a remainder. 8 objects can be evenly divided into groups of 2, so 8 is divisible by 2.

$8 \div 2 = 4$

8 can be evenly divided by 2.
8 is divisible by 2.

The next week, you clean your room and find 9 identical socks. How many pairs of socks can you make? *4.* How many socks are left over? *1.* 9 divided by 2 equals 4, with a remainder of 1.

$9 \div 2 = 4\,R1$

9 cannot be evenly divided by 2.
9 is not divisible by 2.

Point to "R1". **The R stands for *remainder*. The amount left over after division is called the *remainder*, because it's the part that remains. 9 objects can't be evenly divided into groups of 2, so 9 isn't divisible by 2.**

Have your child complete the division problems in part A. After she completes each column, discuss whether the dividend in that column is divisible by 3, 4, and 5. For example: **12 is divisible by 3 and 4, but it's not divisible by 5.**

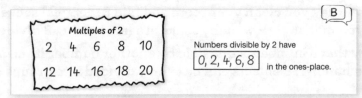

$12 \div 3 =$ [4] $15 \div 3 =$ [5] $16 \div 3 =$ [5 R1] — A

$12 \div 4 =$ [3] $15 \div 4 =$ [3 R3] $16 \div 4 =$ [4]

$12 \div 5 =$ [2 R2] $15 \div 5 =$ [3] $16 \div 5 =$ [3 R1]

If your child has trouble solving these problems mentally, use counters to model the problems. For example, for $12 \div 3$, place 12 counters on the table and have your child split them into groups of 3.

Activity (B): Find Divisibility Rules for 2, 5, and 10

There are patterns that make it easy to tell whether a number is divisible by another number. These patterns are called divisibility rules. We'll find the divisibility rules for 2, 5, and 10.

Point to the multiples of 2. **These numbers are the first 10 multiples of 2. Are these numbers all divisible by 2?** *Yes.* **How do you know?** *Sample answers: They're even. They're the answers to the ×2 facts, so they must be divisible by 2.*

All of these numbers are even. The definition of even numbers is that they can be split evenly into two groups. So, if a number is even and has 0, 2, 4, 6, or 8 in the ones-place, you know that it's divisible by 2. Complete the printed sentence as shown.

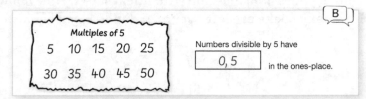

Multiples of 2

2   4   6   8   10

12   14   16   18   20

Numbers divisible by 2 have [0, 2, 4, 6, 8] in the ones-place. — B

Point to the multiples of 5. **These numbers are the first 10 multiples of 5. Are these numbers all divisible by 5?** *Yes.* **How do you know?** *Sample answer: They're the numbers you say when you count by 5s. They're the answers to the ×5 facts, so they must be divisible by 5.*

What do you notice about the ones-place in these numbers? *Sample answer: They all have a 0 or a 5 in the ones-place.* **When you multiply a number by 5, your answer always has a 0 or 5 in the ones-place. So, if a number has a 0 or a 5 in the ones-place, you know that it's divisible by 5.** Complete the printed sentence as shown.

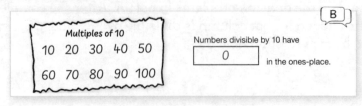

Multiples of 5

5   10   15   20   25

30   35   40   45   50

Numbers divisible by 5 have [0, 5] in the ones-place. — B

Point to the multiples of 10. **These numbers are the first 10 multiples of 10. Are these numbers all divisible by 10?** *Yes.* **How do you know?** *Sample answer: They're the numbers you say when you count by 10s. They're the answers to the ×10 facts, so they must be divisible by 10.*

What do you notice about the ones-place in these numbers? *Sample answer: They all have a 0 in the ones-place.* **When you multiply a number by 10, your answer always has a 0 in the ones-place. So, if a number has a 0 in the ones-place, you know that it's divisible by 10.** Complete the printed sentence as shown.

Multiples of 10

10   20   30   40   50

60   70   80   90   100

Numbers divisible by 10 have [0] in the ones-place. — B

We can use these divisibility rules to tell whether any number is divisible by 2, 5, or 10.
Ask your child the following questions. Encourage her to use the divisibility rules to tell the answers.

- **Is 74 divisible by 2?** *Yes.*
- **Is 374 divisible by 2?** *Yes.*
- **Is 375 divisible by 2?** *No.*
- **Is 95 divisible by 5?** *Yes.*
- **Is 96 divisible by 5?** *No.*
- **Is 100 divisible by 5?** *Yes.*
- **Is 345 divisible by 5?** *Yes.*
- **Is 200 divisible by 10?** *Yes.*
- **Is 225 divisible by 10?** *No.*
- **Is 490 divisible by 10?** *Yes.*

Independent Practice and Review

Have your child complete the Lesson 1.5 Practice and Review workbook pages.

If possible, check your child's work as soon as she finishes, and have her correct any mistakes. Children benefit from immediate accountability, and your prompt attention shows that you value your child's work and effort.

Lesson 1.6
Review Simple Long Division

Purpose	Materials
• Practice memory work • Use hands-on materials to understand the long division algorithm • Practice simple long division	• Memory Work (Blackline Master 1) • Counters • Die

Children often find long division challenging. *Math with Confidence* spreads long division instruction over third and fourth grade so that children are proficient at long division with smaller numbers before they tackle larger numbers.

In this lesson, you'll review the long division process that was introduced in *Third Grade Math with Confidence*. If your child did not use *Third Grade Math with Confidence* or struggled with long division last year, he may need two days for this lesson. Here's a suggested plan for how to split the lesson over two days:

- Day 1: Do the Warm-up, Activity A, and Activity B. Then, have your child complete the Review page only.

- Day 2: Review the steps in Activity B and play Roll and Divide. Then, have your child complete the Practice page. Stay close by as your child completes the Practice page, and encourage him to model the problems with counters as needed.

Warm-up: Practice Memory Work

Have your child read aloud the memory work listed under "Measurement" on Blackline Master 1. (Or, read it aloud to him.) Then, use the following questions to quiz him on the information. Allow him to peek at the list as needed.

- **How many ounces equal 1 pound?** *16.*
- **How many grams equal 1 kilogram?** *1,000.*
- **How many cups equal 1 pint?** *2.*
- **How many pints equal 1 quart?** *2.*
- **How many quarts equal 1 gallon?** *4.*
- **How many milliliters equal 1 liter?** *1,000.*

Discuss any units that are unfamiliar to your child.

Activity (A): Subtract to Find Leftover Chocolates at the Chocolate Shop

In the last lesson, we reviewed remainders. Today, we'll review long division.

Let's pretend you work at a chocolate shop, and I'm the customer. I'll tell you how many chocolates I want and how many chocolates I would like you to pack in each box.

Show your child part A. **I'd like 17 striped chocolates. Please put 5 in each box.** Have your child take 17 counters and organize them into as many groups of 5 as possible. (He will have 2 left over.) **How many boxes can you fill?** *3.* Write 3 as shown.

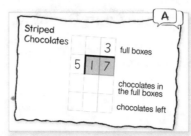

How many chocolates are in the full boxes? *15.* **How do you know?** *Sample answer: 3 times 5 equals 15. 3 times 5 equals 15, so there are 15 chocolates in the full boxes.* Write 15 as shown.

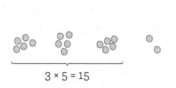
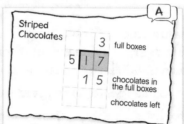

How many chocolates are left? *2.* **How do you know?** *Sample answers: 17 minus 15 equals 2. I see 2 counters left over.* Write a minus sign and horizontal line as shown. **17 minus 15 equals 2, so there are 2 left.** Write 2 as shown.

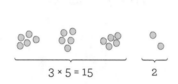
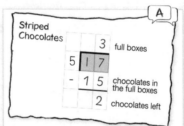

How many boxes of striped chocolates did you pack? *3.* **How many striped chocolates were left over?** *2.*

> Asking this question ensures that your child pays attention to the underlying meaning of the answer.

I have a few more orders today! Act out the rest of the problems in part A in the same way. For example: **There are 18 caramel chocolates. Please put 4 in each box.** For 21 ÷ 3, point out that there is no remainder: **21 is divisible by 3, so there aren't any chocolates left over.**

Activity (B): Practice Long Division

Show your child the list of steps in part B. **We used 3 steps to divide the chocolates in part A: divide, multiply, and subtract.**

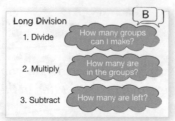

We can use the same steps to solve other division problems. This method is called long division. Later this year, you'll learn another step in long division, and you'll learn how to use long division to divide larger numbers.

I'll show you how to use the steps to divide 14 by 4. Place 14 counters on the table.

The first step is to divide. I think, "How many groups of 4 can I make from 14?" I want to make as many groups as possible, without going over 14. How many groups of 4 can I make? *3.* If your child isn't sure, encourage him to try out some numbers and multiply them by 4. For example: *4 times 5 is 20. 20 is greater than 14, so that's too many groups. Or, 4 times 2 is 8. That's 6 less than 14, so I can make another group of 4.*

Organize the counters in 3 groups of 4, with 2 left over. Write 3 as shown.

Next, I multiply to find out how many are in the groups. 3 times 4 is 12, so I write 12 on the next line. Point to 3 and 4 as you say them, and write 12 as shown.

Last, I subtract to find how many are left. Write a minus sign and horizontal line as shown. **14 minus 12 equals 2, so there is a remainder of 2.** Write 2 as shown.

Have your child complete part B. Talk through the steps for each problem, and model the problems with counters as needed.

Your child can use either mental math or the subtraction algorithm for the subtraction step.

Some children resist using long division because they can easily find the quotients and remainders mentally. If your child does this, explain that practicing the steps in long division with smaller numbers prepares him to solve problems with larger numbers that are difficult to divide mentally.

Cover Part B with your hand or a piece of paper. **Can you remember the three steps in order?** *Divide, multiply, subtract.* If your child can't remember, allow him to peek before telling them to you.

Activity (C): Play Roll and Divide

Use the scorecards to play Roll and Divide. Watch your child carefully as he completes the long division problems to make sure he follows the steps correctly.

Roll and Divide

Materials: Die

Object of the Game: Score the most points by creating greater remainders than your opponent.

On your turn, roll the die. Write the number on the die as the divisor in one of the long division problems on your scorecard. Try to choose a problem that will yield as large a remainder as possible. Then, solve the problem. The remainder is your score for that round. If there is no remainder, your score is 0.

For example, if you roll a 3 on your first turn, you may write 3 as the divisor in any of the long division problems. 17 divided by 3 yields the largest remainder, so it's the best play. $17 \div 3 = 5$ R2, so your score is 2.

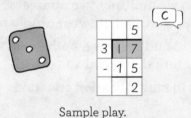

Sample play.

Play until both players have completed their scorecards. Find the sum of each player's remainders. Whoever has the greater total sum wins the game.

Independent Practice and Review

Have your child complete the Lesson 1.6 Practice and Review workbook pages.

Lesson 1.7
Factor Pairs

Purpose	Materials
• Practice memory work • Introduce factors and factor pairs • Identify factors	• Memory Work (Blackline Master 1) • Die • Counters

Warm-up: Practice Memory Work

Have your child read aloud the memory work listed under "Fractions" on Blackline Master 1. (Or, read it aloud to her.) Then, put the list away. Use the following questions to quiz her on the information. Allow her to peek at the list as needed

- **What do we call the top number in a fraction?** *The numerator.*
- **What does the numerator tell?** *The number of parts.*
- **What do we call the bottom number in a fraction?** *The denominator.*
- **What does the denominator tell?** *How many equal parts the whole was split into.*
- **What do we call fractions that look different but have the same value?** *Equivalent fractions.*
- **What do we call numbers that have a whole number and a fraction?** *Mixed numbers.*

If you did not use *Third Grade Math with Confidence* last year and your child did not learn these vocabulary words, skip them for now. You will review these terms in depth in Unit 4.

Activity (A): Introduce Factor Pairs and Factors

What do we call the result when we multiply two numbers? *The product.* **What do we call the numbers in a multiplication equation that we multiply together?** *Factors.*

Show your child part A. **1 times 10 and 2 times 5 both equal 10. We call them** *factor pairs* **of 10, because they are pairs of factors that equal 10.**

1, 2, 5, and 10 can all be factors in multiplication equations equal to 10. We say that 1, 2, 5, and 10 are the *factors* **of 10.**

Let's complete the list of factor pairs that equal 20. Every number has 1 as a factor. 1 times what equals 20? *20.* **So, 1 times 20 is one factor pair of 20.** Write 20 in the blank. Have your child complete the other missing factors in the same way.

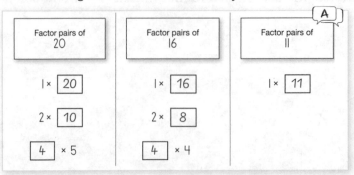

If your child has trouble completing any of the factors, frame the problem as a division problem instead. For example, for __ × 5: **We want to know what times 5 equals 20. So, you can divide 20 by 5 to find the missing factor. What's 20 divided by 5?** *4.*

Point to the completed list for 20. **These are the factor pairs of 20. So, what are the factors of 20?** *1, 20, 2, 10, 4, and 5.*

Is 20 divisible by 1? *Yes.* **By 20?** *Yes.* **By 2?** *Yes.* **By 10?** *Yes.* **By 4?** *Yes.* **By 5?** *Yes.* **Numbers are divisible by all of their factors.**

Is 20 a multiple of 1? *Yes.* **Of 20?** *Yes.* **Of 2?** *Yes.* **Of 10?** *Yes.* **Of 4?** *Yes.* **Of 5?** *Yes.* **Numbers are always a multiple of each of their factors.**

Point to the completed list for 16. **What are the factors of 16?** *1, 16, 2, 8, and 4.* **What numbers is 16 divisible by?** *1, 16, 2, 8, and 4.* **16 is a multiple of what numbers?** *1, 16, 2, 8, and 4.*

Point to the completed list for 11. **What are the factors of 11?** *1 and 11.* **What numbers is 11 divisible by?** *1 and 11.* **11 is a multiple of what numbers?** *1 and 11.*

Your child will learn about prime numbers (numbers that have exactly 2 factors) and composite numbers (numbers with more than 2 factors) in Lesson 1.10.

It's easy to get factors and multiples confused, since they're so closely related. It helps to imagine a multiplication factory. Factors are the smaller numbers that go in to the multiplication factory. They get multiplied together. Multiples are the products. They're the bigger numbers that come out of the multiplication factory.

Activity (B): Play Factors Four in a Row

Play Factors Four in a Row. Encourage your child to use what she knows about factors, multiples, and divisibility as she plays the game. For example: *18 is a multiple of 6, so 6 is a factor of 18.* Or, *40 is divisible by 5, so 5 is a factor of 40.*

This game is very similar to Multiples Four in a Row (from Lesson 1.2) to reinforce the idea that a number is a multiple of each of its factors.

Factors Four in a Row

Materials: Die; counters of two different colors

Object of the Game: Be the first player to fill 4 boxes in a row, either horizontally, vertically, or diagonally.

On your turn, roll the die. Use a counter to cover a number that has the number on the die as a factor. For example, if you roll a 5, you can cover 5, 10, 15, 20, 25, 30, 35, or 40 (since these numbers all have 5 as a factor). If you roll a 1, you may cover any number, since 1 is a factor of every number.

Play then passes to the other player. Continue until one player covers 4 boxes in a row, either horizontally, vertically, or diagonally.

Independent Practice and Review

Have your child complete the Lesson 1.7 Practice and Review workbook pages.

Lesson 1.8
Factor Pairs and Area

Purpose	Materials
• Review how to find the area and perimeter of a rectangle • Practice finding factor pairs • Use factor pairs to find possible dimensions for a rectangle with a given area	• Base-ten blocks • Die • Markers or colored pencils

Warm-up (A): Review Area and Perimeter

Last year, you learned about area and perimeter. What does perimeter measure? *The distance around the outside edge of a shape.* **What does area measure?** *The amount of space that a shape covers.*

To find the distance around the outside edge of a rectangle, we add up all 4 sides. We call the longer side of a rectangle its *length.* **We call the shorter side of a rectangle its** *width.*

The perimeter of a rectangle equals the length plus the width plus the length plus the width. Have your child help you write and solve an addition equation to find the perimeter of the rectangle. **The perimeter of the rectangle is 14 centimeters.**

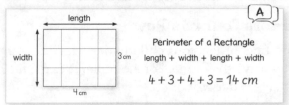

Perimeter of a Rectangle
length + width + length + width
$4 + 3 + 4 + 3 = 14\ cm$

To find the area of a rectangle, we multiply the length times the width to find how many square units it takes to completely cover the rectangle. Have your child help you write and solve a multiplication equation to find the area of the rectangle. **The area of the rectangle is 12 square centimeters.**

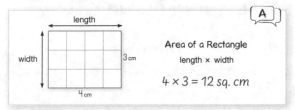

Area of a Rectangle
length × width
$4 \times 3 = 12\ sq.\ cm$

Activity (B): Find Factor Pairs

In the last lesson, you found factor pairs. What are factor pairs? *Sample answer: Pairs of factors that you multiply together to equal a certain number.* **Today, we'll explore the connection between factor pairs and the area of rectangles.**

Let's find the factor pairs that equal 12. Every number has 1 as a factor. 1 times what equals 12? *12.* **So, 1 times 12 is one factor pair of 12.** Write "1 × 12" to start a list.

To find the other factor pairs of a number, we think of multiplication problems that equal the number. What multiplication facts equal 12? *Sample answers: 2 times 6. 3 times 4.* Write these multiplication problems in the list. Repeat with the rest of the problems.

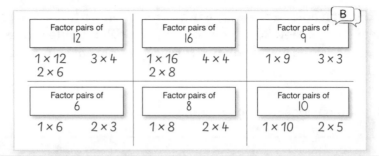

Some children have trouble with how open-ended this question is. If your child has trouble identifying all the factor pairs, allow him to use the multiplication chart to help. For example, to find factors of 12, have him find 12 every place it appears in the chart and identify the matching factor pairs.

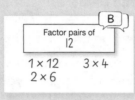

Ask your child the following questions about the completed factor pairs:

- **How many factor pairs does 12 have?** *3.*
- **How many factors does 12 have?** *6.*
- **How many factor pairs does 16 have?** *3.*
- **How many factors does 16 have?** *5.* If your child says 6, point out that the factors are 1, 16, 2, 8, and 4. 4 is listed twice in the list of factor pairs, but it only counts as one factor.
- **How many factors does 9 have?** *3.*

Activity (B): Discuss the Relationship Between Factor Pairs and Area

Let's say I wanted to make a rectangle with an area of 8 square centimeters. You already found that the factor pairs of 8 are 1 times 8 and 2 times 4. So, that means my rectangle could be 1 by 8 or 2 by 4. Give your child 8 unit blocks (from your set of base-ten blocks). Have him arrange them in a 1×8 rectangle. Then, have him arrange them in a 2×4 rectangle.

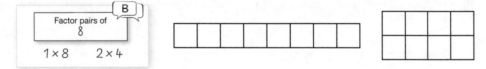

Can you use 8 unit blocks to make a rectangle where one side is 3 centimeters long? *No.* **Why not?** *Sample answer: 3 isn't a factor of 8. You can't multiply 3 by a whole number and get 8.* Arrange the blocks as shown. **3 isn't a factor of 8, so it's not possible to arrange the blocks to make a rectangle with a length of 3 centimeters and an area of 8 square centimeters.**

Activity (C): Play Fill the Garden

We're going to play a game called Fill the Garden. Each square stands for 1 square foot of dirt in a garden. The goal of the game is to fill as much of the garden as you can.

After you roll the die, you color a rectangle in your garden with the matching color and matching number of square feet. So, if you roll a 5, you color a blue rectangle that covers 9 square feet. What dimensions could you use for a rectangle with an area of 9 square feet? *1×9 or 3×3.* If your child's not sure, suggest he look at the factor pairs of 9 in part B.

Play Fill the Garden. Encourage your child to use the matching list of factor pairs in part B to identify the possible dimensions for each rectangle.

Fill the Garden

Materials: Die; markers or colored pencils

Object of the Game: Fill more of your garden than your opponent.

Choose who will go first. Each player chooses a gameboard.

On your turn, roll the die and find the corresponding flower and number of square feet. Then, color a rectangle in your garden with the matching color and number of square feet. For example, if you roll a 2, color either a 1×6 or 2×3 orange rectangle.

Sample play. You could also draw a 1×6 rectangle.

Take turns rolling the die and filling in the garden plan. Place the rectangles close together to fill as much of the garden as possible.

Your game ends once you roll a number and do not have space for the matching rectangle. For example, if you roll a 6, but you do not have room for a 1×10 or 2×5 rectangle, your game is over. The other player may continue until they roll a number and do not have space for the matching rectangle.

Whoever has fewer empty spaces at the end of the game wins.

Cooperative Version: Play together (on one garden plan) and see how many empty spaces you have at the end of the game. Then, play together again (on the other garden plan) and try to have fewer empty spaces.

Independent Practice and Review

Have your child complete the Lesson 1.8 Practice and Review workbook pages.

Lesson 1.9
Factor Pairs, Multiples, and Divisibility

Purpose	Materials
• Practice finding half of a number • Make an organized list to find all the factor pairs for a number	• 2 dice

Warm-up: Mentally Divide Numbers by 2

Dividing a number by 2 is just like splitting it in half.

- **What's 10 divided by 2?** *5.*
- **What's 18 divided by 2?** *9.*
- **What's 20 divided by 2?** *10.*
- **What's 24 divided by 2?** *12.*
- **What's 28 divided by 2?** *14.*
- **What's 30 divided by 2?** *15.*
- **What's 32 divided by 2?** *16.*
- **What's 36 divided by 2?** *18.*

This warm-up prepares your child to find factor pairs in which 2 is one of the factors. If your child has trouble, use base-ten blocks to model the problems. For example, for 32, place 3 rods and 2 unit blocks on the table and have your child split them into 2 equal groups. She will need to trade 1 rod for 10 units.

Activity (A): Find All Factor Pairs of Numbers

In the last two lessons, you learned how to find the factor pairs of a number. **What are factor pairs?** *Sample answer: Pairs of factors that you multiply together to equal a certain number.* **Today, you'll learn how to find every factor pair for a number.**

To find all the factor pairs of 24, we'll check every number from 1 to 9 to see if it's a factor of 24. We'll use this list to make sure we check every number.

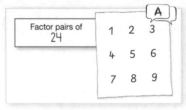

Use the following questions to help your child find all factor pairs for 24.

- **Is 1 a factor of 24?** *Yes.* **What is the other number in the factor pair?** *24.* Write "1 × 24." Cross out 1 in the chart.
- **Is 2 a factor of 24?** *Yes.* **What is the other number in the factor pair?** *12.* Write "2 × 12." Cross out 2 in the chart. If your child has trouble finding the matching factor for 2, suggest she split 24 in half. **12 plus 12 equals 24, so 2 times 12 equals 24.**
- **Is 3 a factor of 24?** *Yes.* **What is the other number in the factor pair?** *8.* Write "3 × 8." Cross out both 3 and 8 in the chart.
- **Is 4 a factor of 24?** *Yes.* **What is the other number in the factor pair?** *6.* Write "4 × 6." Cross out both 4 and 6 in the chart.
- **Is 5 a factor of 24?** *No.* **How do you know?** *Sample answer: 24 doesn't have a 5 or 0 in the ones-place, so it's not divisible by 5.* Cross out 5 in the chart.
- **We've already found that 6 is a factor of 24.**
- **Is 7 a factor of 24?** *No.* **How do you know?** *Sample answer: 7 times 3 equals 21 and 7 times 4 equals 28, so 24 isn't a multiple of 7.* Cross out 7 in the chart.
- **We've already found that 8 is a factor of 24.**
- **Is 9 a factor of 24?** *No.* **How do you know?** *Sample answer: 24 divided by 9 has a remainder, so 24 isn't divisible by 9.* Cross out 9 in the chart.

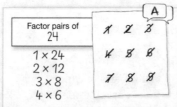

If your child has trouble finding any of the matching factors, frame the problem as a division problem instead. For example, to find the matching factor for 3: **We want to know 3 times what equals 24. So, you can divide 24 by 3 to find the matching factor. What's 24 divided by 3?** *8.*

Find all the factors of 30 in the same way.

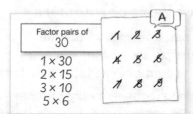

Checking the numbers from 1 to 9 only ensures that you've found every factor if your target number is less than 100. Your child will learn strategies for finding factors for numbers greater than or equal to 100 in future grades.

Activity (B): Play Factor Blast

Play Factor Blast.

Factor Blast

Materials: 2 dice

Object of the Game: Score more points than the other player.

Factor Blast has 3 rounds. On your turn, roll 2 dice and add to find their sum. Find the matching number on the game board and write this number in the first column on your score card. Find all the factor pairs of the number and write them in the second column. Add the factors together and write this total in the third column. This sum is your score for the round.

For example, if you roll a 2 and 1, the matching number is 28. The factor pairs of 28 are 1 × 28, 2 × 14, and 4 × 7. The sum of the factors (1 + 28 + 2 + 14 + 4 + 7) is 56, so you score 56 points.

Number	Factor Pairs	Sum of Factors
28	1 × 28 2 × 14 4 × 7	56

Each factor only counts once in the sum. So, if your number is 25, the factor pairs are 1 × 25 and 5 × 5. The factors of 25 are 1, 25, and 5, so the total of the factors is 31. You do not count the 5 twice.

If you roll a number that has already been used, roll again. You may need to roll again several times until you roll a number that hasn't been used.

Take turns until you have completed 3 rounds. Each player finds their total number of points. Whoever has the greater total wins.

Independent Practice and Review

Have your child complete the Lesson 1.9 Practice and Review workbook pages.

The workbook pages occasionally include optional starred problems. These problems provide extra challenge and give your child the chance to stretch her skills. If your child struggles with the starred problems or feels frustrated by them, feel free to skip them.

Lesson 1.10
Prime and Composite Numbers

Purpose	Materials
• Practice memory work • Introduce prime and composite numbers	• Memory Work (Blackline Master 1) • Playing cards

Warm-up: Practice Memory Work

Have your child read aloud the memory work listed under "Geometry" on Blackline Master 1. (Or, read it aloud to him.) Then, use the following questions to quiz him on the information. Allow him to peek at the list as needed.

- **What do we call an angle that looks like the corner of a piece of paper?** *A right angle.*
- **What do we call a quadrilateral with 4 right angles?** *A rectangle.*
- **What do we call a quadrilateral with 4 right angles and 4 equal sides?** *A square.*
- **What do we call a quadrilateral with 4 equal sides?** *A rhombus.*

Activity (A): Identify Prime and Composite Numbers

In this unit, you've seen that some numbers have many factors, but other numbers only have a few. Mathematicians have special names for numbers depending on how many factors they have.

Read aloud the first definition: *Prime numbers have exactly 2 factors: 1 and the number itself.* 2, 5 and 19 each have exactly 2 factors, so they're all examples of prime numbers.

Read aloud the second definition: *Composite numbers have more than 2 factors.* 4, 12, and 21 each have more than 2 factors, so they're all examples of composite numbers.

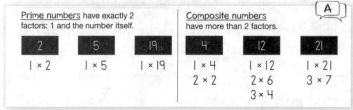

Let's see how many of the numbers up to 20 are prime. We'll go through each number to check.

What are the factors of 1? *Just 1!* **1 only has 1 factor. Prime numbers must have exactly 2 factors, and composite numbers must have more than 2 factors. 1 is an unusual number because it's not prime or composite.** Cross out 1 on the chart.

What are the factors of 2? *1 and 2.* **2 has exactly 2 factors, so it's prime.** Circle 2 on the chart.

Continue with the rest of the numbers in the chart. Encourage your child to use the multiplication facts, division facts, and divisibility rules to decide whether each number is prime or composite.

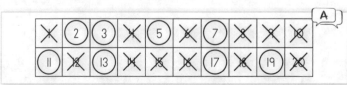

Once your child finishes, ask: **Are the prime numbers mostly odd or even?** *Odd.* **Why do you think the prime numbers are mostly odd?** *Sample answer: Even numbers always have 2 as a factor.* **2 is the only even prime number! Even numbers are divisible by 2, so all the even numbers greater than 2 have more than 2 factors.**

Activity (B): Play Number Knock-Out

Play Number Knock-Out. Encourage your child to use the multiplication facts, division facts, and divisibility rules to decide whether each number is prime or composite.

> If your child isn't sure whether a number is prime, allow him to use the multiplication chart (Blackline Master 2) to check. For example, 37 doesn't appear in the multiplication chart. That means it doesn't have any factors less than 10 (other than 1), so it must be prime.

Number Knock-Out

Materials: Deck of playing cards

Object of the Game: Cross out all the numbers on your gameboard before your opponent.

Shuffle the cards and place them face down in a pile. Choose who will go first. Each player chooses a gameboard.

On your turn, flip over a card. If the card is red, cross out a composite number on your game board. If the card is black, cross out a prime number on your game board. (It doesn't matter what number is on the card.)

If you flip over a card and can't cross out a number, play passes to the other player.

Take turns until one player crosses out all the numbers on their game board.

Cooperative Version: Play together (on one game board) and count how many cards you have to flip over before crossing out all the numbers. Then, play together again (on the other game board) and see if you can flip over fewer cards before crossing out all the numbers.

Independent Practice and Review

Have your child complete the Lesson 1.10 Practice and Review workbook pages.

Lesson 1.11
Enrichment (Optional)

Purpose	Materials
• Practice memory work • Appreciate the many ways math is used in real life • Use factor pairs to divide brownies into equal pieces • Summarize what your child has learned and assess your child's progress	• *I'm Trying to Love Math*, written and illustrated by Bethany Barton • 4 sheets of paper • Pan of brownies or sheet cake, optional

The final lesson in each unit is an optional enrichment lesson. The purpose of these enrichment lessons is to help your child enjoy math, develop a positive attitude toward math, and appreciate how math is used in everyday life. Feel free to adapt the enrichment activity directions to fit your family. Simplify them if you're short on time, or use different materials if you don't have the exact items listed. Or, if your child is particularly excited about a project, make the project more elaborate and spend more time on it.

Warm-up: Review Memory Work

Quiz your child on any of the memory work items that she struggled with during this unit.

Math Picture Book: *I'm Trying to Love Math*

Read *I'm Trying to Love Math*, written and illustrated by Bethany Barton. As you read, discuss the many ways math is used in real life. Encourage your child to think of more examples of math in her own life.

Enrichment Activity: How Should We Cut the Brownies?

Knowing factor pairs helps when you want to cut brownies or a cake into equal pieces. The factor pairs tell you how many rows and columns to make.

Let's pretend we have a rectangular pan of brownies, and we want 24 brownies. What's one factor pair that equals 24? *Possible answers: 1 × 24, 2 × 12, 3 × 8, and 4 × 6.* Have your child draw lines on a sheet of paper to show how she could cut the brownies into the matching number of rows and columns. For example, if she chooses 3 × 8, help her draw lines to divide the paper into 3 rows and 8 columns:

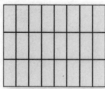

Repeat for the other possible factor pairs for 24.

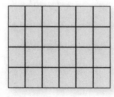

6 × 4

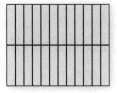

2 × 12

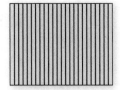

1 × 24

Once your child completes the drawings, discuss which method is most practical. For example: **I think the brownies in the 1 × 24 array would be so skinny that they'd fall apart! I'd rather have a brownie from the 6 × 4 or 3 × 8 array.**

If you have brownies or a sheet cake on hand, have your child use one of the factor pairs to help you cut the treat into 24 equal pieces.

Unit Wrap-Up

Have your child complete the Unit 1 Wrap-Up.

The final lesson in each unit includes an optional Unit Wrap-Up in the Student Workbook. You can use the Unit Wrap-Ups to informally review the material from the unit. Or, you can use them as tests to assess your child's progress more formally. (If you live in a state where you're required to provide evidence of learning, you may want to save them for your child's portfolio.) The Unit Wrap-Ups are completely optional, but children (and parents!) often find it very satisfying to see this concrete evidence of learning and growth.

Unit 1 Answer Key

1.1 Practice

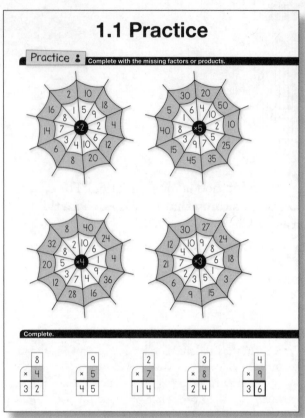

Practice 👤 Complete with the missing factors or products.

Complete.

	8			9			2			3			4	
×	4		×	5		×	7		×	8		×	9	
3	2		4	5		1	4		2	4		3	6	

1.1 Review

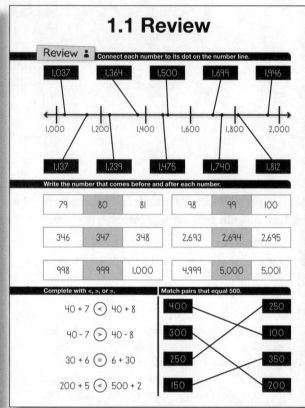

Review 👤 Connect each number to its dot on the number line.

Write the number that comes before and after each number.

79	80	81		98	99	100

346	347	348		2,693	2,694	2,695

998	999	1,000		4,999	5,000	5,001

Complete with <, >, or =.

$40 + 7 \; (<) \; 40 + 8$

$40 - 7 \; (>) \; 40 - 8$

$30 + 6 \; (=) \; 6 + 30$

$200 + 5 \; (<) \; 500 + 2$

Match pairs that equal 500.

1.2 Practice

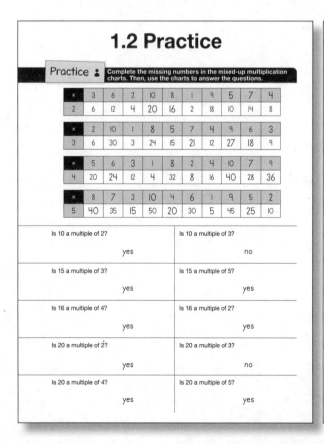

Practice 👤 Complete the missing numbers in the mixed-up multiplication charts. Then, use the charts to answer the questions.

×	3	6	2	10	8	1	9	5	7	4
2	6	12	4	20	16	2	18	10	14	8

×	2	10	1	8	5	7	4	9	6	3
3	6	30	3	24	15	21	12	27	18	9

×	5	6	3	1	8	2	4	10	7	9
4	20	24	12	4	32	8	16	40	28	36

×	8	7	3	10	4	6	1	9	5	2
5	40	35	15	50	20	30	5	45	25	10

Is 10 a multiple of 2?	Is 10 a multiple of 3?
yes	no
Is 15 a multiple of 3?	Is 15 a multiple of 5?
yes	yes
Is 16 a multiple of 4?	Is 16 a multiple of 2?
yes	yes
Is 20 a multiple of 2?	Is 20 a multiple of 3?
yes	no
Is 20 a multiple of 4?	Is 20 a multiple of 5?
yes	yes

1.2 Review

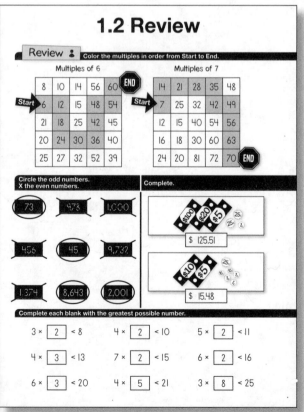

Review 👤 Color the multiples in order from Start to End.

Multiples of 6   Multiples of 7

Circle the odd numbers. X the even numbers.

73   473   1,000

456   45   9,732

1,374   8,643   2,001

Complete.

$ 125.51

$ 15.48

Complete each blank with the greatest possible number.

$3 × \boxed{2} < 8$ $4 × \boxed{2} < 10$ $5 × \boxed{2} < 11$

$4 × \boxed{3} < 13$ $7 × \boxed{2} < 15$ $6 × \boxed{2} < 16$

$6 × \boxed{3} < 20$ $4 × \boxed{5} < 21$ $3 × \boxed{8} < 25$

Unit 1 Answer Key

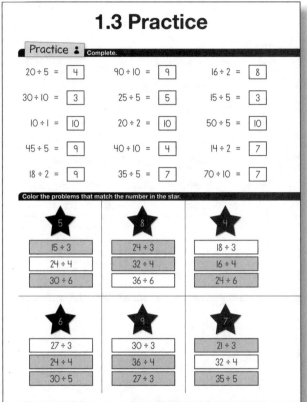

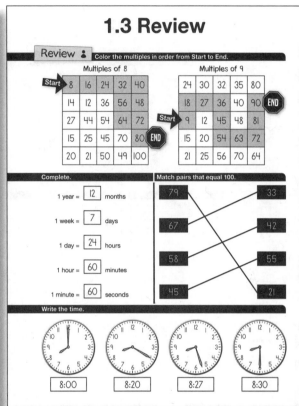

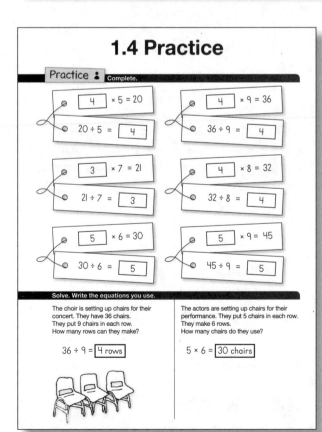

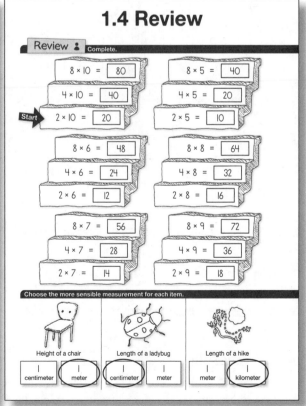

Unit 1 Answer Key

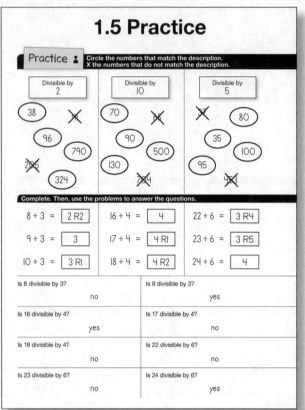

1.5 Practice

Practice 👤 Circle the numbers that match the description.
X the numbers that do not match the description.

Divisible by 2	Divisible by 10	Divisible by 5
(38) ✗	(70) ✗	✗ (80)
(96) (790)	(90) (500)	(35) (100)
✗ 205	(130) ✗ 24	(95) ✗ 43
(324)		

Complete. Then, use the problems to answer the questions.

$8 \div 3 =$	2 R2	$16 \div 4 =$	4	$22 \div 6 =$	3 R4
$9 \div 3 =$	3	$17 \div 4 =$	4 R1	$23 \div 6 =$	3 R5
$10 \div 3 =$	3 R1	$18 \div 4 =$	4 R2	$24 \div 6 =$	4

Is 8 divisible by 3?	Is 9 divisible by 3?
no	yes

Is 16 divisible by 4?	Is 17 divisible by 4?
yes	no

Is 18 divisible by 4?	Is 22 divisible by 6?
no	no

Is 23 divisible by 6?	Is 24 divisible by 6?
no	yes

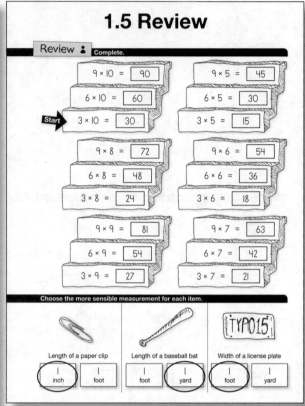

1.5 Review

Review 👤 Complete.

$9 \times 10 =$ 90	$9 \times 5 =$ 45
$6 \times 10 =$ 60	$6 \times 5 =$ 30
Start $3 \times 10 =$ 30	$3 \times 5 =$ 15
$9 \times 8 =$ 72	$9 \times 6 =$ 54
$6 \times 8 =$ 48	$6 \times 6 =$ 36
$3 \times 8 =$ 24	$3 \times 6 =$ 18
$9 \times 9 =$ 81	$9 \times 7 =$ 63
$6 \times 9 =$ 54	$6 \times 7 =$ 42
$3 \times 9 =$ 27	$3 \times 7 =$ 21

Choose the more sensible measurement for each item.

Length of a paper clip	Length of a baseball bat	Width of a license plate
(inch) / foot	foot / (yard)	(foot) / yard

TYPO15

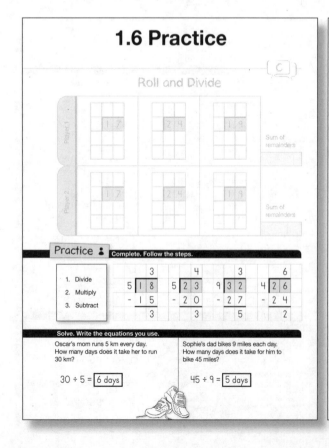

1.6 Practice

Roll and Divide

Player 1: 1 7   2 4   1 9

Sum of remainders

Player 2: 1 7   2 4   1 9

Sum of remainders

Practice 👤 Complete. Follow the steps.

1. Divide
2. Multiply
3. Subtract

3	4	3	6
5) 1 8	5) 2 3	9) 3 2	4) 2 6
− 1 5	− 2 0	− 2 7	− 2 4
3	3	5	2

Solve. Write the equations you use.

Oscar's mom runs 5 km every day. How many days does it take her to run 30 km?

$30 \div 5 =$ 6 days

Sophie's dad bikes 9 miles each day. How many days does it take for him to bike 45 miles?

$45 \div 9 =$ 5 days

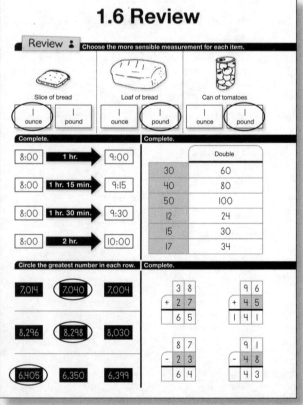

1.6 Review

Review 👤 Choose the more sensible measurement for each item.

Slice of bread	Loaf of bread	Can of tomatoes
(ounce) / pound	ounce / (pound)	ounce / (pound)

Complete.

8:00 → 1 hr.	9:00
8:00 → 1 hr. 15 min.	9:15
8:00 → 1 hr. 30 min.	9:30
8:00 → 2 hr.	10:00

Complete.

	Double
30	60
40	80
50	100
12	24
15	30
17	34

Circle the greatest number in each row.

7,014	(7,040)	7,004
8,296	(8,298)	8,030
(6,405)	6,350	6,399

Complete.

	3 8		9 6
+	2 7	+	4 5
	6 5		1 4 1

	8 7		9 1
−	2 3	−	4 8
	6 4		4 3

Unit 1 Answer Key

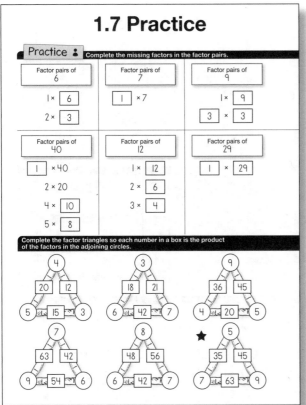

1.7 Practice

Practice 👤 Complete the missing factors in the factor pairs.

Factor pairs of 6	Factor pairs of 7	Factor pairs of 9
1 × **6**	**1** × 7	1 × **9**
2 × **3**		**3** × **3**

Factor pairs of 40	Factor pairs of 12	Factor pairs of 29
1 × 40	1 × **12**	**1** × **29**
2 × 20	2 × **6**	
4 × **10**	3 × **4**	
5 × **8**		

Complete the factor triangles so each number in a box is the product of the factors in the adjoining circles.

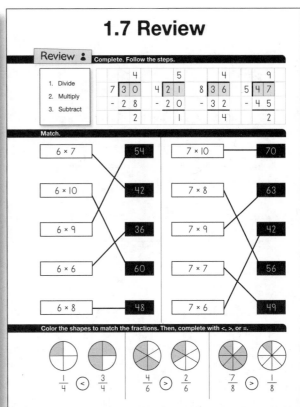

1.7 Review

Review 👤 Complete. Follow the steps.

1. Divide
2. Multiply
3. Subtract

	4	5	4	9
	7 ⟌ 3 0	4 ⟌ 2 1	8 ⟌ 3 6	5 ⟌ 4 7
	− 2 8	− 2 0	− 3 2	− 4 5
	2	1	4	2

Match.

6 × 7 — 54
6 × 10 — 42
6 × 9 — 36
6 × 6 — 60
6 × 8 — 48

7 × 10 — 70
7 × 8 — 63
7 × 9 — 42
7 × 7 — 56
7 × 6 — 49

Color the shapes to match the fractions. Then, complete with <, >, or =.

$\frac{1}{4}$ **<** $\frac{3}{4}$ $\frac{4}{6}$ **>** $\frac{2}{6}$ $\frac{7}{8}$ **>** $\frac{1}{8}$

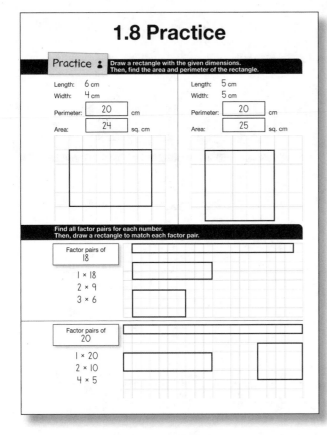

1.8 Practice

Practice 👤 Draw a rectangle with the given dimensions. Then, find the area and perimeter of the rectangle.

Length: 6 cm
Width: 4 cm
Perimeter: **20** cm
Area: **24** sq. cm

Length: 5 cm
Width: 5 cm
Perimeter: **20** cm
Area: **25** sq. cm

Find all factor pairs for each number. Then, draw a rectangle to match each factor pair.

Factor pairs of 18
1 × 18
2 × 9
3 × 6

Factor pairs of 20
1 × 20
2 × 10
4 × 5

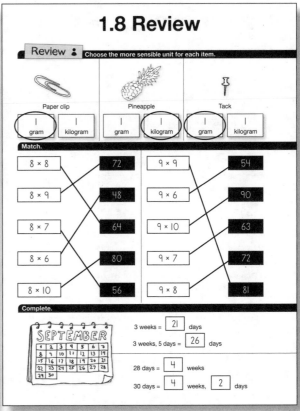

1.8 Review

Review 👤 Choose the more sensible unit for each item.

Paper clip — (gram) | kilogram
Pineapple — gram | (kilogram)
Tack — (gram) | kilogram

Match.

8 × 8 — 72
8 × 9 — 48
8 × 7 — 64
8 × 6 — 80
8 × 10 — 56

9 × 9 — 54
9 × 6 — 90
9 × 10 — 63
9 × 7 — 72
9 × 8 — 81

Complete.

3 weeks = **21** days
3 weeks, 5 days = **26** days
28 days = **4** weeks
30 days = **4** weeks, **2** days

Unit 1 Answer Key

1.9 Practice

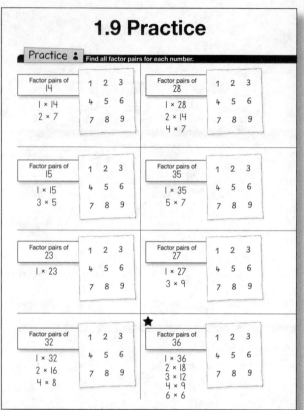

Practice — Find all factor pairs for each number.

Factor pairs of **14**
1 × 14
2 × 7
| 1 2 3 | 4 5 6 | 7 8 9 |

Factor pairs of **28**
1 × 28
2 × 14
4 × 7
| 1 2 3 | 4 5 6 | 7 8 9 |

Factor pairs of **15**
1 × 15
3 × 5
| 1 2 3 | 4 5 6 | 7 8 9 |

Factor pairs of **35**
1 × 35
5 × 7
| 1 2 3 | 4 5 6 | 7 8 9 |

Factor pairs of **23**
1 × 23
| 1 2 3 | 4 5 6 | 7 8 9 |

Factor pairs of **27**
1 × 27
3 × 9
| 1 2 3 | 4 5 6 | 7 8 9 |

Factor pairs of **32**
1 × 32
2 × 16
4 × 8
| 1 2 3 | 4 5 6 | 7 8 9 |

★ Factor pairs of **36**
1 × 36
2 × 18
3 × 12
4 × 9
6 × 6
| 1 2 3 | 4 5 6 | 7 8 9 |

1.9 Review

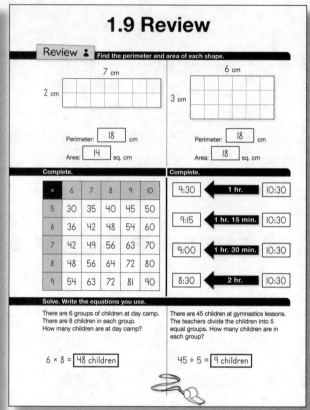

Review — Find the perimeter and area of each shape.

7 cm, 2 cm
Perimeter: 18 cm
Area: 14 sq. cm

6 cm, 3 cm
Perimeter: 18 cm
Area: 18 sq. cm

Complete.

×	6	7	8	9	10
5	30	35	40	45	50
6	36	42	48	54	60
7	42	49	56	63	70
8	48	56	64	72	80
9	54	63	72	81	90

9:30 ← 1 hr. → 10:30
9:15 ← 1 hr. 15 min. → 10:30
9:00 ← 1 hr. 30 min. → 10:30
8:30 ← 2 hr. → 10:30

Solve. Write the equations you use.

There are 6 groups of children at day camp. There are 8 children in each group. How many children are at day camp?

6 × 8 = 48 children

There are 45 children at gymnastics lessons. The teachers divide the children into 5 equal groups. How many children are in each group?

45 ÷ 5 = 9 children

1.10 Practice

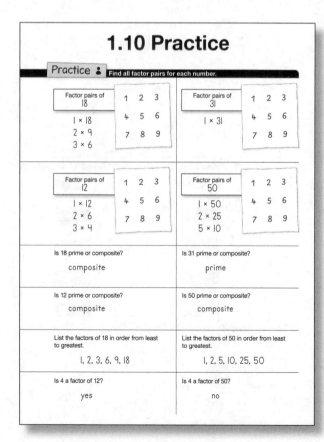

Practice — Find all factor pairs for each number.

Factor pairs of **18**
1 × 18
2 × 9
3 × 6
| 1 2 3 | 4 5 6 | 7 8 9 |

Factor pairs of **31**
1 × 31
| 1 2 3 | 4 5 6 | 7 8 9 |

Factor pairs of **12**
1 × 12
2 × 6
3 × 4
| 1 2 3 | 4 5 6 | 7 8 9 |

Factor pairs of **50**
1 × 50
2 × 25
5 × 10
| 1 2 3 | 4 5 6 | 7 8 9 |

Is 18 prime or composite?
composite

Is 31 prime or composite?
prime

Is 12 prime or composite?
composite

Is 50 prime or composite?
composite

List the factors of 18 in order from least to greatest.
1, 2, 3, 6, 9, 18

List the factors of 50 in order from least to greatest.
1, 2, 5, 10, 25, 50

Is 4 a factor of 12?
yes

Is 4 a factor of 50?
no

1.10 Review

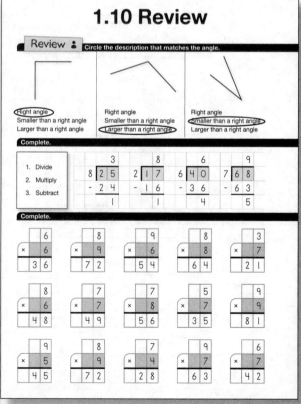

Review — Circle the description that matches the angle.

Right angle (circled)
Smaller than a right angle
Larger than a right angle

Right angle
Smaller than a right angle
Larger than a right angle (circled)

Right angle
Smaller than a right angle (circled)
Larger than a right angle

Complete.

1. Divide
2. Multiply
3. Subtract

3
8) 2 5
− 2 4
1

8
2) 1 7
− 1 6
1

6
6) 4 0
− 3 6
4

9
7) 6 8
− 6 3
5

Complete.

× 6 / 6 = 3 6
× 8 / 9 = 7 2
× 9 / 6 = 5 4
× 8 / 8 = 6 4
× 3 / 7 = 2 1

× 8 / 6 = 4 8
× 7 / 7 = 4 9
× 7 / 8 = 5 6
× 5 / 7 = 3 5
× 9 / 9 = 8 1

× 9 / 5 = 4 5
× 8 / 9 = 7 2
× 7 / 4 = 2 8
× 9 / 7 = 6 3
× 6 / 7 = 4 2

Unit 1 Answer Key

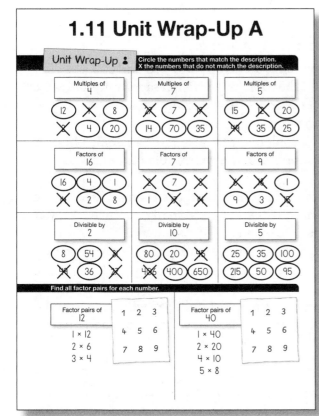

1.11 Unit Wrap-Up A

Unit Wrap-Up 👤 Circle the numbers that match the description.
X the numbers that do not match the description.

Multiples of 4	Multiples of 7	Multiples of 5
⑫ ✗ ⑧	✗ ⑦ ✗	⑮ ✗ ⑳
✗ ④ ⑳	⑭ ⑦⓪ ③⑤	✗ ③⑤ ②⑤

Factors of 16	Factors of 7	Factors of 9
⑯ ④ ①	✗ ⑦ ✗	✗ ✗ ①
✗ ② ⑧	① ✗ ✗	⑨ ③ ✗

Divisible by 2	Divisible by 10	Divisible by 5
⑧ ⑤④ ✗	⑧⓪ ②⓪ ✗	②⑤ ③⑤ ①⓪⓪
✗ ③⑥ ✗	✗ ④⓪⓪ ⑥⑤⓪	②①⑤ ⑤⓪ ⑨⑤

Find all factor pairs for each number.

Factor pairs of 12	1 2 3
1 × 12	4 5 6
2 × 6	7 8 9
3 × 4	

Factor pairs of 40	1 2 3
1 × 40	4 5 6
2 × 20	7 8 9
4 × 10	
5 × 8	

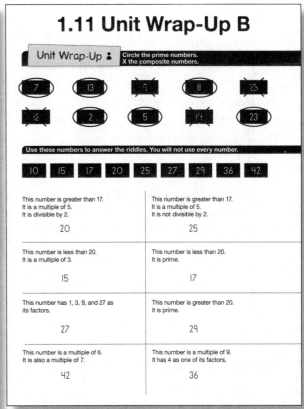

1.11 Unit Wrap-Up B

Unit Wrap-Up 👤 Circle the prime numbers.
X the composite numbers.

⑦ ⑬ ✗ ⑪ ✗

✗ ② ⑤ ✗ ㉓

Use these numbers to answer the riddles. You will not use every number.

| 10 | 15 | 17 | 20 | 25 | 27 | 29 | 36 | 42 |

This number is greater than 17. It is a multiple of 5. It is divisible by 2.	This number is greater than 17. It is a multiple of 5. It is not divisible by 2.
20	25
This number is less than 20. It is a multiple of 3.	This number is less than 20. It is prime.
15	17
This number has 1, 3, 9, and 27 as its factors.	This number is greater than 20. It is prime.
27	29
This number is a multiple of 6. It is also a multiple of 7.	This number is a multiple of 9. It has 4 as one of its factors.
42	36

Unit 1 Checkpoint

What to Expect at the End of Unit 1

By the end of Unit 1, most children will be able to do the following:

- Find answers for the multiplication and division facts (up to 10 × 10 and 100 ÷ 10). Many children will know most of the multiplication and division facts automatically. Many will still need to pause to figure out the more-challenging facts.
- Solve one-step multiplication and division word problems.
- Use long division to solve simple division problems with a remainder. Some children will still need to model the problems with counters or have trouble remembering the steps.
- Use the terms *factor*, *multiple*, and *divisibility* in context and use them to describe relationships between numbers. Some children will still occasionally confuse factor and multiple and need to be reminded of their definitions.
- Know the divisibility rules for 2, 5, and 10 and tell whether a number is divisible by 2, 5, or 10.
- Find all factor pairs for a given number.
- Tell whether a given number is prime or composite. Most children will understand the difference between types of numbers, but many will still be working on memorizing the two terms.

Is Your Child Ready to Move on?

In Unit 2, your child will learn to read, write, compare, add, and subtract numbers to 1,000,000. She'll also learn how to round large numbers and identify them on the number line.

Before moving on to Unit 2, your child should be **mostly fluent at adding and subtracting four-digit numbers with the addition and subtraction algorithms**. It's fine if she sometimes has trouble remembering a few of the addition or subtraction facts or forgets one of the steps.

Your child will continue to practice the multiplication facts (and the other skills she learned in Unit 1) in the Review pages. **She does not need to have fully mastered the multiplication facts or the other Unit 1 skills before moving on to Unit 2.**

What to Do If Your Child Needs More Practice

If your child needs more practice adding and subtracting four-digit numbers, make up a four-digit addition problem and a four-digit subtraction problem for her to solve at the beginning of the lessons in Unit 2. Make sure to include problems that require trading.

Unit 2
Place Value and Large Numbers

Overview

In this unit, your child will learn how to read, write, and compare numbers up to one million. He'll develop number sense with these large numbers as he writes them in expanded form, approximates their positions on the number line, and rounds them to any place. He'll also learn to extend his addition and subtraction skills to larger numbers.

What Your Child Will Learn

In this unit, your child will learn to:

- Read, write, and compare numbers to one million
- Understand place value to the millions-place and write large numbers in expanded form
- Round three- and four-digit numbers to any place
- Round large numbers to the nearest thousand
- Use place-value thinking to mentally add and subtract thousands
- Use the addition and subtraction algorithms to add and subtract five- and six-digit numbers
- Solve multi-step addition and subtraction word problems with large numbers

Lesson List

Lesson 2.1	Review Place Value and Mental Math	Lesson 2.6	Round Large Numbers to the Nearest Thousand
Lesson 2.2	Round Three-Digit Numbers to Any Place	Lesson 2.7	Mental Math with Large Numbers
Lesson 2.3	Round Four-Digit Numbers to Any Place	Lesson 2.8	Add and Subtract Large Numbers
Lesson 2.4	Place Value to the Millions-Place	Lesson 2.9	Word Problems with Large Numbers
Lesson 2.5	Compare Large Numbers	Lesson 2.10	Enrichment (Optional)

Extra Materials Needed for Unit 2

- 6 dice
- 10 slips of paper
- For optional Enrichment Lesson:
  - × *A Million Dots*, written by Andrew Clements and illustrated by Mike Reed. Atheneum Books for Young Readers, 2006.
  - × Almanac or internet access

Teaching Math with Confidence:
How Commas Help Children Understand Large Numbers

In this unit, your child will learn to read and write numbers with 5 or 6 digits. Throughout the unit, you'll emphasize using the commas to help make sense of these numbers. Although commas are small, they serve an important role in helping children understand large numbers.

First, commas make large numbers easier to read. In five- and six-digit numbers, the digits before the comma tell the number of thousands. So, when reading a five- or six-digit number, you read the part before the comma as one number, say "thousand" when you reach the comma, and then read the part after the comma as one number.

35,720

thirty-five thousand seven hundred twenty

The comma separates the number into 2 chunks: 35 thousands and 720 ones.

Besides making numbers easier to read, commas also help us grasp the magnitude of numbers. The digits before the comma tell the number of thousands, so they're usually the most meaningful. The digits after the comma are less important, because their value is so much less relative to the other digits. This helps us comprehend the overall value of the number without getting distracted by the less-important digits. For example, if you see a house listed at $241,589, you'll probably remember that the house costs a little more than $240,000, even if you can't remember every digit.

For Sale
$241,589

The digits before the comma tell that there are 241 thousands in the number.
The digits after the comma tell that there are 589 ones in the number.

As you teach this unit, make sure to emphasize the role of the comma to help your child develop deep number sense with the numbers to one million.

Lesson 2.1
Review Place Value and Mental Math

Purpose	Materials
• Review writing numbers in expanded form • Review mental addition and subtraction with hundreds	• 2 decks of cards

Memory Work	• **What is a prime number?** *A number with exactly 2 factors.* • **What is a composite number?** *A number with more than 2 factors.*

This lesson reviews writing four-digit numbers in expanded form and mental addition and subtraction with hundreds. If your child is very comfortable with these skills, do a quick review and then combine this lesson with Lesson 2.2.

Warm-up (A): Review Writing 4-Digit Numbers in Expanded Form

Show your child the ad in part A. Briefly discuss your child's experiences with any of the vehicles in the ad.

How much does the golf cart cost? *$3,217.* **How many digits are in this number?** *4.* Have your child write 3,217 in the place-value chart.

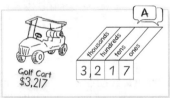

- Point to the 3. **What place is the 3 in?** *The thousands-place.* **What is the value of the 3?** *3,000.*
- Point to the 2. **What place is the 2 in?** *The hundreds-place.* **What is the value of the 2?** *200.*
- Point to the 1. **What place is the 1 in?** *The tens-place.* **What is the value of the 1?** *10.*
- Point to the 7. **What place is the 7 in?** *The ones-place.* **The 7 is in the ones-place so it has a value of 7.**

Point to the comma between the 3 and 2. **Remember, the comma in four-digit numbers separates the thousands-place from the hundreds-place. When we read four-digit numbers, we say "thousand" when we reach the comma.**

Have your child read aloud the other prices and write them in the place-value chart.

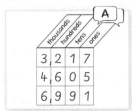

The usual way we write numbers is called *standard form.* **When you stretch the number to show the value of each digit, you write the number in** *expanded form.*

Point to the first line of the chart. **Here's how we write 3,217 in expanded form.** Have your child write the other prices in expanded form. If she has trouble, have her first identify the value of each digit.

Standard Form	Expanded Form
3,217	3,000 + 200 + 10 + 7
4,605	4,000 + 600 + 5
6,991	6,000 + 900 + 90 + 1

Make sure your child writes the addends in expanded form in the same order as the digits, beginning with the digit with the greatest value. She does not need to write the value of any place-holder zeros. For example, for 4,605, she should write 4,000 + 600 + 5, not 4,000 + 600 + 0 + 5.

Activity (B): Review Mental Math with Hundreds

In younger grades, you learned how place-value thinking makes it easier to solve problems with large numbers in our heads.

Have your child read aloud the addition problem: *600 plus 800.* **What's 6 plus 8?** *14.* Write 14 in the blank. **6 plus 8 equals 14, so 6 hundreds plus 8 hundreds equal 14 hundreds. What does 14 hundreds equal?** *1,400.* If your child's not sure, point out that there are 10 hundreds in 1,000 and 4 hundreds in 400. Write 1,400 in the blank.

600 + 800 = [1,400]

6 + 8 = [14]

Have your child read aloud the subtraction problem: *1,200 minus 300.* **How many hundreds equal 1,200?** *12.* **12 hundreds equal 1,200, so you can think of this problem as 12 hundreds minus 3 hundreds.**

What's 12 minus 3? *9.* Write 9 in the blank. **12 minus 3 equals 9, so 12 hundreds minus 3 hundreds equals 9 hundreds.** Write 900 in the blank.

1,200 - 300 = [900]

12 - 3 = [9]

Activity (C): Play Close to 3,000

We're going to play a game called Close to 3,000. I'll show you a sample hand before we play.

In this game, each number card counts for the matching number of hundreds. Aces count for 100. You take 5 cards and find their sum. Place a 7, 4, ace, 10, and 6 from a deck of playing cards on the table. (Any suit is fine.)

What's the value of each card? *700, 400, 100, 1,000, and 600.* **What's the sum of all 5 cards?** *2,800.* Your child may add the cards in order or look for pairs that equal 1,000 (like 400 and 600) to make the mental addition easier.

When we play, we'll each find the sum of our cards. Then, whoever is closer to 3,000 wins a point. How close to 3,000 is 2,800? *200.* **That's a pretty good hand!**

If your child isn't sure, suggest she add up to find the difference: **2,800 plus what equals 3,000?** *200.*

Play Close to 3,000.

Close to 3,000

Materials: 2 decks of playing cards, with jacks, queens, and kings removed (80 cards total).

Object of the Game: Score more points than the other player by creating sums as close to 3,000 as possible.

Shuffle the cards and place the stack face down on the table.

On your turn, take 5 cards off the top of the deck. Each card has the value of the matching number of hundreds. For example, a 7 has a value of 700, or a 10 has a value of 1,000 (10 hundreds). Aces have a value of 100.

Mentally find the sum of your 5 cards and record the sum in the scorecard. For example, if you turn over a 9, 4, 7, ace, and 10, your sum is 3,100 (900 + 400 + 700 + 100 + 1,000).

Play then passes to the other player. Whoever is closer to 3,000 wins a point for the round. If both players are equally close to 3,000, both players win a point.

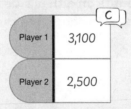

Player 1's total is closer to 3,000, so Player 1 wins the round.

Continue until both players have completed their score cards. Add up each player's total points. The player with more points wins.

Independent Practice and Review

Have your child complete the Lesson 2.1 Practice and Review workbook pages.

Lesson 2.2
Round Three-Digit Numbers to Any Place

Purpose	Materials
• Practice rounding two-digit numbers to the nearest ten • Round three-digit numbers to the nearest hundred or ten	• Counters

Memory Work	• **Name 4 factors of 18.** *Possible answers: 1, 2, 3, 6, 9, 18.* • **Name 4 multiples of 6.** *Sample answers: 6, 30, 42, 60.*

Warm-up: Round Two-Digit Numbers to the Nearest Ten

Have your child round the following numbers to the nearest ten.

- **38.** *40.*
- **62.** *60.*
- **19.** *20.*
- **84.** *80.*

- **65.** *70.* If needed, remind your child that numbers with a 5 in the ones-place round up to the next ten.
- **97.** *100.*

Activity (A): Round Three-Digit Numbers to the Nearest Hundred or Ten

In everyday conversation, we often round numbers instead of telling exact amounts. Last year, you learned how to round three-digit numbers to the nearest hundred. Today, we'll review rounding to the nearest hundred, and you'll learn how to round to the nearest ten.

Point to the first approximately-equal sign (≈). **This symbol is called the approximately-equal sign. It means that the amounts on either side of it are roughly equal to each other. We'll use it when we round numbers to show that the numbers are approximately equal to each other.**

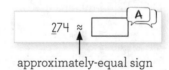

approximately-equal sign

First, we'll round 274 to the nearest hundred. The hundreds-place in 274 is underlined to show what place we're rounding to.

When we say the "nearest hundred," we mean the multiples of 100. They're the numbers that we say when we count by 100s. 274 is between 200 and 300, so this number line goes from 200 to 300. About where does 274 go on this number line? *Child points to approximate position shown below.* **Draw a dot at this position. Is 274 closer to 200 or 300?** *300.* **Write 300 in the blank.**

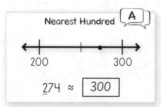

If your child isn't sure, point to the tick mark for 250 (halfway between 200 and 300): **274 is more than 250, so it's closer to 300 than 200.**

Next, we'll round 274 to the nearest ten. When we say the "nearest ten," we mean the multiples of 10, or the numbers we say when we count by 10s.

274 is between 270 and 280, so the next number line goes from 270 to 280. It's like we zoomed in on the first number line. About where does 274 go on this number line? *Child points to approximate position shown below.* **Draw a dot at this position. Is 274 closer to 270 or 280?** *270.* **Write 270 in the blank.**

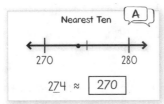

Show your child the next exercise. **The digit in the hundreds-place is underlined, so we will round 445 to the hundreds-place. First, let's label the number line. 445 is between what multiples of 100?** *400 and 500.* **Write 400 and 500 below the tick marks on the number line.** Then, have him draw a dot for 445 on the number line. **Is 445 closer to 400 or 500?** *400.* **Write 400 in the blank.**

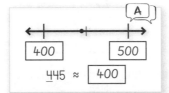

If your child has trouble labeling the number line, say: **To find the lower multiple of 100, imagine that all the digits after the hundreds-place are zeros. What number would you have?** *400.* **To find the higher multiple of 100, add 400 plus 100. What's 400 plus 100?** *500.*

Show your child the next exercise. **The digit in the tens-place is underlined, so this time we'll round 445 to the tens-place. First, let's label the number line. 445 is between what multiples of 10?** *440 and 450.* **Write 440 and 450 below the tick marks on the number line.** Then, have him draw a dot for 445 on the number line.

Is 445 closer to 440 or 450? *It's exactly in between.* **Remember, mathematicians have agreed that we round up when a number is exactly halfway between the two numbers. So, we round 445 up to 450. Write 450 in the blank.**

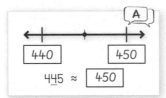

If your child has trouble labeling the number line, say: **To find the lower multiple of ten, imagine that all the digits after the tens-place are zeros. What number would you have?** *440.* **To find the higher multiple of ten, add 440 plus 10. What's 440 plus 10?** *450.*

Repeat with the final two exercises. After your child completes the exercises, point out that both have the same answer. **900 is both a multiple of 10 and a multiple of 100. Sometimes, the nearest ten is also the nearest hundred!**

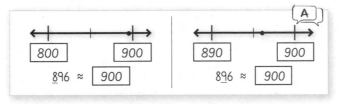

Activity (B): Play Rounding Four in a Row

Play Rounding Four in a Row.

Rounding Four in a Row

Materials: 12 counters per player, with a different color for each player

Object of the Game: Be the first player to place counters in 4 squares in a row, either horizontally, vertically, or diagonally.

On your turn, choose a number with an underlined digit on the board (in one of the darker boxes). Round the number to the underlined digit and find the rounded number (in one of the lighter boxes). Use 2 counters to cover both boxes. For example, if you choose 214, cover both the box with 214 and the box with 210.

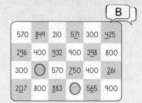

Play then passes to the other player. Continue until one player covers 4 boxes in a row, either horizontally, vertically, or diagonally.

Independent Practice and Review

Have your child complete the Lesson 2.2 Practice and Review workbook pages. If your child has trouble with any of the rounding exercises, have him draw a simple number line as on the Lesson Activities page.

Lesson 2.3
Round Four-Digit Numbers to Any Place

Purpose	Materials
• Practice counting by tens, hundreds, or thousands • Round four-digit numbers to the nearest thousand, hundred, or ten	• Counters • Die

Memory Work	
	• **How do you know if a number is divisible by 2?** *It is even. It has 0, 2, 4, 6, or 8 in the ones-place.* • **How do you know if a number is divisible by 5?** *It has a 0 or 5 in the ones-place.* • **How do you know if a number is divisible by 10?** *It has a 0 in the ones-place.*

Warm-up: Practice Counting by Tens, Hundreds, or Thousands

Have your child count by the following numbers:

- **Start at 1,900 and count by tens.** *1,900, 1,910, 1,920...* Stop your child when she reaches 2,000.
- **Start at 3,600 and count by hundreds.** *3,600, 3,700, 3,800...* Stop your child when she reaches 4,600.
- **Start at 1,000 and count by thousands.** *1,000, 2,000, 3,000...* Stop your child when she reaches 10,000.

These counting sequences prepare your child to round four-digit numbers to the nearest ten, hundred, or thousand.

Activity (A): Round Four-Digit Numbers to the Nearest Thousand, Hundred, or Ten on the Number Line

In the last lesson, you learned how to round three-digit numbers to the nearest hundred or ten. Today, you'll learn how to round four-digit numbers to the nearest thousand, hundred, or ten.

Point to the approximately-equal sign (≈). **What do we call this symbol?** *The approximately-equal sign.* **What does it mean?** *The amounts on either side of it are roughly equal to each other.*

First, we'll round 5,371 to the nearest thousand. 5,371 is between what multiples of 1,000? *5,000 and 6,000.* Write 5,000 and 6,000 below the tick marks on the number line. Then, have your child draw a dot for the approximate location of 5,371 on the number line. **Is 5,371 closer to 5,000 or 6,000?** *5,000.* Write 5,000 in the blank.

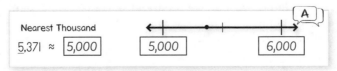

Use the same approach to demonstrate how to round 5,371 to the nearest hundred and nearest ten.

- **5,371 is between what multiples of 100?** *5,300 and 5,400.* Write 5,300 and 5,400 below the tick marks on the number line. **Is 5,371 closer to 5,300 or 5,400?** *5,400.* Write 5,400 in the blank.

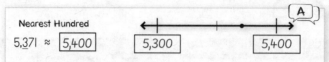

- **5,371 is between what multiples of 10?** *5,370 and 5,380.* Write 5,370 and 5,380 below the tick marks on the number line. **Is 5,371 closer to 5,370 or 5,380?** *5,370.* Write 5,370 in the blank.

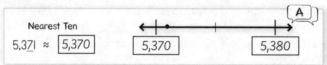

Activity (A): Round Four-Digit Numbers to the Nearest Thousand, Hundred, or Ten without the Number Line

We don't have to draw a number line to round numbers. Instead, we can just look at the digits.

Here's how to round 4,628 to the nearest thousand. I point to the digit that I want to round to. Point to the 4. **Then, I look at the digit in the next-smaller place.** Draw an arrow as shown. **If that digit is less than 5, I round down. If that digit is 5 or greater, I round up.**

The digit in the hundreds-place is a 6, so I round up. I increase the thousands-place by 1 and then write zeros for the smaller places. Write 5,000 in the blank. **4,628 is closer to 5,000 than 4,000.**

$$4{,}628 \approx \boxed{5{,}000}$$

Round 4,628 to the nearest hundred and ten in the same way. To round to the hundreds-place: **There are 2 tens, so I round down. I keep the thousands-place and hundreds-place the same, and then I write zeros for the smaller places.** To round to the tens-place: **There are 8 ones, so I round up. I increase the tens-place by 1 and then write zero for the ones-place.**

$$4{,}628 \approx \boxed{4{,}600}$$
$$4{,}628 \approx \boxed{4{,}630}$$

Have your child round the rest of the numbers in part A in the same way.

$$8{,}409 \approx \boxed{8{,}000} \qquad 6{,}965 \approx \boxed{7{,}000}$$
$$8{,}409 \approx \boxed{8{,}400} \qquad 6{,}965 \approx \boxed{7{,}000}$$
$$8{,}409 \approx \boxed{8{,}410} \qquad 6{,}965 \approx \boxed{6{,}970}$$

If your child has trouble rounding 6,965 to the nearest hundred, say: **There are 6 tens, so we round up. What's 9 increased by 1?** *10.* **10 hundreds equals 1 thousand, so 6,965 rounded to the nearest hundred is 7,000. Sometimes the nearest hundred is also the nearest thousand.** It may also help to draw a simple number line to illustrate.

$$6{,}965 \approx \boxed{7{,}000}$$
6,900   7,000

Activity (B): Play Dice Tic-Tac-Toe

Play Dice Tic-Tac-Toe.

Dice Tic-Tac-Toe

Materials: Die; counters of two different colors

Object of the Game: Be the first player to fill three boxes in a row, either horizontally, vertically, or diagonally.

On your turn, roll the die. Find the column in the game board that matches your roll, and choose a number in that column. Round the number on the gameboard to the underlined place and cover the problem with one of your counters. If you roll a 6, you may choose a problem in any column.

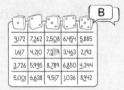

9,172	7,262	2,508	6,454	5,885
1,617	4,210	7,373	3,463	2,193
3,726	5,995	8,789	6,850	4,344
5,001	6,638	9,517	1,036	8,342

Sample play. You may choose any problem in the column that matches your roll.

Play then passes to the other player. Continue until one player covers 3 boxes in a row, either horizontally, vertically, or diagonally.

Note that you only need to place 3 counters in a row to win, even though there are 4 rows and 5 columns on the gameboard. The extra row and columns provide more opportunities to win.

Independent Practice and Review

Have your child complete the Lesson 2.3 Practice and Review workbook pages. If your child has trouble with any of the rounding exercises, have her draw a simple number line as on the Lesson Activities page.

Lesson 2.4
Place Value to the Millions-Place

Purpose	Materials
• Understand that each place in the place-value system is 10 times greater than the next-smaller place • Use a place-value chart to write large numbers • Read large numbers	• None

Memory Work	• **What does perimeter measure?** *The distance around the outside edge of a shape.* • **What does area measure?** *The amount of space that a shape covers.*

Warm-up (A): Review Place Value Relationships

In the last lesson, we reviewed place value in four-digit numbers. Today, you'll learn about place value in numbers up to one million!

Show your child the chart in part A.

- **How many ones equal 1 ten?** *10.*
- **How many tens equal 1 hundred?** *10.*
- **How many hundreds equal 1 thousand?** *10.*

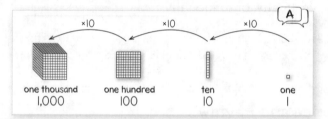

If your child has trouble answering these questions, use base-ten blocks to demonstrate how 10 unit blocks equal 1 rod, 10 rods equal 1 flat, and 10 flats equal 1 large cube.

Why do you think mathematicians sometimes call our place-value system a *base-ten* number system? *Sample answers: It's all based on the number 10. The number 10 is the base of our number system. It's the foundation for place value and for how we read and write numbers. Each place in our number system has 10 times the value of the next-smaller place.*

Activity (B): Use the Place-Value Chart to Write Numbers from Fun Facts

This place-value pattern continues for numbers greater than 1,000 and for numbers less than 1. You'll learn about place value in numbers less than 1 later this year. Today, you'll learn about place value in numbers greater than 1,000.

Show your child the place-value chart in part B. **Each place is 10 times greater than the next-smaller place.**

- Point to the ten-thousands column. **The ten-thousands-place comes after the thousands-place. 10 groups of 1,000 equal 10,000.**
- Point to the hundred-thousands column. **The hundred-thousands-place comes after the ten-thousands-place. 10 groups of 10,000 equal 100,000.**
- Point to the millions column. **The millions-place comes after the hundred-thousands-place. 10 groups of 100,000 equal one million. That's 1,000 thousands!**

I'm going to tell you some fun facts about the world. We'll use the place-value chart to write the numbers.

An adult male elephant usually weighs over 10,000 pounds. Demonstrate how to write 10,000 in the place-value chart. **I write a 1 in the ten-thousands-place, then I write place-holder zeros in the smaller places. Otherwise, the 1 would look like it was in a different place. I write a comma between the thousands and hundreds-place to make the number easier to read.**

A humpback whale weighs around 60,000 pounds. Demonstrate how to write 60,000. **60 equals 6 tens. So, I write a 6 in the ten-thousands-place and zeros in the smaller places.**

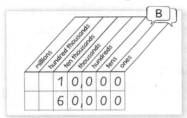

A blue whale can weigh over 300,000 pounds! Demonstrate how to write 300,000. **300 equals 3 hundreds. So, I write a 3 in the hundred-thousands-place and zeros in the smaller places.**

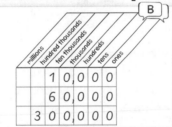

Ireland has a population of about 5 million people. Demonstrate how to write 5,000,000. **I write a 5 in the millions-place and zeros in the smaller places. I write a comma between the thousands and hundreds-place to make the number easier to read. I write a comma between the millions and hundred-thousands-place, too.**

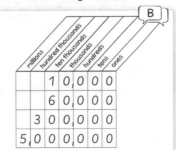

Read your child the following facts. Have him write each number in the place value chart. Remind him to include commas as needed.

- **A few American baseball stadiums have seats for more than 50,000 people.**
- **Some American football fields have seats for more than 100,000 people.**

- The moon is about 200,000 miles away from earth.
- Iceland has a population of about 400,000 people.
- Jamaica has a population of about 3 million people.

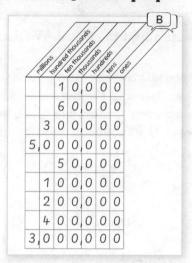

millions	hundred thousands	ten thousands	thousands	hundreds	tens	ones
		1	0	0	0	0
		6	0	0	0	0
	3	0	0	0	0	0
5	0	0	0	0	0	0
		5	0	0	0	0
	1	0	0	0	0	0
	2	0	0	0	0	0
	4	0	0	0	0	0
3	0	0	0	0	0	0

Activity (C): Read Large Numbers

The commas in large numbers help us read them. Point to the price tag for the first car. **The digits before the comma tell the number of thousands.** Underline the 3 and 5. **There's a 3 in the ten-thousands-place and a 5 in the thousands-place, so there are 35 thousands.**

The digits after the comma tell how many ones there are. Underline the 7, 2, and 0. **There's a 7 in the hundreds-place, a 2 in the tens-place, and a 0 in the ones-place, so there are 720 ones.**

$ 35,720

Here's how you read numbers that have one comma. First, read the part before the comma as one number: thirty-five. Then, say "thousand" when you reach the comma. Last, read the part after the comma as one number: seven hundred twenty. This car costs thirty-five thousand seven hundred twenty dollars.

Have your child read aloud the prices of the pick-up truck and sports car. Underline the parts of the number as needed.

$ 47,699 $ 117,200

Thinking of numbers in "chunks" rather than as individual digits helps children make sense of large numbers. See the Unit 2 **Teaching Math with Confidence** for more on how this approach helps children develop number sense with large numbers.

Independent Practice and Review

Have your child complete the Lesson 2.4 Practice and Review workbook pages.

Lesson 2.5
Compare Large Numbers

Purpose	Materials
• Review place-value names • Write large numbers in expanded form • Write large numbers • Use place-value thinking to compare large numbers	• None

Memory Work	• **How many ounces equal 1 pound?** *16.* • **How many grams equal 1 kilogram?** *1,000.*

Warm-up (A): Review Place-Value Names

In the last lesson, you learned about place value in large numbers. Cover the labels at the top of the place-value chart with your hand or a slip of paper so that only the ones-place is showing. **What place comes after ones?** *Tens.* Slide your hand or the paper to reveal the tens-place.

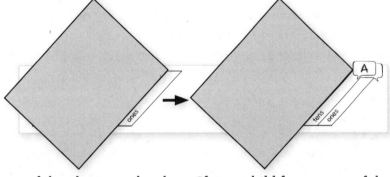

Repeat with the rest of the places on the chart. If your child forgets any of the places, remind her that each place has 10 times the value of the previous place. For example, if your child forgets the name of the hundred-thousands-place: **This place equals 10 groups of ten thousand. 10 times 10 is 100, so what is this place called?** *Hundred thousands.*

Activity (A): Write Large Numbers in Expanded Form

Today, you'll learn how to write large numbers in expanded form and standard form. Writing large numbers in expanded form is just like writing smaller numbers in expanded form. You stretch the number to show the value of its digits.

Before we write the first number in expanded form, let's identify the value of each digit.

- Point to the 4. **What place is the 4 in?** *The ten-thousands-place.* **So, what is the value of the 4?** *40,000.*
- Point to the 6. **What place is the 6 in?** *The thousands-place.* **What is the value of the 6?** *6,000.*
- Point to the 2. **What place is the 2 in?** *The hundreds-place.* **What is the value of the 2?** *200.*
- Point to the 0. **What place is the 0 in?** *The tens-place.* **What is the value of the 0?** *0.* **If a digit has a value of 0, you don't have to include it in the expanded form of the number.**
- Point to the 5. **What place is the 5 in?** *The ones-place.* **What is the value of the 5?** *5.*

Have your child write 46,205 in expanded form in the blank next to the place-value chart. Then, repeat with the other numbers in the chart. If she is overwhelmed by the number of digits in the numbers, encourage her to focus on one digit at a time, from left to right.

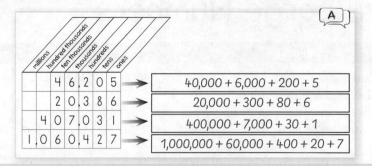

Make sure your child writes the addends in expanded form in the same order as the digits, beginning with the digit with the greatest value. She does not need to write the value of any place-holder zeros.

Activity (B): Write Boat Prices

Boats are expensive, so there are a lot of digits in their prices! To write large numbers, we write each part of the number as we hear it. We write a comma when we hear the word "thousand."

The sailboat costs thirty-two thousand eight hundred ninety dollars. So, I write 32, then a comma, then 890. Write 32,890 below the sailboat.

Read your child the following boat prices. Have her write each number below the corresponding boat.

- Airboat: $40,799
- Speed boat: $185,600
- Yacht: $550,319
- Pontoon boat: $32,005
- Cabin cruiser: $213,058

Activity (B): Use Place-Value Thinking to Compare Boat Prices

Point to the sailboat and airboat. **Which costs more, the sailboat or the airboat?** *The airboat.*
How do you know? *Answers will vary.*

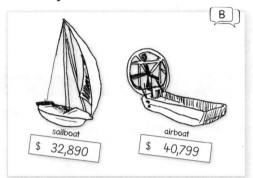

When you compare large numbers, first look at the digits before the comma. The digits
before the comma tell us how many thousands there are in the number. If one number has
more thousands than the other number, you know it's greater! How many thousands are
in 32,890? *32.* How many thousands are in 40,799? *40.* 40 is greater than 32, so 40,799
is greater than 32,890. In this case, we don't have to think about the digits in the hundreds-place, tens-place, or ones-place.

Point to the sailboat and pontoon boat. **Which costs more, the sailboat or the pontoon boat?**
The sailboat. **How do you know?** *Answers will vary.*

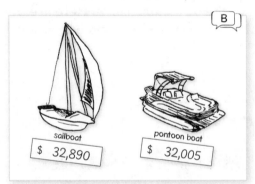

Both the sailboat and pontoon boat prices start with 32 thousand. So, we need to compare
the rest of the number. 890 is greater than 5, so the sailboat costs more.

If the numbers have the same number of thousands, we need to look closely at the hundreds-place, tens-place, and ones-place.

Ask your child the following comparison questions. Encourage her to use the number of thousands in each price to determine which price is greater.

- **Which costs more, the airboat or the speedboat?** *The speedboat.*
- **Which costs less, the yacht or the cabin cruiser?** *The cabin cruiser.*
- **Which costs more, the pontoon boat or the airboat?** *The airboat.*
- **Which of these boats costs the most?** *The yacht.*
- **Which of these boats costs the least?** *The pontoon boat.*

Independent Practice and Review

Have your child complete the Lesson 2.5 Practice and Review workbook pages.

Lesson 2.6
Round Large Numbers to the Nearest Thousand

Purpose	Materials
• Practice reading large numbers • Identify the approximate positions of large numbers on the number line • Round large numbers to the thousands-place	• None

Memory Work	• **What is a prime number?** *A number with exactly 2 factors.* • **What is a composite number?** *A number with more than 2 factors.*

This lesson uses a game show to give context to large numbers and make the lesson more fun. Feel free to ham it up with an over-the-top announcer voice as you teach.

Warm-up (A): Read Large Numbers

In the last two lessons, you learned how to read, write, and compare large numbers. Today, we're going to pretend you're on a game show! Here are the prizes you can win. Have your child read aloud the value of each prize. Remind him as needed to say "thousand" when he reaches the comma.

Which prize is worth the most? *The trip around the world.* **Which prize is worth the least?** *The grand piano.* **Which prize would you most like to win?** *Answers will vary.*

Activity (A): Identify and Compare Numbers on the Number Line

The first game is "Match It!" To win each prize, you have to find where each number belongs on the number line. We'll start with the SUV!

These number lines have increments of 10,000. So, we can count by ten-thousands to see what each tick mark stands for. Have your child count in unison with you by ten-thousands for both number lines. Point to each tick mark as you name it: **Ten thousand, twenty thousand, thirty thousand...**

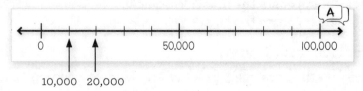

The SUV costs $53,900. Which tick marks must the number be between? *The tick marks for 50,000 and 60,000.* **Is 53,900 closer to 50,000 or 60,000?** *50,000.* **How do you know?** *Answers will vary. 53 is closer to 50 than 60, so 53,900 is closer to 50,000 than 60,000.* Have your child draw a dot at the approximate position for 53,900 and draw a line connecting the number to the dot. Repeat for the other prize values.

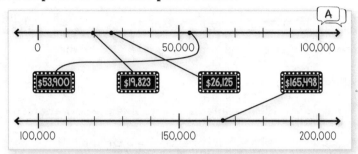

If your child makes a mistake, give him a chance to correct it for another chance to win the prize.

Activity (B): Round Numbers to the Nearest Thousand

In our final game, you round each number to the nearest thousand. If you round each prize value to the nearest thousand, you win the grand prize of $100,000 in cash, plus all the other prizes!

Here's how to round 53,900 to the nearest thousand. I point to the digit that I want to round to. Point to the 3. **Then, I look at the digit in the next-smaller place.** Draw an arrow as shown. **If that digit is less than 5, I round down. If that digit is 5 or greater, I round up.**

The digit in the hundreds-place is a 9, so I round up. I increase the thousands-place by 1 and then write zeros for the smaller places. Write 54,000 in the blank. **53,900 is closer to 54,000 than 53,000.** Have your child round the other numbers in the same way.

$$53{,}900 \approx \boxed{54{,}000}$$

$$19{,}823 \approx \boxed{20{,}000}$$

$$26{,}125 \approx \boxed{26{,}000}$$

$$165{,}498 \approx \boxed{165{,}000}$$

If your child has trouble rounding 19,823 to the nearest thousand, say: **The digit in the hundreds-place is an 8, so we round up. What's 9 increased by 1?** *10.* **10 thousands equals 1 ten-thousand, so 19,823 rounded to the nearest thousand is 20,000.**

If your child correctly rounds the numbers, announce: **Congratulations, you've won all the prizes plus the grand prize!** If he makes a mistake, give him the chance to try again.

Independent Practice and Review

Have your child complete the Lesson 2.6 Practice and Review workbook pages.

Lesson 2.7
Mental Math with Large Numbers

Purpose	Materials
• Practice using place-value thinking to add and subtract hundreds • Mentally add and subtract thousands	• 6 dice

Memory Work	• **What do we call an angle that looks like the corner of a piece of paper?** *A right angle.* • **What do we call a quadrilateral with 4 right angles?** *A rectangle.* • **What do we call a quadrilateral with 4 right angles and 4 equal sides?** *A square.* • **What do we call a quadrilateral with 4 equal sides?** *A rhombus.*

Warm-up: Use Place-Value Thinking to Add and Subtract Hundreds

Ask your child the following mental math questions:

- **400 plus 200.** *600.*
- **800 plus 200.** *1,000.*
- **700 plus 800.** *1,500.*

- **600 minus 100.** *500.*
- **1,000 minus 300.** *700.*
- **1,300 minus 400.** *900.*

These questions prepare your child to use place-value thinking to solve mental math problems with thousands.

Activity (A): Mental Math with Thousands

In the warm-up you used place-value thinking to add and subtract hundreds. Today, you'll learn how to use place-value thinking to add and subtract thousands.

Have your child read aloud the first problem: *35,000 plus 5,000.* **What's 35 plus 5?** *40.* Write 40 in the cloud's answer blank. **So, what does 35 thousand plus 5 thousand equal?** *40 thousand.* Write 40,000 in the blank.

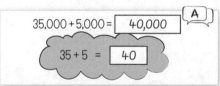

Children are sometimes visually overwhelmed by the sheer number of digits in large numbers. Reading the problem aloud helps your child helps your child see how simple the problem really is: adding 35 plus 5. If your child struggles with this idea, say: **Think of each thousand as 1 group. 35 groups plus 5 groups equals 40 groups. So, 35 thousands plus 5 thousands equals 40 thousands.**

Repeat with the rest of the problems in part A. Make sure to have your child read aloud each problem so she hears the number of thousands in each number. Have her use the problem in each cloud to solve the related problem.

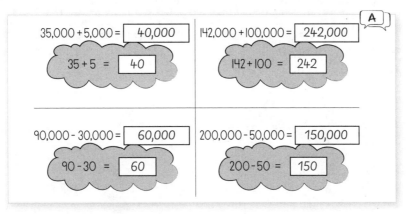

Activity (B): Play Race to 500,000

Play Race to 500,000. Have your child use mental addition to find her new score after each turn.

This game is an adaptation of the classic dice game Farkle (with a little inspiration from Yahtzee). If you're short on time, play until one player reaches 250,000.

Race to 500,000

Materials: 6 dice

Object of the Game: Be the first player to reach 500,000 points by rolling dice that show the same number.

Each player takes turns rolling the dice. You may roll the dice up to 3 times per turn. Your goal is to have as many dice showing the same number as possible by the end of the three rolls.

For your first roll, roll all 6 dice. Set aside any dice that show the same number. (For example, if you roll 3 fives, set those dice aside.) You may only set one group of dice aside. If none of your dice show the same number, don't set any aside and reroll all the dice.

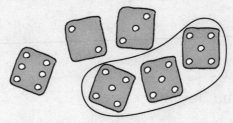

Sample first roll. Set aside the 3 fives.

Directions continued on next page.

For your second roll, roll the remaining dice. Set aside any dice that match the ones you already set aside. (For example, if you rolled 3 fives on your first roll and 1 five on your second roll, set the additional five aside.)

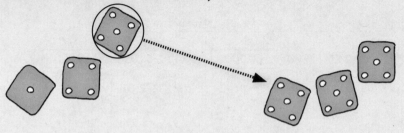

Sample second roll. Set aside the additional 5.

For your third roll, roll the remaining dice. Then, count how many dice show the same number. Use the scoring chart to determine your score and add your score to your previous total. You may only score one group of dice per turn. (For example, if you rolled 3 fives and 3 twos, only score one of the groups. Choose the fives, since they are worth more points.)

Sample third roll. Score 50,000 points, since you have four of a kind.

If you like, you may decide to re-roll dice that you set aside in previous rolls. For example, if you set aside 2 fours after the first roll and then roll 3 twos in your second roll, you may keep the twos and re-roll the fours.

Take turns until one player reaches 500,000 or greater.

Cooperative variation: Play the game together and keep track of how many rounds it takes for you to reach 500,000. Then, play a second time and see if you can reach 500,000 in fewer rounds.

Independent Practice and Review

Have your child complete the Lesson 2.7 Practice and Review workbook pages.

Lesson 2.8
Add and Subtract Large Numbers

Purpose	Materials
• Practice reading and writing large numbers • Add and subtract large numbers with the addition and subtraction algorithms	• 10 slips of paper

Memory Work	
	• **Name 4 factors of 8.** *1, 2, 4, 8.* • **Name 4 multiples of 8.** *Sample answers: 8, 32, 40, 80.*

You will need 10 slips of paper to play Leaf Fight. Use brown paper (or orange, red, and yellow) if you'd like the slips to look more like leaves.

Warm-up: Read and Write Large Numbers

Read the following numbers aloud. (These numbers are also printed in Activity B on the Lesson Activities page.) Have your child write each number on a separate slip of paper.

- 467,890
- 128,365
- 38,704

- 333,333
- 99,999

Then, switch roles. Have your child read aloud the following numbers to you. Write each number on a separate slip of paper.

- 209,999
- 56,001
- 8,998

- 519,786
- 19,643

You will use these slips of paper to play Leaf Fight later in the lesson.

Activity (A): Add and Subtract Large Numbers

You already know how to add and subtract numbers with up to four digits. Today, you'll learn how to add and subtract larger numbers.

Adding and subtracting six-digit numbers is just like adding and subtracting smaller numbers. You can use the exact same steps. Have your child complete both problems in part A. Remind him to begin with the ones-place and work from right to left.

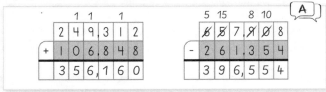

Adding and subtracting large numbers takes a while! Adults often use a calculator or computer when they need to add a bunch of large numbers, but sometimes it comes in handy to know how to add and subtract large numbers without a calculator, too.

Activity (B): Play Leaf Fight

Play Leaf Fight.

> The silliness of this activity makes solving these problems feel more relaxed and fun. But, if you'd rather not encourage throwing (or if you're teaching this lesson in a place where it's not practical), put the paper wads in a bowl and draw 2 wads each turn instead. Replace the wads in the bowl after each turn.

Leaf Fight

Materials: 10 slips of paper (prepared in warm-up)
Object of the Game: Win the most points.

Crumple the slips of paper you prepared in the warm-up and place them on the table.

Both players count down in unison from 10 while throwing the crumpled wads of paper at each other. When you reach 1, both players stop and pick up the 2 closest wads of paper.

Both players unfold their paper wads and write the numbers in neighboring blank grids on the scorecard. If the blank grids have a plus sign, each player finds the sum of the numbers they picked up. Whoever has the greater sum wins a point.

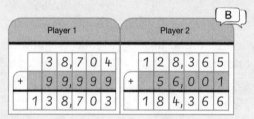

Player 2 wins a point, since he has the greater sum.

If the blank grids have a minus sign, each player finds the difference between their numbers they picked up. Whoever has the greater difference wins the point.

Player 1 wins a point, since she has the greater difference.

Crumple up your numbers and add them back to the pile of "leaves." Repeat until you have filled in all of the blank grids. Whoever wins more points wins the game.

Independent Practice and Review

Have your child complete the Lesson 2.8 Practice and Review workbook pages.

> The Practice section is short, since your child practiced lots of multi-digit addition and subtraction in the Lesson Activities. As a result, there is only 1 page of Practice and Review in this lesson.

Lesson 2.9
Word Problems with Large Numbers

Purpose	Materials
• Practice multiplication facts • Solve multi-step word problems with large numbers	• 2 decks of playing cards

Memory Work	
	• **How many cups equal 1 pint?** *2.* • **How many pints equal 1 quart?** *2.* • **How many quarts equal 1 gallon?** *4.*

Warm-up: Play Multiplication War

Play Multiplication War. See Lesson 1.4 (page 23) for directions.

Activity (A): Solve Word Problems with Large Numbers

In the last lesson, you learned how to add and subtract large numbers. Today, you'll use addition and subtraction to solve word problems with large numbers.

The first word problem has two different questions. You'll use the same information to answer both questions. Read aloud the first problem: *37,406 people came to the baseball game on Thursday. 48,694 people came to the baseball game on Friday. What was the total attendance for both games?*

What's the goal? *Find how many people came to both baseball games.* Then, have your child read the problem again slowly and describe what she imagines. For example: *I imagine two different baseball games. The stands have more people at one game than the other game.*

Sometimes, kids freeze up when they see word problems with large numbers, because the numbers look overwhelming. It helps if you plan what you're going to do *before* you focus on the exact numbers.

In this problem, you know how many people came on Thursday and how many people came on Friday. How do we find the total attendance? *Add the number of people who came on Thursday to the number of people who came on Friday.*

So, you know you're going to add the two numbers together. Now, you can go back to the problem, find the exact numbers, and set up the addition problem. Have your child write the matching addition problem and solve it. If needed, remind her to label her answer and draw a box around it.

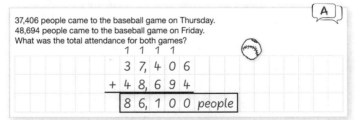

Point to the arrow in front of the second question. **This arrow means that you should use the information from the previous question to answer this question, too.** Have your child follow the same steps to answer the second question.

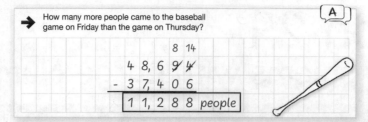

Activity (B): Solve Two-Step Word Problems with Large Numbers

The next problem has two different questions, too. Have your child read the problem and first question aloud, identify the goal, and read the problem again slowly. Then, have her tell you how she plans to solve the problem and solve it.

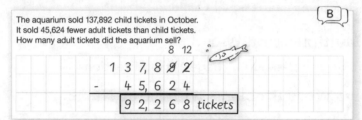

Read aloud the second question: ***How many child and adult tickets did the aquarium sell in all?*** **What's the goal?** *Find the total number of child tickets and adult tickets.*

How do we find the total number of tickets? *Add the number of child tickets to the number of adult tickets.* **Where can you find the number of child tickets?** *Child points to printed problem.* **Where can you find the number of adult tickets?** *Child points to answer to the previous problem.* **This time, you need to use the answer to the first question to answer the second question.**

Have your child write the matching addition problem and solve it.

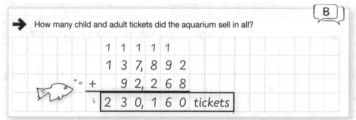

Independent Practice and Review

Have your child complete the Lesson 2.9 Practice and Review workbook pages.

Lesson 2.10
Enrichment (Optional)

Purpose	Materials
• Practice memory work • Understand the magnitude of large numbers • Introduce millions and billions in the context of population numbers • Summarize what your child has learned and assess your child's progress	• *A Million Dots*, written by Andrew Clements and illustrated by Mike Reed • Almanac or internet access

Warm-up: Review Memory Work

Quiz your child on all memory work through Unit 2. See pages 536-537 for the full list.

Math Picture Book: *A Million Dots*

Read *A Million Dots*, written by Andrew Clements and illustrated by Mike Reed. Invite your child to read some of the large numbers in the book.

Enrichment Activity: Find the Population of Your City, State, and Country

Use an almanac or internet search engine to find the population of your town or city, state or province, and country. Discuss whether your child is surprised by any of the numbers.

Then, look up the current population of the entire world. Read the number aloud to your child and explain that 1 billion equals 1,000 millions!

Don't worry if you can only find approximate numbers or numbers that are a few years out of date. The main goal is for your child to understand the magnitude of these large numbers in an important real-life context.

Unit Wrap-Up

Have your child complete the Unit 2 Wrap-Up.

Unit 2 Answer Key

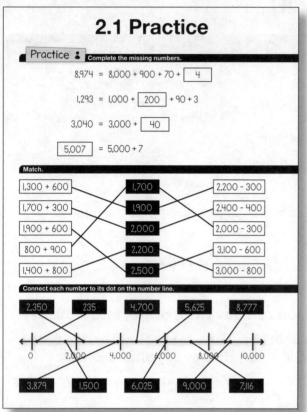

2.1 Practice

Practice Complete the missing numbers.

$8,974 = 8,000 + 900 + 70 + \boxed{4}$

$1,293 = 1,000 + \boxed{200} + 90 + 3$

$3,040 = 3,000 + \boxed{40}$

$\boxed{5,007} = 5,000 + 7$

Match.

1,300 + 600	1,700	2,200 - 300
1,700 + 300	1,900	2,400 - 400
1,900 + 600	2,000	2,000 - 300
800 + 900	2,200	3,100 - 600
1,400 + 800	2,500	3,000 - 800

Connect each number to its dot on the number line.

| 2,350 | 235 | 4,700 | 5,625 | 8,777 |

0   2,000   4,000   6,000   8,000   10,000

| 3,879 | 1,500 | 6,025 | 9,000 | 7,116 |

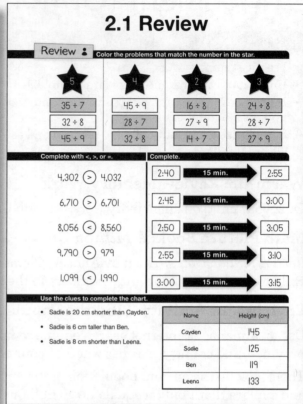

2.1 Review

Review Color the problems that match the number in the star.

★ 5 | ★ 4 | ★ 2 | ★ 3

35 ÷ 7	45 ÷ 9	16 ÷ 8	24 ÷ 8
32 ÷ 8	28 ÷ 7	27 ÷ 9	28 ÷ 7
45 ÷ 9	32 ÷ 8	14 ÷ 7	27 ÷ 9

Complete with <, >, or =.

$4,302 \enspace \boxed{>} \enspace 4,032$

$6,710 \enspace \boxed{>} \enspace 6,701$

$8,056 \enspace \boxed{<} \enspace 8,560$

$9,790 \enspace \boxed{>} \enspace 979$

$1,099 \enspace \boxed{<} \enspace 1,990$

Complete.

2:40	15 min.	2:55
2:45	15 min.	3:00
2:50	15 min.	3:05
2:55	15 min.	3:10
3:00	15 min.	3:15

Use the clues to complete the chart.

- Sadie is 20 cm shorter than Cayden.
- Sadie is 6 cm taller than Ben.
- Sadie is 8 cm shorter than Leena.

Name	Height (cm)
Cayden	145
Sadie	125
Ben	119
Leena	133

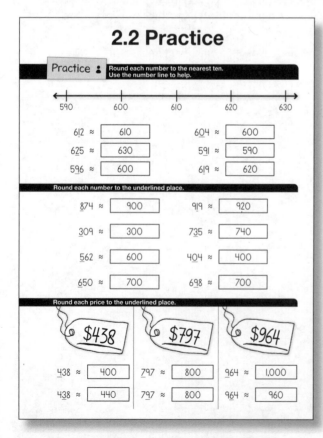

2.2 Practice

Practice Round each number to the nearest ten. Use the number line to help.

590   600   610   620   630

$612 \approx \boxed{610}$ $604 \approx \boxed{600}$

$625 \approx \boxed{630}$ $591 \approx \boxed{590}$

$596 \approx \boxed{600}$ $619 \approx \boxed{620}$

Round each number to the underlined place.

$8\underline{7}4 \approx \boxed{900}$ $9\underline{1}9 \approx \boxed{920}$

$\underline{3}09 \approx \boxed{300}$ $7\underline{3}5 \approx \boxed{740}$

$\underline{5}62 \approx \boxed{600}$ $4\underline{0}4 \approx \boxed{400}$

$\underline{6}50 \approx \boxed{700}$ $6\underline{9}8 \approx \boxed{700}$

Round each price to the underlined place.

$438 $797 $964

$\underline{4}38 \approx \boxed{400}$ $\underline{7}97 \approx \boxed{800}$ $\underline{9}64 \approx \boxed{1,000}$

$4\underline{3}8 \approx \boxed{440}$ $7\underline{9}7 \approx \boxed{800}$ $9\underline{6}4 \approx \boxed{960}$

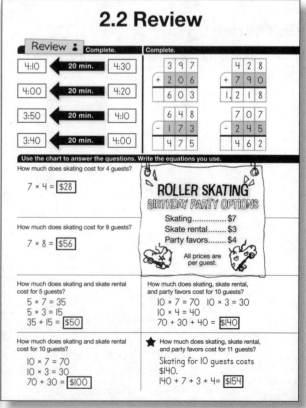

2.2 Review

Review Complete.

4:10	20 min.	4:30
4:00	20 min.	4:20
3:50	20 min.	4:10
3:40	20 min.	4:00

Complete.

```
  3 9 7
+ 2 0 6
-------
  6 0 3
```

```
  4 2 8
+ 7 9 0
-------
1,2 1 8
```

```
  6 4 8
- 1 7 3
-------
  4 7 5
```

```
  7 0 7
- 2 4 5
-------
  4 6 2
```

Use the chart to answer the questions. Write the equations you use.

How much does skating cost for 4 guests?

$7 \times 4 = \boxed{\$28}$

ROLLER SKATING
BIRTHDAY PARTY OPTIONS

Skating............... $7
Skate rental........ $3
Party favors........ $4

All prices are per guest.

How much does skating cost for 8 guests?

$7 \times 8 = \boxed{\$56}$

How much does skating and skate rental cost for 5 guests?

$5 \times 7 = 35$
$5 \times 3 = 15$
$35 + 15 = \boxed{\$50}$

How much does skating, skate rental, and party favors cost for 10 guests?

$10 \times 7 = 70 \quad 10 \times 3 = 30$
$10 \times 4 = 40$
$70 + 30 + 40 = \boxed{\$140}$

How much does skating and skate rental cost for 10 guests?

$10 \times 7 = 70$
$10 \times 3 = 30$
$70 + 30 = \boxed{\$100}$

★ How much does skating, skate rental, and party favors cost for 11 guests?

Skating for 10 guests costs $140.
$140 + 7 + 3 + 4 = \boxed{\$154}$

Unit 2 Answer Key

2.3 Practice

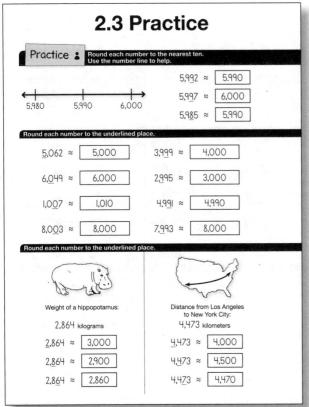

Practice 👤 Round each number to the nearest ten.
Use the number line to help.

$5,992 \approx$ **5,990**

$5,997 \approx$ **6,000**

$5,985 \approx$ **5,990**

Round each number to the underlined place.

$5,062 \approx$ **5,000** $3,999 \approx$ **4,000**

$6,049 \approx$ **6,000** $2,995 \approx$ **3,000**

$1,007 \approx$ **1,010** $4,991 \approx$ **4,990**

$8,003 \approx$ **8,000** $7,993 \approx$ **8,000**

Round each number to the underlined place.

Weight of a hippopotamus:

2,864 kilograms

$2,864 \approx$ **3,000**

$2,864 \approx$ **2,900**

$2,864 \approx$ **2,860**

Distance from Los Angeles to New York City:

4,473 kilometers

$4,473 \approx$ **4,000**

$4,473 \approx$ **4,500**

$4,473 \approx$ **4,470**

2.3 Review

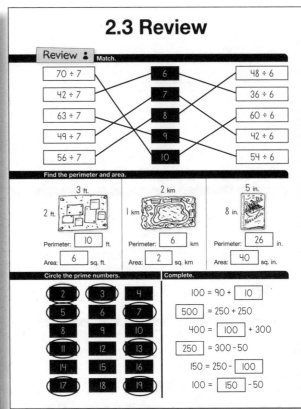

Review 👤 Match.

$70 \div 7$	6
$42 \div 7$	7
$63 \div 7$	8
$49 \div 7$	9
$56 \div 7$	10

$48 \div 6$
$36 \div 6$
$60 \div 6$
$42 \div 6$
$54 \div 6$

Find the perimeter and area.

3 ft. / 2 ft.

Perimeter: **10** ft.

Area: **6** sq. ft.

2 km / 1 km

Perimeter: **6** km

Area: **2** sq. km

5 in. / 8 in.

Perimeter: **26** in.

Area: **40** sq. in.

Circle the prime numbers.

(2) (3) 4
(5) 6 (7)
8 9 10
(11) 12 (13)
14 15 16
(17) 18 (19)

Complete.

$100 = 90 +$ **10**

500 $= 250 + 250$

$400 =$ **100** $+ 300$

250 $= 300 - 50$

$150 = 250 -$ **100**

$100 =$ **150** $- 50$

2.4 Practice

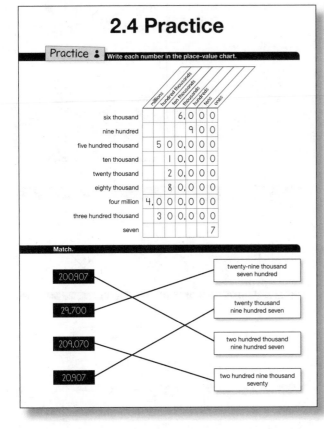

Practice 👤 Write each number in the place-value chart.

	millions	hundred thousands	ten thousands	thousands	hundreds	tens	ones
six thousand				6,	0	0	0
nine hundred					9	0	0
five hundred thousand		5	0	0,	0	0	0
ten thousand			1	0,	0	0	0
twenty thousand			2	0,	0	0	0
eighty thousand			8	0,	0	0	0
four million	4,	0	0	0,	0	0	0
three hundred thousand		3	0	0,	0	0	0
seven							7

Match.

200,907	twenty-nine thousand seven hundred
29,700	twenty thousand nine hundred seven
209,070	two hundred thousand nine hundred seven
20,907	two hundred nine thousand seventy

2.4 Review

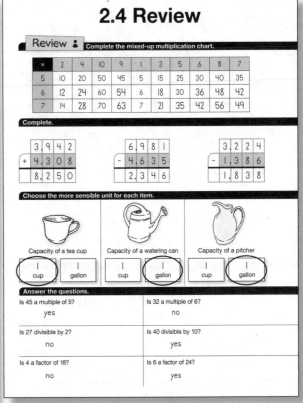

Review 👤 Complete the mixed-up multiplication chart.

×	2	4	10	9	1	3	5	6	8	7
5	10	20	50	45	5	15	25	30	40	35
6	12	24	60	54	6	18	30	36	48	42
7	14	28	70	63	7	21	35	42	56	49

Complete.

```
  3,9 4 2
+ 4,3 0 8
  8,2 5 0
```

```
  6,9 8 1
- 4,6 3 5
  2,3 4 6
```

```
  3,2 2 4
- 1,3 8 6
  1,8 3 8
```

Choose the more sensible unit for each item.

Capacity of a tea cup
(1 cup)   1 gallon

Capacity of a watering can
1 cup   (1 gallon)

Capacity of a pitcher
1 cup   (1 gallon)

Answer the questions.

Is 45 a multiple of 5?	Is 32 a multiple of 6?
yes	no
Is 27 divisible by 2?	Is 40 divisible by 10?
no	yes
Is 4 a factor of 18?	Is 6 a factor of 24?
no	yes

Unit 2 Answer Key

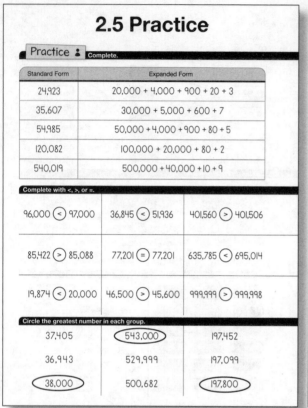

2.5 Practice

Practice 👤 Complete.

Standard Form	Expanded Form
24,923	20,000 + 4,000 + 900 + 20 + 3
35,607	30,000 + 5,000 + 600 + 7
54,985	50,000 + 4,000 + 900 + 80 + 5
120,082	100,000 + 20,000 + 80 + 2
540,019	500,000 + 40,000 + 10 + 9

Complete with <, >, or =.

96,000 < 97,000   36,845 < 51,936   401,560 > 401,506

85,422 > 85,088   77,201 = 77,201   635,785 < 695,014

19,874 < 20,000   46,500 > 45,600   999,999 > 999,998

Circle the greatest number in each group.

37,405	(543,000)	197,452
36,943	529,999	197,099
(38,000)	500,682	(197,800)

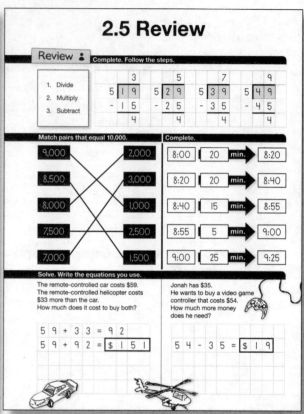

2.5 Review

Review 👤 Complete. Follow the steps.

1. Divide
2. Multiply
3. Subtract

```
        3            5            7            9
5 | 1 9      5 | 2 9      5 | 3 9      5 | 4 9
  - 1 5        - 2 5        - 3 5        - 4 5
      4            4            4            4
```

Match pairs that equal 10,000.

9,000 — 1,000
8,500 — 1,500
8,000 — 2,000
7,500 — 2,500
7,000 — 3,000

Complete.

8:00 → 20 min. → 8:20
8:20 → 20 min. → 8:40
8:40 → 15 min. → 8:55
8:55 → 5 min. → 9:00
9:00 → 25 min. → 9:25

Solve. Write the equations you use.

The remote-controlled car costs $59.
The remote-controlled helicopter costs $33 more than the car.
How much does it cost to buy both?

5 9 + 3 3 = 9 2
5 9 + 9 2 = $ 1 5 1

Jonah has $35.
He wants to buy a video game controller that costs $54. How much more money does he need?

5 4 − 3 5 = $ 1 9

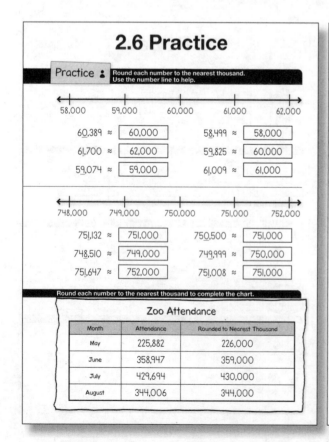

2.6 Practice

Practice 👤 Round each number to the nearest thousand. Use the number line to help.

```
58,000   59,000   60,000   61,000   62,000
```

60,389 ≈ 60,000   58,499 ≈ 58,000
61,700 ≈ 62,000   59,825 ≈ 60,000
59,074 ≈ 59,000   61,009 ≈ 61,000

```
748,000  749,000  750,000  751,000  752,000
```

751,132 ≈ 751,000   750,500 ≈ 751,000
748,510 ≈ 749,000   749,999 ≈ 750,000
751,647 ≈ 752,000   751,008 ≈ 751,000

Round each number to the nearest thousand to complete the chart.

Zoo Attendance

Month	Attendance	Rounded to Nearest Thousand
May	225,882	226,000
June	358,947	359,000
July	429,694	430,000
August	344,006	344,000

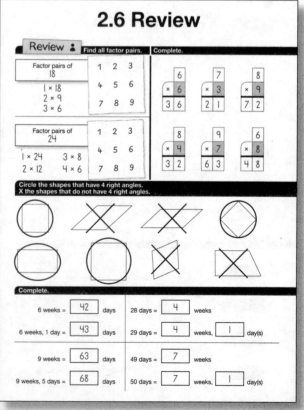

2.6 Review

Review 👤 Find all factor pairs. | Complete.

Factor pairs of 18	1 2 3
1 × 18	4 5 6
2 × 9	7 8 9
3 × 6	

Factor pairs of 24	1 2 3
1 × 24 3 × 8	4 5 6
2 × 12 4 × 6	7 8 9

```
6        7        8
× 6      × 3      × 9
3 6      2 1      7 2

8        9        6
× 4      × 7      × 8
3 2      6 3      4 8
```

Circle the shapes that have 4 right angles.
X the shapes that do not have 4 right angles.

Complete.

6 weeks = 42 days   28 days = 4 weeks
6 weeks, 1 day = 43 days   29 days = 4 weeks, 1 day(s)

9 weeks = 63 days   49 days = 7 weeks
9 weeks, 5 days = 68 days   50 days = 7 weeks, 1 day(s)

Unit 2 Answer Key

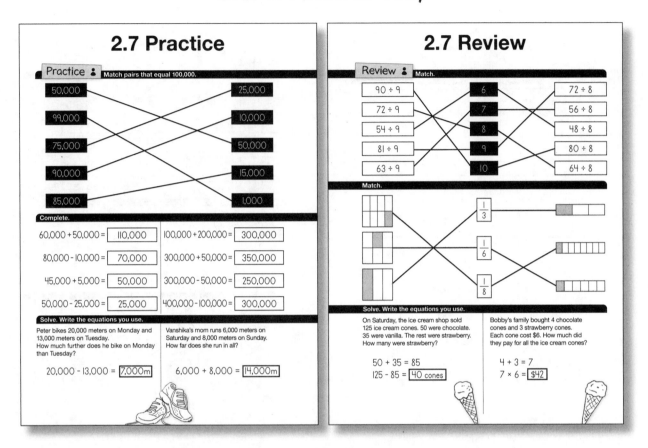

2.7 Practice

Practice **Match pairs that equal 100,000.**

50,000 — 50,000
99,000 — 1,000
75,000 — 25,000
90,000 — 10,000
85,000 — 15,000

Complete.

$60,000 + 50,000 =$ 110,000 $100,000 + 200,000 =$ 300,000

$80,000 - 10,000 =$ 70,000 $300,000 + 50,000 =$ 350,000

$45,000 + 5,000 =$ 50,000 $300,000 - 50,000 =$ 250,000

$50,000 - 25,000 =$ 25,000 $400,000 - 100,000 =$ 300,000

Solve. Write the equations you use.

Peter bikes 20,000 meters on Monday and 13,000 meters on Tuesday. How much further does he bike on Monday than Tuesday?

$20,000 - 13,000 =$ 7,000m

Vanshika's mom runs 6,000 meters on Saturday and 8,000 meters on Sunday. How far does she run in all?

$6,000 + 8,000 =$ 14,000m

2.7 Review

Review **Match.**

$90 ÷ 9$ 6 $72 ÷ 8$
$72 ÷ 9$ 7 $56 ÷ 8$
$54 ÷ 9$ 8 $48 ÷ 8$
$81 ÷ 9$ 9 $80 ÷ 8$
$63 ÷ 9$ 10 $64 ÷ 8$

Match.

$\frac{1}{3}$

$\frac{1}{6}$

$\frac{1}{8}$

Solve. Write the equations you use.

On Saturday, the ice cream shop sold 125 ice cream cones. 50 were chocolate. 35 were vanilla. The rest were strawberry. How many were strawberry?

$50 + 35 = 85$
$125 - 85 =$ 40 cones

Bobby's family bought 4 chocolate cones and 3 strawberry cones. Each cone cost $6. How much did they pay for all the ice cream cones?

$4 + 3 = 7$
$7 × 6 =$ $42

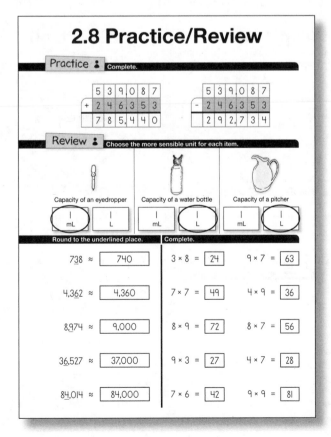

2.8 Practice/Review

Practice **Complete.**

	5	3	9,	0	8	7
+	2	4	6,	3	5	3
	7	8	5,	4	4	0

	5	3	9,	0	8	7
−	2	4	6,	3	5	3
	2	9	2,	7	3	4

Review **Choose the more sensible unit for each item.**

Capacity of an eyedropper: **mL** / L

Capacity of a water bottle: mL / **L**

Capacity of a pitcher: mL / **L**

Round to the underlined place.

$7\underline{3}8 ≈$ 740

$4,\underline{3}62 ≈$ 4,360

$8,\underline{9}74 ≈$ 9,000

$36,\underline{5}27 ≈$ 37,000

$84,\underline{0}14 ≈$ 84,000

Complete.

$3 × 8 =$ 24 $9 × 7 =$ 63

$7 × 7 =$ 49 $4 × 9 =$ 36

$8 × 9 =$ 72 $8 × 7 =$ 56

$9 × 3 =$ 27 $4 × 7 =$ 28

$7 × 6 =$ 42 $9 × 9 =$ 81

Unit 2 Answer Key

2.9 Practice

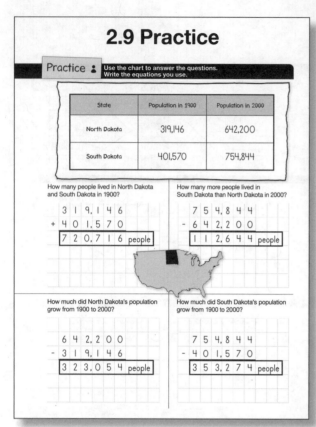

Practice 👤 Use the chart to answer the questions.
Write the equations you use.

State	Population in 1900	Population in 2000
North Dakota	319,146	642,200
South Dakota	401,570	754,844

How many people lived in North Dakota and South Dakota in 1900?

```
   3 1 9 , 1 4 6
 + 4 0 1 , 5 7 0
   7 2 0 , 7 1 6  people
```

How many more people lived in South Dakota than North Dakota in 2000?

```
   7 5 4 , 8 4 4
 - 6 4 2 , 2 0 0
   1 1 2 , 6 4 4  people
```

How much did North Dakota's population grow from 1900 to 2000?

```
   6 4 2 , 2 0 0
 - 3 1 9 , 1 4 6
   3 2 3 , 0 5 4  people
```

How much did South Dakota's population grow from 1900 to 2000?

```
   7 5 4 , 8 4 4
 - 4 0 1 , 5 7 0
   3 5 3 , 2 7 4  people
```

2.9 Review

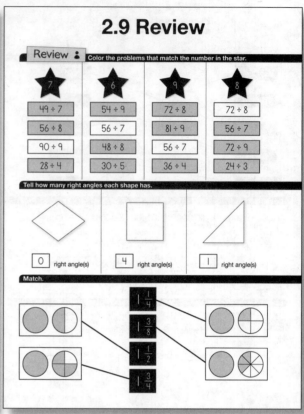

Review 👤 Color the problems that match the number in the star.

★ 7	★ 6	★ 9	★ 8
49 ÷ 7	54 ÷ 9	72 ÷ 8	72 ÷ 8
56 ÷ 8	56 ÷ 7	81 ÷ 9	56 ÷ 7
90 ÷ 9	48 ÷ 8	56 ÷ 7	72 ÷ 9
28 ÷ 4	30 ÷ 5	36 ÷ 4	24 ÷ 3

Tell how many right angles each shape has.

| 0 right angle(s) | 4 right angle(s) | 1 right angle(s) |

Match.

$1\frac{1}{4}$ $1\frac{3}{8}$ $1\frac{1}{2}$ $1\frac{3}{4}$

2.10 Unit Wrap-Up A

Unit Wrap-Up 👤 Write each number in standard form.

Words	Standard Form
five hundred thousand six hundred twenty	500,620
five hundred six thousand twenty	506,020
fifty-six thousand two hundred	56,200
fifty-six thousand two	56,002
five hundred sixty-two thousand	562,000

Write each number in expanded form.

75,978 = 70,000 + 5,000 + 900 + 70 + 8

395,100 = 300,000 + 90,000 + 5,000 + 100

130,891 = 100,000 + 30,000 + 800 + 90 + 1

Round to the underlined place.

3,782 ≈ 3,800

4,961 ≈ 4,960

5,985 ≈ 6,000

36,847 ≈ 37,000

659,285 ≈ 659,000

Use the clues to solve the number riddle.

- I am greater than 80,000 and less than 81,000.
- The digit in my tens-place is 3.
- The digit in my hundreds-place is 2 more than the digit in my tens-place.
- I am divisible by 10.

| 8 | 0 | , | 5 | 3 | 0 |

2.10 Unit Wrap-Up B

Unit Wrap-Up 👤 Complete.

300,000 + 100,000 = 400,000

300,000 + 37,000 = 337,000

99,000 + 3,000 = 102,000

100,000 - 35,000 = 65,000

100,000 - 1,000 = 99,000

150,000 - 25,000 = 125,000

Complete with <, >, or =.

99,999 ⊲ 100,000

74,017 ⊲ 74,701

513,284 ⊲ 531,284

680,562 ⊳ 680,000

739,865 ⊳ 739,864

297,842 ⊜ 297,842

Complete.

```
   5 9 7 , 3 4 6
 + 1 0 2 , 6 5 4
   7 0 0 , 0 0 0
```

```
   6 7 4 , 0 3 9
 - 2 9 1 , 5 2 8
   3 8 2 , 5 1 1
```

```
   2 9 9 , 9 9 9
 + 3 7 5 , 8 6 4
   6 7 5 , 8 6 3
```

```
   5 7 5 , 1 7 5
 - 1 6 2 , 3 8 5
   4 1 2 , 7 9 0
```

Solve. Write the equations you use.

The bookstore had $474,968 in sales this year. It had $439,470 in sales last year. What were its total sales for both years?

```
   4 7 4 , 9 6 8
 + 4 3 9 , 4 7 0
 $ 9 1 4 , 4 3 8
```

➡ How much greater were the bookstore's sales this year than last year?

```
   4 7 4 , 9 6 8
 - 4 3 9 , 4 7 0
 $ 3 5 , 4 9 8
```

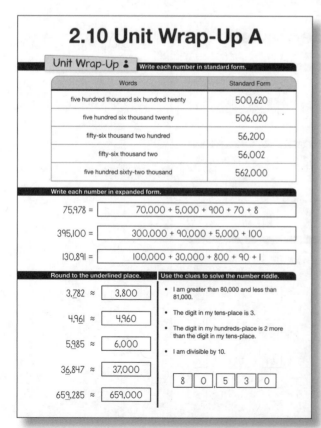
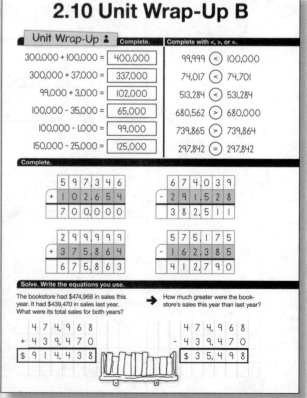

Unit 2 Checkpoint

What to Expect at the End of Unit 2

By the end of Unit 2, most children will be able to do the following:

- Read, write, and compare numbers to one million.
- Understand place value to the millions-place.
- Write numbers with up to six digits in expanded form.
- Round three- or four-digit numbers to any place.
- Round large numbers to the thousands-place.
- Use place-value thinking to mentally add and subtract thousands.
- Use the addition and subtraction algorithms to add and subtract five- and six-digit numbers and solve multi-step addition and subtraction word problems.

Is Your Child Ready to Move on?

In Unit 3, your child will learn several mental multiplication techniques. At this point, your child should be **mostly fluent with the multiplication facts.** It's normal for children to occasionally forget a fact or take a few seconds to find an answer, but most children should be able to tell most of the answers within 3 seconds at this point.

You'll continue to review the division facts with games in the warm-up exercises and review pages, so it's okay if your child isn't completely fluent with the division facts yet.

What to Do If Your Child Needs More Practice

If you're not sure whether your child has mastered the multiplication facts, use Blackline Master 3 to assess his fluency. Then, use the results of the assessment to make a plan to build greater automaticity with the facts.

- If your child can find answers to most of the facts but takes longer than 3 seconds, he needs more practice to build his speed. Play Multiplication War (directions on page 23) or Multiplication Greatest to Least (directions on page 197) a few times per week (either at the beginning of a lesson or at a separate time of day) as you move forward in the program. Encourage your child to respond as quickly as possible as he names the products in the games.
- If your child has just a few facts that stump him, choose 3 of the tricky facts. Write them on a piece of paper and post them in your math lesson area. Have him practice these 3 facts at the beginning of each lesson until he has memorized them. Then, choose 3 new facts to focus on.
- If your child has trouble finding answers to many of the multiplication facts, he likely needs more practice with them to be successful with *Fourth Grade Math with Confidence. Multiplication Facts That Stick* provides a systematic approach to mastering the facts. Use the activities from *Multiplication Facts that Stick* for 5-10 minutes per day outside of your regular math time.

If you find that your child's lack of fluency with the multiplication facts makes lessons long and frustrating, **allow him to use the multiplication chart** (Blackline Master 2) as he completes lessons from this point forward. This will allow him to continue to make progress with new concepts while he works to solidify the multiplication facts.

Unit 3
Mental Multiplication

Overview

In this unit, your child will build on her multiplication and place-value skills to mentally multiply larger numbers. She'll also learn how to solve problems with parentheses, find answers to the ×11 and ×12 facts, and use the distributive property to solve problems.

Later this year, your child will learn the written process for multi-digit multiplication. This unit builds both the conceptual understanding and procedural skills necessary to master this complex process.

What Your Child Will Learn

In this unit, your child will learn to:

- Mentally multiply one-digit numbers by a multiple of 10, 100, or 1,000 (i.e., 4 × 500 or 3,000 × 6)
- Mentally multiply a multiple of 10 by a multiple of 10 (i.e., 40 × 80)
- Write and solve expressions with parentheses
- Understand the distributive property and use it to solve problems
- Find answers for the ×11 and ×12 facts
- Use the area model and box method to multiply two-digit numbers by one-digit numbers
- Solve multiplication word problems, including multiplicative comparison problems and multi-step problems

Lesson List

Lesson 3.1	Comparison Word Problems	Lesson 3.6	×11 Facts
Lesson 3.2	Mental Multiplication, Part 1	Lesson 3.7	×12 Facts
Lesson 3.3	Mental Multiplication, Part 2	Lesson 3.8	The Box Method
Lesson 3.4	Parentheses	Lesson 3.9	Multiplication Word Problems
Lesson 3.5	The Distributive Property	Lesson 3.10	Enrichment (Optional)

Extra Materials Needed for Unit 3

- Tape
- Measuring tape or ruler
- Paper clip
- For optional Enrichment Lesson:
    - *Math Curse*, Jon Scieszka and Lane Smith. Viking, 1995.
    - Large piece of posterboard (or 9 sheets of paper and tape)
    - 9 slips of paper

Teaching Math with Confidence: Understanding the Distributive Property

You may dimly remember memorizing the distributive property sometime in your middle or high school math classes. The property is usually summarized algebraically with letters and then used to "multiply out" or simplify equations.

$$a\,(b+c) = a \times b + a \times c$$

The distributive property expressed algebraically.

If you struggled in your algebra classes (or have blocked out those memories entirely), the idea of teaching the distributive property to your child may feel intimidating. But, don't worry! The distributive property simply expresses a common-sense idea: Multiplying the sum of two numbers yields the same result as if you multiply the numbers separately and then add the products.

For example, say you buy lunch for 3 people at a concession stand. Each person gets a chicken sandwich for $8 and a bottle of water for $2. There are two different ways to find the total cost. One way is to think of the order as 3 combo meals. Each person's combo costs $10, so the total cost for 3 people is $30.

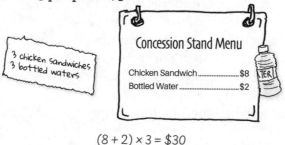

$$(8 + 2) \times 3 = \$30$$

One way to find the total cost is to think of the order as 3 combo meals.
Each meal costs $10, so the total order costs $30.

Another way is to find the cost of the chicken sandwiches, find the cost of the bottles of water, and add them together. The 3 chicken sandwiches cost $24, and the 3 bottles of water cost $6. So, the total cost for lunch is $30. No matter how you calculate it, the total cost is the same.

$$(8 \times 3) + (2 \times 3) = \$30$$

Another way to find the total cost is to find the cost of the chicken sandwiches and water bottles separately, then add. The chicken sandwiches cost $24, and the bottled waters cost $6, so the order costs $30 in all.

In *Third Grade Math with Confidence*, your child informally used the distributive property to learn the multiplication facts and find the areas of large rectangles. In this unit, you'll teach her to use the distributive property to multiply one-digit numbers times two-digit numbers. For example, to find 4 times 16, she'll break 16 into 10 and 6, multiply each part separately by 4, and then add to find the final answer.

	10	6
4	4 × 10	4 × 6

$$4 \times 16 = (4 \times 10) + (4 \times 6) = 64$$

Later in the year, she'll discover that the distributive property also lies at the heart of the traditional written process for multi-digit multiplication. By solidifying her understanding of the distributive property now, you build a solid conceptual foundation for that challenging skill.

Lesson 3.1
Comparison Word Problems

Purpose	Materials
• Practice solving comparison problems with addition and subtraction • Introduce multiplicative comparison word problems • Multiply or divide to find how many times greater (or less) one number is than another	• Tape • Measuring tape or ruler

Memory Work
- **How many ounces equal 1 pound?** *16.*
- **How many grams equal 1 kilogram?** *1,000.*

In previous grades, your child learned to compare numbers and tell "how many more" or "how many less." These types of problems are called *additive comparison* problems, because the quantities are related to each other through addition: the lesser number plus the difference equals the greater number.

In this lesson, you will introduce your child to *multiplicative comparison* word problems, in which the quantities are related to each other through multiplication: the lesser number times a multiplier equals the greater number.

Warm-up: Solve Comparison Age Riddles

Ask your child the following comparison age riddles.

- **Lily is 9. Her uncle is 26 years older than her. How old is her uncle?** *35.*
- **Desmond's grandma is 70. His grandma is 60 years older than him. How old is Desmond?** *10.*
- **Liam is 12. His sister is 6 years younger than him. How old is his sister?** *6.*
- **Evan is 8. He is 31 years younger than his mom. How old is his mom?** *39.*

Activity (A): Compare Animals' Jumps in Two Ways

In earlier grades, you learned how to use addition and subtraction to compare numbers. Today, you'll learn how to use multiplication and division to compare numbers.

Show your child part A. **We'll use the clues in the word problems to complete the bar graph. When it's completed, the bar graph will show how far each type of animal can jump.** Briefly discuss what your child knows about each of the animals listed in the graph.

An impala is a type of antelope found in Africa. A kangaroo rat is a type of rodent found in North American deserts. They jump like kangaroos, by standing on their hind legs and using their tails for balance.

Read aloud the first question: *A bullfrog can jump 6 ft. A snowshoe hare can jump 2 times as far as a bullfrog. How far can a snowshoe hare jump?*

A bullfrog can jump 6 feet. There's no printed line for 6 feet, so I'll approximate the length of the bar and draw it a little longer than 5 feet. Draw a narrow bar as shown.

A snowshoe hare can jump 2 times as far as a bullfrog. So, we multiply 2 times 6 feet to find how far a snowshoe hare can jump. Write "2 × 6 =" in the space below the question. Have your child complete the equation and draw a bar to match.

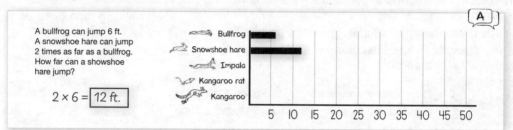

This question told us how many *times* longer the snowshoe hare can jump than the bullfrog. Another way to compare two amounts is to find the difference between them.

Read aloud the next question: *How many feet farther can a snowshoe hare jump than a bullfrog?* **How can we find the answer?** *Subtract 12 minus 6.* Write "12 − 6 =" in the space below the question. Have your child complete the equation.

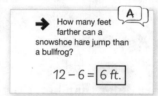

Repeat with the next pair of questions.

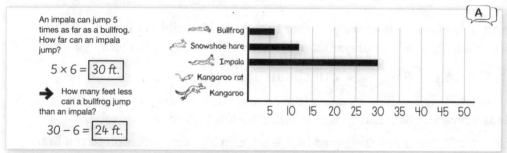

Read aloud the next question: *A kangaroo can jump 45 ft. That's 5 times as far as a kangaroo rat can jump. How far can a kangaroo rat jump?*

A kangaroo can jump 45 feet. Draw a bar as shown. **45 feet is 5 times as far as the kangaroo rat can jump. So, we divide 45 by 5 to find how far a kangaroo rat can jump.** Write "45 ÷ 5 =" in the space below the question. Have your child complete the equation and draw a bar to match. Then, have your child answer the final question.

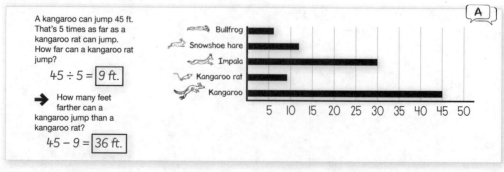

Activity (B): Write Equations to Compare Broad Jump Distances

When you do a broad jump, you start on two feet and land on two feet, with no running or extra jumps. The world record for the broad jump for humans is about 12 feet.

We're going to measure how far you can jump, and then we'll compare your jump with the world record two different ways. Place a piece of tape on the ground. Have your child stand on two feet behind the piece of tape. Have her jump as far as she can and land on both feet. Place another piece of tape just behind her heels. Then, have her use a measuring tape (or ruler) to measure the length of her jump in feet. If needed, help your child round the length to the nearest foot. Record the distance in the blank.

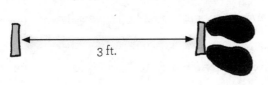 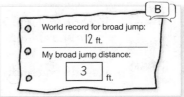

Sample jump.

Your child may want to do a few practice jumps before she measures her "official" jump.

Let's compare your broad jump distance to the world record in two ways. First, we'll find how many feet longer the world record is than your jump. What subtraction equation tells the difference between your jump and the world record jump? *Sample answer: 12 – 3 = 9.* **How many feet longer is the world record jump than your jump?** *Sample answer: 9 feet.* Have your child complete the blank and write the matching subtraction equation below it.

> The world record is _____9_____ feet [B]
> longer than my jump.
>
> $$12 - 3 = 9$$

Sample answer for a 3-foot jump. Your child should use the length of her jump to find the difference.

Now, let's find *how many times* longer the world record is than your jump. We'll divide the world record by the length of your jump to find how many times greater it is. Write an equation showing the length of the world record jump divided by the length of your child's jump. For example, if your child jumped 3 feet, write "$12 \div 3 = 4$" in the space below the question.

> The world record is _____4_____ times [B]
> as long as my jump.
>
> $$12 \div 3 = 4$$

Sample answer for a 3-foot jump.

If your child's division problem has a remainder, help her interpret the answer. For example, if she jumped 5 feet, the world record is between 2 and 3 times the length of her jump.

$$12 \div 5 = 2 \, R \, 2$$

Independent Practice and Review

Have your child complete the Lesson 3.1 Practice and Review workbook pages.

Lesson 3.2
Mental Multiplication, Part 1

Purpose	Materials
• Practice naming the value of groups of 10 or 100 • Tack on place-holder zeros to multiply one-digit numbers by multiples of 10, 100, or 1,000	• Die

| Memory Work | • **How do you know if a number is divisible by 2?** *It is even. It has 0, 2, 4, 6, or 8 in the ones-place.*
• **How do you know if a number is divisible by 5?** *It has a 0 or 5 in the ones-place.*
• **How do you know if a number is divisible by 10?** *It has a 0 in the ones-place.* |

Your child learned how to use place-value thinking to multiply one-digit numbers by multiples of 10 in *Third Grade Math with Confidence.* In this lesson, he'll extend this skill to tack on zeros to multiply one-digit numbers by multiples of 10, 100, or 1,000.

Warm-up: Name the Value of Groups of 10 or 100

Have your child tell the value of the following groups of 10 or 100.

- **9 tens?** *90.*
- **10 tens?** *100.*
- **16 tens?** *160.*
- **38 tens?** *380.*

- **10 hundreds?** *1,000.*
- **12 hundreds?** *1,200.*
- **30 hundreds?** *3,000.*
- **35 hundreds?** *3,500.*

If your child doesn't remember how to find the value of groups of 10, briefly review with base-ten blocks. For example, for 16 times 10, place 16 rods on the table. **How much do 10 tens equal?** *100.* **How much do 6 tens equal?** *60.* **So, you can add 100 plus 60 to find 16 times 10.** He can use the same reasoning for groups of 100.

Activity (A):
Use Place-Value Thinking to Multiply by Multiples of 10, 100, or 1,000

Today, you'll learn how to mentally multiply one-digit numbers by multiples of 10, 100, or 1,000.

Show your child part A. **Have you ever been to an arcade?** *Answers will vary.* Briefly discuss your child's experiences with arcades. **At some arcades, you win tickets with different point values when you play the games. Then, you use the points to earn prizes.**

Let's pretend you're at an arcade and play the same game 3 times. You win 40 points each time. We'll multiply 3 times 40 to see how many points you won.

Point to 3 × 40. **We have 3 groups of tickets. Each group has 4 tens.**

What's 3 times 4? *12.* **So, we have 12 tens.** Write 12 in the cloud answer blank. **12 tens equal how many points?** *120.* Write 120 in the blank.

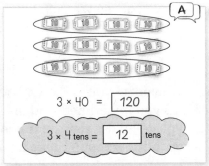

We can use the same reasoning for multiples of 100 or 1,000. Repeat for 4 × 500 and 2 × 8,000.

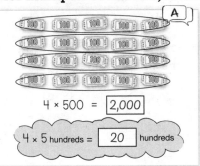

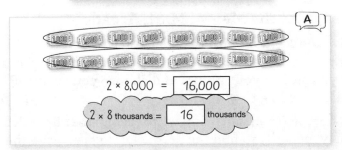

Activity (B): Tack on Zeros to Multiply by Multiples of 10, 100, or 1,000

You can also use the place-holder zeros in the numbers to help you multiply them. These steps show us how.

Point to 4 × 60. **The first step is to underline the place-holder zeros. 60 has one place-holder zero. The place-holder zero holds the ones-place and shows that the 6 is in the tens-place.** Underline the 0 in 60. **Underlining the place-holder zeros reminds us that we're multiplying 6 tens.**

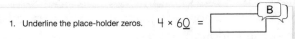

1. Underline the place-holder zeros.   4 × 6<u>0</u> = ⬚

The second step is to multiply the non-zero digits. "Non-zero digits" just means "digits that aren't zero." In this problem, the non-zero digits are 4 and 6. What's 4 times 6? *24.* Write 24 in the answer blank. Leave space for another digit after the 24.

2. Multiply the non-zero digits.   4 × 6<u>0</u> = 24

Does 4 times 60 equal 24? *No.* **We still have to follow the last step. The last step is to tack on the place-holder zeros. This makes sure all the digits are in the right place. In this problem, we multiplied 4 times 6 tens, so we tack on 1 place-holder zero to show that we have 24 *tens*, or 240.** Write 0 after the 24 as shown. **So, 4 times 60 equals 240.**

> 3. Tack on the place-holder zeros. $4 \times 6\underline{0}$ = [240] **B**

Use the steps to demonstrate how to solve 3 × 700 and 5 × 2,000. Make sure you tack on the same number of place-holder zeros as you underlined, and insert a comma. For 5 × 2,000, point out that you need to tack on 3 place-holder zeros: **2 times 5 equals 10. I write a zero in 10, but I still need to tack on 3 zeros to show that 5 times 2 *thousands* equals 10 *thousands*.**

> $3 \times 7\underline{00}$ = [2,100] **B**
>
> $5 \times 2,\underline{000}$ = [10,000]

Have your child complete the problems in part B in the same way. Remind him to leave space for the place-holder zeros when he writes the product of the non-zero digits.

$2 \times 9\underline{0}$ = [180]	$8 \times 4,\underline{000}$ = [32,000] **B**
$5 \times 3,\underline{000}$ = [15,000]	$4 \times 4\underline{00}$ = [1,600]
$8 \times 5\underline{00}$ = [4,000]	$5 \times 6\underline{0}$ = [300]

Activity (C): Multiply at the Mental Math Arcade

Let's pretend we're at the Mental Math Arcade! You win points at the arcade by rolling a die and multiplying the number on the die times one of the ticket amounts. After you roll the die 5 times, you add up your points and choose your prize. Briefly discuss which prize your child would most like to win.

Have your child roll the die. Then, have him write the number he rolled in one of the blank equations and multiply mentally to find the product. (He may write the number on the die in any blank equation.) For example, if your child rolls a 6 and writes it in the first blank equation, his product is 480.

Have your child write the products so that the ones-place is next to the right side of the chart. (This aligns the numbers so it's easier to add them at the end of the activity.)

Have your child continue until he has completed all the equations. Then, have him find the sum of his points and pretend to choose his prize from the printed options. He may choose multiple prizes if he has earned enough points.

Independent Practice and Review

Have your child complete the Lesson 3.2 Practice and Review workbook pages.

Lesson 3.3
Mental Multiplication, Part 2

Purpose	Materials
• Practice tacking on zeros to solve mental multiplication problems • Create arrays to model multiplying multiples of 10 times multiples of 10 • Tack on place-holder zeros to multiply multiples of 10 times multiples of 10	• Base-ten blocks • Paper clip

Memory Work	• **What is a prime number?** *A number with exactly 2 factors.* • **What is a composite number?** *A number with more than 2 factors.*

Warm-up (A): Practice Tacking on Zeros to Multiply

In the last lesson, you learned how to multiply one-digit numbers by multiples of 10, 100, or 1,000. You learned to underline the place-holder zeros, multiply the other digits, and then tack on the place-holder zeros. Have your child use this method to complete the problems in part A.

$3 × 9\underline{00} =$ $\boxed{2,700}$ $4 × 4{,}\underline{000} =$ $\boxed{16,000}$ **A**

Activity (B): Tack on Zeros to Multiply Multiples of 10

Today, you'll learn how to multiply a multiple of 10 times a multiple of 10. First, we'll use the same steps we used in the last lesson. Then, we'll use the array to understand why the steps work.

Point to 20 × 30. **The first step is to underline the place-holder zeros.** Underline the 0 in 20 and the 0 in 30. **Underlining the place-holder zeros reminds us that we're multiplying 2 tens times 3 tens.**

$2\underline{0} × 3\underline{0} =$ $\boxed{}$ **B**

The second step is to multiply the non-zero digits. In this problem, the non-zero digits are 2 and 3. What's 2 times 3? *6.* Write 6 in the answer blank. Leave space for 2 more digits after the 6.

$2\underline{0} × 3\underline{0} =$ $\boxed{6}$ **B**

Does 20 times 30 equal 6? *No.* We still have to tack on the place-holder zeros so the digits are in the right place. In this problem, we underlined 2 place-holder zeros, so we tack on 2 place-holder zeros. Write 2 zeros after the 6 as shown. **2 tens times 3 tens equals 6** *hundreds*, **so the answer is 600.**

$2\underline{0} × 3\underline{0} =$ $\boxed{600}$ **B**

Point to the array. **This array is 20 small squares wide and 30 small squares long. It's another way to think of 20 times 30 and helps show why 20 times 30 equals 600.**

The dark lines divide the array into groups of 100. How many groups of 100 are in the array? 6. **Each group of ten is multiplied by a group of ten to become 1 hundred. There are 2 groups of ten multiplied by 3 groups of ten, so we end up with 6 hundreds.** Write 6 in the blank.

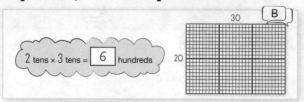

Have your child complete the problems in part B.

$40 \times 40 =$ 1,600 $60 \times 30 =$ 1,800 $80 \times 50 =$ 4,000

If your child has trouble understanding place-value in these problems, use flats from your base-ten blocks to create an array to match each problem. For example, for 40 × 40, create a 4×4 array of flats: **4 tens times 4 tens equal 16 hundreds, or 1,600.**

Activity (C): Play Spin to Win

Use the game board to play Spin to Win.

Spin to Win

Materials: Paper clip

Object of the Game: Score more points than the other player by creating greater products.

Place one end of the paper clip in the middle of the spinner. Place the point of a pencil through the paper clip so that it touches the very middle of the circle.

Spin to Win has 4 rounds. On your turn, hold the pencil upright and spin the paper clip so that it spins freely around the circle. Spin twice. Write the first number you spin as the first factor in your first multiplication problem. Write the second number you spin as the second factor. Then, multiply to find the product. For example, if your first spin is 40 and your second spin is 70, your product is 2,800. This product is your score.

Sample turn.

Then, have the other player spin twice and find the product of her spins.

Continue until you have completed all 4 rounds. Each player adds up their scores from all 4 rounds. Whoever has a higher total score wins the game.

Independent Practice and Review

Have your child complete the Lesson 3.3 Practice and Review workbook pages.

Lesson 3.4
Parentheses

Purpose	Materials
• Practice solving a sequence of math problems in order • Understand parentheses mean to "do this first" • Find the value of equations with parentheses • Write equations with parentheses to solve word problems	• None

Memory Work	• **Name 4 factors of 10.** *1, 2, 5, 10.* • **Name 4 multiples of 10.** *Sample answers: 10, 40, 80, 200.*

Warm-up: Solve Math Problems in Order

Ask your child the following mental math questions.

- **What's 7 times 5?** *35.* **Plus 6?** *41.* **Minus 1?** *40.*
- **What's 3 times 2?** *6.* **Times 4?** *24.* **Divided by 8?** *3.*
- **What's 7 plus 3?** *10.* **Times 10?** *100.* **Minus 50?** *50.*

Activity (A): Introduce Parentheses

The warm-up questions combined addition, subtraction, multiplication, and division. I asked you each step in order, so you knew exactly what to do.

Written equations sometimes combine addition, subtraction, multiplication, or division, too. Mathematicians use symbols called parentheses to show which step to do first.

Parentheses are one of the many conventions that mathematicians use to show order in equations. Your child will learn more about the order of operations in future grades.

Have you ever seen parentheses in a book before? *Answers will vary.* **In books, authors use parentheses to provide extra information. The words in parentheses usually aren't essential. Sometimes, you can even skip them!**

Parentheses in math are different. You definitely can't skip them! When you see parentheses in an equation, it means you should do whatever is in the parentheses first.

Show your child the two equations at the top of part A. **These two equations have the same numbers. They both have a plus sign, multiplication sign, and equals sign. But, they have parentheses in different places.** Point to the parentheses in each equation.

Parentheses mean "do this first!"   A

$(3 + 2) \times 4 =$ ☐ $3 + (2 \times 4) =$ ☐

In the first equation, the parentheses tell us to add 3 plus 2 before we multiply by 4. What's 3 plus 2? *5.* Write 5 below the equation as shown. **Now, we multiply. What's 5 times 4?** *20.* Write 20 in the blank.

$(3 + 2) \times 4 =$ $\boxed{20}$ A
5

Writing the value of the expression in parentheses directly below the equation builds good habits for simplifying algebraic equations in future years.

In the second equation, the parentheses tell us to multiply 2 times 4 first. What's 2 times 4? *8.* **Write 8 below the equation as shown. Now, we add. What's 3 plus 8?** *11.* **Write 11 in the blank.**

$$3 + (2 \times 4) \;=\; \boxed{11}$$
$$8$$

Even though these equations have the same numbers and the same signs, they have different answers because of the parentheses.

Have your child complete the other pairs of equations in the same way. Make sure he writes the value of the step in parentheses below the equation.

$(16 \div 4) - 2 \;=\; \boxed{2}$	$16 \div (4 - 2) \;=\; \boxed{8}$
4	2
$(6 \times 7) + 1 \;=\; \boxed{43}$	$6 \times (7 + 1) \;=\; \boxed{48}$
42	8

Activity (B): Write Equations with Parentheses at the Concession Stand

We can also use parentheses to write equations for problems with multiple steps. Have you ever been to a concession stand at a festival or sports event? *Answers will vary.* **We'll use parentheses to write equations and find the total cost of these concession stand orders.**

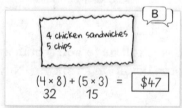

Concession Stand Menu
Chicken Sandwich $8
Veggie Wrap $8
Pizza Slice $4
Hot Dog $3
Chips $3
Bottled Water $2
Candy $2

If your child enjoys pretending, pretend to be the customer placing each order. After your child finds the total cost of your order, pretend to pay him for the order and have him pretend to give you your food.

The first order is for 4 chicken sandwiches and 5 bags of chips. Point to the matching equation. **Each chicken sandwich costs $8, so we multiply 4 times 8 to find the cost of 4 chicken sandwiches. What's 4 times 8?** *32.* **Write 32 below the equation. The 4 chicken sandwiches cost $32.**

Each bag of chips costs $3, so we multiply 5 times 3 to find the cost of 5 bags of chips. What's 5 times 3? *15.* **Write 15 below the equation. The 5 bags of chips cost $15. Now, we can add $32 plus $15 to find the total cost. What's $32 plus $15?** *$47.* **Write $47 in the blank. The total order costs $47.**

4 chicken sandwiches
5 chips

$$(4 \times 8) + (5 \times 3) \;=\; \boxed{\$47}$$
$$32 \qquad\quad 15$$

Point to the next order. **The next order is for 4 pizza slices and 3 bags of chips. What multiplication problem tells the cost of the 4 pizza slices?** *4 times 4.* Write "4 × 4" on the left side of the space below the order. **What multiplication problem tells the cost of the 3 bags of chips?** *3 times 3.* Write "3 × 3" on the right side of the space below the order. **We want to multiply each amount first, then add them together.** Draw parentheses around each multiplication problem and write a plus sign between them.

Have your child solve the problem as shown. Then, have him complete the rest of the problems in part A in the same way.

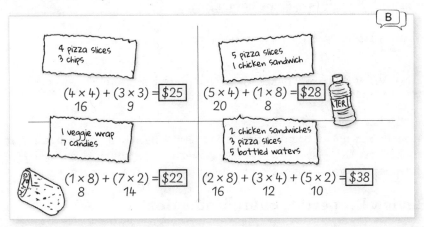

For the orders in which there is only 1 of a certain item, your child may multiply the price of the item times 1, or he may simply add on the cost of the item. For example, for 5 pizza slices and 1 chicken sandwich, your child may write either (5 × 4) + (1 × 8) or (5 × 4) + 8.

Independent Practice and Review

Have your child complete the Lesson 3.4 Practice and Review workbook pages.

Lesson 3.5
The Distributive Property

Purpose	Materials
• Review properties of multiplication • Write equations with parentheses to match multi-step problems • Use the distributive property as a shortcut for solving problems	• None

Memory Work • **What do parentheses mean in a math problem?** *Do this first.*

In this lesson, you'll introduce the distributive property to your child as a shortcut for solving multiplication word problems. Your child is not expected to memorize a formal definition for the distributive property in fourth grade, and she'll learn to apply it in a variety of contexts throughout the year. See the Unit 3 **Teaching Math with Confidence** for more on why the distributive property is so important.

Warm-up: Review Properties of Multiplication

Last year, you learned some multiplication rules that hold true for every number. We call these rules the *properties* of multiplication. We'll warm up today by reviewing some of these properties.

What's 4 times 0? *0.* **What's 100 times 0?** *0.* **What's any number times 0?** *0.* **One property of multiplication is that any number times 0 equals 0.**

What's 4 times 1? *4.* **What's 100 times 1?** *100.* **What's any number times 1?** *The number.* **Another property of multiplication is that any number times 1 equals the same number.**

What's 4 times 3? *12.* **What's 3 times 4?** *12.* **Another property of multiplication is that you can multiply in any order and still get the same answer.**

Activity (A): Introduce the Distributive Property with Concession Stand Orders

Today, you'll learn about a property of multiplication called the *distributive property*. We'll use concession stand equations to learn about this property.

The first order today is for 4 bottled waters and 3 candies. One way to find the total cost is to multiply to find the cost of the bottled waters, multiply to find the cost of the candies, then add the two costs together.

Each bottle of water costs $2, so first we multiply 4 times 2 to find their cost. What's 4 times 2? *8.* **Write 8 below the equation. Each pack of candy costs $2, so we multiply 3 times 2 to find their cost. What's 3 times 2?** *6.* **Write 6 below the equation. Last, we add to find the total cost. What's 8 plus 6?** *14.*

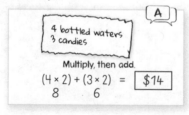

Another way to find the total cost is to first add to find the total number of items. Then, we can multiply the total number of items times 2, since all the items cost $2.

The customer wants 4 bottled waters and 3 candies, so we add 4 plus 3 to find the total number of items. **What's 4 plus 3?** *7.* Write 7 below the equation. **Then, we multiply 7 times 2 to find the total cost. What's 7 times 2?** *14.* Write $14 in the blank.

Add, then multiply. **A**
$$(4 + 3) \times 2 = \boxed{\$14}$$
$$7$$

We get the same answer to this problem no matter which way we solve it. We can multiply and then add. Or, we can add, and then multiply. Either way we get the same answer. This is called the distributive property of multiplication. You'll learn more about the distributive property throughout the rest of the unit.

Activity (B): Use the Distributive Property at the Concession Stand

The next order is for 3 chicken sandwiches and 7 veggie wraps. **How much do chicken sandwiches cost?** *$8.* **How much do veggie wraps cost?** *$8.* Both items cost $8, so we can use the distributive property to quickly find the total cost.

How many items are in the order? *10.* **How do you know?** *Sample answer: I added 3 plus 7.* Write "(3 + 7)" to begin an equation. **Each of the 10 items costs $8, so we can multiply the number of items by 8 to find the total cost of the order.** Write "× 8 =" to continue the equation. Have your child complete the equation. **How much does the order cost?** *$80.*

B
3 chicken sandwiches
7 veggie wraps
$$(3 + 7) \times 8 = \$80$$
$$10$$

The next order is for 5 hot dogs and 4 bags of chips. **How much does each hot dog cost?** *$3.* **How much does each bag of chips cost?** *$3.* Every item costs $3, so we can use the distributive property again to find the total cost. Have your child write and solve an equation to find the cost of the order.

B
5 hot dogs
4 chips
$$(5 + 4) \times 3 = \$27$$
$$9$$

The next order is for 3 chicken sandwiches and 3 bottled waters. **We can use the distributive property in a slightly different way to solve this problem. Let's think of this order as 3 combo meals. Each combo meal has 1 chicken sandwich and 1 bottle of water.**

How much does each combo meal cost? *$10.* **How do you know?** *Sample answer: I added 8 plus 2.* Write "(8 + 2)" to begin an equation. **Each combo meal costs $10, so we multiply 10 times 3 to find the total cost of the order.** Write "× 3 =" to continue the equation. Have your child complete the equation. **How much does the order cost?** *$30.*

B
3 chicken sandwiches
3 bottled waters
$$(8 + 2) \times 3 = \$30$$
$$10$$

Have your child write and solve an equation to find the cost of the final order. Encourage her to think of the order as 5 combo meals, where each combo meal has 1 pizza slice and 1 bag of chips.

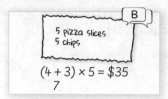

Independent Practice and Review

Have your child complete the Lesson 3.5 Practice and Review workbook pages.

Lesson 3.6
×11 Facts

Purpose	Materials
• Preview the ×11 facts by counting by 11s • Use the distributive property and area model to find answers to the ×11 facts • Practice ×11 facts	• Counters

Memory Work	
	• **What do we call the top number in a fraction?** *The numerator.* • **What does the numerator tell?** *The number of parts.* • **What do we call the bottom number in a fraction?** *The denominator.* • **What does the denominator tell?** *How many equal parts the whole was split into.*

In this lesson, your child will learn to use the distributive property to find answers to the ×11 facts. This method is the same technique your child used to find answers to the multiplication facts in *Third Grade Math with Confidence*. For example, to find 7 × 6, he multiplied 7 × 5 and then added one additional group of 7.

$$7 \times 6 = (7 \times 5) + (7 \times 1) = 42$$

Many children will quickly see the pattern in the answers to ×11 facts. If your child immediately knows the answers to the ×11 facts, make sure to teach the rest of the lesson anyway. He'll use the distributive property to solve more-challenging multiplication problems in the next few lessons, and it helps to practice this strategy first with easy numbers.

Warm-up: Count by 11s

Today, you'll learn the ×11 facts. Let's warm-up by counting by 11s. Have your child count by 11s up to 132. Encourage him to mentally add 11 to each previous number to find the next number. Write each number on a piece of scrap paper as he says it.

11, 22, 33, 44, 55, 66, 77, 88, 99, 110, 121, 132

If your child has trouble, suggest he add the tens and ones separately. For example, to add 44 plus 11: **What's 44 plus 10?** *54.* **Plus 1?** *55.*

What pattern do you notice? *Sample answers: The tens-place and ones-place are the same up to 99!*

Activity (A): Use the Distributive Property to Find Answers for the ×11 Facts

In the last lesson, we used the distributive property to find the total price for concession stand orders. There were two different ways to find the cost of each order. You could multiply the parts of the order separately and then add the two products. Or, you could add the parts first, and then multiply.

Today, we'll use the distributive property to find the answers to the ×11 facts. We'll break the problems into parts, multiply each part separately, and then add the two products.

Show your child the 3×11 array. **This array has 3 rows and 11 columns. Let's use the array to find the answer to 3 times 11. There are 3 rows of 10 on the left side. What's 3 times 10?** *30.* Write 30 on the left side of the array. **There are 3 rows of 1 on the right side. What's 3 times 1?** *3.* Write 3 on the right side of the array. **So, what's 3 times 11?** *33.*

> If your child enjoys using base-ten blocks, have him use 3 rods and 3 units to build a matching array. Point out that the 3 rods equal 30, and the 3 units equal 3. So, the array has a total value of 33.

This equation shows how we used the distributive property to find the number of squares in the array. Read the equation aloud: ***3 times 11 equals 3 times 10 plus 3 times 1.***

3 times 10 equals 30. Write 30 below 3 × 10. **3 times 1 equals 3.** Write 3 below 3 × 1. **30 plus 3 equals 33, so 3 times 11 equals 33.** Write 33 in the final answer blank.

$$3 \times 11 = (3 \times 10) + (3 \times 1) = \boxed{33}$$
$$30 \qquad 3$$

We call 30 and 3 the *partial products* in this problem. Listen to how *partial* starts with the word *part*. We call these numbers partial products because each is part of the total product. We add the partial products to find the total product.

Complete the example for 5 × 11 in the same way.

$$5 \times 11 = (5 \times 10) + (5 \times 1) = \boxed{55}$$
$$50 \qquad 5$$

> If your child is confused by the idea of using two equals signs in the same equation, explain that we can use as many equals signs as we want as long as all the parts of the equation are actually equal to each other.
>
> $5 \times 11 = (5 \times 10) + (5 \times 1) = 55$ $6 \times 4 = 24 + 3 = 27$
>
> This is a valid equation, since the expressions connected by the equals signs all equal each other.   This is not a valid equation, since 6 times 4 equals 24, and the other two parts of the equation equal 27.

Show your child the diagram for 8 × 11. **This picture doesn't show every square. We'll use the lengths of the sides to find the area of each part. Multiplying in parts and then adding the parts together is just like multiplying to find areas and then adding them together to find the area of the whole rectangle. We call diagrams like these *area models* for multiplication.**

> Your child does not need to memorize the terms partial product or area model. Being familiar with the terms simply makes it easier to discuss these problems.

The left side is 8 by 10. What's 8 times 10? *80.* Write 80 on the left side of the rectangle. **The right side is 8 by 1. What's 8 times 1?** *8.* Write 8 on the right side. **So, what's 8 times 11?** *88.* Write 88 in the blank. Have your child find 6 × 11 in the same way.

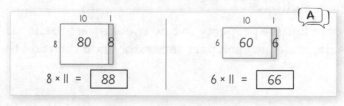

Activity (B): Find Answers to ×11 Facts without Arrays

You can use the distributive property to find answers to the ×11 facts, even if you don't have a printed area model in front of you. You just have to keep the numbers in your head.

Here's how to find 4 × 11. First, I multiply 4 times 10. Point to the 4, and then point to the 1 in the tens-place in 11. **What's 4 times 10?** 40.

4 × 11 = ⬚ **B**   4 × 10 = 40

Then, I multiply 4 times 1. Point to the 4, and then point to the 1 in the ones-place in 11. **What's 4 times 1?** 4.

4 × 11 = ⬚ **B**   4 × 1 = 4

Last, I add. What's 40 plus 4? 44. Write 44 in the final blank.

4 × 11 = 44 **B**   40 + 4 = 44

Have your child use the same method to complete the rest of the problems in part B.

			B
4 × 11 = 44	9 × 11 = 99	2 × 11 = 22	
10 × 11 = 110	11 × 11 = 121	12 × 11 = 132	

If your child is intimidated by 11 × 11 and 12 × 11, encourage him to simply use the same process he used for the one-digit ×11 facts.

11 × 11 = 121

11 × 10 = 110
11 × 1 = 11
110 + 11 = 121

Activity (C): Play Four in a Row

Use the game board to play Four in a Row.

Cover parts A and B with a piece of paper so your child can't refer to the completed problems as you play the game.

Four in a Row

Materials: 20 counters per player, with a different color for each player

Object of the Game: Be the first player to place counters in 4 squares in a row, either horizontally, vertically, or diagonally.

On your turn, choose one problem on the board and say its answer. Use 2 counters to cover the box with the problem as well as the box with the problem's answer. For example, if you choose the box with 6 × 11, cover the box with 6 × 11 and the box with 66.

Play then passes to the other player. Continue until one player covers 4 boxes in a row, either horizontally, vertically, or diagonally.

One square in the game does not have a match (since the gameboard has an odd number of squares). If you discover this square, tell your child that it is a "stopper" and that neither player may play a counter on this square.

Independent Practice and Review

Have your child complete the Lesson 3.6 Practice and Review workbook pages.

Lesson 3.7
×12 Facts

Purpose	Materials
• Preview the ×12 facts by counting by 12s • Use the distributive property to find answers to the ×12 facts • Practice ×12 facts	• 2 dice • Scrap paper

Memory Work	• **How many cups equal 1 pint?** *2.* • **How many pints equal 1 quart?** *2.* • **How many quarts equal 1 gallon?** *4.*

Warm-up: Count by 12s

Today, you'll learn the ×12 facts. Let's warm up by counting by 12s. Have your child count by 12s up to 144. Encourage her to mentally add 12 to each previous number to find the next number. Write each number on a piece of scrap paper as she says it.

12, 24, 36, 48, 60, 72, 84, 96, 108, 120, 132, 144

If your child has trouble, suggest she add the tens and ones separately. For example, to add 48 plus 12: **What's 48 plus 10?** *58.* **Plus 2?** *60.*

What patterns do you notice? *Sample answers: All the answers are even. The ones-place increases by 2 each time. The tens-place increases by 1 each time until you're past 100.*

Activity (A): Use the Distributive Property to Find Answers for the ×12 Facts

In the last lesson, you used the distributive property to find the answers to the ×11 facts. Today, we'll use the same approach to find answers to the ×12 facts.

Show your child the 4×12 array. **Let's use this array to find the answer to 4 times 12. There are 4 rows of 10 on the left side. What's 4 times 10?** *40.* **Write 40 on the left side of the array. There are 4 rows of 2 on the right side. What's 4 times 2?** *8.* **Write 8 on the right side. So, what's 4 times 12?** *48.*

10   2   [A]
4   40   8

If your child enjoys using base-ten blocks, have her use 4 rods and 8 units to build a matching array.

This equation shows how we used the distributive property to find the number of squares in the array. Read the equation aloud: *4 times 12 equals 4 times 10 plus 4 times 2.*

4 times 10 equals 40. Write 40 below 4 × 10. **4 times 2 equals 8.** Write 8 below 4 × 2. **40 plus 8 equals 48, so 4 times 12 equals 48.** Write 48 in the final answer blank.

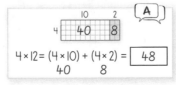

$$4 \times 12 = (4 \times 10) + (4 \times 2) = \boxed{48}$$
40   8

Complete the example for 6 × 12 in the same way.

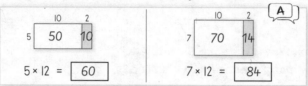

Show your child the area model for 5 × 12. **The left side is 5 by 10. What's 5 times 10?** *50.*
Write 50 on the left side of the rectangle. **The right side is 5 by 2. What's 5 times 2?** *10.* Write
10 on the right side. **So, what's 5 times 12?** *60.* Have your child find 7 × 12 in the same way.

$$5 \times 12 = \boxed{60} \qquad 7 \times 12 = \boxed{84}$$

Activity (B): Find Answers to ×12 Facts without Arrays

**You can use the distributive property to find answers to the ×12 facts in your head, just
like you found answers to the ×11 facts in the last lesson.**

Here's how to find 3 × 12. First, I multiply 3 times 10. Point to the 3, and then point to the 1 in
12. **What's 3 times 10?** *30.*

$$3 \times 12 = \boxed{} \qquad\qquad 3 \times 10 = 30$$

Then, I multiply 3 times 2. Point to the 3, and then point to the 2 in the 12. **What's 3 times 2?** *6.*

$$3 \times 12 = \boxed{} \qquad\qquad 3 \times 2 = 6$$

Last, I add. What's 30 plus 6? *36.* Write 36 in the blank.

$$3 \times 12 = \boxed{36} \qquad\qquad 30 + 6 = 36$$

Have your child use the same method to complete the problems in part B.

$$3 \times 12 = \boxed{36} \qquad 8 \times 12 = \boxed{96} \qquad 9 \times 12 = \boxed{108}$$
$$10 \times 12 = \boxed{120} \qquad 11 \times 12 = \boxed{132} \qquad 12 \times 12 = \boxed{144}$$

If your child is intimidated by 11 × 12 and 12 × 12, encourage her to use the same process she used for the
one-digit ×12 facts.

$$12 \times 12 = \boxed{144}$$

$$12 \times 10 = 120$$
$$12 \times 2 = 24$$
$$120 + 24 = 144$$

Activity (C): Play Egg Scramble

We call 12 of an item a *dozen*. Briefly discuss any items you buy in dozens, such as eggs, soft drinks, bottled water, cupcakes, or hamburger buns. **Let's pretend we have chickens and collect their eggs each day. We'll roll dice to see how many dozens we collect each day. Whoever collects more eggs in 5 days wins!** Play Egg Scramble.

Cover parts A and B with a piece of paper so your child can't refer to the completed problems as you play the game.

As you play Egg Scramble, write the number of eggs so that the ones-place is next to the right side of the scorecard. This aligns the numbers so it's easier to add them at the end of the game.

Egg Scramble

Materials: 2 dice

Object of the Game: Collect the greater total number of eggs.

On your turn, roll 2 dice. Write the sum of the dice in the column labeled "Dozens." Then, multiply the number of dozens by 12 to find the number of eggs collected. Write this product directly in the column labeled "Eggs." For example, if you roll a 7:

Dozens of Eggs	Number of Eggs
7	84

Sample first play.

Take turns rolling the dice and completing the scorecards until each player completes their scorecard. Add the number of eggs to find which player collected more eggs. Whoever collected more eggs wins.

Cooperative variation: Play together (on one scorecard) and see how many eggs you collect. Then, play together again (on a new scorecard) and see if you can beat your previous score.

Independent Practice and Review

Have your child complete the Lesson 3.7 Practice and Review workbook pages.

Lesson 3.8
The Box Method

Purpose	Materials
• Practice mental multiplication • Introduce the box method for multiplying two-digit numbers by one-digit numbers	• Die

Memory Work	
	• **What do we call an angle that looks like the corner of a piece of paper?** *A right angle.* • **What do we call a quadrilateral with 4 right angles?** *A rectangle.* • **What do we call a quadrilateral with 4 right angles and 4 equal sides?** *A square.* • **What do we call a quadrilateral with 4 equal sides?** *A rhombus.*

In *Third Grade Math with Confidence*, your child learned how to split large rectangles into parts, find the area of each part, and then add the parts together to find the total area. This lesson uses a similar visual model to teach your child how to find the product of a two-digit number and a one-digit number. He will learn the traditional written algorithm for these problems in Unit 7.

Warm-up: Practice Mental Multiplication

Ask your child the following mental multiplication problems:

- **4 times 60.** *240.*
- **3 times 70.** *210.*
- **5 times 40.** *200.*
- **7 times 60.** *420.*
- **8 times 80.** *640.*
- **6 times 90.** *540.*

Activity (A): Introduce the Box Method for Multiplication

In the last two lessons, you learned how to find answers for the ×11 and ×12 facts. You split the numbers into parts, multiplied each part, and then added the partial products.

We can use the same approach to multiply any one-digit number times a two-digit number. It can be hard to remember all the numbers, though. Today, you'll learn an approach called the box method to keep track of the partial products as you solve the problems.

Show your child the 4×16 array. **First, let's use the area model to find the answer to 4 times 16. There are 4 rows of 10 on the left side. What's 4 times 10?** *40.* Write 40 on the left side of the array. **There are 4 rows of 6 on the right side. What's 4 times 6?** *24.* Write 24 on the right side. **So, what's 4 times 16?** *64.* Write 64 in the blank.

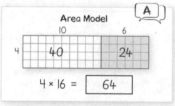

Now, let's solve the same problem with the box method.

- Point to 4 and 10. **What's 4 times 10?** *40.* Write 40 as shown.
- Point to 4 and 6. **What's 4 times 6?** *24.* Write 24 as shown.
- **Now, I add the partial products to find the total product. 40 plus 24 equals 64, so the total product is 64.** Write 64 in the blank.

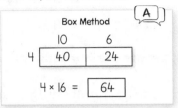

Why do you think people call this method the box method? *Sample answer: Because you record your steps in boxes.*

How is the box method like using the area model? *Sample answers: You get the same partial products and the same answer with both methods.*

Both the area model and the box method involve the same steps and give you the same answer. The box method just gives us an easy way to record the partial products, without having to draw a full area model.

We could have split 16 into 15 and 1, 9 and 7, 8 and 8, or any other pair of numbers whose sum is 16. Splitting numbers into their expanded form usually makes the multiplying and adding steps as easy as possible.

The next problem is 5 times 13. First, we'll solve it with the area model. **What's 5 times 10?** *50.* Write 50 on the left side of the array. **What's 5 times 3?** *15.* Write 15 on the right side. **So, what's 5 times 13?** *65.* Write 65 in the blank.

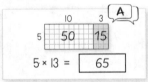

Now, let's solve the same problem with the box method. I write 5 on the left side of the boxes. Write 5 as shown. **I write the expanded form of 13 along the top of the boxes.** Write 10 and 3 as shown.

What's 5 times 10? *50.* Write 50 in the box below 10. **What's 5 times 3?** *15.* Write 15 in the box below 50. **What's 50 plus 15?** *65.* Write 65 in the blank.

	10	3
5	50	15

5 × 13 = 65

Help your child use the box method to solve 7 × 21 and 4 × 35. Remind him as needed to write the expanded form of the two-digit number above the boxes before multiplying.

	20	1
7	140	7

7 × 21 = 147

	30	5
4	120	20

4 × 35 = 140

Activity (B): Play Roll and Multiply

Use the game board to play Roll and Multiply.

Roll and Multiply

Materials: Die

Object of the Game: Have the greater total sum of all your products.

On your turn, roll the die. If you roll a 1, reroll until you roll a different number.

Choose one of the multiplication problems on your scorecard and write the number on the die as the missing factor. (You may write the number in any of the multiplication equations.) Then, use the box method to find the product. The product is your score for that round.

For example, if you roll a 4 and write the 4 in the first multiplication problem, your product is 136, since $4 \times 34 = 136$.

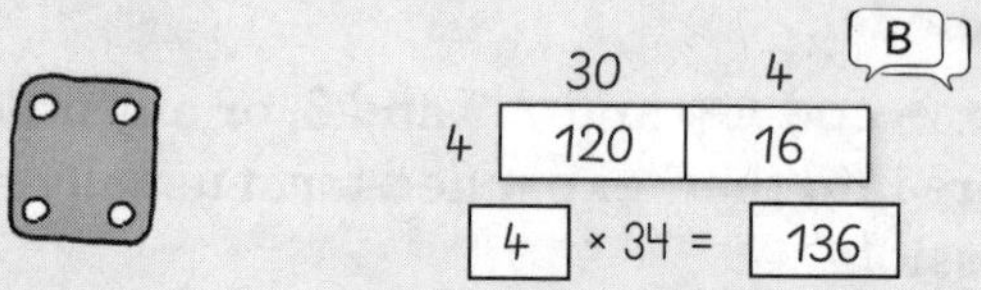

Sample play.

Take turns until both players have completed their scorecards. Each player adds up their products (either mentally or on scrap paper). Whoever has the greater total wins.

Cooperative Variation: Play together on one scorecard. Choose one of the following challenge levels and try to have a greater total than the one listed.

- Math Master: 500 points
- Math Whiz: 600 points
- Math Superstar: 700 points

Independent Practice and Review

Have your child complete the Lesson 3.8 Practice and Review workbook pages.

Lesson 3.9
Multiplication Word Problems

Purpose	Materials
• Practice multiplying two-digit numbers by one-digit numbers with the box method • Use the box method to solve word problems	• None

Memory Work	• **How many centimeters equal 1 meter?** *100.* • **How many meters equal 1 kilometer?** *1,000.*

Warm-up (A): Practice Multiplying with the Box Method

In the last lesson, you learned how to use the box method to multiply one-digit numbers by two-digit numbers. Today, we'll use the box method to solve word problems. We'll warm up by practicing the box method.

The first problem is 6 times 23.

- Point to 6 and 20. **What's 6 times 20?** *120.* Write 120 in the box below 20.
- Point to 6 and 3. **What's 6 times 3?** *18.* Write 18 in the box below 3.
- **Now, we add the partial products to find the total product. What's 120 plus 18?** *138.* Write 138 in the blank.

Help your child use the box method to solve the rest of the problems in part A. Remind her as needed to write the expanded form of the two-digit number above the boxes before multiplying.

Activity (B): Use the Box Method to Solve Word Problems

Have you ever roasted marshmallows over an open fire or made s'mores? *Answers will vary.* **In these word problems, we'll figure out how many marshmallows, graham crackers, and pieces of chocolate we have for making s'mores at a bonfire.**

If your child is not familiar with s'mores, explain that they are a traditional American campfire treat. They're made by sandwiching a roasted marshmallow and piece of chocolate between two graham crackers.

Have your child read aloud the first word problem. **What's the goal of this word problem?** *Find how many marshmallows I buy.* **How can we find the answer?** *Multiply 3 times 38.* Write 3 and 38 as the factors in the equation.

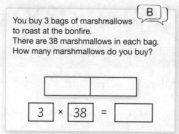

What's the expanded form of 38? *30 plus 8.* Write 3, 30, and 8 as shown around the box diagram. Then, have your child use the box method to solve the problem. **How many marshmallows do you buy?** *114.*

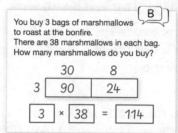

Have your child solve the rest of the word problems in the same way.

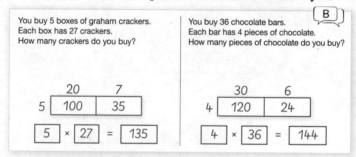

Independent Practice and Review

Have your child complete the Lesson 3.9 Practice and Review workbook pages.

Lesson 3.10
Enrichment (Optional)

Purpose	Materials
• Practice memory work • Appreciate the many ways math is used in daily life • Use mental math in the context of a carnival game • Summarize what your child has learned and assess your child's progress	• *Math Curse*, by Jon Scieszka and Lane Smith • Large piece of posterboard (or 9 sheets of paper and tape) • 9 slips of paper

Warm-up: Review Memory Work

Quiz your child on all memory work through Unit 3. See pages 536-537 for the full list.

Math Picture Book: *Math Curse*

Read *Math Curse*, by Jon Scieszka and Lane Smith. As you read, encourage your child to solve some of the problems that the character encounters.

Your child hasn't learned all the math skills covered in this book (such as measurement conversions), so feel free to simply read those sections without solving the problems.

Enrichment Activity: Make a Mental Multiplication Carnival Game

We're going to make a carnival game today! You'll need to use mental multiplication to find your score. Help your child divide a sheet of poster board into a 3×3 grid of rectangles. Have him label the rectangles with 1,000, 2,000, 3,000, 400, 500, 600, 70, 80, and 90. He may write the numbers in any order.

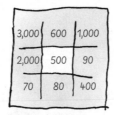

If you don't have posterboard on hand, tape 9 sheets of paper into a 3×3 grid instead.

Write the numbers 1-9 on 9 separate slips of paper.

Crumple each slip of paper into a loose wad. Then, use the wads and board to play a simple carnival-style game. Have your child stand about 10 feet away from the board and toss the wads onto the board. After he throws all 9 wads at the board, have him multiply the number on the wad times the number on the board that it landed on. For example, if the paper slip with 3 lands on the space marked 400, he earns 1,200 points.

Have him add up all his points to find his total score. Then, have him play again and see if he can beat his first score. Or, play yourself and see if you can beat his score!

Unit Wrap-Up

Have your child complete the Unit 3 Wrap-Up.

Unit 3 Answer Key

3.1 Practice

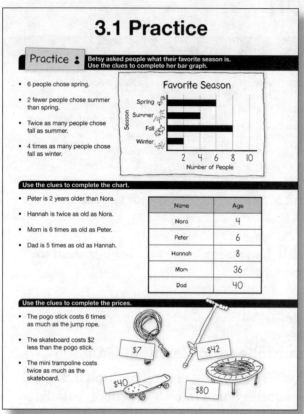

Practice — Betsy asked people what their favorite season is. Use the clues to complete her bar graph.

- 6 people chose spring.
- 2 fewer people chose summer than spring.
- Twice as many people chose fall as summer.
- 4 times as many people chose fall as winter.

Favorite Season

Use the clues to complete the chart.

- Peter is 2 years older than Nora.
- Hannah is twice as old as Nora.
- Mom is 6 times as old as Peter.
- Dad is 5 times as old as Hannah.

Name	Age
Nora	4
Peter	6
Hannah	8
Mom	36
Dad	40

Use the clues to complete the prices.

- The pogo stick costs 6 times as much as the jump rope.
- The skateboard costs $2 less than the pogo stick.
- The mini trampoline costs twice as much as the skateboard.

$7 $42 $40 $80

3.1 Review

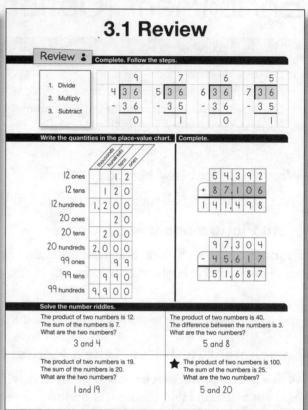

Review — Complete. Follow the steps.

1. Divide
2. Multiply
3. Subtract

Write the quantities in the place-value chart.   **Complete.**

	thousands	hundreds	tens	ones
12 ones			1	2
12 tens		1	2	0
12 hundreds	1,	2	0	0
20 ones			2	0
20 tens		2	0	0
20 hundreds	2,	0	0	0
99 ones			9	9
99 tens		9	9	0
99 hundreds	9,	9	0	0

```
  5 4, 3 9 2
+ 8 7, 1 0 6
1 4 1, 4 9 8
```

```
  9 7, 3 0 4
- 4 5, 6 1 7
  5 1, 6 8 7
```

Solve the number riddles.

The product of two numbers is 12.
The sum of the numbers is 7.
What are the two numbers?
3 and 4

The product of two numbers is 40.
The difference between the numbers is 3.
What are the two numbers?
5 and 8

The product of two numbers is 19.
The sum of the numbers is 20.
What are the two numbers?
1 and 19

★ The product of two numbers is 100.
The sum of the numbers is 25.
What are the two numbers?
5 and 20

3.2 Practice

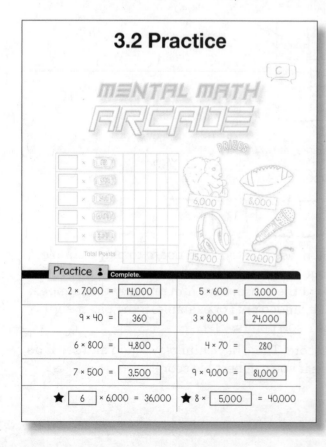

MENTAL MATH ARCADE

Total Points

Practice — Complete.

2 × 7,000 = **14,000**	5 × 600 = **3,000**
9 × 40 = **360**	3 × 8,000 = **24,000**
6 × 800 = **4,800**	4 × 70 = **280**
7 × 500 = **3,500**	9 × 9,000 = **81,000**

★ **6** × 6,000 = 36,000   ★ 8 × **5,000** = 40,000

3.2 Review

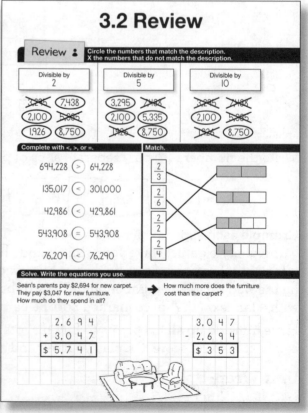

Review — Circle the numbers that match the description. X the numbers that do not match the description.

Divisible by 2	Divisible by 5	Divisible by 10
~~3,295~~ (7,438)	(3,295) ~~7,438~~	~~3,295~~ ~~7,438~~
(2,100) ~~5,335~~	(2,100) (5,335)	(2,100) ~~5,335~~
(1,926) (8,750)	~~1,926~~ (8,750)	~~1,926~~ (8,750)

Complete with <, >, or =.

694,228 > 64,228

135,017 < 301,000

42,986 < 429,861

543,908 = 543,908

76,209 < 76,290

Match.

2/3   2/6   2/2   2/4

Solve. Write the equations you use.

Sean's parents pay $2,694 for new carpet. They pay $3,047 for new furniture. How much do they spend in all?

→ How much more does the furniture cost than the carpet?

```
  2, 6 9 4
+ 3, 0 4 7
$ 5, 7 4 1
```

```
  3, 0 4 7
- 2, 6 9 4
$   3 5 3
```

Unit 3 Answer Key

3.3 Practice

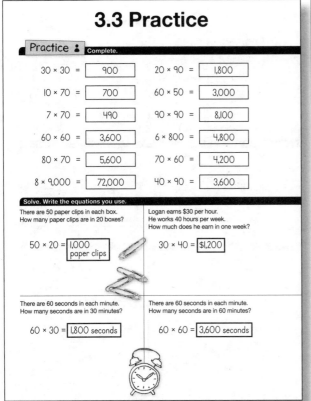

Practice — Complete.

30 × 30 = **900**	20 × 90 = **1,800**
10 × 70 = **700**	60 × 50 = **3,000**
7 × 70 = **490**	90 × 90 = **8,100**
60 × 60 = **3,600**	6 × 800 = **4,800**
80 × 70 = **5,600**	70 × 60 = **4,200**
8 × 9,000 = **72,000**	40 × 90 = **3,600**

Solve. Write the equations you use.

There are 50 paper clips in each box. How many paper clips are in 20 boxes?

50 × 20 = **1,000 paper clips**

Logan earns $30 per hour. He works 40 hours per week. How much does he earn in one week?

30 × 40 = **$1,200**

There are 60 seconds in each minute. How many seconds are in 30 minutes?

60 × 30 = **1,800 seconds**

There are 60 seconds in each minute. How many seconds are in 60 minutes?

60 × 60 = **3,600 seconds**

3.3 Review

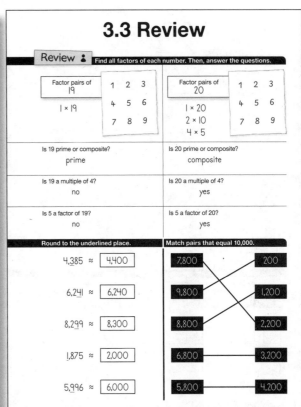

Review — Find all factors of each number. Then, answer the questions.

Factor pairs of 19
1 × 19

Factor pairs of 20
1 × 20
2 × 10
4 × 5

Is 19 prime or composite?
prime

Is 20 prime or composite?
composite

Is 19 a multiple of 4?
no

Is 20 a multiple of 4?
yes

Is 5 a factor of 19?
no

Is 5 a factor of 20?
yes

Round to the underlined place.

4,385 ≈ **4,400**
6,241 ≈ **6,240**
8,299 ≈ **8,300**
1,875 ≈ **2,000**
5,996 ≈ **6,000**

Match pairs that equal 10,000.

7,800 — 2,200
9,800 — 200
8,800 — 1,200
6,800 — 3,200
5,800 — 4,200

3.4 Practice

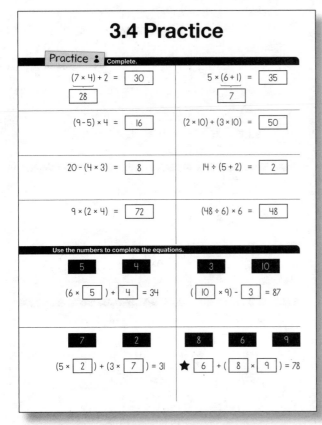

Practice — Complete.

(7 × 4) + 2 = **30**
28

5 × (6 + 1) = **35**
7

(9 − 5) × 4 = **16**

(2 × 10) + (3 × 10) = **50**

20 − (4 × 3) = **8**

14 ÷ (5 + 2) = **2**

9 × (2 × 4) = **72**

(48 ÷ 6) × 6 = **48**

Use the numbers to complete the equations.

5   4

(6 × **5**) + **4** = 34

3   10

(**10** × 9) − **3** = 87

7   2

(5 × **2**) + (3 × **7**) = 31

8   6   9

★ **6** + (**8** × **9**) = 78

3.4 Review

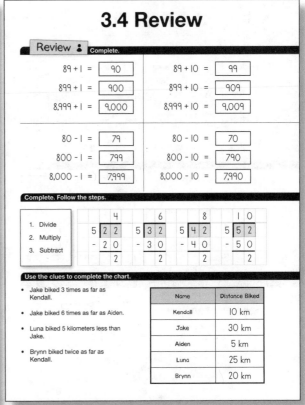

Review — Complete.

89 + 1 = **90**	89 + 10 = **99**
899 + 1 = **900**	899 + 10 = **909**
8,999 + 1 = **9,000**	8,999 + 10 = **9,009**
80 − 1 = **79**	80 − 10 = **70**
800 − 1 = **799**	800 − 10 = **790**
8,000 − 1 = **7,999**	8,000 − 10 = **7,990**

Complete. Follow the steps.

1. Divide
2. Multiply
3. Subtract

```
      4          6          8         1 0
5 | 2 2    5 | 3 2    5 | 4 2    5 | 5 2
  - 2 0      - 3 0      - 4 0      - 5 0
      2          2          2          2
```

Use the clues to complete the chart.

- Jake biked 3 times as far as Kendall.
- Jake biked 6 times as far as Aiden.
- Luna biked 5 kilometers less than Jake.
- Brynn biked twice as far as Kendall.

Name	Distance Biked
Kendall	10 km
Jake	30 km
Aiden	5 km
Luna	25 km
Brynn	20 km

Unit 3 Answer Key

3.5 Practice

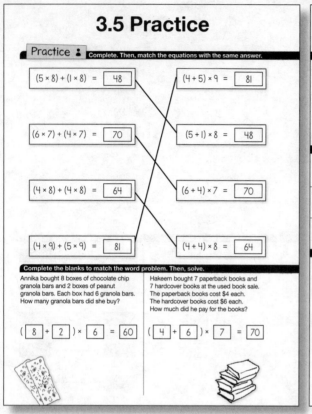

Practice 👤 Complete. Then, match the equations with the same answer.

$(5 \times 8) + (1 \times 8) = \boxed{48}$

$(6 \times 7) + (4 \times 7) = \boxed{70}$

$(4 \times 8) + (4 \times 8) = \boxed{64}$

$(4 \times 9) + (5 \times 9) = \boxed{81}$

$(4 + 5) \times 9 = \boxed{81}$

$(5 + 1) \times 8 = \boxed{48}$

$(6 + 4) \times 7 = \boxed{70}$

$(4 + 4) \times 8 = \boxed{64}$

Complete the blanks to match the word problem. Then, solve.

Annika bought 8 boxes of chocolate chip granola bars and 2 boxes of peanut granola bars. Each box had 6 granola bars. How many granola bars did she buy?

$(\boxed{8} + \boxed{2}) \times \boxed{6} = \boxed{60}$

Hakeem bought 7 paperback books and 7 hardcover books at the used book sale. The paperback books cost $4 each. The hardcover books cost $6 each. How much did he pay for the books?

$(\boxed{4} + \boxed{6}) \times \boxed{7} = \boxed{70}$

3.5 Review

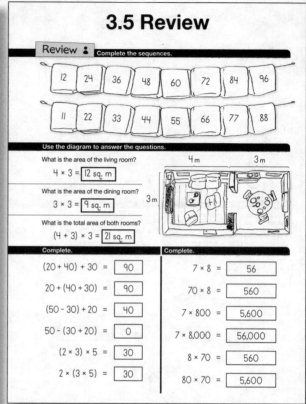

Review 👤 Complete the sequences.

12 24 36 48 60 72 84 96

11 22 33 44 55 66 77 88

Use the diagram to answer the questions.

What is the area of the living room?

$4 \times 3 = \boxed{12 \text{ sq. m}}$

What is the area of the dining room?

$3 \times 3 = \boxed{9 \text{ sq. m}}$

What is the total area of both rooms?

$(4 + 3) \times 3 = \boxed{21 \text{ sq. m}}$

Complete.

$(20 + 40) + 30 = \boxed{90}$

$20 + (40 + 30) = \boxed{90}$

$(50 - 30) + 20 = \boxed{40}$

$50 - (30 + 20) = \boxed{0}$

$(2 \times 3) \times 5 = \boxed{30}$

$2 \times (3 \times 5) = \boxed{30}$

Complete.

$7 \times 8 = \boxed{56}$

$70 \times 8 = \boxed{560}$

$7 \times 800 = \boxed{5,600}$

$7 \times 8,000 = \boxed{56,000}$

$8 \times 70 = \boxed{560}$

$80 \times 70 = \boxed{5,600}$

3.6 Practice

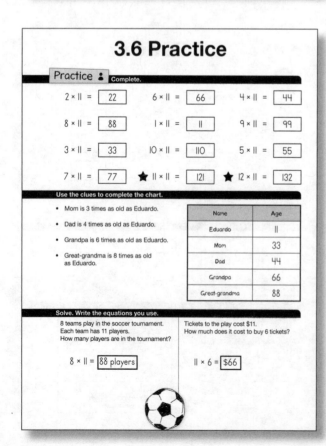

Practice 👤 Complete.

$2 \times 11 = \boxed{22}$ $6 \times 11 = \boxed{66}$ $4 \times 11 = \boxed{44}$

$8 \times 11 = \boxed{88}$ $1 \times 11 = \boxed{11}$ $9 \times 11 = \boxed{99}$

$3 \times 11 = \boxed{33}$ $10 \times 11 = \boxed{110}$ $5 \times 11 = \boxed{55}$

$7 \times 11 = \boxed{77}$ ★ $11 \times 11 = \boxed{121}$ ★ $12 \times 11 = \boxed{132}$

Use the clues to complete the chart.

- Mom is 3 times as old as Eduardo.
- Dad is 4 times as old as Eduardo.
- Grandpa is 6 times as old as Eduardo.
- Great-grandma is 8 times as old as Eduardo.

Name	Age
Eduardo	11
Mom	33
Dad	44
Grandpa	66
Great-grandma	88

Solve. Write the equations you use.

8 teams play in the soccer tournament. Each team has 11 players. How many players are in the tournament?

$8 \times 11 = \boxed{88 \text{ players}}$

Tickets to the play cost $11. How much does it cost to buy 6 tickets?

$11 \times 6 = \boxed{\$66}$

3.6 Review

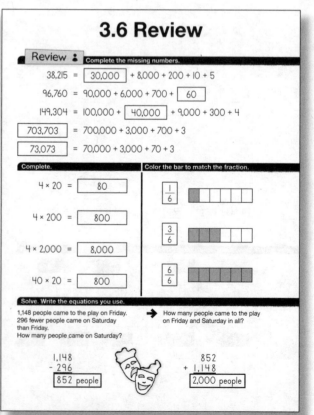

Review 👤 Complete the missing numbers.

$38,215 = \boxed{30,000} + 8,000 + 200 + 10 + 5$

$96,760 = 90,000 + 6,000 + 700 + \boxed{60}$

$149,304 = 100,000 + \boxed{40,000} + 9,000 + 300 + 4$

$\boxed{703,703} = 700,000 + 3,000 + 700 + 3$

$\boxed{73,073} = 70,000 + 3,000 + 70 + 3$

Complete.

$4 \times 20 = \boxed{80}$

$4 \times 200 = \boxed{800}$

$4 \times 2,000 = \boxed{8,000}$

$40 \times 20 = \boxed{800}$

Color the bar to match the fraction.

$\frac{1}{6}$

$\frac{3}{6}$

$\frac{6}{6}$

Solve. Write the equations you use.

1,148 people came to the play on Friday. 296 fewer people came on Saturday than Friday. How many people came on Saturday?

➡ How many people came to the play on Friday and Saturday in all?

$\begin{array}{r} 1,148 \\ - 296 \\ \hline \boxed{852 \text{ people}} \end{array}$

$\begin{array}{r} 852 \\ + 1,148 \\ \hline \boxed{2,000 \text{ people}} \end{array}$

Unit 3 Answer Key

3.7 Practice

Practice 👤 Complete.

$3 \times 12 =$ 36 $7 \times 12 =$ 84 $4 \times 12 =$ 48

$6 \times 12 =$ 72 $10 \times 12 =$ 120 $1 \times 12 =$ 12

$2 \times 12 =$ 24 $5 \times 12 =$ 60 $9 \times 12 =$ 108

$8 \times 12 =$ 96   ★ $11 \times 12 =$ 132   ★ $12 \times 12 =$ 144

Complete the charts.

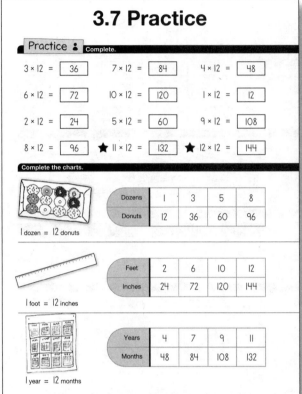

Dozens	1	3	5	8
Donuts	12	36	60	96

1 dozen = 12 donuts

Feet	2	6	10	12
Inches	24	72	120	144

1 foot = 12 inches

Years	4	7	9	11
Months	48	84	108	132

1 year = 12 months

3.7 Review

Review 👤 Complete.

$100 - (5 \times 5) =$ 75

$(10 \times 9) + (2 \times 9) =$ 108

$(10 + 2) \times 9 =$ 108

Draw the missing halves for the symmetric shapes.

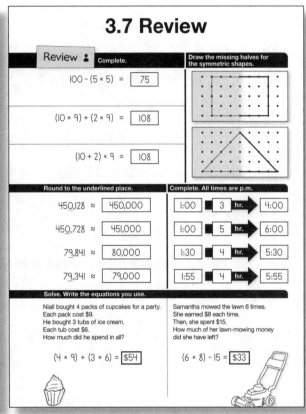

Round to the underlined place.

$450,\underline{1}28 \approx$ 450,000

$450,\underline{7}28 \approx$ 451,000

$7\underline{9},841 \approx$ 80,000

$7\underline{9},341 \approx$ 79,000

Complete. All times are p.m.

1:00	3 hr.	4:00
1:00	5 hr.	6:00
1:30	4 hr.	5:30
1:55	4 hr.	5:55

Solve. Write the equations you use.

Niall bought 4 packs of cupcakes for a party. Each pack cost $9. He bought 3 tubs of ice cream. Each tub cost $6. How much did he spend in all?

$(4 \times 9) + (3 \times 6) =$ $54

Samantha mowed the lawn 6 times. She earned $8 each time. Then, she spent $15. How much of her lawn-mowing money did she have left?

$(6 \times 8) - 15 =$ $33

3.8 Practice

Practice 👤 Complete the boxes to find the product.

	10	8
3	30	24

$3 \times 18 =$ 54

	20	2
9	180	18

$9 \times 22 =$ 198

	30	6
6	180	36

$6 \times 36 =$ 216

	40	7
8	320	56

$8 \times 47 =$ 376

	50	6
7	350	42

$7 \times 56 =$ 392

	9	9
9	810	81

$9 \times 99 =$ 891

Find the missing numbers.

	70	4
6	420	24

6 × 74 = 444

	90	4
5	50	20

5 × 14 = 70

★
	30	2
7	210	14

7 × 32 = 224

★
	80	5
3	240	15

3 × 85 = 255

3.8 Review

Review 👤 Complete.

$3 \times 11 =$ 33 $6 \times 11 =$ 66 $2 \times 11 =$ 22

$7 \times 11 =$ 77 $4 \times 11 =$ 44 $8 \times 11 =$ 88

$5 \times 11 =$ 55 $1 \times 11 =$ 11 $9 \times 11 =$ 99

Write the word that describes all the shapes in each group.

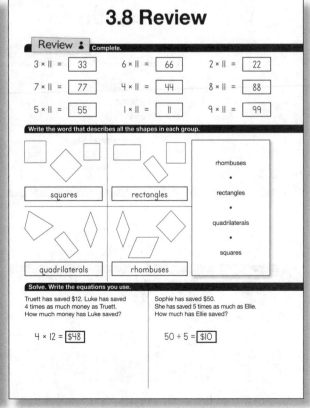

squares

rectangles

quadrilaterals

rhombuses

- rhombuses
- rectangles
- quadrilaterals
- squares

Solve. Write the equations you use.

Truett has saved $12. Luke has saved 4 times as much money as Truett. How much money has Luke saved?

$4 \times 12 =$ $48

Sophie has saved $50. She has saved 5 times as much as Ellie. How much has Ellie saved?

$50 \div 5 =$ $10

Unit 3 Answer Key

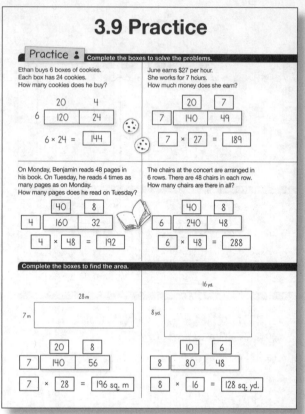

3.9 Practice

Practice 👤 Complete the boxes to solve the problems.

Ethan buys 6 boxes of cookies.
Each box has 24 cookies.
How many cookies does he buy?

	20	4
6	120	24

6 × 24 = **144**

June earns $27 per hour.
She works for 7 hours.
How much money does she earn?

	20	7
7	140	49

7 × 27 = **189**

On Monday, Benjamin reads 48 pages in his book. On Tuesday, he reads 4 times as many pages as on Monday.
How many pages does he read on Tuesday?

	40	8
4	160	32

4 × 48 = **192**

The chairs at the concert are arranged in 6 rows. There are 48 chairs in each row.
How many chairs are there in all?

	40	8
6	240	48

6 × 48 = **288**

Complete the boxes to find the area.

28 m

	20	8
7	140	56

7 m

7 × 28 = **196 sq. m**

16 yd.

8 yd.

	10	6
8	80	48

8 × 16 = **128 sq. yd.**

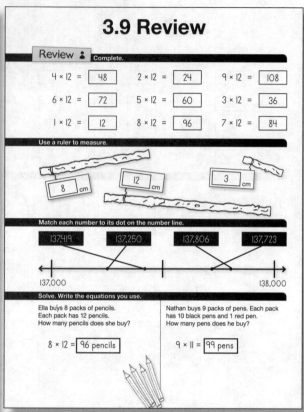

3.9 Review

Review 👤 Complete.

4 × 12 = **48**   2 × 12 = **24**   9 × 12 = **108**

6 × 12 = **72**   5 × 12 = **60**   3 × 12 = **36**

1 × 12 = **12**   8 × 12 = **96**   7 × 12 = **84**

Use a ruler to measure.

8 cm   **12** cm   **3** cm

Match each number to its dot on the number line.

137,419	137,250	137,806	137,723

137,000   138,000

Solve. Write the equations you use.

Ella buys 8 packs of pencils.
Each pack has 12 pencils.
How many pencils does she buy?

8 × 12 = **96 pencils**

Nathan buys 9 packs of pens. Each pack has 10 black pens and 1 red pen.
How many pens does he buy?

9 × 11 = **99 pens**

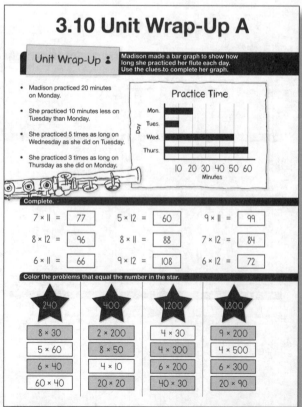

3.10 Unit Wrap-Up A

Unit Wrap-Up 👤 Madison made a bar graph to show how long she practiced her flute each day. Use the clues to complete her graph.

- Madison practiced 20 minutes on Monday.
- She practiced 10 minutes less on Tuesday than Monday.
- She practiced 5 times as long on Wednesday as she did on Tuesday.
- She practiced 3 times as long on Thursday as she did on Monday.

Practice Time

Day: Mon., Tues., Wed., Thurs.

10 20 30 40 50 60
Minutes

Complete.

7 × 11 = **77**   5 × 12 = **60**   9 × 11 = **99**

8 × 12 = **96**   8 × 11 = **88**   7 × 12 = **84**

6 × 11 = **66**   9 × 12 = **108**   6 × 12 = **72**

Color the problems that equal the number in the star.

⭐ 240	⭐ 400	⭐ 1,200	⭐ 1,800
8 × 30	2 × 200	4 × 30	9 × 200
5 × 60	8 × 50	4 × 300	4 × 500
6 × 40	4 × 10	6 × 200	6 × 300
60 × 40	20 × 20	40 × 30	20 × 90

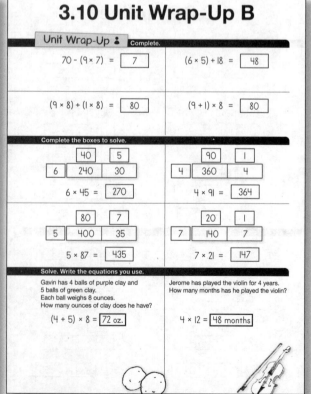

3.10 Unit Wrap-Up B

Unit Wrap-Up 👤 Complete.

70 − (9 × 7) = **7**   (6 × 5) + 18 = **48**

(9 × 8) + (1 × 8) = **80**   (9 + 1) × 8 = **80**

Complete the boxes to solve.

	40	5
6	240	30

6 × 45 = **270**

	90	1
4	360	4

4 × 91 = **364**

	80	7
5	400	35

5 × 87 = **435**

	20	1
7	140	7

7 × 21 = **147**

Solve. Write the equations you use.

Gavin has 4 balls of purple clay and 5 balls of green clay.
Each ball weighs 8 ounces.
How many ounces of clay does he have?

(4 + 5) × 8 = **72 oz.**

Jerome has played the violin for 4 years.
How many months has he played the violin?

4 × 12 = **48 months**

Unit 3 Checkpoint

What to Expect at the End of Unit 3

By the end of Unit 3, most children will be able to do the following:

- Mentally multiply one-digit numbers by a multiple of 10, 100, or 1,000.
- Mentally multiply a multiple of 10 by a multiple of 10.
- Understand that parentheses mean "do this first," and write and solve expressions with parentheses.
- Understand the distributive property and use it to solve problems.
- Find answers for the ×11 and ×12 facts. Some children will have memorized many of the ×11 facts, and most will need much more practice to become fluent with the ×12 facts. Your child will continue to practice these facts in the Review workbook pages.
- Use the area model and box method to multiply two-digit numbers by one-digit numbers. Some children will still need help setting up problems when using the box method.
- Solve multiplication word problems, including multiplicative comparison problems and multi-step problems.

Is Your Child Ready to Move on?

In Unit 4, your child will learn to add and subtract fractions and mixed numbers. Your child does not need to have fully mastered the skills from Unit 3 before moving on to Unit 4.

Unit 4
Fractions and Mixed Numbers

Overview

In this unit, your child will study fractions and mixed numbers. He'll first review reading, writing, and comparing fractions and mixed numbers. Then, he'll learn to convert mixed numbers to fractions, convert fractions to mixed numbers, multiply fractions by whole numbers, and add and subtract mixed numbers with the same denominator.

This unit is the first of two fraction units in *Fourth Grade Math with Confidence*. In Unit 12, your child will learn to identify equivalent fractions and use equivalent fractions to compare fractions with different denominators. In fifth grade, he'll build on these skills to add and subtract fractions and mixed numbers with different denominators.

What Your Child Will Learn

In this unit, your child will learn to:

- Identify and compare fractions and mixed numbers on the number line
- Convert whole numbers and mixed numbers to fractions
- Convert fractions to mixed numbers or whole numbers
- Multiply fractions by whole numbers
- Add and subtract fractions and mixed numbers with the same denominator

Lesson List

Lesson 4.1	Fractions on the Number Line	Lesson 4.6	Convert Fractions to Mixed Numbers
Lesson 4.2	Mixed Numbers on the Number Line	Lesson 4.7	Add and Subtract Fractions
Lesson 4.3	Express Whole Numbers as Fractions	Lesson 4.8	Multiply Fractions by Whole Numbers
Lesson 4.4	Express Fractions as Whole Numbers or Mixed Numbers	Lesson 4.9	Add Mixed Numbers
		Lesson 4.10	Subtract Mixed Numbers
Lesson 4.5	Convert Mixed Numbers to Fractions	Lesson 4.11	Fraction Word Problems
		Lesson 4.12	Enrichment (Optional)

Extra Materials Needed for Unit 4

- Paper clip
- For optional Enrichment Lesson:
  - × *The Wishing Club: A Story About Fractions*, written by Donna Jo Napoli and illustrated by Anna Currey. Henry Holt and Co., 2007.
  - × Recipe with mixed numbers and fractions.

You will also need pattern blocks for the first time in Unit 4.

Teaching Math with Confidence:
Adding "Like to Like" (and Subtracting "Like from Like") with Mixed Numbers

Your child spent many hours mastering the addition and subtraction algorithms for whole numbers during the past few years. He's learned that you add "like to like" (or subtract "like from like") when you use these algorithms. When you use the addition algorithm, you add ones to ones, tens to tens, and so on. When you use the subtraction algorithm, you subtract ones from ones, tens from tens, and so on.

In this unit, your child will learn step-by-step algorithms for adding and subtracting mixed numbers. He'll find that these algorithms are very similar to the whole number addition and subtraction algorithms. Just as you add ones to ones or tens to tens, you add fractions to fractions and whole numbers to whole numbers. If you end up with a fraction greater than one whole, you trade it for one whole (in the same way that you trade 10 ones for 1 ten).

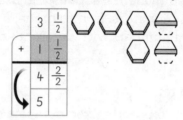

In this problem, you first add 1/2 plus 1/2 and 3 wholes plus 1 whole.
Then, you trade 2 halves for 1 whole to find the final sum.

Or, just as you subtract ones from ones and tens from tens, you subtract fractions from fractions and whole numbers from whole numbers. If you don't have enough fractional parts to subtract, you trade 1 whole for fractional parts.

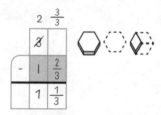

In this problem, you trade 1 whole for 3 thirds before subtracting.
Then, you subtract 2/3 from 3/3 and 1 whole from 2 wholes.

Adding and subtracting items of the same kind is a fundamental principle of arithmetic. Your child will use a similar approach in Unit 9 to add and subtract compound measures (like 3 feet 8 inches + 4 feet 9 inches, or 3 liters 400 milliliters – 1 liter 800 milliliters). In fifth grade, he'll see the same principle at work when he learns to find a common denominator before adding or subtracting fractions with different denominators. And, when he learns to simplify and solve equations in algebra, he'll learn to add and subtract "like terms." By teaching your child the algorithms for adding and subtracting mixed numbers, you help him understand this deep foundational concept.

Lesson 4.1
Fractions on the Number Line

Purpose	Materials
• Identify fractional parts with pattern blocks • Review reading, writing, and comparing fractions • Identify fractions on the number line	• Pattern blocks • 2 decks of playing cards • Counters

Memory Work
- **How many ounces equal 1 pound?** *16.*
- **How many grams equal 1 kilogram?** *1,000.*

Many of the lessons in this unit (including this one) begin with informal pattern block activities that preview the concept covered in the lesson. This gives your child concrete, hands-on experience with the new concept before he applies it to written fractions.

Warm-up: Find Fractional Parts with Pattern Blocks

We're beginning a unit on fractions today! What are 3 things you remember about fractions from last year? *Answers will vary.*

We will use pattern blocks to model fractions and mixed numbers in this unit. Spread a handful of pattern blocks on the table. Briefly review the name of each block:

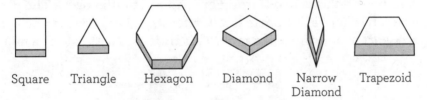

Square   Triangle   Hexagon   Diamond   Narrow Diamond   Trapezoid

The hexagon always represents one whole in this unit. Arrange 2 trapezoids on top of a hexagon. **2 trapezoids cover 1 hexagon completely. The trapezoids split the hexagon into halves.**

2 trapezoids equal 1 hexagon. Since one hexagon represents one whole, each trapezoid represents one-half.

Let's see which other blocks split the hexagon into equal parts. Give your child a few moments to experiment with the other blocks and see which ones can be put together to cover the hexagon completely. **Which blocks don't split the hexagon into equal parts?** *The narrow diamond and square.* **Which blocks do split the hexagon into equal parts?** *The diamond and triangle.*

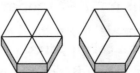

Both the diamond and triangle cover the hexagon completely.

3 diamonds equal 1 hexagon, so the diamonds split the hexagon into thirds. 6 triangles equal 1 hexagon, so the triangles split the hexagon into sixths.

> You'll use the hexagons, trapezoids, diamonds, and triangles to represent fractions and mixed numbers in this unit. You won't use the squares or narrow diamonds, since they don't split the hexagon into equal parts.

Activity (A): Review Fractions

Remember, a fraction is a number that represents part of a whole. Point to 2/3. **How do we read this fraction?** *Two-thirds.* **3 diamonds equal 1 whole. So, each diamond equals one-third of the whole. 2 diamonds equal two-thirds of the whole hexagon.**

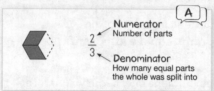

> When you read fractions, always point to the corresponding numbers as you name them. For example, when you say "one-sixth," point to the 1 as you say "one" and the 6 as you say "sixth."

2 is the numerator in this fraction. It tells the number of parts. Do you hear how *numerator* **starts like the word** *number***? That's because it tells the number of parts.**

3 is the denominator in this fraction. It tells how many equal parts the whole was split into. *Denominator* **comes from a Latin word that means "to name something". That's because it names what kind of parts the whole was split into, like fourths, halves, or sixths.**

Discuss how each picture shows two-thirds. For example, for the pizza: **The pizza was cut into 3 equal parts, and there are 2 parts left.** Or, for the hiking trail: **If you split one mile into 3 parts, each part is one-third of a mile. This trail is two-thirds of a mile long.**

Have your child write fractions to match the pattern block pictures. Encourage her to think about the meaning of the numerator and denominator as she writes each fraction. For example, for 1/6: **How many parts are colored in?** *1.* **So, 1 is the numerator. How many equal parts was the hexagon split into?** *6.* **So, 6 is the denominator. One triangle is one-sixth of the hexagon.** Model the problems with real pattern blocks as needed.

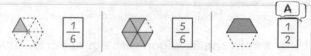

> When you write fractions, always write the fraction bar horizontally (and not diagonally). Writing the fraction bar horizontally makes it easier to see which number is the numerator and which number is the denominator.

Activity (B): Identify Fractions on the Number Line

We can also use the number line to model fractions. The distance between 0 and 1 is split into equal parts. We use fractions to label the parts.

Show your child the first number line in part B. **The tick mark in the middle of the number line divides the distance from 0 to 1 into 2 equal parts. So, this tick mark divides the distance into halves.**

Place a counter on the tick mark for 0/2. **Zero-halves is the same as zero.** Then, move the counter to the tick mark for 1/2. **From 0 to this tick mark is one-half of the distance from 0 to 1.**

Move the counter to the tick mark for 2/2. **From 0 to this tick mark is two-halves of the distance. Two-halves equals 1 whole, so we can label this tick mark with either two-halves or 1.** Just like two-halves of a pizza equal the whole pizza, two-halves of the distance equals the whole distance.

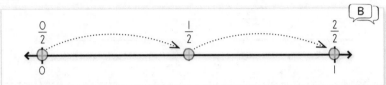

Place a counter on the tick mark for 0 on the next number line. **How many spaces are there from 0 to 1 on this number line?** *3.* **So, what fractional part is this number line split into?** *Thirds.* Move the counter to each tick mark on the number line. Have your child tell you the matching fraction. Write the fraction above the tick mark. Repeat with the other number lines.

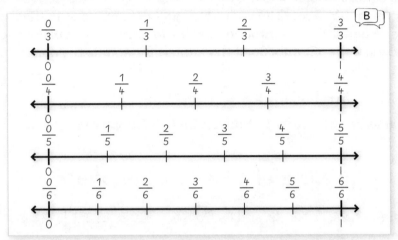

Activity (B): Compare Fractions on the Number Line

We can use number lines to compare fractions, just like we use the number line to compare whole numbers. Place counters on 2/6 and 5/6. **Imagine two ants were walking along this number line. One ant walked from zero to two-sixths. The other ant walked from zero to five-sixths. Which ant walked farther?** *The ant that walked to five-sixths.* **Five-sixths is farther to the right on the number line than two-sixths, so it's greater than two-sixths.**

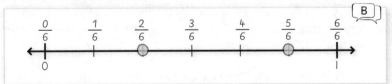

Place counters on 1/4 and 1/3. **Which fraction is less, one-fourth or one-third?** *One-fourth.* **One-fourth is farther to the left on the number line than one-third, so one-fourth is less than one-third.**

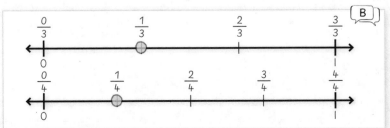

Place counters on 1/2 and 3/6. **Which fraction is greater, one-half or three-sixths?** *They're equal.* **One-half and three-sixths have the same position on the number line, so they are equal.**

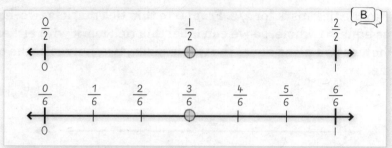

We call fractions that look different but have the same value *equivalent fractions.* **Can you find another fraction that's equivalent to one-half?** *Two-fourths.*

Your child will study equivalent fractions in depth in Unit 12.

Which fractions equal 1 whole? *Two-halves, three-thirds, four-fourths, five-fifths, and six-sixths.* **What do you notice about the numerator and denominator in these fractions?** *They're the same.* **When the numerator equals the denominator, it means you have all the parts that the whole was split into. So, if the numerator equals the denominator, the fraction is equal to 1 whole.**

Activity (B): Play Number Line Fraction War

Use the number lines in part B to play Number Line Fraction War.

Number Line Fraction War

Materials: Aces, 2s, 3s, 4s, 5s, and 6s from two decks of cards (48 cards total); counters of two colors

Object of the Game: Win the most counters.

Give 8 counters of one color t o Player 1. Give 8 counters of another color to Player 2. Shuffle the cards and place them in a face-down pile.

To play, draw two cards off the top of the deck. Use the numbers on the cards to create a fraction. (The numerator must be less than or equal to the denominator. For example, if you flip over a 4 and 6, make 4/6, not 6/4.) Place a counter on the matching fraction on the number lines. Then, the other player draws 2 cards, creates a fraction, and places a counter on the matching fraction.

Aces count as ones. If you draw two aces, discard one of them and choose a new card.

Directions continued on next page.

Whoever has the greater fraction wins both counters and places them in her "Won" pile. Counters in the "Won" pile are now out of the game and cannot be used again.

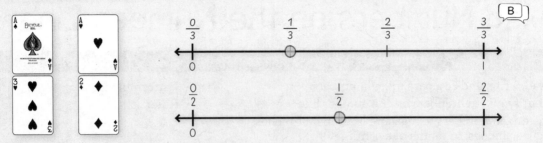

Sample play. The player with 1/2 wins, since 1/2 is greater than 1/3.

If the fractions are equal, leave both counters on the board and play again. Whoever has the greater fraction in the next round wins all the counters on the board.

Play until both players use up their original pile of counters. Whoever has more counters in their "Won" pile wins the game.

Independent Practice and Review

Have your child complete the Lesson 4.1 Practice and Review workbook pages.

Lesson 4.2
Mixed Numbers on the Number Line

Purpose	Materials
• Read, write, and compare mixed numbers • Identify mixed numbers on the number line • Use mixed numbers to measure lines in half-inches, quarter-inches, or tenths of a centimeter	• Pattern blocks • Ruler

Memory Work	• **What do we call the top number in a fraction?** *The numerator.* • **What does the numerator tell?** *The number of parts.* • **What do we call the bottom number in a fraction?** *The denominator.* • **What does the denominator tell?** *How many equal parts the whole was split into.*

Warm-up (A): Review Mixed Numbers

In the last lesson, we reviewed fractions and labeled fractions on the number line. Today, we'll review mixed numbers and label mixed numbers on the number line.

Place 2 hexagons and 1 triangle on the table to match the picture in part A. **We have 2 hexagons and 1 triangle. The 2 hexagons equal 2 wholes. The triangle equals one-sixth. 2 wholes plus one-sixth equals 2 and one-sixth.** Point to the matching equation in part A.

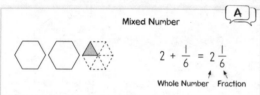 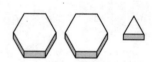

In real life, we often have a mix of whole objects and parts of an object. Numbers like 1, 2, and 3 are called *whole numbers,* because they stand for whole things. Numbers that show a whole number and a fraction are called *mixed numbers.* That's because they're a mix of a whole number and a fraction.

Make sure to say "and" between the whole number and fraction in mixed numbers.

Have your child write a mixed number to match each pattern block picture. Model the mixed numbers with real pattern blocks as needed.

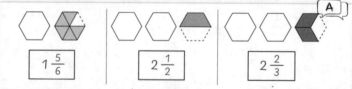

Which is greater, 1 and five-sixths or 2 and one-half? *2 and one-half.* If your child isn't sure, point to the matching pattern block pictures in part A. **How do you know?** *Sample answer: 2 and one-half is more than 2 wholes, but 1 and five-sixths is less than 2 wholes.*

Which is greater, 2 and one-sixth or 2 and one-half? *2 and one-half.* If your child isn't sure, point to the matching pattern block pictures in part A. **How do you know?** *Sample answer: Both numbers have 2 wholes. One-half is greater than one-sixth, so 2 and one-half is greater than 2 and one-sixth.*

Activity (B): Identify Mixed Numbers on the Number Line

In the last lesson, we used the number line to model fractions. We can also use the number line to model mixed numbers.

Point to the number line. **How many spaces are there from 0 to 1 on this number line?** *4.* **So, what fractional part is this number line split into?** *Fourths.*

Point to the following tick marks on the number line. Have your child tell you the matching fraction or mixed number for each tick mark. If he has trouble, encourage him to use the whole numbers to help. For example, for 1 1/4: **This tick mark is one-fourth greater than 1, so it must be 1 and one-fourth.**

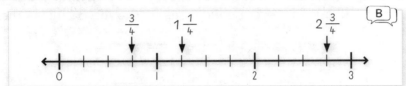

Then, name the following numbers (one at a time): 2/4, 1, 1 3/4, 2, 2 1/4, 2 2/4, 3. Have your child point to the matching tick mark for each.

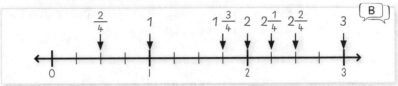

Activity (C): Write Mixed Numbers for Lengths

We often use mixed numbers to measure lengths. Show your child the first inch-ruler and line in part C. **This ruler measures in inches. Each inch is divided into what fractional part?** *Fourths.* **So, this line is 1 and three-fourths inches long.** Write 1 3/4 in the blank.

Have your child measure the second line in the same way. **Two-fourths equal one-half. So, we can write 2 and two-fourths or 2 and one-half inches for this measurement.**

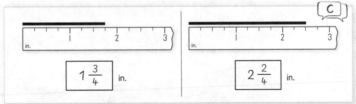

> Your child will learn more about equivalent fractions in Unit 12. Your child does not need to simplify (or "reduce") any of his answers in this unit. He will learn how to simplify fractions in fifth grade.

Show your child a real ruler marked in inches. **Real rulers have tick marks on them for halves, fourths, eighths, and sixteenths of an inch. Can you find the tick mark that splits each inch into halves?** *Child points to half-inch tick marks.*

Can you find the tick marks that split each inch into fourths? *Child points to quarter-inch tick marks.* **We sometimes call one-fourth of an inch a quarter-inch, just like we call one-fourth of an hour a quarter-hour.**

Show your child the first centimeter-ruler and line in part C. **This ruler measures in centimeters. Each centimeter is divided into what fractional part?** *Tenths.* Have your child count the spaces between the lines if he's not sure. **So, this line is 1 and nine-tenths centimeters long.** Write 1 9/10 in the blank. Have your child measure the second line in the same way.

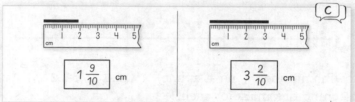

Show your child a real ruler marked in centimeters. **These tiny parts of a centimeter are called millimeters. You'll learn about them later in the year.**

Independent Practice and Review

Have your child complete the Lesson 4.2 Practice and Review workbook pages.

Lesson 4.3
Express Whole Numbers as Fractions

Purpose	Materials
• Draw lines with mixed-number lengths • Introduce improper fractions • Use concrete materials to express whole numbers as fractions	• Ruler • Pattern blocks • Counters • 2 decks of playing cards

Memory Work	• **What do we call the top number in a fraction?** *The numerator.* • **What does the numerator tell?** *The number of parts.* • **What do we call the bottom number in a fraction?** *The denominator.* • **What does the denominator tell?** *How many equal parts the whole was split into.*

This lesson gives your child a gentle, concrete introduction to expressing whole numbers as fractions. She'll learn the written process in Lesson 4.5.

Warm-up: Draw Lines with Mixed-Number Lengths

In the last lesson, you learned how to measure lines with half-inches, quarter-inches, or tenths of a centimeter. Show your child a ruler. On the inch side, have her identify the half-inch and quarter-inch tick marks. On the centimeter side, have her identify the tick marks that divide each centimeter into tenths.

Have your child use a ruler to draw lines with the following lengths on scrap paper:

- 4 1/2 in.
- 2 3/4 in.
- 5 1/4 in.
- 6 5/10 cm
- 3 1/10 cm

Activity (A): Express Amounts of Pie with Mixed Numbers and Fractions

In the last two lessons, we reviewed fractions and mixed numbers. In most fractions, the numerator was less than the denominator. People sometimes call fractions like these *proper fractions.*

You can also write fractions where the numerator is greater than or equal to the denominator. People sometimes call fractions like these *improper fractions.*

We see proper fractions more often in everyday life. But there's nothing wrong with improper fractions! In fact, they can be very helpful when you add, subtract, multiply, or divide fractions. Today, you'll learn how to write improper fractions to match whole numbers.

Your child does not need to memorize the terms *proper fractions* and *improper fractions*. The distinction between the two types of fractions is rarely helpful, and the terms tend to make children view improper fractions as somehow bad or inferior. *Math with Confidence* refers to both types as simply *fractions* unless the distinction is helpful.

Show your child part A. **These chocolate pies are left over after a party. One way to express the amount of leftover pie is with a mixed number. How many whole pies are left?** *1.* **What fraction of a pie is left?** *Three-eighths.* **So, there are 1 and three-eighths of a pie left.** Point to 1 3/8.

We can also express the amount of leftover pie with a fraction. How many slices of pie are left? *11.* **Each slice is one-eighth of a pie, so we have eleven-eighths left.** Point to 11/8.

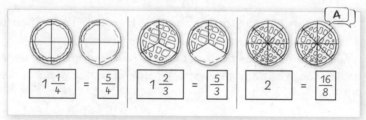

Both the mixed number and fraction tell how much pie is left over. They just express the amount in different ways.

Have your child write a mixed number and fraction to tell how much pie is left in each picture.

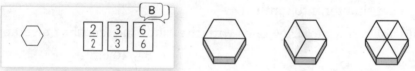

Activity (B): Express Whole Numbers as Fractions

We can also write fractions equal to whole numbers. We'll use pattern blocks to find the fractions that equal these whole numbers.

Place 1 hexagon on the table to match the first exercise. **How many halves does it take to equal 1 whole?** *2.* Write 2 as the numerator for the first fraction. Have your child arrange 2 trapezoids on the table to match. Repeat with thirds and sixths.

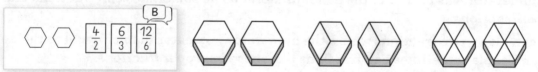

Place 2 hexagons on the table to match the next exercise. **How many halves does it take to equal 2 wholes?** *4.* Write 4 for the numerator for the first fraction. If your child's not sure, say: **Each whole equals 2 halves. So, you can multiply 2 times 2 to find the total number of halves you need to make 2 wholes.** Then, have her put together 4 trapezoids to create 2 whole hexagons. Repeat with thirds and sixths.

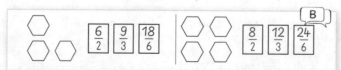

Have your child complete the rest of the exercises in the same way. Encourage her to predict the number of halves, thirds, or sixths before she models the problems with pattern blocks.

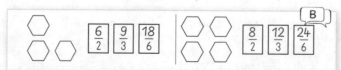

When you change a whole number into a fraction, we say that you *convert* **the whole number into a fraction. Even though the whole number and fraction look very different from each other, they both mean the same amount.**

Activity (C): Play Fraction Crash

Play Fraction Crash.

Your child can look back at the previous section for help converting the fractions to whole numbers.

If you own transparent counters, use them for this game (so you can see the fractions under the counters).

Fraction Crash

Materials: Aces, 2s, 3s, and 4s from two decks of playing cards (32 cards total); 10 counters of two different colors

Object of the Game: Have the most counters on the game board at the end of the game.

Shuffle the cards and place the stack face down on the table. Give 10 counters of one color to one player and 10 counters of a different color to the other player.

On your turn, flip over the top card. Choose a fraction on the game board that equals the whole number on the card. Place a counter on the matching square. For example, if you flip over a 3, you may place a counter on 6/2, 18/6, or 9/3. Aces count as 1s.

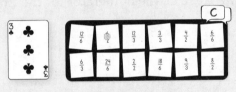

Sample play.

If the other player already has a counter on the square, you may "crash" into their counter, remove it, and place your own counter on the square. Continue until all the squares are filled. Whoever has more counters on the board at the end wins the game.

Independent Practice and Review

Have your child complete the Lesson 4.3 Practice and Review workbook pages.

Lesson 4.4
Express Fractions as Whole Numbers or Mixed Numbers

Purpose	Materials
• Practice expressing whole numbers as fractions • Use concrete materials to express fractions as whole numbers or mixed numbers	• Pattern blocks • Die

Memory Work
- **Name 4 factors of 12.** *Possible answers: 1, 2, 3, 4, 6, 12.*
- **Name 4 multiples of 12.** *Sample answers: 12, 24, 36, 48.*

This lesson gives your child concrete experience with converting fractions to mixed numbers before you teach him the written process in Lesson 4.6.

Warm-up (A): Practice Expressing Whole Numbers as Fractions

Show your child part A. **There are 2 whole pizzas. If I split each pizza into fourths, how many fourths would I get?** *8.* Write 8 as the numerator for the first fraction. Repeat with the rest of the fractions.

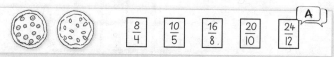

If your child's not sure, draw 2 circles on scrap paper and have him draw lines to split each circle into the matching fractional part.

$$2 = \frac{8}{4}$$

Activity (B): Express Fractions as Mixed Numbers or Whole Numbers

In the last lesson, you learned how to express whole numbers as fractions. Today, we'll go in the other direction. You'll learn how to express fractions as whole numbers or mixed numbers. We'll use pattern blocks to model the fractions.

Show your child the chart. **We'll use pattern blocks to express these fractions as whole numbers or mixed numbers. One-third and two-thirds are less than 1 whole, so we can't express those fractions as a whole number or mixed number.** Write an X below 1/3 and 2/3.

Point to 3/3. Place 3 diamonds on the table, then push them together to create a hexagon. **What does three-thirds equal?** *1 whole.* Write 1 below 3/3.

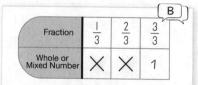

Point to 4/3. Add 1 diamond to the previous arrangement. **What mixed number does four-thirds equal?** *1 and one-third.* Write 1 1/3 below 4/3.

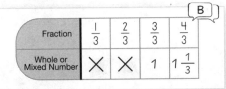

Fraction	$\frac{1}{3}$	$\frac{2}{3}$	$\frac{3}{3}$	$\frac{4}{3}$
Whole or Mixed Number	✗	✗	1	$1\frac{1}{3}$

Repeat with the rest of the chart.

Fraction	$\frac{1}{3}$	$\frac{2}{3}$	$\frac{3}{3}$	$\frac{4}{3}$	$\frac{5}{3}$	$\frac{6}{3}$	$\frac{7}{3}$	$\frac{8}{3}$	$\frac{9}{3}$
Whole or Mixed Number	✗	✗	1	$1\frac{1}{3}$	$1\frac{2}{3}$	2	$2\frac{1}{3}$	$2\frac{2}{3}$	3

If your child immediately understands how to complete the rest of the chart, allow him to complete it without modeling all the problems with pattern blocks.

This number line shows the fractions from the top line of the chart. We'll label the whole numbers on this number line. Where does 1 whole go? *At three-thirds.* Circle 3/3 and write 1 as shown. Repeat for 2 and 3.

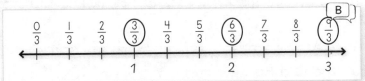

What do you notice about the numerator and denominator in the circled fractions? *Sample answers: The numerator divided by the denominator equals the whole number. The numerator is divisible by the denominator.* **If you divide the numerator by the denominator in these fractions, you get the matching whole number!**

Your child will learn how to use division to convert fractions to whole or mixed numbers in Lesson 4.6.

Activity (C): Play Pizza Roll

Play Pizza Roll.

Pizza Roll

Materials: Die

Object of the Game: Be the first player to fill 4 pizzas.

On your turn, roll the die and color the corresponding number of slices of pizza on your gameboard. Color the pizzas in order, from left to right. Color one whole pizza before moving on to the next pizza.

Name the total amount of pizza that you have colored, both as a fraction and as a whole number or mixed number (if possible).

Directions continued on next page.

For example, if your first roll is a 3, color 3 slices of the first pizza. You have 3/6 of a pizza, so you say "Three-sixths."

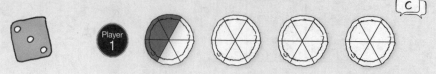

Sample first play.

If you roll a 4 on your second turn, color in 4 more slices of pizza. You now have colored 7 slices of pizza (or 1 whole pizza plus 1/6 of a pizza), so say, "Seven-sixths. One and one-sixth."

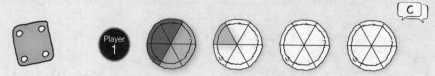

Sample second play.

Take turns until one player completes all 4 pizzas. For the final turn, you may have more than 4 pizzas.

Independent Practice and Review

Have your child complete the Lesson 4.4 Practice and Review workbook pages.

The fraction bars on the Practice page give your child a different visual model for understanding fractions. If your child dislikes coloring, reassure him that he does not need to color every bar perfectly. A swipe of a highlighter over the correct number of parts is fine.

Lesson 4.5
Convert Mixed Numbers to Fractions

Purpose	Materials
• Concretely convert mixed numbers to fractions with pattern blocks • Multiply and add to convert mixed numbers to fractions	• Pattern blocks • Die • Counters

Memory Work · **What do we call numbers that have a whole number and a fraction?** *Mixed numbers.*

Warm-up: Convert Mixed Numbers to Fractional Parts with Pattern Blocks

This warm-up gives your child concrete experience with converting mixed numbers to fractions before you teach her the more abstract written process.

Place 1 hexagon and 1 trapezoid on the table. **How many halves equal 1 and one-half?** *3.* **How do you know?** *Sample answer: Each hexagon equals 2 halves, plus we already have 1 half.* Have your child arrange 3 trapezoids to match your original blocks.

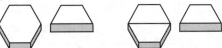

Place 3 hexagons and 2 diamonds on the table. **How many thirds equal 3 and two-thirds?** *11.* Have your child arrange 11 diamonds to match your original blocks.

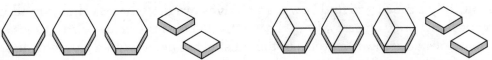

Place 2 hexagons and 3 triangles on the table. **How many sixths equal 2 and three-sixths?** *15.* Have your child arrange 15 triangles to match your original blocks.

Activity (A): Convert Whole Numbers and Mixed Numbers to Fractions

In the last two lessons, we've explored the relationships between fractions, whole numbers, and mixed numbers. Today, you'll learn how to use multiplication and addition to convert whole numbers and mixed numbers to fractions.

Point to the first problem. **First, we'll convert 2 wholes to sixths. Each whole equals 6 sixths. So we can multiply 2 times 6 to find how many sixths are in 2 wholes.**

What's 2 times 6? *12.* Write 12 in the blank in the cloud. **So, 2 equals 12 sixths.** Write 12 for the fraction's numerator.

$$2 = \frac{12}{6}$$
$$2 \times 6 = 12$$

Point to the next problem. **Next, we'll convert 2 and one-sixth to sixths. First, we multiply 2 times 6 to find how many sixths are in 2 wholes. Then, we add on the 1 extra sixth.**

What's 2 times 6? *12.* **Plus 1?** *13.* Write 13 in the blank in the cloud. **So, 2 and one-sixth equals 13 sixths.** Write 13 as the fraction's numerator.

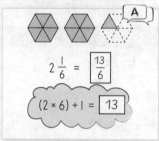

Point to the next problem. **This problem means "3 equals how many halves?" We can multiply 2 times 3 to find the answer, since there are 2 halves in each of the 3 wholes.** Draw an arrow from the 2 to the 3. Label the arrow with a times sign as shown. **What's 2 times 3?** *6.* Write 6 in the blank.

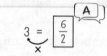

Let's use pattern blocks to check the answer. Place 6 trapezoids on the table. Have your child put them together to confirm that they equal 3 whole hexagons.

Point to the next problem. **This problem means "3 and one-half equals how many halves?" First, we multiply 2 times 3 to find how many halves are in 3 wholes. Then, we add on the extra one-half.** Draw an arrow from the 2 to the 3. Label the arrow with a times sign as shown. Then, draw an arrow from the 3 to the 1. Label the arrow with a plus sign as shown. **What's 2 times 3?** *6.* **Plus 1?** *7.* Write 7 in the blank.

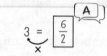

Let's use pattern blocks to check the answer. Place 7 trapezoids on the table. Have your child put them together to confirm that they equal 3 1/2 whole hexagons.

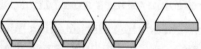

One way to remember that you multiply to convert whole numbers or mixed numbers to fractions is to think of this rhyme: *Whole to parts? Multiply to start!* **This means that if you have whole numbers that you want to convert to fractional parts, start by multiplying. Then, add on any extra fractional parts.**

Have your child repeat the rhyme with you. Use the following hand motions:

- For "whole," spread your hands several feet apart.
- For "parts," move your hands so that they're several inches apart.
- For "multiply," cross your arms in front of you like a multiplication sign.

Whole...   ...to parts?   Multiply to start!

Your child will learn the next part of this rhyme in Lesson 4.6.

Repeat with the other problems in part B. Have your child use multiplication (and addition, if needed) to solve each problem.

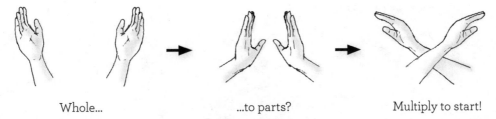

If your child has trouble converting 3 or 3 1/4 to fourths, draw a simple circle sketch to help her visualize the problem.

$$3 = \frac{12}{4}$$

$$3\frac{1}{4} = \frac{13}{4}$$

Activity (B): Play Fraction Three in a Row

Play Fraction Three in a Row. Encourage your child to multiply and add to convert the mixed numbers to fractions. If your child has trouble, model the problems with pattern blocks or draw a simple circle sketch.

Fraction Three in a Row

Materials: Die, counters of two colors

Object of the Game: Be the first player to place 3 counters in a row (horizontally, vertically, or diagonally) in the circles in the center of the game board.

Have each player choose a different-colored counter to use as a game token and place it on one of the Start squares.

Directions continued on next page.

On your turn, roll the die and advance your token the corresponding number of squares clockwise around the path. When you land on a square, read the mixed number aloud. Convert the mixed number to a fraction and place one of your counters on the corresponding circle in the middle of the game board. For example, if you land on 5 3/4, place a counter on 23/4.

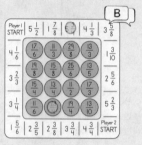

If there is already a counter on the matching circle, play passes to the other player. If you land on one of the start squares, roll again.

Play until one player covers three circles in a row, either horizontally, vertically, or diagonally.

Crash variation: If you land on a mixed number and your opponent already has a counter on the matching circle, "crash" into your opponent's counter and replace it with one of your own. This variation works best if you own transparent counters, so it's easy to see the numbers under the counters.

Independent Practice and Review

Have your child complete the Lesson 4.5 Practice and Review workbook pages.

Lesson 4.6
Convert Fractions to Mixed Numbers

Purpose	Materials
• Concretely convert fractions to mixed numbers with pattern blocks • Convert fractions to mixed numbers by dividing	• Pattern blocks • Die • Counters

Memory Work	• **What is a prime number?** *A number with exactly 2 factors.* • **What is a composite number?** *A number with more than 2 factors.*

This lesson gently previews the idea that the fraction bar can also be thought of as a division sign. (For example, one way to think of 1/3 is 1 divided by 3, or one-third.) Your child is not expected to understand this connection now. He will explore this concept more as he learns different ways to write equations in later grades.

Warm-up: Practice Mental Division with Remainders

Ask your child the following mental division questions:

- **6 divided by 3?** *2.*
- **7 divided by 3?** *2, with a remainder of 1.*
- **8 divided by 3?** *2, with a remainder of 2.*
- **3 divided by 3?** *1.*
- **4 divided by 3?** *1, with a remainder of 1.*
- **10 divided by 3?** *3, with a remainder of 1.*
- **14 divided by 3?** *4, with a remainder of 2.*

Activity (A): Convert Fractions to Mixed Numbers

In the last lesson, you learned how to multiply to convert whole numbers and mixed numbers to fractions. Do you remember the rhyme you learned to help you remember to multiply? *Whole to parts, multiply to start.*

In this lesson, you'll do the opposite. You'll learn how to divide to convert fractions to mixed numbers.

Point to the first problem. **First, we'll convert 6 thirds to a whole number. Each group of 3 thirds equals 1 whole. So, we divide 6 by 3 to find how many groups of 3 we can make.**

What's 6 divided by 3? *2.* Write 2 in the blank in the cloud. **So, 6 thirds equal 2 wholes.** Write 2 in the blank.

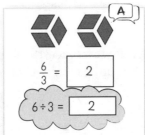

Point to the next problem. **Next, we'll convert 7 thirds to a mixed number. Each group of 3 thirds equals 1 whole. So, we divide 7 by 3 to find how many groups of 3 we can make.**

What's 7 divided by 3? *2, with a remainder of 1.* **Write "2 R1" in the blank in the cloud. So, seven-thirds equals 2 wholes, with 1 third left over.** Write 2 1/3 in the blank.

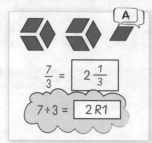

One way to remember that you divide to convert fractional parts to whole numbers or mixed numbers to fractions is to think of this rhyme: *Parts to whole? Division's in control!* **This means that if you have fractional parts that you want to convert to a whole number or mixed number, start by dividing.**

Have your child repeat the rhyme with you. Use the following hand motions:

- For "parts," move your hands so that they're several inches apart.
- For "whole," spread your hands several feet apart.
- For "divide," hold your arm horizontally in front of you like the bar in a division symbol.

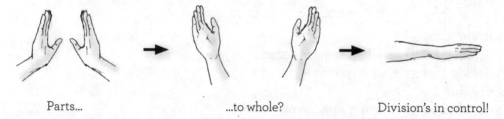

Parts...   ...to whole?   Division's in control!

If your child finds this rhyme and the rhyme he learned in Lesson 4.5 helpful, encourage him to use them as he works on the Practice and Review pages. If he finds the rhymes confusing, don't require him to use them. Instead, encourage him to visualize the fraction problems as he decides whether to multiply or divide.

In Unit 9, your child will learn that he can use the same rhyme to help decide whether to multiply or divide when converting measurements.

Point to the next problem. **This problem means "Eleven-thirds equals what whole number or mixed number?" We can divide 11 by 3 to find the answer, since each group of 3 thirds equals 1 whole.** Draw an arrow from the 11 to the 3. Label the arrow with a division sign as shown. **What's 11 divided by 3?** *3, with a remainder of 2.* **So, eleven-thirds equals 3 and two-thirds.** Write 3 2/3 in the blank.

$$ \div \left(\frac{11}{3} \right. = \boxed{3 \frac{2}{3}} $$

Let's use pattern blocks to check the answer. Place 11 diamonds on the table. Have your child put them together to confirm that they equal 3 whole hexagons, with 2 diamonds left over.

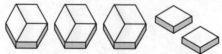

Have your child use similar reasoning for the rest of the problems. Encourage him to use division to find the answers.

$$\div \Big(\frac{11}{3} = \boxed{3\,\frac{2}{3}} \qquad \frac{13}{6} = \boxed{2\,\frac{1}{6}} \qquad \frac{8}{2} = \boxed{4}^{\,\text{A}}$$

$$\frac{9}{4} = \boxed{2\,\frac{1}{4}} \qquad \frac{19}{8} = \boxed{2\,\frac{3}{8}} \qquad \frac{8}{5} = \boxed{1\,\frac{3}{5}}$$

Use pattern blocks as needed to model 13/6 and 8/2. If your child has trouble with any of the problems in the second row, draw a simple sketch to help him visualize the problem.

 $\frac{9}{4} = 2\,\frac{1}{4}$

Activity (B): Play Fraction Three in a Row

Play Fraction Three in a Row. The rules are the same as in Lesson 4.5. The only difference is that the fractions are on the game track, while the mixed numbers and whole numbers are in the middle of the board. When you land on a square, read the fraction aloud. Convert the fraction to a mixed number or whole number and place one of your counters on the corresponding circle in the middle of the game board. See Lesson 4.5 (pages 141-142) for full directions.

Encourage your child to divide the numerator by the denominator to convert the fractions to mixed numbers.

Independent Practice and Review

Have your child complete the Lesson 4.6 Practice and Review workbook pages.

Lesson 4.7
Add and Subtract Fractions

Purpose	Materials
• Practice division facts • Add and subtract fractions with the same denominator	• Pattern blocks • Counters • Die

Memory Work	
	• **What do we call an angle that looks like the corner of a piece of paper?** *A right angle.* • **What do we call a quadrilateral with 4 right angles?** *A rectangle.* • **What do we call a quadrilateral with 4 right angles and 4 equal sides?** *A square.* • **What do we call a quadrilateral with 4 equal sides?** *A rhombus.*

Your child learned how to add and subtract fractions in *Third Grade Math with Confidence.* This lesson provides a brief review so she's ready to add and subtract mixed numbers in Lessons 4.9 and 4.10. She'll learn how to add and subtract fractions with different denominators in fifth grade.

Warm-up: Practice Division Facts

We'll warm up with some division facts today. Look for a pattern in the questions. Have your child solve the following division problems.

- **35 divided by 7?** *5.*
- **42 divided by 7?** *6.*
- **49 divided by 7?** *7.*
- **56 divided by 7?** *8.*
- **63 divided by 7?** *9.*

- **80 divided by 8?** *10.*
- **72 divided by 8?** *9.*
- **64 divided by 8?** *8.*
- **56 divided by 8?** *7.*
- **48 divided by 8?** *6.*

Your child will study mental division techniques in Unit 5. Reviewing this pattern reminds your child that she can use related facts to solve division problems if she forgets an answer.

Activity (A): Add and Subtract Fractions

Today, we'll review adding and subtracting fractions with the same denominator. Organize pattern blocks on the table as shown so that your child can see at a glance which block represents each fractional part.

Have your child read aloud the first addition problem: *Two-sixths plus three-sixths.* Arrange a group of 2 triangles and a group of 3 triangles on the table to match the picture. Push the triangles together as shown.

Each triangle is one-sixth. What's two-sixths plus three-sixths? *Five-sixths.* If your child's not sure, point out that there are 5 triangles, and each triangle represents one-sixth. Write 5/6 in the blank.

$$\frac{2}{6} + \frac{3}{6} = \boxed{\frac{5}{6}}$$

Just like 2 stickers plus 3 stickers equal 5 stickers, two-sixths plus three-sixths equals five-sixths. When fractions have the same denominator, we add the numerators just like whole numbers.

Why does the denominator stay the same? *Sample answer: The denominator just tells us what kind of parts the whole was split into.* **When you add fractions, you don't add the denominators. In this problem, we added groups of sixths, so the answer is a group of sixths, too. The denominator is like a label for the answer, because it tells what kind of fractional parts we added together.**

$$\frac{2}{6} + \frac{3}{6} = \boxed{\frac{5}{6}}$$

Total number of parts
What kind of fractional parts were added together

Have your child read aloud the first subtraction problem: *Seven-sixths minus three-sixths.* Arrange 7 triangles on the table to match the picture. Then, take away 3. **What's seven-sixths minus three-sixths?** *Four-sixths.* If your child's not sure, point out that there are 4 triangles left, and each triangle represents one-sixth. Write 4/6 in the blank.

$$\frac{7}{6} - \frac{3}{6} = \boxed{\frac{4}{6}}$$

Just like 7 stickers minus 3 stickers equals 4 stickers, seven-sixths minus three-sixths equals four-sixths. When fractions have the same denominator, we subtract the numerators just like whole numbers.

When you subtract fractions, you don't subtract the denominators. In this problem, we subtracted groups of sixths, so the answer is a group of sixths as well. The denominator is like a label for the answer. It tells what kind of fractional parts we have left.

$$\frac{7}{6} - \frac{3}{6} = \boxed{\frac{4}{6}}$$

Number of parts left
What kind of fractional parts are left

Have your child use the same reasoning to complete the problems in part A.

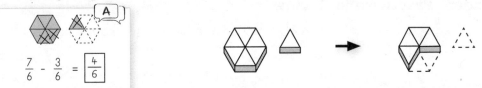

$$\frac{5}{3} + \frac{2}{3} = \boxed{\frac{7}{3}} \qquad \frac{3}{8} + \frac{4}{8} = \boxed{\frac{7}{8}}$$

$$\frac{4}{2} - \frac{1}{2} = \boxed{\frac{3}{2}} \qquad \frac{6}{4} - \frac{3}{4} = \boxed{\frac{3}{4}}$$

Your child does not need to convert any improper fractions to mixed numbers in this lesson, since the focus is on adding and subtracting fractions. She also does not need to simplify (or "reduce") any of her answers.

Activity (B): Play Climb and Slide

Play Climb and Slide. Encourage your child to use what she knows about addition and subtraction to solve the problems. For example, for 5/6 – 1/6: **What's 5 marbles minus 1 marble?** *4 marbles.* **So, what's 5 sixths minus 1 sixth?** *4 sixths.*

Climb and Slide

Materials: 2 different-colored counters to use as game tokens; die

Object of the Game: Be the first player to reach the Finish square.

Each player chooses a counter to use as a game token and places it on the Start Square.

On your turn, roll the die and advance your token the corresponding number of squares. Say the answer to the problem on your landing square.

If you land on a square at the bottom of a ladder, "climb" the ladder and place your game token on the square at the top of the ladder. If you land on a square at the top of a slide, slide down the slide and place your game token on the square at the bottom of the slide.

The first player to reach Finish wins the game.

Independent Practice and Review

Have your child complete the Lesson 4.7 Practice and Review workbook pages.

Lesson 4.8
Multiply Fractions by Whole Numbers

Purpose	Materials
• Practice repeated fraction addition with pattern blocks • Multiply fractions by whole numbers • Practice converting fractions to mixed numbers	• Pattern blocks • Die

Memory Work · **What do parentheses mean in a math problem?** *Do this first.*

Warm-up: Practice Repeated Fraction Addition with Pattern Blocks

In the last lesson, you practiced adding and subtracting fractions.

Arrange 2 triangles on the table. **Each triangle is one-sixth of a hexagon. What's one-sixth plus one-sixth?** *Two-sixths.*

Add 1 triangle to the arrangement. **Plus one-sixth?** *Three-sixths.*

Add 1 more triangle. **Plus one-sixth?** *Four-sixths.*

Activity (A): Multiply Fractions by Whole Numbers

Today, you'll learn how to multiply fractions by a whole number. Multiplication is repeated addition of equal groups, so you can use what you know about fraction addition to solve fraction multiplication problems.

Point to the repeated addition problem. **In the warm-up, you used pattern blocks to add one-sixth plus one-sixth plus one-sixth plus one-sixth. What was the sum?** *Four-sixths.* Write 4/6 in the blank.

Repeated Addition

$$\frac{1}{6} + \frac{1}{6} + \frac{1}{6} + \frac{1}{6} = \boxed{\frac{4}{6}}$$

We have 4 equal groups of one-sixth, so we can also think of this problem as 4 times one-sixth. 4 is the number of groups, and one-sixth is the size of each group.

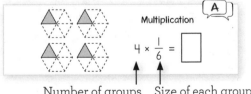

Multiplication

$$4 \times \frac{1}{6} = \boxed{}$$

Number of groups   Size of each group

4 times 1 equals 4. There are 4 parts, so the numerator is 4. Write 4 as the numerator for the answer. **The whole was split into 6 equal parts, so the denominator is 6.** Write 6 as the denominator for the answer. **4 times one-sixth equals four-sixths.**

$$4 \times \frac{1}{6} = \frac{4}{6}$$

Multiplication

Just like 4 groups of 1 sticker equal 4 stickers, **4 groups of one-sixth equal four-sixths. When we multiply a whole number times a fraction, we multiply the whole number times the numerator to find the total number of parts.**

When you multiply a whole number times a fraction, **you don't change the denominator. It's just like in the addition problems you solved in the last lesson. We multiplied groups of sixths, so the answer is a group of sixths, too.**

Have your child complete the first column of problems in part A.

$$2 \times \frac{1}{3} = \frac{2}{3}$$

$$5 \times \frac{1}{6} = \frac{5}{6}$$

$$3 \times \frac{1}{4} = \frac{3}{4}$$

For 2 × 1/3 and 5 × 1/6, model the problems with pattern blocks if needed. For 3 × 1/4, draw a sketch like the following if your child has trouble understanding the problem.

$$3 \times \frac{1}{4} = \frac{3}{4}$$

If the product is an improper fraction, we convert the fraction to a whole number or mixed number to make it easier to understand. Have your child complete the second column of problems. After he multiplies to find a fraction, have him convert the fraction to a whole number or mixed number.

$$4 \times \frac{2}{6} = \frac{8}{6} = 1\frac{2}{6}$$

$$3 \times \frac{1}{2} = \frac{3}{2} = 1\frac{1}{2}$$

$$3 \times \frac{3}{8} = \frac{9}{8} = 1\frac{1}{8}$$

For 4 × 2/6 and 3 × 1/2, model the problems with pattern blocks if needed. For 3 × 3/8, draw a sketch like the following if your child has trouble understanding the problem.

$$3 \times \frac{3}{8} = \frac{9}{8} = 1\frac{1}{8}$$

Activity (B): Play Roll and Multiply

Use the game board to play Roll and Multiply.

Model the problems with pattern blocks as needed. For example, for 8 × 1/3, place 8 diamonds on the table.

Roll and Multiply

Materials: 2 dice

Object of the Game: Score more points than the other player.

Roll and Multiply has 5 rounds. In each round, each player rolls two dice and writes the sum of the dice as the missing factor in the multiplication problem on their score-card. Then, they find the product of the printed number and the written fraction (and convert the result to a mixed number, if needed). Write an X in the rightmost box if you can't convert it to a whole number or mixed number.

Whoever has the greater product wins a point. If the products are equal, both players win a point.

For example, if Player 1 rolls an 8 and Player 2 rolls a 5 in the first round:

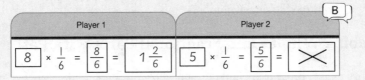

Player 1 wins the point, since 1 2/6 is greater than 5/6.

Play until you have completed the entire scorecard. Complete the blanks in order. Whoever has won more points wins the game.

Independent Practice and Review

Have your child complete the Lesson 4.8 Practice and Review workbook pages.

Have your child use pattern blocks to model the final problems on the Practice page (2 × 5/6 and 8 × 1/2) if he has trouble with them.

Lesson 4.9
Add Mixed Numbers

Purpose	Materials
• Use pattern blocks to regroup whole numbers and fractions into mixed numbers • Use the mixed number addition algorithm to add mixed numbers	• Pattern blocks • Paper clip

Memory Work	• **What do we call the number to be divided?** *The dividend.* • **What do we call the number we divide by?** *The divisor.* • **What do we call the result when we divide two numbers?** *The quotient.* • **What do we call an amount that is left over after division?** *The remainder.*

Some children are able to add and subtract mixed numbers mentally and find the algorithms tedious and unnecessary. If your child falls into this category, make sure to introduce the steps in the algorithms anyway so that she has the chance to observe the similarities between the algorithms for mixed numbers and whole numbers. Allow her to use whichever method she prefers as she solves the problems on the worksheets. See the Unit 4 **Teaching Math with Confidence** for more on why it's so important for your child to understand the algorithms for adding and subtracting mixed numbers.

Warm-up: Combine Wholes and Fractional Parts with Pattern Blocks

Adding mixed numbers requires that your child regroup wholes and fractional parts into mixed numbers. This activity introduces this skill so your child can use it later in the lesson.

Place 2 hexagons and 2 trapezoids on the table. **How many wholes can you make from 2 and two-halves?** *3.* **How many fractional parts will be left?** *None.* **2 and two-halves equal 3 wholes.**

Place 1 hexagon and 4 diamonds on the table. **1 and four-thirds equals what mixed number?** *2 and one-third.*

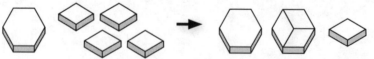

Place 2 hexagons and 7 triangles on the table. **2 and seven-sixths equals what mixed number?** *3 and one-sixth.*

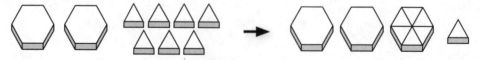

Activity (A): Add Mixed Numbers with the Mixed Number Addition Algorithm

You already know how to add fractions with the same denominator. Today, you'll learn how to add mixed numbers where the fractions have the same denominator.

Adding mixed numbers is a lot like adding whole numbers. We'll use the Mixed Number Addition Algorithm diagram as a guide.

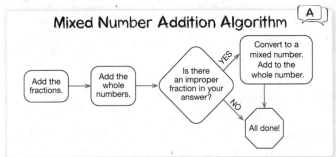

Read aloud the first problem: **2 and one-third plus 2 and one-third.** Arrange pattern blocks on the table to match the diagram.

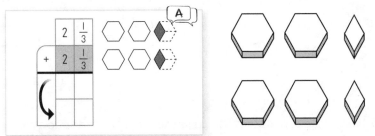

The first step says: *Add the fractions.* **What's one-third plus one-third?** *Two-thirds.* Write 2/3 as shown.

The next step says: *Add the whole numbers.* **What's 2 plus 2?** *4.* Write 4 as shown.

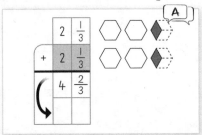

Point to the next step in the diagram. **The next step is a question:** *Is there an improper fraction in your answer? No.* If needed, remind your child that an improper fraction is a fraction where the numerator is greater than or equal to the denominator. **So, we follow the path labeled "No." Trace your finger along the "No" arrow until you reach the final step. You're done! 2 and one-third plus 2 and one-third equals 4 and two-thirds.** Leave the final space below the problem blank.

The extra space provides room for the final answer, in case the answer needs to be regrouped. See the next problem for an example of why this is sometimes necessary.

Read aloud the next problem: **3 and one-half plus 1 and one-half.** Arrange pattern blocks on the table to match the diagram. Have your child follow the first two steps in the algorithm to add the fractions and whole numbers.

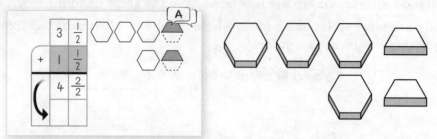

The next step is a question: *Is there an improper fraction in your answer?* Yes. **So, we follow the path labeled "Yes."** Trace your finger along the "Yes" arrow until you reach the next step. *Convert to a mixed number. Add to the whole number.* **What does 2/2 equal?** *1 whole.* Push the two trapezoids together to make 1 whole. What's 4 wholes plus 1 whole? 5. Write 5 as shown. **Now, you're done! So, what's 3 and one-half plus 1 and one-half?** *5.*

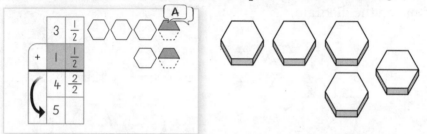

Have your child solve the next problem in the same way. Help her convert the fraction to a mixed number when she reaches that step. **What mixed number does 7/6 equal?** *1 and one-sixth.* Push 6 diamonds together to make 1 whole. **What's 3 wholes plus 1 and one-sixth?** *4 and one-sixth.* Write 4 1/6 to complete the problem.

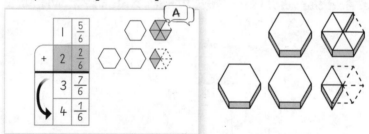

The last problem involves adding eighths, so we can't model this problem with pattern blocks. Instead, we'll draw a simple circle sketch. Draw circles next to 1 5/8 and 2 5/8 as shown. Then, have your child complete the problem.

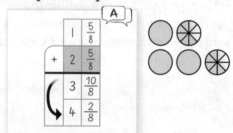

Drawing a sketch is a great way to visualize fraction problems and make sense of them. Make sure to draw a sketch if you ever feel confused by a fraction or mixed number addition problem.

How is the mixed number addition algorithm like the usual process for adding whole numbers? *Sample answers: You start at the right. You add the smaller units and then the larger units. You trade if you need to.*

How is the mixed number addition algorithm different from the usual process for adding whole numbers? *Sample answers: You add whole numbers and fractions instead of tens and ones. When you trade, you trade 1 whole for fractional pieces instead of 1 ten for 10 ones. You trade after you finish the adding.*

Activity (B): Play Spin to Win

Use the game board to play Spin to Win. Model the problems with pattern blocks as needed.

Spin to Win

Materials: Paper clip

Object of the Game: Win the most points.

Place one end of the paper clip in the middle of the top spinner. Place the point of a pencil through the paper clip so that it touches the very middle of the circle.

Spin to Win has 4 rounds. On your turn, hold the pencil upright and spin the paper clip so that it spins freely around the circle. Write the number from the left-hand spinner as the top addend in the first blank addition problem. Write the number from the right-hand spinner as the bottom addend in the problem. Then, add to find the sum. For example, if your first spin is 1 5/6 and your second spin is 1 2/6, your sum is 3 1/6.

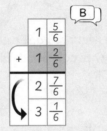

Then, have the other player spin twice and find the sum of her spins. Whoever has the greater sum wins a point for that round.

Continue until you have completed 4 rounds. Whoever has won more points wins the game.

Independent Practice and Review

Have your child complete the Lesson 4.9 Practice and Review workbook page. If your child has trouble with any of the mixed number addition problems, encourage her to draw a sketch to match the problem.

Lesson 4.10
Subtract Mixed Numbers

Purpose	Materials
• Concretely subtract mixed numbers with pattern blocks • Use the mixed number subtraction algorithm to subtract mixed numbers	• Pattern blocks • Paper clip

Memory Work
- **What do we call the top number in a fraction?** *The numerator.*
- **What does the numerator tell?** *The number of parts.*
- **What do we call the bottom number in a fraction?** *The denominator.*
- **What does the denominator tell?** *How many equal parts the whole was split into.*

Warm-up: Subtract from Multiple Wholes with Pattern Blocks

In the last lesson, you learned how to add mixed numbers. Today, you'll learn how to subtract mixed numbers. First, we'll solve some problems with pattern blocks. Then, I'll show you how to solve them with the Fraction Subtraction Algorithm.

Place 3 hexagons on the table. **Let's pretend the pattern blocks are pizzas. There are 3 pizzas. I'd like one-third of a pizza, so I'll cut one of the pizzas into thirds.** Trade 1 of the hexagons for 3 diamonds. Then, take 1 diamond and pretend to eat it. **How many whole pizzas are left?** *2.* **What part of a pizza is left?** *Two-thirds.* **So, 2 and two-thirds are left.**

Place 2 hexagons on the table. **I have 2 pizzas. I eat one-half of a pizza.** Trade 1 hexagon for 2 trapezoids and remove 1 trapezoid. **How much pizza is left?** *One and one-half pizzas.*

Place 4 hexagons on the table. **I have 4 pizzas. I eat 2 and one-sixth pizzas.** Trade 1 hexagon for 6 diamonds. Then, remove 2 hexagons and 1 diamond. **How much pizza is left?** *One and five-sixths.*

Activity (A):
Subtract Mixed Numbers with the Mixed Number Subtraction Algorithm

Subtracting mixed numbers is a lot like subtracting whole numbers. We'll use the Mixed Number Subtraction Algorithm diagram as a guide.

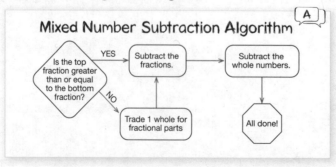

Read aloud the first problem: **2 and five-sixths minus 1 and one-sixth.** Model 2 5/6 with pattern blocks to match the diagram.

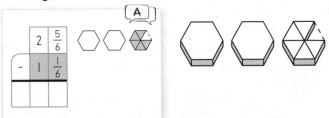

Is the top fraction greater than or equal to the bottom fraction? Yes. **So, we follow the path labeled "Yes."** Trace your finger along the "Yes" arrow until you reach the next step.

The next step says: *Subtract the fractions.* **What's five-sixths minus one-sixth?** *Four-sixths.* Remove 1 triangle (1/6). Write 4/6 as shown.

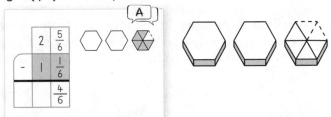

The next step says: *Subtract the whole numbers.* **What's 2 minus 1?** *1.* Remove 1 hexagon (1 whole). Write 1 as shown. **2 and five-sixths minus 1 and one-sixth equals 1 and four-sixths.**

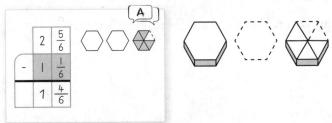

Mixed number subtraction problems do not require regrouping at the end of the problem, so these problems do not have a final answer blank.

Read aloud the next problem: **3 minus 1 and two-thirds.** Arrange 3 hexagons on the table to match the diagram.

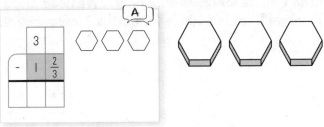

The first step is a question: *Is the top fraction greater than or equal to the bottom fraction?* *No.* **There is no top fraction, so it's definitely not greater than the bottom fraction! We follow the "No" arrow.** Trace your finger along the "No" arrow until you reach the next step. **The next step says:** *Trade 1 whole for fractional parts.* **We need more thirds before we can subtract the fractions. So, we'll trade 1 whole for thirds. How many thirds equal 1 whole?** *3.* Trade 1 hexagon for 3 diamonds. Have your child draw lines on the printed hexagon to show splitting it into thirds.

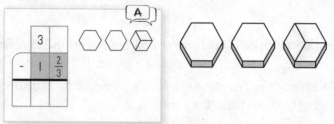

We need to record our trade before we subtract. How many wholes do we have now? *2.* Cross out the 3 and write 2 above it. **How many thirds do we have now?** *3.* Write 3/3 next to the 2.

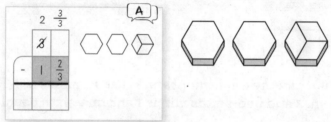

Now, we're ready to subtract. Have your child follow the steps in the algorithm to finish the problem.

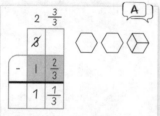

Read aloud the next problem: **2 and one-sixth minus five-sixths.** Arrange pattern blocks to match the diagram. *Is the top fraction greater than or equal to the bottom fraction?* *No.* **The next step says:** *Trade 1 whole for fractional parts.* **We need more sixths before we can subtract the fractions. So, we'll trade 1 whole for sixths. How many sixths equal 1 whole?** *6.* Trade 1 hexagon for 6 triangles. Have your child draw lines on the printed hexagon to show splitting it into sixths.

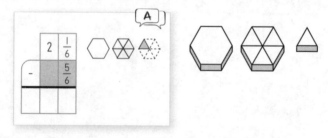

How many wholes do we have now? *1.* Cross out the 2 and write 1 above it. **How many sixths do we have now?** *7.* Cross out 1/6 and write 7/6 above it. **Now, we're ready to subtract.** Have your child follow the steps in the algorithm to finish the problem.

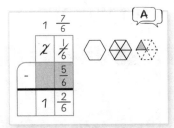

The last problem involves subtracting fourths, so we can't model this problem with pattern blocks. Instead, we'll draw a simple circle sketch. Draw circles as shown to model 5 1/4. Then, have your child complete the problem. Have him draw lines to split one whole into fourths to model the trading.

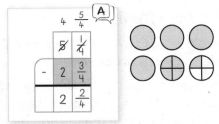

Remember, drawing a sketch is a great way to visualize fraction problems and make sense of them. Make sure to draw a sketch if you ever feel confused by a fraction or mixed number subtraction problem.

How is the mixed number subtraction algorithm like the usual process for subtracting whole numbers? *Sample answers: You start at the right. You subtract the smaller units and then the larger units. You trade if you need to.*

How is the mixed number subtraction algorithm different from the usual process for subtracting whole numbers? *Sample answers: You subtract whole numbers and fractions instead of tens and ones. When you trade, you trade 1 whole for fractional parts instead of 1 ten for 10 ones.*

Activity (B): Play Spin to Win

Use the game board to play Spin to Win. Game play is the same as in Lesson 4.9. See Lesson 4.9 (page 155) for full directions. Write the number from the left-hand spinner as the top number in your subtraction problem and the number from the right-hand spinner as the bottom number in your subtraction problem. Whoever has the greater answer wins the point. Use pattern blocks to model the problems as needed.

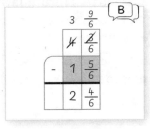

Sample play.

Independent Practice and Review

Have your child complete the Lesson 4.10 Practice and Review workbook pages. If your child has trouble, encourage him to draw a sketch to match the problem.

Lesson 4.11
Fraction Word Problems

Purpose	Materials
• Practice fraction skills • Solve fraction word problems	• None

Memory Work	
	• **How do you know if a number is divisible by 2?** *It is even. It has 0, 2, 4, 6, or 8 in the ones-place.* • **How do you know if a number is divisible by 5?** *It has a 0 or 5 in the ones-place.* • **How do you know if a number is divisible by 10?** *It has a 0 in the ones-place.*

Warm-up (A): Practice Fraction Skills

You've learned a lot of fraction skills in this unit! Today, you'll review what you've learned and use your skills to solve fraction word problems.

Have your child complete the problems in part A. If she forgets how to complete any of the problems, use a real-life example to help her think about the underlying meaning of the problem. For example, for 5 × 3/4: **This problem means you have 5 groups of 3/4. That's like having 5 boxes with 3/4 of a pizza in each box.**

Activity (B): Solve Fraction Word Problems

Have your child read aloud the first word problem. **What's the goal of this word problem?** *Find how many pounds of apples she used.*

Word problems with fractions sometimes feel intimidating! If you ever feel confused by a fraction word problem, just ignore the fractions and think about how you would solve the problem if the fractions were whole numbers.

For example, if Emmett's mom used 4 pounds of red apples and 3 pounds of green apples, how would you find the number of pounds she used in all? *Sample answer: Add 4 plus 3.*

When we want to find a total amount, we add the two numbers together—no matter whether they're whole numbers or fractions! Have your child write and solve the matching addition problem. Repeat with the other word problems.

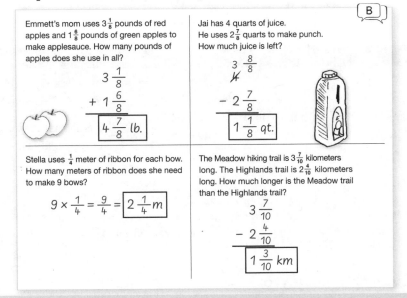

If your child has trouble with any of the problems, temporarily substitute any fractions with whole numbers and ask your child what operation she would use to solve the problem. Then, have her write an equation with the fractions and correct operation.

For example, for the problem about Stella: **Let's not worry about the fraction in the problem for a second. Stella uses some ribbon for each bow. We want to know how much ribbon it takes for her to make 9 bows. If she used 2 meters of ribbon for each bow, how would you find out how much ribbon she needs?** *Multiply 9 times 2.* **You'd multiply the number of bows times the amount of ribbon she needs for each bow. She needs one-fourth meter of ribbon for each bow, so multiply 9 times one-fourth to find the total amount.**

Independent Practice and Review

Have your child complete the Lesson 4.11 Practice and Review workbook pages.

Lesson 4.12
Enrichment (Optional)

Purpose	Materials
• Practice memory work • Discover a fraction rule in the context of wishes • Add mixed numbers and fractions to double a recipe • Summarize what your child has learned and assess your child's progress	• *The Wishing Club: A Story About Fractions*, written by Donna Jo Napoli and illustrated by Anna Currey • Recipe with mixed numbers and fractions

In the enrichment activity, your child will double a recipe. Choose a recipe for the enrichment activity that involves lots of fractions and mixed numbers. If your family celebrates American Thanksgiving, make this enrichment activity more seasonal by using a recipe for one of your family's favorite holiday dishes, such as cranberry sauce, stuffing, or gravy.

Warm-up: Review Memory Work

Quiz your child on all memory work through Unit 4. See pages 536-537 for the full list.

Math Picture Book: *The Wishing Club: A Story About Fractions*

Read *The Wishing Club: A Story About Fractions*, written by Donna Jo Napoli and illustrated by Anna Currey. After you read, ask your child what he might wish for (and how he would need to phrase his wish according to the wishing comet's rules!)

Enrichment Activity: Double a Recipe

When people make food for a large gathering, they often need to double the recipe to make sure they have enough. Show your child a family recipe and work together to double the recipe. Encourage your child to use his fraction addition skills as he works. For example: **The stuffing recipe calls for 1 and three-fourths of a cup of celery. So, add 1 and three-fourths plus 1 and three-fourths to double the amount.**

Unit Wrap-Up

Have your child complete the Unit 4 Wrap-Up.

Unit 4 Answer Key

4.1 Practice

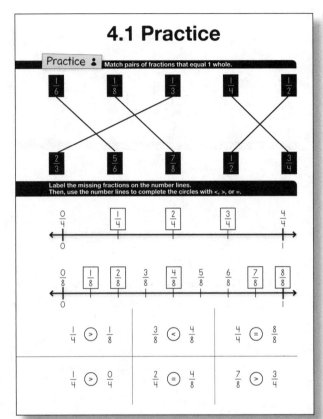

4.1 Review

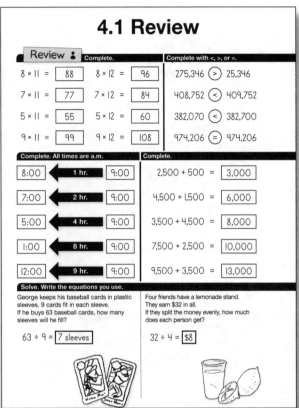

4.2 Practice

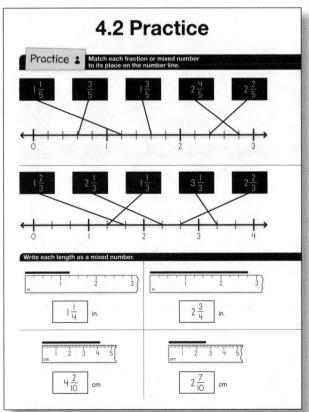

4.2 Review

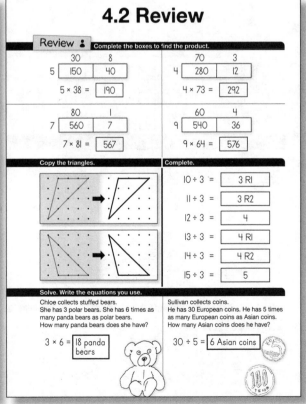

Unit 4 Answer Key

4.3 Practice

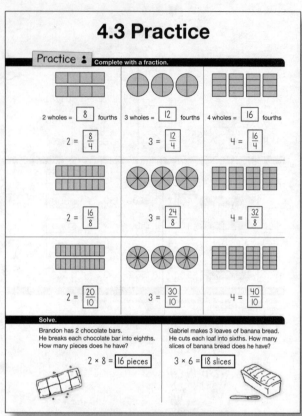

4.3 Review

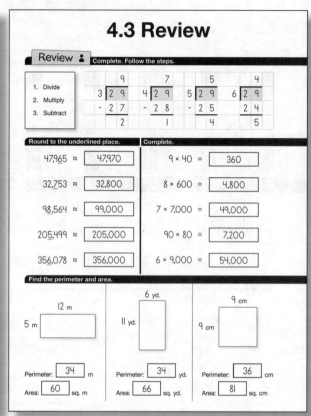

4.4 Practice

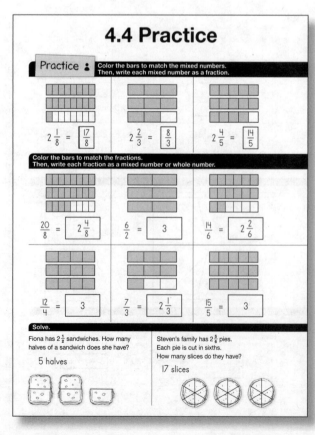

4.4 Review

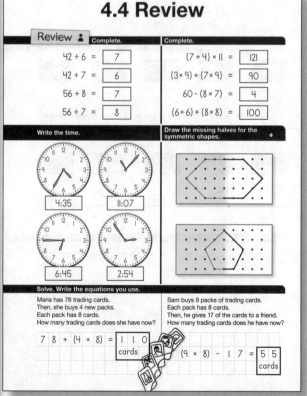

Unit 4 Answer Key

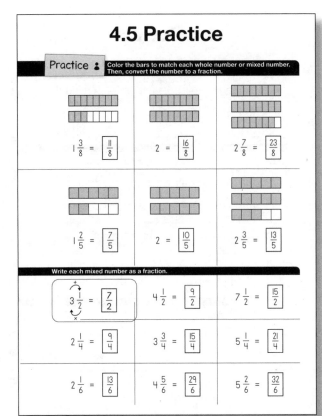

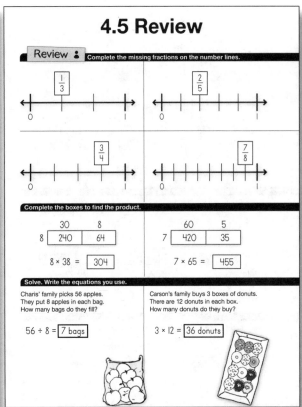

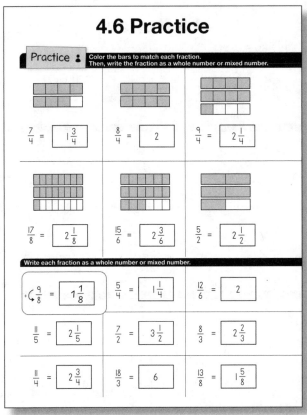

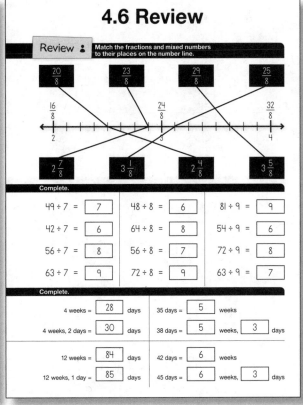

Unit 4 Answer Key

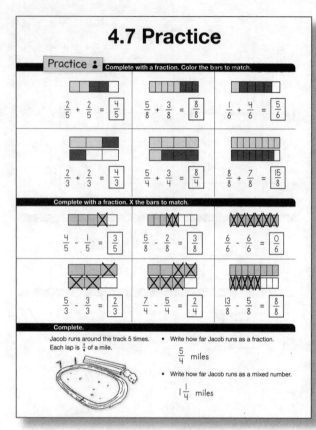

4.7 Practice

Practice 👤 Complete with a fraction. Color the bars to match.

$\frac{2}{5} + \frac{2}{5} = \boxed{\frac{4}{5}}$ $\frac{5}{8} + \frac{3}{8} = \boxed{\frac{8}{8}}$ $\frac{1}{6} + \frac{4}{6} = \boxed{\frac{5}{6}}$

$\frac{2}{3} + \frac{2}{3} = \boxed{\frac{4}{3}}$ $\frac{5}{4} + \frac{3}{4} = \boxed{\frac{8}{4}}$ $\frac{8}{8} + \frac{7}{8} = \boxed{\frac{15}{8}}$

Complete with a fraction. X the bars to match.

$\frac{4}{5} - \frac{1}{5} = \boxed{\frac{3}{5}}$ $\frac{5}{8} - \frac{2}{8} = \boxed{\frac{3}{8}}$ $\frac{6}{6} - \frac{6}{6} = \boxed{\frac{0}{6}}$

$\frac{5}{3} - \frac{3}{3} = \boxed{\frac{2}{3}}$ $\frac{7}{4} - \frac{5}{4} = \boxed{\frac{2}{4}}$ $\frac{13}{8} - \frac{5}{8} = \boxed{\frac{8}{8}}$

Complete.

Jacob runs around the track 5 times. Each lap is $\frac{1}{4}$ of a mile.

• Write how far Jacob runs as a fraction.

$\frac{5}{4}$ miles

• Write how far Jacob runs as a mixed number.

$1\frac{1}{4}$ miles

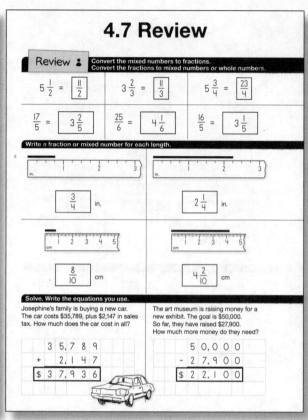

4.7 Review

Review 👤 Convert the mixed numbers to fractions. Convert the fractions to mixed numbers or whole numbers.

$5\frac{1}{2} = \boxed{\frac{11}{2}}$ $3\frac{2}{3} = \boxed{\frac{11}{3}}$ $5\frac{3}{4} = \boxed{\frac{23}{4}}$

$\frac{17}{5} = \boxed{3\frac{2}{5}}$ $\frac{25}{6} = \boxed{4\frac{1}{6}}$ $\frac{16}{5} = \boxed{3\frac{1}{5}}$

Write a fraction or mixed number for each length.

$\boxed{\frac{3}{4}}$ in. $\boxed{2\frac{1}{4}}$ in.

$\boxed{\frac{8}{10}}$ cm $\boxed{4\frac{2}{10}}$ cm

Solve. Write the equations you use.

Josephine's family is buying a new car. The car costs $35,789, plus $2,147 in sales tax. How much does the car cost in all?

$$\begin{array}{r} 3\,5,7\,8\,9 \\ +\ \ \ 2,1\,4\,7 \\ \hline \$\ 3\,7,9\,3\,6 \end{array}$$

The art museum is raising money for a new exhibit. The goal is $50,000. So far, they have raised $27,900. How much more money do they need?

$$\begin{array}{r} 5\,0,0\,0\,0 \\ -\ 2\,7,9\,0\,0 \\ \hline \$\ 2\,2,1\,0\,0 \end{array}$$

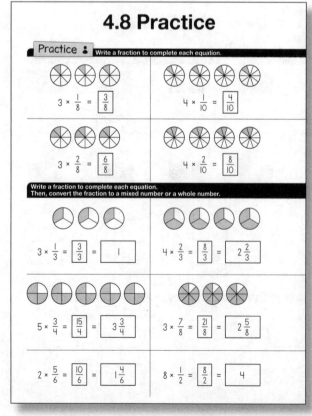

4.8 Practice

Practice 👤 Write a fraction to complete each equation.

$3 \times \frac{1}{8} = \boxed{\frac{3}{8}}$ $4 \times \frac{1}{10} = \boxed{\frac{4}{10}}$

$3 \times \frac{2}{8} = \boxed{\frac{6}{8}}$ $4 \times \frac{2}{10} = \boxed{\frac{8}{10}}$

Write a fraction to complete each equation. Then, convert the fraction to a mixed number or a whole number.

$3 \times \frac{1}{3} = \boxed{\frac{3}{3}} = \boxed{1}$ $4 \times \frac{2}{3} = \boxed{\frac{8}{3}} = \boxed{2\frac{2}{3}}$

$5 \times \frac{3}{4} = \boxed{\frac{15}{4}} = \boxed{3\frac{3}{4}}$ $3 \times \frac{7}{8} = \boxed{\frac{21}{8}} = \boxed{2\frac{5}{8}}$

$2 \times \frac{5}{6} = \boxed{\frac{10}{6}} = \boxed{1\frac{4}{6}}$ $8 \times \frac{1}{2} = \boxed{\frac{8}{2}} = \boxed{4}$

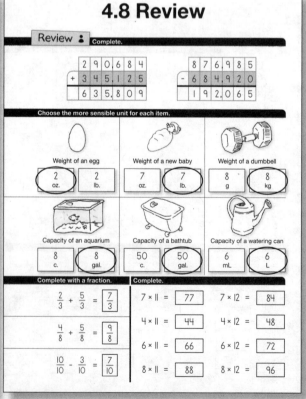

4.8 Review

Review 👤 Complete.

$$\begin{array}{r} 2\,9\,0,6\,8\,4 \\ +\ 3\,4\,5,1\,2\,5 \\ \hline 6\,3\,5,8\,0\,9 \end{array}$$

$$\begin{array}{r} 8\,7\,6,9\,8\,5 \\ -\ 6\,8\,4,9\,2\,0 \\ \hline 1\,9\,2,0\,6\,5 \end{array}$$

Choose the more sensible unit for each item.

Weight of an egg: (2 oz.) 2 lb.

Weight of a new baby: 7 oz. (7 lb.)

Weight of a dumbbell: 8 g (8 kg)

Capacity of an aquarium: 8 c. (8 gal.)

Capacity of a bathtub: 50 c. (50 gal.)

Capacity of a watering can: 6 mL (6 L)

Complete with a fraction.

$\frac{2}{3} + \frac{5}{3} = \boxed{\frac{7}{3}}$

$\frac{4}{8} + \frac{5}{8} = \boxed{\frac{9}{8}}$

$\frac{10}{10} - \frac{3}{10} = \boxed{\frac{7}{10}}$

Complete.

$7 \times 11 = \boxed{77}$ $7 \times 12 = \boxed{84}$

$4 \times 11 = \boxed{44}$ $4 \times 12 = \boxed{48}$

$6 \times 11 = \boxed{66}$ $6 \times 12 = \boxed{72}$

$8 \times 11 = \boxed{88}$ $8 \times 12 = \boxed{96}$

Unit 4 Answer Key

4.9 Practice/Review

Practice Complete.

	2	$\frac{3}{8}$
+	4	$\frac{7}{8}$
↻	6	$\frac{10}{8}$
→	7	$\frac{2}{8}$

	2	$\frac{7}{10}$
+	1	$\frac{2}{10}$
↻	3	$\frac{9}{10}$

	6	$\frac{3}{4}$
+	2	$\frac{2}{4}$
↻	8	$\frac{5}{4}$
→	9	$\frac{1}{4}$

	3	$\frac{3}{5}$
+	2	$\frac{2}{5}$
↻	5	$\frac{5}{5}$
→	6	

Review Write a fraction to complete each equation. Then, convert the fraction to a mixed number or whole number.

$4 \times \frac{2}{5} = \boxed{\frac{8}{5}} = \boxed{1\frac{3}{5}}$

$2 \times \frac{4}{6} = \boxed{\frac{8}{6}} = \boxed{1\frac{2}{6}}$

$3 \times \frac{3}{8} = \boxed{\frac{9}{8}} = \boxed{1\frac{1}{8}}$

$6 \times \frac{2}{3} = \boxed{\frac{12}{3}} = \boxed{4}$

Use the clues to find the secret number.

★
- The number has 6 digits.
- There is a 5 in the thousands place.
- There is a 6 in the ten thousands place.
- The sum of the digit in the tens place and the digit in the thousands place is 8.
- The product of the digit in the tens place and the digit in the ones place is 27.
- The digit in the ones place is the same as the digit in the hundreds place.
- The number is greater than 400,000 and less than 500,000.

Secret Number: | 4 | 6 | 5, | 9 | 3 | 9 |

4.10 Practice

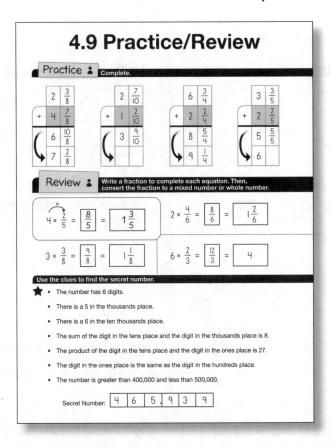

SPIN TO WIN!   B

Practice Complete.

		4
-	2	$\frac{2}{3}$
	1	$\frac{1}{3}$

	4	$\frac{2}{10}$
-	3	$\frac{5}{10}$
		$\frac{7}{10}$

	5	$\frac{1}{6}$
-	2	$\frac{4}{6}$
	2	$\frac{3}{6}$

	3	$\frac{7}{8}$
-	1	$\frac{3}{8}$
	2	$\frac{4}{8}$

4.10 Review

Review Color the multiples in order from Start to End.

Multiples of 11

Start → 11	22	33	36	40
17	24	44	45	42
21	48	55	66	72
30	56	60	77	110 END
36	63	72	88	99

Multiples of 12

24	36	42	64	80
Start → 12	48	60	72	77
8	56	54	84	92
4	16	40	96	108
6	20	28	110	120 END

Complete.

$400,000 + 27,000 = \boxed{427,000}$ $8 \times 3,000 = \boxed{24,000}$

$125,000 + 125,000 = \boxed{250,000}$ $7 \times 6,000 = \boxed{42,000}$

$76,000 + 4,000 = \boxed{80,000}$ $8 \times 8,000 = \boxed{64,000}$

$100,000 - 10,000 = \boxed{90,000}$ $4 \times 5,000 = \boxed{20,000}$

$500,000 - 50,000 = \boxed{450,000}$ $9 \times 10,000 = \boxed{90,000}$

Complete the missing mixed numbers.

| $1\frac{1}{5}$ | $1\frac{3}{5}$ | $2\frac{2}{5}$ | $2\frac{4}{5}$ |

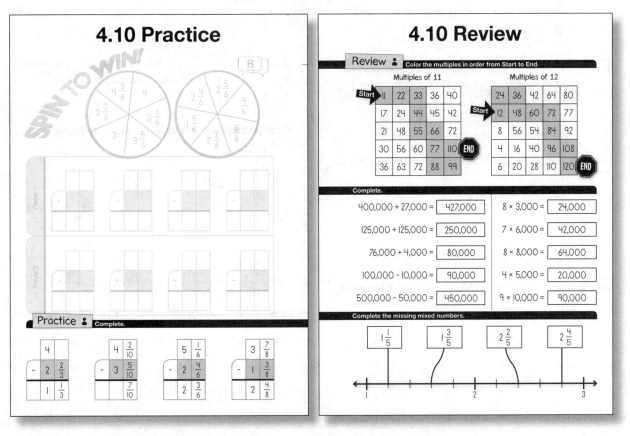

Unit 4 Answer Key

4.11 Practice

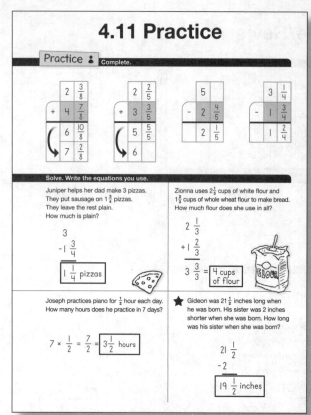

Practice Complete.

$$2 \frac{3}{8}$$
$$+ 4 \frac{7}{8}$$
$$6 \frac{10}{8}$$
$$7 \frac{2}{8}$$

$$2 \frac{2}{5}$$
$$+ 3 \frac{3}{5}$$
$$5 \frac{5}{5}$$
$$6$$

$$5 \frac{}{}$$
$$- 2 \frac{4}{5}$$
$$2 \frac{1}{5}$$

$$3 \frac{1}{4}$$
$$- 1 \frac{3}{4}$$
$$1 \frac{2}{4}$$

Solve. Write the equations you use.

Juniper helps her dad make 3 pizzas. They put sausage on $1\frac{3}{4}$ pizzas. They leave the rest plain. How much is plain?

$$3$$
$$-1 \frac{3}{4}$$
$$1 \frac{1}{4} \text{ pizzas}$$

Zionna uses $2\frac{1}{3}$ cups of white flour and $1\frac{2}{3}$ cups of whole wheat flour to make bread. How much flour does she use in all?

$$2 \frac{1}{3}$$
$$+1 \frac{2}{3}$$
$$3 \frac{3}{3} = \boxed{4 \text{ cups of flour}}$$

Joseph practices piano for $\frac{1}{2}$ hour each day. How many hours does he practice in 7 days?

$$7 \times \frac{1}{2} = \frac{7}{2} = \boxed{3\frac{1}{2} \text{ hours}}$$

★ Gideon was $21\frac{1}{2}$ inches long when he was born. His sister was 2 inches shorter when she was born. How long was his sister when she was born?

$$21 \frac{1}{2}$$
$$-2$$
$$\boxed{19 \frac{1}{2} \text{ inches}}$$

4.11 Review

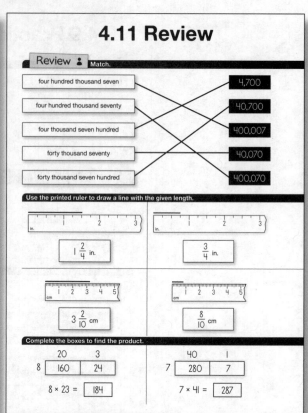

Review Match.

four hundred thousand seven — 400,007
four hundred thousand seventy — 400,070
four thousand seven hundred — 4,700
forty thousand seventy — 40,070
forty thousand seven hundred — 40,700

Use the printed ruler to draw a line with the given length.

$$1 \frac{2}{4} \text{ in.}$$

$$\frac{3}{4} \text{ in.}$$

$$3 \frac{2}{10} \text{ cm}$$

$$\frac{8}{10} \text{ cm}$$

Complete the boxes to find the product.

	20	3
8	160	24

$$8 \times 23 = \boxed{184}$$

	40	1
7	280	7

$$7 \times 41 = \boxed{287}$$

4.12 Unit Wrap-Up A

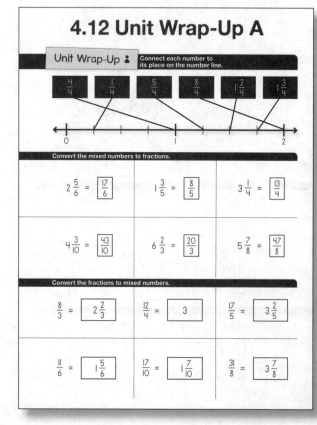

Unit Wrap-Up Connect each number to its place on the number line.

$$\frac{4}{4} \quad \frac{1}{4} \quad \frac{5}{4} \quad \frac{8}{4} \quad 1\frac{2}{4} \quad 1\frac{3}{4}$$

Convert the mixed numbers to fractions.

$$2 \frac{5}{6} = \boxed{\frac{17}{6}} \qquad 1 \frac{3}{5} = \boxed{\frac{8}{5}} \qquad 3 \frac{1}{4} = \boxed{\frac{13}{4}}$$

$$4 \frac{3}{10} = \boxed{\frac{43}{10}} \qquad 6 \frac{2}{3} = \boxed{\frac{20}{3}} \qquad 5 \frac{7}{8} = \boxed{\frac{47}{8}}$$

Convert the fractions to mixed numbers.

$$\frac{8}{3} = \boxed{2 \frac{2}{3}} \qquad \frac{12}{4} = \boxed{3} \qquad \frac{17}{5} = \boxed{3 \frac{2}{5}}$$

$$\frac{11}{6} = \boxed{1 \frac{5}{6}} \qquad \frac{17}{10} = \boxed{1 \frac{7}{10}} \qquad \frac{31}{8} = \boxed{3 \frac{7}{8}}$$

4.12 Unit Wrap-Up B

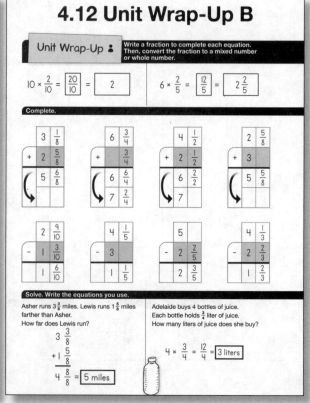

Unit Wrap-Up Write a fraction to complete each equation. Then, convert the fraction to a mixed number or whole number.

$$10 \times \frac{2}{10} = \boxed{\frac{20}{10}} = \boxed{2} \qquad 6 \times \frac{2}{5} = \boxed{\frac{12}{5}} = \boxed{2 \frac{2}{5}}$$

Complete.

$$3 \frac{1}{8}$$
$$+ 2 \frac{5}{8}$$
$$5 \frac{6}{8}$$

$$6 \frac{3}{4}$$
$$+ \frac{3}{4}$$
$$6 \frac{6}{4}$$
$$7 \frac{2}{4}$$

$$4 \frac{1}{2}$$
$$+ 2 \frac{1}{2}$$
$$6 \frac{2}{2}$$
$$7$$

$$2 \frac{5}{8}$$
$$+ 3$$
$$5 \frac{5}{8}$$

$$2 \frac{9}{10}$$
$$- 1 \frac{3}{10}$$
$$1 \frac{6}{10}$$

$$4 \frac{1}{5}$$
$$- 3$$
$$1 \frac{1}{5}$$

$$5 \frac{}{}$$
$$- 2 \frac{2}{5}$$
$$2 \frac{3}{5}$$

$$4 \frac{1}{3}$$
$$- 2 \frac{2}{3}$$
$$1 \frac{2}{3}$$

Solve. Write the equations you use.

Asher runs $3\frac{3}{8}$ miles. Lewis runs $1\frac{5}{8}$ miles farther than Asher. How far does Lewis run?

$$3 \frac{3}{8}$$
$$+1 \frac{5}{8}$$
$$4 \frac{8}{8} = \boxed{5 \text{ miles}}$$

Adelaide buys 4 bottles of juice. Each bottle holds $\frac{3}{4}$ liter of juice. How many liters of juice does she buy?

$$4 \times \frac{3}{4} = \frac{12}{4} = \boxed{3 \text{ liters}}$$

Unit 4 Checkpoint

What to Expect at the End of Unit 4

By the end of Unit 4, most children will be able to do the following:

- Identify and compare fractions and mixed numbers on the number line.
- Use multiplication to convert whole numbers and mixed numbers to fractions.
- Use division to convert fractions to whole numbers or mixed numbers.
- Multiply fractions by whole numbers and understand what it means to multiply a fraction by a whole number. Some children will still need to use manipulatives to make sense of these multiplication problems.
- Add and subtract fractions and mixed numbers with the same denominator. Most children will be fluent at adding and subtracting fractions, but many will still be working on learning the algorithms for adding and subtracting mixed numbers. Subtracting mixed numbers has many steps to learn, so don't worry if your child still mixes up the steps sometimes. He'll have many more opportunities for review and practice.

Is Your Child Ready to Move on?

In Unit 5, your child will review the division facts and learn several mental division techniques. This unit will reinforce your child's multiplication and division skills. He does not need to have fully mastered the division facts before moving on to Unit 5.

Your child does not need to have fully mastered the fraction skills in Unit 4 before moving on to Unit 5. He'll get more practice with fractions and mixed numbers in the Review workbook pages to reinforce these skills.

Unit 5
Mental Division

Overview

In this unit, your child will learn how to mentally divide larger numbers. She'll also review remainders, use multiplication to check division, and learn the ÷11 and ÷12 facts.

Later this year, your child will learn the written process for multi-digit long division. This unit builds both the conceptual understanding and mental math skills necessary for mastering the multi-digit division algorithm.

What Your Child Will Learn

In this unit, your child will learn to:

- Mentally find remainders
- Solve division word problems and interpret remainders depending on the context
- Use multiplication (and addition) to check answers to division problems
- Find answers for the ÷11 and ÷12 facts
- Mentally divide multiples of 10, 100, or 1,000 by one-digit numbers (for example, 60 ÷ 3 or 3,000 ÷ 5)

Lesson List

Lesson 5.1	Review Division Facts	Lesson 5.5	Mentally Divide Tens
Lesson 5.2	Find Remainders	Lesson 5.6	Mentally Divide Hundreds
Lesson 5.3	Check and Interpret		and Thousands
	Remainders	Lesson 5.7	Enrichment (Optional)
Lesson 5.4	÷11 and ÷12 Facts		

Extra Materials Needed for Unit 5

- Paper clip
- For optional Enrichment Lesson:
  - × *The Great Divide: A Mathematical Marathon*, written by Dayle Ann Dodds and illustrated by Tracy Mitchell. Candlewick, 2005.
  - × 4 pieces of yarn of different colors, each 36 inches long
  - × Ruler
  - × Scissors
  - × Wooden stick, about 1 foot long

Teaching Math with Confidence:
Using "The Price is Right" Approach to Find Quotients

If you grew up in the United States, you're probably familiar with *The Price is Right*, a long-running television game show. In the show, the contestants guess the prices of items ranging from toothpaste to trips around the world. The player whose guess is as close as possible to the actual price wins. However, there's one important condition: Your guess must be less than or equal to the actual price. If your guess is greater than the actual price, you lose!

Finding the quotient for a division problem is a lot like being a contestant on *The Price is Right*. Just like the contestants, the goal is to find a multiple of the divisor that's as close as possible to the dividend. But, you can't go over!

For example, say your child is dividing 30 by 7. To find the quotient, she needs to figure out how many groups of 7 are in 30. Here's what her thought process might look like:

- *7 times 3 is 21. That's too low.*
- *7 times 5 is 35. That's too high.*
- *7 times 4 is 28. That's as close as I can get without going over.*
- *So, 30 divided by 7 equals 4, with a remainder of 2.*

If your child's familiar with the game show, encourage her to use "Price is Right" thinking as she solves division problems in this unit. If she's not familiar with the show, simply encourage her to use multiplication to find a multiple of the divisor that's as close as possible to the dividend, without going over it.

In Unit 10, your child will learn how to use long division to divide multi-digit numbers. The mental math skills your child learns in this unit (and the "Price is Right" thinking process that she develops) will help her estimate and find the digits in the quotient when she tackles this complicated process.

Lesson 5.1
Review Division Facts

Purpose	Materials
• Practice division facts • Understand that the remainder must always be less than the divisor	• Die • Counters

Memory Work	• **What do we call the number to be divided?** *The dividend.* • **What do we call the number we divide by?** *The divisor.* • **What do we call the result when we divide two numbers?** *The quotient.* • **What do we call an amount that is left over after division?** *The remainder.*

Warm-up (A): Play Dice Tic-Tac-Toe

We're starting a new unit on division! Today, we'll review the division facts and explore remainder patterns.

Play Dice Tic-Tac-Toe. If the game goes quickly, play 2 rounds.

Dice Tic-Tac-Toe

Materials: Die; counters of two different colors

Object of the Game: Be the first player to fill three boxes in a row, either horizontally, vertically, or diagonally.

On your turn, roll the die. Find the column in the game board that matches your roll, and choose a division problem in that column. Say the answer and cover the problem with one of your counters. If you roll a 6, you may choose a problem in any column.

Play then passes to the other player. Continue until one player covers 3 boxes in a row, either horizontally, vertically, or diagonally.

Activity (B): Explore Remainder Patterns

Let's pretend some children are playing a game and want to split into 2 equal teams. If 12 children divide into 2 equal teams, how many children are on each team? *6.* Write 6 in the blank.

$$12 \div 2 = \boxed{6} \; ^{\text{B}}$$

If 13 children divide into 2 equal teams, how many children are on each team? *6, but there's one left over.* Write "6 R1" in the blank. **How do you think the children might handle having one person left?** *Sample answers: They might have one person be the referee or take turns sitting out. They might decide it's okay for one team to have more people than the other team.*

$$13 \div 2 = \boxed{6 \text{ R1}} \; ^{\text{B}}$$

If your child has trouble mentally dividing 13 by 2, place 13 counters on the table and have her split them into 2 equal groups. She will find that there is 1 counter left after she makes 2 groups of 6.

Your child will learn more about finding and interpreting remainders in the next two lessons.

Continue with the same way with the rest of the division problems in the column.

What patterns do you notice? *Sample answers: The problems switch between having remainders and not having remainders. The even dividends don't have remainders, but the odd dividends do have remainders.*

What's the only possible remainder if you divide by 2? *1.* Write 1 in the box. **Why can't the remainder be greater than 1 when you divide by 2?** *Sample answer: If you have a remainder of 2 or greater, you could split the children up between the two teams.*

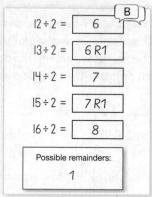

Now, let's pretend the children want to divide into 3 equal groups. Have your child complete the problems in the middle column. **What are the only possible remainders if you divide by 3?** *1 or 2.* Write 1 and 2 in the box.

Repeat with the final column. **What are the only possible remainders if you divide by 4?** *1, 2, or 3.* Write 1, 2, and 3 in the box.

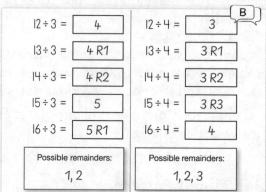

If I divided a number by 10, what's the greatest possible remainder that I could get? *9.* **How do you know?** *Sample answer: If you get 10 or more for your remainder, it means you didn't divide everything up as much as you could.* **The remainder in a problem must always be less than the divisor. If you get a remainder that's greater than the divisor, you know you need to check your work.**

Independent Practice and Review

Have your child complete the Lesson 5.1 Practice and Review workbook pages.

Lesson 5.2
Find Remainders

Purpose	Materials
• Practice adding up to find differences • Solve mental division problems with remainders	• Playing cards

Memory Work	• **What do we call numbers that have a whole number and a fraction?** *Mixed numbers.*

In this lesson, your child will use multiplication to solve division problems. This reinforces the connection between the two operations and prepares your child to use multiplication to check answers in the next lesson.

Warm-up: Practice Adding Up to Find Differences

Ask your child the following mental subtraction problems. Encourage him to add up to find the differences. For example, for 80 – 76: **76 plus what is 80?** *4.* **So, 80 minus 76 equals 4.**

- 80 – 76 = *4*
- 90 – 87 = *3*
- 75 – 72 = *3*

- 61 – 59 = *2*
- 42 – 38 = *4*

Your child will use this skill to find remainders later in the lesson.

Activity (A): Find Remainders at the Toy Store

In the last lesson, you practiced the division facts and explored remainder patterns. Today, we'll focus more on remainders. We'll review how to find remainders mentally, and you'll learn how to check division problems with remainders.

Congratulations, you've won a $30 gift card to the toy store! Show your child the toys and briefly discuss which toy he'd like most. **The yo-yos cost $7 each. Let's find how many you could buy if you only bought yo-yos.**

To divide 30 by 7, I think, "What number can I multiply by 7 to get as close as possible to 30 without going over?"
- **If I multiply 7 by 5, I get 35. That's more than 30, so that's too much.**
- **If I multiply 7 by 3, I get 21. I can get closer to 30.**
- **If I multiply 7 by 4, I get 28. That's as close as I can get to 30 without going over. So, the quotient is 4.** Write 4 as shown.

Now, I need to find the difference between 28 and 30. When two numbers are close together, it's usually easiest to add up to find the difference between them. 28 plus 2 equals 30, so the remainder is 2. Write "R2" as shown.

So, how many yo-yos could you buy with $30? *4.* **How much money would be left on the gift card?** *$2.*

If your child is familiar with the game show *The Price is Right*, explain that this method is similar to what the contestants do on the show: Guess the price of the prizes as accurately as possible, but without going over. See the Unit 5 **Teaching Math with Confidence** for more on this approach.

Have your child solve the remaining division problems in the same way. Encourage him to multiply to find how many of each item he can buy. Then, have him add up to find the remainder.

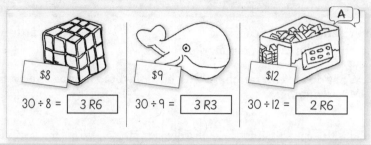

Frame each problem in terms of the toy store gift card. For example: **How many stuffed animals can you buy with $30?**

Activity (B): Play Flip and Divide

Play Flip and Divide.

Flip and Divide

Materials: 6s, 7s, 8s, and 9s from a deck of playing cards (16 cards in all)

Object of the Game: Score the most points by creating greater remainders than your opponent.

Shuffle the cards and place them in a face-down pile. On your turn, flip over the top card. Write the number on the card as the divisor for one of the division problems on your scorecard. Try to choose a problem that will yield as large a remainder as possible. Then, solve the problem. The remainder is your score for that round. If there is no remainder, your score is 0.

For example, if you flip over a 9 on your first turn, you may write 9 as the divisor for any of the problems. 60 ÷ 9 yields the greatest possible remainder, so writing the 9 in the final division problem is the best play. 60 ÷ 9 = 6 R6, so your score is 6.

$$60 \div \boxed{9} = \boxed{6 \text{ R}6}$$ B

Play until both players have completed their scorecards. Find the sum of each player's remainders. Whoever has the greater sum wins the game.

Cooperative Variation: Play together on just one game board. After you finish one round, play again on the other game board. See if you can beat your first score.

Independent Practice and Review

Have your child complete the Lesson 5.2 Practice and Review workbook pages.

Lesson 5.3
Check and Interpret Remainders

Purpose	Materials
• Practice mental division with a remainder • Multiply and add to check division problems with a remainder • Review how to interpret remainders in a sensible way depending on the context	• None

Memory Work · **What do parentheses mean in a math problem?** *Do this first.*

In real life, solving problems with remainders is more complex than simply writing "R1" after the quotient. In this lesson, you'll review how to interpret remainders according to the context.

Warm-up: Solve Division Problems with a Remainder

In the last lesson, you solved division problems with a remainder in your head. Ask your child the following mental division problems. Encourage her to multiply to find each quotient. Then, have her add up to find the remainder.

- 31 ÷ 10 = *3 R1*
- 31 ÷ 5 = *6 R1*

- 31 ÷ 4 = *7 R3*
- 31 ÷ 8 = *3 R7*

If your child has trouble keeping the numbers in her head, write the problems horizontally on a piece of scrap paper.

Activity (A): Multiply and Add to Check Division Problems with a Remainder

Today, you'll learn how to check your answers to division problems with remainders. You'll also practice solving division word problems and interpreting the remainder in a sensible way.

Let's say I have 21 marbles. I want to divide them into 3 equal groups. How many marbles will be in each group? *7.* Write 7 in the blank.

Multiplication is the opposite of division. So, I can use multiplication to check my answer. I want to make sure that 3 groups of 7 equal 21, so I multiply 3 times 7. Write "3 × 7 =" in the blank. **3 times 7 equals 21, so 21 divided by 3 equals 7.** Write 21 to complete the equation.

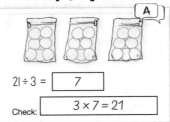

I changed my mind. I have 21 marbles, but now I want to divide them into 4 equal groups. How many marbles will be in each group? *5.* **How many marbles will be left over?** *1.* Write "5 R1" in the blank.

Let's use multiplication to check this answer, too. First, I'll multiply 4 times 5 to see how many marbles are in the 4 groups of 5. Write "(4 × 5)" in the blank. **Then, I'll add on the extra marble.** Continue the equation with "+ 1" as shown. **What's 4 times 5?** *20.* **Plus 1?** *21.* Write 21 to complete the equation.

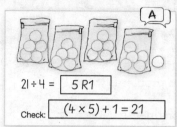

Have your child mentally solve the rest of the division problems in part A. Then, have her multiply and add to check the answers. Model the problems with counters as needed.

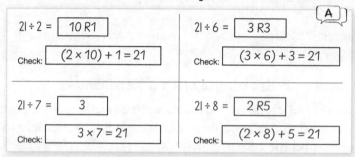

Activity (B): Interpret Remainders in a Sensible Way

Have your child read aloud the first word problem: *19 children play kickball. They make 2 teams. They make the teams as equal as possible. How many children are on each team?*

What equation matches the problem? *19 divided by 2.* Write "19 ÷ 2 =" in the space below the problem. Have your child complete the problem: 19 ÷ 2 = 9 R1.

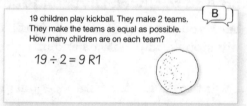

What is the goal of this problem? *Find how many children are on each team.* **Are there 9 remainder 1 children on each team?** *No.* **In real life, what do you think the children would do?** *Sample answer: They would have one team be a little bigger than the other team.*

To make the teams as even as possible, they would probably have the last child just join one of the teams. So, one team will have 9 children and the other group will have 10 children. Write "9 or 10 children" in the space below the problem and draw a box around it. **It's funny to have 2 answers, isn't it? But that's the most logical way to handle the remainder in this problem.**

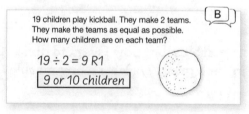

Have your child read aloud the next word problem: *19 children are at tennis practice. The coach splits them into pairs. How many pairs does he make?*

What equation matches the problem? *19 divided by 2.* **That's the same equation you used for the last problem! You already found the answer is 9 with a remainder of 1.**

The remaining problems all involve dividing 19 by 2. You can simply write the answers to these problems rather than writing out the matching equation again.

What is the goal of this problem? *Find how many pairs there are.* **Are there 9 remainder 1 pairs?** *No!* **In real life, what do you think the children would do?** *Sample answers: They might take turns sitting out so that everyone can play.*

The coach can make 9 pairs. Maybe the players will take turns sitting out so that everyone can play. Write "9 pairs" in the space below the problem and draw a box around it. **In this problem, the remainder isn't part of the answer.**

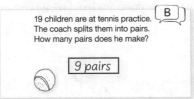

In the kickball problem, you divided 19 by 2 to find the number of people in each group. In the tennis problem, you divided to find how many groups you could make. We use division to find answers to both kinds of problems.

Have your child solve the remaining two word problems in the same way.

- For the costume problem, point out that the remainder is the answer: **The quotient isn't part of the answer for this problem!**
- For the lemonade stand problem, point out that the friends could share the extra dollar. **If the friends split the extra dollar, how many cents will each of them get?** *50 cents.* **So, how much money will each friend get in all?** *$9.50.* **In this problem, we split the remainder equally, too.**

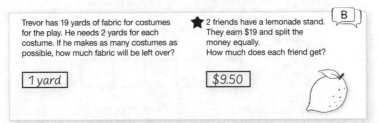

Encourage your child to use her knowledge of dollars and cents to solve the final problem, and model it with play money if needed. She is not expected to be able to divide decimals at this point.

Independent Practice and Review

Have your child complete the Lesson 5.3 Practice and Review workbook pages.

Lesson 5.4
÷11 and ÷12 Facts

Purpose	Materials
• Practice ×12 facts • Use the ×12 facts to find answers to the ÷12 facts • Use the ×11 facts to find answers to the ÷11 facts	• Deck of playing cards • Counters

Memory Work
- **How many centimeters equal 1 meter?** *100.*
- **How many meters equal 1 kilometer?** *1,000.*

Warm-up (A): Play Multiplication Crash (×12)

Play Multiplication Crash.

Multiplication Crash (×12)

Materials: Deck of playing cards with jacks, queens, and kings removed (40 cards total); 10 counters of two different colors

Object of the Game: Have the most counters on the game board at the end of the game.

Shuffle the cards and place the stack face down on the table. Give 10 counters of one color to one player and 10 counters of a different color to the other player.

On your turn, flip over the top card. Multiply the card by 12, say the matching multiplication fact, and place a counter on the matching square. For example, if you flip over a 7, say "7 times 12 equals 84" and place a counter on 84.

If the other player already has a counter on the square, you may "crash" into their counter, remove it, and place your own counter on the square. Continue until all the squares are filled. Whoever has more counters on the board at the end wins the game.

If your child has trouble recalling any of the ×12 facts, draw a quick box diagram to help him find the answer (as in Lesson 3.8). For example, for 7 × 12: **7 times 10 is 70. 7 times 2 is 14. So, you can add 70 plus 14 to find that the answer is 84.**

	10	2
7	70	14

Activity (B): Use Related ×12 Facts to Find Answers for the ÷12 Facts

In Unit 3, you learned the ×11 and ×12 facts. Today, you'll use the ×11 and ×12 facts to find answers to the ÷11 and ÷12 facts.

Let's pretend you have chickens and collect their eggs each day. You put each group of 12 eggs in a carton. We call 12 of an item a *dozen*.

One day, you collect 48 eggs. **What times 12 equals 48?** *4.* **4 times 12 equals 48, 48 divided by 12 equals 4.** Write 4 in both blanks. Have your child solve the rest of the division problems in the same way.

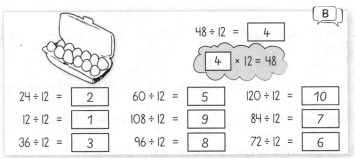

If your child has trouble with any of the problems, encourage him to try a number and then adjust his guess based on the result. For example, for 72 ÷ 12: **Let's try 5. What's 5 times 12?** *60.* **That's too low, so try multiplying 12 by a larger number.**

Activity (C): Use ×11 Facts to Find Answers for the ÷11 Facts

You can use the same approach to find answers to the ÷11 facts. Let's pretend you're arranging flowers for a party. You have 55 flowers, and you put 11 flowers in each vase. We'll divide 55 by 11 to find how many vases you can fill.

What times 11 equals 55? *5.* **5 times 11 equals 55, so 55 divided by 11 equals 5.** Write 5 in both blanks. Have your child solve the rest of the division problems in the same way.

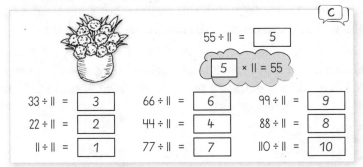

Independent Practice and Review

Have your child complete the Lesson 5.4 Practice and Review workbook pages.

Lesson 5.5
Mentally Divide Tens

Purpose	Materials
• Practice multiplying one-digit numbers by multiples of 10 • Use place-value thinking to divide multiples of 10 by one-digit numbers	• Play money • Paper clip

| Memory Work | • **What do we call an angle that looks like the corner of a piece of paper?** *A right angle.*
• **What do we call a quadrilateral with 4 right angles?** *A rectangle.*
• **What do we call a quadrilateral with 4 right angles and 4 equal sides?** *A square.*
• **What do we call a quadrilateral with 4 equal sides?** *A rhombus.* |

Warm-up: Practice Multiplying by Multiples of 10

Have your child solve the following multiplication problems.

- 3 × 20 = *60*
- 2 × 40 = *80*
- 5 × 20 = *100*

- 5 × 30 = *150*
- 4 × 50 = *200*

> Remind your child to use place-value thinking to solve these problems. For example, for 5 times 30: **5 times 3 equals 15, so 5 times 3 tens equals 15 tens, or 150.**

Activity (A): Use Place-Value Thinking to Mentally Divide Multiples of 10

Today, you'll learn how to mentally divide multiples of 10 by one-digit numbers.

Place 8 ten-dollar bills on the table to match the picture. **Let's pretend 4 friends did yard work and earned $80 in all. They want to divide the money evenly.**

We have 8 tens to split into 4 equal groups. What's 8 divided by 4? *2.* Have your child split the 8 ten-dollar bills into 4 equal groups. **8 tens divided by 4 equals 2 tens.** Write 2 in the cloud's blank. **So, 80 divided by 4 equals 2 tens, or 20.** Write 20 in the blank.

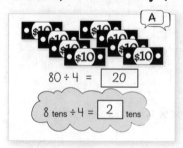

Now, let's pretend 5 friends do yard work and earn $150 in all. $150 equals 15 tens. What's 15 divided by 5? *3.* **15 tens divided by 5 equals 3 tens.** Write 5 in the cloud's blank. **So, 150 divided by 5 equals 3 tens, or 30. Each friend gets $30.** Write 30 in the blank.

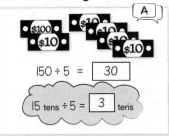

If your child has trouble understanding the problem, model $150 with 15 ten-dollar bills and have her split the bills into 5 equal groups.

Have your child use this approach to solve the division problems in part A. Encourage her to use place-value thinking, and model the problems with ten-dollar bills as needed.

90 ÷ 3 = 30		160 ÷ 8 = 20
60 ÷ 2 = 30		180 ÷ 6 = 30
100 ÷ 5 = 20		240 ÷ 4 = 60

Activity (B): Use Division to Choose Prizes at the Mental Math Arcade

Let's pretend we're at the Mental Math Arcade again! This time, you'll spin the spinner to find how many tickets you win. Then, you choose a prize to buy with your tickets. You may only choose one type of prize per spin.

Before you spin, we'll discuss a few examples. Let's pretend I spin and win 120 tickets. Place a paper clip on the spinner so that it points to 120. **I decide to spend my tickets on stickers. Each sticker costs 3 tickets. How many stickers can I buy?** *40.* **How do you know?** *120 divided by 3 equals 40.*

If your child has trouble keeping the numbers in her head, write the matching horizontal equation on a piece of scrap paper: 120 ÷ 3 = 40.

Place one end of a paper clip in the middle of the spinner. Place the point of a pencil through the paper clip so that it touches the very middle of the circle. Then, have your child spin 5 times. After each spin, have her choose one prize to buy. Then, have her divide to find how many of the prize she can buy. For example, if she lands on 240 and wants to buy bouncy balls: *240 divided by 6 equals 40, so I would get 40 bouncy balls!*

The lollipops (at 10 tickets apiece) preview dividing by multiples of 10. If your child has trouble with these questions, point out that she can use place-value thinking. For example, for 120 ÷ 10: **120 equals 12 tens. There are 12 groups of 10 in 120, so 120 divided by 10 equals 12.** Your child will learn more about dividing by multiples of 10 in fifth grade.

Independent Practice and Review

Have your child complete the Lesson 5.5 Practice and Review workbook pages.

Lesson 5.6
Mentally Divide Hundreds and Thousands

Purpose	Materials
• Review mentally dividing multiples of 10 • Use related multiplication problems to divide multiples of 10, 100, or 1,000 by one-digit numbers	• Play money • Playing cards

Memory Work	• **What do we call the number to be divided?** *The dividend.* • **What do we call the number we divide by?** *The divisor.* • **What do we call the result when we divide two numbers?** *The quotient.* • **What do we call an amount that is left over after division?** *The remainder.*

Warm-up: Practice Mentally Dividing Multiples of 10

In the last lesson, you learned how to use place-value thinking to mentally divide groups of tens. Have your child solve the following problems.

- 60 ÷ 3 = *20*
- 80 ÷ 2 = *40*
- 100 ÷ 5 = *20*

- 160 ÷ 4 = *40*
- 240 ÷ 3 = *80*

Activity (A): Mentally Divide Hundreds

In this lesson, you'll use place-value thinking to divide groups of hundreds or thousands.

Let's pretend 4 people worked together to earn $800. Place 8 hundred-dollar bills on the table. **If you split the money evenly between 4 people, how many hundreds will each person get?** *2.* Have your child split the 8 hundred-dollar bills into 4 equal groups.

8 hundreds divided by 4 equals 2 hundreds. Write 2 in the cloud's blank. **So, 800 divided by 4 equals 2 hundreds, or 200.** Write 200 in the blank.

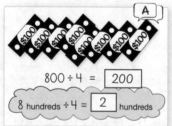
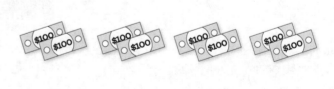

Now, let's pretend 4 friends earned $200. Place 2 hundred-dollar bills on the table. **There aren't enough bills to divide the bills evenly. How could you split the money between 4 people?** *Sample answer: I'd trade the hundred-dollar bills for smaller bills.*

Let's trade the 2 hundred-dollar bills for 20 ten-dollar bills. Trade the 2 hundred-dollar bills for 20 ten-dollar bills. **How many tens do we have now?** *20.* **If you split them evenly between 4 people, how many tens will each person get?** *5.* **20 tens divided by 4 equals 5 tens.** Write 5 in the cloud's blank. **So, 200 divided by 4 equals 50.** Write 50 in the blank.

If your child readily grasps that 200 equals 20 tens, you can skip physically trading the 2 hundred-dollar bills for 20 ten-dollar bills.

Have your child complete part A.

400 ÷ 2 = ⬚ 200	300 ÷ 3 = ⬚ 100
400 ÷ 4 = ⬚ 100	300 ÷ 5 = ⬚ 60
400 ÷ 5 = ⬚ 80	300 ÷ 6 = ⬚ 50

Activity (B): Mentally Divide Thousands

We can mentally divide thousands in the same way. Imagine 3 people work together to earn $6,000. **If you split 6 thousands evenly between 3 people, how many thousands will each person get?** *2.* Write 2 in the cloud's blank. **So, what's 6,000 divided by 3?** *2,000.* Write 2,000 in the blank.

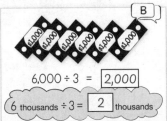

Imagine 4 friends work together to earn $2,000. **We can't divide 2 thousand-dollar bills into 4 equal groups. Instead, we think of the 2 thousands as 20 hundreds. If you split 20 hundreds evenly between 4 people, how many hundreds does each person get?** *5.* **20 hundreds divided by 4 equals 5 hundreds.** Write 5 in the cloud's blank. **So, 2,000 divided by 4 equals 500.** Write 500 in the blank.

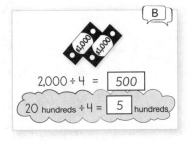

Have your child complete part B.

4,000 ÷ 2 = **2,000**	3,000 ÷ 5 = **600**
6,000 ÷ 2 = **3,000**	4,000 ÷ 5 = **800**
8,000 ÷ 2 = **4,000**	5,000 ÷ 5 = **1,000**

Activity (C): Play Flip and Divide

We're going to play Flip and Divide again. In this version, the goal is to create quotients that are as large as possible. We'll use the 2s, 3s, and 6s from a deck of cards as the divisors.

Using only 2s, 3s, and 6s ensures that your child can solve the problems mentally.

Point to the final row of the score card. **Which divisor gives you the largest quotient for this problem: 2, 3, or 6?** *2.* **How do you know?** *Sample answer: 6,000 divided by 3 is 2,000. 6,000 divided by 6 is 1,000. 6,000 divided by 2 is 3,000, so that's the largest quotient possible.* **When we divide by a smaller divisor, we get a bigger quotient!**

6,000 ÷ ☐ = ☐

Play Flip and Divide. See Lesson 5.2 (page 176) for the general directions. Use only the 2s, 3s, and 6s from a deck of cards (12 cards in all). Instead of trying to create the largest possible remainders, try to create the largest possible quotients. The player who has the greater sum of their quotients wins the game.

Independent Practice and Review

Have your child complete the Lesson 5.6 Practice and Review workbook pages.

Lesson 5.7
Enrichment (Optional)

Purpose	Materials
• Practice memory work • Use mental division to divide by 2 • Use division to measure yarn for a craft • Summarize what your child has learned and assess your child's progress	• *The Great Divide: A Mathematical Marathon,* written by Dayle Ann Dodds and illustrated by Tracy Mitchell • 4 pieces of yarn of different colors, each 36 inches long • Ruler • Scissors • Wooden stick, about 1 foot long

In the enrichment activity, your child will wrap yarn around a stick to make a craft. Look outdoors for a stick about 1 foot long. The stick can be mostly straight or have several small side branches. Your stick should be about 1 foot long and a half-inch wide.

Warm-up: Review Memory Work

Quiz your child on all memory work through Unit 5. See pages 536-537 for the full list.

Math Picture Book: *The Great Divide: A Mathematical Marathon*

Read *The Great Divide: A Mathematical Marathon,* written by Dayle Ann Dodds and illustrated by Tracy Mitchell. As you read, have your child predict how many runners will be left after each division.

Enrichment Activity: Cut Yarn into Equal Pieces to Make a Craft

We're going to use division to make a craft today. We'll divide the yarn into different-sized lengths and then wrap the yarn around a stick.

Give your child 4 pieces of yarn, each 36 inches long. **Each piece of yarn is 36 inches long. Let's cut the first piece into 4 equal pieces. How long should each piece be?** *9 inches.* **How do you know?** *36 divided by 4 equals 9.* Have your child use a ruler to cut the yarn into 4 nine-inch pieces.

9 inches

Have your child use a ruler to cut the other pieces of yarn into the following lengths:

- **Cut the next piece into 3 equal pieces. How long should each piece be?** *12 inches.*
- **Cut the next piece into 6 equal pieces. How long should each piece be?** *6 inches.*
- **Cut the last piece into 2 equal pieces. How long should each piece be?** *18 inches.*

12 inches   6 inches   18 inches

Tie the end of one piece of yarn around the end of a stick. Then, have your child begin wrapping the yarn around the stick. She may wrap it tightly (so that little of the stick is showing), or she may wrap it loosely (so that much of the stick is showing). Once she has wrapped the entire piece of yarn around the stick, help her tie a new piece of yarn to the end of the old one. She can use a random order for the colors or create a pattern.

Continue until she has wrapped yarn around the whole stick, including any side branches. Help her tie the end of the yarn around the stick and tuck the loose end under the wrapped yarn.

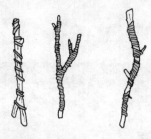

If your child enjoys wrapping the yarn, encourage her to cover several sticks this way. Put them in a vase as a centerpiece or decoration.

Unit Wrap-Up

Have your child complete the Unit 5 Wrap-Up.

Unit 5 Answer Key

5.1 Practice

Practice **Complete.**

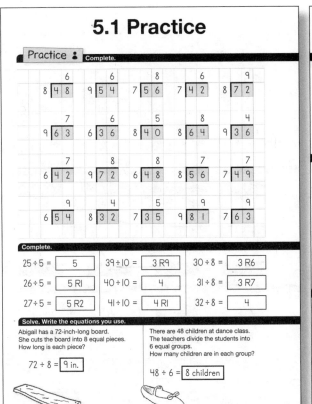

8 $\overline{4\ 8}$ ⁶	9 $\overline{5\ 4}$ ⁶	7 $\overline{5\ 6}$ ⁸	7 $\overline{4\ 2}$ ⁶	8 $\overline{7\ 2}$ ⁹
9 $\overline{6\ 3}$ ⁷	6 $\overline{3\ 6}$ ⁶	8 $\overline{4\ 0}$ ⁵	8 $\overline{6\ 4}$ ⁸	9 $\overline{3\ 6}$ ⁴
6 $\overline{4\ 2}$ ⁷	9 $\overline{7\ 2}$ ⁸	6 $\overline{4\ 8}$ ⁸	8 $\overline{5\ 6}$ ⁷	7 $\overline{4\ 9}$ ⁷
6 $\overline{5\ 4}$ ⁹	8 $\overline{3\ 2}$ ⁴	7 $\overline{3\ 5}$ ⁵	9 $\overline{8\ 1}$ ⁹	7 $\overline{6\ 3}$ ⁹

Complete.

$25 \div 5 =$ [5] $39 \div 10 =$ [3 R9] $30 \div 8 =$ [3 R6]

$26 \div 5 =$ [5 R1] $40 \div 10 =$ [4] $31 \div 8 =$ [3 R7]

$27 \div 5 =$ [5 R2] $41 \div 10 =$ [4 R1] $32 \div 8 =$ [4]

Solve. Write the equations you use.

Abigail has a 72-inch-long board.
She cuts the board into 8 equal pieces.
How long is each piece?

$72 \div 8 =$ [9 in.]

There are 48 children at dance class.
The teachers divide the students into
6 equal groups.
How many children are in each group?

$48 \div 6 =$ [8 children]

5.1 Review

Review **Complete. Use the example to help.**

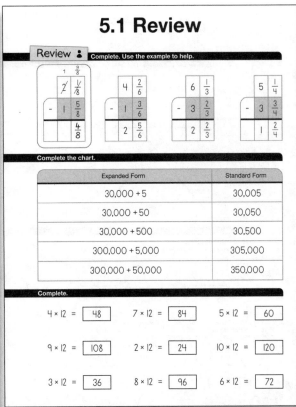

Complete the chart.

Expanded Form	Standard Form
30,000 + 5	30,005
30,000 + 50	30,050
30,000 + 500	30,500
300,000 + 5,000	305,000
300,000 + 50,000	350,000

Complete.

$4 \times 12 =$ [48] $7 \times 12 =$ [84] $5 \times 12 =$ [60]

$9 \times 12 =$ [108] $2 \times 12 =$ [24] $10 \times 12 =$ [120]

$3 \times 12 =$ [36] $8 \times 12 =$ [96] $6 \times 12 =$ [72]

5.2 Practice

Practice **Complete.**

$49 \div 10 =$ [4 R9] $38 \div 5 =$ [7 R3]

$34 \div 4 =$ [8 R2] $43 \div 7 =$ [6 R1]

$39 \div 6 =$ [6 R3] $50 \div 8 =$ [6 R2]

$35 \div 8 =$ [4 R3] $94 \div 9 =$ [10 R4]

Solve. Write the equations you use.

Soren has 60 centimeters of yarn.
He cuts the yarn into pieces that are 8
centimeters long.
- How many pieces does he make?
  $60 \div 8 = 7$ R4
  [7 pieces]
- How much yarn is left over?
  [4 cm]

Mina has 46 shells.
She puts 9 shells on each shelf.
- How many shelves does she fill?
  $46 \div 9 = 5$ R1
  [5 shelves]
- How many shells are left over?
  [1 shell]

5.2 Review

Review **Complete. Use the example to help.**

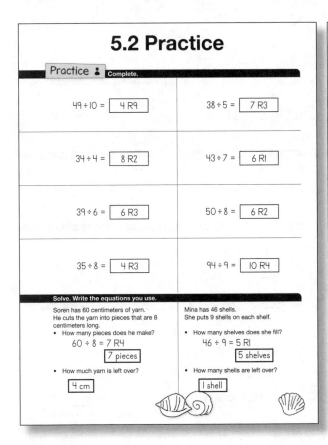

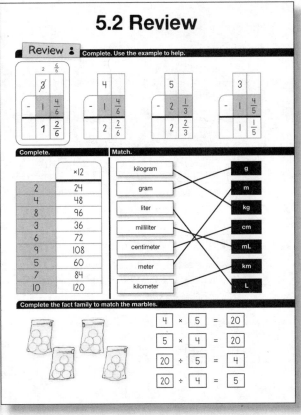

Complete.

	×12
2	24
4	48
8	96
3	36
6	72
9	108
5	60
7	84
10	120

Match.

kilogram	g
gram	m
liter	kg
milliliter	cm
centimeter	mL
meter	km
kilometer	L

Complete the fact family to match the marbles.

$4 \times 5 =$ [20]

$5 \times 4 =$ [20]

$20 \div 5 =$ [4]

$20 \div 4 =$ [5]

Unit 5 Answer Key

5.3 Practice

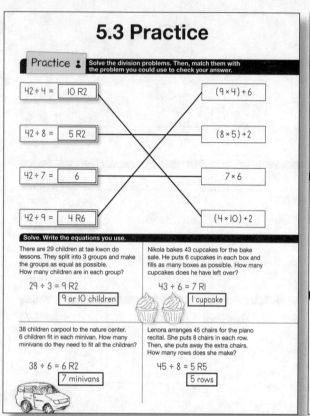

Practice : Solve the division problems. Then, match them with the problem you could use to check your answer.

$42 \div 4 = $ | 10 R2

$42 \div 8 = $ | 5 R2

$42 \div 7 = $ | 6

$42 \div 9 = $ | 4 R6

$(9 \times 4) + 6$

$(8 \times 5) + 2$

7×6

$(4 \times 10) + 2$

Solve. Write the equations you use.

There are 29 children at tae kwon do lessons. They split into 3 groups and make the groups as equal as possible. How many children are in each group?

$29 \div 3 = 9$ R2

9 or 10 children

Nikola bakes 43 cupcakes for the bake sale. He puts 6 cupcakes in each box and fills as many boxes as possible. How many cupcakes does he have left over?

$43 \div 6 = 7$ R1

1 cupcake

38 children carpool to the nature center. 6 children fit in each minivan. How many minivans do they need to fit all the children?

$38 \div 6 = 6$ R2

7 minivans

Lenora arranges 45 chairs for the piano recital. She puts 8 chairs in each row. Then, she puts away the extra chairs. How many rows does she make?

$45 \div 8 = 5$ R5

5 rows

5.3 Review

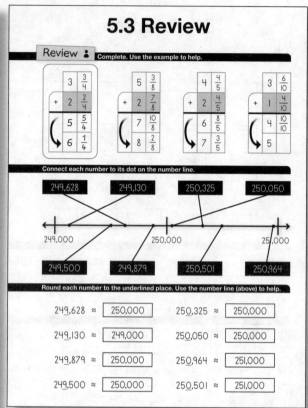

Review : Complete. Use the example to help.

$3 \frac{3}{4}$ + $2 \frac{2}{4}$ → $5 \frac{5}{4}$ → $6 \frac{1}{4}$

$5 \frac{3}{8}$ + $2 \frac{7}{8}$ → $7 \frac{10}{8}$ → $8 \frac{2}{8}$

$4 \frac{4}{5}$ + $2 \frac{4}{5}$ → $6 \frac{8}{5}$ → $7 \frac{3}{5}$

$3 \frac{6}{10}$ + $1 \frac{4}{10}$ → $4 \frac{10}{10}$ → 5

Connect each number to its dot on the number line.

249,628   249,130   250,325   250,050

249,000   250,000   250,000

249,500   249,879   250,501   250,964

Round each number to the underlined place. Use the number line (above) to help.

$24\underline{9},628 \approx$ | 250,000

$24\underline{9},130 \approx$ | 249,000

$249,\underline{8}79 \approx$ | 250,000

$249,\underline{5}00 \approx$ | 250,000

$25\underline{0},325 \approx$ | 250,000

$25\underline{0},050 \approx$ | 250,000

$250,\underline{9}64 \approx$ | 251,000

$250,\underline{5}01 \approx$ | 251,000

5.4 Practice

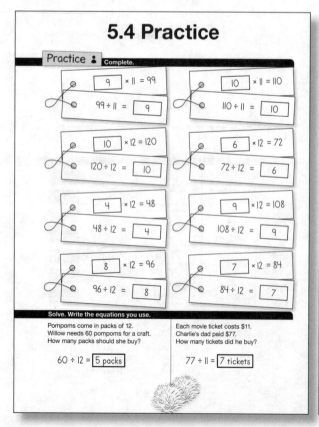

Practice : Complete.

9 × 11 = 99
99 ÷ 11 = 9

10 × 11 = 110
110 ÷ 11 = 10

10 × 12 = 120
120 ÷ 12 = 10

6 × 12 = 72
72 ÷ 12 = 6

4 × 12 = 48
48 ÷ 12 = 4

9 × 12 = 108
108 ÷ 12 = 9

8 × 12 = 96
96 ÷ 12 = 8

7 × 12 = 84
84 ÷ 12 = 7

Solve. Write the equations you use.

Pompoms come in packs of 12. Willow needs 60 pompoms for a craft. How many packs should she buy?

$60 \div 12 = $ 5 packs

Each movie ticket costs $11. Charlie's dad paid $77. How many tickets did he buy?

$77 \div 11 = $ 7 tickets

5.4 Review

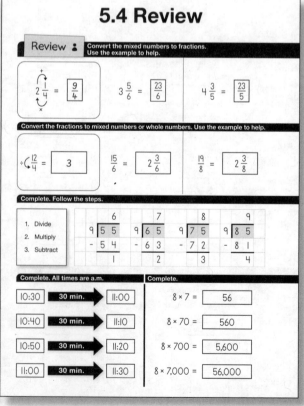

Review : Convert the mixed numbers to fractions. Use the example to help.

$2 \frac{1}{4} = \frac{9}{4}$

$3 \frac{5}{6} = \frac{23}{6}$

$4 \frac{3}{5} = \frac{23}{5}$

Convert the fractions to mixed numbers or whole numbers. Use the example to help.

$\frac{12}{4} = 3$

$\frac{15}{6} = 2 \frac{3}{6}$

$\frac{19}{8} = 2 \frac{3}{8}$

Complete. Follow the steps.

1. Divide
2. Multiply
3. Subtract

$9 \overline{) 5\,5}$ 6
$- 5\,4$
1

$9 \overline{) 6\,5}$ 7
$- 6\,3$
2

$9 \overline{) 7\,5}$ 8
$- 7\,2$
3

$9 \overline{) 8\,5}$ 9
$- 8\,1$
4

Complete. All times are a.m.

10:30 → 30 min. → 11:00

10:40 → 30 min. → 11:10

10:50 → 30 min. → 11:20

11:00 → 30 min. → 11:30

Complete.

$8 \times 7 = $ 56

$8 \times 70 = $ 560

$8 \times 700 = $ 5,600

$8 \times 7,000 = $ 56,000

Unit 5 Answer Key

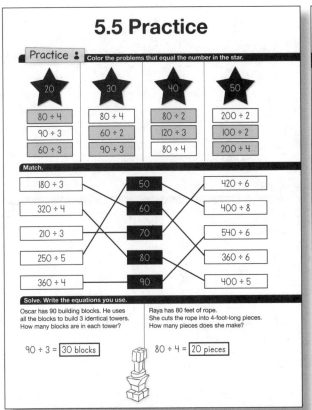

5.5 Practice

Practice 👤 Color the problems that equal the number in the star.

★ 20 ★ 30 ★ 40 ★ 50

80 ÷ 4	80 ÷ 4	80 ÷ 2	200 ÷ 2
90 ÷ 3	60 ÷ 2	120 ÷ 3	100 ÷ 2
60 ÷ 3	90 ÷ 3	80 ÷ 4	200 ÷ 4

Match.

180 ÷ 3 — 50 — 420 ÷ 6
320 ÷ 4 — 60 — 400 ÷ 8
210 ÷ 3 — 70 — 540 ÷ 6
250 ÷ 5 — 80 — 360 ÷ 6
360 ÷ 4 — 90 — 400 ÷ 5

Solve. Write the equations you use.

Oscar has 90 building blocks. He uses all the blocks to build 3 identical towers. How many blocks are in each tower?

90 ÷ 3 = 30 blocks

Raya has 80 feet of rope. She cuts the rope into 4-foot-long pieces. How many pieces does she make?

80 ÷ 4 = 20 pieces

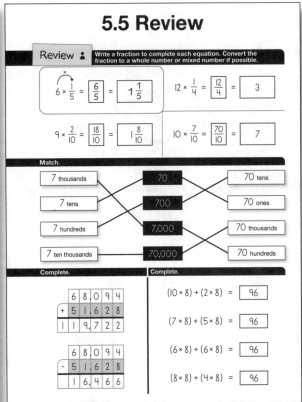

5.5 Review

Review 👤 Write a fraction to complete each equation. Convert the fraction to a whole number or mixed number if possible.

$6 \times \frac{1}{5} = \frac{6}{5} = 1\frac{1}{5}$ $12 \times \frac{1}{4} = \frac{12}{4} = 3$

$9 \times \frac{2}{10} = \frac{18}{10} = 1\frac{8}{10}$ $10 \times \frac{7}{10} = \frac{70}{10} = 7$

Match.

7 thousands — 70 — 70 tens
7 tens — 700 — 70 ones
7 hundreds — 7,000 — 70 thousands
7 ten thousands — 70,000 — 70 hundreds

Complete.

```
  6 8, 0 9 4
+ 5 1, 6 2 8
1 1 9, 7 2 2
```

```
  6 8, 0 9 4
- 5 1, 6 2 8
  1 6, 4 6 6
```

Complete.

$(10 \times 8) + (2 \times 8) = 96$

$(7 \times 8) + (5 \times 8) = 96$

$(6 \times 8) + (6 \times 8) = 96$

$(8 \times 8) + (4 \times 8) = 96$

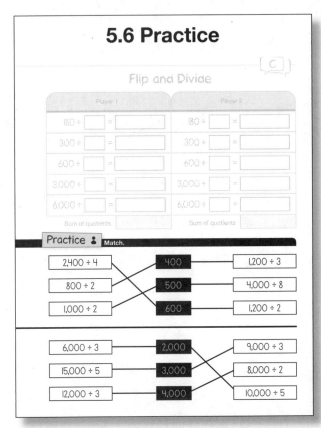

5.6 Practice

Flip and Divide

Player 1	Player 2
180 ÷ ▢ = ▢	180 ÷ ▢ = ▢
300 ÷ ▢ = ▢	300 ÷ ▢ = ▢
600 ÷ ▢ = ▢	600 ÷ ▢ = ▢
3,000 ÷ ▢ = ▢	3,000 ÷ ▢ = ▢
6,000 ÷ ▢ = ▢	6,000 ÷ ▢ = ▢
Sum of quotients	Sum of quotients

Practice 👤 Match.

2,400 ÷ 4 — 400 — 1,200 ÷ 3
800 ÷ 2 — 500 — 4,000 ÷ 8
1,000 ÷ 2 — 600 — 1,200 ÷ 2

6,000 ÷ 3 — 2,000 — 9,000 ÷ 3
15,000 ÷ 5 — 3,000 — 8,000 ÷ 2
12,000 ÷ 3 — 4,000 — 10,000 ÷ 5

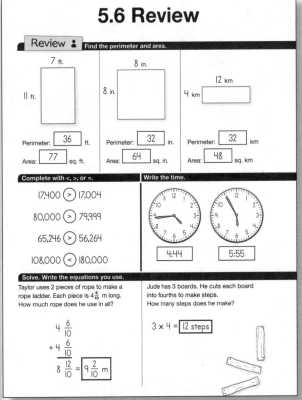

5.6 Review

Review 👤 Find the perimeter and area.

7 ft. / 11 ft.
Perimeter: 36 ft.
Area: 77 sq. ft.

8 in. / 8 in.
Perimeter: 32 in.
Area: 64 sq. in.

12 km / 4 km
Perimeter: 32 km
Area: 48 sq. km

Complete with <, >, or =.

17,400 > 17,004
80,000 > 79,999
65,246 > 56,264
108,000 < 180,000

Write the time.

4:44   5:55

Solve. Write the equations you use.

Taylor uses 2 pieces of rope to make a rope ladder. Each piece is $4\frac{6}{10}$ m long. How much rope does he use in all?

$4\frac{6}{10}$
$+ 4\frac{6}{10}$
$8\frac{12}{10} = 9\frac{2}{10}$ m

Jude has 3 boards. He cuts each board into fourths to make steps. How many steps does he make?

$3 \times 4 = 12$ steps

Unit 5 Answer Key

5.7 Unit Wrap-Up A

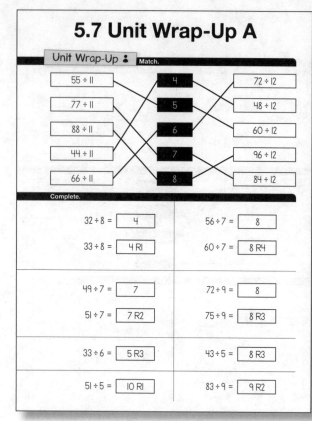

Unit Wrap-Up 👤 **Match.**

55 ÷ 11	4	72 ÷ 12
77 ÷ 11	5	48 ÷ 12
88 ÷ 11	6	60 ÷ 12
44 ÷ 11	7	96 ÷ 12
66 ÷ 11	8	84 ÷ 12

Complete.

32 ÷ 8 = 4		56 ÷ 7 = 8
33 ÷ 8 = 4 R1		60 ÷ 7 = 8 R4
49 ÷ 7 = 7		72 ÷ 9 = 8
51 ÷ 7 = 7 R2		75 ÷ 9 = 8 R3
33 ÷ 6 = 5 R3		43 ÷ 5 = 8 R3
51 ÷ 5 = 10 R1		83 ÷ 9 = 9 R2

5.7 Unit Wrap-Up B

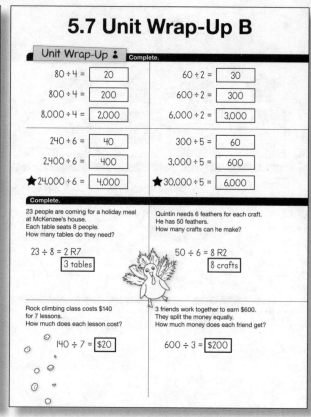

Unit Wrap-Up 👤 **Complete.**

80 ÷ 4 = 20	60 ÷ 2 = 30
800 ÷ 4 = 200	600 ÷ 2 = 300
8,000 ÷ 4 = 2,000	6,000 ÷ 2 = 3,000
240 ÷ 6 = 40	300 ÷ 5 = 60
2,400 ÷ 6 = 400	3,000 ÷ 5 = 600
★ 24,000 ÷ 6 = 4,000	★ 30,000 ÷ 5 = 6,000

Complete.

23 people are coming for a holiday meal at McKenzee's house. Each table seats 8 people. How many tables do they need?

23 ÷ 8 = 2 R7

3 tables

Quintin needs 6 feathers for each craft. He has 50 feathers. How many crafts can he make?

50 ÷ 6 = 8 R2

8 crafts

Rock climbing class costs $140 for 7 lessons. How much does each lesson cost?

140 ÷ 7 = $20

3 friends work together to earn $600. They split the money equally. How much money does each friend get?

600 ÷ 3 = $200

Unit 5 Checkpoint

What to Expect at the End of Unit 5

By the end of Unit 5, most children will be able to do the following:

- Mentally divide two-digit numbers by a one-digit number and add up to find the remainder.
- Solve division word problems and interpret remainders depending on the context. Some children will still need to model division problems with counters in order to make sense of the remainders.
- Use multiplication (and addition) to check answers to division problems. Most children will understand that they can multiply to check answers to division problems, but some will still be hazy on why they need to add the remainder.
- Find answers for the ÷11 and ÷12 facts. Most children will be fairly fluent with the ÷11 facts and the ÷12 facts with smaller dividends (like 36 ÷ 12 or 48 ÷ 12). Many children will need more practice with the ÷12 facts with larger dividends (like 96 ÷ 12 or 108 ÷ 12).
- Use multiplication or place-value strategies to mentally divide multiples of 10, 100, or 1,000 by one-digit numbers (for example, 60 ÷ 3 or 4,000 ÷ 4). Some children will still be working on solving problems that involve regrouping hundreds as tens or thousands as hundreds (for example, 300 ÷ 6 or 2,000 ÷ 5).

Is Your Child Ready to Move on?

In Unit 6, your child will learn more about area and perimeter. Your child does not need to have mastered any specific skills from Unit 5 before beginning Unit 6. She'll continue to practice mental division in the Review pages.

Unit 6
Area and Perimeter

Overview

In *Third Grade Math with Confidence*, your child learned how to find the area and perimeter of rectangles (and shapes made by combining rectangles). In this unit, he'll go deeper with these concepts as he solves more challenging area and perimeter problems. He'll learn how to write equations with parentheses to find perimeter or area. He'll also deepen his problem-solving skills as he solves a variety of multi-step perimeter and area word problems.

What Your Child Will Learn

In this unit, your child will learn to:

- Use correct units to calculate perimeter and area
- Find the perimeter of shapes with straight sides and understand how to use multiplication to add sides with equal lengths more efficiently
- Understand how to split shapes composed of rectangles into parts and add or subtract to find total area
- Write equations with parentheses to find perimeter or area
- Solve multi-step perimeter and area word problems

Lesson List

Lesson 6.1	Review Perimeter	Lesson 6.5	Area Units
Lesson 6.2	Find Perimeter of Shapes with Equal Sides	Lesson 6.6	Write Equations with Parentheses for Area
Lesson 6.3	Perimeter Word Problems	Lesson 6.7	Area Word Problems
Lesson 6.4	Review Area	Lesson 6.8	Enrichment (Optional)

Extra Materials Needed for Unit 6

- 8 toothpicks, craft sticks, or straws
- Large piece of paper (at least 12 inches by 12 inches)
- Ruler
- Scissors
- Yardstick, optional
- Meterstick, optional
- For optional Enrichment Lesson:
  - × *Spaghetti and Meatballs for All!*, written by Marilyn Burns and illustrated by Debbie Tilley. Scholastic, 2008.
  - × 2 pieces of centimeter graph paper
  - × Scissors

Teaching Math with Confidence:
Developing Perseverance and Flexibility in Problem-Solving

In this unit, your child will study area and perimeter. While the content is similar to the skills covered in the area and perimeter unit in *Third Grade Math with Confidence,* you'll find that the lessons move more quickly and are significantly more challenging.

Some of the lessons introduce your child to writing equations with parentheses to find area or perimeter. Others include a variety of multi-step perimeter and area word problems. Altogether, they nudge your child to think about perimeter and area more abstractly, and they teach your child how to apply these concepts to more complex real-life situations.

The lessons are designed not only to help your child understand perimeter and area more deeply but also to help him develop greater perseverance and flexibility with problem-solving. Children often mistakenly think they're bad at math if they don't know immediately how to solve a problem. As you teach this unit, use the following tips to help your child develop his problem-solving skills.

- Reassure your child that he's not expected to immediately know how to solve every problem (especially the multi-step word problems in Lessons 6.3 and 6.7). Explain that you value careful thinking more than speed.
- Make sure you follow the usual steps for understanding word problems before providing any help: Read the problem, identify the goal, then read the problem again slowly. Imagine what's happening in the problem, and stop after every sentence to make sure you understand it.
- Many children immediately ask for help when confronted with an unfamiliar word problem. Help your child understand what each problem is asking, but then ask him to spend a minute or two thinking about the problem before jumping in to help him solve it.
- If your child's stuck, encourage him to discuss his thinking and try out a couple of different ways to tackle the problem. Explain that mathematicians often try out several problem-solving strategies that don't work before they find the strategy that does work.

Lesson 6.1
Review Perimeter

Purpose	Materials
• Practice multiplication facts • Review how to add the sides of a shape to find its perimeter • Use logical reasoning to find the length of a shape's sides	• 2 decks of playing cards

Memory Work
- **What is a prime number?** *A number with exactly 2 factors.*
- **What is a composite number?** *A number with more than 2 factors.*

Warm-up: Play Multiplication Greatest to Least

Play Multiplication Greatest to Least.

Multiplication Greatest to Least

Materials: 2 decks of cards, with jacks, queens, and kings removed (80 cards total)

Object of the Game: Win the most cards.

Shuffle the cards and deal 5 cards to each player. Place the rest of the deck in a face-down pile.

Choose who will go first. Player 1 chooses two cards from his hand, places them face-up on the table, and names the product. For example, if you play a 4 and a 9, the product is 36. Then, Player 1 picks up two new cards to replenish his hand.

Player 2 chooses any two cards from her hand whose product is less than Player 1's product. (The products may not be equal.) She places her cards on top of Player 1's cards, names their product, and takes two new cards to replenish her hand. For example, if Player 1 played a 4 and a 9, Player 2 may play any two cards with a product less than 36.

Continue alternating turns until one player can no longer play a lower product. The player who last played takes all of the face-up cards. These cards go into the player's "Won" pile, and the cards are out of the game. The player who was unable to play new cards starts a new round.

Play until you have used all the cards. Whoever has won the most cards wins the game.

Cooperative Variation: Take turns playing pairs of cards. Try to play as many cards as possible before one player can no longer play a lower product. Count how many cards both players played, and see if you can play more cards in the next round.

Activity (A): Review Perimeter

We're starting a new unit on perimeter and area today. Today, we'll review perimeter. What do you remember about perimeter from last year? *Answers will vary.*

The perimeter of an object is the distance around its outside edge. Trace your finger around the sandbox in part A to show its perimeter. **If you build a sandbox, you need to know the perimeter so you know the length of the boards to buy for the sides.**

To find the perimeter of an object, we add up the length of all its sides. We'll start at the top left corner of the sandbox and add the side lengths in order, to make sure we don't miss any. Draw a star at the top left corner of the diagram to mark your starting place. Trace your finger clockwise around the rectangle. Have your child tell the length of each side as you trace it. As she tells you the length of each side, record the length in an addition equation.

What's the total of all the sides? *20 feet.* Write "20 ft." to complete the equation. **So, it would take boards that are 20 feet long to build the sides of the sandbox.**

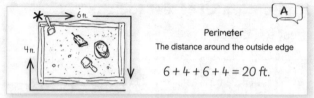

Perimeter
The distance around the outside edge

$$6 + 4 + 6 + 4 = 20 \text{ ft.}$$

If needed, remind your child that opposite sides of a rectangle are equal to each other. The right side of the sandbox has the same length as the left side, and the bottom side has the same length as the top side.

Show your child the plans for the family room and office. **Architects draw plans like these when they design a house. The builder uses the perimeter of each room to help figure out how much baseboard or ceiling trim is needed for each room.**

Let's find the perimeter of the family room. We'll start at the top left corner and add the side lengths in order again. Start at the top left corner and trace your finger clockwise around the family room. Have your child tell the length of each side as you trace it. (Make sure not to include the office. Disregard any doors or windows.)

As your child tells you the length of each side, record the length in an addition equation. Then, have your child add to complete the equation. **What's the perimeter of the family room?** *46 feet.* Repeat with the office.

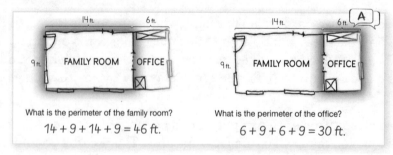

What is the perimeter of the family room?
$$14 + 9 + 14 + 9 = 46 \text{ ft.}$$

What is the perimeter of the office?
$$6 + 9 + 6 + 9 = 30 \text{ ft.}$$

The next drawing shows a backyard. The pool is the smaller inner rectangle, and it's surrounded by a wooden pool deck. Have your child find the perimeter of both the deck and the pool.

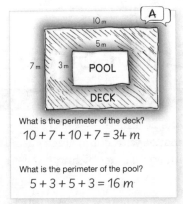

What is the perimeter of the deck?
$10 + 7 + 10 + 7 = 34$ m

What is the perimeter of the pool?
$5 + 3 + 5 + 3 = 16$ m

Activity (B): Find the Perimeter of Rooms with Unlabeled Sides

This kitchen has one side that's unlabeled. What must its length be? *4 yards.* Write "4 yd." below the unlabeled side.

If your child's not sure, use a crayon or colored pencil to trace the top side of the diagram. **The top side is 7 yards long.** Trace the other 2 horizontal sides. **These two sides added together equal the top side, so their sum must be 7 yards. The labeled side is 3 yards long, so the unlabeled side must be 4 yards.**

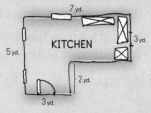

Then, have your child write and solve an addition equation to find the perimeter of the kitchen.

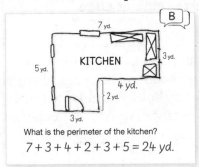

What is the perimeter of the kitchen?
$7 + 3 + 4 + 2 + 3 + 5 = 24$ yd.

Repeat with the bedroom. Make sure your child finds the lengths of the unlabeled sides before adding to find the total perimeter.

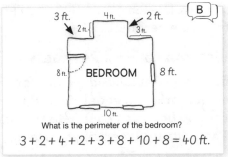

What is the perimeter of the bedroom?
$3 + 2 + 4 + 2 + 3 + 8 + 10 + 8 = 40$ ft.

Independent Practice and Review

Have your child complete the Lesson 6.1 Practice and Review workbook pages.

Lesson 6.2
Find Perimeter of Shapes with Equal Sides

Purpose	Materials
• Make different shapes with the same perimeter • Multiply to find the perimeter of shapes with equal sides • Divide the perimeter of shapes with equal sides to find the length of each side	• 8 toothpicks, craft sticks, or straws

Memory Work	
	• **How do you know if a number is divisible by 2?** *It is even. It has 0, 2, 4, 6, or 8 in the ones-place.* • **How do you know if a number is divisible by 5?** *It has a 0 or 5 in the ones-place.* • **How do you know if a number is divisible by 10?** *It has a 0 in the ones-place.*

Warm-up: Create Different Shapes with the Same Perimeter

In the last lesson, you found the perimeter of different shapes. Today, you'll solve perimeter problems about shapes where all the sides are equal to each other.

We usually measure perimeter with length units like inches and feet or centimeters and meters. We'll start with a different kind of unit today—toothpicks!

If you don't have toothpicks, use craft sticks or straws instead. If you are using round objects, place them on a small towel to prevent them from rolling.

Arrange 8 toothpicks as shown. **The perimeter of this rectangle is 8 toothpicks, since it takes 8 toothpicks to go around the outside edge.**

What other shapes can you make that have a perimeter of 8 toothpicks? Give your child a few minutes to build 3-5 shapes with toothpicks. Each shape should be made with exactly 8 toothpicks, with the points of the toothpicks as close to touching as possible. If your child is stuck, suggest he try making an octagon, square, or pentagon.

These shapes look very different from each other. But, they are all made from exactly 8 toothpicks, so they all have the same perimeter!

Activity (A): Use Multiplication to Find Perimeter

Let's pretend we work at a mirror store and build frames for the mirrors. Our mirror store is a little unusual! We only sell mirrors with equal sides. Our customers choose how many sides they want on their mirror and how long each side should be. Our first customer ordered a mirror with 6 sides. Each side is 20 centimeters long.

One way to find the perimeter is to add up all the sides. Have your child write the corresponding addition equation and add to find the mirror's perimeter. He should find the mirror has a perimeter of 120 cm.

It takes a while to add all those numbers! Multiplication is a faster way to add equal groups. Since all the sides are the same length, we can multiply the number of sides times the length of each side to find the perimeter more quickly. **Write "6 × 20 =" and have your child complete the equation.**

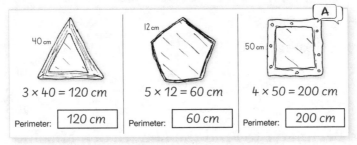

Both equations have the same answer. No matter which method we use, the mirror still has the same perimeter. Have your child multiply to find the perimeters of the other mirrors in part A. Have him write his equations in the space below the mirrors.

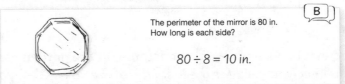

Activity (B): Divide Perimeter to Find Side Length

Have your child read the word problem aloud: *The perimeter of the mirror is 80 in. How long is each side?* **What's the goal of this problem?** *Find the length of the sides.*

In this problem, we know the perimeter and how many sides the mirror has. We want to find the length of each side.

How many sides does this mirror have? *8.* **How can we find the length of each side?** *Divide 80 by 8.* **Write "80 ÷ 8 =" in the space below the problem. Have your child complete the equation. How long is each side of the mirror?** *10 in.*

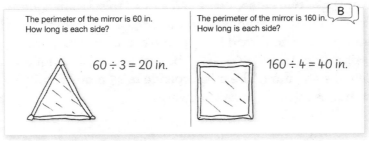

We can divide the perimeter by the number of sides to find how long each side is. This only works if the shape has equal sides, though! Have your child solve the other word problems in the same way.

Independent Practice and Review

Have your child complete the Lesson 6.2 Practice and Review workbook pages.

Lesson 6.3
Perimeter Word Problems

Purpose	Materials
• Practice ÷12 facts • Use perimeter to find the length of a missing side • Solve multi-step perimeter word problems • Develop perseverance and flexibility in problem-solving	• None

Memory Work
  • **How many ounces equal 1 pound?** *16.*
  • **How many grams equal 1 kilogram?** *1,000.*

Warm-up: Practice ÷12 Facts

Ask your child the following ÷12 facts.

- $36 \div 12 = 3$
- $60 \div 12 = 5$
- $24 \div 12 = 2$

- $72 \div 12 = 6$
- $48 \div 12 = 4$
- $84 \div 12 = 7$

- $96 \div 12 = 8$
- $120 \div 12 = 10$
- $108 \div 12 = 9$

Activity (A): Use Perimeter to Find the Length of a Missing Side

Today, we'll pretend you work at the Landscaping Help Desk at a garden center. Your job is to answer the customers' questions about their yards. I'll pretend to be the customers! Briefly discuss your child's experiences with garden centers or home improvement stores.

These customers all have different questions, so you'll need to solve each problem in a different way. It's okay if you don't see how to solve a problem right away and you need to take a couple of minutes to figure it out.

For each problem, help your child understand what the problem is asking. Then, give her a minute to see if she can figure out how to solve it. Use the suggested questions only if she's stuck or needs more support. See the Unit 6 **Teaching Math with Confidence** for more tips on helping your child develop greater perseverance and flexibility with problem-solving.

Read aloud the first question as if you were a customer at the garden center. **What's the goal?** *Find how much fence you need for the last side of the yard.* Give your child a minute to think about how to solve the problem. If she's unsure what to do, guide her with the following questions.

- **Two sides of the yard already have a fence. First, let's add 20 plus 15 to find the total length of those two sides.** Write "20 + 15 = " to start an equation and have your child complete it. **These two sides account for 35 meters of the perimeter.**
- **The perimeter of the whole yard is 60 meters. So, we can subtract 60 minus 35 to find the missing side.** Write "60 – 35 = " below the previous equation, and have your child complete the equation. **The missing side is 25 meters long, so I need 25 meters more of fencing.** Label and box the answer.

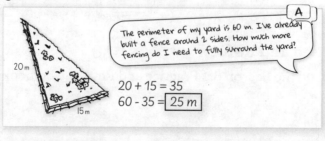

Activity (B): Solve Multi-Step Perimeter Word Problems

Read aloud the next question as if you were a different customer at the garden center. **What's the goal?** *Find how much fence it takes to make 3 beds.* Give your child a minute to think about how to solve the problem. If she's stuck, suggest she first find the perimeter of one garden bed. Then, ask: **How can you use the perimeter of 1 bed to find the perimeter of all 3 beds?** *Multiply the perimeter of one garden bed by 3.*

Read aloud the next question as if you were a different customer. **What's the goal?** *Find how many fence panels it will take to go around the whole yard.* Give your child a minute to think about how to solve the problem. If she's stuck, suggest she first find the perimeter of the yard. Then, say: **The perimeter is 28 meters, and each panel is 2 meters wide. How can you find how many panels it will take to go all the way around the yard?** *Divide 28 by 2.*

Read aloud the last question as if you were a different customer. **What's the goal?** *Find how much it costs to buy bricks to go around the garden.* Give your child a minute to think about how to solve the problem. If she's stuck, suggest she first find the perimeter of the garden. Then, ask: **How many bricks does the customer need to enclose the yard?** *30.* **How can you find the total cost of 30 bricks?** *Multiply 30 times 2.*

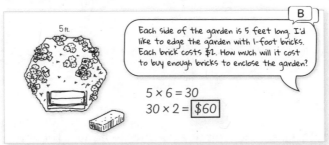

Your child may use a different method to find the answer. For example, she might first find how much it costs to put bricks along one side of the garden. Then, she can multiply that cost times 6 to find the total cost of enclosing the garden.

Independent Practice and Review

Have your child complete the Lesson 6.3 Practice and Review workbook pages.

Lesson 6.4
Review Area

Purpose	Materials
• Review the ÷11 facts • Review how to find area • Reason about rectangles' dimensions and build spatial skills	• 2 dice

Memory Work
- **Name 4 factors of 20.** *Possible answers: 1, 2, 4, 5, 10, 20.*
- **Name 4 multiples of 20.** *Sample answers: 20, 40, 80, 140.*

Warm-up: Practice ÷11 Facts

Ask your child the following ÷11 facts.

- $55 \div 11 = 5$
- $33 \div 11 = 3$
- $66 \div 11 = 6$
- $22 \div 11 = 2$
- $77 \div 11 = 7$

- $99 \div 11 = 9$
- $44 \div 11 = 4$
- $88 \div 11 = 8$
- $110 \div 11 = 10$
- $11 \div 11 = 1$

Activity (A): Review Area

In the last few lessons, you reviewed perimeter. Today, we'll review area. **What do you remember about area from last year?** *Answers will vary.* **The area of an object is the amount of flat space it covers.**

Each square in this shape is 1 centimeter on each side. So, each square covers an area of 1 square centimeter. **What is the area of this shape?** *6 square centimeters.* **How do you know?** *Sample answer: I counted how many squares are in the shape.* Write 6 in the blank.

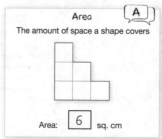

The next shape is a rectangle. **The area of a rectangle equals the length times the width. We call the longer side of a rectangle its *length*. We call the shorter side of a rectangle its *width*.**

What's the length of this rectangle? *6 centimeters.* **What's the width of this rectangle?** *2 centimeters.* **So, what's its area?** *12 square centimeters.* Write 12 in the blank.

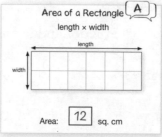

Have your child find the area of the other shapes in part A.

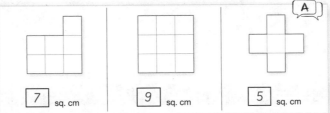

| 7 | sq. cm | 9 | sq. cm | 5 | sq. cm |

Activity (B): Play Area Capture

In this game, we'll draw rectangles and try to cover as much of our gameboards as possible. Try to draw your rectangles so that they completely fill the grid. It's usually best to draw the rectangles so that their sides touch, with no space between them. Play Area Capture.

Area Capture

Materials: 2 dice

Object of the Game: Fill more of the squares in your grid than your opponent.

Choose who will go first. Each player chooses a gameboard.

On your turn, roll 2 dice. Outline and color a rectangle with the matching dimensions on your grid. For example, if you roll a 2 and 4, outline and color a 2×4 rectangle. Your rectangle may be oriented horizontally or vertically.

You may not draw any shape other than a rectangle (or square). Your rectangles may touch, but they may not overlap.

If you cannot fit a rectangle with the matching dimensions on your gameboard, you get a strike. Write a check mark in one of the circles below your game board, and play passes to the other player.

Your game is over once you have 3 strikes. The other player may continue until they have 3 strikes as well.

Count how many squares on the grid you left empty. Whoever has fewer empty squares at the end of the game wins the game.

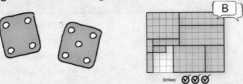

Strikes: ✓✓✓

Sample final play. This player already has 2 strikes and cannot fit a 4×5 rectangle on his gameboard. There are 10 empty squares on his gameboard, so his final score is 10.

Cooperative Variation: Play together (on one grid) and see how many empty squares you have at the end of the game. Then, play together again (on the other grid) and try to have fewer empty squares.

Independent Practice and Review

Have your child complete the Lesson 6.4 Practice and Review workbook pages.

Lesson 6.5
Area Units

Purpose	Materials
• Review the difference between the units used to measure perimeter and area • Find the number of square inches in a square foot • Find the number of square feet in a square yard • Find the number of square centimeters in a square meter	• Base-ten blocks • Pattern blocks • Large piece of paper (at least 12 inches by 12 inches) • Ruler • Scissors • Yardstick, optional • Meterstick, optional

Memory Work
- **How many inches equal 1 foot?** *12.*
- **How many feet equal 1 yard?** *3.*
- **How many inches equal 1 yard?** *36.*
- **How many centimeters equal 1 meter?** *100.*
- **How many meters equal 1 kilometer?** *1,000.*

Your child will make a paper square foot in this lesson. Newspaper, wrapping paper, scrapbooking paper, or 4 pages of copy paper taped together work well for this activity.

Note to families that use the metric system: Your child will make a paper square foot in this lesson. She'll use the paper square foot to estimate and measure the area of real objects for the exercises on the Practice page, so don't skip this activity. The hands-on practice is very valuable even if square feet aren't a common unit for your family.

Warm-up (A): Review Units for Perimeter and Area

To warm-up, we'll review the difference between the units we use for perimeter and the units we use for area.

The perimeter of an object is a distance, so we measure perimeter with the same units that we use to measure other distances. Read aloud the perimeter units in the chart.

Area measures the amount of flat surface that a shape covers, so we use square units to measure area. Read aloud the area units.

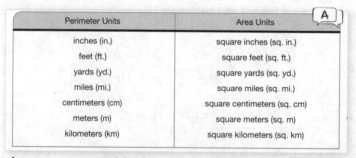

Perimeter Units	Area Units
inches (in.)	square inches (sq. in.)
feet (ft.)	square feet (sq. ft.)
yards (yd.)	square yards (sq. yd.)
miles (mi.)	square miles (sq. mi.)
centimeters (cm)	square centimeters (sq. cm)
meters (m)	square meters (sq. m)
kilometers (km)	square kilometers (sq. km)

Place a unit block and square pattern block on the table. **Each side of the unit block is 1 centimeter long. The unit block covers a square that is 1 centimeter on each side, so it covers 1 square centimeter.**

Each side of the square pattern block is 1 inch long. The pattern block covers a square that is 1 inch on each side, so it covers 1 square inch. **Which is larger, a square inch or a square centimeter?** *A square inch.*

1 unit block covers an area of 1 square centimeter.

1 square pattern block covers an area of 1 square inch.

Activity (B): Find the Number of Square Inches in a Square Foot

In the last lesson, you measured area in square centimeters. Today, you'll learn more about square feet, square yards, and square meters.

Let's make a paper square foot, so we can see how many square inches equal 1 square foot. Help your child use a ruler to measure and cut a square foot out of paper.

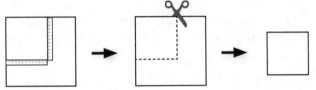

Place 1 square pattern block in a corner of the paper square foot. **Imagine covering the whole square foot with pattern blocks. How many inches long is each side of the square?** *12 inches.* **So, how can we find the area in square inches?** *Multiply 12 times 12.* **12 times 12 equals 144, so 1 square foot equals 144 square inches!** Show your child the matching diagram in part B and write 144 in the blank.

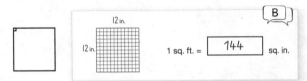

> If your child is confused as to why 12 square inches do not equal 1 square foot, show her 12 square pattern blocks. **Each square pattern block is 1 square inch, so 12 square pattern blocks cover an area of 12 square inches. They don't come close to covering a whole square foot.**

> Your child is not expected to memorize any of the square unit equivalencies she discovers in this lesson.

 Save the square foot for the Lesson 6.5 Practice page. Your child will use it to estimate the area of items in your home.

Activity (C): Find the Number of Square Feet in a Square Yard and the Number of Square Centimeters in a Square Meter

Next, let's find how many square feet equal 1 square yard. Use a yardstick to show your child the approximate size of a square yard on the floor. (Or, use your hands to approximate it.)

How many feet equal 1 yard? *3.* Show your child the printed square yard. **Each side of a square yard is 3 feet long. So, how can we find the area in square feet?** *Multiply 3 times 3.* **What's 3 times 3?** *9.* **1 square yard equals 9 square feet!** Write 9 in the blank.

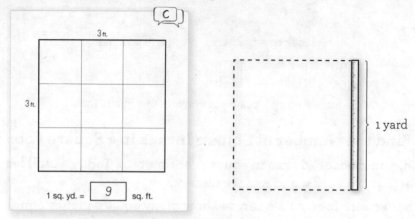

1 square yard.

Last, let's find how many square centimeters equal 1 square meter. Use a meterstick to show your child the approximate size of a square meter on the floor. (Or, use your hands to approximate it.)

How many centimeters equal 1 meter? *100.* Show your child the printed square meter. **Each side is 100 centimeters long. So, how can we find the area in square centimeters?** *Multiply 100 times 100.* **100 times 100 equals 10,000, so 1 square meter equals 10,000 square centimeters!** Write 10,000 in the blank.

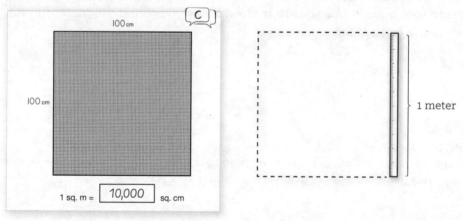

1 square meter.

If you have time, use yarn or masking tape to outline a full-size square yard and square meter on the floor. Or, if weather permits, draw a square yard and square meter on pavement with chalk.

Independent Practice and Review

Have your child complete the Lesson 6.5 Practice and Review workbook pages. Your child will need the paper square foot (created during the lesson in part B) to complete the Practice page.

Lesson 6.6
Write Equations with Parentheses for Area

Purpose	Materials
• Practice multiplication facts • Split shapes into parts and add or subtract the parts' areas to find total area • Use parentheses to write equations for area	• 2 decks of playing cards

Memory Work	
	• **How many cups equal 1 pint?** *2.* • **How many pints equal 1 quart?** *2.* • **How many quarts equal 1 gallon?** *4.*

Warm-up: Play Multiplication Greatest to Least

Play Multiplication Greatest to Least. See Lesson 6.1 (page 197) for directions.

Activity (A): Split Areas into Parts and Add to Find Total Area

In the last lesson, you learned about the square units we use to measure area. Today, we'll use those units to find the area of different rooms in a house.

Show your child the room plans. **These are the same building plans we used in Lesson 6.1. In that lesson, we found the perimeter of each room. Today, we'll find the area of each room. The builder uses the area of each room to figure out how much flooring is needed.**

Let's figure out how much carpet is needed to cover the floor of the bedroom. Draw a line as shown. **This line splits the room into 2 rectangles. We'll find the area of each rectangle, then add to find the total area.**

Use these questions to write an equation to find the total area of the room:

- **How can we find the area of the larger rectangle?** *Multiply 8 times 10.* Write "(8 × 10)" to begin an equation. **How can we find the area of the smaller rectangle?** *Multiply 2 times 4.* Continue the equation as shown.
- **What do the parentheses mean?** *Do this first.* Point to the plus sign. **Why is there a plus sign between the two multiplication problems?** *Sample answer: The plus sign shows that you add the two products.*
- Have your child multiply and add to complete the equation. **How many square feet of carpet do you need to cover the bedroom floor?** *88 square feet.*

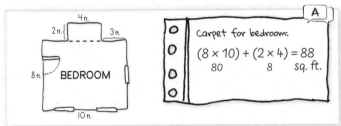

Next, let's figure out how much tile is needed for the kitchen floor. Again, we'll split the room into rectangles, find the area of each rectangle, then add to find the total area. Draw a line as shown.

How can we find the area of the larger rectangle? *Multiply 3 times 7.* Write "(3 × 7)" to begin an equation. **How can we find the area of the smaller rectangle?** *Multiply 2 times 3.* Continue the equation as shown. Then, have your child multiply and add to complete the equation. **How many square yards of tile are needed for the kitchen floor?** *27 square yards.*

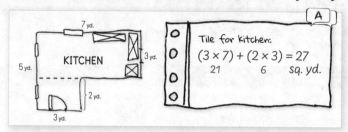

Activity (B): Use the Distributive Property to Find Area

Next, we'll find how much wood flooring is needed for the family room and office. We could find the area of each room separately and then add them. But, the calculations will be easier if we combine the rooms and find the area of both rooms at once.

What's the total length of the two rooms? *20 feet.* **How do you know?** *14 plus 6 is 20.* Write "(14 + 6)" to begin an equation. **What is the width of the two rooms?** *9 feet.* **So, we can multiply the length times the width to find the area of both rooms.** Continue the equation as shown. Then, have your child add and multiply to complete the equation. **How many square feet of wood flooring are needed for the family room and office?** *180 square feet.*

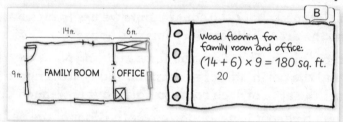

This is an example of the distributive property. Instead of multiplying and then adding, we added and then multiplied.

It's fine if your child doesn't fully understand the connection to the distributive property.

Activity (C): Subtract to Find an Area

The last drawing shows a backyard. The pool is the smaller inner rectangle, and it's surrounded by a wooden pool deck.

Let's figure out how much wooden decking is needed for the deck. We could divide the deck into smaller parts, but we'd have a lot of small parts to add together. Instead, let's find the area of the entire large rectangle and then subtract the area of the pool.

How can we find the area of the larger rectangle? *Multiply 10 times 7.* Write "(10 × 7)" to begin an equation. **How can we find the area of the pool?** *Multiply 5 times 3.* Continue the equation as shown.

Point to the minus sign. **Why is there a minus sign between the two multiplication problems?** *Sample answer: The minus sign shows that you subtract the area of the pool from the area of the larger rectangle.*

Have your child multiply and subtract to complete the equation. **How many square meters of wooden decking do you need to cover the border around the pool?** *55 square meters.*

Independent Practice and Review

Have your child complete the Lesson 6.6 Practice and Review workbook pages.

Lesson 6.7
Area Word Problems

Purpose	Materials
• Practice mental division • Use area to find the length of a missing side of a rectangle • Solve multi-step area word problems • Develop perseverance and flexibility in problem-solving	• None

Memory Work	• **What do we call the result when we multiply two numbers?** *The product.* • **What do we call the numbers in a multiplication equation that we multiply together?** *Factors.*

Warm-up: Practice Mental Division

Have your child solve the following mental division problems.

- $60 \div 3 = 20$
- $80 \div 4 = 20$
- $150 \div 3 = 50$

- $270 \div 3 = 90$
- $300 \div 6 = 50$
- $420 \div 7 = 60$

Activity (A): Use Area to Find the Length of a Missing Side of a Rectangle

Today, we'll pretend you work at a Fabric Store Help Desk. Your job is to answer the customers' questions about their sewing projects. I'll pretend to be the customers. Briefly discuss your child's experiences with fabric stores.

If you're experienced at sewing, you'll notice that this lesson simplifies typical fabric store conventions to make the word problems more straightforward.

These customers all have different questions, so you'll need to solve each problem in a different way. It's okay if you don't see how to solve a problem right away and need to take a few minutes to figure out how to solve it.

As in Lesson 6.3, adjust your level of guidance to match your child's needs. Give your child a minute to think about each problem before you offer any help. Use the suggested questions only if she's stuck or needs more support.

Read aloud the first question as if you were a customer at the fabric store. **What's the goal?** *Find how long a piece of fabric you should buy.* Give your child a minute to think about how to solve the problem. If she's unsure what to do, say: **Length times width equals area. We know the width and the area, but not the length.** Write "__ × 4 = 36." **The blank stands for the missing length. The width is 4 feet, and the area is 36 square feet.**

How can we find the missing number? *Divide 36 by 4.* Write "36 ÷ 4 =" and have your child complete both equations. **So, how long a piece should I buy?** *9 ft.* Have your child label and box her answer.

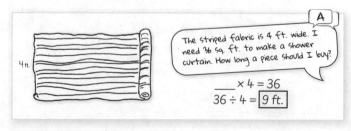

Activity (B): Solve Multi-Step Area Word Problems

Read aloud the next question as if you were a different customer at the fabric store. **What's the goal?** *Find how much the fabric costs.* Give your child a minute to think about how to solve the problem. If she's stuck, suggest she first find the area of the fabric. Then, ask: **Each square yard costs $7. How can you use the area to find the cost of the fabric?** *Multiply the area times 7.*

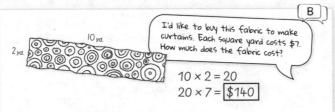

Read aloud the next question as if you were a different customer at the fabric store. **What's the goal?** *Find the area of each piece of the fabric.* Give your child a minute to think about how to solve the problem. If she's stuck, suggest she first find the total area of the fabric. Then, ask: **Imagine cutting the fabric into 4 equal pieces. How can you find the area of each piece?** *Divide the area by 4.*

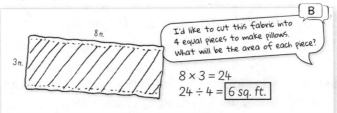

Read aloud the last question as if you were a different customer at the fabric store. **What's the goal?** *Find the area of the fabric that's left.* Give your child a minute to think about how to solve the problem. If she's stuck, suggest she first find the area of the original piece of fabric (before it was cut). Then, have her find the area of the fabric that was cut off and subtract it from the original area.

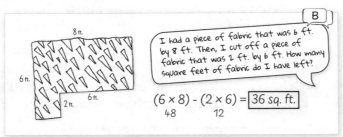

Your child may use a different method to find the answers. For example, another way to solve the last problem is to split the remaining fabric into parts, find the area of each part, and then add the areas.

Independent Practice and Review

Have your child complete the Lesson 6.7 Practice and Review workbook pages.

Lesson 6.8
Enrichment (Optional)

Purpose	Materials
• Practice memory work • Understand how perimeter changes when shapes are put together or taken apart • Draw a scale model of a room and its furniture • Summarize what your child has learned and assess your child's progress	• *Spaghetti and Meatballs for All!,* written by Marilyn Burns and illustrated by Debbie Tilley • 2 pieces of centimeter graph paper • Scissors

If you don't have centimeter graph paper, search online for printable graph paper.

Warm-up: Review Memory Work

Quiz your child on all memory work through Unit 6. See pages 536-537 for the full list.

Math Picture Book: *Spaghetti and Meatballs for All!*

Read *Spaghetti and Meatballs for All!,* written by Marilyn Burns and illustrated by Debbie Tilley. After you finish the story, read aloud the mathematical explanation at the back of the book. Discuss how the area of the eight tables stays the same throughout the story, but the perimeter changes as the tables are put together or taken apart.

Enrichment Activity: Make a Scale Drawing of a Room and Its Furniture

Today, we'll draw one of the rooms in our house. We'll draw the furniture on separate pieces of paper so we can try out different ways to arrange the furniture. It's a lot easier to try out different arrangements with paper than it is to move all the real furniture!

Have your child choose a room in your house. Encourage him to choose a room in which several different furniture arrangements are possible, such as a bedroom or playroom.

With your child, use a tape measure to measure the length of each wall. Round each length to the nearest foot and draw the outline of the room on a piece of centimeter graph paper. Use 1 centimeter to represent each foot. For example, if the room is 12 feet by 18 feet, draw a 12 cm by 18 cm rectangle. Draw rough approximations of the locations of any doors or windows.

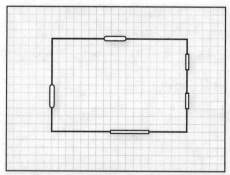

Measure the major pieces of furniture and draw them on a separate piece of graph paper. Use 1 centimeter to represent 1 foot, just as you did for the room outline. (For example, if your child's bed is 3 feet by 6 feet, draw a 3 cm by 6 cm rectangle to represent it.) Cut out each item and label it.

Have your child arrange the furniture in the room to match its current arrangement. Then, have him experiment with other ways to arrange the furniture.

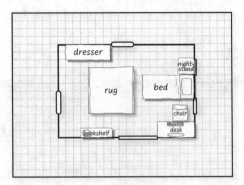

Unit Wrap-Up

Have your child complete the Unit 6 Wrap-Up.

Unit 6 Answer Key

6.1 Practice

Practice ▲ Find the perimeter of each shape. Include the correct units.

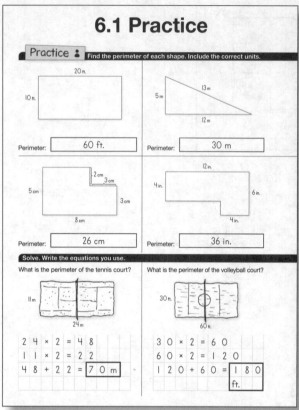

Perimeter: 60 ft.   Perimeter: 30 m

Perimeter: 26 cm   Perimeter: 36 in.

Solve. Write the equations you use.

What is the perimeter of the tennis court?

2 4 × 2 = 4 8
1 1 × 2 = 2 2
4 8 + 2 2 = 7 0 m

What is the perimeter of the volleyball court?

3 0 × 2 = 6 0
6 0 × 2 = 1 2 0
1 2 0 + 6 0 = 1 8 0 ft.

6.1 Review

Review ▲ Complete.

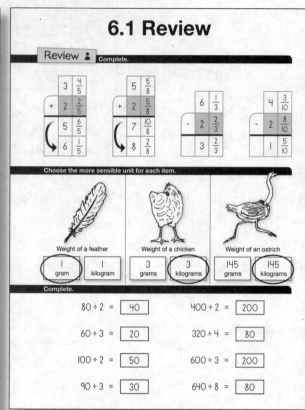

Choose the more sensible unit for each item.

Weight of a feather: **1 gram**
Weight of a chicken: **3 kilograms**
Weight of an ostrich: **145 kilograms**

Complete.

80 ÷ 2 = 40   400 ÷ 2 = 200

60 ÷ 3 = 20   320 ÷ 4 = 80

100 ÷ 2 = 50   600 ÷ 3 = 200

90 ÷ 3 = 30   640 ÷ 8 = 80

6.2 Practice

Practice ▲ Find the perimeter of each shape.
All the sides of each shape are equal.

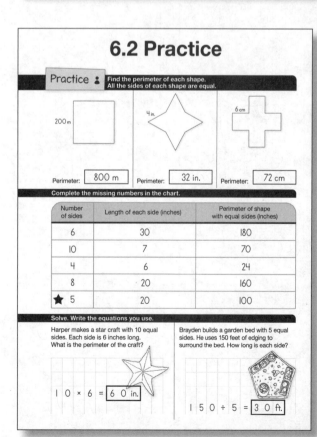

Perimeter: 800 m   Perimeter: 32 in.   Perimeter: 72 cm

Complete the missing numbers in the chart.

Number of sides	Length of each side (inches)	Perimeter of shape with equal sides (inches)
6	30	180
10	7	70
4	6	24
8	20	160
★ 5	20	100

Solve. Write the equations you use.

Harper makes a star craft with 10 equal sides. Each side is 6 inches long. What is the perimeter of the craft?

1 0 × 6 = 6 0 in.

Brayden builds a garden bed with 5 equal sides. He uses 150 feet of edging to surround the bed. How long is each side?

1 5 0 ÷ 5 = 3 0 ft.

6.2 Review

Review ▲ Convert the mixed numbers to fractions.
Convert the fractions to whole numbers or mixed numbers.

$2\frac{7}{8} = \frac{23}{8}$ $5\frac{1}{10} = \frac{51}{10}$ $6\frac{5}{6} = \frac{41}{6}$

$\frac{19}{6} = 3\frac{1}{6}$ $\frac{28}{4} = 7$ $\frac{67}{10} = 6\frac{7}{10}$

Complete.

9 × 300 = 2,700   9 × 7,000 = 63,000

8 × 700 = 5,600   6 × 8,000 = 48,000

12 × 300 = 3,600   11 × 9,000 = 99,000

11 × 400 = 4,400   12 × 4,000 = 48,000

10 × 500 = 5,000   10 × 10,000 = 100,000

Solve. Write the equations you use.

Poppy has 20 flowers to plant. She plants them in 3 groups. She makes the groups as equal as possible. How many flowers are in each group?

2 0 ÷ 3 = 6 R 2

6 or 7 flowers

Amrut's family has 2 pizzas. They eat $1\frac{3}{8}$ pizzas. What fraction of a pizza is left?

2
− 1 3/8
5/8 of a pizza

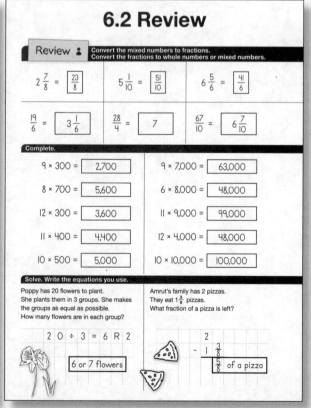

Unit 6 Answer Key

6.3 Practice

Practice Find the length of the missing sides.

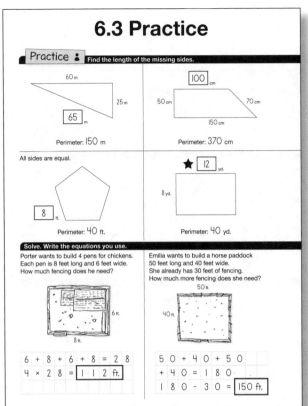

60 m
25 m
65 m

Perimeter: 150 m

100 cm
50 cm
70 cm
150 cm

Perimeter: 370 cm

All sides are equal.

8 ft.

Perimeter: 40 ft.

★ **12** yd.
8 yd.

Perimeter: 40 yd.

Solve. Write the equations you use.

Porter wants to build 4 pens for chickens. Each pen is 8 feet long and 6 feet wide. How much fencing does he need?

6 + 8 + 6 + 8 = 2 8
4 × 2 8 = **1 1 2 ft.**

Emilia wants to build a horse paddock 50 feet long and 40 feet wide. She already has 30 feet of fencing. How much more fencing does she need?

5 0 + 4 0 + 5 0 + 4 0 = 1 8 0
1 8 0 - 3 0 = **150 ft.**

6.3 Review

Review Complete.

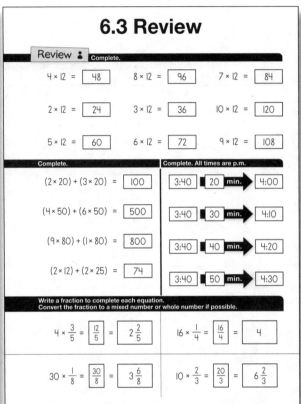

4 × 12 = **48**   8 × 12 = **96**   7 × 12 = **84**

2 × 12 = **24**   3 × 12 = **36**   10 × 12 = **120**

5 × 12 = **60**   6 × 12 = **72**   9 × 12 = **108**

Complete.

(2 × 20) + (3 × 20) = **100**

(4 × 50) + (6 × 50) = **500**

(9 × 80) + (1 × 80) = **800**

(2 × 12) + (2 × 25) = **74**

Complete. All times are p.m.

3:40 → **20** min. → 4:00

3:40 → **30** min. → 4:10

3:40 → **40** min. → 4:20

3:40 → **50** min. → 4:30

Write a fraction to complete each equation. Convert the fraction to a mixed number or whole number if possible.

$4 \times \frac{3}{5} = \frac{12}{5} = 2\frac{2}{5}$ $16 \times \frac{1}{4} = \frac{16}{4} = 4$

$30 \times \frac{1}{8} = \frac{30}{8} = 3\frac{6}{8}$ $10 \times \frac{2}{3} = \frac{20}{3} = 6\frac{2}{3}$

6.4 Practice

Practice Find the area of each shape.

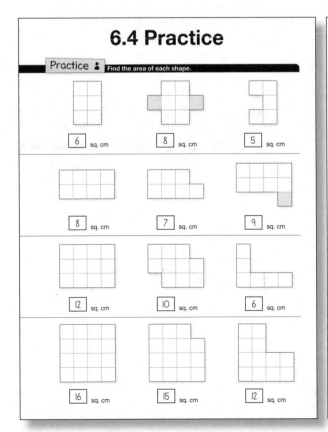

6 sq. cm   **8** sq. cm   **5** sq. cm

8 sq. cm   **7** sq. cm   **9** sq. cm

12 sq. cm   **10** sq. cm   **6** sq. cm

16 sq. cm   **15** sq. cm   **12** sq. cm

6.4 Review

Review Complete the boxes to find the product.

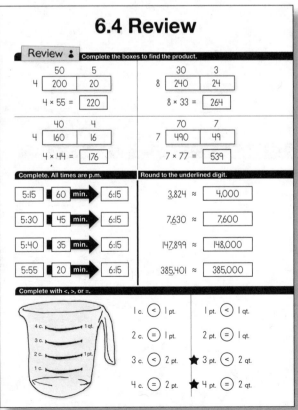

	50	5
4	200	20

4 × 55 = **220**

	30	3
8	240	24

8 × 33 = **264**

	40	4
4	160	16

4 × 44 = **176**

	70	7
7	490	49

7 × 77 = **539**

Complete. All times are p.m.

5:15 → **60** min. → 6:15

5:30 → **45** min. → 6:15

5:40 → **35** min. → 6:15

5:55 → **20** min. → 6:15

Round to the underlined digit.

3,824 ≈ **4,000**

7,630 ≈ **7,600**

147,899 ≈ **148,000**

385,401 ≈ **385,000**

Complete with <, >, or =.

1 c. **<** 1 pt.   1 pt. **<** 1 qt.

2 c. **=** 1 pt.   2 pt. **=** 1 qt.

3 c. **<** 2 pt.   ★ 3 pt. **<** 2 qt.

4 c. **=** 2 pt.   ★ 4 pt. **=** 2 qt.

Unit 6 Answer Key

6.5 Practice

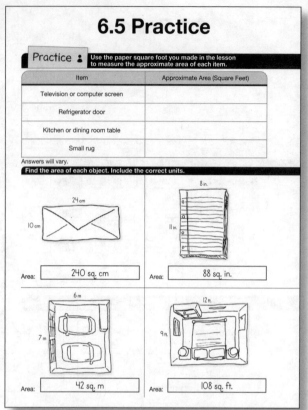

Practice 👤 Use the paper square foot you made in the lesson to measure the approximate area of each item.

Item	Approximate Area (Square Feet)
Television or computer screen	
Refrigerator door	
Kitchen or dining room table	
Small rug	

Answers will vary.

Find the area of each object. Include the correct units.

24 cm / 10 cm

Area: 240 sq. cm

8 in. / 11 in.

Area: 88 sq. in.

6 m / 7 m

Area: 42 sq. m

12 ft. / 9 ft.

Area: 108 sq. ft.

6.5 Review

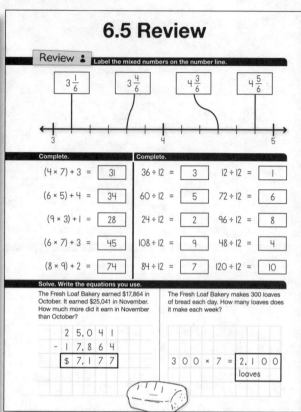

Review 👤 Label the mixed numbers on the number line.

$3\frac{1}{6}$ $3\frac{4}{6}$ $4\frac{3}{6}$ $4\frac{5}{6}$

3   4   5

Complete.

$(4 \times 7) + 3 =$ 31	$36 \div 12 =$ 3	$12 \div 12 =$ 1
$(6 \times 5) + 4 =$ 34	$60 \div 12 =$ 5	$72 \div 12 =$ 6
$(9 \times 3) + 1 =$ 28	$24 \div 12 =$ 2	$96 \div 12 =$ 8
$(6 \times 7) + 3 =$ 45	$108 \div 12 =$ 9	$48 \div 12 =$ 4
$(8 \times 9) + 2 =$ 74	$84 \div 12 =$ 7	$120 \div 12 =$ 10

Solve. Write the equations you use.

The Fresh Loaf Bakery earned $17,864 in October. It earned $25,041 in November. How much more did it earn in November than October?

```
  2 5, 0 4 1
- 1 7, 8 6 4
  $ 7, 1 7 7
```

The Fresh Loaf Bakery makes 300 loaves of bread each day. How many loaves does it make each week?

$300 \times 7 =$ 2,100 loaves

6.6 Practice

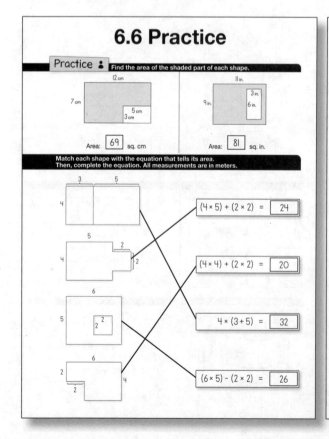

Practice 👤 Find the area of the shaded part of each shape.

12 cm / 7 cm / 5 cm 3 cm

Area: 69 sq. cm

11 in. / 9 in. / 3 in. 6 in.

Area: 81 sq. in.

Match each shape with the equation that tells its area. Then, complete the equation. All measurements are in meters.

3 5 / 4

5 / 4   2 2

6 / 5   2 2

6 / 2   2 2   4

$(4 \times 5) + (2 \times 2) =$ 24

$(4 \times 4) + (2 \times 2) =$ 20

$4 \times (3 + 5) =$ 32

$(6 \times 5) - (2 \times 2) =$ 26

6.6 Review

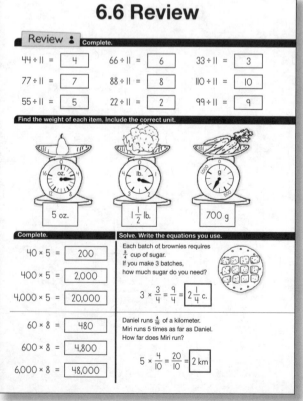

Review 👤 Complete.

$44 \div 11 =$ 4	$66 \div 11 =$ 6	$33 \div 11 =$ 3
$77 \div 11 =$ 7	$88 \div 11 =$ 8	$110 \div 11 =$ 10
$55 \div 11 =$ 5	$22 \div 11 =$ 2	$99 \div 11 =$ 9

Find the weight of each item. Include the correct unit.

5 oz. $1\frac{1}{2}$ lb.   700 g

Complete.

$40 \times 5 =$ 200
$400 \times 5 =$ 2,000
$4,000 \times 5 =$ 20,000
$60 \times 8 =$ 480
$600 \times 8 =$ 4,800
$6,000 \times 8 =$ 48,000

Solve. Write the equations you use.

Each batch of brownies requires $\frac{3}{4}$ cup of sugar. If you make 3 batches, how much sugar do you need?

$3 \times \frac{3}{4} = \frac{9}{4} = 2\frac{1}{4}$ c.

Daniel runs $\frac{4}{10}$ of a kilometer. Miri runs 5 times as far as Daniel. How far does Miri run?

$5 \times \frac{4}{10} = \frac{20}{10} =$ 2 km

Unit 6 Answer Key

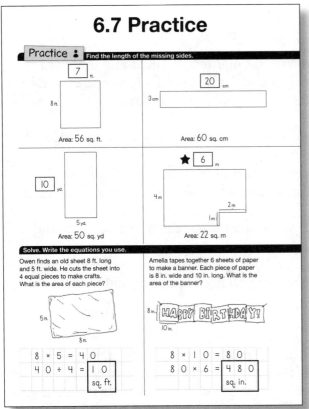

6.7 Practice

Practice Find the length of the missing sides.

7 ft.
8 ft.
Area: 56 sq. ft.

20 cm
3 cm
Area: 60 sq. cm

10 yd.
5 yd.
Area: 50 sq. yd

★ 6 m
4 m
2 m
1 m
Area: 22 sq. m

Solve. Write the equations you use.

Owen finds an old sheet 8 ft. long and 5 ft. wide. He cuts the sheet into 4 equal pieces to make crafts. What is the area of each piece?

5 ft.
8 ft.

8 × 5 = 4 0
4 0 ÷ 4 = 1 0 sq. ft.

Amelia tapes together 6 sheets of paper to make a banner. Each piece of paper is 8 in. wide and 10 in. long. What is the area of the banner?

8 in. HAPPY BIRTHDAY!
10 in.

8 × 1 0 = 8 0
8 0 × 6 = 4 8 0 sq. in.

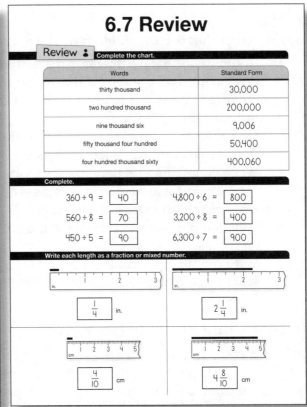

6.7 Review

Review Complete the chart.

Words	Standard Form
thirty thousand	30,000
two hundred thousand	200,000
nine thousand six	9,006
fifty thousand four hundred	50,400
four hundred thousand sixty	400,060

Complete.

360 ÷ 9 = 40   4,800 ÷ 6 = 800
560 ÷ 8 = 70   3,200 ÷ 8 = 400
450 ÷ 5 = 90   6,300 ÷ 7 = 900

Write each length as a fraction or mixed number.

$\frac{1}{4}$ in. $2\frac{1}{4}$ in.

$\frac{4}{10}$ cm $4\frac{8}{10}$ cm

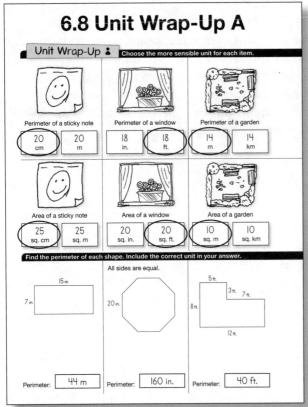

6.8 Unit Wrap-Up A

Unit Wrap-Up Choose the more sensible unit for each item.

Perimeter of a sticky note
(20 cm)   20 m

Perimeter of a window
18 in.   (18 ft.)

Perimeter of a garden
(14 m)   14 km

Area of a sticky note
(25 sq. cm)   25 sq. m

Area of a window
20 sq. in.   (20 sq. m)

Area of a garden
(10 sq. m)   10 sq. km

Find the perimeter of each shape. Include the correct unit in your answer.

15 m
7 m
Perimeter: 44 m

All sides are equal.
20 in.
Perimeter: 160 in.

5 ft.
3 ft.
7 ft.
8 ft.
12 ft.
Perimeter: 40 ft.

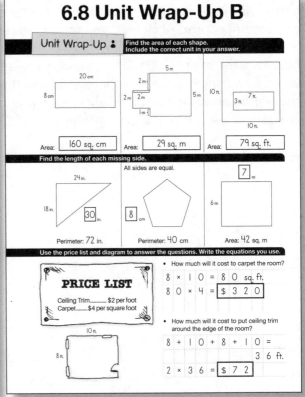

6.8 Unit Wrap-Up B

Unit Wrap-Up Find the area of each shape. Include the correct unit in your answer.

20 cm
8 cm
Area: 160 sq. cm

5 m
2 m
2 m
2 m
1 m
5 m
Area: 29 sq. m

10 ft.
7 ft.
3 ft.
10 ft.
Area: 79 sq. ft.

Find the length of each missing side.

24 in.
18 in.
30 in.
Perimeter: 72 in.

All sides are equal.
8 cm
Perimeter: 40 cm

7 m
6 m
Area: 42 sq. m

Use the price list and diagram to answer the questions. Write the equations you use.

PRICE LIST
Ceiling Trim........ $2 per foot
Carpet........ $4 per square foot

10 ft.
8 ft.

• How much will it cost to carpet the room?

8 × 1 0 = 8 0 sq. ft.
8 0 × 4 = $ 3 2 0

• How much will it cost to put ceiling trim around the edge of the room?

8 + 1 0 + 8 + 1 0 = 3 6 ft.
2 × 3 6 = $ 7 2

Unit 6 Checkpoint

What to Expect at the End of Unit 6

By the end of Unit 6, most children will be able to do the following:

- Understand that perimeter is measured with regular length units and that area is measured with square units. Many children will occasionally forget to include "square" when writing units for area problems, even if they understand the underlying concept.
- Find the perimeter of shapes with straight sides. Understand how to use multiplication to add sides with equal lengths more efficiently.
- Write equations with parentheses to find perimeter or area. Some children will be very comfortable writing equations with parentheses, while others will still prefer to write each step as its own equation.
- Split complex shapes into parts and add or subtract the areas of the parts to find total area.
- Solve multi-step perimeter and area word problems. Some children will confidently solve these problems on their own, while others will need lots of coaching and parent support.

Is Your Child Ready to Move on?

In Unit 7, your child will learn the written algorithm for multi-digit multiplication. Before moving on to Unit 7, your child should be mostly fluent with the multiplication facts. It's normal for children to occasionally forget a fact or take a few seconds to find an answer, but most children should be able to tell most of the answers within 3 seconds at this point.

What to Do If Your Child Needs More Practice

Some children will still be working on mastering the multiplication facts, especially the challenging ×7 and ×8 facts. If your child often needs more than a few seconds to find answers to the multiplication facts, **allow him to use the multiplication chart** (Blackline Master 2) as he solves the multi-digit multiplication problems in Unit 7. Otherwise, he'll spend so much energy figuring out the multiplication facts that he'll struggle to remember all the steps in these problems. Make sure he also keeps practicing the multiplication facts to develop greater fluency. See the Unit 2 Checkpoint (page 85) for practice suggestions.

Unit 7
Written Multiplication, Part 1

Overview

Your child will learn how to multiply multi-digit numbers by one-digit numbers with the traditional written process. You'll use play money and base-ten blocks to help her understand why this algorithm works, and you'll give her lots of practice to build fluency and accuracy.

In Unit 13, your child will learn how to multiply two-digit numbers by two-digit numbers with the written algorithm.

What Your Child Will Learn

In this unit, your child will learn to:

- Understand the steps in the written multiplication algorithm and model them with base-ten blocks or play money
- Multiply a two-, three-, or four-digit number by a one-digit number
- Use multi-digit multiplication to solve word problems
- Use multi-digit multiplication to find area or perimeter

Lesson List

Lesson 7.1 Introduce the Multiplication Algorithm

Lesson 7.2 Compare the Box Method and Multiplication Algorithm

Lesson 7.3 Multiply Three-Digit Numbers by One-Digit Numbers

Lesson 7.4 Multiply Four-Digit Numbers by One-Digit Numbers

Lesson 7.5 Multiply to Find Area or Perimeter

Lesson 7.6 Enrichment (Optional)

Extra Materials Needed for Unit 7

- Colored pencils or markers
- 8 slips of paper
- Paper clip
- For optional Enrichment Lesson:
  - × *365 Penguins*, written by Jean-Luc Fromental and illustrated by Joëlle Jolivet. Harry N. Abrams, 2006.
  - × Calculator or calculator app

Teaching Math with Confidence: How Using the Addition Algorithm and Box Method Helps Your Child Understand the Multiplication Algorithm

In this unit, your child will learn how to multiply multi-digit numbers by one-digit numbers with the traditional written algorithm. She'll find that the algorithm is a logical extension of both the addition algorithm and the box method. You'll explore both connections to help your child understand this complicated process.

First, you'll demonstrate how the steps in the multiplication algorithm are similar to the steps in the addition algorithm: start with the ones-place, multiply the numbers in each place, and trade as needed. Multiplication is simply a more efficient way to add equal groups, so the steps in the multiplication algorithm reflect this relationship between multiplication and addition.

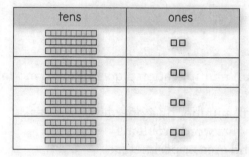 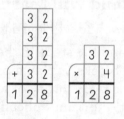

Adding 4 groups of 32 is equivalent to multiplying 32 by 4.
4 groups of 2 ones equal 8 ones, and 4 groups of 3 tens equal 12 tens.

Then, you'll demonstrate how the steps in the multiplication algorithm correspond to the partial products in the box method. With both methods, you split a number into its expanded form, multiply the parts, and add the partial parts. You keep track of the parts differently and add the parts in a different order, but the underlying concept is the same. In the box method, you add the partial products as the final step in the problem. In the multiplication algorithm, you add on any traded digits after you multiply the digits for the corresponding place.

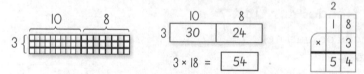

When you use the box method to multiply 18 × 3, you add 30 and 24 to find the product.
When you use the algorithm, you split the 24 into 2 tens and 4 ones and record and add the digits separately.

Connecting the multiplication algorithm to familiar skills helps your child develop both deep conceptual understanding and procedural fluency with the new skill. In this unit, your child will use the multiplication algorithm to multiply multi-digit numbers by one-digit numbers. Then, in Unit 13, she'll learn how to extend the process to multiply two-digit numbers by two-digit numbers.

Lesson 7.1
Introduce the Multiplication Algorithm

Purpose	Materials
• Practice multiplying and adding • Use the multiplication algorithm to multiply two-digit numbers by one-digit numbers • Compare and contrast the addition algorithm and multiplication algorithm	• Play money • Place-Value Chart (Blackline Master 4) • Colored pencils or markers

Memory Work	• **What do we call the top number in a fraction?** *The numerator.* • **What does the numerator tell?** *The number of parts.* • **What do we call the bottom number in a fraction?** *The denominator.* • **What does the denominator tell?** *How many equal parts the whole was split into.*

In this lesson, you'll introduce the multiplication algorithm and show your child how the multiplication algorithm is a logical extension of the addition algorithm. Children sometimes have trouble recalling the multiplication facts as they master this new process. If you find your child struggling with the facts, allow her to refer to the multiplication chart (Blackline Master 2). She'll likely need it less once she becomes more skilled with the multiplication algorithm.

Warm-up: Practice Multiplying and Adding

The written multiplication process requires your child to multiply two numbers, hold the product in her head, and then add an additional number to the product. This warm-up gives her practice with this skill.

Have your child solve the following problems orally.

- **What's 4 times 3?** *12.* **Plus 2?** *14.*
- **What's 2 times 7?** *14.* **Plus 1?** *15.*
- **What's 8 times 3?** *24.* **Plus 2?** *26.*
- **What's 8 times 7?** *56.* **Plus 4?** *60.*
- **What's 9 times 4?** *36.* **Plus 3?** *39.*

Activity (A):
Use Play Money to Model the Multiplication Algorithm (without Trading)

Today, you'll learn how to use the multiplication algorithm to multiply two-digit numbers by one-digit numbers.

Read aloud the word problem in part A: *Tickets to the concert cost $21. How much do 3 tickets cost?* **One way to find the answer is to add 21 plus 21 plus 21.** Have your child complete the addition problem.

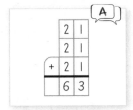

Arrange 3 groups of $21 (2 ten-dollar bills and 1 one-dollar bill) on the Place-Value Chart. **Multiplication is a more efficient way to add equal groups. First, we find the number of ones.** Use a colored pencil or marker to draw rings around the ones-place digits in both problems as shown. **Adding 1 plus 1 plus 1 is the same as multiplying 1 times 3. What's 1 times 3?** *3.* Write 3 in the answer's ones-place.

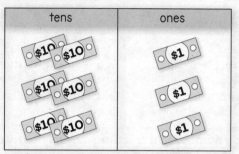
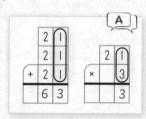

Next, we find the number of tens. Use a different colored pencil or marker to draw rings around the tens-place digits as shown. **Adding 2 plus 2 plus 2 is the same as multiplying 2 times 3. What's 2 times 3?** *6.* Write 6 in the answer's tens-place. **21 times 3 equals 63.**

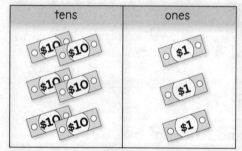
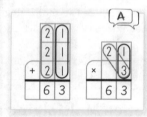

Have your child complete the addition and multiplication problems in part A in the same way. Make sure your child starts with the ones-place for every problem.

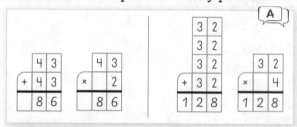

For 32 × 4, explain as needed how to record 12 tens in the answer: **12 tens equal 1 hundred and 2 tens, so you write a 1 in the hundreds-place and a 2 in the tens-place.**

Activity (B):
Use Play Money to Model the Multiplication Algorithm (with Trading)

In the problems in part A, we didn't need to trade any ones for tens. In the problems in part B, we'll need to trade ones for tens.

Read aloud the word problem in part B: *Tickets to the game cost $24. How much do 3 tickets cost?* **One way to find the answer is to add 24 plus 24 plus 24.** Arrange 3 groups of $24 (2 ten-dollar bills and 4 one-dollar bills) on the Place-Value Chart to model the problem.

Have your child complete the addition problem. **Why did you write a 1 above the tens-place?** *Sample answer: It shows I traded 10 ones for 1 ten.*

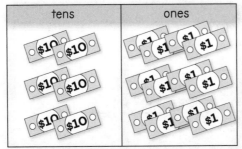
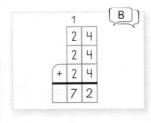

Now, let's use the multiplication algorithm to multiply 24 times 3. First, we find the number of ones. Use a colored pencil or marker to draw rings around the ones-place digits in both problems as shown. **Adding 4 plus 4 plus 4 is the same as multiplying 4 times 3.**

What's 4 times 3? *12.* **12 ones equal 1 ten and 2 ones.** Trade 10 one-dollar bills for 1 ten-dollar bill and place the ten-dollar bill in the tens-column. **I write 1 above the tens-place to show that I traded for 1 ten. I write 2 in the answer's ones-place to show that I have 2 ones.** Write 1 above the tens-place and 2 in the answer's ones-place.

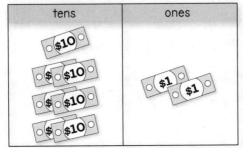
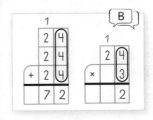

Next, we find the number of tens. Use a different colored pencil or marker to draw rings around the tens-place digits as shown. **Adding 2 plus 2 plus 2 is the same as multiplying 2 times 3.**

I multiply 2 tens by 3, then add on the extra traded ten. What's 2 times 3? *6.* **Plus 1?** *7.* **There are a total of 7 tens.** Write 7 in the answer's tens-place. **24 times 3 equals 72.**

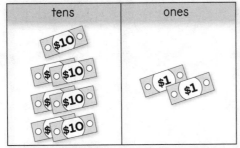
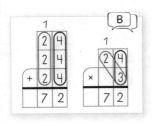

With both algorithms, we add on any traded digits. When we use the addition algorithm, we usually add any traded digits first. When we use the multiplication algorithm, we multiply first, then add the traded digits.

If your child wonders why this is true, have her try adding the traded tens before multiplying and comparing the result with the actual answer. **If you add first in this problem, you end up with 9 tens! That's too many! The traded tens aren't multiplied by 3. They're just added on to the product of 2 times 3.**

Have your child complete the addition and multiplication problems in part B in the same way. Remind her to multiply before adding any traded digits. Model the problems with play money as needed.

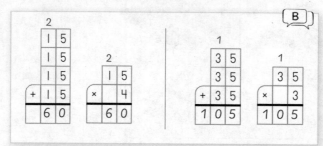

Children often forget to add the traded tens after they multiply. If your child makes this common mistake, have her cross out the traded digit after she adds it. This visual and physical cue will help her remember to add it.

Independent Practice and Review

Have your child complete the Lesson 7.1 Practice and Review workbook pages.

Encourage your child to refer to the example at the top of the Practice page as she completes the problems. If she needed lots of help in the lesson, complete the Practice page with her and model the problems with play money.

Lesson 7.2
Compare the Box Method and Multiplication Algorithm

Purpose	Materials
• Practice multiplying and adding • Compare and contrast the box method with the multiplication algorithm • Use the multiplication algorithm to multiply two-digit numbers by one-digit numbers	• Colored pencils or markers • Die

Memory Work · **How many grams equal 1 kilogram?** *1,000.*

In this lesson, you'll show your child how the multiplication algorithm and box method are related. See the Unit 7 **Teaching Math with Confidence** for more on the benefit of understanding this connection.

Warm-up: Practice Multiplying and Adding

Have your child solve the following problems orally. For each problem, first ask the multiplication part of the problem. After he names the product, ask the addition part of the problem.

- **What's 4 times 9?** *36.* **Plus 4?** *40.*
- **What's 2 times 8?** *16.* **Plus 6?** *22.*
- **What's 7 times 3?** *21.* **Plus 4?** *25.*
- **What's 5 times 7?** *35.* **Plus 6?** *41.*
- **What's 6 times 9?** *54.* **Plus 3?** *57.*

Activity (A): Compare the Box Method and the Multiplication Algorithm

In the last lesson, you learned how to use the multiplication algorithm to multiply a two-digit number by a one-digit number. Today, we'll see how the box method and the multiplication algorithm are related.

First, let's find 3 times 18 with the box method. Remember, we use the expanded form of 18 to make the multiplying and adding easier.

- Point to 3 and 10. **What's 3 times 10?** *30.* Write 30 as shown.
- Point to 3 and 8. **What's 3 times 8?** *24.* Write 24 as shown.
- **Now, we add the partial products to find the total product. What's 30 plus 24?** *54.* Write 54 in the blank.

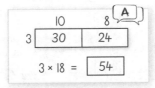

Now, let's use the multiplication algorithm to solve the problem. First, we find the ones. Use a colored pencil or marker to draw a ring around the 8 and 3 as shown. **What's 8 times 3?** *24.* **24 ones equal 2 tens and 4 ones.** Write 2 above the tens-place and 4 in the answer's ones-place.

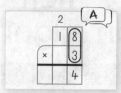

If your child has trouble understanding the trading, use real base-ten blocks to model trading 20 ones for 2 tens.

Next, we find the tens. Use a different colored pencil or marker to draw a ring around the 1 and 3 as shown. **We multiply 1 ten by 3, then add on the extra traded 2 tens. What's 1 times 3?** *3.* **Plus 2?** *5.* **There are a total of 5 tens.** Write 5 in the answer's tens-place. **18 times 3 equals 54.**

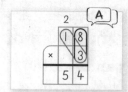

We found the product of 18 times 3 in two different ways. What do the two ways have in common? *Sample answers: You get the same answer. You multiply the numbers in parts and then add them.*

How are the two ways different from each other? *Sample answers: You have to add the partial products when you use the box method. You have to show trading when you use the algorithm.*

Both ways involve splitting the numbers into tens and ones, multiplying the parts, and then adding the parts. We just keep track of the parts differently and add them in a different order.

In the box method, we find two partial products and add them. In the algorithm, we break the first partial product into tens and ones. We add the traded tens as we go.

Which method do you like better, the box method or the multiplication algorithm? *Answers will vary.*

When you study topics like fractions, decimals, and algebra in future grades, you'll find that it's helpful to understand both methods. Sometimes, the multiplication algorithm is faster. Other times, it's more helpful to use the box method to multiply in parts. In this unit, you'll focus on mastering the multiplication algorithm.

Have your child find 35 × 7 with both methods.

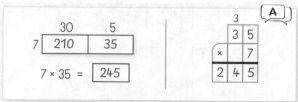

Activity (B): Play Roll and Multiply

Play Roll and Multiply.

Roll and Multiply

Materials: Die

Object of the Game: Have the greater total sum of all your products.

On your turn, roll the die. Choose one of the multiplication problems on your score-card and write the number on the die as the missing factor. (You may write the number in any of the multiplication problems.) Then, multiply to find the product.

For example, if you roll a 4 on your first turn and write the 4 in the first multiplication problem, your product is 112.

Take turns until both players have completed their scorecards. Each player adds up their products on a piece of scrap paper. Whoever has the greater total wins.

Cooperative Variation: Play together on one gameboard. Try to reach as high a score as possible:

- Math Master: 500 points
- Math Whiz: 750 points
- Math Superstar: 1,000 points

Independent Practice and Review

Have your child complete the Lesson 7.2 Practice and Review workbook pages.

Lesson 7.3
Multiply Three-Digit Numbers by One-Digit Numbers

Purpose	Materials
• Practice multiplying one-digit numbers by multiples of 100 • Use the multiplication algorithm to multiply three-digit numbers by one-digit numbers	• Play money • Place-Value Chart (Blackline Master 4) • Colored pencils or markers • 8 slips of paper

Memory Work	
	• **What do we call the number to be divided?** *The dividend.* • **What do we call the number we divide by?** *The divisor.* • **What do we call the result when we divide two numbers?** *The quotient.* • **What do we call an amount that is left over after division?** *The remainder.*

You will need 8 slips of paper to play Snowball Fight. Use white paper if you'd like the slips to look like snowflakes.

Warm-up: Practice Multiplying One-Digit Numbers by Multiples of 100

Have your child solve the following multiplication problems.

- **3 times 300.** *900.*
- **2 times 400.** *800.*
- **6 times 100.** *600.*
- **0 times 900.** *0.*

- **5 times 200.** *1,000.*
- **5 times 300.** *1,500.*
- **8 times 400.** *3,200.*

Activity (A): Multiply Three-Digit Numbers by One-Digit Numbers with the Multiplication Algorithm

In the last two lessons, you learned how to use the multiplication algorithm to multiply a two-digit number by a one-digit number. Today, you'll use the algorithm to multiply three-digit numbers by one-digit numbers. We'll follow the same steps.

We'll pretend we work at a furniture store today. Our first customer would like 3 of these lamps. Each lamp costs $142, so we'll multiply 3 times 142 to find the total cost. We'll use play money to model the problems today. Arrange play money as shown on the Place-Value Chart.

Which place do we start with? *The ones-place.* Use a colored pencil or marker to draw a ring around the 2 and 3 as shown. **What's 2 times 3?** *6.* Write a 6 in the answer's ones-place.

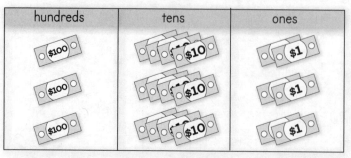

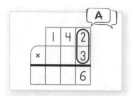

What do we do next? *Multiply 4 tens by 3.* Use a different colored pencil or marker to draw a ring around the 4 and 3 as shown. **What's 4 times 3?** *12.* Trade 10 ten-dollar bills for 1 hundred-dollar bill, and place the hundred-dollar bill in the hundreds-column.

We added 1 hundred to the hundreds-place, so I write a 1 above the hundreds-place. Write a 1 above the hundreds-place. **There are 2 tens left in the tens-place, so I write a 2 in the tens-place.** Write a 2 in the answer's tens-place.

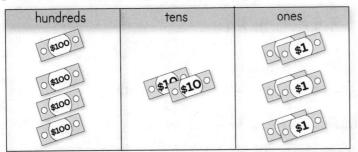
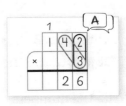

Last, we follow the same steps for the hundreds-place. Point to the hundred-dollar bills. Use a different colored pencil or marker to draw a ring around the 1 and 3 as shown. **We have 3 groups of 1 hundred. What's 1 times 3?** *3.* **We have 1 extra hundred to add. 3 plus 1 is 4, so there are a total of 4 hundreds.** Write 4 in the answer's hundreds-place.

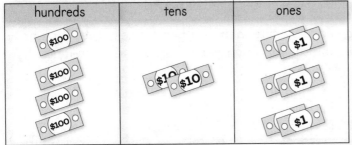
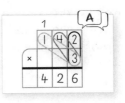

Have your child solve the rest of the problems in the same way. Model the problems with play money and draw rings around the digits as needed.

- For 470 × 2, point out that your child should multiply the zero just as she multiplies any other number. **Zero times 2 is zero, so write a zero in the ones-place.**
- For 153 × 8, remind your child that 10 hundreds equal 1 thousand. **12 hundreds equal 1 thousand and 2 hundreds. So, write a 1 in the answer's thousands-place and a 2 in the answer's hundreds-place.**

How much do 3 bookshelves cost?	How much do 2 armchairs cost?	How much do 8 chairs cost?
$286	$470	$153
2 1		+ 2
2 8 6	4 7 0	1 5 3
× 3	× 2	× 8
8 5 8	9 4 0	1,2 2 4

If your child often forgets to add the traded digits after she multiplies, have her cross out the traded digit after she adds it.

$$\begin{array}{ccc} \cancel{2} & \cancel{1} & \\ 2 & 8 & 6 \\ \times & & 3 \\ \hline 8 & 5 & 8 \end{array}$$

Activity (B): Play Snowball Fight

Play Snowball Fight.

If you'd rather avoid throwing, put the paper wads in a bowl and draw 2 wads each turn instead. Replace the wads in the bowl after each turn.

Snowball Fight

Materials: 8 slips of paper

Object of the Game: Have the greater sum of all your products.

Write the numbers on the snowballs on separate slips of paper:

Crumple the slips of paper and place them on the table. Both players count down in unison from 10 while throwing the crumpled wads of paper at each other. When you reach 1, both players stop and pick up the closest wad of paper.

Both players unfold their paper wad and write their number in one of the blank grids on their scorecards. Both players multiply to find the product of the written number and printed number.

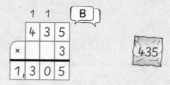

Sample play.

Crumple up your numbers and add them back to the pile of "snowballs." Repeat until both players have filled in all of the blank grids. Each player adds up their products on a piece of scrap paper. Whoever has the greater total wins.

Independent Practice and Review

Have your child complete the Lesson 7.3 Practice and Review workbook pages.

Lesson 7.4
Multiply Four-Digit Numbers by One-Digit Numbers

Purpose	Materials
• Practice rounding to the nearest thousand • Use the multiplication algorithm to multiply four-digit numbers by one-digit numbers • Estimate products and compare the estimate with the exact answer	• Play money, optional • Paper clip

Memory Work   • **How many milliliters equal 1 liter?** *1,000.*

Warm-up: Practice Rounding to the Nearest Thousand

Have your child orally round each number to the nearest thousand.

- **7,001.** *7,000.*
- **7,231.** *7,000.*
- **7,499.** *7,000.*

- **7,500.** *8,000.*
- **7,501.** *8,000.*
- **7,999.** *8,000.*

Activity (A): Multiply Four-Digit Numbers by One-Digit Numbers with the Multiplication Algorithm

In the last lesson, you used the multiplication algorithm to multiply three-digit numbers by one-digit numbers. Today, you'll use the same steps to multiply four-digit numbers by one-digit numbers.

Before we solve the first problem, let's estimate the answer. Estimating the answer helps you know whether your answer is reasonable.

What's 1,846 rounded to the nearest thousand? *2,000.* Write 2,000 × 3 as shown. **What's 2,000 times 3?** *6,000.* Write 6,000 as shown. **Do you think the exact answer will be higher or lower than 6,000? Why?** *Sample answer: 1,846 is less than 2,000, so the exact answer will be less than the estimate.*

We estimate the product will be about 6,000. Now, let's multiply to find the exact answer. We'll use the same steps that we use to multiply two- or three-digit numbers by a one-digit number. Have your child use the multiplication algorithm to find the product. If he has trouble, model the problem with play money.

If your child has trouble remembering which digits to multiply, use colored pencils or markers to draw rings around the digits (as in Lesson 7.3).

We estimated the product would be about 6,000. You found that the exact product is 5,538, so that seems like a reasonable answer. It's a little less than the estimate, since we rounded 1,846 up to 2,000.

Don't worry if your child doesn't fully understand why the exact answer is less than the estimate. Whether or not an answer is "reasonable" depends on the numbers involved. The product of a four-digit number times a one-digit number can be several thousand off from the estimate and still be a reasonable answer.

Repeat with the next problem. First, have your child round 3,058 to the nearest thousand and estimate the product. Then, have him use the multiplication algorithm to find the exact product. If he has trouble with the final step, say: **18 thousands equal 1 ten-thousand and 8 thousands. So, write a 1 in the answer's ten-thousands place and an 8 in the answer's thousands-place.**

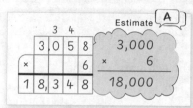

Activity (B): Play Spin to Win

Play Spin to Win.

Spin to Win

Materials: Paper clip

Object of the Game: Win the most points.

On your turn, place one end of the paper clip in the center of the top spinner. Place the point of a pencil through the paper clip so that it touches the center of the circle. Spin the paper clip and write this number on the top line of your first blank grid. Then, move the paper clip and pencil to the bottom spinner. Spin again, and write this number on the next line. Find the product of the two numbers.

Then, have the other player spin twice, write the value of each spin in their next blank grid, and find the product. Whoever has the greater product wins a point.

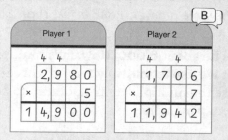

Player 1 has a greater product than Player 2, so Player 1 wins the point.

Continue until you have filled in all the blank grids. Whoever has won more points wins the game.

Independent Practice and Review

Have your child complete the Lesson 7.4 Practice and Review workbook pages.

Lesson 7.5
Multiply to Find Area or Perimeter

Purpose	Materials
• Practice multiplying a four-digit number by a one-digit number • Use multi-digit multiplication to find area or perimeter	• None

| Memory Work | • **What do we call an angle that looks like the corner of a piece of paper?** *A right angle.*
• **What do we call a quadrilateral with 4 right angles?** *A rectangle.*
• **What do we call a quadrilateral with 4 right angles and 4 equal sides?** *A square.*
• **What do we call a quadrilateral with 4 equal sides?** *A rhombus.* |

Warm-up (A): Practice the Steps in Multi-Digit Multiplication

In this unit, you've learned how to use the multiplication algorithm to multiply multi-digit numbers by one-digit numbers. Today, you'll practice with a silent activity. Then, you'll apply what you've learned to area and perimeter.

Watch as I solve the first problem. Tap your pencil on the table each time I write a correct number. We'll do this completely silently so we can both concentrate.

Silent teaching may feel strange, but children often enjoy the change of pace (and concentrate more intently, too). Having your child tap her pencil after you write each number ensures that she carefully observes how you solve the problem. If you and your child don't enjoy this activity, it's fine for your child to simply solve the problems instead.

Slowly and deliberately solve the first problem. Your child should tap her pencil on the table after you write each number.

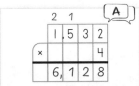

Reverse roles for the other two problems. Have your child solve each problem. Tap your pencil on the table every time she writes a correct number. If she makes a mistake, do not tap the table. Instead, give her a puzzled look to prompt her to check her work.

Activity (B): Use the Multiplication Algorithm to Find the Perimeter of Shapes with Equal Sides

In Unit 6, you learned how to multiply to find the perimeter of shapes with equal sides. You multiply the length of each side by the number of sides.

This nature preserve is shaped like a square, with 4 equal sides. Each side is 1,762 feet long. So, we multiply 1,762 times 4 to find its perimeter. Have your child complete the multiplication problem. **What's the perimeter of the nature preserve?** *7,048 square feet.*

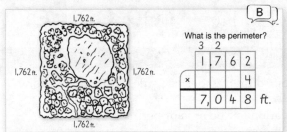

This mirror has 5 equal sides. Each side is 38 centimeters. How can you use multiplication to find its perimeter? *Multiply 38 times 5.* Have your child write and solve a multiplication problem to find the perimeter of the mirror.

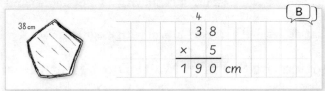

Activity (C): Use the Multiplication Algorithm to Find the Area of Rectangles

In Unit 6, you also learned how to multiply length times width to find area. This driveway is 27 meters long and 4 meters wide, so you can multiply 27 times 4 to find its area. Have your child solve the matching multiplication problem. **What's the area of the driveway?** *108 square meters.*

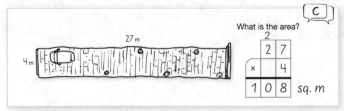

Have your child find the area of the other driveway in the same way.

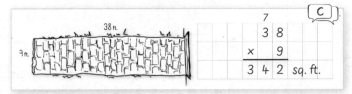

Independent Practice and Review

Have your child complete the Lesson 7.5 Practice and Review workbook pages.

Lesson 7.6
Enrichment (Optional)

Purpose	Materials
• Practice memory work • Use addition and multiplication to reason about days of the year and groups of penguins • Use multiplication to convert years to days • Summarize what your child has learned and assess your child's progress	• *365 Penguins*, written by Jean-Luc Fromental and illustrated by Joëlle Jolivet • Calculator or calculator app

Warm-up: Review Memory Work

Quiz your child on all memory work through Unit 7. See pages 536-537 for the full list.

Math Picture Book: *365 Penguins*

Read *365 Penguins*, written by Jean-Luc Fromental and illustrated by Joëlle Jolivet. As you read, discuss the addition and multiplication equations that match the various penguin arrangements.

Enrichment Activity: How Many Days Old Am I?

There are usually 365 days in each year. So, you can multiply a person's age times 365 to find about how many days old they were at their last birthday.

Make a simple chart with the names and ages of the people in your family. For anyone 9 years old or younger, have your child multiply the person's age by 365 to find approximately how many days old they were at their last birthday. For example, if your child is 9 years old, he was approximately 3,285 days old at his last birthday. For anyone older than 9, show your child how to use a calculator to multiply the person's age times 365.

Name	Age (in Years) at Last Birthday	Approximate Age (in Days) at Last Birthday
Liza	6	2,190
Nate	9	3,285
Mom	35	12,775
Dad	36	13,140

Sample chart.

Some years are called leap years. They happen every 4 years, and they have 366 days in them. So, we'd have to find the number of leap years each person has been alive to find the exact number of days old they were at their last birthday.

If your child is interested, figure out how many leap years your child has been alive. For each leap year, add 1 extra day to your child's total.

Leap Years: 2012, 2016, 2020, 2024, 2028, 2032, 2036, ...

If your child would like to make his total even more exact, give him a calendar and challenge him to find how many days it has been since his birthday. Then, add that number to the previous total to find exactly how many days he has been alive.

Unit Wrap-Up

Have your child complete the Unit 7 Wrap-Up.

Unit 7 Answer Key

7.1 Practice

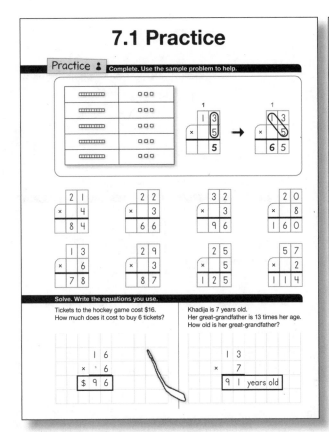

7.1 Review

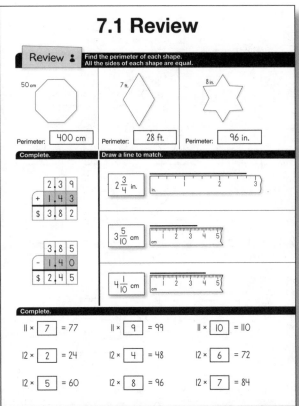

7.2 Practice

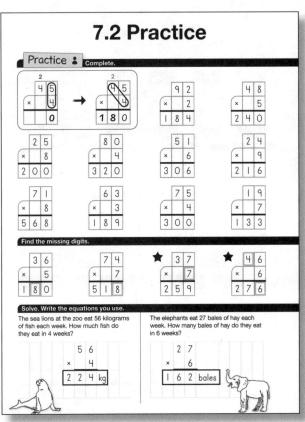

7.2 Review

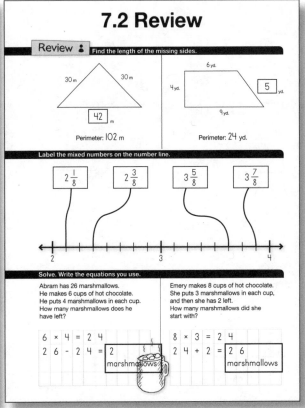

Unit 7 Answer Key

7.3 Practice

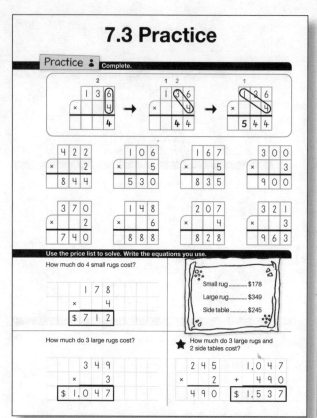

7.3 Review

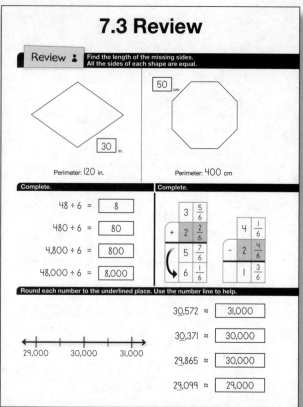

7.4 Practice

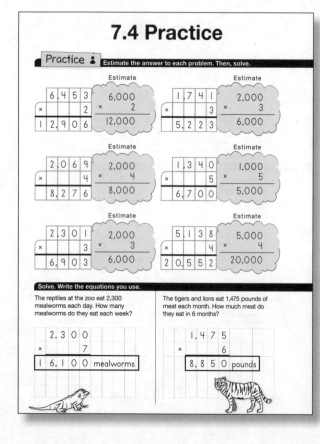

7.4 Review

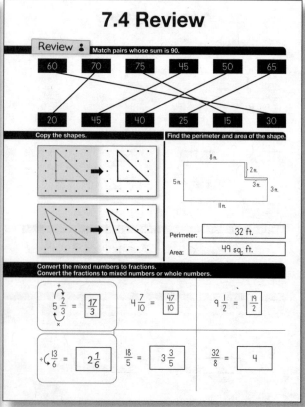

Unit 7 Answer Key

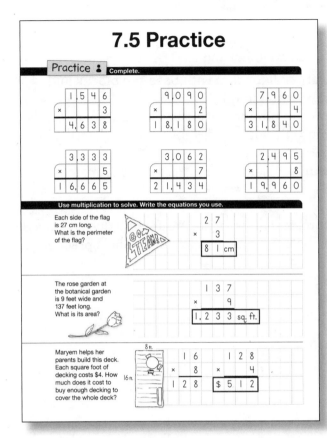

7.5 Practice

Practice 👤 **Complete.**

	1	5	4	6
×				3
4	6	3	8	

	9	0	9	0
×				2
18	1	8	0	

	7	9	6	0
×				4
31	8	4	0	

	3	3	3	3
×				5
16	6	6	5	

	3	0	6	2
×				7
21	4	3	4	

	2	4	9	5
×				8
19	9	6	0	

Use multiplication to solve. Write the equations you use.

Each side of the flag is 27 cm long. What is the perimeter of the flag?

$$\begin{array}{r} 2\ 7 \\ \times\quad 3 \\ \hline \boxed{8\ 1}\ \text{cm} \end{array}$$

The rose garden at the botanical garden is 9 feet wide and 137 feet long. What is its area?

$$\begin{array}{r} 1\ 3\ 7 \\ \times\quad\ 9 \\ \hline \boxed{1,2\ 3\ 3}\ \text{sq. ft.} \end{array}$$

Maryem helps her parents build this deck. Each square foot of decking costs $4. How much does it cost to buy enough decking to cover the whole deck?

8 ft. · 16 ft.

$$\begin{array}{r} 1\ 6 \\ \times\ 8 \\ \hline 1\ 2\ 8 \end{array} \qquad \begin{array}{r} 1\ 2\ 8 \\ \times\quad 4 \\ \hline \boxed{\$\ 5\ 1\ 2} \end{array}$$

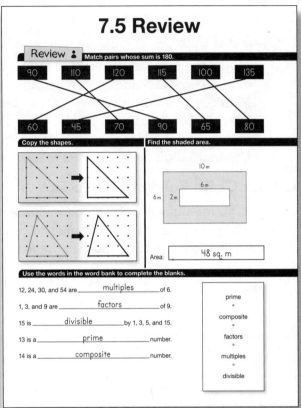

7.5 Review

Review 👤 **Match pairs whose sum is 180.**

90	110	120	115	100	135

60	45	70	90	65	80

Copy the shapes.

Find the shaded area.

10 m · 6 m · 6 m · 2 m

Area: 48 sq. m

Use the words in the word bank to complete the blanks.

12, 24, 30, and 54 are ___multiples___ of 6.

1, 3, and 9 are ___factors___ of 9.

15 is ___divisible___ by 1, 3, 5, and 15.

13 is a ___prime___ number.

14 is a ___composite___ number.

- prime
- composite
- factors
- multiples
- divisible

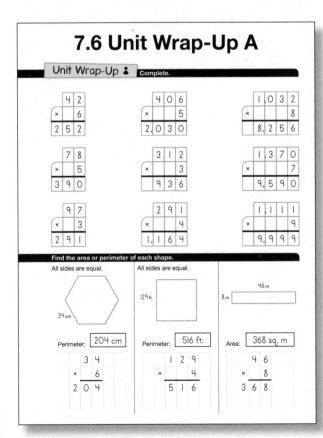

7.6 Unit Wrap-Up A

Unit Wrap-Up 👤 **Complete.**

	4	2
×		6
2	5	2

	4	0	6
×			5
2,	0	3	0

	1,	0	3	2
×				8
8,	2	5	6	

	7	8
×		5
3	9	0

	3	1	2
×			3
9	3	6	

	1,	3	7	0
×				7
9,	5	9	0	

	9	7
×		3
2	9	1

	2	9	1
×			4
1,	1	6	4

	1,	1	1	1
×				9
9,	9	9	9	

Find the area or perimeter of each shape.

All sides are equal.

34 cm

Perimeter: 204 cm

$$\begin{array}{r} 3\ 4 \\ \times\quad 6 \\ \hline 2\ 0\ 4 \end{array}$$

All sides are equal.

129 ft.

Perimeter: 516 ft.

$$\begin{array}{r} 1\ 2\ 9 \\ \times\quad\ 4 \\ \hline 5\ 1\ 6 \end{array}$$

8 m · 46 m

Area: 368 sq. m

$$\begin{array}{r} 4\ 6 \\ \times\quad 8 \\ \hline 3\ 6\ 8 \end{array}$$

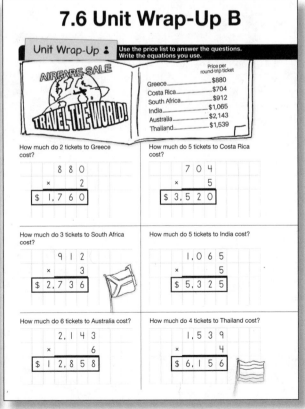

7.6 Unit Wrap-Up B

Unit Wrap-Up 👤 **Use the price list to answer the questions. Write the equations you use.**

AIRFARE SALE · TRAVEL THE WORLD!

Price per round-trip ticket	
Greece	$880
Costa Rica	$704
South Africa	$912
India	$1,065
Australia	$2,143
Thailand	$1,539

How much do 2 tickets to Greece cost?

$$\begin{array}{r} 8\ 8\ 0 \\ \times\quad\ 2 \\ \hline \boxed{\$\ 1,7\ 6\ 0} \end{array}$$

How much do 5 tickets to Costa Rica cost?

$$\begin{array}{r} 7\ 0\ 4 \\ \times\quad\ 5 \\ \hline \boxed{\$\ 3,5\ 2\ 0} \end{array}$$

How much do 3 tickets to South Africa cost?

$$\begin{array}{r} 9\ 1\ 2 \\ \times\quad\ 3 \\ \hline \boxed{\$\ 2,7\ 3\ 6} \end{array}$$

How much do 5 tickets to India cost?

$$\begin{array}{r} 1,0\ 6\ 5 \\ \times\quad\ 5 \\ \hline \boxed{\$\ 5,3\ 2\ 5} \end{array}$$

How much do 6 tickets to Australia cost?

$$\begin{array}{r} 2,1\ 4\ 3 \\ \times\quad\ 6 \\ \hline \boxed{\$\ 1\ 2,8\ 5\ 8} \end{array}$$

How much do 4 tickets to Thailand cost?

$$\begin{array}{r} 1,5\ 3\ 9 \\ \times\quad\ 4 \\ \hline \boxed{\$\ 6,1\ 5\ 6} \end{array}$$

Unit 7 Checkpoint

What to Expect at the End of Unit 7

By the end of Unit 7, most children will be able to do the following:

- Model the steps in the written multiplication algorithm with base-ten blocks and explain how the blocks correspond to the written digits.
- Multiply a two-digit, three-digit, or four-digit number by a one-digit number, mostly fluently. Some children will be able to multiply with ease, while others will still need to stop and think as they progress through the steps.
- Use multi-digit multiplication to solve word problems or find area and perimeter.

Is Your Child Ready to Move on?

In Unit 8, your child will learn to identify, measure, and draw angles. Your child does not need to have fully mastered multi-digit multiplication before moving on to Unit 8. She'll practice the multiplication algorithm more in the Review pages.

Unit 8
Angles

Overview

In this unit, your child will learn how to measure angles with degrees. First, you will use visual comparisons and a hands-on Degree Wheel to help him develop a concrete sense of what degrees measure. Then, you'll teach him how to use a protractor to measure angles and draw angles with a given measure. You'll also teach your child how to add and subtract angles to solve angle puzzles and find unknown angles.

What Your Child Will Learn

In this unit, your child will learn to:

- Estimate angle measures in degrees
- Identify acute, right, obtuse, and straight angles
- Measure angles with a protractor
- Draw angles with a given measure
- Add or subtract to find the measure of an unknown angle

Lesson List

Lesson 8.1   Label and Compare Angles

Lesson 8.2   Degrees

Lesson 8.3   Acute, Right, Obtuse, and Straight Angles

Lesson 8.4   Measure Angles with a Protractor

Lesson 8.5   Draw Angles with a Protractor

Lesson 8.6   Add Angles with Pattern Blocks

Lesson 8.7   Add and Subtract Angles

Lesson 8.8   Enrichment (Optional)

Extra Materials Needed for Unit 8

- 2 pencils
- Colored pencils or markers
- Paper clip
- For optional Enrichment Lesson:
  - × *Sir Cumference and the Great Knight of Angleland,* written by Cindy Neuschwander and illustrated by Wayne Geehan.
  - × 2 pencils

You will need a protractor for the first time in this unit. Any clear, plastic protractor with degree markings will work for the lessons.

You will also need the Degree Wheel (Blackline Master 5) for this unit. Make sure to copy it onto sturdy paper and cut it out before Lesson 8.2.

Teaching Math with Confidence: The Challenges of Measuring in Degrees

In this unit, you'll teach your child to measure angles in degrees with a protractor. Measuring angles presents several new challenges to children. First, children have to understand what degrees measure: the amount of "spread" between two lines. The angle is the space between the two lines, so children have to get used to the idea of measuring this empty space.

Second, children need to become comfortable with the unit that we use to measure angles: degrees. When you taught your child about length units in *Kindergarten* and *First Grade Math with Confidence,* you lined up square pattern blocks or centimeter cubes to help your child develop a concrete understanding of inches or centimeters. This approach doesn't work when it comes to angles, though! One degree is very small, so it's not practical to line them up to measure angles.

Instead, you'll use a tool called the Degree Wheel to help your child develop a sense of degrees. By moving the Degree Wheel, your child will see how moving one side of the angle changes its degree measure. This helps your child get a sense for the size of different angles and begin to estimate angles' sizes in degrees. He'll also learn that he can use right angles as an important benchmark for estimating angles' sizes. For example, this angle is a bit larger than a right angle. Right angles measure 90 degrees, so a reasonable estimate for this angle is around 110 degrees.

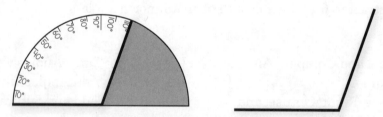

The Degree Wheel helps your child learn to estimate angle measures.

After your child understands what degrees measure and can approximate angle measurements with degrees, he'll finally be ready to learn to use a protractor. Children often struggle when it comes to the mechanics of using this complex tool. You'll demonstrate step-by-step how to align the protractor with the angle and choose the correct scale so that your child learns how to measure angles with confidence.

Lesson 8.1
Label and Compare Angles

Purpose	Materials
• Use hands-on materials to create angles • Introduce the term *vertex* • Label angles in two ways • Identify angles and visually compare their sizes	• 2 pencils • Colored pencils or markers

Memory Work	• **How do you know if a number is divisible by 10?** *It has a 0 in the ones-place.* • **How do you know if a number is divisible by 5?** *It has a 0 or 5 in the ones-place.* • **How do you know if a number is divisible by 2?** *It is even. It has 0, 2, 4, 6, or 8 in the ones-place.*

Warm-up: Make Angles with Pencils

We're starting a new unit on angles today! What do you remember about angles that you learned in younger grades? *Answers will vary.*

When two lines meet, they form an angle. Arrange 2 pencils in a V on the table, with their points touching. **These two pencils meet to form an angle. The angle is the space between the pencils.**

The space between the pencils is the angle.

If I move the pencils to make the V narrower, the angle becomes smaller. Move the pencils to make the V narrower. (Keep the points of the pencils touching.)

If I move the pencils to make the V wider, the angle between them becomes larger. Move the pencils to make the V larger.

Give your child a minute to move the pencils and explore the angles she can make between them.

Activity (A): Identify Angles in Two Ways

An angle is formed when two lines meet. We call the point where the two lines meet the *vertex* of the angle. The two lines form the sides of the angle, and the angle is the space between the lines.

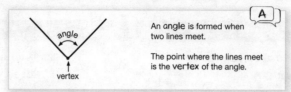

We're going to study a lot of different angles in this unit, so it's important that we know how to name and label them. One way to name an angle is with its vertex. In this angle, the sides meet at point M. So, this angle is angle M.

Point to the angle symbol. **This symbol is called the angle symbol. It stands for the word angle, so say "angle" whenever you see it.** Have your child trace the label for ∠M. Then, have her label ∠R in the same way.

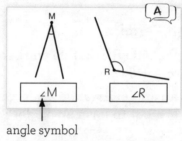

angle symbol

Make sure your child draws the angle symbol from top to bottom.

Another way to name an angle is to label it with a number. To label an angle in this way, you write a number inside the angle. This angle is labeled with a 1, so we call it angle 1. Have your child trace the label for ∠1 and label ∠2 in the same way.

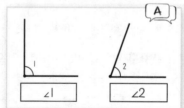

Right angles are angles like the corner of a square or piece of paper. Which angle is a right angle? *Angle 1.* Tear off a corner of a piece of paper. Have your child place the corner in ∠1 to check that it is a right angle.

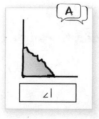

Which angle is larger than a right angle? *Angle R.* Have your child place the torn corner in ∠R to check that it is larger than a right angle.

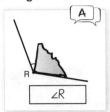

Which angles are smaller than a right angle? *Angle M and angle 2.* Have your child place the torn corner in these angles to verify that they are smaller than a right angle.

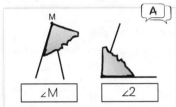

Which angle is smaller, angle M or angle 2? *Angle M.* **How do you know?** *Sample answers: Angle M is pointier than angle 2. Angle 2 looks wider than angle M.*

Activity (B): Find Angles in Your Child's Name

I wonder how many angles we can find in your name! Have your child write her name in capital letters on the graph paper in part B. If her name is longer than 5-6 letters, have her split the letters over two lines.

Let's draw a small arc in every angle we can find. Have your child draw an arc in each angle with a marker or colored pencil (as in ∠1 and ∠2 in part A). Have her use different colors for neighboring angles to help distinguish them.

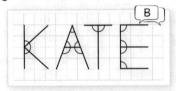

Sample name and angles.

Your child will learn about angles greater than or equal to 180° in the next lesson. For this activity, focus only on angles that are less than 180° since these angles are easiest to see and understand.

After your child has identified as many angles as she can find, use the following questions to discuss the angles.

- **Are there any curved lines in your name?** *Answers will vary.* **Curved lines change direction like angles, but they're not angles. Angles must be made from straight lines.**
- **Are there any right angles in your name?** *Answers will vary.*
- **Which angles in your name are smaller than a right angle?** *Answers will vary.*
- **What's the smallest angle in your name?** *Answers will vary.* If your child's not sure, encourage her to look for the "pointiest" angle in her name.
- **Which angles in your name are larger than a right angle?** *Answers will vary.*

Use a torn corner of a piece of paper as needed to check whether the angles are bigger, smaller, or equal to a right angle.

Independent Practice and Review

Have your child complete the Lesson 8.1 Practice and Review workbook pages.

Lesson 8.2
Degrees

Purpose	Materials
• Introduce degrees as a unit for measuring angles • Understand that 360° equal 1 full turn • Estimate and measure angles in degrees with the Degree Wheel	• Degree Wheel (Blackline Master 5), cut out

Memory Work	• **What is a prime number?** *A number with exactly 2 factors.* • **What is a composite number?** *A number with more than 2 factors.*

In this lesson, you will use a paper Degree Wheel to introduce the concept of measuring angles in degrees. The Degree Wheel helps your child develop a concrete sense of what degrees measure before he deals with the challenge of manipulating a protractor. See the Unit 8 **Teaching Math with Confidence** for more on the importance of learning to estimate with degrees before introducing protractors.

Warm-up: Introduce Degrees with Turns

We use different units of measurements depending on what we're measuring. You already know about many different kinds of units, like feet, kilograms, and gallons.

Today, you'll learn about the units we use to measure angles. To measure angles, we use a unit called *degrees*. Degrees measure how spread apart the sides of the angle are.

Have your child stand up. **Make one full turn to the right, so that you end up facing the same way you started.** *Child makes a full turn to the right.* **You just turned 360 degrees. In sports, athletes sometimes say they "did a 360." What they mean is that they turned a full 360 degrees and ended up facing the same direction that they started.**

One full turn equals 360 degrees. So, if you divide a full turn into 360 equal small turns, each turn is 1 degree. Imagine dividing up your full turn into 360 equal parts. Show me how far a 1 degree turn to the right might look. *Child turns very slightly to the right.* **One degree is very small!**

One thing that's confusing about degrees is that we measure temperature with degrees, too. We use the same word, but we mean different things. Angles aren't hot or cold!

Ancient Babylonians invented degrees about 3,000 years ago. They noticed that the stars moved back to the same position in the sky after about 360 days, so they decided that 1 full turn would equal 360 degrees. Their number system was based on the number 60, so this may have also played a factor in their decision to use 360 as the foundation for their angle measurement system rather than the full 365 days it takes the stars to return to a particular position in the sky.

Activity: Introduce the Degree Wheel

Show your child the white part of the Degree Wheel. **This is the Degree Wheel. We will use it to make and measure angles. The white circle is divided into increments of 10 degrees.**

Imagine you were so small that you could stand in the center of the wheel and face the 0-degree mark. If you turned all the way around, you'd turn 360 degrees.

Place the gray circle on top of the white circle with the slits aligned. Then, rotate the gray circle clockwise (without moving the white circle). Tuck the labeled edge of the gray circle under the slit in the white circle. Make sure both dark lines remain visible. **The angle is the white opening between the two dark lines.**

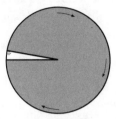

If I move the gray circle clockwise, the angle becomes larger. If I move the gray circle counter-clockwise, the angle becomes smaller. Demonstrate how to rotate the gray circle in both directions. Keep the white circle stationary, and use one hand to gently hold the two pieces together. Use the thumb of your other hand to gently push the gray circle clockwise and then counter-clockwise. Also give your child a chance a few minutes to explore rotating the Degree Wheel.

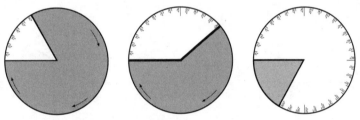

As you push the gray circle clockwise, you'll form a larger angle
between the two dark lines and see more of the white circle below.

From this point forward, you and your child will use the Degree Wheel to show angles with a measure of 180° or less. To save space, the illustrations will only show the top half of the Degree Wheel.

Rotate the gray circle to form a 40° angle. **What is the measure of this angle?** *40 degrees.* Repeat with 70°, 90°, 120°, and 170° angles and have your child tell the measure of each angle.

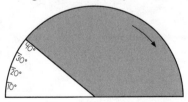

Move the gray circle to form a 130° angle. *Child rotates gray wheel to form a 130° angle.* Have your child also use the Degree Wheel to create 60°, 110°, 140°, and 180° angles.

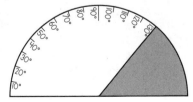

Activity (A): Measure Angles with the Degree Wheel

The angles on the Lesson Activities page are 180 degrees or less, so only the top half of the Degree Wheel is printed. What is the measure of angle 1? *50 degrees.* **Write "50" in the blank.**

Point to the degree symbol. **This little circle is the degree symbol.** Point to the m. **This little m stands for measure. To read the whole equation, we say:** *The measure of angle 1 equals 50 degrees.*

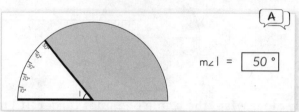

Have your child use the printed Degree Wheels to find the measures of ∠2 and ∠3. Make sure he writes the degree sign for each measurement. Have him read each equation aloud after he completes it: *The measure of angle 2 equals 110 degrees. The measure of angle 3 equals 150 degrees.*

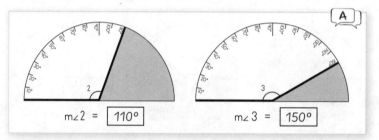

Activity (B): Estimate Angle Measures with the Degree Wheel

We can also use the Degree Wheel to estimate angles' measures. Move the Degree Wheel to make an angle that looks like angle A. *Child moves the Degree Wheel to match ∠A.*

What do you estimate is the measure of angle A? *Answers will vary.* Write your child's estimate in the chart. **The actual measure of angle A is 30 degrees.** Discuss how close your child's estimate is to the actual measure.

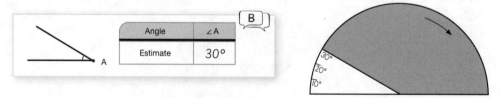

Sample matching approximate angle on degree wheel and estimate.
Your child's angle and estimate may be different.

Don't worry if your child's estimates aren't very accurate. He'll learn to estimate angles' measures more accurately as he gains more experience with degrees.

Repeat for ∠B and ∠C. Discuss how your child's estimates compare to the actual measures for the angles: **Angle B's actual measure is 130 degrees. Angle C's actual measure is 90 degrees. Angle C is a right angle, like the corner of a square. Right angles always have a measure of 90 degrees.**

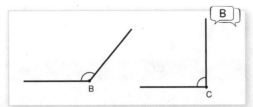

For Angle D, let's tilt the page to make it easier to estimate with the Degree Wheel. Turn the page clockwise so that one side of the angle is horizontal and the angle opens to the left. Have your child model the angle on the Degree Wheel and estimate its measure. **Angle D's actual measure is 70 degrees.**

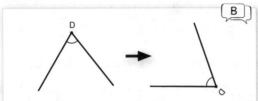

Let's tilt the page for angle E, too. Have your child tilt the page to make one side of ∠E horizontal. Then, have him model the angle on the Degree Wheel and estimate its measure. **Angle E's actual measure is 90 degrees, just like angle C! It's just tilted in a different direction.**

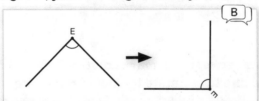

In Angle F, the two lines meet to create a straight line. We call angles like this one *straight angles.* Have your child model ∠F with the Degree Wheel and estimate its measure. **Angle F's actual measure is 180 degrees. Straight angles always measure 180 degrees.**

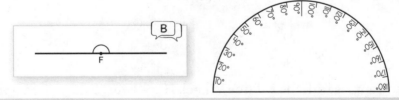

Your child will learn more about straight angles (as well as acute, obtuse, and right angles) in the next lesson.

Independent Practice and Review

Have your child complete the Lesson 8.2 Practice and Review workbook pages.

Lesson 8.3
Acute, Right, Obtuse, and Straight Angles

Purpose	Materials
• Measure angles with the Degree Wheel • Identify acute, right, obtuse, and straight angles	• Degree Wheel (Blackline Master 5) • Counters • Die

Memory Work	• **How many cups equal 1 pint?** *2.* • **How many pints equal 1 quart?** *2.* • **How many quarts equal 1 gallon?** *4.*

Warm-up: Measure Angles with the Degree Wheel

Rotate the gray circle on the Degree Wheel to form a 20° angle. **What is the measure of this angle?** *20 degrees.* Repeat with 60°, 90°, 100°, and 160° angles.

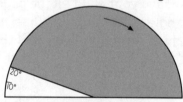

When the side of the angle is between the marks on the Degree Wheel, you can use what you know about the number line to estimate its measure. Rotate the gray circle so that the dark line is halfway between the 40° and 50° mark. **The side of the angle is halfway between 40 degrees and 50 degrees. What number is halfway between 40 and 50 on the number line?** *45.* **So, this angle measures about 45 degrees.**

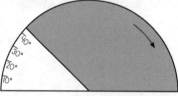

Make the following angles with the Degree Wheel. Have your child estimate the measure of each angle. Accept any reasonable answer.

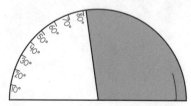

About 82°.

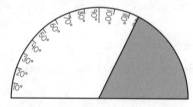

About 117°.

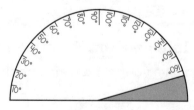

About 163°.

Activity (A): Introduce Acute, Right, Obtuse, and Straight Angles

Mathematicians classify angles based on their measures. Today, you'll learn the names for four different types of angles.

Right angles measure 90 degrees. Have your child create a 90° angle with the Degree Wheel. Point to the small square in the corner of the printed angle. **This square means that the angle is a right angle.**

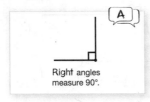   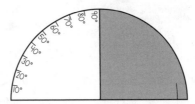

Acute angles measure less than 90 degrees. Any angle less than 90 degrees is an acute angle. Have your child rotate the Degree Wheel to approximately match the printed acute angle.

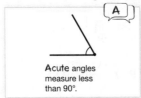   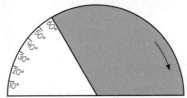

Obtuse angles measure greater than 90 degrees and less than 180 degrees. Any angle greater than 90 degrees and less than 180 degrees is an obtuse angle. Have your child rotate the Degree Wheel to match the printed obtuse angle.

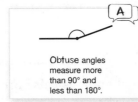   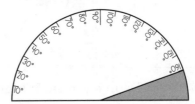

Straight angles measure 180 degrees. Have your child rotate the Degree Wheel to match the printed straight angle.

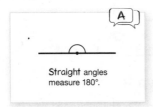   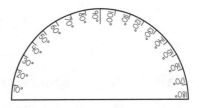

Activity: Show Acute, Right, Obtuse, and Straight Angles with the Degree Wheel

Make the smallest angle possible with the Degree Wheel. **Which type of angle is this?** *Acute.* Gradually rotate the gray circle clockwise. Stop just before you reach 90°. **All of these angles are acute angles.**

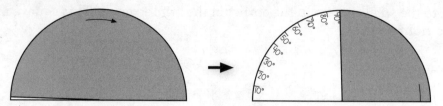

Make a 90° angle with the Degree Wheel. **Which type of angle is this?** *Right.*

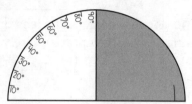

Rotate the Degree Wheel slightly past 90°. **Which type of angle is this?** *Obtuse.* Gradually rotate the gray circle clockwise. Stop just before you reach 180°. **All of these angles are obtuse angles.**

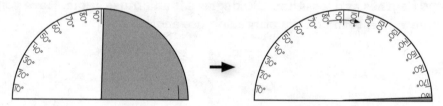

Make a 180° angle with the Degree Wheel. **Which type of angle is this?** *Straight.*

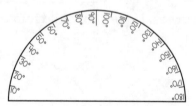

Activity (B): Prepare to Play Angle Four in a Row

Show your child the Angle Four in a Row game board. **In this game, we'll take turns rolling a die and placing a counter on an angle that matches the roll.**

Sometimes, it can be hard to identify angles when they're turned in different directions. It helps to compare the angle to a right angle. If the angle is open wider than a right angle, it's obtuse. If the angle is open less than a right angle, it's acute. Point to several angles on the page and have your child tell whether the angle is acute, right, obtuse, or straight.

Activity (B): Play Angle Four in a Row

Play Angle Four in a Row.

Angle Four in a Row

Materials: Counters of two different colors; die

Object of the Game: Be the first player to place counters in 4 squares in a row, either horizontally, vertically, or diagonally.

Give 12 counters of one color to Player 1. Give 12 counters of another color to Player 2.

On your turn, roll the die. Use the key to see what type of angle you can cover. For example, if you roll a 4, you can cover any straight angle on the game board. Cover that type of angle with one of your counters.

If you roll a 4, cover any straight angle.

If you roll a 6, you may remove one of your opponent's counters. If you roll a number and all the matching angles are already covered, you lose your turn and do not place a new counter.

Play then passes to the other player. Continue until one player covers 4 boxes in a row, either horizontally, vertically, or diagonally.

Answer Key:

Angle Four in a Row B

Independent Practice and Review

Have your child complete the Lesson 8.3 Practice and Review workbook pages.

Lesson 8.4
Measure Angles with a Protractor

Purpose	Materials
• Practice creating and identifying acute, right, obtuse, and straight angles • Measure angles with a protractor • Extend angles' sides in order to accurately measure the angle	• Degree Wheel (Blackline Master 5) • Protractor

Memory Work	
	• **What do we call an angle with a measure less than 90 degrees?** *Acute.* • **What do we call an angle with a measure equal to 90 degrees?** *Right.* • **What do we call an angle with a measure greater than 90 degrees and less than 180 degrees?** *Obtuse.* • **What do we call an angle with a measure equal to 180 degrees?** *Straight.*

Warm-up: Play "Simon Says" with Angles

In the last lesson, you learned about acute, right, obtuse, and straight angles. Make each of the following angles with the Degree Wheel and have your child tell whether it is acute, right, obtuse, or straight.

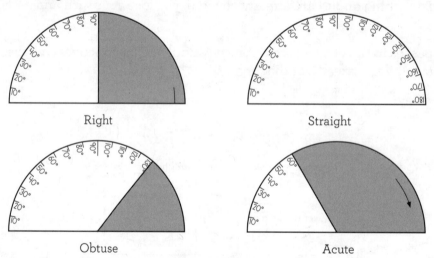

Right   Straight

Obtuse   Acute

Let's play Simon Says with angles. If I say "Simon says" first, make the angle with the Degree Wheel. But if I don't say "Simon says," don't make the angle.

- **Simon says make an acute angle.** *Child makes an acute angle with the Degree Wheel.* Any angle measure less than 90° is fine.
- **Simon says make a right angle.** *Child makes a right angle with the Degree Wheel.*
- **Make a straight angle.** *Child doesn't move.*

Repeat 8-10 times with different types of angles. Keep the game fun and fast-paced.

If your child doesn't enjoy Simon Says, challenge him to make the angles as fast as possible instead.

Activity (A): Introduce Measuring Angles with a Printed Protractor

Today, you'll learn how to use a protractor to measure angles. A protractor is a bit like a curved ruler. But instead of measuring in inches or centimeters, it measures in degrees!

This printed protractor is lined up on top of the angle so we can measure it. Point to the midpoint. **This is the protractor's midpoint. When we measure an angle, we put the angle's vertex here.**

Point to the zero line (the line that connects the two 0° marks on either side of the protractor). **This is the protractor's zero line. When we measure an angle, we line up one side of the angle with the zero line.**

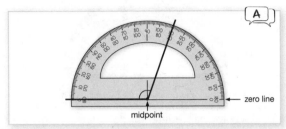

Point to the numbers and tick marks along the edge of the protractor. **After we line up one side of the angle with the zero line, we find where the other side intersects these numbers and tick marks. The numbers and tick marks are the scale. They tell us the angle's measure. The protractor is labeled every 10 degrees, and each tick mark stands for 1 degree.**

The tricky part of using a protractor is that protractors have two scales. This angle intersects one scale at 110 degrees and the other scale at 70 degrees. We have to decide which scale to use.

One way to tell is to use estimation. Is this angle acute, right, or obtuse? *Obtuse.* **Obtuse angles have a measure greater than 90 degrees, so this angle couldn't measure 70 degrees. It must measure 110 degrees.**

Another way is to look for where the bottom side of the angle intersects the scale. The bottom side of the angle touches the 0-degree mark of the scale on the left side of the protractor. So, we use the scale that starts with zero on the left side. Point to the 0° mark on the left side of the protractor.

I move my finger along the scale from the 0-degree mark until it reaches the place where the other side of the angle intersects this scale. Point to the 0-degree mark and sweep your finger along the scale until you reach the other side of the angle. **The other side of the angle intersects this scale at the 110-degree mark. So, this angle measures 110 degrees, not 70 degrees.**

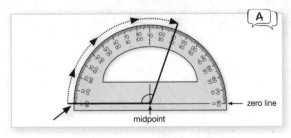

Activity (B): Measure Angles with a Real Protractor

Show your child a real protractor. Have him find the protractor's midpoint and zero line. If your protractor has numbers and tick marks for measuring inches or centimeters, point them out. **These numbers and tick marks are for measuring inches and centimeters, not degrees. We'll ignore them when we measure angles.**

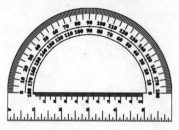

Ignore the inch and centimeter marks when measuring angles.

Let's use the protractor to measure angle 1. We'll follow these steps.

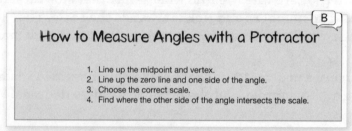

How to Measure Angles with a Protractor

1. Line up the midpoint and vertex.
2. Line up the zero line and one side of the angle.
3. Choose the correct scale.
4. Find where the other side of the angle intersects the scale.

The first step is: *Line up the midpoint and vertex.* **Make sure you put the vertex right in the center of the midpoint.** *Child places the protractor's midpoint on top of the vertex.*

The second step is: *Line up the zero line and one side of the angle.* **Make sure to keep the vertex lined up with the midpoint.** *Child aligns protractor's zero line with angle's bottom side.*

The third step is: *Choose the correct scale.* **Which scale should we use?** *Child points to scale whose 0-degree mark is aligned with the bottom side of the angle.* **The bottom side of the angle touches the 0-degree mark of the scale on the right side of the protractor. So, we use the scale that starts with zero on the right side.** Point to the 0° mark on the right side of the protractor.

The last step is: *Find where the other side of the angle intersects the scale.* **What is the angle's measurement?** *30 degrees.* If your child isn't sure, have him point to the 0-degree mark and sweep his finger along the scale until he reaches the other side of the angle.

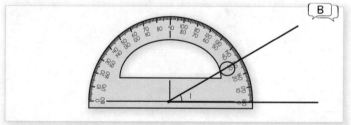

Angle 1's side intersects the other scale at the 150-degree mark. Why wouldn't it make sense for this angle to measure 150 degrees? *Sample answer: It's an acute angle, not an obtuse angle.* **When you use a protractor to measure an angle, always stop and think about whether the measurement makes sense. If you get a number more than 90 degrees for an acute angle, or if you get a measurement less than 90 degrees for an obtuse angle, you're probably using the wrong scale!**

Have your child measure ∠2 in the same way. **The side of this angle intersects the scale halfway between 60 and 70 degrees. What number is halfway between 60 and 70 on the number line?** *65.* **So, this angle measures 65 degrees.**

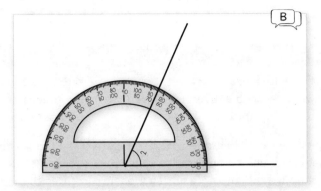

Align the protractor on ∠3. **Angle 3's side doesn't reach all the way to the scale. We need to extend the side so we can measure it correctly.**

Demonstrate how to align the straight edge of the protractor along this side of the angle. Draw a line along the protractor to extend the side. Then, have your child use the protractor to measure the angle. He should find that ∠3 measures 105°.

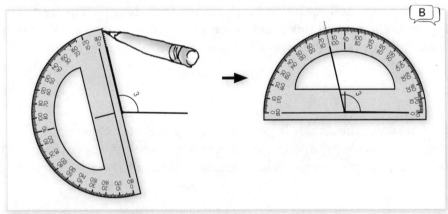

You do not need to extend the bottom side of the angle, since you can align it with the protractor's zero line no matter how long it is.

Have your child measure ∠4 with the protractor. (He may need to extend one side.) He should find that the angle measures 120°.

Independent Practice and Review

Have your child complete the Lesson 8.4 Practice and Review workbook pages.

Lesson 8.5
Draw Angles with a Protractor

Purpose	Materials
• Practice measuring angles with a protractor • Use a protractor to draw angles with a given measure • Introduce the concept of adding angles	• Protractor • 2 pieces of paper • Paper clip

Memory Work	• **What do we call an angle with a measure less than 90 degrees?** *Acute.* • **What do we call an angle with a measure equal to 90 degrees?** *Right.* • **What do we call an angle with a measure greater than 90 degrees and less than 180 degrees?** *Obtuse.* • **What do we call an angle with a measure equal to 180 degrees?** *Straight.*

Warm-up (A): Practice Measuring Angles to the Nearest Degree with a Protractor

In the last lesson, you learned how to measure angles with a protractor. Point to the part of the protractor shown below, from 30 degrees to 40 degrees. **The protractor is labeled in increments of 10 degrees, and each tick mark stands for 1 degree. The first tick mark after 30 is for 31 degrees. The second tick mark is for 32 degrees, and so on. Can you point to the tick mark for 39 degrees? 35 degrees? 36 degrees?** *Child points to matching tick marks.*

Have your child measure the angles in part A with a protractor. She should find the first angle measures approximately 37° and the second angle measures approximately 113°. **Which angle is acute?** *The 37-degree angle.* **Which angle is obtuse?** *The 113-degree angle.*

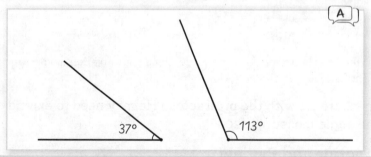

Accept any answer within several degrees of the given measure. Slight shifts in the protractor can quickly cause the measurements to be off.

Activity (B): Draw Angles with a Protractor

Today, you'll learn how to draw angles with a protractor. First, we'll draw a 155-degree angle. Will this angle be acute, right, obtuse, or straight? *Obtuse.* **We'll use the printed line for one of its sides and the marked point for its vertex.**

Using the marked point for the vertex ensures that the angles fit on the page. As you draw this angle, it may look like it overlaps the space for the next angle. The next angle is quite small, so both will fit.

First, we need to line up the protractor, just like we do to measure angles. Demonstrate how to place the protractor on the page. Make sure to align the protractor's midpoint with the vertex (the marked point) and the protractor's zero line with the printed line.

Next, we choose the correct scale and draw a point at the correct measure. The bottom side of the angle touches the zero-degree mark on the left side of the protractor, so we'll use the scale where the zero mark is on the left. Point to the correct 0° mark. Sweep your finger along the numbers until you reach the 155-degree mark. Draw a point at this spot.

Last, we connect the point and the vertex with a straight line. Use the edge of the protractor to draw a straight line connecting the point and vertex.

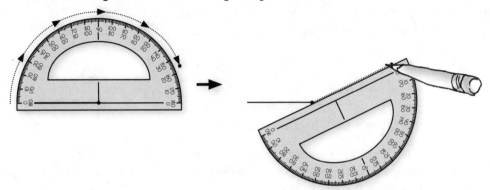

Have your child draw a 15° angle in the remaining space in part B. Have her use the printed line for one of the angle's sides and the marked point for its vertex.

Activity (C): Play Race to 180°

What do we call 180° angles? *Straight angles.* **What do straight angles look like?** *A straight line.*

We're going to play a game called Race to 180°. In this game, we'll add angles next to each together and add to find the total measure of all the angles. The first person to create a straight angle and reach 180° wins!

Make sure to draw the angles (and not just add their measures) so that your child gets more practice at drawing angles with a protractor. Your child will learn more about adding angles in Lessons 8.6 and 8.7.

Race to 180°

Materials: 2 pieces of paper, paper clip, protractor, ruler (optional)

Object of the Game: Be the first player to draw an angle with a total measure greater than or equal to 180°.

Give each player a piece of paper. Before beginning the game, each player orients their paper horizontally and draws a dot in the bottom middle as shown. Then, each player uses a ruler or protractor edge to draw a straight line from the dot toward the right edge of the paper.

Each player needs a piece of paper with a dot and straight line as shown.

Directions continued on next page.

Place one end of the paper clip in the middle of the spinner. Place the point of a pencil through the paper clip so that it touches the very middle of the circle.

On your turn, hold the pencil upright and spin the paper clip so that it spins freely around the circle. Draw an angle with this measure on your paper. For example, if you spin 35° for your first turn, draw a 35° angle on your paper. Use the point you marked for the vertex, and use the horizontal line you drew for one side of the angle. Label the angle measure, and record your angle's measure (35°) in the first line of your score card.

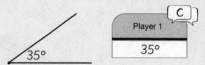

The other player then takes a turn in the same way.

On your following turns, spin the paper clip. Add an angle with this measure to the previous angle you drew. Use the marked point for the vertex. Use the line you drew **during your previous turn** for one of the sides.

Add the new angle measure to your previous score. Record the running total of your angle measures on your score card. For example, if you spin 35° for your first turn and 20° for your second turn:

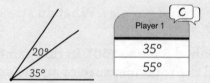

Continue in this way until one player has a total angle measure greater than or equal to 180°. The first player to do so wins.

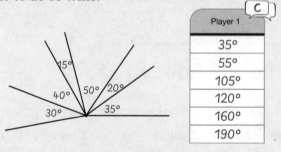

Sample final drawing and scorecard.

Cooperative variation: Play the game together and keep track of how many rounds it takes for you to reach 180°. Then, play a second time and see if you can reach 180° in fewer rounds.

Independent Practice and Review

Have your child complete the Lesson 8.5 Practice and Review workbook pages.

Lesson 8.6
Add Angles with Pattern Blocks

Purpose	Materials
• Practice drawing angles with a protractor • Understand that you can add angles and their measures • Understand that there are multiple ways to split an angle into smaller angles	• Protractor • Pattern blocks

| Memory Work | • **What do we call an angle with a measure equal to 180 degrees?** *Straight.*
• **What do we call an angle with a measure equal to 90 degrees?** *Right.*
• **What do we call an angle with a measure less than 90 degrees?** *Acute.*
• **What do we call an angle with a measure greater than 90 degrees and less than 180 degrees?** *Obtuse.* |

In this lesson, your child will put pattern blocks together to concretely add angles. He'll add angles more abstractly in the next lesson.

Warm-up: Draw Angles with a Protractor

Have your child use a protractor to draw the following angles on scrap paper: 25°, 60°, 125°, 90°. After your child draws each angle, have him tell whether it is acute, right, obtuse, or straight.

Activity (A): Use Pattern Blocks to Add Angles

In the last few lessons, you've learned how to measure angles with a protractor. Today, you'll learn how to add angles and use logical reasoning to find angles' measures without a protractor.

This chart shows the size of the angles in some of the pattern blocks. We'll use these pattern blocks to measure angles today.

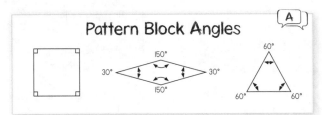

Pattern Block Angles

What do the little squares in the corner of the square pattern block mean? *The angles measure 90 degrees. They are right angles.* **Which of the labeled angles has the greatest measure?** *The 150-degree angle.* **Which of the labeled angles has the smallest measure?** *The 30-degree angle.*

Place a small pile of squares, narrow diamonds, and triangles on the table. You won't need the other types of pattern blocks.

Place a square and narrow diamond inside ∠A as shown. **The square's angle measures 90 degrees. The narrow diamond's angle measures 30 degrees. So, what must angle A measure?** *120 degrees.* If your child's not sure, suggest he add 90 plus 30. Write "90 + 30 = 120" in the Equations box. Write 120° in the blank. Then, have your child measure the angle with a protractor to check.

I wonder how many ways we could put pattern blocks inside angle A to show that it equals 120 degrees. Have your child experiment with the pattern blocks and find several other ways to fill in the 120° angle. Have him write an addition equation to match each arrangement.

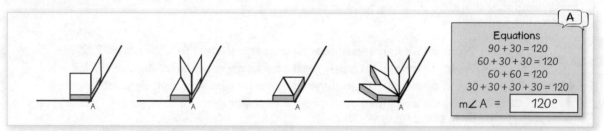

All possible ways to create a 120° angle with the available pattern block angles.

Your child does not need to rearrange the numbers in the equations in multiple ways. For example, if he writes 60 + 30 + 30, he does not need to also write 30 + 60 + 30 and 30 + 30 + 60.

Repeat for ∠B and ∠C. Have your child find several different ways to fill each angle with the available pattern blocks and write an addition equation to match each arrangement. He does not need to find every possible way to fill each angle.

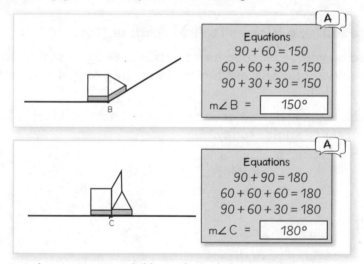

Sample answers. Your child may find other ways to fill the angles.

For ∠B, have your child use a protractor to check that he found the correct measure. For ∠C, ask: **How can you be sure that angle C is 180° without measuring it?** *Angle C is a straight angle, so it must measure 180°.*

Independent Practice and Review

Have your child complete the Lesson 8.6 Practice and Review workbook pages.

The purple triangle on the Practice page is not a standard pattern block. It is included to give your child experience with reasoning about 45° angles. These angles are created any time you cut a square along a diagonal, so they often come up in real-life contexts.

Lesson 8.7
Add and Subtract Angles

Purpose	Materials
• Practice estimating angle measures • Add or subtract angles to find the measure of unknown angles • Solve angle puzzles with right angles and straight angles	• Degree Wheel (Blackline Master 5) • Colored pencils or markers

| Memory Work | • **What do we call an angle with a measure equal to 180 degrees?** *Straight.*
• **What do we call an angle with a measure equal to 90 degrees?** *Right.*
• **What do we call an angle with a measure greater than 90 degrees and less than 180 degrees?** *Obtuse.*
• **What do we call an angle with a measure less than 90 degrees?** *Acute.* |

Warm-up: Estimate Angles with the Degree Wheel

Use a marker or colored pencil to quickly shade the back of the white circle (with the degree marks) from your Degree Wheel.

Shading the back of the Degree Wheel allows your child to better see the angles it forms when you flip the Degree Wheel in this activity.

Assemble the Degree Wheel as usual. Secretly make a 75° angle. Then, flip the Degree Wheel and show your child the back only. Have her trace the non-shaded part of the wheel with her finger. **What's your estimate for this degree's measure?** *Answers will vary.*

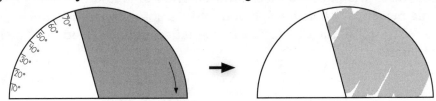

Show your child the back of the Degree Wheel so that she can estimate the secret angle.

Flip the Degree Wheel to the front (without rotating either circle) so your child can see the degree markings. **What's the exact measure for this angle?** *75°.* Briefly discuss how your child's estimate compares to the actual measure.

Repeat with the following angles: 120°, 180°, 170°, 90°, 45°, 10°.

Activity (A): Add and Subtract to Solve Angle Puzzles

You've learned a lot about angles in this unit! Today, you'll use what you've learned to solve angle puzzles. In the puzzles, some of the angles are marked. Your job is to use the marked angles to figure out the measure of the unknown angle.

In the first puzzle, two angles are put together to make a larger angle. You want to find the measure of this larger angle.

- Trace the 40° angle with a marker or colored pencil. **This angle measures 40°.**
- Trace the 30° angle with a different marker or colored pencil. **This angle measures 30°.**
- Trace the large angle with a different marker or colored pencil. **So, what must the measure of this larger angle be?** *70 degrees.* If your child's not sure, suggest she add 30 plus 40. Write 70° in the blank.

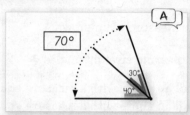

Tracing the angles with different colors makes it easier to see the relationships between the angles. If your child can easily see the angle relationships, she does not need to trace the angles before solving the puzzles.

Have your child find the unknown angle in the next puzzle in the same way. Remind her as needed that the small square symbol means that the angle measures 90°. **What is the measure of the unknown angle?** *120°.* **How do you know?** *Sample answer: 30 plus 90 equals 120.*

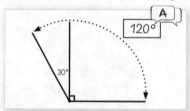

In the next puzzle, you know the measure of the largest angle and the measure of one of the smaller angles. You want to find the measure of the other smaller angle.

- Trace the 80° angle with a marker or colored pencil. **This angle measures 80°.**
- Trace the labeled 40° angle with a different marker or colored pencil. **This angle measures 40°.**
- Trace the unknown angle with a different marker or colored pencil. **So, what must this angle measure?** *40 degrees.* If your child's not sure, suggest she subtract 40 from 80. Write 40° in the blank. **The two smaller angles are equal. The larger angle is split in half.**

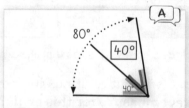

Have your child find the unknown angle in the next puzzle in the same way. **What is the measure of the unknown angle?** *20°.* **How do you know?** *Sample answer: 110 minus 90 equals 20.*

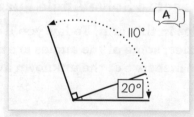

Activity (B): Solve Angle Puzzles with Right Angles and Straight Angles

In the next puzzle, two angles are put together to make a right angle. What is the measure of a right angle? *90 degrees.* **How can you find the measure of the unknown angle?** *Subtract 45 from 90.* **What's the measure of the unknown angle?** *45 degrees.* **Write 45° in the blank. This right angle is split in half.**

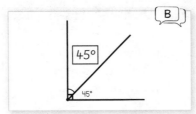

In the next puzzle, two angles are put together to make a straight angle. What is the measure of a straight angle? *180 degrees.* **How can you find the measure of the unknown angle?** *Subtract 100 from 180.* **What's the measure of the unknown angle?** *80 degrees.* **Write 80° in the blank.**

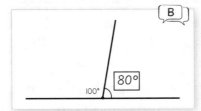

Activity (C): Make Your Own Angle Puzzles

Now, you get to make two angle puzzles for me to solve. Have your child draw a straight line that splits the right angle into two smaller angles. Have her use a protractor to measure and label one of the smaller angles.

Subtract the angle measure from 90° to find the measure of the unknown angle. For example: **Hmm, you drew a 32° angle. 90 minus 32 equals 58, so the unknown angle must measure 58 degrees.** Use a protractor to measure the unknown angle and confirm your answer.

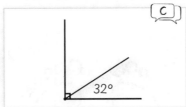

Sample puzzle. The unknown angle must equal 58°, since 90 – 32 = 58.

Repeat with the straight angle.

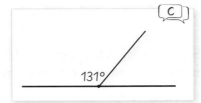

Sample puzzle. The unknown angle must equal 49°, since 180 – 131 = 49.

Independent Practice and Review

Have your child complete the Lesson 8.7 Practice and Review workbook pages.

Lesson 8.8
Enrichment (Optional)

Purpose	Materials
• Practice memory work • Understand degrees in the context of following directions • Turn a given number of degrees to reach a secret object • Summarize what your child has learned and assess your child's progress	• *Sir Cumference and the Great Knight of Angleland*, written by Cindy Neuschwander and illustrated by Wayne Geehan • 2 pencils

Warm-up: Review Memory Work

Quiz your child on all memory work through Unit 8. See pages 536-537 for the full list.

Math Picture Book: *Sir Cumference and the Great Knight of Angleland*

Read *Sir Cumference and the Great Knight of Angleland*, written by Cindy Neuschwander and illustrated by Wayne Geehan. As you read, discuss the different angles that the knight makes as he pursues his quest.

Enrichment Activity: Describe Turns with Degrees to Find the Secret Object

In this unit, we've used degrees to measure angles formed by two lines. We can also use degrees to measure turns.

Have your child stand. **The direction you're facing is like the zero-line on the protractor. I'll put a pencil on the floor to mark this direction.** Place a pencil on the floor in front of your child's feet. Align the pencil's tip so that it points in the same direction as his feet.

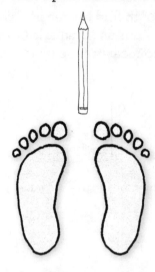

Give your child another pencil. Have him hold the pencil in front of him, directly above the other pencil. **We'll use this pencil to help see how far you turn.**

Turn to the right until the two pencils make a 90-degree angle. *Child turns 90 degrees to the right.* **You just turned 90 degrees to the right.**

Have your child return to the starting position (so the two pencils are aligned again). **This time, turn to the left until the two pencils make an angle that's about 45 degrees.** *Child turns 45 degrees to the left.* **You just turned 45 degrees to the left.**

Accept any reasonable approximation for 45 degrees. If your child's not sure how far to turn, encourage him to use logical thinking to approximate the turn: **45 degrees is half of 90, so turn half as far as you did to make a 90-degree angle.**

Repeat with the following directions. Have your child return to the starting position (with the pencils aligned) before you give each direction.

- **Turn 75 degrees to the right.** *Child turns 75° to the right.*
- **Turn 180 degrees to the right.** *Child turns 180° to the right (so that he makes a half-turn and ends up facing the opposite direction).*
- **Turn 10 degrees to the left.** *Child turns 10° to the left.* **10 degrees is a pretty small turn!**
- **Turn 100 degrees to the left.** *Child turns 100° to the left.* If your child isn't sure how far to turn, say: **100 degrees is a little more than 90 degrees, so you should turn a little more than 90 degrees.**
- **Turn 360 degrees to the left.** *Child turns 360° to the left (so that he makes one full turn and ends up facing the same direction again).* If your child isn't sure how far to turn, say: **Think about the Degree Wheel. How many degrees equal one full turn?** *360.* **When you turn 360 degrees, you make one full turn.**

Now, I'm going to choose something in the room and give you directions for how to get to it. See if you can figure out which object I choose! Secretly choose an item in the room. Give your child directions (like the ones in the previous activity) that guide him to the secret object. Once your child arrives, have him guess which object you chose. Sample directions:

- **Turn 90 degrees to the left.**
- **Take 2 steps forward.**
- **Turn 30 degrees to the left.**
- **Take 3 steps forward.**
- **Turn 50 degrees to the right.**
- **Take 1 step forward.**
- **You've arrived! Can you guess which object I chose?**

Repeat this activity several times, choosing a different secret object each time. Then, switch roles: have your child choose a secret object and direct you to it.

Unit Wrap-Up

Have your child complete the Unit 8 Wrap-Up.

Unit 8 Answer Key

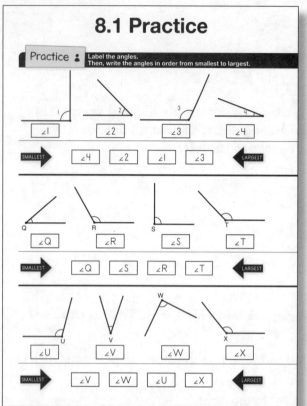

8.1 Practice

Practice : Label the angles.
Then, write the angles in order from smallest to largest.

∠1 ∠2 ∠3 ∠4

SMALLEST → ∠4 ∠2 ∠1 ∠3 ← LARGEST

∠Q ∠R ∠S ∠T

SMALLEST → ∠Q ∠S ∠R ∠T ← LARGEST

∠U ∠V ∠W ∠X

SMALLEST → ∠V ∠W ∠U ∠X ← LARGEST

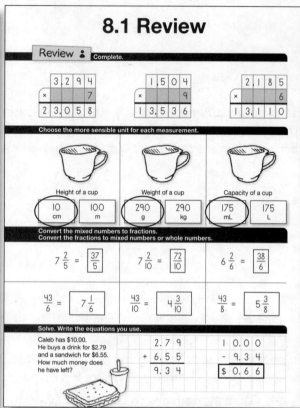

8.1 Review

Review : Complete.

	3,	2	9	4
×				7
2	3,	0	5	8

	1,	5	0	4
×				9
1	3,	5	3	6

	2,	1	8	5
×				6
1	3,	1	1	0

Choose the more sensible unit for each measurement.

Height of a cup: (10 cm) 100 m

Weight of a cup: (290 g) 290 kg

Capacity of a cup: (175 mL) 175 L

Convert the mixed numbers to fractions.
Convert the fractions to mixed numbers or whole numbers.

$7\frac{2}{5} = \frac{37}{5}$ $7\frac{2}{10} = \frac{72}{10}$ $6\frac{2}{6} = \frac{38}{6}$

$\frac{43}{6} = 7\frac{1}{6}$ $\frac{43}{10} = 4\frac{3}{10}$ $\frac{43}{8} = 5\frac{3}{8}$

Solve. Write the equations you use.

Caleb has $10.00.
He buys a drink for $2.79
and a sandwich for $6.55.
How much money does
he have left?

	2.	7	9
+	6.	5	5
	9.	3	4

	1	0.	0	0
−		9.	3	4
	$	0.	6	6

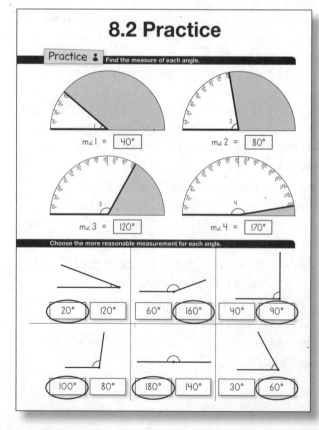

8.2 Practice

Practice : Find the measure of each angle.

m∠1 = 40°   m∠2 = 80°

m∠3 = 120°   m∠4 = 170°

Choose the more reasonable measurement for each angle.

(20°) 120°

60° (160°)

40° (90°)

(100°) 80°

(180°) 140°

30° (60°)

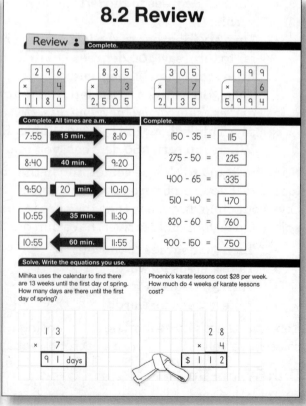

8.2 Review

Review : Complete.

	2	9	6
×			4
1,	1	8	4

	8	3	5
×			3
2,	5	0	5

	3	0	5
×			7
2,	1	3	5

	9	9	9
×			6
5,	9	9	4

Complete. All times are a.m.

7:55 → 15 min. → 8:10

8:40 → 40 min. → 9:20

9:50 → 20 min. → 10:10

10:55 ← 35 min. ← 11:30

10:55 ← 60 min. ← 11:55

Complete.

150 − 35 = 115

275 − 50 = 225

400 − 65 = 335

510 − 40 = 470

820 − 60 = 760

900 − 150 = 750

Solve. Write the equations you use.

Mihika uses the calendar to find there
are 13 weeks until the first day of spring.
How many days are there until the first
day of spring?

	1	3
×		7
9	1	days

Phoenix's karate lessons cost $28 per week.
How much do 4 weeks of karate lessons
cost?

	2	8
×		4
$	1	1	2

Unit 8 Answer Key

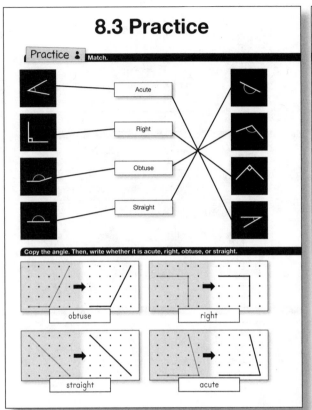

8.3 Practice

Practice Match.

Acute
Right
Obtuse
Straight

Copy the angle. Then, write whether it is acute, right, obtuse, or straight.

obtuse

right

straight

acute

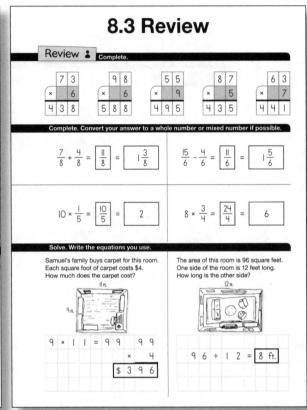

8.3 Review

Review Complete.

	7	3
×		6
4	3	8

	9	8
×		6
5	8	8

	5	5
×		9
4	9	5

	8	7
×		5
4	3	5

	6	3
×		7
4	4	1

Complete. Convert your answer to a whole number or mixed number if possible.

$$\frac{7}{8} + \frac{4}{8} = \boxed{\frac{11}{8}} = \boxed{1\frac{3}{8}}$$

$$\frac{15}{6} - \frac{4}{6} = \boxed{\frac{11}{6}} = \boxed{1\frac{5}{6}}$$

$$10 \times \frac{1}{5} = \boxed{\frac{10}{5}} = \boxed{2}$$

$$8 \times \frac{3}{4} = \boxed{\frac{24}{4}} = \boxed{6}$$

Solve. Write the equations you use.

Samuel's family buys carpet for this room. Each square foot of carpet costs $4. How much does the carpet cost?

11 ft.

9 ft.

$9 \times 11 = 99$

		9	9
×			4
$	3	9	6

The area of this room is 96 square feet. One side of the room is 12 feet long. How long is the other side?

12 ft.

$9 6 \div 1 2 = \boxed{8 \text{ ft.}}$

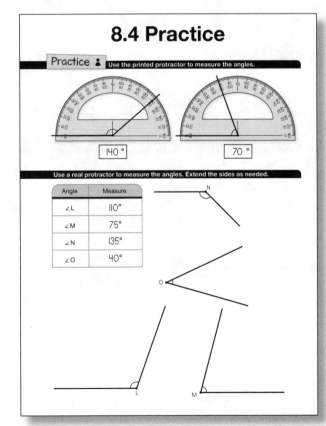

8.4 Practice

Practice Use the printed protractor to measure the angles.

$\boxed{140}$ °

$\boxed{70}$ °

Use a real protractor to measure the angles. Extend the sides as needed.

Angle	Measure
∠L	110°
∠M	75°
∠N	135°
∠O	40°

N

O

L

M

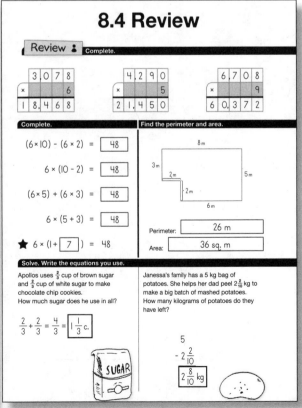

8.4 Review

Review Complete.

	3,	0	7	8
×				6
1	8,	4	6	8

	4,	2	9	0
×				5
2	1,	4	5	0

	6,	7	0	8
×				9
6	0,	3	7	2

Complete.

$$(6 \times 10) - (6 \times 2) = \boxed{48}$$

$$6 \times (10 - 2) = \boxed{48}$$

$$(6 \times 5) + (6 \times 3) = \boxed{48}$$

$$6 \times (5 + 3) = \boxed{48}$$

★ $6 \times (1 + \boxed{7}) = 48$

Find the perimeter and area.

8 m

3 m

2 m

2 m

5 m

6 m

Perimeter: $\boxed{26 \text{ m}}$

Area: $\boxed{36 \text{ sq. m}}$

Solve. Write the equations you use.

Apollos uses $\frac{2}{3}$ cup of brown sugar and $\frac{2}{3}$ cup of white sugar to make chocolate chip cookies. How much sugar does he use in all?

$$\frac{2}{3} + \frac{2}{3} = \frac{4}{3} = \boxed{1\frac{1}{3} \text{ c.}}$$

SUGAR

Janessa's family has a 5 kg bag of potatoes. She helps her dad peel $2\frac{2}{10}$ kg to make a big batch of mashed potatoes. How many kilograms of potatoes do they have left?

$$\begin{array}{r} 5 \\ - 2\frac{2}{10} \\ \hline \boxed{2\frac{8}{10} \text{ kg}} \end{array}$$

Unit 8 Answer Key

8.5 Practice

Practice : Use a protractor to draw an angle with the given measure. Use the printed line for one side. Use the dot for the vertex.

80°   35°

140°   105°

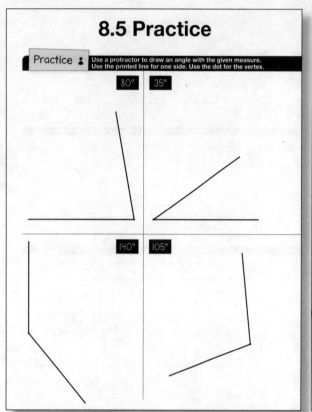

8.5 Review

Review : Complete. Follow the steps.

1. Divide
2. Multiply
3. Subtract

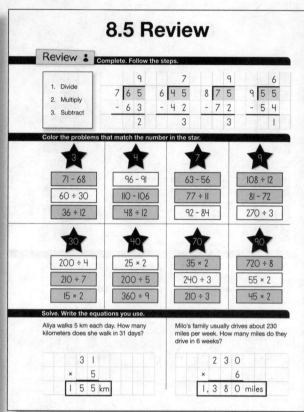

Color the problems that match the number in the star.

★ 3	★ 4	★ 7	★ 9
71 - 68	96 - 91	63 - 56	108 ÷ 12
60 ÷ 30	110 - 106	77 ÷ 11	81 - 72
36 ÷ 12	48 ÷ 12	92 - 84	270 ÷ 3

★ 30	★ 40	★ 70	★ 90
200 ÷ 4	25 × 2	35 × 2	720 ÷ 8
210 ÷ 7	200 ÷ 5	240 ÷ 3	55 × 2
15 × 2	360 ÷ 9	210 ÷ 3	45 × 2

Solve. Write the equations you use.

Aliya walks 5 km each day. How many kilometers does she walk in 31 days?

```
    3 1
  ×   5
  1 5 5 km
```

Milo's family usually drives about 230 miles per week. How many miles do they drive in 6 weeks?

```
    2 3 0
  ×     6
  1, 3 8 0 miles
```

8.6 Practice

Practice : Use the labeled angles to find the missing angle measures.

45°   60°   30°

m∠ F = 75°

m∠ G = 90°

m∠ H = 105°

m∠ I = 105°

m∠ J = 135°

m∠ K = 180°

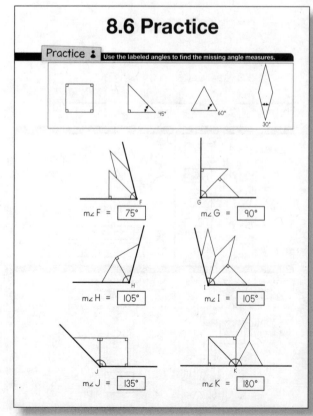

8.6 Review

Review : Complete.

```
    8 4 5      9 3 7      8 2 5      7 0 7
  ×     7    ×     4    ×     8    ×     7
  5, 9 1 5    3, 7 4 8    6, 6 0 0    4, 9 4 9
```

Write whether each angle is acute, right, obtuse, or straight.

obtuse

acute

straight

right

Circle the prime numbers. X the composite numbers.

⊠ ⊠ ⑰ ⊠
⑲ ⊠ ⊠ ⊠
㉓ ⊠ ⊠ ⊠
⊠ ⊠ ㉙ ⊠

Solve. Write the equations you use.

Evie sews together 5 pieces of fabric to make a blanket. Each piece of fabric is 30 in. long and 8 in. wide. What is the total area of the blanket?

8 in.
30 in.

```
    3 0        2 4 0
  ×   8      ×     5
  2 4 0      1, 2 0 0 sq. in.
```

Eliana's backyard is shaped like a square. Each side is 76 feet long. What is the perimeter of her yard?

76 ft.

```
      7 6
  ×     4
  3 0 4 ft.
```

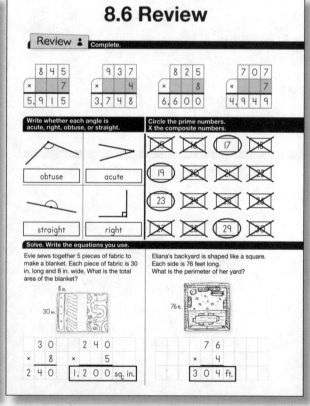

Unit 8 Answer Key

8.7 Practice

Practice 👤 Find the missing angle measures.

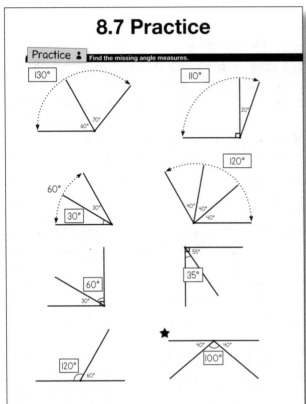

8.7 Review

Review 👤 Complete.

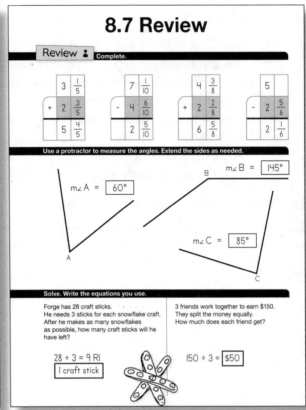

8.8 Unit Wrap-Up A

Unit Wrap-Up 👤 Choose the more reasonable measurement for each angle.

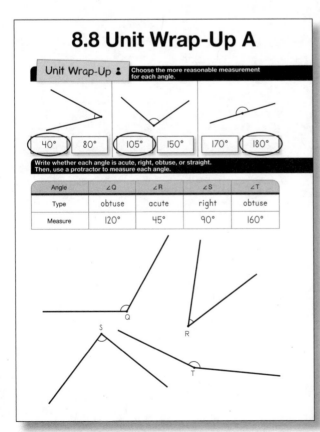

8.8 Unit Wrap-Up B

Unit Wrap-Up 👤 Use a protractor to draw an angle with the given measure. Use the printed line for one side. Use the dot for the vertex.

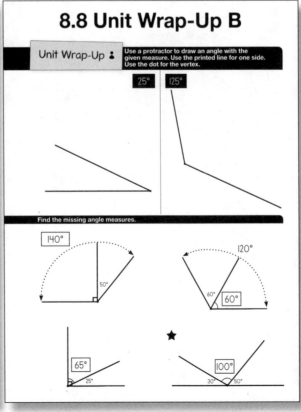

Unit 8 Checkpoint

What to Expect at the End of Unit 8

By the end of Unit 8, most children will be able to do the following:

- Estimate angle measures in degrees with a reasonable level of accuracy. Most children will be able to estimate angles' measures within about 20°.
- Identify acute, right, obtuse, and straight angles. Some children will still be working on memorizing these terms.
- Correctly align a protractor to measure angles or draw angles with a given measure. Many children will occasionally use the wrong scale when using a protractor.
- Add or subtract angle measures to find the measure of an unknown angle.

Is Your Child Ready to Move on?

In Unit 9, your child will learn how to convert length units and solve problems involving compound length units. Your child does not need to have mastered any specific skills before moving on to Unit 9.

Unit 9
Length

Overview

Your child will learn how to convert length units within both the U.S. customary system (inches, feet, yards, and miles) and within the metric system (millimeters, centimeters, meters, and kilometers). She'll learn how to add and subtract compound units, and she'll also learn how to solve two-step length word problems that require conversions.

What Your Child Will Learn

In this unit, your child will learn to:

- Convert length measurements within the U.S. customary system (inches, feet, yards, and miles)
- Add and subtract feet and inches
- Convert length measurements within the metric system (millimeters, centimeters, meters, and kilometers)
- Measure with a ruler in centimeters and millimeters
- Add and subtract compound units in the metric system
- Solve two-step word problems that involve converting units

Lesson List

Lesson 9.1	Feet and Inches	Lesson 9.6	Millimeters and Centimeters
Lesson 9.2	Add Feet and Inches	Lesson 9.7	Meters
Lesson 9.3	Subtract Feet and Inches	Lesson 9.8	Kilometers
Lesson 9.4	Yards and Miles	Lesson 9.9	Add and Subtract Metric Units
Lesson 9.5	Two-Step Word Problems with Feet and Inches	Lesson 9.10	Two-Step Word Problems with Metric Length Units
		Lesson 9.11	Enrichment (Optional)

Extra Materials Needed for Unit 9

- Tape measure marked in feet and inches (at least 10 feet long)
- 2 slips of paper
- 2 paper clips
- Colored pencils or markers
- Tape measure marked in meters and centimeters, or knowledge of your child's height (in either meters and centimeters or feet and inches)
- For optional Enrichment Lesson:
    - *Millions to Measure*, written by David M. Schwartz and illustrated by Steven Kellogg. HarperCollins, 2003.
    - Cardboard strip, about 1 in. wide and 3 ft. long (or 3 cm wide and 1 m long)
    - Scissors

Note for Families that Use the Metric System

This unit is split into two parts. The first part focuses on the U.S. customary system, while the second part focuses on the metric system. If your family uses the metric system as your main measurement system, teach the metric system lessons first (Lessons 9.6 through 9.10). Then, go back to the beginning of the unit and teach the lessons on the U.S. customary system (Lessons 9.1 through 9.5). Even if your child rarely encounters the U.S. customary system in everyday life, the lessons will reinforce important concepts and stretch her skills as she works with a less-familiar measurement system.

Teaching Math with Confidence:
How to Help Your Child Make Sense of Measurement Conversions

In this unit, your child will learn to convert length measurements to different units and solve problems that involve adding, subtracting, multiplying, or dividing lengths. She'll first study the measurement system that's more familiar to her (either the U.S. customary system or the metric system). Once she's learned how to convert measurements and solve problems within the more-familiar system, she'll revisit these skills with the less-familiar system.

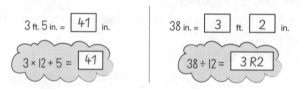

Sample measurement conversions.

Children sometimes feel overwhelmed by the variety of different units that we use to measure length. If your child struggles with the measurement conversions in this unit, use these tips to help her make sense of them:

- Keep the measurement equivalencies on the Memory Work page (Blackline Master 1) available for your child to refer to as she completes the lessons. Even if she has already memorized these equivalencies, she may temporarily forget them when confronted with so many different units of measurement.

- If your child gives you a nonsensical answer when converting measurements, give her a concrete sense of the length involved. For example: **We want to convert 53 millimeters to centimeters. One millimeter is tiny, so 53 millimeters is a very small length. It's about as long as my pinky. It definitely couldn't be equal to 530 centimeters!** Often, just remembering the physical meaning of a measurement is enough to help a child make sense of a problem.

- If your child has trouble deciding whether to multiply or divide when converting measurements, help her identify whether she's converting from a whole unit to part of a unit (for example, feet to inches) or whether she's converting from part of a unit to a whole unit (for example, centimeters to meters). Then, help her use the rhyme she learned in Unit 4 to decide whether to multiply or divide. **Whole to parts, multiply to start! Parts to whole, division's in control!** You'll review this rhyme and teach your child how to apply it to measurement conversions in Lessons 9.1 and 9.6.

Lesson 9.1
Feet and Inches

Purpose	Materials
• Review feet and inches with a tape measure • Convert feet to inches • Convert inches to feet	• Tape measure marked in feet and inches • 1-foot ruler • Die • Counters

Memory Work	• **How many inches equal 1 foot?** *12.* • **How many feet equal 1 yard?** *3.* • **How many inches equal 1 yard?** *36.*

If your family uses the metric system, teach the metric system lessons first (Lessons 9.6 through 9.10). Then, come back to this lesson and teach the lessons on the U.S. customary system (Lessons 9.1 through 9.5).

Warm-up: Use a Tape Measure to Measure in Feet and Inches

We're starting a new unit on length today. In this lesson and the next few lessons, we'll study U.S. customary units, like inches, feet, yards, and miles. These units are used in the United States, and sometimes in the United Kingdom and Canada. Today, you'll learn how to convert feet and inches.

Show your child a tape measure marked in feet and inches. **Tape measures are very helpful when we measure lengths that are longer than a foot.** Briefly discuss a few ways you have used a tape measure. For example: **When I bought a new rug, I used a tape measure to measure the floor to see whether the rug would fit. I used a tape measure to measure the wood when I built the fence.**

Extend the tape measure about 5 feet. If you have a metal tape measure, lock the tape into place. Point out the foot-marks and inch-marks on the tape measure. Help your child to find the following markings on the tape measure:

- 2 feet
- 4 feet
- 4 inches

- 36 inches
- 38 inches

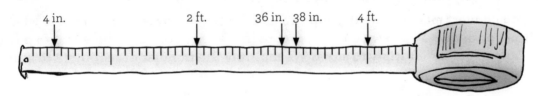

If you have a metal tape measure, demonstrate how to unlock the tape and hold the end of the tape as it retracts. Tape measures' edges are a little sharp, so it's important to pull the tape out slowly and hold the end of the tape as it goes back into the case.

Activity (A): Convert Feet to Inches and Inches to Feet

Cora and Liam had a jumping contest. Cora measured her jump in feet and inches, and Liam measured his jump in inches.

Cora jumped 3 feet 5 inches. Let's convert Cora's jump to inches so we can see who jumped farther. 3 feet equal 3 groups of 12 inches. So, we multiply 3 times 12 to find how many inches are in 3 feet. Then, we add on the extra 5 inches. What's 3 times 12? *36.* Plus 5? *41.* So, 3 feet 5 inches equal 41 inches. Write 41 in both blanks.

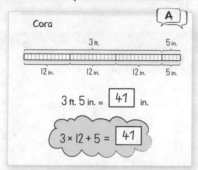

Who jumped farther, Cora or Liam? *Cora.* How much farther did Cora jump than Liam? *3 inches.* How do you know? *Sample answer: 41 minus 38 equals 3.*

Liam measured his jump in inches. Another way to compare the jumps is to convert his jump to feet and inches. Every group of 12 inches equals 1 foot. So, we can divide 38 by 12 to find how many whole feet Liam jumped.

How many groups of 12 can you make from 38 inches? *3.* How many inches are left over? *2.* Write "3 R2" in the division equation blank. So, 38 inches equal 3 feet 2 inches. Write 3 and 2 as shown.

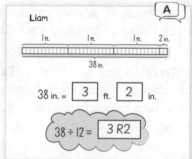

Liam jumped 3 feet 2 inches, and Cora jumped 3 feet 5 inches. No matter which units we use, Cora jumped 3 inches farther than Liam. Have your child find the length of both jumps on the tape measure to confirm that 3 feet 5 inches is 3 inches longer than 38 inches.

In Unit 4, you learned a rhyme to help you remember whether to multiply or divide when you convert mixed numbers to fractions and fractions to mixed numbers. It went: *Whole to parts? Multiply to start! Parts to whole? Division's in control!*

When you convert measurements, you can use the same rhyme to help decide whether to multiply or divide. When we convert feet to inches, we convert whole feet to parts of feet. *Whole to parts? Multiply to start!* We multiply the number of feet by 12 to start the conversion.

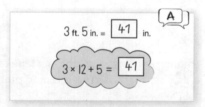

Whole to parts? Multiply to start.

When we convert inches to feet, we convert parts of feet to whole feet. *Parts to whole? Division's in control!* **We divide the number of inches by 12.**

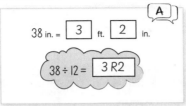

38 in. = [3] ft. [2] in.

38 ÷ 12 = [3 R2]

Parts to whole? Division's in control!

See the Unit 9 **Teaching Math with Confidence** for more tips on helping your child convert measurements.

Have your child complete the measurement conversions in part A. Encourage her to use the first problem in each pair to help solve the second one.

2 ft. = [24] in.   36 in. = [3] ft.

2 ft. 10 in. = [34] in.   37 in. = [3] ft. [1] in.

Activity (B): Play Length Three in a Row

Play Length Three in a Row.

If you own transparent counters, use them for this game (so you can see the numbers under the counters).

Length Three in a Row

Materials: Die, counters of two colors

Object of the Game: Be the first player to place 3 counters in a row (horizontally, vertically, or diagonally) in the spaces in the center of the game board.

Have each player choose a different-colored counter to use as a game token and place it on one of the Start squares.

On your turn, roll the die and advance your token the corresponding number of squares clockwise around the path. If you land on a space with feet (or feet and inches), convert the measure to inches. If you land on a space with inches, convert the measure to feet (or feet and inches). Place one of your counters on the corresponding square in the middle of the game board. For example, if you land on 1 ft. 4 in. place a counter on 16 in. If you land on 51 in., place a counter on 4 ft. 3 in.

If your opponent already has a counter on the matching square, remove your opponent's counter and replace it with your counter. If you land on one of the start squares, roll again.

Play until one player covers three squares in a row, either horizontally, vertically, or diagonally.

Independent Practice and Review

Have your child complete the Lesson 9.1 Practice and Review workbook pages.

Lesson 9.2
Add Feet and Inches

Purpose	Materials
• Convert feet and inches with a tape measure • Practice converting feet and inches • Add feet and inches	• Tape measure marked in feet and inches (at least 10 feet long) • 2 slips of paper

Memory Work	• **How many inches equal 1 foot?** *12.* • **How many feet equal 1 yard?** *3.* • **How many inches equal 1 yard?** *36.*

For the hands-on activity in this lesson, you will need a tape measure marked in feet and inches, with a minimum length of 10 feet. You will also need at least 10 feet of floor space and enough room to safely throw a small wad of paper. If you don't have a tape measure or enough room, see the game description for an alternative way to play.

Warm-up: Convert Feet and Inches with a Tape Measure

In the last lesson, you learned how to convert feet and inches. Extend a tape measure approximately 4 feet and lock the tape into place. Have your child find the following measurements on the tape measure. Then, have him convert the measurement to feet and inches.

- **15 inches.** *1 foot 3 inches.*
- **26 inches.** *2 feet 2 inches.*
- **39 inches.** *3 feet 3 inches.*

This activity previews the regrouping your child will do when adding lengths.

Activity (A): Add Feet and Inches

Today, you'll learn how to add feet and inches. We'll add feet and inches to play a game called Paper Toss later in the lesson. On your turn, you'll throw two wads of paper and add the two measurements to find your total distance. Whoever has the longer total distance in each round wins the round.

First, I'll show you how to add feet and inches so you're ready to play Paper Toss. Show your child part A. **This person tossed one paper wad 3 feet 10 inches and the other paper wad 2 feet 7 inches. We'll add the lengths to find the total distance of both throws.**

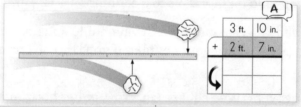

If your child immediately finds the answer mentally, demonstrate how to solve the problem with the written process anyway. Ask him to use the written process to solve the problems in the Lesson Activities so that he's familiar with it, but allow him to use whichever method makes more sense to him when he solves problems on the Practice page.

Adding measurements is a lot like adding whole numbers. First, we add the smaller units. What's 10 inches plus 7 inches? *17 inches.* **Write "17 in." as shown. Next, we add the larger units. What's 3 feet plus 2 feet?** *5 feet.* **Write "5 ft." as shown.**

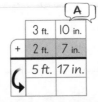

Now, we check whether we can trade any of the smaller units for larger units. Do we have enough inches to trade some for feet? *Yes.* **How many feet and inches can I make from 17 inches?** *1 foot 5 inches.*

5 feet plus 1 foot 5 inches equals 6 feet 5 inches. **Write "6 ft. 5 in." in the second box below the problem.**

	A	
	3 ft.	10 in.
+	2 ft.	7 in.
	5 ft.	17 in.
	6 ft.	5 in.

The second box below the problem is there in case you need to trade after you add. If you don't need to trade, leave it blank. Have your child solve the other problems in the same way.

	2 ft.	9 in.		3 ft.	8 in.			6 ft.	5 in.
+	5 ft.	4 in.	+	3 ft.	4 in.	+	7 ft.	2 in.
	7 ft.	13 in.		6 ft.	12 in.		13 ft.	7 in.
	8 ft.	1 in.		7 ft.				

How is adding feet and inches like adding whole numbers? *Sample answers: You start at the right. You add the inches and then the feet. You trade if you need to.*

How is adding feet and inches different from adding whole numbers? *Sample answers: You add feet and inches instead of tens and ones. When you trade, you trade inches for feet instead of trading tens and ones. You trade after you finish the adding instead of in the middle of the problem.*

Activity (B): Play Paper Toss

Play Paper Toss.

This activity works best if you use a small slip of light paper and crumple it loosely. A 2- inch-by-2-inch sticky note or square of regular copy paper works well. Make sure your child throws the wad of paper over-hand, not underhand, so that the wad is less likely to slide a long distance on the floor.

Paper Toss

Materials: Tape measure marked in feet and inches, at least 10 feet long; 2 small slips of paper (each about 2 inches by 2 inches)

Object of the Game: Win the most points.

Lay a measuring tape on the floor. Extend the measuring tape at least 10 feet. (15 feet is ideal.) Take 2 small slips of paper and crumple each into a loose ball.

Paper Toss is played in 3 rounds. On your turn, stand behind the zero-mark on the tape measure. Throw one paper wad overhand in the same direction as the tape measure. Then, throw the other paper wad in the same way. Find the point on the tape measure closest to where each paper wad lands. Write these measurements in your next blank addition problem. Add the two measurements to find the total length of both throws.

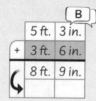

Then, have the other player take a turn in the same way. Whoever has the greater total length for that round wins a point.

Play two more rounds in the same way. Whoever wins more points wins the game.

Variation for families that don't have a long measuring tape or enough space: Write the following distances on separate slips of paper and place them in a bowl. On your turn, draw 2 slips of paper from the bowl. Use the distances on the slips as the addends in your addition problem. Return the slips to the bowl before you draw again.

- 8 ft. 3 in.
- 6 ft. 2 in.
- 7 ft. 11 in.
- 5 ft. 4 in.
- 9 ft. 8 in.

- 10 ft. 9 in.
- 8 ft. 7 in.
- 9 ft. 6 in.
- 7 ft. 5 in.
- 6 ft. 10 in.

Independent Practice and Review

Have your child complete the Lesson 9.2 Practice and Review workbook pages.

Lesson 9.3
Subtract Feet and Inches

Purpose	Materials
• Use a tape measure to measure height in feet and inches • Subtract feet and inches • Subtract to find differences between heights	• Tape measure marked in feet and inches

Memory Work
- **How many inches equal 1 foot?** *12.*
- **How many feet equal 1 yard?** *3.*
- **How many inches equal 1 yard?** *36.*

Warm-up (A): Measure Heights in Feet and Inches

Later in the lesson, we'll use subtraction to find the difference between the heights of people in our family. Have your child stand against a wall. Use a tape measure to measure her height in feet and inches. Record her name and height in the first row of the chart. Record your own name and height in the chart as well.

Have your child choose two more family members or friends to add to the chart. Approximate their height as best you can and write it in the chart. (Or, if the people your child chooses are in your home, measure their heights with the tape measure.)

A

Name	Height (Feet and Inches)
Emily	4 ft. 1 in.
Mom	5 ft. 8 in.
Dad	6 ft. 1 in.
George	4 ft. 10 in.

Sample completed chart.

If you don't own a tape measure that measures in feet and inches, approximate the heights instead. If you know the heights in centimeters only, use a calculator to divide each height by 2.54 to find the equivalent number of inches. Then, divide the result by 12 to find the height in feet and inches.

Activity (B): Subtract Feet and Inches

In the last lesson, you learned how to add feet and inches. Today, you'll learn how to subtract feet and inches. Read the word problem aloud.

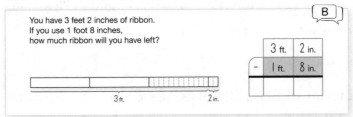

You have 3 feet 2 inches of ribbon.
If you use 1 foot 8 inches,
how much ribbon will you have left?

Subtracting measurements is a lot like subtracting whole numbers. First, we look at the inches and check that we have enough inches to subtract. Point to the inches column. **Can we subtract 8 inches from 2 inches?** *No.* **Before we subtract, we need to trade to get more inches.**

1 foot equals 12 inches. So, we can trade 1 foot for 12 inches and add the 12 inches to the 2 inches we already have. What's 12 inches plus 2 inches? *14 inches.* Draw a bracket and label it as shown.

Here's how we record the trade. We traded 1 foot for inches, so we only have 2 feet left. Cross out 3 ft. and write "2 ft." above it. **We added 12 inches to the 2 inches we already had. Now, we have 14 inches.** Cross out 2 in. and write "14 in." above it.

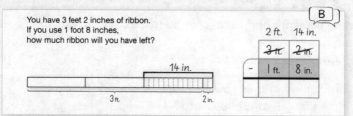

Is 2 feet 14 inches really the same length as 3 feet 2 inches? *Yes.* **How do you know?** *Sample answer: 14 inches is 1 foot 2 inches. If I add that to 2 feet, I get 3 feet 2 inches.* **Trading 1 foot for 12 inches is like trading 1 ten for 10 ones. You don't change the amount. You just express it in a different way.**

Now, we're ready to subtract. What's 14 inches minus 8 inches? *6 inches.* Write "6 in." as shown. **What's 2 feet minus 1 foot?** *1 foot.* Write "1 ft." as shown.

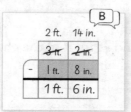

Have your child solve the rest of the subtraction problems in the same way. Help her as needed, especially with the trading.

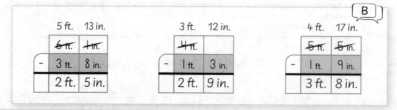

> If your child has trouble with the trading, draw a simple diagram for each problem (as in the sample problem) to help her visualize and record the trades.

How is subtracting feet and inches like subtracting whole numbers? *Sample answers: You start at the right. You subtract the inches and then the feet. You trade if you need to.*

How is subtracting feet and inches different from subtracting whole numbers? *Sample answers: You subtract feet and inches instead of tens and ones. When you trade, you trade feet for inches instead of trading tens for ones.*

> This process is also very similar to the process your child learned in Unit 4 for subtracting mixed numbers.

Activity (C): Subtract to Find Differences Between Heights

Let's subtract to find the differences between some of the heights we recorded in the warm-up activity. Have your child choose two heights from the chart in part A. Have her write both heights in the first blank subtraction problem. Make sure she writes the taller height on the top line of the problem.

Then, have her subtract to find the difference between the two heights. Discuss the meaning of the answer. For example: **I'm 1 foot 7 inches taller than you right now.** Repeat with two other pairs of heights. Your child can compare her height to the other people or choose to compare two of the other people's heights.

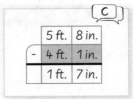

Sample subtraction problem to compare two heights. Use the heights from the chart in part A.

Independent Practice and Review

Have your child complete the Lesson 9.3 Practice and Review workbook pages.

Lesson 9.4
Yards and Miles

Purpose	Materials
• Review benchmarks for yards and miles • Convert yards to feet • Convert feet to yards • Convert miles to feet	• 2 paper clips • Counters

Memory Work	
	• **How many inches equal 1 foot?** *12.* • **How many feet equal 1 yard?** *3.* • **How many inches equal 1 yard?** *36.*

Warm-up: Review Yards and Miles

In the last few lessons, you have learned about feet and inches. Today, you'll learn about yards and miles.

Use your hands to show me how long a yard is. *Child holds his hands about one yard (or 3 feet) apart.* **1 yard equals 3 feet. A yard is about as long as a baseball bat, or about as wide as a doorway.**

5,280 feet equal 1 mile. You'll memorize the number of feet in a mile as part of your memory work. Briefly discuss a few familiar trips to give your child a sense of the length of a mile. For example: **The bike path by the creek is 3 miles long. The grocery store is about 1 mile away.**

If your family doesn't use the U.S. customary system in daily life, tell your child how each unit compares to a more-familiar unit from the metric system: **One yard is a little shorter than one meter. A kilometer is a little more than half a mile.**

Activity (A): Convert Yards to Feet and Feet to Yards

Sam and Liza both threw a football. Sam measured the length of his throw in yards, and Liza measured the length of her throw in feet.

Sam threw the football 8 yards. 8 yards equal 8 groups of 3 feet, so we multiply 8 times 3. What's 8 times 3? *24. 8 yards equal 24 feet.* Write 24 in both blanks.

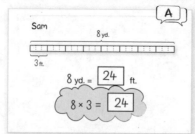

We could also use the rhyme to help remember to multiply. When we convert yards to feet, we convert yards to parts of yards. *Whole to parts? Multiply to start!* **We multiply the number of yards by 3.**

Liza threw the football 21 feet. Who threw the football farther, Sam or Liza? *Sam.* **How much farther did Sam throw the football than Liza?** *3 feet.* **How do you know?** *Sample answer: 24 minus 21 equals 3.*

Liza measured her throw in feet. Another way to compare the throws is to convert her throw to yards. Every group of 3 feet equals 1 yard. So, we can divide 21 by 3 to find how many yards Liza threw the football.

What's 21 divided by 3? *7.* **So, 21 feet equal 7 yards.** Write 7 in both blanks.

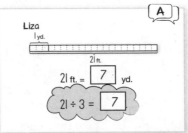

We could also use the rhyme to help remember to multiply. When we convert feet to yards, we convert parts of yards to yards. *Parts to whole? Division's in control!* We divide the number of feet by 3.

Activity (B): Play Measurement War

We're going to use these spinners to play Measurement War in a minute. Each of us will spin one spinner. Whoever's spinner shows the greater measurement will win counters.

Before we play, we need to finish the spinners. To make the game fair, both spinners need to have the same measurements. Point to 4 yd. on the left-hand spinner. **4 yards equal how many feet?** *12.* Write 12 in the blank on the corresponding space on the other spinner. Repeat with the other blanks.

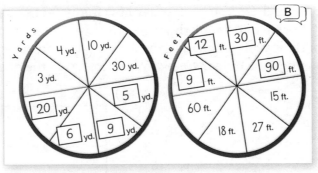

Completed spinners.

Measurement War

Materials: Counters of two colors; 2 paper clips

Object of the Game: Win the most counters.

Give 5 counters of one color to Player 1. Give 5 counters of another color to Player 2.

Measurement War has 5 rounds. At the beginning of each round, both players place a counter in the middle of the table.

Then, Player 1 places one end of a paper clip in the middle of the spinner labeled in yards. He places a pencil through the paper clip so that it touches the middle and spins the paper clip. Player 2 does the same on the spinner labeled in feet.

Directions continued on next page.

Have your child decide which player's spinner shows a longer distance. The player whose spinner shows a longer distance wins both counters and places them in his "Won" pile. If the distances are the same, leave both counters on the table and spin again until one player wins them. Counters in the "Won" pile are now out of the game and cannot be used again.

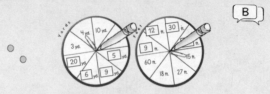

The player who spun 15 ft. wins both counters, since 15 ft. is longer than 4 yd.

Play until both players use up their original pile of counters. Whoever has more counters in their "Won" pile wins the game.

Activity (C): Convert Miles to Feet

This map shows the length of the hiking trails at a park. Briefly discuss your child's experiences with hiking or trail maps. **We'll use this map to take a pretend hike today.**

We start at the parking lot. We first hike to Stillwater Pond, and then we hike to Forest Falls for a snack. Have your child trace the route on the map with his finger. **How far have we hiked?** *2 miles*. Write 2 in the chart as shown. **Let's figure out how many feet equal 2 miles.**

Cover the map with your hand. **Do you remember how many feet equal 1 mile?** *5,280*. **Each mile equals 5,280 feet. So, we multiply 2 times 5,280 to find how many feet equal 2 miles.** Write the matching multiplication problem in the work space and have your child solve the problem. **How many feet equal 2 miles?** *10,560*. Write 10,560 in the chart as shown.

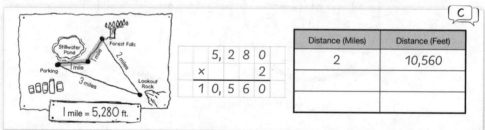

After Forest Falls, we hike to Lookout Rock and have lunch. How far have we hiked now? *4 miles*. Have your child write and solve a multiplication problem to find how many feet equal 4 miles. **How many feet equal 4 miles?** *21,220*. Write 4 and 21,220 in the next line of the chart.

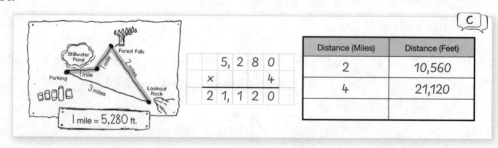

Time to head home! After Lookout Rock, we hike back to the parking lot. How far have we hiked now? *7 miles.* Have your child write and solve a multiplication problem to find how many feet equal 7 miles. **How many feet equal 7 miles?** *36,960.* Write 7 and 36,960 in the next line of the chart. **That was a long hike. Time for a rest!**

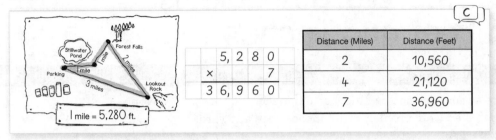

$$\begin{array}{r} 5{,}2\,8\,0 \\ \times\qquad 7 \\ \hline 3\,6{,}9\,6\,0 \end{array}$$

Distance (Miles)	Distance (Feet)
2	10,560
4	21,120
7	36,960

1 mile = 5,280 ft.

Independent Practice and Review

Have your child complete the Lesson 9.4 Practice and Review workbook pages.

Lesson 9.5
Two-Step Word Problems with Feet and Inches

Purpose	Materials
• Practice adding and subtracting feet and inches • Solve two-step word problems with inches, feet, and yards	• None

Memory Work	• **How many inches equal 1 foot?** *12.* • **How many feet equal 1 yard?** *3.* • **How many inches equal 1 yard?** *36.* • **How many feet equal 1 mile?** *5,280.*

The word problems in this lesson all require two steps. In each problem, your child will need to convert a measurement as well as add, subtract, multiply, or divide. Adjust your level of support to match your child's needs. Some children may be able to solve these problems with little help, while others will need a lot of coaching.

Warm-up (A): Practice Adding and Subtracting Feet and Inches

Have your child complete the addition and subtraction problems. Guide her as needed with the trading.

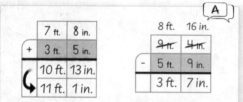

Activity (B): Solve Two-Step Word Problems at the Craft Store Help Desk

In the last few lessons, you've learned how to convert measurements and add and subtract them. Today, we'll pretend you work at a Craft Store Help Desk. You'll use what you've learned about measurement to answer the customers' questions about their craft projects. **I'll pretend to be the customers.** Briefly discuss your child's experiences with craft stores.

The customers all have different questions, so you'll need to solve each problem in a different way. It's okay if you don't see how to solve a problem right away and need to take a few minutes to figure out how to solve it.

Read aloud the first question as if you were a customer at the craft store. **What's the goal?** *Find how much ribbon the customer has.* **What unit are we supposed to use for our answer?** *Feet.* **What information do we know?** *There are 4 yards of striped ribbon and 8 feet of solid-colored ribbon.* Underline "4 yards" and "8 feet" in the word problem.

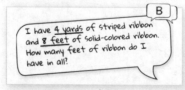

Underlining the measurements encourages your child to think about their units and not simply add 4 plus 8.

Some kids might read this problem and say the answer is 12, because 8 plus 4 equals 12. Why isn't that correct? *Sample answer: The 8 and 4 don't have the same units.* **We want the final answer to be in feet, so let's start by converting the yards to feet.**

4 yards equal how many feet? *12.* Write "4 yd. = 12 ft." **So, we add 12 plus 8 to find the total number of feet.** Write "12 ft. + 8 ft. =" Have your child complete the equation and label and box the final answer. **How many feet of ribbon does the customer have?** *20 feet.*

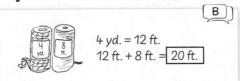

Read aloud the next question as if you were a different customer. **What's the goal?** *Find how many more inches the customer needs to knit.* **What unit are we supposed to use for our answer?** *Inches.* **What information do we know?** *The scarf is 18 inches so far. The person wants it to be 5 feet long.* Underline "18 inches" and "5 feet" in the problem.

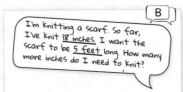

We want the final answer to be in inches, so let's start by converting the feet to inches. 5 feet equal how many inches? *60.* Write "5 ft. = 60 in." **So, we subtract 60 minus 18 to find how many inches the customer still needs to knit.** Write "60 in. – 18 in. =" Have your child complete the equation and label and box the final answer. **How many more inches does the customer need to knit?** *42 inches.*

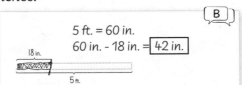

Read aloud the next question. **What's the goal?** *Find the perimeter of the picture frame in feet and inches.* **What unit are we supposed to use for our answer?** *Feet and inches.* **What information do we know?** *Each side is 16 inches.* Underline "16 inches" in the problem.

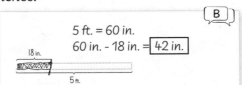

How can we find the perimeter? *Multiply the length of each side times 4.* **It's easier to multiply inches than feet and inches. So, let's find the perimeter of the picture frame in inches and then convert the perimeter to feet and inches.** Have your child multiply 16 × 4 to find the perimeter of the picture frame in inches. Then, have her convert the perimeter from inches to feet and inches.

Read aloud the final question. **What's the goal?** *Find the length of each piece of string.* **What unit are we supposed to use for our answer?** *Inches.* **What information do we know?** *The person has 3 feet of string.* Underline "4 equal pieces" and "3 feet" in the word problem.

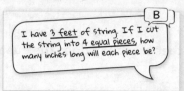

We want to find our answer in inches, so let's convert 3 feet to inches before dividing. **3 feet equal how many inches?** *36.* Write "3 ft. = 36 in." **So, we divide 36 inches by 4 to find the length of each piece in inches.** Write "36 ÷ 4 =" Have your child complete the equation and label and box the final answer. **How many inches long will each piece be?** *9 inches.*

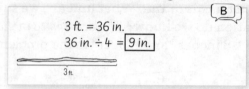

Independent Practice and Review

Have your child complete the Lesson 9.5 Practice and Review workbook pages.

Lesson 9.6
Millimeters and Centimeters

Purpose	Materials
• Review benchmarks for metric units • Introduce millimeters • Convert millimeters to centimeters and centimeters to millimeters • Draw and measure lines in centimeters and millimeters	• 30-cm (1-foot) ruler • Colored pencils or markers

Memory Work	
	• **How many feet equal 1 mile?** *5,280.* • **How many centimeters equal 1 meter?** *100.* • **How many meters equal 1 kilometer?** *1,000.*

If your family uses the metric system, teach Lessons 9.6 through 9.10 (on the metric system) before you teach Lessons 9.1 through 9.5 (on the U.S. customary system). The memory work in these lessons includes the number of feet in a mile. Briefly explain to your child that a mile equals about 1 2/3 kilometers. Then, help him memorize the number of feet in 1 mile as part of his memory work. He will use it when you teach him more about miles in Lesson 9.4.

Warm-up: Review Metric Units

In the last few lessons, you studied inches, feet, yards, and miles. These units are used in the United States, and sometimes in the United Kingdom and Canada. But in most of the world, people use a measurement system called the metric system. In the next few lessons, you'll study metric units of length.

In younger grades, you learned about centimeters, meters, and kilometers.

- Have your child hold his thumb and forefinger about one centimeter apart. **A centimeter is about as wide as your pinky finger, or as long as a ladybug.**
- Have your child hold his hands about one meter apart. **100 centimeters equal 1 meter. Refrigerators are usually about a meter wide, and kitchen chairs are often about a meter high.**
- **1,000 meters equal 1 kilometer.** Tell your child the length of some familiar distances in kilometers. For example: **The bike race that I did was 30 kilometers long. Uncle Charlie and Aunt Louise live about 100 kilometers away.**

If your family doesn't use the metric system in daily life, tell your child how each metric unit compares to a more-familiar unit from the U.S. customary system:

- **One centimeter is a little shorter than half an inch.**
- **A meter is a little longer than a yard.**
- **A kilometer is a little longer than half of a mile.**

Activity (A): Convert Millimeters and Centimeters

Today, you'll learn about a new metric length unit: millimeters. Point out the millimeter marks on the printed ruler. **Each centimeter is split into 10 equal parts. We call these units *millimeters*. 10 millimeters equal 1 centimeter.**

Millimeters are very small! The tip of a pencil is about 1 millimeter across. Have your child hold the tip of his pencil between the millimeter marks on the printed ruler to verify that the tip is about 1 millimeter wide.

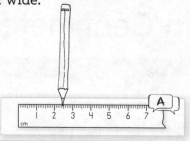

The ruler printed on the Lesson Activities page is actual size.

Engineers use centimeters and millimeters when they design electronics. They draw precise plans and use exact measurements to make sure all the small parts and wires fit together correctly. Let's pretend we're engineers drawing plans for a robot. We need to draw lines to match each of these measurements.

Here's how to draw a line that's 4 centimeters 3 millimeters long. Demonstrate how to use a real ruler to draw a line with this length. **First, I draw a line that's 4 centimeters long. Then, I continue it for 3 more millimeters.**

Let's convert this length to millimeters. In Unit 4, you learned a rhyme to help you remember whether to multiply or divide when you convert mixed numbers to fractions and fractions to mixed numbers. It went: *Whole to parts? Multiply to start! Parts to whole? Division's in control!*

When you convert measurements, you can use the same rhyme to help decide whether to multiply or divide. When we convert centimeters to millimeters, we convert whole centimeters to parts of centimeters. Whole to parts, multiply to start!

You multiply 4 times 10 to find how many millimeters are in 4 centimeters. Then, you add on the extra 3 millimeters. What's 4 times 10? *40.* **Plus 3?** *43.* **So, this line is 43 millimeters long.** Write 43 in both blanks.

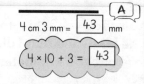

Next, we'll draw a line that's 37 millimeters long. Let's convert 37 millimeters to centimeters first. When we convert millimeters to centimeters, we convert parts of centimeters to whole centimeters. Parts to whole? Division's in control!

Every group of 10 millimeters equals 1 centimeter. So, we divide 37 by 10. How many groups of 10 millimeters can you make from 37 millimeters? *3.* **How many millimeters are left over?** *7.* **Write "3 R7" in the division equation blank. So, 37 millimeters equal 3 centimeters 7 millimeters.** Write 3 and 7 as shown. Have your child draw a matching line in the space above the printed measurement.

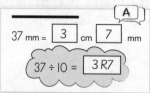

See the Unit 9 **Teaching Math with Confidence** for tips on helping your child convert measurements.

Now, we have some wires to measure for our robot. Have your child use a ruler to measure the wires in centimeters and millimeters. (He should include the exposed tips of the wires.) Record each measurement in the chart. Then, have him convert the measurement to millimeters.

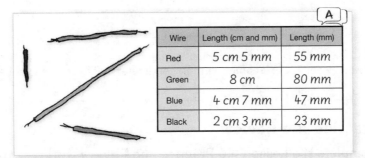

Wire	Length (cm and mm)	Length (mm)
Red	5 cm 5 mm	55 mm
Green	8 cm	80 mm
Blue	4 cm 7 mm	47 mm
Black	2 cm 3 mm	23 mm

Accept any answer that's within 1 or 2 millimeters of the above answers, since small slips of the ruler can cause the measurements to be slightly off. Encourage your child to measure the wires as accurately as possible, but keep the focus on understanding the relationship between centimeters and millimeters.

Activity (B): Play Measurement Tag with Centimeters and Millimeters

Play Measurement Tag. **This game is like Tag, but on paper! One of us will be "it." The person who's "it" is the tagger and tries to catch the other person.**

Measurement Tag

Materials: 2 dice; ruler; colored pencils or markers

Object of the Game: If you are the tagger (or "it"), your goal is to tag your opponent by landing within 1 cm of the end of their path. If you are not the tagger, your goal is to draw a path that avoids getting tagged for as long as possible.

Decide which player will be the tagger. The tagger is Player 1 and goes first. Each player chooses a different colored pencil or marker to use to draw their line.

On your turn, roll 2 dice. Use the numbers on the dice to make a two-digit number of millimeters. Use the ruler to draw a straight line of that length, beginning at your starting dot. For example, if you roll a 2 and a 4, you may draw either a 24 mm or a 42 mm line. Draw a dot at the end of the line. You will start your next line at this dot. Then the other player takes a turn in the same way.

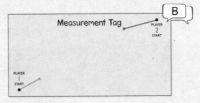

Sample first move by each player. Player 1 (the tagger) should try to draw a line towards the other player's position. Player 2 should try to draw a line that moves away from the tagger's position.

All lines must be straight and fit inside the game board. Lines may go in any direction, and they may cross any previously-drawn lines.

Directions continued on next page.

Take turns rolling the dice and drawing lines. The game ends when the tagger's line comes within 1 centimeter of the other player's current end dot.

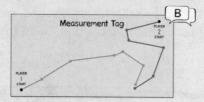

Sample final game board.
Player 1 wins when his line comes within 1 centimeter of Player 2's current end dot.

Independent Practice and Review

Have your child complete the Lesson 9.6 Practice and Review workbook pages.

Lesson 9.7
Meters

Purpose	Materials
• Find your child's height in meters and centimeters • Convert meters to centimeters • Convert centimeters to meters	• Tape measure marked in meters and centimeters, or knowledge of your child's height (in either meters and centimeters or feet and inches)

Memory Work	
	• **How many feet equal 1 mile?** *5,280.* • **How many millimeters equal 1 centimeter?** *10.* • **How many centimeters equal 1 meter?** *100.* • **How many meters equal 1 kilometer?** *1,000.*

Warm-up: Find Your Child's Height in Meters and Centimeters

Today, you'll learn how to convert centimeters and meters. Have your child hold her hands about one meter apart. **Refrigerators are usually about a meter wide, and kitchen chairs are often about a meter high. A meter is a little longer than a yard.**

Choose from one of the following options to find your child's height in meters and centimeters:

- If you own a centimeter tape measure, have your child stand against a wall. Use a tape measure to measure her height in meters and centimeters. For example: **You're 1 meter and 48 centimeters tall.**
- If your family uses the metric system and you don't own a metric tape measure, simply tell your child her approximate height in meters and centimeters. For example: **At your last doctor's appointment, you were 1 meter and 42 centimeters tall.**
- If your family uses the U.S. customary measurement system and you don't own a centimeter tape measure, use the following chart to tell your child her approximate height in meters and centimeters.

48 in.	49 in.	50 in.	51 in.	52 in.	53 in.	54 in.	55 in.	56 in.	57 in.	58 in.
1 m 22 cm	1 m 24 cm	1 m 27 cm	1 m 30 cm	1 m 32 cm	1 m 35 cm	1 m 37 cm	1 m 40 cm	1 m 42 cm	1 m 45 cm	1 m 47 cm

The metric equivalencies in the chart are rounded to the nearest centimeter. If your child's height isn't on the chart, multiply her height (in inches) by 2.54 to find the equivalent number of centimeters.

Activity (A): Convert Meters and Centimeters for Olympic Track Records

Have you ever watched the Olympics? *Answers will vary.* **At the Olympics, the judges use metric units to measure the results in the jumping events.**

The Olympic records in this lesson are rounded to the nearest centimeter and correct as of 2023.

The Olympic record for women's high jump is 2 meters 6 centimeters. Each meter equals 100 centimeters. To convert meters to centimeters, we multiply the number of meters times 100 then add on the extra centimeters. What's 2 times 100? *200.* **Plus 6?** *206.* **Write 206 in both blanks. 2 meters 6 centimeters equals 206 centimeters.**

> If your family uses the U.S. customary system, explain that 2 meters 6 centimeters is approximately 6 feet 9 inches.

The Olympic record for men's high jump is 239 centimeters. To convert centimeters to meters, we divide the number of centimeters by 100. How many groups of 100 can you make from 239 centimeters? *2.* **How many centimeters are left over?** *39.* **Write "2 R39" in the division equation blank. So, 239 centimeters equal 2 meters 39 centimeters.** Write 2 and 39 as shown.

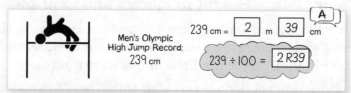

> If your family uses the U.S. customary system, explain that 2 meters 39 centimeters is approximately 7 feet 10 inches.

Have your child complete the Olympic records charts.

Women's Olympic Records

Event	Pole Vault	Long Jump	Triple Jump
Record (m and cm)	5 m 5 cm	7 m 40 cm	15 m 67 cm
Record (cm)	505 cm	740 cm	1,567 cm

Men's Olympic Records

Event	Pole Vault	Long Jump	Triple Jump
Record (m and cm)	6 m 3 cm	8 m 90 cm	18 m 9 cm
Record (cm)	603 cm	890 cm	1,809 cm

> The pole vault records are roughly equivalent to jumping over an adult giraffe. The long jump records are roughly equal to the width of a two-car garage. In the triple jump, Olympians take a running start and perform a hop, step, and jump. The triple jump records are roughly equal to the length of a semi-truck trailer!

Independent Practice and Review

Have your child complete the Lesson 9.7 Practice and Review workbook pages.

Lesson 9.8
Kilometers

Purpose	Materials
• Draw lines with a given length in centimeters and millimeters • Convert kilometers to meters • Convert meters to kilometers • Practice converting metric units	• 30-cm (1-foot) ruler

Memory Work	• **How many feet equal 1 mile?** *5,280.* • **How many millimeters equal 1 centimeter?** *10.* • **How many centimeters equal 1 meter?** *100.* • **How many meters equal 1 kilometer?** *1,000.*

Warm-up: Draw Lines with Centimeters and Millimeters

Have your child use a ruler to draw lines with the following lengths on scrap paper. Then, have him convert each measurement to millimeters.

- **5 centimeters.** *50 millimeters.*
- **5 centimeters 6 millimeters.** *56 millimeters.*
- **9 centimeters 8 millimeters.** *98 millimeters.*

Activity (A): Convert Kilometers and Meters

Today, you'll learn how to convert kilometers and meters. We'll convert the heights of seven mountains called the Seven Summits. They are the highest mountains on each continent. Some people try to climb to the top of all of them!

The mountains' heights in this lesson are accurate as of 2022. (Earthquakes and tectonic plate movements sometimes change the heights slightly, so they vary over time.) There are several different versions of the Seven Summits list, depending on how you define the boundaries of the continents.

Mount Everest is the highest mountain in Asia and in the world. It's 8 kilometers 849 meters high. We'll find its elevation in meters.

Each kilometer equals 1,000 meters. To convert kilometers to meters, we multiply the number of kilometers times 1,000. Then, we add the extra meters. What's 8 times 1,000? *8,000.* **Plus 849?** *8,849.* **Write "8,849" in both blanks.**

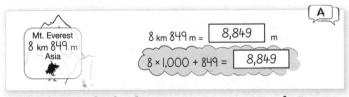

Denali is 6,190 meters high. It's the highest mountain in North America. We'll find its elevation in kilometers and meters.

To convert meters to kilometers, we divide the number of meters by 1,000. **How many thousands are in 6,190?** *6.* **How many extra meters are left over?** *190.* Write "6 R190" in the division equation blank. **So, 6,190 meters equal 6 kilometers 190 meters.** Write 6 and 190 as shown.

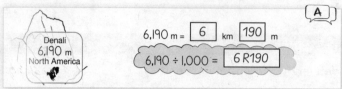

Have your child use similar reasoning to complete the chart.

Continent	Mountain	Elevation (km and m)	Elevation (m)
South America	Aconcagua	6 km 961 m	6,961 m
Africa	Kilimanjaro	5 km 895 m	5,895 m
Antarctica	Mount Vinson	4 km 892 m	4,892 m
Europe	Mont Blanc	4 km 810 m	4,810 m
Australia	Mount Kosciuszko	2 km 228 m	2,228 m

Activity (B): Convert Millimeters, Centimeters, Meters, and Kilometers

You've learned about four different metric units in this unit: millimeters, centimeters, meters, and kilometers. We'll solve a riddle to review how to convert measurements with these units. The question is: *Why did the obtuse angle lose the argument?*

When you do lots of different conversions, it's normal to sometimes get confused about whether you multiply or divide. If you aren't sure, think of the rhyme you learned earlier in the unit: *Whole to parts? Multiply to start! Parts to whole? Division's in control.*

Point to the first problem. **The first problem is to convert 7 centimeters to millimeters. 7 centimeters equal how many millimeters?** *70.* Have your child find the blank labeled "70 mm" and write V in the blank.

If your child has trouble with the conversion, say: **When you convert centimeters to millimeters, do you convert wholes to parts or parts to wholes?** *Wholes to parts.* **So, do you multiply or divide?** *Multiply.*

Repeat until your child has completed all the blanks. **Why did the obtuse angle lose the argument?** *Because it's never right!*

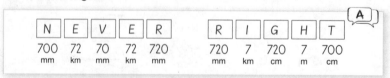

Independent Practice and Review

Have your child complete the Lesson 9.8 Practice and Review workbook pages.

Lesson 9.9
Add and Subtract Metric Units

Purpose	Materials
• Practice converting metric units • Add and subtract metric units	• None

Memory Work
- **How many feet equal 1 mile?** *5,280.*
- **How many millimeters equal 1 centimeter?** *10.*
- **How many centimeters equal 1 meter?** *100.*
- **How many meters equal 1 kilometer?** *1,000.*

Warm-up (A): Find Metric Unit Equivalents

This activity previews the trading your child will do as she adds and subtracts metric units.

Earlier in this unit, you learned how to add feet and inches. Today, you'll learn how to add and subtract metric units. Have your child complete the metric equivalencies in the blue box.

$$1\ cm = \boxed{10}\ mm$$
$$1\ m = \boxed{100}\ cm$$
$$1\ km = \boxed{1{,}000}\ m$$

When we add and subtract metric units, we sometimes need to trade units. Read aloud the first conversion: **6 centimeters and 13 millimeters equal 7 centimeters and how many millimeters?** *3 millimeters.* If your child isn't sure, ask: **13 millimeters equal how many centimeters and millimeters?** *1 centimeter and 3 millimeters.* **So, add 6 centimeters plus 1 centimeter and 3 millimeters to find the total.** Repeat with the second exercise.

$$6\ cm\ 13\ mm = 7\ cm\ \boxed{3}\ mm$$
$$7\ m\ 140\ cm = 8\ m\ \boxed{40}\ cm$$

To make this problem more concrete, use a ruler to show your child that 6 cm 13 mm equals 7 cm 3 mm.

Read aloud the next problem: **4 centimeters and 5 millimeters equal 3 centimeters and how many millimeters?** *15 millimeters.* If your child isn't sure, say: **1 centimeter equals how many millimeters?** *10 millimeters.* **So, if you have 4 centimeters and 5 millimeters, and you trade 1 centimeter for millimeters, how many millimeters will you get?** *15.* Repeat with the final exercise.

$$4\ cm\ 5\ mm = 3\ cm\ \boxed{15}\ mm$$
$$2\ m\ 30\ cm = 1\ m\ \boxed{130}\ cm$$

To make this problem more concrete, use a ruler to show your child that 4 cm 5 mm equals 3 cm 15 mm.

Activity (B): Add and Subtract Metric Units

If your child can immediately find the answers in her head for these problems, demonstrate how to solve them with the written process anyway. Ask her to use the written process to solve the problems in the Lesson Activities so that she's familiar with it, but allow her to use whichever method makes more sense to her when she solves problems on the Practice page.

Adding and subtracting metric units is a lot like adding or subtracting feet and inches or whole numbers.

Read aloud the first problem and first question. **We want to add 7 centimeters 4 millimeters plus 2 centimeters 8 millimeters. First, we add the smaller units. What's 4 millimeters plus 8 millimeters?** *12 millimeters.* Write "12 mm" as shown. **Next, we add the larger units. What's 7 centimeters plus 2 centimeters?** *9 centimeters.* Write "9 cm" as shown.

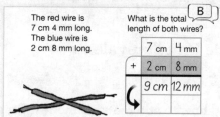

Now, we check whether we can trade the smaller units for larger units. Do we have enough millimeters to trade some for centimeters? *Yes.* **How many millimeters equal 1 centimeter?** *10.* **How many centimeters and millimeters equal 12 millimeters?** *1 centimeter 2 millimeters.*

Last, we add 1 centimeter 2 millimeters to the 9 centimeters. What's 9 centimeters plus 1 centimeter 2 millimeters? *10 centimeters 2 millimeters.* Write "10 cm 2 mm" in the final box below the problem.

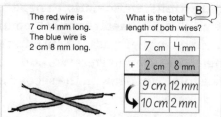

Read aloud the second question. **Now, we want to subtract 7 centimeters 4 millimeters minus 2 centimeters 8 millimeters. First, we look at the smaller unit and check that we have enough of them to subtract.** Point to the millimeters column. **Can we subtract 8 millimeters from 4 millimeters?** *No.* **Before we subtract, we need to trade to get more millimeters.**

We trade 1 centimeter for 10 millimeters. Cross out 7 cm and write "6 cm" above it. **We trade 1 centimeter for 10 millimeters and add the 10 millimeters to the 4 millimeters we already have. Now, we have 14 millimeters.** Cross out 4 mm and write "14 mm" above it.

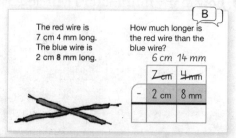

If your child has trouble understanding the trade, use a ruler to demonstrate. Show her 7 cm 4 mm on the ruler. **7 centimeters 4 millimeters is the same length as 6 centimeters 14 millimeters.**

Now, we're ready to subtract! What's 14 millimeters minus 8 millimeters? *6 millimeters.* Write "6 mm" as shown." **What's 6 centimeters minus 2 centimeters?** *4 centimeters.* Write "4 cm" as shown.

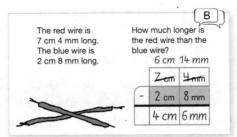

Have your child solve the other problems in the same way. Help her as needed to trade the correct units in each problem.

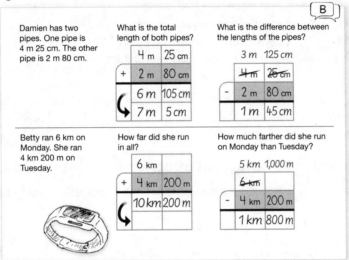

Independent Practice and Review

Have your child complete the Lesson 9.9 Practice and Review workbook pages.

The second box below the problem is there in case your child needs to trade after she adds. If she does not need to trade, she should leave it blank.

Lesson 9.10
Two-Step Word Problems
with Metric Length Units

Purpose	Materials
• Practice adding and subtracting metric length units • Solve two-step word problems with millimeters, centimeters, meters, and kilometers	• None

Memory Work	• **How many feet equal 1 mile?** *5,280.* • **How many millimeters equal 1 centimeter?** *10.* • **How many centimeters equal 1 meter?** *100.* • **How many meters equal 1 kilometer?** *1,000.*

These word problems in this lesson are similar to the word problems in Lesson 9.5. In each problem, your child will need to convert a measurement as well as add, subtract, multiply, or divide. As in Lesson 9.5, adjust your level of support to match your child's needs.

Warm-up (A): Practice Adding and Subtracting Metric Units

Have your child complete the addition and subtraction problems. Guide him as needed with the trading.

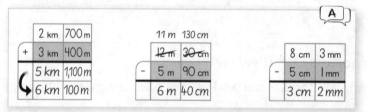

Activity (B): Solve Two-Step Word Problems with Metric Units

In the last few lessons, you learned how to convert metric measurements and add and subtract them. Today, we'll solve word problems with metric measurements.

Read aloud the first question. **What's the goal?** *Find how far Mateo runs.* **What unit are we supposed to use for our answer?** *Meters.* **What information do we know?** *He ran 3 kilometers on Monday and 750 meters on Tuesday.* Underline "3 km" and "750 m" in the word problem.

> On Monday, Mateo runs <u>3 km.</u>
> On Tuesday, he runs <u>750 m.</u>
> How many meters does he run in all?

Some kids might read this problem and say the answer is 753, because 3 plus 750 equals 753. Why isn't that correct? *Sample answer: The 3 and 750 don't have the same units.* **We want the final answer to be in meters, so let's start by converting the kilometers to meters.**

3 kilometers equal how many meters? *3,000.* **Write "3 km = 3,000 m" So, you can add 3,000 plus 750 to find the total number of meters that Mateo runs.** Write "3,000 + 750 = " Have your child complete the equation and label and box the answer.

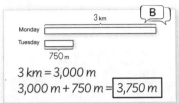

Read aloud the next question. **What's the goal?** *Find how much farther Hazel needs to run.* **What unit are we supposed to use for our answer?** *Meters.* **What information do we know?** *Hazel wants to run 2 kilometers. She's run 800 meters so far.* Underline "2 km" and "800 m" in the problem.

> [B]
> Hazel wants to run 2 km.
> So far, she has run 800 m.
> How many more meters does she need to
> run to accomplish her goal?

We want the final answer to be in meters, so let's start by converting the kilometers to meters. 2 kilometers equal how many meters? *2,000.* **Write "2 km = 2,000 m" So, we subtract 2,000 minus 800 to find how many meters she has left to run.** Write "2,000 m – 800 m =" Have your child complete the equation and label and box the final answer. **How much farther does Hazel need to run?** *1,200 meters.*

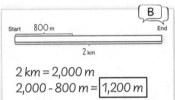

Read aloud the next question. **What's the goal?** *Find the length of the banner.* **What unit are we supposed to use for our answer?** *Meters and centimeters.* **What information do we know?** *Each piece of paper is 30 centimeters long. There are 6 pieces of paper.* Underline "6 pieces" and "30 cm" in the problem.

> [B]
> Gianna tapes together 6 pieces of paper
> to make a banner.
> Each piece of paper is 30 cm long.
> What is the total length of the banner in
> meters and centimeters?

Give your child a minute to think about how to solve the problem. If he's stuck, suggest he first find the length of the banner in centimeters: **Each piece of paper is 30 centimeters long, so multiply 30 times 6 to find the length of the banner in centimeters.** Then, have him convert the length from centimeters to meters and centimeters.

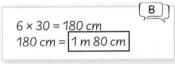

Read aloud the final question. **What's the goal?** *Find the length of each piece of wire.* **What unit are we supposed to use for our answer?** *Millimeters.* **What information do we know?** *He starts with 3 centimeters of wire. He cuts it into 2 pieces.* Underline "3 cm" and "2 equal pieces" in the word problem.

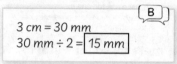

Muhammad uses wire to make jewelry.
He has a piece of wire 3 cm long.
He cuts the wire into 2 equal pieces.
How long is each piece in millimeters?

We want to find our answer in millimeters, so let's convert 3 centimeters to millimeters before dividing. **3 centimeters equal how many millimeters?** *30.* Write "3 cm = 30 mm" **So, we divide 30 millimeters by 2 to find the length of each piece in millimeters.** Write "30 ÷ 2 =" Have your child complete the equation and label and box the final answer. **How long is each piece?** *15 millimeters.*

3 cm = 30 mm
30 mm ÷ 2 = 15 mm

Independent Practice and Review

Have your child complete the Lesson 9.10 Practice and Review workbook pages.

Lesson 9.11
Enrichment (Optional)

Purpose	Materials
• Practice memory work • Understand the importance of having standard units for measurement • Create two new units for measuring length and measure items around the house with the new units • Summarize what your child has learned and assess your child's progress	• *Millions to Measure*, written by David M. Schwartz and illustrated by Steven Kellogg • Cardboard strip, about 1 in. wide and 3 ft. long (or 3 cm wide and 1 m long) • Scissors

Your child will invent her own length units and make a ruler with her units in this enrichment activity. Before the lesson, cut a piece of cardboard or cardstock into 1-inch (or 3-centimeter) strips and tape them together to form a strip about 3 feet (or 1 meter) long.

Warm-up: Review Memory Work

Quiz your child on all memory work through Unit 9. See pages 536-537 for the full list.

Math Picture Book: *Millions to Measure*

Read *Millions to Measure*, written by David M. Schwartz and illustrated by Steven Kellogg. As you read, discuss the importance of having standard units of measurement.

Your child will learn more about units for weight and capacity in Unit 15.

Enrichment Activity: Create Your Own Length Units

In this unit, you've learned about many different units for measuring length. All of the units you've learned about were invented by people to make it easier to compare lengths and communicate about them.

Today, you get to invent two of your own length units. One unit will be a longer unit, like feet or meters. The other unit will be a shorter unit, like inches or centimeters.

What would you like to name your longer unit? *Answers will vary.* Give your child a cardboard strip about 1 in. wide and 3 ft. long. **You get to choose the length of your unit.** Have her choose where to cut the strip to form one unit. Label the ruler with the name she chose for the unit. **We'll use this strip as a ruler to measure with your made-up unit.**

1 grob

Sample ruler and unit. Label the ruler with the name your child invents for her unit.

The rest of the activity will work best if the unit is at least 8 inches (or 20 centimeters) long.

What would you like to name your shorter unit? *Answers will vary.* **Let's subdivide the ruler into your made-up shorter units. How many of your shorter unit equal 1 of your longer unit?** *Answers will vary.* On the other side of the paper strip, help your child divide the ruler into her chosen number of shorter units. For example, if your child decides that 6 of her shorter units equal 1 of her longer units, draw lines on the paper ruler to divide it into 6 equal parts. Number the lines and label them with the name your child invents for this shorter unit.

| 1 bloop | 2 bloops | 3 bloops | 4 bloops | 5 bloops | 6 |

Encourage your child to choose a small number to make it easier to subdivide the longer unit. Make the subdivisions as equal as possible, but it's fine if they aren't exactly even.

Have your child use the paper strip to measure a few items in the room with both of her invented units. For example: *The table is about 3 grobs high. The pencil is about 3 bloops long. The chair is 4 grobs and 1 bloop high.*

Help your child make a table to show how to convert the larger unit to the smaller unit. For example:

Grobs	1	2	3	4	5	6
Bloops	6	12	18	24	30	36

Then, have your child make up an addition and subtraction problem that involves her two units. Help her solve the problems. Trade 1 larger unit for smaller units as needed.

```
                                          4 grobs   7 bloops
    4 grobs    3 bloops               5̶ ̶g̶r̶o̶b̶s̶   1̶ ̶b̶l̶o̶o̶p̶s̶
 +  2 grobs    5 bloops            -    2 grobs    4 bloops
 ⤷  6 grobs    8 bloops                 2 grobs    3 bloops
 ↳  7 grobs    2 bloops
```

Sample addition and subtraction problems for a measurement system in which 1 grob equals 6 bloops.

Unit Wrap-Up

Have your child complete the Unit 9 Wrap-Up.

Unit 9 Answer Key

9.1 Practice

Practice 👤 **Complete the chart.**

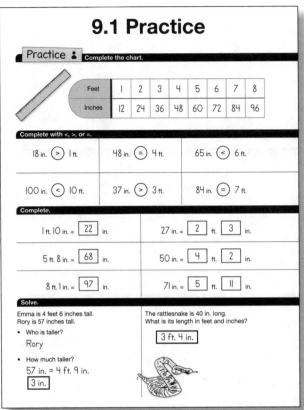

Feet	1	2	3	4	5	6	7	8
Inches	12	24	36	48	60	72	84	96

Complete with <, >, or =.

18 in. ⊙> 1 ft.   48 in. ⊙= 4 ft.   65 in. ⊙< 6 ft.

100 in. ⊙< 10 ft.   37 in. ⊙> 3 ft.   84 in. ⊙= 7 ft.

Complete.

1 ft. 10 in. = **22** in.   27 in. = **2** ft. **3** in.

5 ft. 8 in. = **68** in.   50 in. = **4** ft. **2** in.

8 ft. 1 in. = **97** in.   71 in. = **5** ft. **11** in.

Solve.

Emma is 4 feet 6 inches tall.
Rory is 57 inches tall.

- Who is taller?

  Rory

- How much taller?

  57 in. = 4 ft. 9 in.
  3 in.

The rattlesnake is 40 in. long.
What is its length in feet and inches?

3 ft. 4 in.

9.1 Review

Review 👤 **Convert the mixed numbers to fractions.**

$2\frac{1}{3} = \frac{7}{3}$ $1\frac{5}{6} = \frac{11}{6}$ $5\frac{1}{10} = \frac{51}{10}$

$3\frac{3}{4} = \frac{15}{4}$ $4\frac{1}{2} = \frac{9}{2}$ $2\frac{3}{8} = \frac{19}{8}$

Complete. | **Complete.**

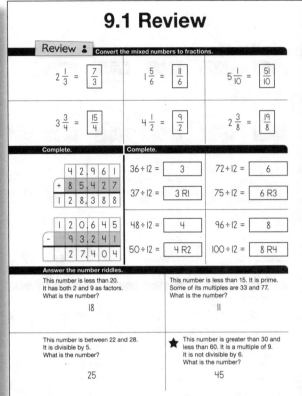

```
  4 2 9 6 1
+ 8 5,4 2 7
1 2 8,3 8 8
```

```
  1 2 0 6 4 5
-   9 3,2 4 1
    2 7,4 0 4
```

36 ÷ 12 = **3**   72 ÷ 12 = **6**

37 ÷ 12 = **3 R1**   75 ÷ 12 = **6 R3**

48 ÷ 12 = **4**   96 ÷ 12 = **8**

50 ÷ 12 = **4 R2**   100 ÷ 12 = **8 R4**

Answer the number riddles.

This number is less than 20.
It has both 2 and 9 as factors.
What is the number?

18

This number is less than 15. It is prime.
Some of its multiples are 33 and 77.
What is the number?

11

This number is between 22 and 28.
It is divisible by 5.
What is the number?

25

★ This number is greater than 30 and
less than 60. It is a multiple of 9.
It is not divisible by 6.
What is the number?

45

9.2 Practice

Practice 👤 **Match the equal lengths.**

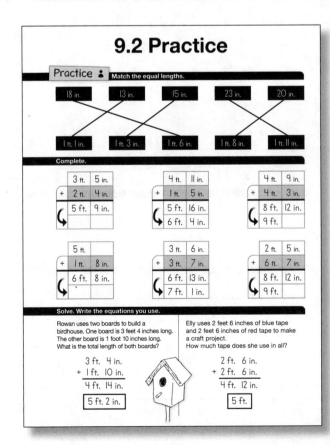

18 in.	13 in.	15 in.	23 in.	20 in.

| 1 ft. 1 in. | 1 ft. 3 in. | 1 ft. 6 in. | 1 ft. 8 in. | 1 ft. 11 in. |

Complete.

```
  3 ft.  5 in.
+ 2 ft.  4 in.
  5 ft.  9 in.
```

```
  4 ft. 11 in.
+ 1 ft.  5 in.
  5 ft. 16 in.
  6 ft.  4 in.
```

```
  4 ft.  9 in.
+ 4 ft.  3 in.
  8 ft. 12 in.
  9 ft.
```

```
  5 ft.
+ 1 ft.  8 in.
  6 ft.  8 in.
```

```
  3 ft.  6 in.
+ 3 ft.  7 in.
  6 ft. 13 in.
  7 ft.  1 in.
```

```
  2 ft.  5 in.
+ 6 ft.  7 in.
  8 ft. 12 in.
  9 ft.
```

Solve. Write the equations you use.

Rowan uses two boards to build a
birdhouse. One board is 3 feet 4 inches long.
The other board is 1 foot 10 inches long.
What is the total length of both boards?

```
  3 ft.  4 in.
+ 1 ft. 10 in.
  4 ft. 14 in.
  5 ft.  2 in.
```

Elly uses 2 feet 6 inches of blue tape
and 2 feet 6 inches of red tape to make
a craft project.
How much tape does she use in all?

```
  2 ft.  6 in.
+ 2 ft.  6 in.
  4 ft. 12 in.
  5 ft.
```

9.2 Review

Review 👤 **Complete.**

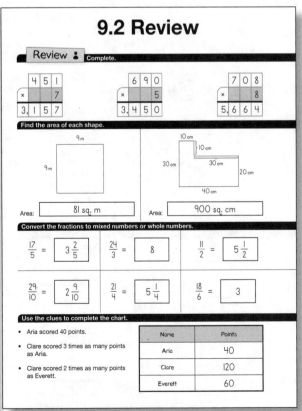

```
    4 5 1
×       7
  3,1 5 7
```

```
    6 9 0
×       5
  3,4 5 0
```

```
    7 0 8
×       8
  5,6 6 4
```

Find the area of each shape.

Area: **81 sq. m**

Area: **900 sq. cm**

Convert the fractions to mixed numbers or whole numbers.

$\frac{17}{5} = 3\frac{2}{5}$ $\frac{24}{3} = 8$ $\frac{11}{2} = 5\frac{1}{2}$

$\frac{29}{10} = 2\frac{9}{10}$ $\frac{21}{4} = 5\frac{1}{4}$ $\frac{18}{6} = 3$

Use the clues to complete the chart.

- Aria scored 40 points.

- Clare scored 3 times as many points
  as Aria.

- Clare scored 2 times as many points
  as Everett.

Name	Points
Aria	40
Clare	120
Everett	60

Unit 9 Answer Key

9.3 Practice

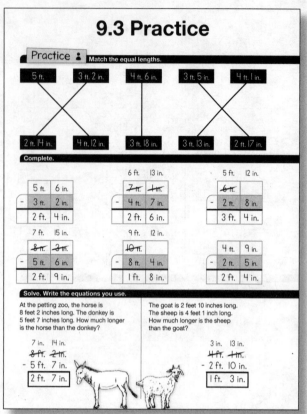

9.3 Review

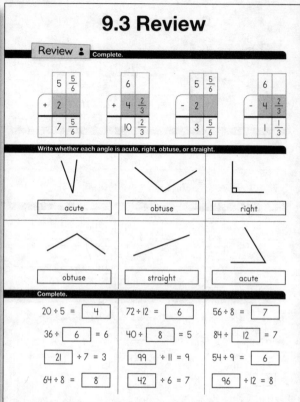

9.4 Practice

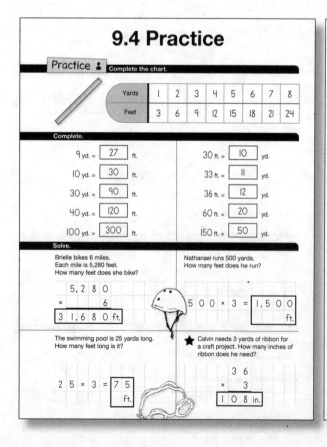

9.4 Review

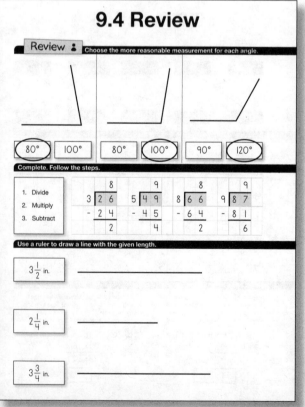

Unit 9 Answer Key

9.5 Practice

Practice 👤 Complete.

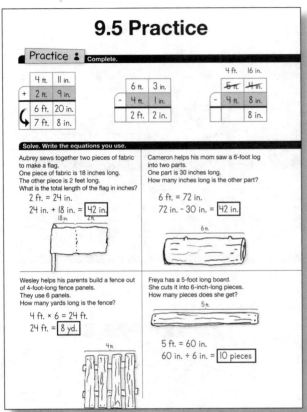

	4 ft.	11 in.
+	2 ft.	9 in.
	6 ft.	20 in.
↰	7 ft.	8 in.

	6 ft.	3 in.
-	4 ft.	1 in.
	2 ft.	2 in.

	4 ft.	16 in.
	~~5 ft.~~	~~4 in.~~
-	4 ft.	8 in.
		8 in.

Solve. Write the equations you use.

Aubrey sews together two pieces of fabric to make a flag.
One piece of fabric is 18 inches long.
The other piece is 2 feet long.
What is the total length of the flag in inches?

2 ft. = 24 in.
24 in. + 18 in. = ☐ 42 in.

Cameron helps his mom saw a 6-foot log into two parts.
One part is 30 inches long.
How many inches long is the other part?

6 ft. = 72 in.
72 in. - 30 in. = ☐ 42 in.

Wesley helps his parents build a fence out of 4-foot-long fence panels.
They use 6 panels.
How many yards long is the fence?

4 ft. × 6 = 24 ft.
24 ft. = ☐ 8 yd.

Freya has a 5-foot long board.
She cuts it into 6-inch-long pieces.
How many pieces does she get?

5 ft. = 60 in.
60 in. ÷ 6 in. = ☐ 10 pieces

9.5 Review

Review 👤 Use a protractor to measure the angles.

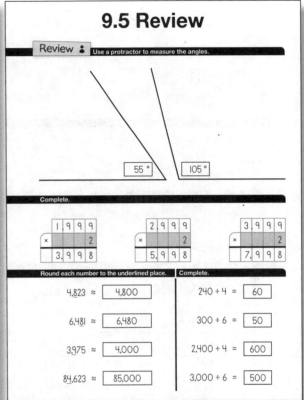

55 °   105 °

Complete.

	1	9	9	9
×				2
	3,	9	9	8

	2	9	9	9
×				2
	5,	9	9	8

	3	9	9	9
×				2
	7,	9	9	8

Round each number to the underlined place.

4,823 ≈ ☐ 4,800

6,481 ≈ ☐ 6,480

3,975 ≈ ☐ 4,000

84,623 ≈ ☐ 85,000

Complete.

240 ÷ 4 = ☐ 60

300 ÷ 6 = ☐ 50

2,400 ÷ 4 = ☐ 600

3,000 ÷ 6 = ☐ 500

9.6 Practice

Practice 👤 Draw a line that matches each measurement. Then, complete the conversion.

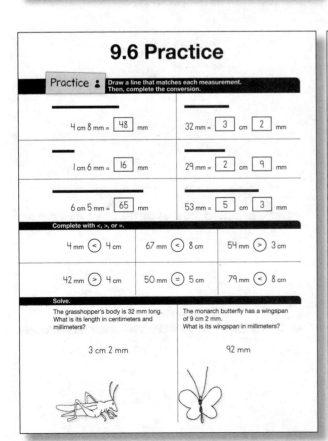

4 cm 8 mm = ☐ 48 mm

32 mm = ☐ 3 cm ☐ 2 mm

1 cm 6 mm = ☐ 16 mm

29 mm = ☐ 2 cm ☐ 9 mm

6 cm 5 mm = ☐ 65 mm

53 mm = ☐ 5 cm ☐ 3 mm

Complete with <, >, or =.

4 mm ⊘ < 4 cm   67 mm ⊘ < 8 cm   54 mm ⊘ > 3 cm

42 mm ⊘ > 4 cm   50 mm ⊘ = 5 cm   79 mm ⊘ < 8 cm

Solve.

The grasshopper's body is 32 mm long.
What is its length in centimeters and millimeters?

3 cm 2 mm

The monarch butterfly has a wingspan of 9 cm 2 mm.
What is its wingspan in millimeters?

92 mm

9.6 Review

Review 👤 Complete.

	9	9
×		5
4	9	5

	9	9
×		6
5	9	4

	9	9
×		7
6	9	3

	9	9
×		8
7	9	2

	9	9
×		9
8	9	1

Complete.

11:00 a.m.	☐ 2 hr. →	1:00 p.m.
11:00 a.m.	☐ 4 hr. →	3:00 p.m.
9:00 a.m.	☐ 5 hr. →	2:00 p.m.
9:00 a.m.	☐ 7 hr. →	4:00 p.m.
8:00 a.m.	☐ 9 hr. →	5:00 p.m.

Complete.

700 ÷ 100 = ☐ 7

400 ÷ 100 = ☐ 4

1,000 ÷ 100 = ☐ 10

2,000 ÷ 1,000 = ☐ 2

5,000 ÷ 1,000 = ☐ 5

9,000 ÷ 1,000 = ☐ 9

Solve. Write the equations you use.

Edith has 16 feet of rope. She cuts the rope into as many 3-foot pieces as she can.
How many feet of rope does she have left over?

16 ÷ 3 = 5 R1
☐ 1 ft.

Elliot throws the frisbee $9\frac{6}{10}$ m. Ahren throws the frisbee $2\frac{3}{10}$ m farther than Elliot.
How far does Ahren throw the frisbee?

$9\frac{6}{10}$
$+ 2\frac{3}{10}$
☐ $11\frac{9}{10}$ m

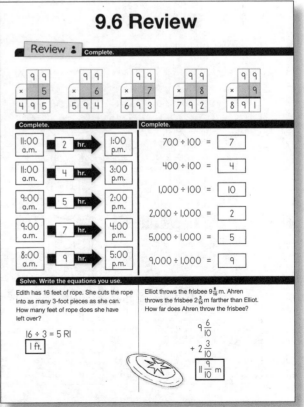

Unit 9 Answer Key

9.7 Practice

Practice 🔖 Complete the chart.

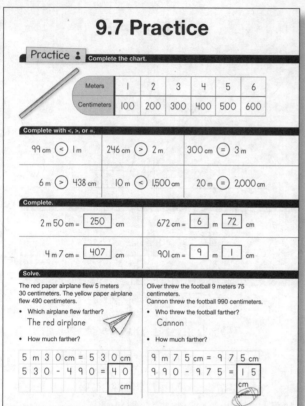

Meters	1	2	3	4	5	6
Centimeters	100	200	300	400	500	600

Complete with <, >, or =.

99 cm (<) 1 m   246 cm (>) 2 m   300 cm (=) 3 m

6 m (>) 438 cm   10 m (<) 1,500 cm   20 m (=) 2,000 cm

Complete.

2 m 50 cm = [250] cm   672 cm = [6] m [72] cm

4 m 7 cm = [407] cm   901 cm = [9] m [1] cm

Solve.

The red paper airplane flew 5 meters 30 centimeters. The yellow paper airplane flew 490 centimeters.

• Which airplane flew farther?

The red airplane

• How much farther?

5	m	3	0	cm	=	5	3	0	cm
5	3	0	-	4	9	0	=	[4 0]	
								cm	

Oliver threw the football 9 meters 75 centimeters. Cannon threw the football 990 centimeters.

• Who threw the football farther?

Cannon

• How much farther?

9	m	7	5	cm	=	9	7	5	cm
9	9	0	-	9	7	5	=	[1 5]	
								cm	

9.7 Review

Review 🔖 Find the missing angle measures.

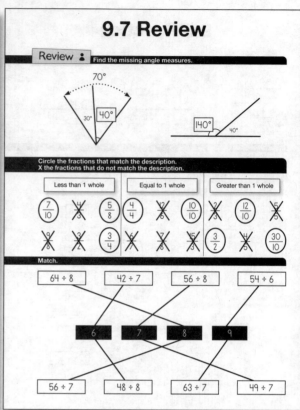

70°   30° [40°]   [140°] 40°

**Circle the fractions that match the description.
X the fractions that do not match the description.**

Less than 1 whole	Equal to 1 whole	Greater than 1 whole

Less than 1 whole: (7/10) ✗4/3 (5/8)   ✗9/8 ✗ (3/4)

Equal to 1 whole: (4/4) ✗10/10 ✗ ✗ ✗5/3

Greater than 1 whole: ✗2/3 (12/10) ✗5/5 (3/2) ✗5/3 (30/10)

Match.

64 ÷ 8   42 ÷ 7   56 ÷ 8   54 ÷ 6

[6]   [7]   [8]   [9]

56 ÷ 7   48 ÷ 8   63 ÷ 7   49 ÷ 7

9.8 Practice

Practice 🔖 Complete with <, >, or =.

4,070 m (>) 4 km   6,000 m (=) 6 km   1,999 m (<) 2 km

3,600 m (>) 3 km   9,587 m (<) 12 km   8,000 m (=) 8 km

Complete.

4 km = [4,000] m   5,000 m = [5] km

4 km 128 m = [4,128] m   5,315 m = [5] km [315] m

7 km = [7,000] m   10,000 m = [10] km

7 km 9 m = [7,009] m   10,030 m = [10] km [30] m

Asher made a chart of how many laps he ran each day. Complete the chart to show how far he ran each day.

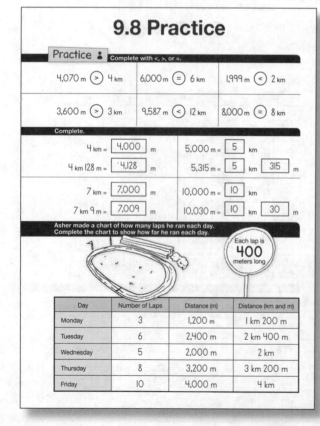

Each lap is **400** meters long

Day	Number of Laps	Distance (m)	Distance (km and m)
Monday	3	1,200 m	1 km 200 m
Tuesday	6	2,400 m	2 km 400 m
Wednesday	5	2,000 m	2 km
Thursday	8	3,200 m	3 km 200 m
Friday	10	4,000 m	4 km

9.8 Review

Review 🔖 Use a protractor to draw an angle with the given measure. Use the printed line for one side. Use the dot for the vertex.

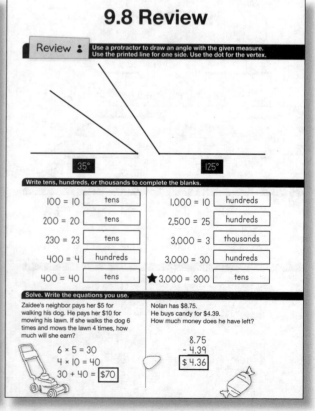

[35°]   [125°]

Write tens, hundreds, or thousands to complete the blanks.

100 = 10 [tens]   1,000 = 10 [hundreds]

200 = 20 [tens]   2,500 = 25 [hundreds]

230 = 23 [tens]   3,000 = 3 [thousands]

400 = 4 [hundreds]   3,000 = 30 [hundreds]

400 = 40 [tens]   ★ 3,000 = 300 [tens]

Solve. Write the equations you use.

Zaidee's neighbor pays her $5 for walking his dog. He pays her $10 for mowing his lawn. If she walks the dog 6 times and mows the lawn 4 times, how much will she earn?

6 × 5 = 30
4 × 10 = 40
30 + 40 = [$70]

Nolan has $8.75. He buys candy for $4.39. How much money does he have left?

8.75
- 4.39
[$ 4.36]

Unit 9 Answer Key

9.9 Practice

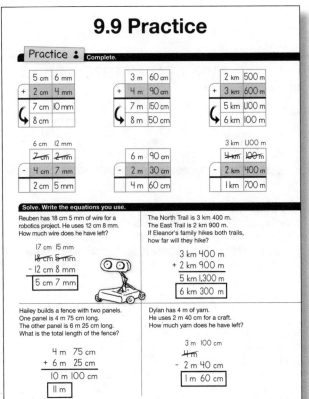

Practice — Complete.

5 cm	6 mm
+ 2 cm	4 mm
7 cm	10 mm
8 cm	

3 m	60 cm
+ 4 m	90 cm
7 m	150 cm
8 m	50 cm

2 km	500 m
+ 3 km	600 m
5 km	1,100 m
6 km	100 m

6 cm	12 mm
7 cm	2 mm
− 4 cm	7 mm
2 cm	5 mm

6 m	90 cm
− 2 m	30 cm
4 m	60 cm

3 km	1,100 m
4 km	100 m
− 2 km	400 m
1 km	700 m

Solve. Write the equations you use.

Reuben has 18 cm 5 mm of wire for a robotics project. He uses 12 cm 8 mm. How much wire does he have left?

17 cm 15 mm
18 cm 5 mm
− 12 cm 8 mm
5 cm 7 mm

The North Trail is 3 km 400 m. The East Trail is 2 km 900 m. If Eleanor's family hikes both trails, how far will they hike?

3 km 400 m
+ 2 km 900 m
5 km 1,300 m
6 km 300 m

Hailey builds a fence with two panels. One panel is 4 m 75 cm long. The other panel is 6 m 25 cm long. What is the total length of the fence?

4 m 75 cm
+ 6 m 25 cm
10 m 100 cm
11 m

Dylan has 4 m of yarn. He uses 2 m 40 cm for a craft. How much yarn does he have left?

3 m 100 cm
4 m
− 2 m 40 cm
1 m 60 cm

9.9 Review

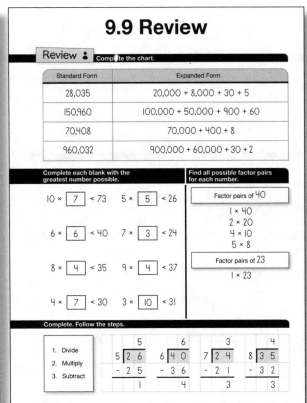

Review — Complete the chart.

Standard Form	Expanded Form
28,035	20,000 + 8,000 + 30 + 5
150,960	100,000 + 50,000 + 900 + 60
70,408	70,000 + 400 + 8
960,032	900,000 + 60,000 + 30 + 2

Complete each blank with the greatest number possible.

10 × 7 < 73   5 × 5 < 26

6 × 6 < 40   7 × 3 < 24

8 × 4 < 35   9 × 4 < 37

4 × 7 < 30   3 × 10 < 31

Find all possible factor pairs for each number.

Factor pairs of 40
1 × 40
2 × 20
4 × 10
5 × 8

Factor pairs of 23
1 × 23

Complete. Follow the steps.

1. Divide
2. Multiply
3. Subtract

```
    5          6          3          4
5 ) 2 6    6 ) 4 0    7 ) 2 4    8 ) 3 5
  − 2 5      − 3 6      − 2 1      − 3 2
      1          4          3          3
```

9.10 Practice

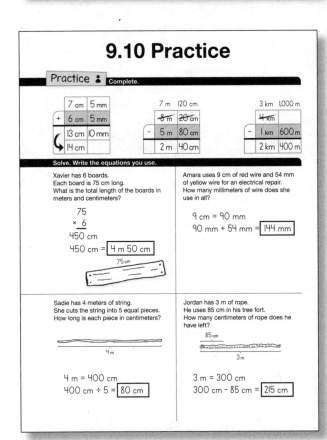

Practice — Complete.

7 cm	5 mm
+ 6 cm	5 mm
13 cm	10 mm
14 cm	

7 m	120 cm
8 m	20 cm
− 5 m	80 cm
2 m	40 cm

3 km	1,000 m
4 km	
− 1 km	600 m
2 km	400 m

Solve. Write the equations you use.

Xavier has 6 boards. Each board is 75 cm long. What is the total length of the boards in meters and centimeters?

75
× 6
450 cm
450 cm = 4 m 50 cm

75 cm

Amara uses 9 cm of red wire and 54 mm of yellow wire for an electrical repair. How many millimeters of wire does she use in all?

9 cm = 90 mm
90 mm + 54 mm = 144 mm

Sadie has 4 meters of string. She cuts the string into 5 equal pieces. How long is each piece in centimeters?

4 m

4 m = 400 cm
400 cm ÷ 5 = 80 cm

Jordan has 3 m of rope. He uses 85 cm in his tree fort. How many centimeters of rope does he have left?

85 cm

3 m

3 m = 300 cm
300 cm − 85 cm = 215 cm

9.10 Review

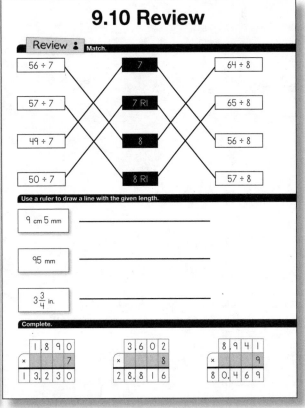

Review — Match.

56 ÷ 7   7   64 ÷ 8
57 ÷ 7   7 R1   65 ÷ 8
49 ÷ 7   8   56 ÷ 8
50 ÷ 7   8 R1   57 ÷ 8

Use a ruler to draw a line with the given length.

9 cm 5 mm _____

95 mm _____

$3\frac{3}{4}$ in. _____

Complete.

	1,	8	9	0
×				7
	1 3,	2	3	0

		3,	6	0	2
×					8
	2	8,	8	1	6

		8,	9	4	1
×					9
	8	0,	4	6	9

Unit 9 Answer Key

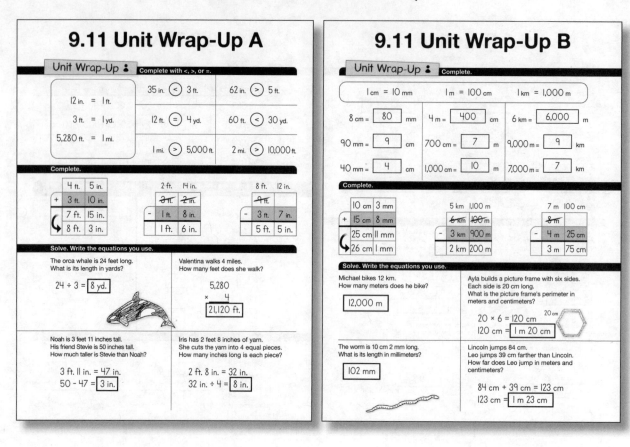

9.11 Unit Wrap-Up A

Unit Wrap-Up · Complete with <, >, or =.

12 in. = 1 ft.	35 in. (<) 3 ft.	62 in. (>) 5 ft.
3 ft. = 1 yd.	12 ft. (=) 4 yd.	60 ft. (<) 30 yd.
5,280 ft. = 1 mi.	1 mi. (>) 5,000 ft.	2 mi. (>) 10,000 ft.

Complete.

	4 ft.	5 in.
+	3 ft.	10 in.
↻	7 ft.	15 in.
	8 ft.	3 in.

	2 ft.	14 in.
-	~~3 ft.~~	~~2 in.~~
	1 ft.	8 in.
	1 ft.	6 in.

	8 ft.	12 in.
	~~9 ft.~~	
-	3 ft.	7 in.
	5 ft.	5 in.

Solve. Write the equations you use.

The orca whale is 24 feet long.
What is its length in yards?

24 ÷ 3 = [8 yd.]

Valentina walks 4 miles.
How many feet does she walk?

5,280
× 4
[21,120 ft.]

Noah is 3 feet 11 inches tall.
His friend Stevie is 50 inches tall.
How much taller is Stevie than Noah?

3 ft. 11 in. = 47 in.
50 − 47 = [3 in.]

Iris has 2 feet 8 inches of yarn.
She cuts the yarn into 4 equal pieces.
How many inches long is each piece?

2 ft. 8 in. = 32 in.
32 in. ÷ 4 = [8 in.]

9.11 Unit Wrap-Up B

Unit Wrap-Up · Complete.

1 cm = 10 mm	1 m = 100 cm	1 km = 1,000 m
8 cm = [80] mm	4 m = [400] cm	6 km = [6,000] m
90 mm = [9] cm	700 cm = [7] m	9,000 m = [9] km
40 mm = [4] cm	1,000 cm = [10] m	7,000 m = [7] km

Complete.

	10 cm	3 mm
+	15 cm	8 mm
↻	25 cm	11 mm
	26 cm	1 mm

	5 km	1,100 m
	~~6 km~~	~~100 m~~
	3 km	900 m
	2 km	200 m

	7 m	100 cm
	~~8 m~~	
-	4 m	25 cm
	3 m	75 cm

Solve. Write the equations you use.

Michael bikes 12 km.
How many meters does he bike?

[12,000 m]

Ayla builds a picture frame with six sides.
Each side is 20 cm long.
What is the picture frame's perimeter in
meters and centimeters?

20 × 6 = 120 cm
120 cm = [1 m 20 cm]

The worm is 10 cm 2 mm long.
What is its length in millimeters?

[102 mm]

Lincoln jumps 84 cm.
Leo jumps 39 cm farther than Lincoln.
How far does Leo jump in meters and
centimeters?

84 cm + 39 cm = 123 cm
123 cm = [1 m 23 cm]

Unit 9 Checkpoint

What to Expect at the End of Unit 9

By the end of Unit 9, most children will be able to do the following:

- Convert length measurements within the U.S. customary system (inches, feet, yards, and miles) and within the metric system (millimeters, centimeters, meters, and kilometers). Many children will occasionally have trouble knowing whether to multiply or divide to perform the conversions.
- Add and subtract feet and inches and compound metric units. Some children will still need help, especially with subtraction problems that require trading.
- Measure with a ruler in centimeters and millimeters.
- Solve two-step word problems that involve converting units. Many children will still need help with these problems, especially ones that involve multiplication or division.

Is Your Child Ready to Move on?

In Unit 10, your child will learn how to use long division to divide multi-digit numbers by one-digit numbers. Before moving on to Unit 10, your child should have already mastered the following skills:

- Tell answers to most of the multiplication and division facts within 3 seconds.
- Know the steps in long division and use written long division to solve simple division problems with a remainder. (For example, $19 \div 4$ or $45 \div 7$.)
- Mentally divide numbers with a remainder. (For example, $38 \div 6$ or $53 \div 10$.)
- Use place-value thinking to divide multiples of 10 or 100 by one-digit numbers. (For example, $120 \div 3$ or $800 \div 4$.)

Your child does not need to have fully mastered measurement conversions or measurement addition and subtraction before moving on to Unit 10. She'll continue to practice solving length problems in the Review pages, and she'll learn how to convert weight and capacity units in Unit 15.

What to Do If Your Child Needs More Practice

Some children will still be working on mastering the multiplication and division facts. Most of the problems in Unit 10 involve the easier multiplication facts (like the ×2, ×3, ×4, and ×5 facts), but your child will also encounter problems that involve the harder facts. **If your child often needs more than a few seconds to find answers to the multiplication facts, allow her to use the multiplication chart (Blackline Master 2) as she solves the long division problems in Unit 10.** Otherwise, she'll spend so much mental energy on the basic facts that she'll struggle to remember all the steps in this complex process. Make sure she also keeps practicing the multiplication and division facts to develop greater fluency.

If your child needs a refresher with any of the other skills, spend a day or two practicing them before moving on to Unit 10.

Activity for Practicing Written Long Division
- Roll and Divide (Lesson 1.6)

Activity for Practicing Mental Division with a Remainder
- Flip and Divide (Lesson 5.2)

Activities for Practicing Dividing Multiples of 10 or 100 by a One-Digit Number
- Mental Math Arcade (Lesson 5.5)
- Flip and Divide (Lesson 5.6)

Unit 10
Long Division

Overview

Your child will learn how to use long division to divide multi-digit numbers by one-digit numbers. He'll begin by dividing two-digit numbers and gradually progress to three- and four-digit numbers. He'll also review how to use multiplication to check division and how to interpret quotients and remainders in division word problems.

This year, your child will solve long division problems with one-digit divisors. In fifth grade, he will extend this skill to long division problems with two-digit divisors.

What Your Child Will Learn

In this unit, your child will learn to:

- Use long division to solve division problems (up to four digits divided by one digit)
- Use multiplication (and addition) to check answers to division problems
- Use long division to solve word problems

Lesson List

Lesson 10.1 Divide Small Numbers	Lesson 10.6 Divide Three-Digit Numbers with Long Division
Lesson 10.2 Review Simple Long Division	
Lesson 10.3 Divide Two-Digit Numbers without Trading	Lesson 10.7 Multiply and Add to Check Long Division
Lesson 10.4 Divide Two-Digit Numbers with Trading	Lesson 10.8 Divide Four-Digit Numbers with Long Division
Lesson 10.5 Predict the Number of Digits in the Quotient	Lesson 10.9 Solve Word Problems with Long Division
	Lesson 10.10 Enrichment (Optional)

Extra Materials Needed for Unit 10

- 5 pieces of paper
- Highlighter or light-colored marker
- For optional Enrichment Lesson:
  - × *The Multiplying Menace Divides,* written by Pam Calvert and illustrated by Wayne Geehan. Charlesbridge, 2011.
  - × Nutrition labels for several different types of cookies or crackers

Teaching Math with Confidence:
How to Make Long Division as Painless as Possible

In Unit 10, your child will learn how to use long division to divide multi-digit numbers by one-digit numbers. By this point, he's spent a lot of time practicing the necessary prerequisite skills, especially place-value, the multiplication and division facts, and the three steps of simple long division. You'll do a brief review of these skills in the first two lessons to make sure your child is well-prepared to master this challenging algorithm.

However, even with a solid foundation, learning long division can be a slog. The main reason is right in the name: it's a loooong process. It can take up to eleven individual steps to divide a three-digit number, or fifteen different steps to divide a four-digit number! Plus, if you make a small mistake at the beginning of a long division problem, all the rest of your work may be incorrect. No wonder many children find long division tedious and discouraging.

You'll find games, hands-on activities, and even silly word problems in this unit to make learning long division feel more fun and relaxed. Use the following suggestions as well to help make learning long division as painless as possible:

- **Adjust your use of manipulatives** to match your child's needs. Some children will only need hands-on materials to model the first few problems in each lesson, while others will need them for most problems.
- If your child doesn't have the stamina to complete both the Lesson Activities page and Practice page in one session, **split the lesson over two days.** Or, if your child has good mastery of the new skill, have him complete just a few problems on the Practice page and allow him to skip the rest.
- If your child often needs more than a second or two to find answers to the multiplication and division facts, **allow him to use the multiplication chart** (Blackline Master 2). Otherwise, he'll spend so much energy figuring out the multiplication and division facts that he'll struggle to remember all the steps.
- Make sure your child uses a **pencil with a good eraser.** Learning long division often involves making mistakes, and it's much easier to cope with the frustration of mistakes if you can easily erase them.
- Watch carefully as your child solves the problems on the Lesson Activities pages and help him **correct any errors immediately.** If you find that he needs lots of coaching and support, sit with him as he completes the Practice pages, too. This is especially important when he's first learning the process.
- Encourage your child to treat zeros **like any other number.** You'll find several warm-ups and discussions about zeros in different positions in long division problems to help your child confidently solve problems involving zeros.
- **Acknowledge that long division is hard.** Many children find long division the most difficult skill they learn in fourth grade. Let your child know that most kids find long division very challenging, and that it's normal to get mixed up or feel confused at first.

Lesson 10.1
Divide Small Numbers

Purpose	Materials
• Practice solving problems with simple long division • Divide small numbers • Understand that the quotient is zero if the dividend is less than the divisor	• Counters • Die

Memory Work	
	• **What do we call the number to be divided?** *The dividend.* • **What do we call the number we divide by?** *The divisor.* • **What do we call the result when we divide two numbers?** *The quotient.* • **What do we call an amount that is left over after division?** *The remainder.*

Warm-up (A): Review Simple Long Division

We're starting a new unit on long division today. You've already learned a simple version of the long division algorithm. Later in the unit, you'll learn the full version and use it to divide numbers with up to four digits! Have your child follow the steps to solve the long division problems.

1. Divide
2. Multiply
3. Subtract

Activity (B): Divide Small Numbers

Long division problems often involve dividing small numbers. Dividing small numbers can sometimes be confusing, so we'll practice dividing small numbers today.

In the first problem, 4 children want to share 5 candies. Place 5 counters on the table. **Imagine the counters are candies, and there are 4 people who want to share them. How many candies will each person get?** *1.* **How many candies will be left over?** *1.* Have your child complete the matching long division problem.

In the next problem, 5 children want to share 4 candies. Place 4 counters on the table. **Imagine the counters are candies, and there are 5 people who want to share them. How many candies will each person get?** *0.* **There aren't enough candies for everyone, so all 4 candies will be left over.** Have your child solve the matching long division problem.

It may seem silly to use long division to solve such simple problems. But knowing how to write out the steps will make problems with larger numbers easier.

Have your child solve the other long division problems in the same way. Model the problems with counters as needed.

	1		0		2		0		0		8 B
3	5	5	3	2	4	4	2	8	1	1	8
−	3	−	0	−	4	−	0	−	0	−	8
	2		3		0		2		1		0

Which of the problems have 0 as a quotient? *3 divided by 5, 2 divided by 4, and 1 divided by 8.* **What do you notice about the dividend and divisor in these problems?** *The dividend is less than the divisor.* **If the dividend is less than the divisor, the quotient is zero.**

This principle only holds true if all numbers involved are whole numbers. In future grades, your child will learn that she can also find fractional quotients for problems like these. For example: 4 ÷5 = 4/5.

Activity (C): Play Zero or One?

Play Zero or One?

Zero or One?

Materials: Two different-colored counters to use as game tokens; counters; die

Object of the Game: Have the most treasure when one player reaches the Finish square.

Each player chooses a counter to use as a game token and places it on the Start square. Place a few handfuls of counters in a pile next to the game board. These counters are the treasure chest.

On your turn, roll the die and advance your token the corresponding number of squares. Say the answer to the problem, including the remainder. If the quotient is 0, do not take any counters from the treasure chest. If the quotient is 1, take 1 counter from the treasure chest.

For example, if you land on 5 ÷ 6, say "5 divided by 6 is 0, with a remainder of 5." Do not take any counters from the treasure chest.

$$6 \overline{)5} \ \text{B}$$

Take turns until one player reaches Finish. Whoever has collected more treasure wins the game.

Directions continued on next page.

Answer Key:

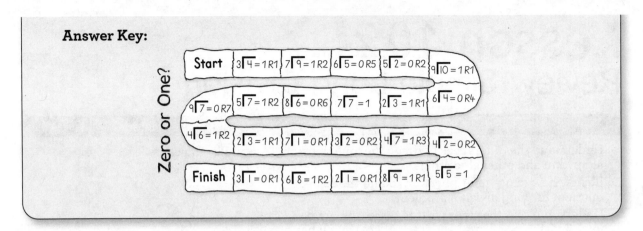

Independent Practice and Review

Have your child complete the Lesson 10.1 Practice and Review workbook pages.

Lesson 10.2
Review Simple Long Division

Purpose	Materials
• Understand the differences between the long division algorithm and other algorithms • Review how to use multiplication to find the correct quotient for long division problems • Understand that the steps written below the dividend in long division problems keep track of how much has been divided	• Playing cards

Memory Work	
	• **What do we call an angle that looks like the corner of a piece of paper?** *A right angle.* • **What do we call a quadrilateral with 4 right angles?** *A rectangle.* • **What do we call a quadrilateral with 4 right angles and 4 equal sides?** *A square.* • **What do we call a quadrilateral with 4 equal sides?** *A rhombus.*

Warm-up (A): Contrast Long Division with the Addition, Subtraction, and Multiplication Algorithms

You have learned algorithms for solving addition, subtraction, multiplication, and division problems. Remember, algorithms are step-by-step methods for solving problems. They're like recipes for math. Have your child use the usual steps to solve the problems in part A.

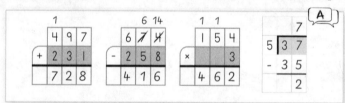

The way we record our work when we use the long division algorithm is quite different from the way we record our work when we use the addition, subtraction, and multiplication algorithms.

- When you use the addition, subtraction, and multiplication algorithms, you always start on the *right*. When you use the long division algorithm, you start on the *left*.
- For the addition, subtraction, and multiplication algorithms, you write your answers *below* the line. When you use the long division algorithm, you write your answer *above* the line.
- For the addition, subtraction, and multiplication algorithms, you keep track of your trades *above* the numbers. When you use the long division algorithm, you keep track of how much you have divided *below* the numbers.

Activity (B): Multiply to Find Quotients

In Unit 5, your child learned how to use multiplication to find quotients. In this activity, you'll review this important skill. If your child is familiar with the game show "The Price is Right," remind him that this method is similar to what the contestants do on the show: Guess the price of the prizes as accurately as possible, but without going over the actual price. See the Unit 5 **Teaching Math with Confidence** (page 172) for more on this approach.

Read aloud the word problem. **What do we want to find?** *How many candy hearts are in each group.*

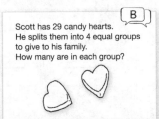

We need to divide 29 by 4. To find the quotient, I think, "What number can I multiply by 4 to get as close as possible to 29 without going over?"

- **What's 4 times 6?** *24.* Write 24 in the blank. **24 is 5 less than 29, so that's too low. Scott could give everyone another candy heart.**
- **What's 4 times 8?** *32.* Write 32 in the blank. **32 is greater than 29, so that's too high. Scott doesn't have enough candy hearts to put 8 in each group.**
- **What's 4 times 7?** *28.* Write 28 in the blank. **That's as close as we can get to 29 without going over. So, the quotient is 7.** Write 7 as shown.

Have your child write 7 as the quotient and complete the long division problem.

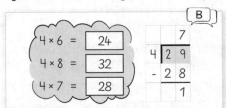

If Scott puts 7 candy hearts in each group, how many candy hearts will he use? *28.* **How do you know?** *4 times 7 equals 28.* **How many candy hearts will be left over?** *1.*

Point to the bottom part of the problem. **The space below the dividend shows how many candy hearts Scott used up, and how many candy hearts are left over. We multiply to find how much we've already used up or divided, and we subtract to find out how much is left. In the next lesson, you'll see how we use this space to keep track of our work in problems with larger quotients.**

Activity (C): Play Don't Go Over!

We're going to play a game called Don't Go Over! In this game, you pick a card and write the number on the card as the divisor for one of the problems on the game board. Your goal is to create a long division problem with a remainder that is as small as possible.

Place a playing card with a 7 on the table. (Any suit is fine). **Let's pretend I turned over a 7.** Point to the problem with 26 as the dividend. **I wonder if this problem would be a good choice. 7 times what number gets me as close as possible to 26, without going over?** *3.* If your child's not sure, have him skip-count by 7s: *7, 14, 21, 28.* **21 is the multiple that's as close as possible to 26 without going over. 7 times 3 equals 21. That's 5 less than 26, so I'd have a remainder of 5.**

Point to the problem with 22 as the dividend. **7 times 3 is 21. That's only 1 less than 22, so that's a better problem to choose.** Then, play Don't Go Over!

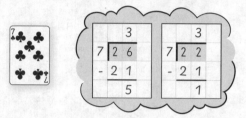

Dividing 22 by 7 yields a smaller remainder than dividing 26 by 7.

You will use 4s, 5s, 6s, 7s, 8s, and 9s for this game. None of the numbers on the game board are divisible by any of these numbers, so every problem will have a remainder.

Don't Go Over!

Materials: 4s, 5s, 6s, 7s, 8s, and 9s from 1 deck of cards (24 cards total)

Object of the Game: Win the fewest points by creating division problems with as low a remainder as possible.

Shuffle the cards. Place the cards in a face-down pile. Choose who will go first. On your turn, flip over the top card. Write this number as the divisor in one of the long division problems on the game board. Complete the long division problem. The remainder is your score. Write this score in the next blank line in your score card.

For example, if you turn over a 7, the best choices are the long division problems with 22, 29, or 43 as the dividend, since each of those problems yields a remainder of 1.

Take turns. Continue until all the long division problems are complete. Each player finds the sum of their points. Whoever has won fewer total points wins the game.

Independent Practice and Review

Have your child complete the Lesson 10.2 Practice and Review workbook pages.

Lesson 10.3
Divide Two-Digit Numbers without Trading

Purpose	Materials
• Concretely divide tens and ones with play money • Use the long division algorithm to divide tens and ones without trading	• 3 pieces of paper • Play money

Memory Work	• **What do we call the result when we subtract two numbers?** *The difference.* • **What do we call the result when we add two numbers?** *The sum.*

In this lesson, you will introduce your child to the full version of the long division algorithm. Every problem involves numbers that can be evenly divided without trading. Your child will learn how to solve problems that involve trading in the next lesson.

Warm-up: Divide Tens and Ones with Play Money

Let's pretend you run a lemonade stand with two friends. Which two friends would you like to run the lemonade stand with? *Answers will vary.* **The three of you agree to evenly split the money you earn each day. If there are any dollars left over, you leave them in your money box to use as change the next day.**

We'll use three pieces of paper as mats to divide the money you earn. Write your child's name and the two friends' names on separate pieces of paper.

One day, the lemonade stand earns $39. Give your child 3 ten-dollar bills and 9 one-dollar bills. Have her divide the bills into 3 equal groups on the mats.

- **How many ten-dollar bills do each of you get?** *1.*
- **How many one-dollar bills do each of you get?** *3.*
- **So, how much money does each person earn in all?** *$13.*

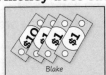 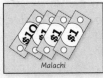 

Repeat with $69 and $96.

$69 divided by 3 equals $23.

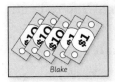  

$96 divided by 3 equals $32.

Leave out the mats and play money for the next activity.

Activity (A): Introduce the Full Version of the Long Division Algorithm

Today, you'll learn the full version of the long division algorithm. Show your child the steps for the full version of the algorithm. **Which step is new?** *Bring down the next digit (if needed).*

To remember the steps, just think, "Dirty Monkeys Smell Bad." The first letter of each word matches the first letter of each step.

Show your child the first printed problem. Point to the space below the dividend. **We'll use this space to keep track of how much we've already divided and how much is left to divide.** Point to the 3 in 37. **This 3 stands for 3 tens, not 3 ones. Every digit that we write in the orange tens-column will stand for a group of ten.**

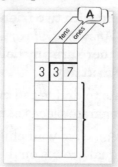

This area is for recording how much has already been divided (or used up)
and how much is left to divide (or use up).

Now, let's solve this problem! One day, the lemonade stand earns $37. Give your child 3 ten-dollar bills and 7 one-dollar bills. Place the 3 labeled mats (from the warm-up) on the table.

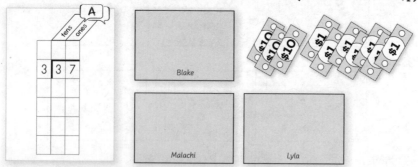

We'll use play money and long division to divide 37 by 3. You're in charge of the play money, and I'm in charge of the writing.

First, we'll divide the tens. Then, we'll divide the ones. It's just like you divided the money in the warm-up.

What's the first step? *Divide.* **Let's divide the 3 tens into 3 equal groups.** Have your child place 1 ten-dollar bill on each mat.

3 divided by 3 equals 1. Point to the numbers as you say them. **Each person gets 1 ten-dollar bill, so I write a 1 in the quotient's tens-place.** Write 1 as shown.

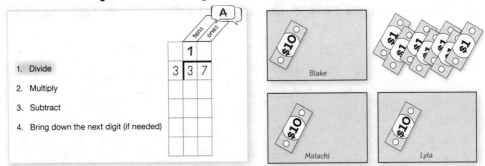

What's the next step? *Multiply.* **1 times 3 equals 3.** Point to the 1 and 3 as you say them, and write 3 as shown. **You used up 3 tens.**

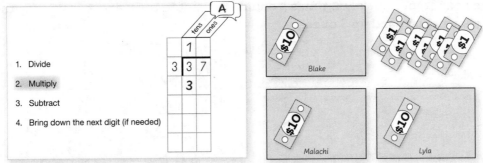

What's the next step? *Subtract.* Write a minus sign and horizontal line as shown. **3 minus 3 equals 0.** Write 0 as shown. **The zero means that you dealt out all the ten-dollar bills, and you don't have any tens left.**

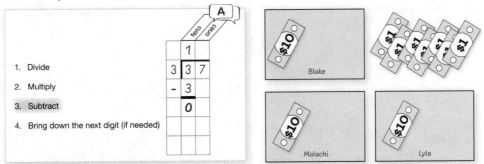

We've divided the tens. How much money do you have left to divide? *$7.*

What's the next step? *Bring down the next digit (if needed).* Draw an arrow and write 7 as shown. **Remember, the space below the dividend is for keeping track of how much is left to divide. Bringing down the 7 shows that we still have 7 dollars to divide.**

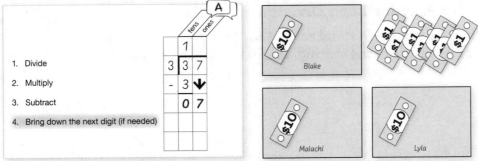

Point to the arrow on the left side of the printed steps. **Now, we repeat the steps for the ones.**

What's the first step? *Divide.* **Let's divide the 7 ones into 3 equal groups. 3 times 2 is 6. That's as close as I can get to 7 without going over.** Have your child place 2 one-dollar bills on each mat. **Each person gets 2 one-dollar bills, so I write a 2 in the quotient's ones-place.** Write 2 as shown.

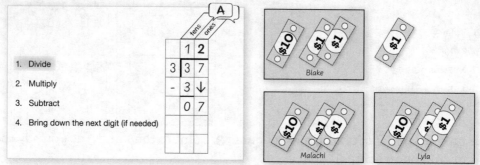

What's the next step? *Multiply.* **2 times 3 equals 6.** Point to the 2 and 3 as you say them, and write 6 as shown. **You used up 6 ones.**

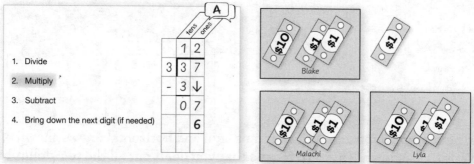

What's the next step? *Subtract.* Write a minus sign and horizontal line as shown. **7 minus 6 equals 1.** Write 1 as shown. **There's a remainder of 1. Do you have 1 one-dollar bill left over?** *Yes.*

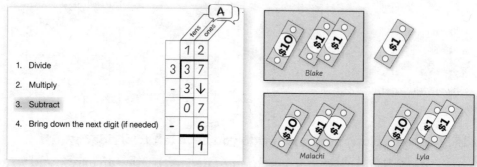

We've divided the ones, so we're done! There are no more digits left to bring down, so we stop after the subtraction step. How much money does each person get? *$12.*

Activity (B): Practice Long Division

The next day, the lemonade stand earns $64. This time, I'll be in charge of the play money, and you'll be in charge of the writing. Take 6 ten-dollar bills and 4 one-dollar bills.

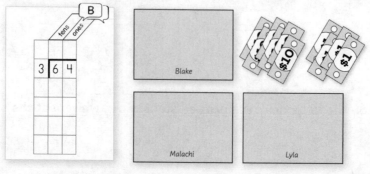

First, we'll divide the tens. Then, we'll divide the ones.

What's the first step? *Divide.* **What's 6 divided by 3?** *2.* Point to the numbers as you say them. Place 2 ten-dollar bills on each mat. Have your child write 2 as shown.

What's the next step? *Multiply.* **What's 2 times 3?** *6.* **I used up 6 tens.**

What's the next step? *Subtract.* Have your child write a minus sign and horizontal line and complete the subtraction problem. **I gave out all the ten-dollar bills. I don't have any tens left.**

What's the next step? *Bring down the next digit (if needed).* Have your child draw an arrow and write 4 as shown. Show your child the remaining 4 one-dollar bills. **We've divided the tens, and we still have $4 left to divide.**

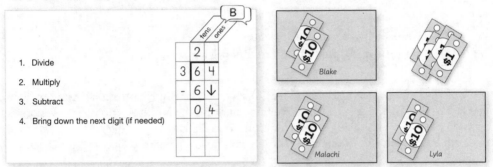

Now, it's time to divide the ones. Repeat the steps for the ones-place and one-dollar bills. **How much money does each person get?** *$21.* **How much money is left over?** *$1.*

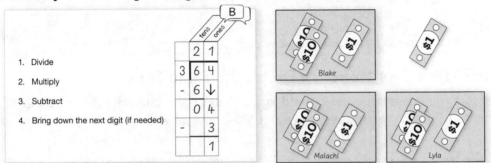

Have your child solve the other problems in the same way. Talk through each step and model each step with play money as needed.

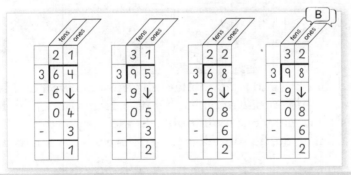

If your child can easily solve the problems mentally, explain that practicing the steps with smaller numbers prepares her to solve problems with three- and four-digit dividends later in the unit.

 Save the labeled mats for Lesson 10.4.

Independent Practice and Review

Have your child complete the Lesson 10.3 Practice and Review workbook pages.

Lesson 10.4
Divide Two-Digit Numbers with Trading

Purpose	Materials
• Trade play money to concretely divide tens and ones • Use the long division algorithm to divide tens and ones with trading	• Play money • Labeled mats from Lesson 10.3 • 2 pieces of paper • Die

Memory Work
- **Name 4 factors of 15.** *1, 3, 5, 15.*
- **Name 4 multiples of 15.** *Sample answers: 15, 30, 45, 60.*

Keeping track of all the steps in long division requires a lot of concentration and working memory. Don't be surprised if your child sometimes has trouble remembering the multiplication and division facts as he learns long division. Allow him to refer to the multiplication chart (Blackline Master 2) as needed. See the Unit 10 **Teaching Math with Confidence** for more tips on making long division as painless as possible.

In the last lesson, your child was able to evenly divide the tens in every long division problem. In this lesson, he'll learn how to solve problems that require trading.

You will need 25 one-dollar bills for this lesson. If you don't have enough play money bills, simply write $1 on slips of paper to create as many bills as needed.

Warm-up: Trade Play Money to Divide Tens and Ones

We'll pretend you run a lemonade stand again today. We'll use the three pieces of paper again as mats to divide the money you earn. Place the labeled mats (from Lesson 10.3) on the table.

One day, the lemonade stand earns $42. Give your child 4 ten-dollar bills and 2 one-dollar bills. **How many ten-dollar bills do each of you get?** *1.* Have him place 1 ten-dollar bill on each mat.

You still have 1 ten-dollar bill and 2 one-dollar bills. How can you divide them as evenly as possible? *Trade the ten-dollar bill for one-dollar bills.* Help your child trade 1 ten-dollar bill for 10 one-dollar bills. **How many one-dollar bills do each of you get?** *4.* Have him place 4 one-dollar bills on each mat. **So, how much money does each person earn in all?** *$14.*

Repeat with $78. **How much money does each person get?** *$26.*

Leave out the mats and play money for the next activity.

Activity (A): Divide Tens and Ones with Trading

In the last lesson, you learned how to use long division to divide tens and ones. Have your child use long division to complete the first problem. Guide him through the steps, and model the problem with play money if needed.

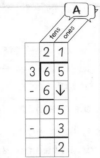

In this problem, you could evenly divide the tens. Today, you'll learn how to solve problems where you can't evenly divide the tens. We'll use the same steps.

One day, the lemonade stand earns $53. One friend is sick and can't help, so you divide the money between you and just one other friend. Give your child 5 ten-dollar bills and 3 one-dollar bills. Place 2 of the labeled mats (from Lesson 10.3) on the table.

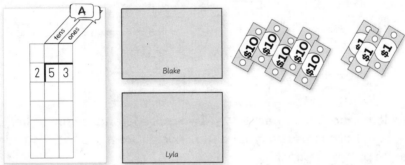

First, we'll divide the tens. Then, we'll divide the ones. I'll do the writing, and you're in charge of the play money.

What's the first step? *Divide.* **Let's divide the 5 tens into 2 equal groups. 2 times what gets us as close to 5 as possible?** *2.* Have your child place 2 ten-dollar bills on each mat. **Each person gets 2 ten-dollar bills, so I write a 2 in the quotient's tens-place.** Write 2 as shown.

What's the next step? *Multiply.* **2 times 2 equals 4.** Point to the numbers as you say them, and write 4 as shown. **You used up 4 tens.**

What's the next step? *Subtract.* Write a minus sign and horizontal line as shown. **5 minus 4 equals 1.** Write 1 as shown.

What's the next step? *Bring down the next digit (if needed).* Draw an arrow and write 3 as shown.

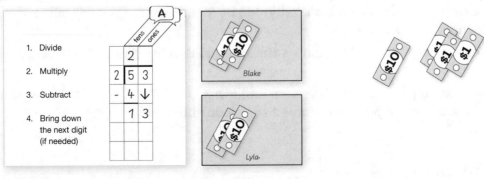

Remember, the space below the dividend is for keeping track of how much is left to divide. The 1 in the tens-place shows that we still have 1 ten left to divide. The 3 in the ones-place shows that we still have 3 ones to divide. So, how much money is left to divide in all? *$13.* Let's trade the 1 ten-dollar bill for 10 one-dollar bills so we can divide the 13 dollars as evenly as possible. Help your child trade 1 ten-dollar bill for 10 one-dollar bills.

Now, we go back to the first step. What's the first step? *Divide.* 2 times what gets us as close to 13 as possible? *6.* Have your child place 6 one-dollar bills on each mat. Each person gets 6 one-dollar bills, so I write a 6 in the quotient's ones-place. Write 6 as shown.

What's the next step? *Multiply.* 2 times 6 equals 12. You used up 12 ones.

What's the next step? *Subtract.* Write a minus sign and horizontal line as shown. 13 minus 12 equals 1. Write 1 as shown. We've divided the ones, so we're done! There are no more digits left to bring down, so we stop after the subtraction step. How much money does each person get? *$26.* How much money is left over? *$1.*

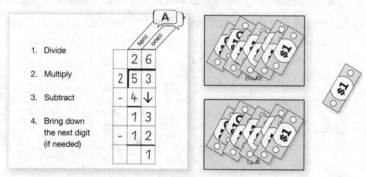

The next day, the lemonade stand earns $75. Two more friends come to help, so you divide the money into 5 equal groups. Have your child choose two more friends and write their names on 2 separate pieces of paper.

This time, I'll be in charge of the play money, and you'll be in charge of the writing. Take 7 ten-dollar bills and 5 one-dollar bills. First, we'll divide the tens. Then, we'll divide the ones.

What's the first step? *Divide.* What's 7 divided by 5? *1.* Place 1 ten-dollar bill on each mat. Have your child write 1 as shown.

What's the next step? *Multiply.* What's 1 times 5? *5.* I used up 5 tens. Have your child write 5 as shown.

What's the next step? *Subtract.* Have your child write a minus sign and horizontal line and complete the subtraction problem. I have 2 ten-dollar bills left.

What's the next step? *Bring down the next digit (if needed).* Have your child draw an arrow and write a 5 as shown.

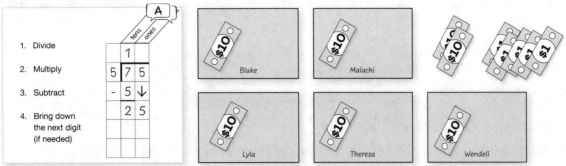

The 2 in the tens-place shows that we still have 2 tens to divide. The 5 in the ones-place shows that we still have 5 ones to divide. So, how much money is left to divide in all? *$25.* **Let's trade the 2 ten-dollar bills for 20 one-dollar bills so we can divide the 25 dollars evenly.** Trade the 2 ten-dollar bills for 20 one-dollar bills.

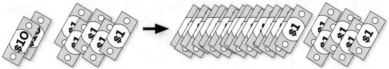

Now, it's time to divide the ones. Repeat the steps for the ones-place and one-dollar bills. **How much money does each person get?** *$15.* **How much money is left over?** *$0.*

Activity (B): Play Roll and Divide

Play Roll and Divide.

Roll and Divide

Materials: Die

Object of the Game: Score more points than your opponent by creating larger remainders.

On your turn, roll the die. Write the number on the die as the divisor in the first long division problem on your scorecard. Then, solve the problem. The remainder is your score for that problem. If there is no remainder, your score is 0.

For example, if you roll a 3 in the first problem, write 3 as the divisor. 83 ÷ 3 = 27 R2, so your score is 2.

Directions continued on next page.

Take turns completing the problems. Play until both players have completed their entire scorecard. Find the sum of each player's remainders. Whoever has the greater sum wins the game.

Advanced variation: Instead of completing the problems in order, choose which problem to complete for each roll. Try to choose a problem that will yield the greatest possible remainder.

Independent Practice and Review

Have your child complete the Lesson 10.4 Practice and Review workbook pages.

Lesson 10.5
Predict the Number of Digits in the Quotient

Purpose	Materials
• Practice multiplying and dividing with zeros • Use long division to divide two-digit numbers by one-digit numbers • Predict the number of digits and correctly place digits in one- and two-digit quotients	• Highlighter or light-colored marker • Die • Counters • Play money, optional

Memory Work	• **How many millimeters equal 1 centimeter?** *10.* • **How many centimeters equal 1 meter?** *100.* • **How many meters equal 1 kilometer?** *1,000.*

Children often write the digits in the quotient in the wrong place, especially when they begin dividing three- or four-digit numbers. In this lesson, you'll teach your child how to predict the number of digits in the quotient and place the digits correctly so that she's ready to tackle these harder problems with confidence.

Warm-up: Review Multiplying and Dividing with Zeros

Long division problems often involve multiplying or dividing with zeros. Let's review the rules for multiplying and dividing with zeros so that you're ready for these problems.

What's 300 times 0? *0.* What's 0 times 5,698? *0.* What's 0 times 0? *0.* **Any number times zero equals zero.**

What's 0 divided by 4? *0.* What's 0 divided by 694? *0.* **Zero divided by any other number equals zero. Imagine dividing zero cookies. No matter how many people share the cookies, they'll all get zero cookies.**

What's 4 divided by 0? *Sample answer: You can't divide a number by zero.* **This problem is like asking how to divide 4 cookies between 0 people. It's not possible to split cookies with people that don't exist, no matter how many cookies there are!**

Mathematicians say that dividing by zero is "undefined." You can't divide by zero, and zero isn't allowed to be the divisor for a division problem.

Activity (A):
Use Long Division to Solve Problems with Two-Digit or One-Digit Quotients

One of the most common mistakes kids make with long division is writing the digits in the quotient in the wrong place. Today, you'll learn how to predict how many digits will be in the quotient so you always know where to write the digits.

In the last lesson, you learned how to use the long division algorithm to divide tens and ones with trading. Have your child use long division to complete the first problem. Guide her through the steps, and model the problem with play money if needed. **What's the quotient in this problem?** *16.* **How many digits are in the quotient?** *2.*

Now, let's try the next problem. This time, you'll divide 48 by 5 instead of by 3. It's as if you earned $48 and had to split it with 5 friends instead of 3 friends. Do you expect the quotient will be larger or smaller than the first problem? Why? *Sample answer: The quotient will be smaller, since the 48 is divided into more groups.*

The first step is to divide. What's 4 divided by 5? *Sample answers: 0. We can't divide 4 into 5 equal groups.*

If your child has trouble with this question, model 48 with 4 ten-dollar bills and 8 one-dollar bills.

We don't have enough tens to evenly divide the tens into 4 groups. Instead, we divide 48 ones by 5. Highlight the 48. **The first digit in the quotient will go in the ones-place.**

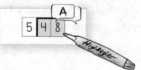

Highlighting the digits in the dividend helps your child know where to write the digits in the quotient.

5 times what is as close as possible to 48 without going over? *9.* Write 9 in the quotient. **Always write the digit in the quotient directly above the rightmost of the digits you're dividing. You divided 48 by 5. The rightmost digit in 48 is 8, so you write the 5 directly above the 8. 48 ones divided by 5 equals 9 ones.**

Now, we follow the usual steps to finish the problem. Have your child multiply and subtract to complete the problem.

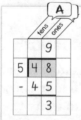

What's 48 divided by 5? *9, with a remainder of 3.* **What's the quotient in this problem?** *9.* **How many digits are in the quotient?** *1.*

Look back at both problems with your child. **In the first problem, we were able to divide the tens. So, we wrote the first digit in the quotient in the tens-place, and the quotient has two digits. In the second problem, we were not able to divide the tens. So, we wrote the first digit in the quotient in the ones-place, and the quotient has only one digit.**

Activity (A): Predict the Number of Digits in the Quotient

Have your child use long division to solve the rest of the problems in part A. Before she solves each problem, have her highlight the digits she will divide first, tell where she will write the first digit in the quotient, and tell how many digits each quotient will have. Use play money to model the problems as needed.

For 74 ÷ 7, discuss why there is a zero in the quotient's ones-place: **After you divide the tens, there are 4 ones left. 4 divided by 7 equals 0, so we write a 0 in the quotient's ones-place. Otherwise, the quotient would look like 1 instead of 10.**

Children sometimes have trouble remembering where to write the first digit in the quotient, especially in problems where the first digit goes in the ones-place. If your child has trouble with this, have her draw a capital X in the quotient's tens-place to remind her not to write the first digit there.

Activity (B): Play How Many Digits?

Play How Many Digits?

In this game, you decide whether the quotient for each problem has 1 or 2 digits. Your child does not need to solve the problems.

How Many Digits?

Materials: Two different-colored counters to use as game tokens; counters; die

Object of the Game: Have the most treasure when a player reaches the Finish square.

Each player chooses a counter to use as a game token and places it on the Start square. Place a few handfuls of counters in a pile next to the game board. These counters are the treasure chest.

On your turn, roll the die and advance your token the corresponding number of squares. Decide whether the quotient for the division problem has 1 or 2 digits. You do not have to solve the problem.

- If the quotient has 1 digit, take 1 counter from the treasure chest.
- If the quotient has 2 digits, take 2 counters from the treasure chest.

Take turns until one player reaches Finish. Whoever has collected more treasure wins the game.

Directions continued on next page.

Answer Key

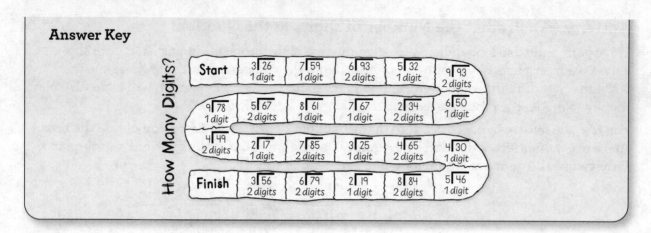

Independent Practice and Review

Have your child complete the Lesson 10.5 Practice and Review workbook pages.

Lesson 10.6
Divide Three-Digit Numbers with Long Division

Purpose	Materials
• Pratice solving division problems with small numbers • Use long division to divide three-digit numbers by one-digit numbers • Understand that dividing a number by a smaller divisor yields a larger quotient	• Highlighter or light-colored marker • Base-ten blocks • Place-Value Chart (Blackline Master 4) • 5 small pieces of paper or index cards • Playing cards

Memory Work	• **What do we call an angle with a measure equal to 180 degrees?** *Straight.* • **What do we call an angle with a measure equal to 90 degrees?** *Right.* • **What do we call an angle with a measure greater than 90 degrees and less than 180 degrees?** *Obtuse.* • **What do we call an angle with a measure less than 90 degrees?** *Acute.*

If you find that your child doesn't have the stamina to complete this lesson in one session, split the lesson over two days:

- Day 1: Do the Warm-up, Activity A, and Activity B. Then, have your child complete the Review page only.
- Day 2: Review the steps in Activity A. Then, have your child complete the Practice page. Stay close by as he completes the Practice page, and encourage him to model the problems with play money as needed.

Warm-up: Practice Solving Division Problems with 0 or 1 as the Quotient

Ask your child the following oral division problems. If your child has trouble with any of the problems, model them with unit blocks from your set of base-ten blocks. For example, for 2 divided by 5, place 2 units on the table: **We can't divide 2 units into 5 equal groups. So, the answer is 0, with a remainder of 2.**

- **2 divided by 5.** *0, with a remainder of 2.*
- **6 divided by 5.** *1, with a remainder of 1.*
- **4 divided by 5.** *0, with a remainder of 4.*
- **1 divided by 3.** *0, with a remainder of 1.*
- **8 divided by 6.** *1, with a remainder of 2.*

Activity (A):
Use Long Division to Divide Three-Digit Numbers by One-Digit Numbers

In the last few lessons, you divided two-digit numbers by one-digit numbers. You learned how to predict how many digits were in the quotient so you knew where to write the digits.

Today, you'll learn how to use long division to divide three-digit numbers by one-digit numbers. We follow the same steps we used for dividing two-digit numbers.

Show your child the two long division problems in part A. **We're going to divide 235 by 2. Then, we're going to divide 235 by 3. Which quotient do you expect to be greater? Why?** *Sample answer: I expect 235 divided by 2 to be greater, since we only have to divide 235 into two parts.*

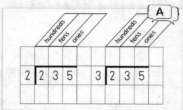

Let's solve both problems and see! First, we'll use long division to divide 235 by 2. Place 2 flats, 3 rods and 5 units on the Place-Value Chart. Place 2 small pieces of paper or index cards above the Place-Value Chart to use as a mat for each group.

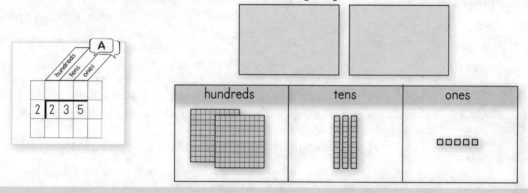

If your child prefers using money to model math problems, use play money instead of base-ten blocks.

First, we divide the hundreds. Can we divide 2 hundreds by 2? *Yes.* Highlight the 2 in 235. **The first digit in the quotient will go in the hundreds-place.**

What's 2 hundreds divided by 2? *1 hundred.* Place 1 flat on each piece of paper. **We put 1 hundred in each group, so I write 1 in the quotient's hundreds-place.** Write 1 in the quotient as shown.

The second step is to multiply to find how many hundreds we used. We put 1 hundred in each group, and there are 2 groups. 1 hundred times 2 equals 2 hundreds, so I write a 2 in the hundreds-column. Write 2 as shown.

The third step is to subtract. Write a minus sign and horizontal line. **2 hundreds minus 2 hundreds equals 0. We have 0 hundreds left.** Write 0 as shown.

We're done dividing the hundreds. Now, we bring down the next digit to get ready to divide the tens. Draw an arrow and write 3 as shown.

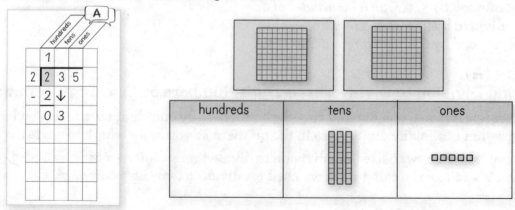

Now, we divide the tens. What's 3 divided by 2? *1.* Place 1 rod on each piece of paper. **We put 1 ten in each group, so I write 1 in the quotient's tens-place.** Write 1 as shown.

Next, we multiply. We put 1 ten in each group, and there are 2 groups. 1 ten times 2 equals 2 tens. Write 2 as shown.

Next, we subtract. Write a minus sign and horizontal line. **3 tens minus 2 tens equals 1 ten. We have 1 ten left.** Write 1 as shown.

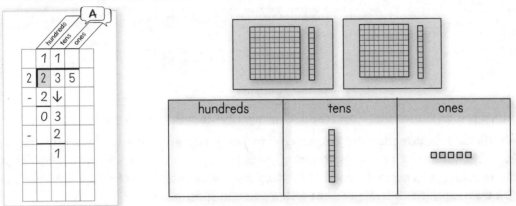

We're done dividing the tens. Now, we bring down the next digit to get ready to divide the ones. Draw an arrow and write 5 as shown. **1 ten and 5 ones equal 15 ones.** Trade the 1 left-over rod for 10 units and place them in the ones-column of the Place-Value Chart.

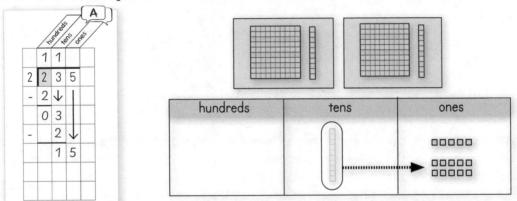

Follow the steps in the long division process to divide the ones and complete the problem.

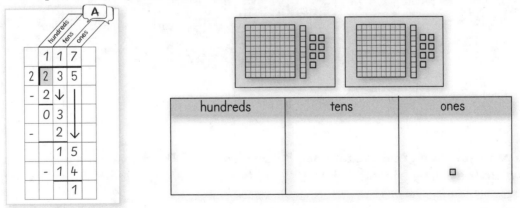

We've brought down the digit in the ones-place and divided the ones, so we're finally done! What's 235 divided by 2? *117, with a remainder of 1.*

Now, let's use long division to divide 235 by 3. Return the 2 flats, 3 rods, and 5 units to the Place-Value Chart. Add 1 more piece of paper above the Place-Value Chart, for a total of 3.

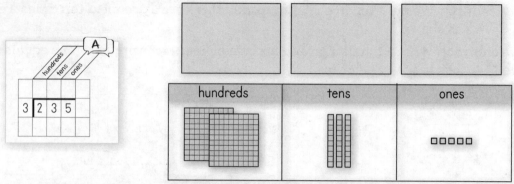

The first step is to divide the hundreds. Can we divide 2 flats into 3 equal groups? *No.*

We can't divide 2 hundreds into 3 equal groups, so we need to trade the 2 hundreds for 20 tens. Trade the 2 flats for 20 rods and place them in the tens-column of the Place-Value Chart. **2 hundreds and 3 tens equal 23 tens. We start by dividing 23 tens by 3.** Highlight the 2 and 3 in 235. **The first digit in the quotient will go in the tens-place.**

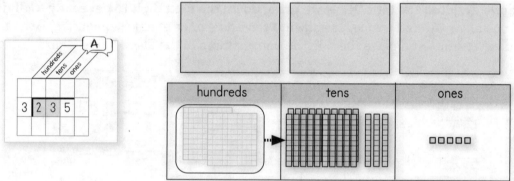

Demonstrate how to follow the steps for the tens-place and ones-place and complete the problem. Model each step with the base-ten blocks. After you finish, ask: **What's 235 divided by 3?** *78, with a remainder of 1.*

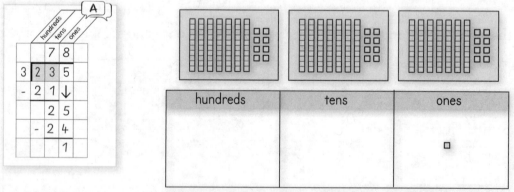

Which problem has a greater quotient? *235 divided by 2.* **Why do we get a greater quotient when we divide 235 by 2 instead of by 3?** *Sample answer: We split it into only 2 parts, instead of 3 parts.*

Imagine dividing \$235 between 2 people. Now, imagine dividing \$235 between 3 people. When you divide a number between fewer people, each person gets more. You'll want to keep this idea in mind for the Quotient Game in part B!

Activity (B): Play the Quotient Game

Play the Quotient Game.

As you play, encourage your child to use estimation and logical reasoning to create the division problem that yields the greatest possible quotient. It's generally best to try to make as large a three-digit number as possible and divide it by as small of a one-digit number as possible.

The Quotient Game

Materials: Deck of playing cards, with aces, 10s, jacks, queens, and kings removed (32 cards total)

Object of the Game: Score more points than the other player by creating greater quotients.

Shuffle the cards and place the stack face down on the table. On your turn, take 4 cards off the top of the deck. Use them to make a three-digit number and a one-digit number. Use the numbers to create a long division problem. Write the problem on your scorecard and solve it. The quotient is your score.

For example, if you have an 8, 2, 4, and 3, you could write division problems like 428 ÷ 3, 342 ÷ 8, or 843 ÷ 2. The best choice is 843 ÷ 2, since that problem yields the greatest quotient. 843 divided by 2 equals 421 R1, so your score is 421.

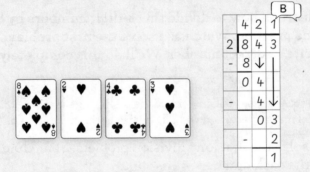

Sample play.

Play then passes to the other player. Continue until both players have completed both rounds. Add up each player's total points, either mentally or on scrap paper. The player with more points wins.

Independent Practice and Review

Have your child complete the Lesson 10.6 Practice and Review workbook pages.

Lesson 10.7
Multiply and Add to Check Long Division

Purpose	Materials
• Practice dividing three-digit numbers by one-digit numbers with long division • Multiply and add to check division problems with a remainder • Solve division word problems and interpret remainders	• Base-ten blocks, optional

Memory Work	• **What's zero times any number?** *Zero.* • **What's zero divided by any other number?** *Zero.* • **What's any number divided by zero?** *Undefined.*

If you find that your child doesn't have the stamina to complete this lesson in one session, split the lesson over two days:

• Day 1: Do the Warm-up, Activity A, and Activity B. Then, have your child complete the Review page only.

• Day 2: Review the problems in Activity B. Then, have your child complete the Practice page.

Warm-up (A): Practice Long Division

In the last lesson, you learned how to divide three-digit numbers by one-digit numbers. Let's warm up with some practice. Watch as I solve the first problem. Tap your pencil on the table each time I write a correct number. We'll do this completely silently so we can both concentrate.

If your child is not ready to solve these problems without help, skip the silent portion of this activity. Instead, use base-ten blocks to model the problems and verbally guide her through the steps (as in Lesson 10.6).

Slowly and deliberately solve the first long division problem. Your child should tap her pencil on the table after you write each number.

Then, reverse roles for the other two problems. Have your child solve each problem. Tap your pencil on the table every time she writes a correct number. If she makes a mistake, do not tap the table. Instead, give her a puzzled look to prompt her to check her work.

Activity (B): Multiply and Add to Check Division Problems with a Remainder

In Unit 5, you learned how to multiply and add to check your answers for division problems with small numbers. Today, you'll learn how to multiply and add to check your answers for division problems with larger numbers. You'll also practice solving division word problems.

Read aloud the first word problem: *Two friends work together to earn $764. They split the money equally. How much does each friend earn?* Which long division problem in part **A** matches this problem? *764 divided by 2.*

764 divided by 2 equals 382. So, how much money does each friend earn? *$382.* Write $382 in the space below the problem.

Multiplication is the opposite of division, so we can use multiplication to check the answer. We want to make sure that 2 groups of 382 equal 764, so we multiply 382 times 2. Write 382 × 2 vertically in the blank grid. Have your child complete the multiplication problem. **382 times 2 equals 764, so 764 divided by 2 equals 382. Our answer is correct.**

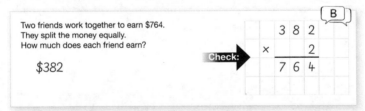

Read aloud the next word problem: *A baker makes 419 cookies. She arranges the cookies on 4 trays and puts the same number of cookies on each tray.* Which long division problem in part **A** matches this problem? *419 divided by 4.* **419 divided by 4 equals 104, with a remainder of 3.**

This word problem has 2 questions. The first question is: *How many cookies are on each tray?* *104.* Write "104 cookies" below the first question.

The second question is: *How many cookies are left over?* *3.* Write "3 cookies" below the second question.

Let's use multiplication to check this answer. First, we'll multiply 104 times 4 to find the number of cookies on the trays. Write 104 × 4 vertically in the blank grid. Have your child complete the multiplication problem.

104 times 4 equals 416. There are 416 cookies on the trays. Now, we add on the 3 leftover cookies. Write a 3 below the ones-place in the problem. Write a plus sign and horizontal line. Have your child complete the addition problem. **104 times 4 plus 3 equals 419, so our answer is correct.**

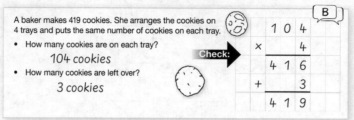

Have your child answer the final word problem (using the matching long division problem in part A). Then, have her multiply and add to check her answer.

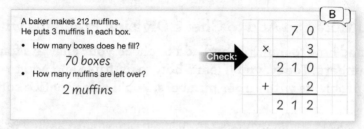

Independent Practice and Review

Have your child complete the Lesson 10.7 Practice and Review workbook pages.

Lesson 10.8
Divide Four-Digit Numbers with Long Division

Purpose	Materials
• Practice mental multiplication and division • Use long division to divide four-digit numbers by one-digit numbers • Multiply to estimate quotients	• Highlighter or light-colored marker • Play money • Counters

Memory Work   • **How many feet equal 1 mile?** *5,280.*

You will need 3 thousand-dollar bills for this lesson. If you don't have any in your play money set, simply write $1,000 on 3 slips of paper.

If you find that your child doesn't have the stamina to complete this lesson in one session, split the lesson over two days:

- Day 1: Do the Warm-up, Activity A, and Activity B. Then, have your child complete the Review page only.
- Day 2: Review how to use multiplication to estimate quotients (in Activity B). Then, have your child complete the Practice page.

Warm-up: Practice Mental Multiplication and Division

Ask your child the following mental math questions:

- **400 times 2?** *800.*
- **4,000 times 2?** *8,000.*
- **500 times 2?** *1,000.*
- **500 times 3?** *1,500.*

- **500 times 5?** *2,500.*
- **1,000 divided by 2?** *500.*
- **1,000 divided by 5?** *200.*
- **2,000 divided by 5?** *400.*

Activity (A):
Use Long Division to Divide Four-Digit Numbers by One-Digit Numbers

Today, you'll learn how to use long division to divide four-digit numbers by one-digit numbers.

Dividing four-digit numbers with long division is just like dividing three-digit numbers or two-digit numbers. You start with the thousands, and you repeat the steps until you have divided the ones.

Let's pretend 4 friends worked together to earn $3,813. They want to divide the money equally. Place 3 thousand-dollar bills, 8 hundred-dollar bills, 1 ten-dollar bill, and 3 one-dollar bills on the table.

Modeling the dividend with money makes the problem more concrete and helps your child make sense of the meaning of the dividend, divisor, and quotient.

About how much money do you expect each person will get? *Sample answer: About $1,000.* **How do you know?** *Sample answer: 3,813 is close to 4,000, and 4,000 divided by 4 equals 1,000.*

> If your child is confused by this question, move on to finding the exact quotient. You'll further discuss how to estimate quotients in part B.

The first step is to divide. We start with the thousands-place. Can we divide 3 thousands into 4 equal groups? *No.* **Instead, we'll think of the 3 thousands as 30 hundreds. 3 thousands and 8 hundreds equal 38 hundreds. We start by dividing 38 hundreds by 4.** High-light the 3 and 8 in 3,813. **The first digit in the quotient will go in the hundreds-place.**

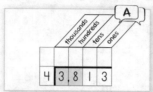

What's 38 hundreds divided by 4? *9 hundreds.* Write 9 in the quotient. Then, demonstrate how to follow the steps until you complete the problem.

$$
\begin{array}{r}
9\,5\,3 \\
4\ \overline{)3{,}8\,1\,3} \\
-3\,6 \\
\hline
2\,1 \\
-2\,0 \\
\hline
1\,3 \\
-1\,2 \\
\hline
1
\end{array}
$$

> At this point, most children will be ready to solve long division problems without directly modeling each step. If your child gets confused by any of the steps, use the play money to model each step in the same way as in the previous lessons.

After you finish, ask: **So, what's 3,813 divided by 4?** *953, with a remainder of 1.* **How many whole dollars will each person get?** *$953.* **What do you think they'll do with the leftover dollar?** *Sample answer: Trade it for quarters and give each person 25¢.*

Activity (B): Multiply to Estimate Quotients

> This activity uses a game show context to make practicing long division more fun. Feel free to ham it up with an over-the-top announcer voice as you teach.

Now, you get to appear on the famous game show, "Guess the Quotient!" In this game, you win money each time you accurately predict which number the quotient will be closest to. Your choices are 500, 1,000, 1,500, and 2,000.

The division problem for the first round is 3,138 divided by 2. Let's multiply to see which choice will be closest to the actual quotient.

- **What's 2 times 500?** *1,000.* **That's pretty far from 3,138.**
- **What's 2 times 1,000?** *2,000.* **Getting closer!**
- **What's 2 times 1,500?** *3,000.* **Pretty close!**
- **What's 2 times 2,000?** *4,000.* **That's further away from 3,138.**

The product of 2 times 1,500 is closest to 3,138, so 1,500 is the best guess. Have your child put a counter on 1,500 to mark the guess. **Now, divide 3,138 by 2 to find the exact quotient.** Have your child complete the division problem.

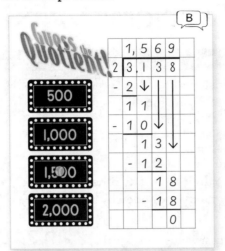

Once he finishes, say: **You found that 3,138 divided by 2 equals 1,569. 1,500 is the number closest to the quotient, so you were correct! You win $1,500!** Give your child $1,500 in play money.

Repeat with the other two long division problems. Encourage your child to use multiplication to predict which printed number will be closest to the quotient. For 2,546 ÷ 5, the best guess is 500. For 6,470 ÷ 3, the best guess is 2,000. **Congratulations, and thanks for appearing on Guess the Quotient!**

Independent Practice and Review

Have your child complete the Lesson 10.8 Practice and Review workbook pages.

Lesson 109
Solve Word Problems with Long Division

Purpose	Materials
• Practice the steps in long division • Practice using long division to divide four-digit numbers by one-digit numbers • Solve division word problems and interpret remainders	• None

Memory Work	• **What's zero times any number?** *Zero.* • **What's zero divided by any other number?** *Zero.* • **What's any number divided by zero?** *Undefined.*

In this lesson, your child will suggest words to create silly division word problems (as in the game Mad Libs). The problems also include ridiculous and unrealistic quantities to make them more relaxed and fun.

If you find that your child doesn't have the stamina to complete this lesson in one session, split the lesson over two days:

- Day 1: Do the Warm-up and Activity A. Then, have your child complete the Review page only.
- Day 2: Repeat the Warm-up. Then, have your child complete the Practice page.

Warm-up: Practice the Steps in Long Division

Earlier in the unit, you learned a silly sentence to remember the steps in long division. Do you remember the sentence? *Dirty monkeys smell bad.*

Remember, the first letter of each word matches the steps. Write the first letter of each word on a piece of scrap paper. **What step does the D stand for?** *Divide.* Complete the word. Then, repeat with the other letters.

> *Divide*
> *Multiply*
> *Subtract*
> *Bring down*

We'll keep this piece of paper nearby. You can look at it any time you need help remembering the steps. Keep the paper nearby for your child to refer to when she solves long division problems in this lesson.

Activity (A): Fill in the Blanks to Create Silly Division Word Problems

In the last lesson, you learned how to divide four-digit numbers by one-digit numbers. Today, you'll use long division to solve silly word problems.

Keep the Lesson Activities page hidden as you introduce the first activity.

Have you ever played the game Mad Libs? *Answers will vary.* **In this game, people suggest words to complete the blanks in a story. They don't know what the story is about, so the story often ends up pretty silly.**

I'm going to ask you to tell me some words, and I'll write your answers in the blanks in the word problems.

First, tell me the name of a boy. *Sample answer: Bob.* Write the name in the first blank in the first word problem. **Next, tell me an object. It can be any sort of object.** *Sample answer: Bowling ball.* Write the plural form of the object (for example, "bowling balls") in the next blank.

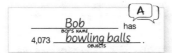

Sample completed problem.

Continue in the same way with the rest of the word problems. Keep the page hidden while you complete the blanks so that your child doesn't know the context for each problem. Once you've completed all the blanks, read and enjoy the completed word problems together.

Activity (A): Divide Four-Digit Numbers to Solve Silly Word Problems

Now, let's use long division to solve these silly word problems. Remember, you can look at the steps we wrote in the warm-up if you forget any of them.

Read the first completed word problem aloud. Have your child use long division to solve the matching problem. Once she completes the division problem, have her use the quotient and remainder to answer the word problem. For example: *Bob has 1,357 bowling balls in each group, with 3 left over.* Repeat with the other word problems.

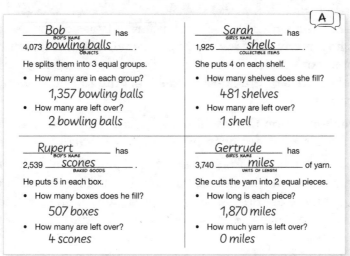

Completed long division problems.

Sample answers. Have your child label her answers based on the words she used to complete the word problems.

Independent Practice and Review

Have your child complete the Lesson 10.9 Practice and Review workbook pages.

Lesson 10.10
Enrichment (Optional)

Purpose	Materials
• Practice memory work • Preview division with a fractional result • Use long division to calculate the number of calories in crackers or cookies • Summarize what your child has learned and assess your child's progress	• *The Multiplying Menace Divides*, written by Pam Calvert and illustrated by Wayne Geehan • Nutrition labels for several different types of cookies or crackers

You will need nutrition labels for several different types of cookies or crackers for the enrichment activity. You can print these off the internet if you don't have several kinds handy. The activity will work best if the nutrition label lists 9 or fewer cookies or crackers per serving.

Warm-up: Review Memory Work

Quiz your child on all memory work through Unit 10. See pages 536-537 for the full list.

Math Picture Book: *The Multiplying Menace Divides*

Read *The Multiplying Menace Divides*, written by Pam Calvert and illustrated by Wayne Geehan. As you read, discuss what division problem matches the magic of the Great Divide wand.

This book previews the idea that the result of division can be a fraction. Your child will learn more about this in fifth grade.

Enrichment Activity: Find the Number of Calories in Each Cookie or Cracker

Have you ever looked at the nutrition label on packaged foods? *Answers will vary.* Briefly discuss your child's experiences with nutrition labels. **Nutrition labels tell us how many calories are in one serving. Calories measure how much energy food gives us.**

Show your child the nutrition labels for several different types of cookies or crackers. **The nutrition label tells how many calories are in one serving, but it doesn't tell how many calories are in each cookie or cracker. We need to divide the number of calories in one serving by the number of cookies or crackers in each serving to find how many calories are in each cookie or cracker.**

Which cookie or cracker do you think will have the most calories per item? Which do you think will have the fewest calories per item? *Answers will vary.*

Help your child use long division to find the number of calories in each cookie or cracker. He should divide the number of calories per serving by the number of cookies or crackers in one serving. For example, if there are 80 calories and 5 crackers in one serving: **80 divided by 5 equals 16, so there are 16 calories per cracker.** Help your child round as needed.

After your child finds the number of calories in each type of cookie or cracker, compare the results to his prediction.

If the number of cookies or crackers per serving is greater than 10, show your child how to use a calculator to find the number of calories per cookie or cracker.

Unit Wrap-Up

Have your child complete the Unit 10 Wrap-Up.

Unit 10 Answer Key

10.1 Practice

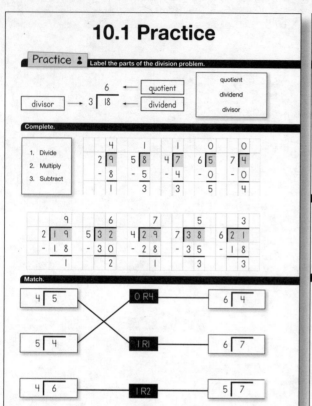

Practice — Label the parts of the division problem.

10.1 Review

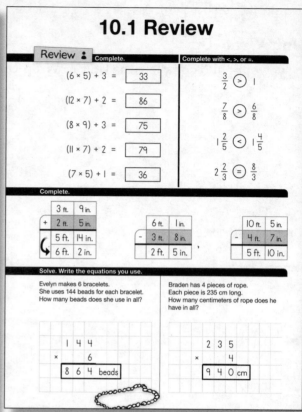

Review — Complete.

$(6 \times 5) + 3 = \boxed{33}$

$(12 \times 7) + 2 = \boxed{86}$

$(8 \times 9) + 3 = \boxed{75}$

$(11 \times 7) + 2 = \boxed{79}$

$(7 \times 5) + 1 = \boxed{36}$

Complete with <, >, or =.

$\frac{3}{2} \enspace > \enspace 1$

$\frac{7}{8} \enspace > \enspace \frac{6}{8}$

$1\frac{2}{5} \enspace < \enspace 1\frac{4}{5}$

$2\frac{2}{3} \enspace = \enspace \frac{8}{3}$

10.2 Practice

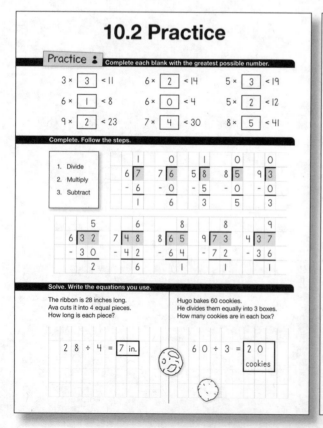

Practice — Complete each blank with the greatest possible number.

10.2 Review

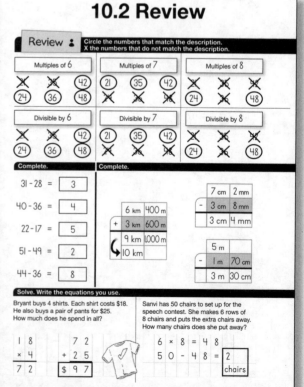

Review — Circle the numbers that match the description. X the numbers that do not match the description.

Unit 10 Answer Key

10.3 Practice

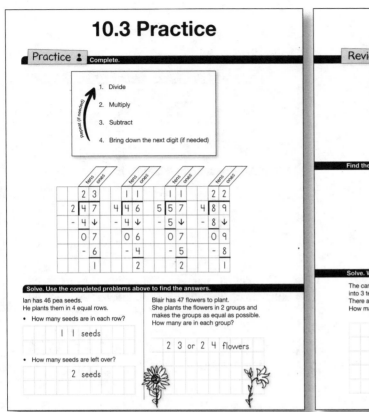

Practice Complete.

1. Divide
2. Multiply
3. Subtract
4. Bring down the next digit (if needed)

Repeat (if needed)

		tens	ones			tens	ones			tens	ones			tens	ones
		2	3			1	1			1	1			2	2
2		4	7	4		4	6	5		5	7	4		8	9
-		4	↓	-		4	↓	-		5	↓	-		8	↓
		0	7			0	6			0	7			0	9
	-		6		-		4		-		5		-		8
			1				2				2				1

Solve. Use the completed problems above to find the answers.

Ian has 46 pea seeds.
He plants them in 4 equal rows.

• How many seeds are in each row?

| 1 | 1 | seeds |

• How many seeds are left over?

| 2 | seeds |

Blair has 47 flowers to plant.
She plants the flowers in 2 groups and
makes the groups as equal as possible.
How many are in each group?

| 2 | 3 | or | 2 | 4 | flowers |

10.3 Review

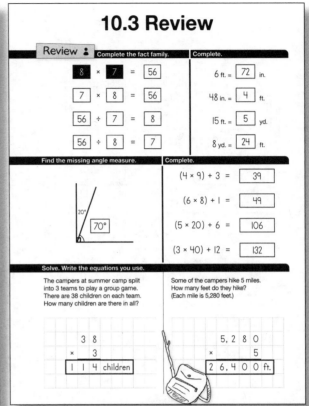

Review Complete the fact family. | Complete.

8	×	7	=	56
7	×	8	=	56
56	÷	7	=	8
56	÷	8	=	7

6 ft. = | 72 | in.

48 in. = | 4 | ft.

15 ft. = | 5 | yd.

8 yd. = | 24 | ft.

Find the missing angle measure. | Complete.

20°
| 70° |

$(4 × 9) + 3$ = | 39 |

$(6 × 8) + 1$ = | 49 |

$(5 × 20) + 6$ = | 106 |

$(3 × 40) + 12$ = | 132 |

Solve. Write the equations you use.

The campers at summer camp split
into 3 teams to play a group game.
There are 38 children on each team.
How many children are there in all?

		3	8
×			3
1	1	4	children

Some of the campers hike 5 miles.
How many feet do they hike?
(Each mile is 5,280 feet.)

	5,	2	8	0
×				5
2	6,	4	0	0	ft.

10.4 Practice

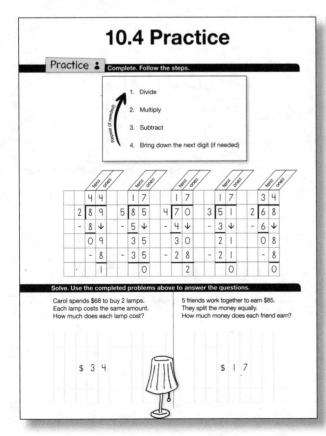

Practice Complete. Follow the steps.

1. Divide
2. Multiply
3. Subtract
4. Bring down the next digit (if needed)

Repeat (if needed)

		tens	ones			tens	ones			tens	ones			tens	ones			tens	ones
		4	4			1	7			1	7			1	7			3	4
2		8	9	5		8	5	4		7	0	3		5	1	2		6	8
-		8	↓	-		5	↓	-		4	↓	-		3	↓	-		6	↓
		0	9			3	5			3	0			2	1			0	8
	-		8		-	3	5		-	2	8		-	2	1		-		8
			1				0				2				0				0

Solve. Use the completed problems above to answer the questions.

Carol spends $68 to buy 2 lamps.
Each lamp costs the same amount.
How much does each lamp cost?

$ | 3 | 4 |

5 friends work together to earn $85.
They split the money equally.
How much money does each friend earn?

$ | 1 | 7 |

10.4 Review

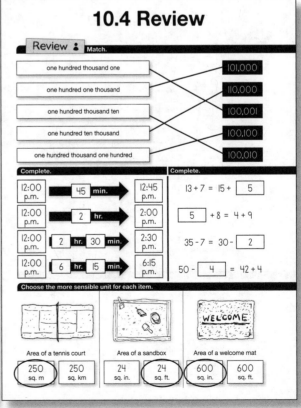

Review Match.

one hundred thousand one
one hundred one thousand
one hundred thousand ten
one hundred ten thousand
one hundred thousand one hundred

101,000
110,000
100,001
100,100
100,010

Complete. | **Complete.**

12:00 p.m. | 45 min. | 12:45 p.m.

12:00 p.m. | 2 hr. | 2:00 p.m.

12:00 p.m. | 2 hr. 30 min. | 2:30 p.m.

12:00 p.m. | 6 hr. 15 min. | 6:15 p.m.

$13 + 7 = 15 +$ | 5 |

| 5 | $+ 8 = 4 + 9$

$35 - 7 = 30 -$ | 2 |

$50 -$ | 4 | $= 42 + 4$

Choose the more sensible unit for each item.

Area of a tennis court
(250 sq. m) | 250 sq. km

Area of a sandbox
24 sq. in. | (24 sq. ft.)

Area of a welcome mat
(600 sq. in.) | 600 sq. ft.

Unit 10 Answer Key

10.5 Practice

Practice 👤 Complete. Follow the steps.

1. Divide
2. Multiply
3. Subtract
4. Bring down the next digit (if needed)

repeat (if needed)

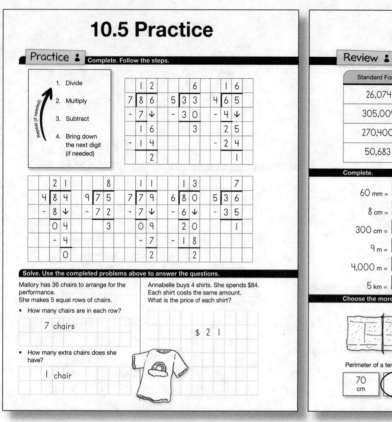

	1	2				6		1	6
7	8	6	5	3	3		4	6	5
−	7	↓	−	3	0		−	4	↓
	1	6			3			2	5
−	1	4					−	2	4
		2							1

	2	1			8		1	1		1	3			7
4	8	4	9	7	5	7	7	9	6	8	0	5	3	6
−	8	↓	−	7	2	−	7	↓	−	6	↓	−	3	5
	0	4			3		0	9		2	0			1
	−	4					−	7		−	1	8		
		0						2			2			

Solve. Use the completed problems above to answer the questions.

Mallory has 36 chairs to arrange for the performance.
She makes 5 equal rows of chairs.

• How many chairs are in each row?

    7 chairs

• How many extra chairs does she have?

    1 chair

Annabelle buys 4 shirts. She spends $84.
Each shirt costs the same amount.
What is the price of each shirt?

    $ 2 1

10.5 Review

Review 👤 Complete the chart.

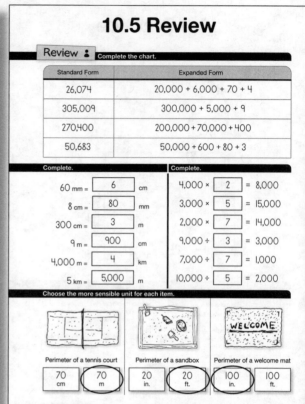

Standard Form	Expanded Form
26,074	20,000 + 6,000 + 70 + 4
305,009	300,000 + 5,000 + 9
270,400	200,000 + 70,000 + 400
50,683	50,000 + 600 + 80 + 3

Complete.

60 mm = **6** cm
8 cm = **80** mm
300 cm = **3** m
9 m = **900** cm
4,000 m = **4** km
5 km = **5,000** m

Complete.

4,000 × **2** = 8,000
3,000 × **5** = 15,000
2,000 × **7** = 14,000
9,000 ÷ **3** = 3,000
7,000 ÷ **7** = 1,000
10,000 ÷ **5** = 2,000

Choose the more sensible unit for each item.

Perimeter of a tennis court
70 cm   (70 m)

Perimeter of a sandbox
20 in.   (20 ft.)

Perimeter of a welcome mat
(100 in.)   100 ft.

10.6 Practice

Practice 👤 Complete. Follow the steps.

1. Divide
2. Multiply
3. Subtract
4. Bring down the next digit (if needed)

repeat (if needed)

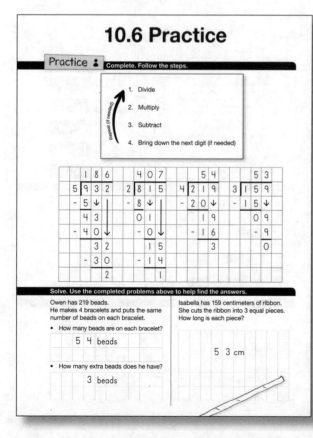

	1	8	6		4	0	7			5	4			5	3
5	9	3	2	2	8	1	5	4	2	1	9	3	1	5	9
−	5	↓		−	8	↓		−	2	0	↓	−	1	5	↓
	4	3			0	1			1	9			0	9	
−	4	0	↓	−	0	↓		−	1	6		−	9		
		3	2		1	5				3			0		
	−	3	0	−	1	4									
			2			1									

Solve. Use the completed problems above to help find the answers.

Owen has 219 beads.
He makes 4 bracelets and puts the same number of beads on each bracelet.

• How many beads are on each bracelet?

    5 4 beads

• How many extra beads does he have?

    3 beads

Isabella has 159 centimeters of ribbon.
She cuts the ribbon into 3 equal pieces.
How long is each piece?

    5 3 cm

10.6 Review

Review 👤 Complete.

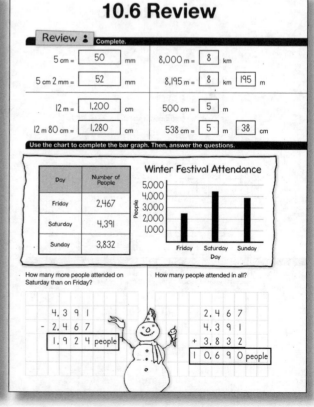

5 cm = **50** mm
5 cm 2 mm = **52** mm
12 m = **1,200** cm
12 m 80 cm = **1,280** cm

8,000 m = **8** km
8,195 m = **8** km **195** m
500 cm = **5** m
538 cm = **5** m **38** cm

Use the chart to complete the bar graph. Then, answer the questions.

Day	Number of People
Friday	2,467
Saturday	4,391
Sunday	3,832

Winter Festival Attendance

How many more people attended on Saturday than on Friday?

    4,391
  − 2,467
   1,924 people

How many people attended in all?

    2,467
    4,391
  + 3,832
  1 0,6 9 0 people

Unit 10 Answer Key

10.7 Practice

Practice Complete. Follow the steps.
Then, multiply (or multiply and add) to check your answers.

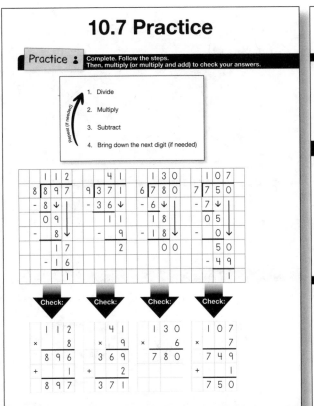

10.7 Review

Review Find the perimeter or area.

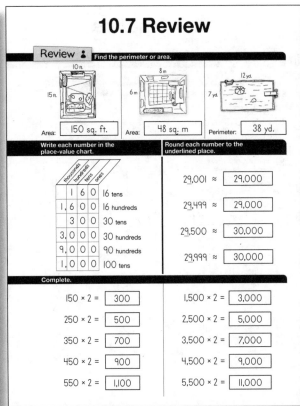

Area: 150 sq. ft.   Area: 48 sq. m   Perimeter: 38 yd.

Write each number in the place-value chart.

thousands	hundreds	tens	ones	
1	6	0		16 tens
1,	6	0	0	16 hundreds
	3	0	0	30 tens
3,	0	0	0	30 hundreds
9,	0	0	0	90 hundreds
1,	0	0	0	100 tens

Round each number to the underlined place.

29,001 ≈ 29,000

29,499 ≈ 29,000

29,500 ≈ 30,000

29,999 ≈ 30,000

Complete.

150 × 2 = 300

250 × 2 = 500

350 × 2 = 700

450 × 2 = 900

550 × 2 = 1,100

1,500 × 2 = 3,000

2,500 × 2 = 5,000

3,500 × 2 = 7,000

4,500 × 2 = 9,000

5,500 × 2 = 11,000

10.8 Practice

Practice Circle the more accurate estimate for each quotient.

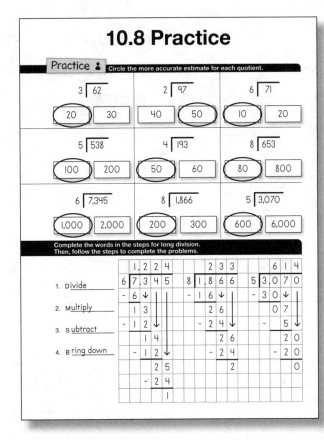

**Complete the words in the steps for long division.
Then, follow the steps to complete the problems.**

1. D ivide
2. M ultiply
3. S ubtract
4. B ring down

10.8 Review

Review Write whether each angle is acute, right, obtuse, or straight.

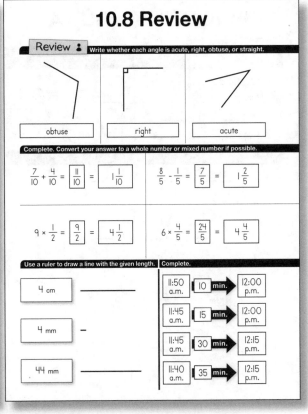

obtuse   right   acute

Complete. Convert your answer to a whole number or mixed number if possible.

$\frac{7}{10} + \frac{4}{10} = \frac{11}{10} = 1\frac{1}{10}$

$\frac{8}{5} - \frac{1}{5} = \frac{7}{5} = 1\frac{2}{5}$

$9 \times \frac{1}{2} = \frac{9}{2} = 4\frac{1}{2}$

$6 \times \frac{4}{5} = \frac{24}{5} = 4\frac{4}{5}$

Use a ruler to draw a line with the given length.

4 cm ——————

4 mm —

44 mm ——————

Complete.

11:50 a.m. →10 min.→ 12:00 p.m.

11:45 a.m. →15 min.→ 12:00 p.m.

11:45 a.m. →30 min.→ 12:15 p.m.

11:40 a.m. →35 min.→ 12:15 p.m.

Unit 10 Answer Key

10.9 Practice

Practice Use long division to solve.
Write the long division problems in the work space.

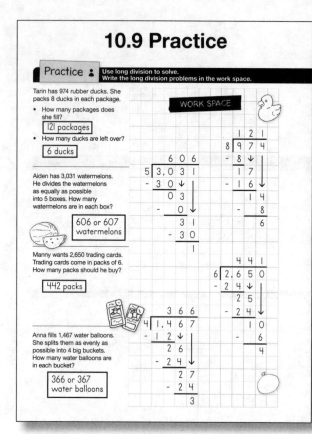

Tarin has 974 rubber ducks. She packs 8 ducks in each package.
- How many packages does she fill?

  121 packages
- How many ducks are left over?

  6 ducks

Aiden has 3,031 watermelons. He divides the watermelons as equally as possible into 5 boxes. How many watermelons are in each box?

606 or 607 watermelons

Manny wants 2,650 trading cards. Trading cards come in packs of 6. How many packs should he buy?

442 packs

Anna fills 1,467 water balloons. She splits them as evenly as possible into 4 big buckets. How many water balloons are in each bucket?

366 or 367 water balloons

WORK SPACE

10.9 Review

Review Use a protractor to measure the angles.

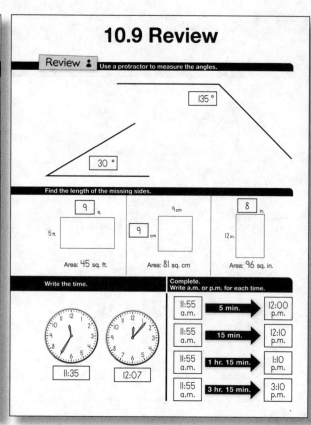

135°

30°

Find the length of the missing sides.

9 ft. 5 ft. Area: 45 sq. ft.

9 cm 9 cm Area: 81 sq. cm

8 in. 12 in. Area: 96 sq. in.

Write the time.

11:35   12:07

Complete. Write a.m. or p.m. for each time.

11:55 a.m.	5 min.	12:00 p.m.
11:55 a.m.	15 min.	12:10 p.m.
11:55 a.m.	1 hr. 15 min.	1:10 p.m.
11:55 a.m.	3 hr. 15 min.	3:10 p.m.

10.10 Unit Wrap-Up A

Unit Wrap-Up Write the steps for long division in order.

1. Divide
2. Multiply
3. Subtract
4. Bring down

Circle the more accurate estimate for each division problem.

4) 167   30   (40)

5) 614   (100)   200

6) 1,236   (200)   2,000

Use long division to complete.
Then, multiply (or multiply and add) to check your answer.

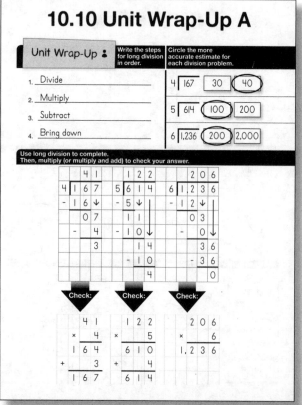

Check: Check: Check:

10.10 Unit Wrap-Up B

Unit Wrap-Up Use long division to solve.
Write the long division problems in the work space.

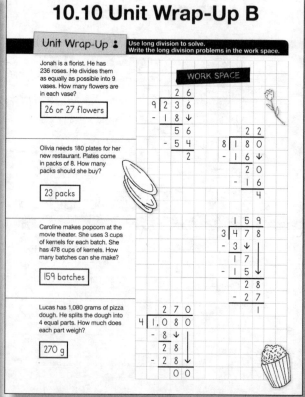

Jonah is a florist. He has 236 roses. He divides them as equally as possible into 9 vases. How many flowers are in each vase?

26 or 27 flowers

Olivia needs 180 plates for her new restaurant. Plates come in packs of 8. How many packs should she buy?

23 packs

Caroline makes popcorn at the movie theater. She uses 3 cups of kernels for each batch. She has 478 cups of kernels. How many batches can she make?

159 batches

Lucas has 1,080 grams of pizza dough. He splits the dough into 4 equal parts. How much does each part weigh?

270 g

WORK SPACE

Unit 10 Checkpoint

What to Expect at the End of Unit 10

By the end of Unit 10, most children will be able to do the following:

- Use long division to solve division problems (up to four digits divided by one digit). Most children will be able to use the steps to solve long division problems independently, but some will still need coaching and support. Many children will make occasional mistakes, especially in problems involving zero.
- Use multiplication (and addition) to check answers to division problems.

Is Your Child Ready to Move on?

In Unit 11, your child will study geometry. Your child does not need to have fully mastered multi-digit long division before moving on. He'll continue to practice long division on the Review workbook pages.

Unit 11
Geometry

Overview

Your child will study geometry, with a focus on relationships between lines. After a brief introduction to geometry vocabulary, she'll learn to identify quadrilaterals based on whether they have right angles, pairs of parallel sides, or equal sides. She'll also learn to categorize triangles based on their angles and find lines of symmetry in triangles and quadrilaterals.

Children often enjoy this shift in focus from numbers to spatial skills. Your child will practice long division in the review pages so that she continues to build fluency.

What Your Child Will Learn

In this unit, your child will learn to:

- Identify and label points, rays, lines, and line segments
- Identify parallel, perpendicular, and intersecting lines
- Identify, construct, and draw trapezoids, parallelograms, squares, rectangles, and rhombuses
- Identify and draw right triangles, obtuse triangles, and acute triangles
- Find lines of symmetry in triangles and quadrilaterals

Lesson List

Lesson 11.1   Points, Rays, Lines, and Line Segments

Lesson 11.2   Parallel, Perpendicular, and Intersecting Lines

Lesson 11.3   Identify Quadrilaterals

Lesson 11.4   Properties of Quadrilaterals

Lesson 11.5   Identify Triangles by Their Angles

Lesson 11.6   Symmetry in Triangles and Quadrilaterals

Lesson 11.7   Enrichment (Optional)

Extra Materials Needed for Unit 11

- 4 craft sticks or narrow strips of paper
- 2 pencils
- For optional Enrichment Lesson:
    - *Seeing Symmetry*, written and illustrated by Loreen Leedy. Holiday House, 2013.
    - Paper square, approximately 6 inches by 6 inches
    - Ruler
    - Scissors
    - Tape or glue
    - Pushpin
    - Pencil

Teaching Math with Confidence:
More Sophisticated Ways to Analyze and Reason About Shapes

In this unit, your child will learn how to identify quadrilaterals based on the relationships between the shapes' sides. She'll look for pairs of parallel sides, right angles, and equal sides as she determines whether the shapes are parallelograms, trapezoids, squares, rectangles, or rhombuses.

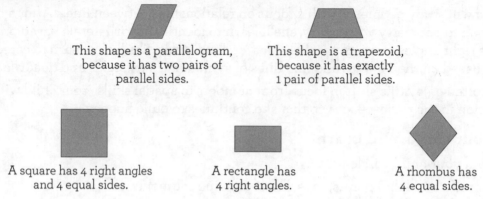

This shape is a parallelogram, because it has two pairs of parallel sides.

This shape is a trapezoid, because it has exactly 1 pair of parallel sides.

A square has 4 right angles and 4 equal sides.

A rectangle has 4 right angles.

A rhombus has 4 equal sides.

Your child will also learn how to analyze triangles' angles in order to categorize them.

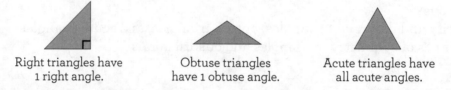

Right triangles have 1 right angle.

Obtuse triangles have 1 obtuse angle.

Acute triangles have all acute angles.

Analyzing shapes helps your child reason about shapes more abstractly and not just rely on their overall "look" to identify them. Most children need many concrete examples and hands-on experiences to fully grasp these properties and definitions. Your child will construct shapes from craft sticks, draw shapes, play guessing games, and fold paper shapes throughout the unit to help her kinesthetically understand these basic principles of geometry.

Lesson 11.1
Points, Rays, Lines, and Line Segments

Purpose	Materials
• Practice drawing angles with a protractor • Learn the definitions of points, rays, lines, and line segments • Label and draw points, rays, lines, and line segments	• Protractor

| Memory Work | • **What do we call an angle with a measure less than 90 degrees?** *Acute.*
• **What do we call an angle with a measure equal to 90 degrees?** *Right.*
• **What do we call an angle with a measure greater than 90 degrees and less than 180 degrees?** *Obtuse.*
• **What do we call an angle with a measure equal to 180 degrees?** *Straight.* |

Warm-up: Draw Angles with a Protractor

Have your child draw a 45° angle and a 160° angle on a piece of scrap paper. After your child draws each angle, have her tell whether it is acute, right, obtuse, or straight.

The 45° angle is acute. The 160° angle is obtuse.

Activity (A): Introduce Points, Lines, Line Segments, and Rays

We're starting a new unit on geometry today. In Unit 8, you learned about angles. In this unit, you'll learn how we put together lines and angles to make shapes. Today, you'll learn about the building blocks of shapes: points, lines, line segments, and rays.

A *point* marks a specific location. This point is labeled with an R, so we call it "point R."

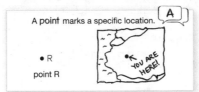

Point R marks a specific place on the paper, just like a "You are here" sign on a map tells you exactly where you are.

A *line* is a straight line that connects two points. It has no endpoints. Mathematicians imagine that lines continue forever in either direction, even though we can't really draw a line like that! Point to the arrows at either end of the line. **The arrows remind us that the line continues beyond what's drawn on the page.**

We use two points on the line to label it. **This line connects points E and F, so we call it "line EF."**

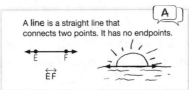

Have you ever watched the sun go down over the ocean? Or seen it in a picture or movie? *Answers will vary.* The horizon line between the ocean and sky is like a line in geometry. It's straight, and you can't see the end of it in either direction.

A *line segment* is part of a line. It has two endpoints. Point to the endpoints at either end of the line segment. **We use the endpoints of the line segment to label it. The endpoints of this line segment are points A and B, so we call it "line segment AB."**

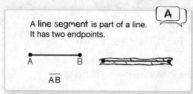

A piece of ribbon is like a line segment. It's one part of a longer piece of ribbon, just like a line segment is one part of a longer line.

A *ray* is also part of a line. It has only one endpoint and continues forever in the other direction. We label rays with their endpoint and another point on the ray. This ray has point X as its endpoint, and it goes through point Y, so we call it "ray XY." Point to the arrow at the right end of the ray. **The arrow reminds us that the ray continues beyond what's drawn on the page.**

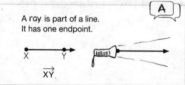

A flashlight is like a ray. The light begins at the flashlight and then extends in the other direction for a long way.

Activity (B): Label Lines, Line Segments, and Rays

Now, I'll show you how to label lines, line segments, and rays. Point to $\overleftrightarrow{MN}$. **This line goes through points M and N, so first I write MN. Mathematicians always write capital letters when they label points.** Write "MN" in the box below the line, with no space between the letters.

Then, I draw a line above the letters with two arrows. Draw a line above the letters with two arrows, as shown.

Can you find another line in part B? *Child points to $\overleftrightarrow{KL}$.* Have your child label this line in the same way.

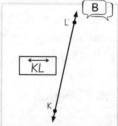

Point to $\overline{IJ}$. **This line segment ends at points I and J, so first I write IJ.** Write "IJ" in the box below the line segment. **Then, I draw a line segment symbol over the letters.** Draw a line over the letters, as shown. **The line segment symbol doesn't have arrows, since line segments don't continue forever.**

Can you find another line segment in part B? *Child points to* $\overline{GH}$. Have your child label this line segment in the same way.

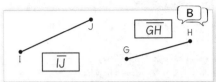

Point to $\overrightarrow{CD}$. **When we label rays, we first write the endpoint. Then, we write the other point that the ray goes through. This ray begins at point C and goes through point D, so I write CD.** Write "CD" in the box next to the ray. **Then, I draw a ray symbol over the letters.** Draw a line with one arrow over the letters, as shown. **The arrow shows that the ray continues in the direction of D.**

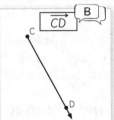

Can you find another ray in part B? *Child points to* $\overrightarrow{RQ}$. **Which point is the ray's endpoint?** *Point R.* **What other point does the ray go through?** *Q.* **When we label rays, we first write the endpoint. So, write R first, then Q.** Have your child label the ray as shown.

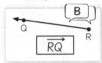

Activity (C): Draw Lines, Line Segments, and Rays

Now, you get to draw some lines, line segments, and rays. Once you finish drawing them, you'll find a secret word. Point to the first line in the list. **What's the name of the first item to draw?** *Line BN.* Help your child find points B and N. Then, have her draw a line to connect the two dots. Remind her to extend the line slightly beyond the points and draw arrows at both ends.

Continue in the same way with the rest of the lines, line segments, and rays. Once she finishes, have her turn the page upside down to find the secret word.

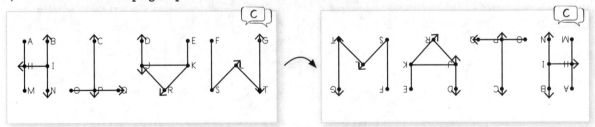

Your child may use a ruler to draw the lines or draw them freehand.

Independent Practice and Review

Have your child complete the Lesson 11.1 Practice and Review workbook pages.

Lesson 11.2
Parallel, Perpendicular, and Intersecting Lines

Purpose	Materials
• Practice identifying points, lines, line segments, and rays • Identify parallel, perpendicular, and intersecting lines • Construct quadrilaterals and analyze the relationships between the sides	• 4 craft sticks or narrow strips of paper • 2 dice

Memory Work	• **What's zero times any number?** *Zero.* • **What's zero divided by any other number?** *Zero.* • **What's any number divided by zero?** *Undefined.*

Warm-up (A): Identify Points, Lines, Line Segments, and Rays

In the last lesson, you learned about points, lines, line segments, and rays. Point to each figure in part A and have your child tell whether it is a point, line, line segment, or ray.

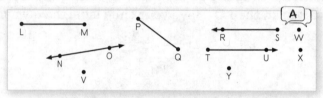

V, Y, W, and X are points. $\overleftrightarrow{NO}$ is a line. $\overrightarrow{SR}$ and $\overrightarrow{TU}$ are rays. $\overline{LM}$ and $\overline{PQ}$ are line segments.

Activity (B): Introduce Parallel, Perpendicular, and Intersecting Lines

Today, you'll learn three ways to describe relationships between lines.

Parallel lines are always the same distance apart, like railroad tracks. No matter how far you continue the lines, they never cross. Have your child arrange two craft sticks or narrow strips of paper to match the parallel lines.

Point to the parallel lines symbol (∥). **This symbol means "is parallel to." We read this statement as "Line AB is parallel to line CD."**

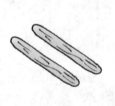

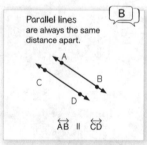

Intersecting lines cross each other. Line EF intersects line GH. Have your child identify the 4 angles that the two lines create where they intersect. Then, have him arrange two craft sticks to match the intersecting lines.

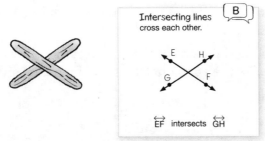

Point at $\overleftrightarrow{NO}$ in part A. **Remember, mathematicians imagine that lines continue forever. If you extended line NO, it would intersect line segment PQ, even though the printed lines don't cross on the paper.**

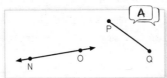

Perpendicular lines are intersecting lines that intersect to create 4 right angles. Draw a small square in the corner of one angle. **Remember, the small square means that the angle is a right angle.** Have your child arrange two craft sticks to match the perpendicular lines.

Point to the perpendicular lines symbol (⊥). **This symbol means "is perpendicular to." We read this statement as "Line IJ is perpendicular to line KL."**

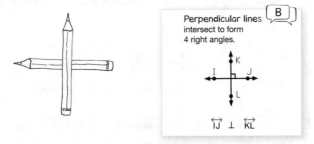

Activity (C): Identify Parallel Sides in Quadrilaterals

Show your child part C. **These shapes are made from parallel, perpendicular, and intersecting lines. All of them are quadrilaterals.** *Quadrilaterals* are flat, closed shapes with 4 straight sides.

> You will briefly introduce your child to the names of different quadrilaterals in this activity. Your child does not need to memorize these names, and he will learn more about the shapes' properties in the next lesson. For now, keep the focus on identifying pairs of parallel sides.

Show your child the first set of lines in part C. Arrange 2 craft sticks horizontally on the table to match the top and bottom sides. Then, arrange 2 more sticks on top of the other pair to form the lines on the left and right sides. Overlap the sticks as shown.

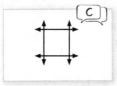

Where do the lines intersect to form right angles? *Child points to four corners of the square.* Draw a right angle symbol in each corner of the square on the page. **This shape is a square, because it has 4 right angles and 4 equal sides.**

Point to the line that forms the top side of the shape. **Which line is parallel to this line?** *The line that forms the bottom side.*

Point to the line that forms the right side of the shape. **Which line is parallel to this line?** *The line that forms the left side.* **So, the shape has 2 pairs of parallel sides.** Write 2 in the blank.

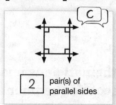

Repeat with the next set of lines. Have your child first identify where the lines intersect to form right angles. Then, have him identify the pairs of parallel sides. **This shape is a rectangle, because it has 4 right angles. The sides of the rectangle are perpendicular to each other.**

Repeat with the rest of the quadrilaterals. (None of the remaining shapes have right angles.) Tell your child the name of each shape after he builds it from craft sticks and identifies the pairs of parallel sides.

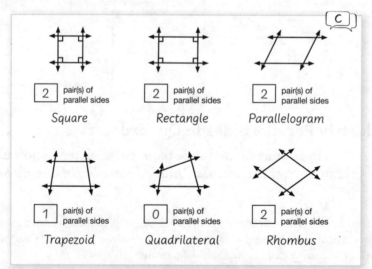

Your child will learn the definitions of these shapes in the next lesson. If he's interested, you can share them with him in this lesson as well:

- Parallelograms have 2 pairs of parallel sides.
- Trapezoids have 1 pair of parallel sides.
- Quadrilaterals have 4 sides.
- Rhombuses have 2 pairs of parallel sides and 4 equal sides.

Independent Practice and Review

Have your child complete the Lesson 11.2 Practice and Review workbook pages.

Lesson 11.3
Identify Quadrilaterals

Purpose	Materials
• Review parallel, perpendicular, and intersecting lines • Introduce quadrilateral definitions • Sort quadrilaterals based on their properties	• 4 craft sticks or narrow strips of paper • Die • Quadrilateral Cards (Blackline Master 6, cut apart on the dotted lines)

Memory Work · **How many feet equal 1 mile?** *5,280.*

The definition of trapezoids is surprisingly controversial! In the U.S. and Canada, some math books define trapezoids as quadrilaterals with *at least* 1 pair of parallel sides, while others define them as quadrilaterals with *exactly* 1 pair of parallel sides. *Math with Confidence* uses this second definition.

In British English, a *trapezoid* is defined as a quadrilateral with no pairs of parallel sides, while *trapezium* is used to describe quadrilaterals with at least 1 pair of parallel sides. If you live in the U.K. or another country that uses British English, explain both meanings to your child.

Warm-up: Review Parallel, Perpendicular, and Intersecting Lines

In the last lesson, you learned about parallel, perpendicular, and intersecting lines. Have your child use craft sticks to create an example of each. For the intersecting lines, have her arrange the sticks so that they are intersecting but not perpendicular.

Activity (A): Introduce Definitions of Quadrilaterals

Today, you'll learn the definitions for different quadrilaterals. Read aloud the definitions and briefly discuss each definition.

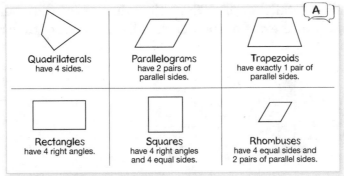

- **Any flat, closed shape with 4 straight sides is a quadrilateral. This picture is one example of a quadrilateral.**
- **Parallelograms have 2 pairs of parallel sides.** Point to the top side of the parallelogram. **Which side is parallel to this side?** *The bottom side.* Point to the left side of the parallelogram. **Which side is parallel to this side?** *The right side.*

- **Trapezoids have exactly 1 pair of parallel sides. Which two sides are parallel in the example?** *The top and bottom sides.*
- **Rectangles have 4 right angles.** Have your child point to the 4 right angles in the rectangle.
- **Squares have 4 right angles and 4 equal sides.** Have your child point to the 4 right angles in the square.
- **Rhombuses have 4 equal sides and 2 pairs of parallel sides. It can be hard to tell whether the sides are equal. It's easier to tell whether the sides are equal if you tilt the paper until the shape looks like a diamond.** Tilt the paper until the rhombus looks like a diamond, as shown. **Do the sides all look like they match each other?** *Yes.*

Activity (B): Sort Quadrilaterals

Spread the Quadrilateral Cards (from Blackline Master 6) on the table. **In part C, we're going to play a game where we roll a die and take a card that matches the category we roll.**

Let's pretend I rolled a 1 and got the Quadrilateral category. What do all quadrilaterals have to have? *4 sides.* **So, which of the cards could I take?** *All of them!*

All of the shapes on the cards have 4 sides, so they're all quadrilaterals. Write the letters of all the shapes in the space below Quadrilaterals.

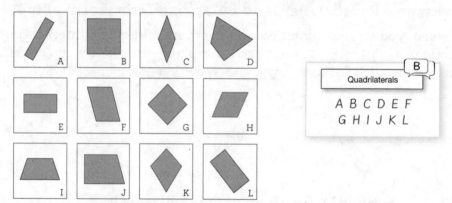

Let's pretend I rolled a 2 and got the Parallelogram category. What do all parallelograms have to have? *2 pairs of parallel sides.* Go through each card with your child and have her identify whether the shape has 2 pairs of parallel sides. Write the letter for these cards in the space below Parallelograms. **Even though some of these shapes have more specific names, they all fit the definition of a parallelogram. So, they're in the parallelogram category.**

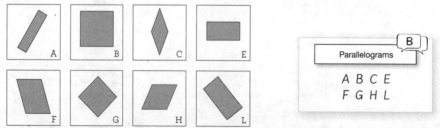

If your child has trouble telling whether two lines are parallel to each other, encourage her to trace the lines with 2 different fingers, at the same time. **Think about whether your fingers move in the same direction as you trace the line. If they do, the lines are parallel.**

Repeat for the other categories.

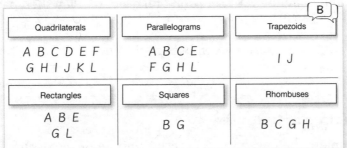

After your child finishes sorting the shapes, use the following questions to discuss which categories have shapes in common.

- **Are there any shapes in both the Parallelogram and Trapezoid categories?** *No.* **Why not?** *Shapes can't have 2 pairs of parallel sides and exactly 1 pair of parallel sides.*
- **Are there any shapes in both the Rectangle and Parallelogram categories?** *Yes.* **Which ones?** *All the rectangles are in the Parallelogram category, too.* **Why?** *Rectangles all have 2 pairs of parallel sides.* **We can think of rectangles as a special kind of parallelogram.**
- **Are there any shapes in both the Rectangle and Square categories?** *Yes.* **Which ones?** *All the squares are in the Rectangle category, too.* **Why?** *Squares all have 4 right angles.* **We can think of squares as a special kind of rectangle.**
- **Are there any shapes in both the Square and Rhombus categories?** *Yes.* **Which ones?** *All the squares are in the Rhombus category, too.* **Why?** *Squares all have 4 equal sides, so they fit the definition of a rhombus.* **We can also think of squares as a special kind of rhombus.**

Activity (C): Play Quadrilateral Capture

Cover parts A and B with a piece of paper. **Try to remember the definition for each category of shape, but you can peek if you forget one.** Play Quadrilateral Capture.

Covering the top of the page helps your child begin to memorize the definitions. If you find that she's not ready to recall the definitions from memory, leave them uncovered.

Quadrilateral Capture

Materials: Quadrilateral Cards; die

Object of the Game: Capture the most cards.

Spread the Quadrilateral Cards face-up on the table.

On your turn, roll the die. You may take any card that belongs to the matching category. For example, if you roll a 4, you may take cards A, B, E, G or L (since they all have 4 right angles and fit the definition of a rectangle.)

If you roll a 4, you may take any of the cards that fit the definition of a rectangle.

Directions continued on next page.

If no card remaining matches your roll, don't take a card. Play then passes to the other player.

Take turns until all the cards have been captured. Whoever has captured more cards wins the game.

Independent Practice and Review

Have your child complete the Lesson 11.3 Practice and Review workbook pages.

Lesson 11.4
Properties of Quadrilaterals

Purpose	Materials
• Review quadrilateral definitions • Identify properties of different types of quadrilaterals • Identify quadrilaterals based on their properties	• Geometry Reference Page (Blackline Master 7) • Quadrilateral Cards (Blackline Master 6, cut apart on the dotted lines)

Memory Work	
	• **What do we call an angle with a measure less than 90 degrees?** *Acute.* • **What do we call an angle with a measure equal to 90 degrees?** *Right.* • **What do we call an angle with a measure greater than 90 degrees and less than 180 degrees?** *Obtuse.* • **What do we call an angle with a measure equal to 180 degrees?** *Straight.*

Warm-up: Review Quadrilateral Definitions

In the last lesson, you learned the definitions of different kinds of quadrilaterals. Let's see how many you remember. It's okay if you don't have them all memorized yet!

- **What do all quadrilaterals have?** *4 sides.*
- **What do all rectangles have?** *4 right angles.*
- **What do all squares have?** *4 right angles and 4 equal sides.*
- **What do all trapezoids have?** *1 pair of parallel sides.*
- **What do all parallelograms have?** *2 pairs of parallel sides.*
- **What do all rhombuses have?** *4 equal sides and 2 pairs of parallel sides.*

Show your child the Geometry Reference page (Blackline Master 7). **Trying to recall the definitions from memory as much as you can will help you memorize them. But you can check this page if you ever forget a definition or aren't sure.**

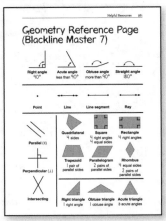

Activity (A): Identify Properties of Quadrilaterals

Today, we'll investigate the properties of each type of quadrilateral.

Point to the group of rectangles. **All of these shapes are rectangles. Let's see what properties they all have in common.** Ask your child the following questions about the shapes:

- **Do all these shapes have 4 sides?** *Yes.* Circle "4 sides" in the list below the shapes.
- **Do all these shapes have exactly 1 pair of parallel sides?** *No.* Cross out "exactly 1 pair of parallel sides."

- **Do all these shapes have 2 pairs of parallel sides?** *Yes.* Circle "2 pairs of parallel sides."
- **Do all these shapes have 4 right angles?** *Yes.* Circle "4 right angles."
- **Do all these shapes have 4 equal sides?** *No. One of the shapes has 4 equal sides, but they don't all have 4 equal sides.* Cross out "4 equal sides."

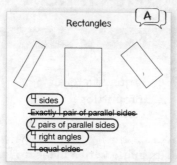

The definition of a rectangle is that it has 4 right angles. Why do you think the definition leaves out the fact that all rectangles have 4 sides and 2 pairs of parallel sides? *Answers will vary.* **If a quadrilateral has 4 right angles, it automatically has 4 sides and 2 pairs of parallel sides. So, we don't have to include those properties in the definition. That makes it easier to remember the definition for each shape.**

If your child is curious why a quadrilateral with 4 right angles automatically has 2 pairs of parallel sides, give him a few moments to try to draw a quadrilateral with 4 right angles that does not have 2 pairs of parallel sides or 4 sides. He'll see that it's impossible.

Repeat with the other groups of shapes. Compare the definition of each shape on the Geometry Reference page with its circled properties.

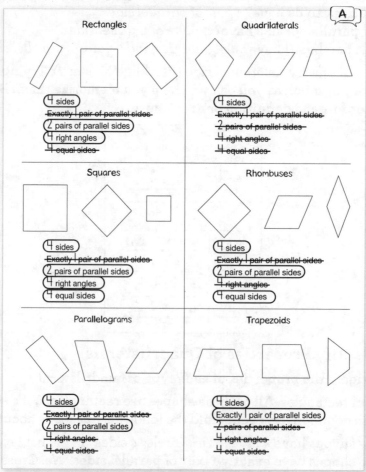

Activity: Play What's My Quadrilateral?

We're going to use the Quadrilateral Cards to play a game. Show your child shape A. **This shape has 4 sides, 2 pairs of parallel sides, and 4 right angles. So, it fits the definition for quadrilaterals, parallelograms, and rectangles! But, in everyday conversation, we usually use the most specific name possible for shapes. What's the most specific name possible for this shape?** *Rectangle.*

Let's make sure we agree on the most specific name for each shape before we play the game. Have your child tell you the name of each shape. Allow him to refer to the Geometry Definitions page as needed.

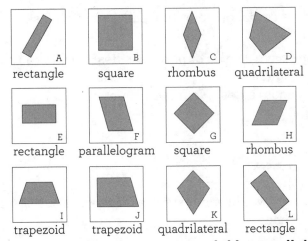

Then, play What's My Quadrilateral? Encourage your child to recall the definitions and properties of the quadrilaterals from memory, but allow him to refer to the Lesson Activities page and Geometry Reference Page if needed.

Make sure you go first in this game, so that you can model how to ask yes/no questions about the shapes.

What's My Quadrilateral?

Materials: Quadrilateral Cards; counters

Object of the Game: Win fewer points by identifying quadrilaterals with as few questions as possible.

Shuffle the Quadrilateral Cards and stack them in a face-down pile on the table. Place a pile of counters on the table.

This game has three rounds. Each player takes one turn per round and identifies one quadrilateral. The instructor goes first in each round.

Directions continued on next page.

On your turn, take the top card in the pile without looking at it. Hold it next to your forehead, so that the other player can see the shape, but you can't.

Ask yes/no questions about the quadrilateral until you guess the most-specific name possible for the quadrilateral. Take one counter from the pile each time you ask a question.

For example, if you have card L on your forehead, you might ask the following questions:

- **Does the shape have 2 pairs of parallel sides?** *Yes.* Take 1 counter.
- **Does it have 4 right angles?** *Yes.* Take 1 counter.
- **Does it have 4 equal sides?** *No.* Take 1 counter.
- **It's a rectangle!**

In the above example, you would end up with 3 counters, since you asked 3 questions before identifying the shape.

Then, the other player takes a turn. Continue until both players have had the chance to guess 3 quadrilaterals. Whoever has fewer counters wins.

Independent Practice and Review

Have your child complete the Lesson 11.4 Practice and Review workbook pages.

Lesson 11.5
Identify Triangles by Their Angles

Purpose	Materials
• Practice identifying types of angles • Identify acute, right, and obtuse triangles • Understand that all triangles have at least 2 acute angles	• 2 pencils • Counters • Die

Memory Work	
	• **What do we call a quadrilateral with 4 right angles?** *A rectangle.* • **What do we call a quadrilateral with 4 right angles and 4 equal sides?** *A square.* • **What do we call a quadrilateral with 4 equal sides?** *A rhombus.* • **What do we call a quadrilateral with 2 pairs of parallel sides?** *A parallelogram.* • **What do we call a quadrilateral with exactly 1 pair of parallel sides?** *A trapezoid.*

Warm-up: Play "Simon Says" with Angles

Let's review the different kinds of angles with Simon Says. Place 2 pencils on the table for your child to use to make the angles. **If I say "Simon says" first, make the angle between the 2 pencils. But if I don't say "Simon says," don't make the angle.**

- **Simon says make an acute angle.** *Child makes an acute angle between the pencils. Any angle measure less than 90° is fine.*
- **Simon says make a straight angle.** *Child makes a straight angle.*
- **Make an obtuse angle.** *Child doesn't move.*

Repeat 8-10 times with different types of angles. Keep the game fun and fast-paced.

> If your child doesn't enjoy Simon Says, challenge her to make the angles as fast as possible instead.

Activity (A): Introduce Right, Obtuse, and Acute Triangles

In the last lesson, you learned about different types of quadrilaterals. Today, you'll learn about different types of triangles.

We can use triangles' angles to sort them into different groups. Triangles with one right angle are called *right triangles*. Which angle in this triangle is right? *Child points to the right angle.*

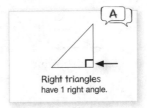

Right triangles
have 1 right angle.

Triangles with one obtuse angle are called *obtuse triangles.* **Which angle in this triangle is obtuse?** *Child points to the obtuse angle.*

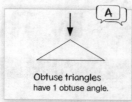

Obtuse triangles
have 1 obtuse angle.

Triangles with 3 acute angles are called *acute triangles.* **Are all the angles in this triangle acute?** *Yes.*

Acute triangles
have 3 acute angles.

How many acute angles does the right triangle have? *2.* **How many acute angles does this obtuse triangle have?** *2.* **All triangles have some acute angles, so it's important to remember that the angles in acute triangles must** *all* **be acute.**

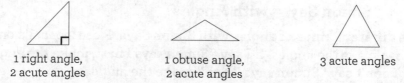

1 right angle,
2 acute angles

1 obtuse angle,
2 acute angles

3 acute angles

Let's see if it's possible to draw a triangle with 2 right angles. Have your child try drawing a triangle with 2 right angles on a piece of scrap paper. **Once you draw 2 right angles, it's impossible for the 3 sides to meet! It's impossible to draw a triangle with 2 right angles.**

Sample drawing.

Let's see if it's possible to draw a triangle with 2 obtuse angles. Have your child try drawing a triangle with 2 obtuse angles on a piece of scrap paper. **We can't draw a triangle with 2 obtuse angles, either. Once you draw 2 obtuse angles, it's impossible for the 3 sides to meet.**

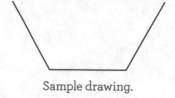

Sample drawing.

Activity (B): Play Triangle Four in a Row

Play Triangle Four in a Row.

Triangle Four in a Row

Materials: Counters; die

Object of the Game: Be the first player to place counters in 4 squares in a row, either horizontally, vertically, or diagonally.

On your turn, roll the die. Use the key to see what type of triangle you can cover. For example, if you roll a 1, you can cover any acute triangle on the game board. Cover that type of triangle with one of your counters.

If you roll a 1, cover any acute triangle.

If you roll a 5, you may cover any triangle. If you roll a 6, you may remove one of your opponent's counters. If you roll a number and all the matching triangles are already covered, you lose your turn and do not place a new counter.

Play then passes to the other player. Continue until one player covers 4 boxes in a row, either horizontally, vertically, or diagonally.

Answer Key:

Triangle Four in a Row

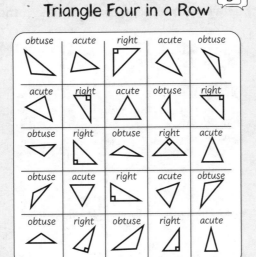

Independent Practice and Review

Have your child complete the Lesson 11.5 Practice and Review workbook pages.

Lesson 11.6
Symmetry in Triangles and Quadrilaterals

Purpose	Materials
• Review symmetry • Identify lines of symmetry in quadrilaterals and triangles	• Shapes for Folding (Blackline Master 8), cut out according to the directions

Memory Work	
	• **What is an acute triangle?** *A triangle with 3 acute angles.* • **What is a right triangle?** *A triangle with a right angle.* • **What is an obtuse triangle?** *A triangle with an obtuse angle.*

Warm-up (A): Review Symmetry

When you were younger, you learned about symmetry. Do you remember what makes a shape symmetric? *Sample answers: The two sides line up with each other. The two sides are a mirror image of each other.*

Shapes and objects are symmetric if they have two halves that exactly mirror each other. Draw a line down the middle of the A. **This line is called a *line of symmetry*. It splits the A into two matching halves.**

Some letters have one line of symmetry, some have two lines of symmetry, and some don't have any lines of symmetry. Have your child draw lines of symmetry for the rest of the letters in the alphabet.

If your child has trouble with this activity, skip it for now and come back to it after you complete the rest of the Lesson Activities page.

Some letters have a type of symmetry called rotational symmetry. Your child will learn about rotational symmetry in the enrichment activity in Lesson 11.7.

Activity (B): Fold Shapes to Identify Lines of Symmetry

Today, we'll investigate symmetry in quadrilaterals and triangles. Show your child part B. **One way to check whether two parts of a shape are symmetric is to see if the two parts line up when you fold them together. We'll fold paper versions of these shapes to see how many lines of symmetry each shape has.**

Point to the first shape. **What's the name of this shape?** *Square*. Allow your child to look at the Geometry Definitions page if needed.

Show your child the matching paper square from Blackline Master 8. Demonstrate how to fold the square in half vertically, as shown. **The two sides of the square line up with each other when I fold it along this line, so this fold line is a line of symmetry.** Trace the fold line with a pencil and draw a matching line across the printed square.

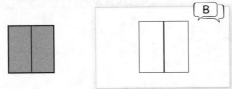

Have your child experiment with folding the square to find more lines of symmetry. Have him trace each line on the paper square and then draw a matching line across the printed square. **How many lines of symmetry did we find for this square?** *4*. Write 4 in the blank.

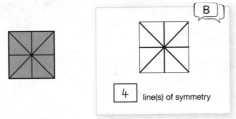

Repeat with the rest of the shapes in part B.

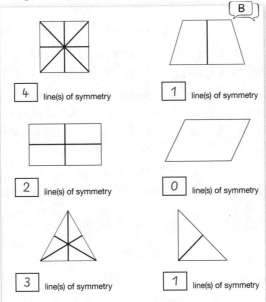

Some shapes have more than one line of symmetry, some have one line of symmetry, and some have none.

Parallelograms have a type of symmetry called rotational symmetry. Your child will learn about rotational symmetry in the enrichment activity in Lesson 11.7.

Independent Practice and Review

Have your child complete the Lesson 11.6 Practice and Review workbook pages.

Lesson 11.7
Enrichment (Optional)

Purpose	Materials
• Practice memory work • Find examples of symmetry in a variety of real-life contexts • Create a craft with rotational symmetry • Summarize what your child has learned and assess your child's progress	• *Seeing Symmetry*, written and illustrated by Loreen Leedy • Paper square, approximately 6 inches by 6 inches • Ruler • Scissors • Tape or glue • Pushpin • Pencil with eraser

Warm-up: Review Memory Work

Quiz your child on all memory work through Unit 11. See pages 536-537 for the full list.

Math Picture Book: *Seeing Symmetry*

Read *Seeing Symmetry*, written and illustrated by Loreen Leedy. As you read, find the lines of symmetry in the images.

Enrichment Activity: Make a Pinwheel with Rotational Symmetry

In this unit, you found lines of symmetry in letters and shapes. The two halves of the objects were mirror images of each other. This kind of symmetry is called line symmetry.

There's also another kind of symmetry called rotational symmetry. Listen to how the word rotational has the word *rotate* in it. A shape has rotational symmetry if the shape looks the same after you rotate it or spin it around its center. Today, we'll make a pinwheel with rotational symmetry.

Take a paper square about 6 inches by 6 inches. Use a ruler to draw diagonal lines from corner to corner across the square. Cut a 3-inch slit along each diagonal, starting at the corners of the square.

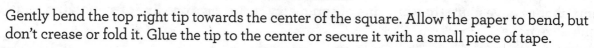

Gently bend the top right tip towards the center of the square. Allow the paper to bend, but don't crease or fold it. Glue the tip to the center or secure it with a small piece of tape.

Start with this tip and bend it toward the center.

Then, repeat with the other 3 tips.

Push a pushpin through the center of the pinwheel. Hold a pencil behind the pinwheel and push the pushpin into the eraser. Leave a little space between the pinwheel and eraser to allow the pinwheel to spin freely.

Demonstrate how to turn the pinwheel a quarter-turn. **The pinwheel looks just the same after I turn it! It has rotational symmetry.** Have your child experiment with turning the pinwheel and blowing on it to make it spin.

Unit Wrap-Up

Have your child complete the Unit 11 Wrap-Up.

Unit 11 Answer Key

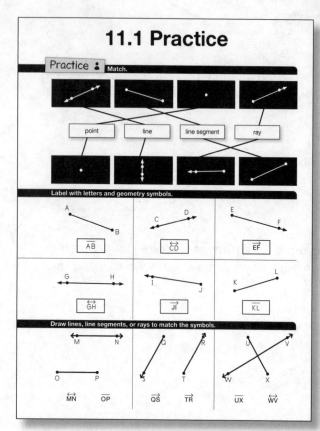

11.1 Practice

Practice — Match.

Label with letters and geometry symbols.

$\overrightarrow{AB}$ $\overleftrightarrow{CD}$ $\overrightarrow{EF}$

$\overleftrightarrow{GH}$ $\overrightarrow{JI}$ $\overline{KL}$

Draw lines, line segments, or rays to match the symbols.

$\overleftrightarrow{MN}$ $\overline{OP}$ $\overrightarrow{QS}$ $\overrightarrow{TR}$ $\overleftrightarrow{UX}$ $\overleftrightarrow{WV}$

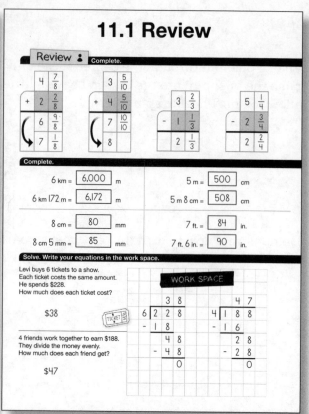

11.1 Review

Review — Complete.

Complete.

6 km = **6,000** m   5 m = **500** cm

6 km 172 m = **6,172** m   5 m 8 cm = **508** cm

8 cm = **80** mm   7 ft. = **84** in.

8 cm 5 mm = **85** mm   7 ft. 6 in. = **90** in.

Solve. Write your equations in the work space.

Levi buys 6 tickets to a show.
Each ticket costs the same amount.
He spends $228.
How much does each ticket cost?

$38

4 friends work together to earn $188.
They divide the money evenly.
How much does each friend get?

$47

WORK SPACE

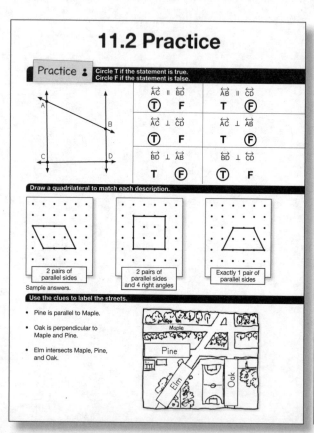

11.2 Practice

Practice — Circle T if the statement is true.
Circle F if the statement is false.

$\overrightarrow{AC} \parallel \overrightarrow{BD}$ **T** F $\overrightarrow{AB} \parallel \overleftrightarrow{CD}$ T **F**

$\overrightarrow{AC} \perp \overleftrightarrow{CD}$ **T** F $\overrightarrow{AC} \perp \overrightarrow{AB}$ T **F**

$\overrightarrow{BD} \perp \overrightarrow{AB}$ T **F** $\overrightarrow{BD} \perp \overleftrightarrow{CD}$ **T** F

Draw a quadrilateral to match each description.

2 pairs of parallel sides

2 pairs of parallel sides and 4 right angles

Exactly 1 pair of parallel sides

Sample answers.

Use the clues to label the streets.

- Pine is parallel to Maple.
- Oak is perpendicular to Maple and Pine.
- Elm intersects Maple, Pine, and Oak.

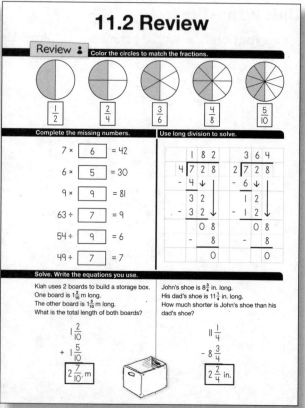

11.2 Review

Review — Color the circles to match the fractions.

$\frac{1}{2}$ $\frac{2}{4}$ $\frac{3}{6}$ $\frac{4}{8}$ $\frac{5}{10}$

Complete the missing numbers.

$7 \times$ **6** $= 42$

$6 \times$ **5** $= 30$

$9 \times$ **9** $= 81$

$63 \div$ **7** $= 9$

$54 \div$ **9** $= 6$

$49 \div$ **7** $= 7$

Use long division to solve.

Solve. Write the equations you use.

Kiah uses 2 boards to build a storage box.
One board is $1\frac{2}{10}$ m long.
The other board is $1\frac{5}{10}$ m long.
What is the total length of both boards?

$1\frac{2}{10}$
$+ 1\frac{5}{10}$
$2\frac{7}{10}$ m

John's shoe is $8\frac{3}{4}$ in. long.
His dad's shoe is $11\frac{1}{4}$ in. long.
How much shorter is John's shoe than his dad's shoe?

$11\frac{1}{4}$
$- 8\frac{3}{4}$
$2\frac{2}{4}$ in.

Unit 11 Answer Key

11.3 Practice

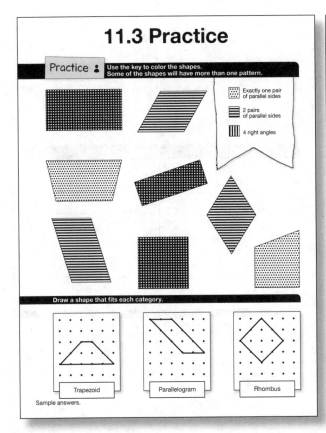

Practice : Use the key to color the shapes.
Some of the shapes will have more than one pattern.

Key:
- ▦ Exactly one pair of parallel sides
- ▤ 2 pairs of parallel sides
- ▥ 4 right angles

Draw a shape that fits each category.

| Trapezoid | Parallelogram | Rhombus |

Sample answers.

11.3 Review

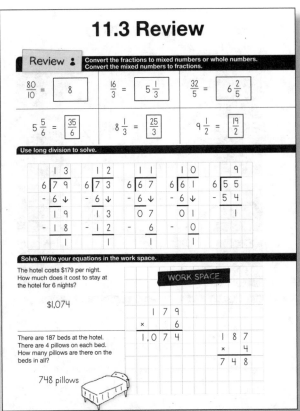

Review : Convert the fractions to mixed numbers or whole numbers. Convert the mixed numbers to fractions.

$\frac{80}{10} = 8$ $\frac{16}{3} = 5\frac{1}{3}$ $\frac{32}{5} = 6\frac{2}{5}$

$5\frac{5}{6} = \frac{35}{6}$ $8\frac{1}{3} = \frac{25}{3}$ $9\frac{1}{2} = \frac{19}{2}$

Use long division to solve.

Solve. Write your equations in the work space.

The hotel costs $179 per night. How much does it cost to stay at the hotel for 6 nights?

$1,074

There are 187 beds at the hotel. There are 4 pillows on each bed. How many pillows are there on the beds in all?

748 pillows

11.4 Practice

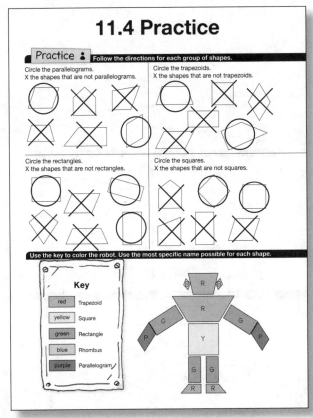

Practice : Follow the directions for each group of shapes.

Circle the parallelograms.
X the shapes that are not parallelograms.

Circle the trapezoids.
X the shapes that are not trapezoids.

Circle the rectangles.
X the shapes that are not rectangles.

Circle the squares.
X the shapes that are not squares.

Use the key to color the robot. Use the most specific name possible for each shape.

Key
- red — Trapezoid
- yellow — Square
- green — Rectangle
- blue — Rhombus
- purple — Parallelogram

11.4 Review

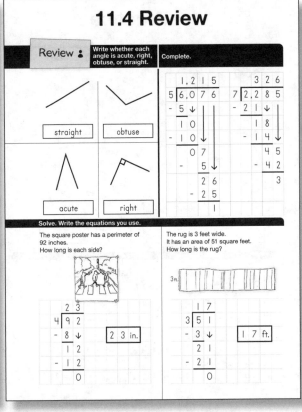

Review : Write whether each angle is acute, right, obtuse, or straight.

straight   obtuse

acute   right

Complete.

Solve. Write the equations you use.

The square poster has a perimeter of 92 inches. How long is each side?

2 3 in.

The rug is 3 feet wide. It has an area of 51 square feet. How long is the rug?

1 7 ft.

Unit 11 Answer Key

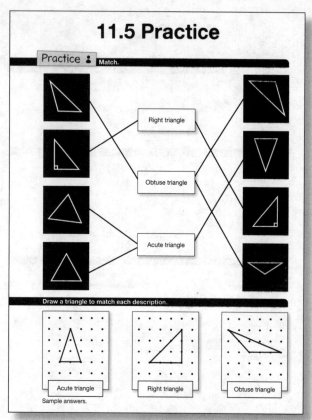

11.5 Practice

Practice 👤 Match.

Right triangle

Obtuse triangle

Acute triangle

Draw a triangle to match each description.

| Acute triangle | Right triangle | Obtuse triangle |

Sample answers.

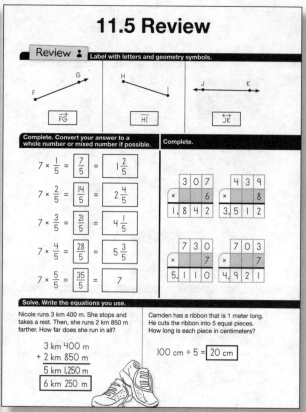

11.5 Review

Review 👤 Label with letters and geometry symbols.

$\overrightarrow{FG}$ $\overline{HI}$ $\overleftrightarrow{JK}$

Complete. Convert your answer to a whole number or mixed number if possible.

$7 \times \frac{1}{5} = \frac{7}{5} = 1\frac{2}{5}$

$7 \times \frac{2}{5} = \frac{14}{5} = 2\frac{4}{5}$

$7 \times \frac{3}{5} = \frac{21}{5} = 4\frac{1}{5}$

$7 \times \frac{4}{5} = \frac{28}{5} = 5\frac{3}{5}$

$7 \times \frac{5}{5} = \frac{35}{5} = 7$

Complete.

| × | 3 0 7 | 6 |
| 1, 8 4 2 |

| × | 4 3 9 | 8 |
| 3, 5 1 2 |

| × | 7 3 0 | 7 |
| 5, 1 1 0 |

| × | 7 0 3 | 7 |
| 4, 9 2 1 |

Solve. Write the equations you use.

Nicole runs 3 km 400 m. She stops and takes a rest. Then, she runs 2 km 850 m farther. How far does she run in all?

3 km 400 m
+ 2 km 850 m
5 km 1,250 m
6 km 250 m

Camden has a ribbon that is 1 meter long. He cuts the ribbon into 5 equal pieces. How long is each piece in centimeters?

100 cm ÷ 5 = 20 cm

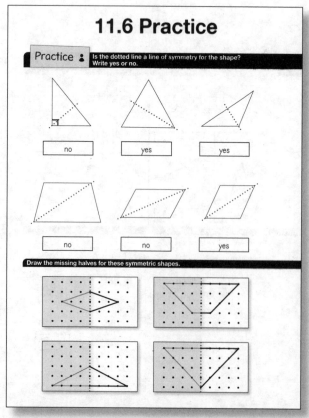

11.6 Practice

Practice 👤 Is the dotted line a line of symmetry for the shape? Write yes or no.

no   yes   yes

no   no   yes

Draw the missing halves for these symmetric shapes.

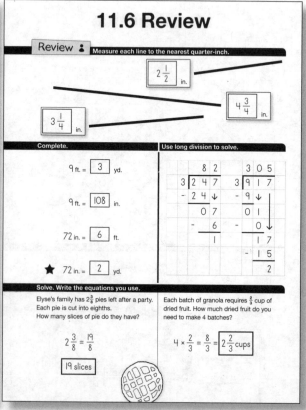

11.6 Review

Review 👤 Measure each line to the nearest quarter-inch.

$2\frac{1}{2}$ in.

$4\frac{3}{4}$ in.

$3\frac{1}{4}$ in.

Complete.

9 ft. = 3 yd.

9 ft. = 108 in.

72 in. = 6 ft.

★ 72 in. = 2 yd.

Use long division to solve.

	8 2
3	2 4 7
-	2 4 ↓
	0 7
-	6
	1

	3 0 5
3	9 1 7
-	9 ↓
	0 1
-	0
	1 7
-	1 5
	2

Solve. Write the equations you use.

Elyse's family has $2\frac{3}{8}$ pies left after a party. Each pie is cut into eighths. How many slices of pie do they have?

$2\frac{3}{8} = \frac{19}{8}$

19 slices

Each batch of granola requires $\frac{2}{3}$ cup of dried fruit. How much dried fruit do you need to make 4 batches?

$4 \times \frac{2}{3} = \frac{8}{3} = 2\frac{2}{3}$ cups

Unit 11 Answer Key

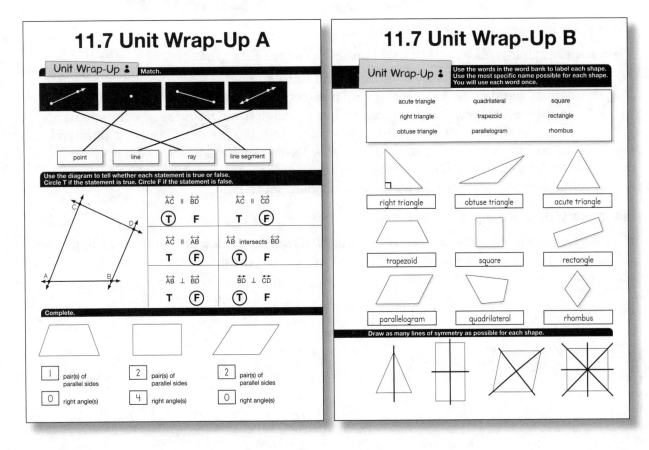

11.7 Unit Wrap-Up A

Unit Wrap-Up 👤 Match.

point | line | ray | line segment

Use the diagram to tell whether each statement is true or false. Circle T if the statement is true. Circle F if the statement is false.

$\overleftrightarrow{AC} \parallel \overleftrightarrow{BD}$ (T) F

$\overleftrightarrow{AC} \parallel \overleftrightarrow{CD}$ T (F)

$\overleftrightarrow{AC} \parallel \overleftrightarrow{AB}$ T (F)

$\overleftrightarrow{AB}$ intersects $\overleftrightarrow{BD}$ (T) F

$\overleftrightarrow{AB} \perp \overleftrightarrow{BD}$ T (F)

$\overleftrightarrow{BD} \perp \overleftrightarrow{CD}$ (T) F

Complete.

1 pair(s) of parallel sides
0 right angle(s)

2 pair(s) of parallel sides
4 right angle(s)

2 pair(s) of parallel sides
0 right angle(s)

11.7 Unit Wrap-Up B

Unit Wrap-Up 👤 Use the words in the word bank to label each shape. Use the most specific name possible for each shape. You will use each word once.

acute triangle	quadrilateral	square
right triangle	trapezoid	rectangle
obtuse triangle	parallelogram	rhombus

right triangle | obtuse triangle | acute triangle

trapezoid | square | rectangle

parallelogram | quadrilateral | rhombus

Draw as many lines of symmetry as possible for each shape.

Unit 11 Checkpoint

What to Expect at the End of Unit 11

By the end of Unit 11, most children will be able to do the following:

- Identify and label points, rays, lines, and line segments.
- Identify parallel, perpendicular, and intersecting lines.
- Identify, construct, and draw trapezoids, parallelograms, squares, rectangles, and rhombuses. Many children will have trouble keeping the definitions straight and sometimes need to refer to the Geometry Reference Page as a reminder.
- Identify and draw right triangles, obtuse triangles, and acute triangles.
- Find lines of symmetry in triangles and quadrilaterals.

Is Your Child Ready to Move on?

In Unit 12, your child will study equivalent fractions and learn new strategies for comparing fractions. Your child does not need to have fully mastered the geometry vocabulary in Unit 11 before moving on to the next unit.

Unit 12
Equivalent Fractions

Overview

In this unit, your child will learn how to create equivalent fractions by multiplying the numerator and denominator by the same number. He will also learn how to use equivalent fractions to compare fractions with different denominators, including fractions of an inch or meter.

In *Fifth Grade Math with Confidence*, your child will build on this skill to add or subtract fractions with different denominators. He will also learn how to divide the numerator and denominator by the same number in order to simplify fractions.

What Your Child Will Learn

In this unit, your child will learn to:

- Multiply the numerator and denominator of a fraction by the same number to create an equivalent fraction
- Find missing numerators or denominators in pairs of equivalent fractions
- Use equivalent fractions to identify and compare fractions of an inch or fractions of a meter
- Use common denominators to compare fractions with different denominators

Lesson List

Lesson 12.1   Review Equivalent Fractions

Lesson 12.2   Multiply to Create Equivalent Fractions

Lesson 12.3   Find Missing Numbers in Equivalent Fractions

Lesson 12.4   Equivalent Fractions of an Inch

Lesson 12.5   Equivalent Fractions of a Meter

Lesson 12.6   Use Common Denominators to Compare Fractions

Lesson 12.7   Enrichment (Optional)

Extra Materials Needed for Unit 12

- Paper
- Colored pencils or markers
- For optional Enrichment Lesson:
  - *Fractions in Disguise: A Math Adventure*, written by Edward Einhorn and illustrated by David Clark. Charlesbridge, 2014.
  - 5 different colors of paper
  - Small bowl or cup (for tracing)
  - Scissors
  - Glue

Teaching Math with Confidence: Understanding Equivalent Fractions

In this unit, your child will learn about equivalent fractions. Equivalent fractions are fractions that have the same value but have different numbers for their numerators and denominators. For example, 3/6, 4/8, and 10/20 are all equivalent to each other. They have different numerators and denominators, but they all equal one-half.

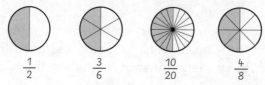

1/2, 3/6, 10/20, and 4/8 are equivalent fractions.
Even though they have different numerators and denominators, they all describe the same amount of the circle.

Your child will discover that he can *multiply* the numerator and denominator of a fraction by the same number to create an equivalent fraction. For example, say you put green peppers on 2/3 of a pizza. If you cut each third into 2 equal parts, 4/6 of the pizza now has green peppers. Multiplying the numerator and denominator by 2 yields the equivalent fraction.

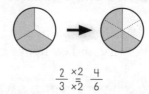

$$\frac{2}{3} \begin{array}{c} \times 2 \\ = \\ \times 2 \end{array} \frac{4}{6}$$

Children often associate splitting things into parts with division. As a result, they sometimes find it confusing that you *split* each piece into more parts but *multiply* to find the new number of parts. If your child has trouble with this idea, try to avoid saying that you "split" the fractional parts. Instead, describe the process as "creating more fractional parts." Or, if your child enjoys fantasy and magic, pretend to wave a magic wand that multiplies each fractional part into more parts.

This unit focuses solely on multiplying the numerator and denominator by the same number so that your child develops deep conceptual understanding of creating equivalent fractions in this way. In fifth grade, your child will learn that he can also create equivalent fractions (or simplify or "reduce" them) by dividing the numerator and denominator by the same number.

Lesson 12.1
Review Equivalent Fractions

Purpose	Materials
• Review the concept of equivalency • Review equivalent fractions • Fold paper to create equivalent fractions • Preview the idea that you can multiply both the numerator and denominator by the same number to create an equivalent fraction	• 2 pieces of paper • Colored pencils or markers

Memory Work
- **What do we call the top number in a fraction?** *The numerator.*
- **What does the numerator tell?** *The number of parts.*
- **What do we call the bottom number in a fraction?** *The denominator.*
- **What does the denominator tell?** *How many equal parts the whole was split into.*

In this lesson, your child will fold paper and draw lines to make rectangles into more fractional parts. She'll discover that she can use multiplication to predict her results. In the next lesson, she'll extend this concept to multiplying a fraction's numerator and denominator by the same number to create an equivalent fraction.

Warm-up: Review the Concept of Equivalency

We're beginning a new unit on equivalent fractions today. What does it mean when we say two things are equivalent? *Sample answer: They're basically the same as each other.*

Things that are equivalent have the same value or serve the same purpose, but they're not exactly alike. For example, 1 meter and 100 centimeters are equivalent. They're different measurements, but they both mean the same length. Or, 4 plus 3 and 6 plus 1 are equivalent. They both have the same value, but they express that value in different ways.

What are some mathematical expressions that are equivalent to 12? *Sample answers: 6 times 2. 96 divided by 8. 12 inches equal 1 foot. 10 plus 2. 1 dozen. Half of a day is 12 hours.*

Activity (A): Review Equivalent Fractions

Last year, you learned that equivalent fractions have the same value but look different from each other. They have different numerators and denominators.

One-half of the top bar is colored. What fraction of the bottom bar is colored? *Two-fourths.*
Write 2/4 in the blank.

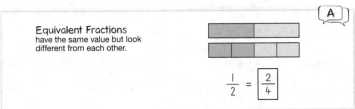

Are one-half and two-fourths equivalent? *Yes.* **How do you know?** *Sample answer: The colored parts of the two bars are equal.* **Both fractions mean the same amount of the bar, so they are equivalent to each other.**

Activity (B): Fold Paper to Create Equivalent Fractions

Now, we'll fold paper to create equivalent fractions. First, we'll find several fractions equivalent to one-third.

Fold a piece of paper into thirds to match the first diagram, then open it up. **What fractional part is this piece of paper split into?** *Thirds.* Use a colored pencil or marker to draw dark lines on top of the fold lines to make them more visible. Have your child color 1/3 of the paper.

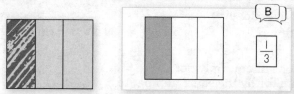

Your child does not need to carefully fill the entire third of the paper. A quick scribble in any color is fine.

Refold the paper. Then, fold it in half in the other direction. **What fractional part do you predict we have now?** *Sixths.* **How many of the parts do you think will be shaded?** *2.*

Open up the paper and have your child check her prediction. Draw dark lines on top of the fold lines. **What fraction of the paper is colored now?** *Two-sixths.* Have your child draw a horizontal line across the next diagram to match the fold lines. Then, have her write 2/6 in the box.

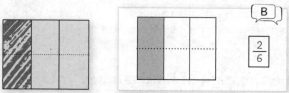

Repeat twice more. For the third diagram, refold the paper into sixths, then fold it in half one more time to create twelfths.

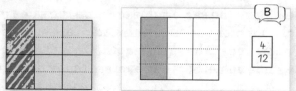

For the fourth diagram, refold the paper into twelfths, then fold it in half one more time to create twenty-fourths.

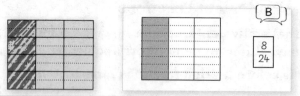

It's okay if your paper ends up with different fold lines than shown in the sample diagrams, as long as the total number of fractional parts are the same.

In this unit, you and your child will often add lines to diagrams in the Student Workbook. These lines are dotted in the Instructor Guide so that it's easier to distinguish between the printed and handwritten lines when teaching.

We ususally say "th" after the number in the denominator to name the fractional part. When the diagram is divided into 12 parts, we say it's divided into twelfths. When the diagram is divided into 24 parts, we say it's divided into twenty-fourths.

We found that one-third, two-sixths, four-twelfths, and eight-twenty-fourths are all equivalent to each other. What do you notice about these fractions? *Sample answer: The denominator is always 3 times the numerator. The numerator and denominator in each new fraction are twice the numerator and denominator of the previous fraction.*

Now, we'll fold paper to find fractions equivalent to three-fourths. Take a new piece of paper. This time, fold the paper into fourths as shown. **What fractional part is this piece of paper split into?** *Fourths.* Use a colored pencil or marker to draw dark lines on top of the fold lines to make them more visible. Have your child color 3/4 of the paper.

Repeat the process of folding the paper in the other direction and identifying the new fraction. Each time, add one additional fold. Make sure to have your child predict what fraction of the paper will be colored before you open it up.

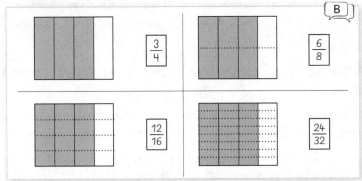

We found that three-fourths, six-eighths, twelve-sixteenths, and twenty-four-thirty-seconds are all equivalent to each other. What do you notice about these fractions? *Sample answer: The numerators are pretty close to the denominators. The numerator and denominator in each new fraction are twice the numerator and denominator of the previous fraction.*

Independent Practice and Review

Have your child complete the Lesson 12.1 Practice and Review workbook pages.

Lesson 12.2
Multiply to Create Equivalent Fractions

Purpose	Materials
• Understand that cutting a whole into more fractional parts creates smaller fractional parts • Multiply the numerator and denominator of a fraction by the same number to create an equivalent fraction	• 1 sheet of paper • Colored pencils or markers

Memory Work	• **What do we call the result when we multiply two numbers?** *The product.* • **What do we call the numbers in a multiplication equation that we multiply together?** *Factors.*

Warm-up: Understand the Relationship Between the Denominator and the Size of Fractional Parts

In the last lesson, we reviewed equivalent fractions. What are equivalent fractions? *Fractions that have the same value but different numerators and denominators.*

Place a piece of paper on the table. Draw a line as shown to split it in half. **Let's pretend the paper is a cake that the two of us are sharing. We each get a big slice of cake!**

Then, 4 more people come. Who should we pretend has come over for cake? *Answers will vary.* **How can we cut the cake so that all 6 of us can have some?** *Sample answer: Cut each half into 3 pieces.* Draw lines on the paper as shown. **What fractional part is the cake split into now?** *Sixths.* **Our slices are still pretty big.**

Then, 6 more people come. Who should we pretend has come now? *Answers will vary.* **How can we cut the cake so that all 12 of us can have some?** *Sample answer: Cut each piece in half.* Draw lines on the paper as shown. **What fractional part is the cake split into now?** *Twelfths.* **These slices are a lot smaller than the sixths.**

Finally, 12 more people come to eat cake with us. How can we cut the cake so that all 24 of us can have some? *Sample answer: Cut each piece in half.* Draw lines on the paper as shown. **What fractional part is the cake split into now?** *Twenty-fourths.* **The slices are pretty small now!**

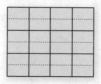

When we cut the cake into more parts, what happens to the size of the parts? *They get smaller.* What happens to the size of the whole cake? *Nothing.* Cutting the cake into more parts doesn't change the total amount of cake, but it changes the size of the slices.

Activity (A): Choose a Multiplier to Create Equivalent Fractions

Today, you'll learn how to use multiplication to create equivalent fractions.

One-half of this pizza has pepperoni. What's the numerator in this fraction? *1.* What does the numerator tell? *The number of parts with pepperoni.* What's the denominator in this fraction? *2.* What does the denominator tell? *How many parts the whole pizza was cut into.*

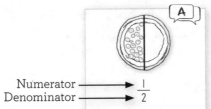

If we wanted to share this pizza with more people, we'd need to cut it into more slices. For the first pizza, I'll cut each half into 4 slices. Draw lines on the pizza as shown.

Each half of the pizza becomes 4 equal slices. Write "×4" two times as shown.

- Point to the numerators. **1 times 4 equals 4. The 1 part with pepperoni becomes 4 parts.** Write 4 as the numerator in the blank fraction.
- Point to the denominators. **2 times 4 equals 8. The 2 parts of the whole pizza become 8 parts.** Write 8 as the denominator in the blank fraction.
- **So, what fraction of the pizza has pepperoni?** *Four-eighths.*

Point to the "×4." **We call this number the multiplier. Multiplier is another word for factor. You can choose any number you want to multiply by the numerator and denominator. As long as you multiply the numerator and denominator by the same number, you'll end up with an equivalent fraction!**

Math with Confidence uses the term *multiplier* in this context because multiplier conveys a greater sense of action than *factor.* This word choice helps children better understand that the multiplier acts on the numerator and denominator.

Children sometimes find it confusing that you *split* each piece into more parts but *multiply* to find the new number of parts. To avoid this confusion, try to describe this process as "creating more fractional parts" rather than "splitting it into parts." See the Unit 12 **Teaching Math with Confidence** for more on the relationship between equivalent fractions and multiplication.

For the next pizza, let's use 3 as the multiplier. We'll cut each half into 3 slices. Draw lines on the pizza and write "×3" twice as shown. Have your child complete the equivalent fraction. **What fraction of the pizza has pepperoni?** *Three-sixths.*

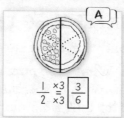

Have your child choose a new multiplier for the final pizza in the row. Then, have him multiply to create a fraction equivalent to 1/2. For example, if he chooses 5: *1 times 5 is 5. 2 times 5 is 10. If you cut each half of the pizza into 5 equal parts, five-tenths of the pizza will have pepperoni!*

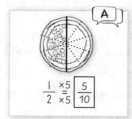

Sample answer.

> If your child chooses a large number, he does not have to draw matching lines on the pizza.

Have your child choose multipliers to create equivalent fractions for the rest of the pizzas in part A.

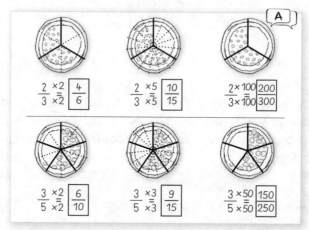

Sample answers. Your child may choose different numbers to multiply by the numerator and denominator.

> If your child is still grasping the idea of equivalent fractions, encourage him to choose small multipliers (like 2, 3, or 4) and draw lines on the pizza to match the multiplier. If your child understands the concept well, encourage him to choose a larger multiplier. He does not need to draw lines on the pizzas to match larger multipliers.

Activity (B): Play Equivalent Fraction Tic-Tac-Toe

Play two rounds of Equivalent Fraction Tic-Tac-Toe. Use fractions equivalent to 1/2 for the first round and fractions equivalent to 3/4 for the second round.

Your child may choose any multiplier he'd like for the equivalent fractions in the game. Allow him to write the multiplication problems on scrap paper, if needed.

Equivalent Fraction Tic-Tac-Toe

Materials: Colored pencils or markers

Object of the Game: Write 3 equivalent fractions in a row, either horizontally, vertically, or diagonally.

Give each player a different-colored marker or colored pencil. Decide who will go first.

On your turn, choose a space on the game board. Use your marker or colored pencil to write a fraction equivalent to the target fraction (the fraction in the box next to the game board). For example, the target fraction for the first round is 1/2. So, you may write any fraction equivalent to 1/2, such as 4/8, 30/60, or 18/36.

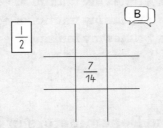

Sample first play.

Take turns writing equivalent fractions. The first player to write 3 equivalent fractions in a row (either horizontally, vertically, or diagonally) wins the game.

Independent Practice and Review

Have your child complete the Lesson 12.2 Practice and Review workbook pages.

Lesson 12.3
Find Missing Numbers in Equivalent Fractions

Purpose	Materials
• Practice identifying missing multipliers in multiplication riddles • Find missing numerators or denominators in pairs of equivalent fractions	• None

Memory Work
- **How many ounces equal 1 pound?** *16.*
- **How many grams equal 1 kilogram?** *1,000.*

Warm-up: Solve Multiplication Riddles

Ask your child the following multiplication riddles.

- **I'm thinking of a multiplier. 4 times my multiplier equals 12. What's my multiplier?** *3.*
- **I'm thinking of a multiplier. 5 times my multiplier equals 30. What's my multiplier?** *6.*
- **I'm thinking of a multiplier. 8 times my multiplier equals 16. What's my multiplier?** *2.*
- **I'm thinking of a multiplier. 7 times my multiplier equals 28. What's my multiplier?** *4.*

Your child will use similar thinking to find missing numerators and denominators in the next activity.

Activity (A):
Find Missing Numerators and Denominators in Equivalent Fractions

In the last lesson, you **learned** how to multiply the numerator and denominator by the same number to create **equivalent fractions.** Today, you'll learn how to find missing numerators and denominators in equivalent fraction puzzles.

In the first puzzle, one-fourth of the bar is colored. Someone started to find an equivalent fraction and wrote 8 for the denominator. But, they stopped before they found the numerator.

First, let's find the multiplier. 4 times what equals 8? *2.* Write "×2" as shown. Draw lines to make each fourth into 2 equal parts. **4 times 2 equals 8. The fourths became eighths.**

To create an equivalent fraction, we multiply the numerator by the same number as the denominator. Write "×2" as shown. **What's 1 times 2?** *2.* Write 2 in the blank. **The 1 shaded part became 2 shaded parts. One-fourth is equivalent to two-eighths.**

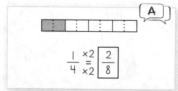

In the next puzzle, two-thirds of the bar is colored. Someone started to find an equivalent fraction and wrote 10 for the numerator.

First, let's find the multiplier. 2 times what equals 10? *5.* Write "×5" as shown. Have your child draw lines to make each third into 5 equal parts.

Each part became 5 parts. So, we need to multiply the denominator by 5 as well. Write "×5" as shown. **What's 3 times 5?** *15.* Write 15 in the blank. **The thirds became fifteenths. Two-thirds is equivalent to ten-fifteenths.**

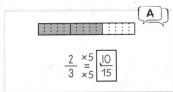

$$\frac{2}{3} \; \begin{matrix} \times 5 \\ = \\ \times 5 \end{matrix} \; \frac{10}{15}$$

Encourage your child to space the lines as evenly as possible, but it's okay if the parts aren't quite equal to each other. Many children assume that they need to draw 5 lines to create 5 equal parts, so it may also help to point out that she only needs to draw 4 lines to create 5 fractional parts.

Have your child complete the other puzzles in the same way.

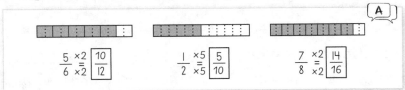

$$\frac{5}{6} \; \begin{matrix} \times 2 \\ = \\ \times 2 \end{matrix} \; \frac{10}{12} \qquad \frac{1}{2} \; \begin{matrix} \times 5 \\ = \\ \times 5 \end{matrix} \; \frac{5}{10} \qquad \frac{7}{8} \; \begin{matrix} \times 2 \\ = \\ \times 2 \end{matrix} \; \frac{14}{16}$$

Activity (B): Play Fill the Fractions

In this game, you win as many points as the number you write. Keep that in mind as you choose which puzzles to complete!

Play Fill the Fractions. As your child solves each problem, have her first find the multiplier and write it above and below the equals sign. Then, have her multiply to find the missing number in the equivalent fraction.

Your child may also draw lines on the fraction bars to help complete the equivalent fractions.

Fill the Fractions

Materials: None

Object of the Game: Complete equivalent fractions to win the most points.

Start a simple scorecard on a separate piece of paper. Choose who will go first.

On your turn, choose a puzzle on the gameboard. Find the missing number in the equivalent fraction. The missing number is your score. Add this score to your previous total.

For example, if you complete the following problem on your first turn, you score 30 points.

$$\frac{7}{10} = \frac{21}{30}$$

Joan	Mom
30	

Take turns until all problems have been completed. Whoever has the higher score wins the game.

Directions continued on next page.

Answer Key:

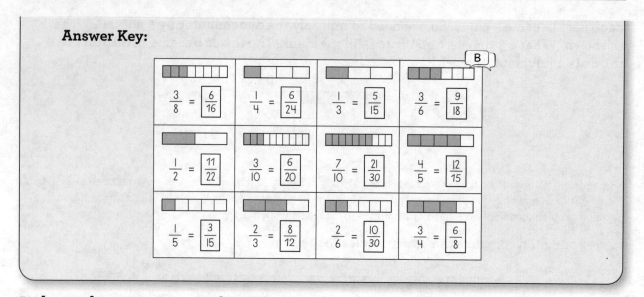

Independent Practice and Review

Have your child complete the Lesson 12.3 Practice and Review workbook pages.

Lesson 12.4
Equivalent Fractions of an Inch

Purpose	Materials
• Observe the different lengths of the tick marks on rulers • Identify the tick marks on a ruler for halves, fourths, eighths, and sixteenths of an inch • Use a ruler to draw lines that are fractions of an inch	• 1-foot ruler • Colored pencils or markers

Memory Work	• **How many inches equal 1 foot?** *12.* • **How many feet equal 1 yard?** *3.* • **How many inches equal 1 yard?** *36.* • **How many feet equal 1 mile?** *5,280.*

Your child will learn how to use common denominators to compare fractions in Lesson 12.6. Measuring with fractional parts of an inch in this lesson previews that skill.

Warm-up: Examine Tick Marks on a Ruler

In the last lesson, you learned how to find missing numbers in equivalent fractions. Today, you'll learn how equivalent fractions help us measure fractions of an inch.

The tick marks on the ruler divide each inch into fractional parts. We're going to focus on the tick marks between 0 and 1 inch today. Have your child look closely at the tick marks from 0 to 1 inch on a ruler.

This ruler (and the others in the Instructor Guide for this lesson) are enlarged to make the tick marks easier to see. If your child has trouble seeing the tick marks on the real ruler, show him these diagrams as well.

What are three things you notice about the tick marks? *Sample answers: There are a lot of them! They divide the inch into very small parts. Some of the tick marks are longer than the others.*

Which tick mark between 0 and 1 is the longest? *Child points to half-inch mark.*

Which tick marks between 0 and 1 are the shortest? *Child points to the sixteenth-inch marks.*

You and your child will identify the value of each tick mark in the next activity.

Activity (A): Identify Halves, Fourths, Eighths, and Sixteenths on a Ruler

Rulers usually have tick marks that divide each inch into halves, fourths, eighths, and sixteenths. Knowing about equivalent fractions helps you use a ruler correctly.

In this lesson, you'll focus on how the ruler's tick marks show equivalent fractions. Your child can also find the multiplier and check that both the numerator and denominator are multiplied by the same number.

Point to the tick mark in the middle of the first ruler. **This tick mark splits the inch into halves. It shows a length of half an inch.** Have your child find the corresponding tick mark on the real ruler. **The longest tick mark on the ruler divides the inch into halves.**

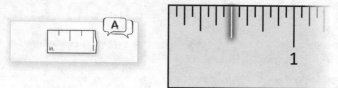

The next-longest tick marks divide each half into 2 equal parts to make fourths.

- **Which tick mark shows one-fourth of an inch?** *Child points to one-fourth mark.*
- **Which tick mark shows two-fourths of an inch?** *Child points to one-half mark.* **One-half is equivalent to two-fourths. So, the same tick mark stands for two-fourths and for one-half.** Write 2 as the numerator for the equivalent fraction.
- **Which tick mark shows three-fourths of an inch?** *Child points to three-fourths mark.*
- Have your child find the quarter-inch marks on the real ruler.

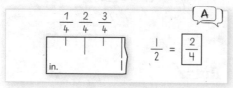

Point to the next printed ruler. **The next-longest tick marks divide each fourth into 2 equal parts to make eighths.** Have your child find the tick marks for 1/8, 2/8, 3/8, and so on. Complete the matching equivalent fractions as your child finds them. For example: **The tick mark for two-eighths is also the tick mark for one-fourth. One-fourth is equivalent to two-eighths.** Then, have your child find the eighth-inch tick marks on the real ruler.

Point to the next printed ruler. **The shortest tick marks divide each eighth into 2 equal parts to make sixteenths.** Have your child find the tick marks for 1/16, 2/16, 3/16, and so on. Complete the matching equivalent fractions as your child finds them.

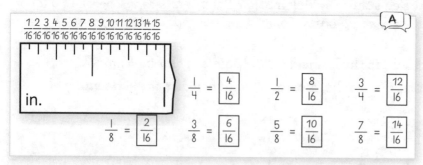
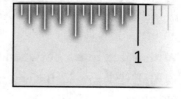

Activity (B): Draw Lines with Fractional Lengths

Understanding what the tick marks on a ruler mean is very important for measuring correctly.

First, we'll draw a line that's **five-sixteenths of an inch long. We want to use sixteenths to draw the line. Which tick marks show sixteenths?** *All of them!* **It takes all the tick marks to divide the inch into sixteenths, so you simply count 5 tick marks from 0.** Have your child draw a line that's 5/16 in. long.

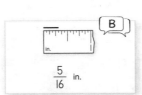

Next, we'll draw a line that's **five-eighths of an inch long. We want to use eighths of an inch to draw the line, so we look for the tick marks that divide the inch into 8 equal parts.** Have your child draw a line that's 5/8 in. long.

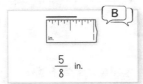

Now, we need to use the ruler to measure this line. **Look at the tick mark at the end of the line. What type of fractional part of an inch does it measure?** *Eighths.* **How many eighths of an inch long is the line?** *7.* Write 7/8 in the blank. Repeat with the final line.

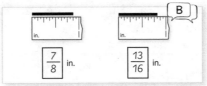

Which line is the shortest? *The one that's 5/16 of an inch.* **Which line is the longest?** *The one that's 7/8 of an inch.*

Activity (C): Play Fraction War

Play Fraction War. Encourage your child to use the equivalent fractions in part A to compare the fractions. For example, to compare 5/8 and 9/16: **Five-eighths equals ten-sixteenths, so it's greater than nine-sixteenths.**

Fraction War

Materials: Counters of two colors, 2 dice

Object of the Game: Win the most counters.

Give 7 counters of one color to Player 1. Give 7 counters of another color to Player 2.

On your turn, roll 2 dice. Add the numbers on the two dice and place a counter on the matching square on the game board. For example, if you roll a 6 and a 3, place your counter on the square labeled with a 9.

Directions continued on next page.

Then, the other player rolls, adds the numbers on the dice, and places a counter on the matching square. Have your child decide which player's counter is on the square with a greater fraction. The player whose counter is on the square with the greater fraction wins both counters and places them in his "Won" pile. Counters in the "Won" pile are now out of the game and cannot be used again.

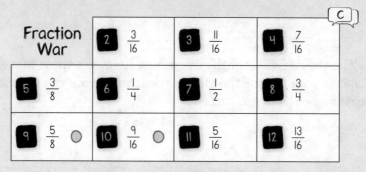

Sample play. The player whose counter is on 5/8 wins, since 5/8 is greater than 9/16.

If both counters are on the same square, leave them on the game board and play another round. Whoever wins the next round wins all 4 counters.

Play until both players use up their original pile of counters. Whoever has more counters in their "Won" pile wins the game.

Independent Practice and Review

Have your child complete the Lesson 12.4 Practice and Review workbook pages.

Lesson 12.5
Equivalent Fractions of a Meter

Purpose	Materials
• Practice identifying measurements on a (printed) meterstick • Write fractions with tenths and hundredths to describe parts of a meter • Use equivalent fractions to compare tenths and hundredths	• Meterstick, optional • Counters • 2 dice

Memory Work	• **How many millimeters equal 1 centimeter?** *10.* • **How many centimeters equal 1 meter?** *100.* • **How many meters equal 1 kilometer?** *1,000.*

Your child will learn how to use common denominators to compare fractions in Lesson 12.6. Measuring with fractional parts of a meter in this lesson previews that skill.

This lesson also previews decimals. Your child will learn about tenths and hundredths of a meter in the context of decimals in Unit 14.

Warm-up: Identify Measurements on a Meterstick

Today, you'll learn how to use fractions to describe parts of a meter. Have your child hold her hands about one meter apart. **Remember, refrigerators are usually about a meter wide, and kitchen chairs are often about a meter high. A meter is a little longer than a yard.**

100 centimeters equal 1 meter. This meterstick diagram (which is much smaller than a real meterstick!) is split into 100 centimeters. There's a longer tick mark every 10 centimeters to make the meterstick easier to read.

Either show your child a real meterstick or the printed meterstick on the page. (If you're using the printed meterstick, cover the fractions above and below it with a piece of paper.) Then, have your child point to the tick marks for the locations for the following measurements: 1 cm, 10 cm, 30 cm, 37 cm, 43 cm, 60 cm, 90 cm, 99 cm.

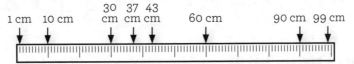

If your child has trouble, encourage her to think of the meterstick like a number line. For example: **49 is 1 less than 50. Each tick mark stands for 1 centimeter, so the tick mark for 49 must be the one before 50.**

Activity (A): Write Fractions for Parts of a Meter

Uncover the fractions above the meterstick. Leave the fractions below the meterstick covered (or cover them now).

If you divide 1 meter into 100 equal parts, each part is 1 centimeter long. So, each centimeter is one-hundredth of a meter. Remember, a real meterstick is much bigger than the one shown here. On a real meterstick, a centimeter is about the width of your little finger. Point to the tick mark for 10 cm. **From 0 to this tick mark is 10 centimeters, or ten-hundredths of a meter.**

Read the fractions from left to right. Have your child complete the missing numerators as you reach them.

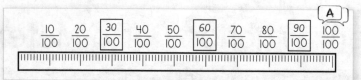

Point to the tick mark for 1 centimeter. **From 0 to this tick mark is 1 centimeter. What fraction of a meter is that?** *One-hundredth.* Repeat with 37 cm, 43 cm, and 99 cm.

Cover the fractions above the printed meterstick with a piece of paper, and uncover the ones below it. **If you divide 1 meter into 10 equal parts, each part is 10 centimeters long. So, each group of 10 centimeters is one-tenth of a meter.** Point to the tick mark for 10 cm. **From 0 to this tick mark is one-tenth of a meter.**

Read the fractions from left to right. Have your child complete the missing numerators as you reach them.

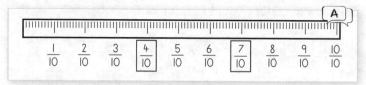

Activity (B): Find Equivalent Fractions with Tenths and Hundredths

Cover part A with a piece of paper.

> Covering part A prevents your child from completing the equivalent fractions by simply looking at the meterstick diagram.

Have your child complete the first pair of equivalent fractions. **Seven-tenths of a meter and seventy-hundredths of a meter are the same length. If I have a ribbon that's seven-tenths of a meter long, how many centimeters long is it?** *70.* If your child's not sure, uncover part A and have her find the matching tick mark on the printed meterstick. Repeat with the rest of the equivalent fractions.

$$\frac{7}{10} = \boxed{\frac{70}{100}} \qquad \frac{5}{10} = \boxed{\frac{50}{100}} \qquad \frac{4}{10} = \boxed{\frac{40}{100}}$$

$$\frac{6}{10} = \boxed{\frac{60}{100}} \qquad \frac{3}{10} = \boxed{\frac{30}{100}} \qquad \frac{8}{10} = \boxed{\frac{80}{100}}$$

Activity (C): Play Fraction War

Play Fraction War. See Lesson 12.4 (pages 403-404) for directions. Encourage your child to use the equivalent fractions in part B to compare the fractions. For example, to compare 6/10 and 56/100: **Six-tenths equals sixty-hundredths, so it's greater than fifty-six-hundredths.** Or, she may refer to the meterstick diagram in part A.

Independent Practice and Review

Have your child complete the Lesson 12.5 Practice and Review workbook pages.

Lesson 12.6
Use Common Denominators to Compare Fractions

Purpose	Materials
• Practice comparing fractions with common denominators • Use equivalent fractions to compare fractions with different denominators • Solve fraction comparison word problems	• None

Memory Work · **How many milliliters equal 1 liter?** *1,000.*

Warm-up (A): Practice Comparing Fractions with the Same Denominator

Have your child write <, >, or = in the circles to compare the fractions.

$$\frac{2}{5} \;\textcircled{<}\; \frac{4}{5} \qquad \frac{9}{10} \;\textcircled{>}\; \frac{8}{10} \qquad \frac{14}{16} \;\textcircled{<}\; \frac{15}{16} \quad \boxed{A}$$

What do you notice about the denominators in these fractions? *Sample answer: The fractions in each pair have the same denominator.* **When fractions have the same denominator, we know that they're cut into the same fractional parts. So, whichever fraction has more parts is the greater fraction.**

Activity (B): Use Common Denominators to Compare Two Fractions

Today, you'll learn how to use equivalent fractions to compare fractions with different denominators.

Read the first word problem aloud: *Jeremy has 3/4 cup of flour. He needs 5/8 cup to make muffins. Does he have enough flour?*

What are we trying to find in this problem? *Whether Jeremy has enough flour.* **To find the answer, we need to compare three-fourths and five-eighths. If three-fourths of a cup is less than five-eighths of a cup, Jeremy doesn't have enough.**

If the fractions had the same denominators, it would be easy to compare them. So, we'll find how many eighths equal three-fourths of a cup. Have your child multiply to find the missing numerator.

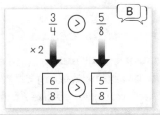

If your child has trouble with the vertical format, have him write the equivalent fractions and multipliers horizontally on a piece of scrap paper.

Three-fourths equals six-eighths. Six-eighths is greater than five-eighths. So, three-fourths is greater than five-eighths. Write > in both circles. **Does Jeremy have enough flour to make the muffins?** *Yes.* Write "Yes" to complete the problem.

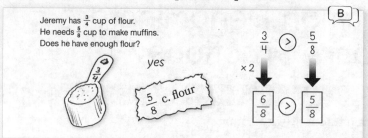

When two fractions have the same denominator, we say they have *common denominators.* **We used 8 as the common denominator for the fractions in this problem, because it's easy to change fourths into eighths. In this book, we'll always use the larger denominator in the pair as the common denominator in fraction comparison problems. Next year, you'll learn more ways to find common denominators.**

If your child wonders why we use the larger number for the common denominator, draw a fraction bar to match 5/8. Then, draw darker lines dividing the bar into fourths. **Five-eighths doesn't equal a whole number of fourths, so it's easier to change three-fourths to eighths than five-eighths to fourths.**

Read the next word problem aloud: ***The purple ribbon is 7/10 meter long. The orange ribbon is 4/5 meter long. Which ribbon is longer?***

What are we trying to find in this problem? *Which ribbon is longer.* **To find the answer, we need to compare seven-tenths and four-fifths. 10 is the greater denominator, so we'll use 10 as our common denominator.** Write 10 as the denominators for both blank fractions. Then, have your child find the missing numerators.

Four-fifths equals eight-tenths. Which is greater: seven-tenths or four-fifths? *Four-fifths.* Write < in both circles. **Which ribbon is longer?** *The orange ribbon.* Write "Orange" to complete the problem.

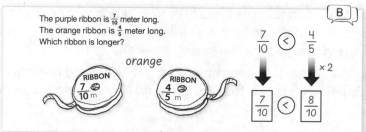

Activity (C): Use Common Denominators to Compare Three Fractions

We can also use common denominators to compare more than two fractions. Read the next word problem aloud: ***Etta has 2/3 kg of red modeling clay, 5/6 kg of blue modeling clay, and 7/12 kg of green modeling clay. Which color does she have the least of?***

What are we trying to find in this problem? *Which color she has the least of.* **To find the answer, we need to compare thirds, sixths, and twelfths. 12 is the greatest denominator, so we'll use 12 as our common denominator.** Write 12 as the denominators for all three blank fractions. Then, have your child find the missing numerators.

Which color does she have the least of? *Green.* **How do you know?** *Sample answer: Seven-twelfths is less than eight-twelfths and ten-twelfths.* Write "Green" to complete the problem.

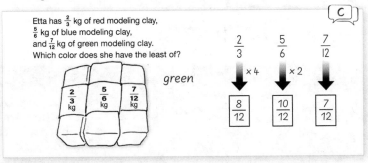

Independent Practice and Review

Have your child complete the Lesson 12.6 Practice and Review workbook pages.

Lesson 12.7
Enrichment (Optional)

Purpose	Materials
• Practice memory work • Introduce the concept of simplifying fractions • Create an equivalent fraction collage • Summarize what your child has learned and assess your child's progress	• *Fractions in Disguise: A Math Adventure*, written by Edward Einhorn and illustrated by David Clark • 5 different colors of paper • Small bowl or cup (for tracing) • Scissors • Glue

Warm-up: Review Memory Work

Quiz your child on all memory work through Unit 12. See pages 536-537 for the full list.

Math Picture Book: *Fractions in Disguise: A Math Adventure*

Read *Fractions in Disguise: A Math Adventure*, written by Edward Einhorn and illustrated by David Clark. As you read, explain that the "Reducer" created by George in the book doesn't change the value of the fraction. Instead, it reduces the *numbers* for the numerator and denominator so that the fraction is easier to understand.

Your child will learn how to simplify fractions (or "reduce" them) in *Fifth Grade Math with Confidence.*

Enrichment Activity: Equivalent Fraction Collage

We're going to make an equivalent fraction collage today! Have your child choose 5 different colors of paper. Help her cut a large square out of 1 piece of paper, about 8 inches on each side.

Then, help her cut two circles out of each of the other 4 colors of paper. To make the circles, place a small bowl or cup on top of each piece of paper and trace it twice. Aim to make the circles about 3 or 4 inches wide.

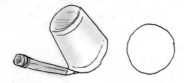

Have your child cut 2 of the circles into halves, 2 of the circles into fourths, 2 of the circles into eighths, and 2 of the circles into sixteenths.

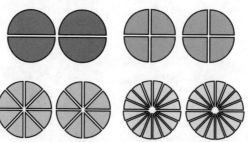

Now, you get to arrange the pieces to make a collage! Here are the rules for your collage:

- **You must use all the pieces.**
- **The pieces may overlap.**
- **Your finished piece must have two lines of symmetry. The top side must be a mirror image of the bottom side, and the left side must be a mirror image of the right side.**

Have your child arrange the fraction pieces on the paper square. Once she's pleased with her arrangement, have her glue the pieces to the square.

Sample collage.

Unit Wrap-Up

Have your child complete the Unit 12 Wrap-Up.

Unit 12 Answer Key

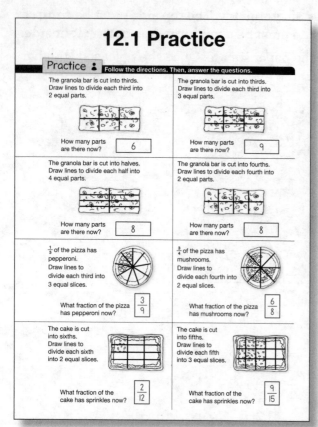

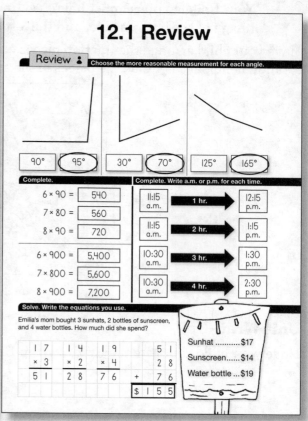

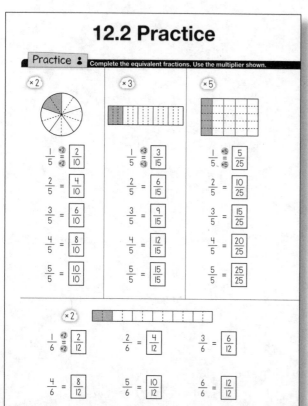

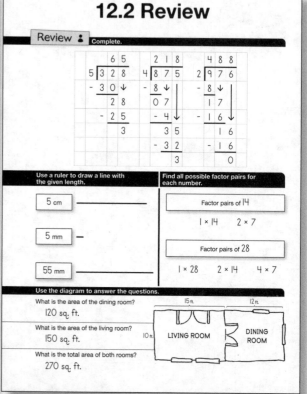

Unit 12 Answer Key

12.3 Practice

Practice 👤 Use the pictures to complete the equivalent fractions.

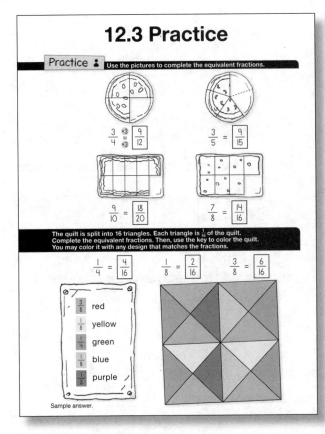

$$\frac{3}{4} \overset{\times 3}{\underset{\times 3}{=}} \frac{9}{12}$$ $$\frac{3}{5} = \frac{9}{15}$$

$$\frac{9}{10} = \frac{18}{20}$$ $$\frac{7}{8} = \frac{14}{16}$$

The quilt is split into 16 triangles. Each triangle is $\frac{1}{16}$ of the quilt. Complete the equivalent fractions. Then, use the key to color the quilt. You may color it with any design that matches the fractions.

$$\frac{1}{4} = \frac{4}{16}$$ $$\frac{1}{8} = \frac{2}{16}$$ $$\frac{3}{8} = \frac{6}{16}$$

$\frac{3}{8}$	red
$\frac{1}{8}$	yellow
$\frac{1}{4}$	green
$\frac{1}{8}$	blue
$\frac{1}{8}$	purple

Sample answer.

12.3 Review

Review 👤 Label with letters and geometry symbols.

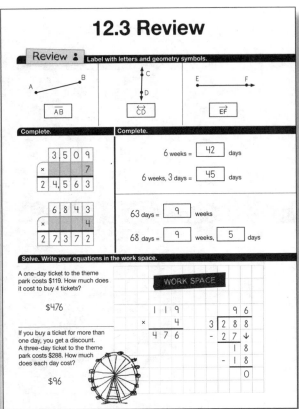

$\overline{AB}$ $\overleftrightarrow{CD}$ $\overrightarrow{EF}$

Complete.

$$\begin{array}{c} 3\,5\,0\,9 \\ \times \qquad 7 \\ \hline 2\,4\,5\,6\,3 \end{array}$$

$$\begin{array}{c} 6\,8\,4\,3 \\ \times \qquad 4 \\ \hline 2\,7\,3\,7\,2 \end{array}$$

Complete.

6 weeks = 42 days

6 weeks, 3 days = 45 days

63 days = 9 weeks

68 days = 9 weeks, 5 days

Solve. Write your equations in the work space.

A one-day ticket to the theme park costs $119. How much does it cost to buy 4 tickets?

$476

WORK SPACE

$$\begin{array}{c} 1\,1\,9 \\ \times \quad 4 \\ \hline 4\,7\,6 \end{array}$$

If you buy a ticket for more than one day, you get a discount. A three-day ticket to the theme park costs $288. How much does each day cost?

$96

$$\begin{array}{r} 9\,6 \\ 3\,\overline{)2\,8\,8} \\ -\,2\,7\,\downarrow \\ \hline 1\,8 \\ -\,1\,8 \\ \hline 0 \end{array}$$

12.4 Practice

Practice 👤 Use a ruler to draw lines that match each length. Then, write <, >, or = to complete the fractions.

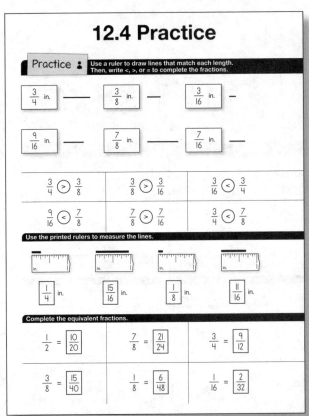

$\frac{3}{4}$ in. ____ $\frac{3}{8}$ in. ____ $\frac{3}{16}$ in. ____

$\frac{9}{16}$ in. ____ $\frac{7}{8}$ in. ____ $\frac{7}{16}$ in. ____

$$\frac{3}{4} > \frac{3}{8}$$ $$\frac{3}{8} > \frac{3}{16}$$ $$\frac{3}{16} < \frac{3}{4}$$

$$\frac{9}{16} < \frac{7}{8}$$ $$\frac{7}{8} > \frac{7}{16}$$ $$\frac{3}{4} < \frac{7}{8}$$

Use the printed rulers to measure the lines.

$\frac{1}{4}$ in. $\frac{15}{16}$ in. $\frac{1}{8}$ in. $\frac{11}{16}$ in.

Complete the equivalent fractions.

$$\frac{1}{2} = \frac{10}{20}$$ $$\frac{7}{8} = \frac{21}{24}$$ $$\frac{3}{4} = \frac{9}{12}$$

$$\frac{3}{8} = \frac{15}{40}$$ $$\frac{1}{8} = \frac{6}{48}$$ $$\frac{1}{16} = \frac{2}{32}$$

12.4 Review

Review 👤 Complete.

$$20 \times 30 = 600$$

$$40 \times 40 = 1{,}600$$

$$50 \times 60 = 3{,}000$$

$$80 \times 50 = 4{,}000$$

$$70 \times 70 = 4{,}900$$

Draw as many lines of symmetry as possible for each shape.

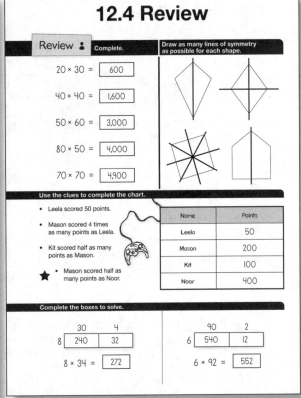

Use the clues to complete the chart.

- Leela scored 50 points.
- Mason scored 4 times as many points as Leela.
- Kit scored half as many points as Mason.
- Mason scored half as many points as Noor.

Name	Points
Leela	50
Mason	200
Kit	100
Noor	400

Complete the boxes to solve.

8	30	4
	240	32

$$8 \times 34 = 272$$

6	90	2
	540	12

$$6 \times 92 = 552$$

Unit 12 Answer Key

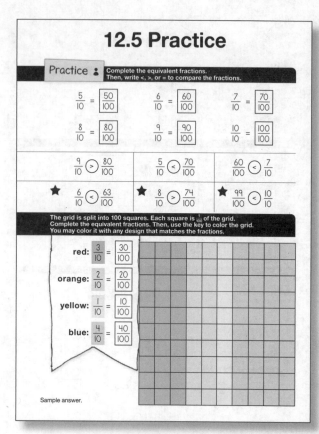

12.5 Practice

Practice 👤 Complete the equivalent fractions.
Then, write <, >, or = to compare the fractions.

$$\frac{5}{10} = \frac{50}{100} \qquad \frac{6}{10} = \frac{60}{100} \qquad \frac{7}{10} = \frac{70}{100}$$

$$\frac{8}{10} = \frac{80}{100} \qquad \frac{9}{10} = \frac{90}{100} \qquad \frac{10}{10} = \frac{100}{100}$$

$$\frac{9}{10} > \frac{80}{100} \qquad \frac{5}{10} < \frac{70}{100} \qquad \frac{60}{100} < \frac{7}{10}$$

★ $\frac{6}{10} < \frac{63}{100}$ ★ $\frac{8}{10} > \frac{74}{100}$ ★ $\frac{99}{100} < \frac{10}{10}$

The grid is split into 100 squares. Each square is $\frac{1}{100}$ of the grid.
Complete the equivalent fractions. Then, use the key to color the grid.
You may color it with any design that matches the fractions.

red: $\frac{3}{10} = \frac{30}{100}$

orange: $\frac{2}{10} = \frac{20}{100}$

yellow: $\frac{1}{10} = \frac{10}{100}$

blue: $\frac{4}{10} = \frac{40}{100}$

Sample answer.

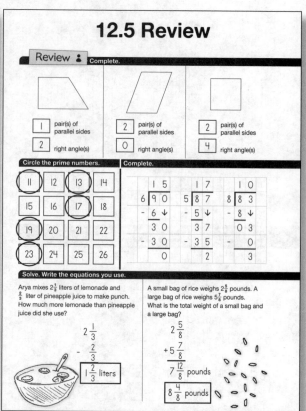

12.5 Review

Review 👤 Complete.

☐ 1 pair(s) of parallel sides   ☐ 2 pair(s) of parallel sides   ☐ 2 pair(s) of parallel sides

☐ 2 right angle(s)   ☐ 0 right angle(s)   ☐ 4 right angle(s)

Circle the prime numbers.

⑪	12	⑬	14
15	16	⑰	18
⑲	20	21	22
㉓	24	25	26

Complete.

```
    1 5        1 7        1 0
 6) 9 0     5) 8 7     8) 8 3
  - 6 ↓      - 5 ↓      - 8 ↓
    3 0        3 7        0 3
  - 3 0      - 3 5      -   0
      0          2          3
```

Solve. Write the equations you use.

Arya mixes $2\frac{1}{3}$ liters of lemonade and $\frac{2}{3}$ liter of pineapple juice to make punch. How much more lemonade than pineapple juice did she use?

$$2\frac{1}{3} - \frac{2}{3} = 1\frac{2}{3} \text{ liters}$$

A small bag of rice weighs $2\frac{5}{8}$ pounds. A large bag of rice weighs $5\frac{7}{8}$ pounds. What is the total weight of a small bag and a large bag?

$$2\frac{5}{8} + 5\frac{7}{8} = 7\frac{12}{8} \text{ pounds} = 8\frac{4}{8} \text{ pounds}$$

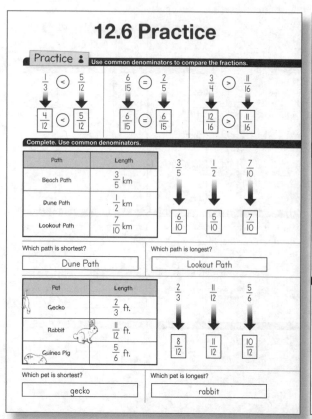

12.6 Practice

Practice 👤 Use common denominators to compare the fractions.

$$\frac{1}{3} < \frac{5}{12} \qquad \frac{6}{15} = \frac{2}{5} \qquad \frac{3}{4} > \frac{11}{16}$$

$$\frac{4}{12} < \frac{5}{12} \qquad \frac{6}{15} = \frac{6}{15} \qquad \frac{12}{16} > \frac{11}{16}$$

Complete. Use common denominators.

Path	Length
Beach Path	$\frac{3}{5}$ km
Dune Path	$\frac{1}{2}$ km
Lookout Path	$\frac{7}{10}$ km

$$\frac{3}{5} \quad \frac{1}{2} \quad \frac{7}{10}$$
$$\downarrow \quad \downarrow \quad \downarrow$$
$$\frac{6}{10} \quad \frac{5}{10} \quad \frac{7}{10}$$

Which path is shortest?
Dune Path

Which path is longest?
Lookout Path

Pet	Length
Gecko	$\frac{2}{3}$ ft.
Rabbit	$\frac{11}{12}$ ft.
Guinea Pig	$\frac{5}{6}$ ft.

$$\frac{2}{3} \quad \frac{11}{12} \quad \frac{5}{6}$$
$$\downarrow \quad \downarrow \quad \downarrow$$
$$\frac{8}{12} \quad \frac{11}{12} \quad \frac{10}{12}$$

Which pet is shortest?
gecko

Which pet is longest?
rabbit

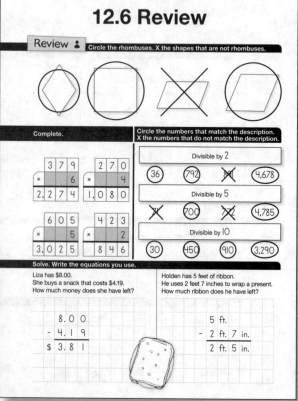

12.6 Review

Review 👤 Circle the rhombuses. X the shapes that are not rhombuses.

Complete.

Circle the numbers that match the description.
X the numbers that do not match the description.

```
  3 7 9        2 7 0
×     6      ×     4
2,2 7 4      1,0 8 0

  6 0 5        4 2 3
×     5      ×     2
3,0 2 5        8 4 6
```

Divisible by 2			
㊱	⑦⑨②	☒	④,⑥⑦⑧

Divisible by 5			
☒	⑦⓪⓪	☒	④,⑦⑧⑤

Divisible by 10			
㉚	④⑤⓪	⑨①⓪	③,②⑨⓪

Solve. Write the equations you use.

Liza has $8.00. She buys a snack that costs $4.19. How much money does she have left?

```
   8.0 0
 - 4.1 9
 $ 3.8 1
```

Holden has 5 feet of ribbon. He uses 2 feet 7 inches to wrap a present. How much ribbon does he have left?

```
   5 ft.
 - 2 ft. 7 in.
   2 ft. 5 in.
```

Unit 12 Answer Key

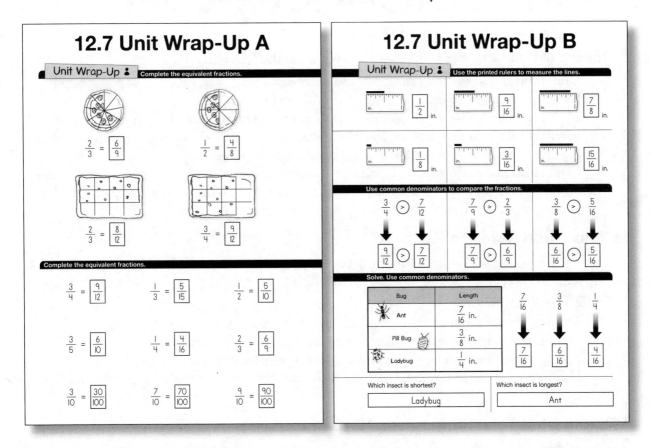

12.7 Unit Wrap-Up A

Unit Wrap-Up 🔧 Complete the equivalent fractions.

$\dfrac{2}{3} = \dfrac{6}{9}$ $\dfrac{1}{2} = \dfrac{4}{8}$

$\dfrac{2}{3} = \dfrac{8}{12}$ $\dfrac{3}{4} = \dfrac{9}{12}$

Complete the equivalent fractions.

$\dfrac{3}{4} = \dfrac{9}{12}$ $\dfrac{1}{3} = \dfrac{5}{15}$ $\dfrac{1}{2} = \dfrac{5}{10}$

$\dfrac{3}{5} = \dfrac{6}{10}$ $\dfrac{1}{4} = \dfrac{4}{16}$ $\dfrac{2}{3} = \dfrac{6}{9}$

$\dfrac{3}{10} = \dfrac{30}{100}$ $\dfrac{7}{10} = \dfrac{70}{100}$ $\dfrac{9}{10} = \dfrac{90}{100}$

12.7 Unit Wrap-Up B

Unit Wrap-Up 🔧 Use the printed rulers to measure the lines.

$\dfrac{1}{2}$ in. $\dfrac{9}{16}$ in. $\dfrac{7}{8}$ in.

$\dfrac{1}{8}$ in. $\dfrac{3}{16}$ in. $\dfrac{15}{16}$ in.

Use common denominators to compare the fractions.

$\dfrac{3}{4} \, \bigcirc\!\!>\! \, \dfrac{7}{12}$ $\dfrac{7}{9} \, \bigcirc\!\!>\! \, \dfrac{2}{3}$ $\dfrac{3}{8} \, \bigcirc\!\!>\! \, \dfrac{5}{16}$

⬇   ⬇   ⬇   ⬇   ⬇   ⬇

$\dfrac{9}{12} \, \bigcirc\!\!>\! \, \dfrac{7}{12}$ $\dfrac{7}{9} \, \bigcirc\!\!>\! \, \dfrac{6}{9}$ $\dfrac{6}{16} \, \bigcirc\!\!>\! \, \dfrac{5}{16}$

Solve. Use common denominators.

Bug	Length
🐜 Ant	$\dfrac{7}{16}$ in.
Pill Bug 🪲	$\dfrac{3}{8}$ in.
Ladybug 🐞	$\dfrac{1}{4}$ in.

$\dfrac{7}{16}$ $\dfrac{3}{8}$ $\dfrac{1}{4}$

⬇   ⬇   ⬇

$\dfrac{7}{16}$ $\dfrac{6}{16}$ $\dfrac{4}{16}$

Which insect is shortest?

Ladybug

Which insect is longest?

Ant

Unit 12 Checkpoint

What to Expect at the End of Unit 12

By the end of Unit 12, most children will be able to do the following:

- Understand that you can multiply the numerator and denominator of a fraction by the same number to create an equivalent fraction.
- Multiply to find missing numerators or denominators in pairs of equivalent fractions.
- Identify and compare halves, fourths, eighths, and sixteenths of an inch on a ruler.
- Identify and compare tenths and hundredths of a meter.
- Use common denominators to compare fractions with different denominators. Some children will need help with this process or have trouble remembering to use the larger denominator when comparing.

Is Your Child Ready to Move on?

In Unit 13, your child will learn to multiply two-digit numbers by two-digit numbers with the multiplication algorithm. Before moving on to Unit 13, your child should have already mastered the following skills:

- Tell answers to most of the multiplication facts within 3 seconds.
- Mentally multiply one-digit numbers by a multiple of 10 or multiple of 100.
- Multiply two-digit numbers by one-digit numbers with the box method.
- Multiply a two-digit number by a one-digit number with the multiplication algorithm, mostly fluently.

What to Do If Your Child Needs More Practice

Some children will still be working on mastering the multiplication facts, especially the challenging ×7 and ×8 facts. **If your child often needs more than a few seconds to find answers to the multiplication facts, allow him to use the multiplication chart (Blackline Master 2) as he solves the multi-digit multiplication problems in Unit 13.** Otherwise, he'll spend so much energy figuring out the multiplication facts that he'll struggle to remember all the steps in these processes. Make sure he also keeps practicing the multiplication facts to develop greater fluency. See the Unit 2 Checkpoint (page 85) for practice suggestions.

If your child is having trouble with any of the other skills, spend a day or two practicing them before moving on to Unit 13.

Activities for Mentally Multiplying with Multiples of 10 or 100

- Multiply at the Mental Math Arcade (Lesson 3.2)
- Spin to Win (Lesson 3.3)

Activities for Multiplying Two-Digit Numbers by One-Digit Numbers with the Box Method

- Roll and Multiply (Lesson 3.8)

Activities for Multiplying Two-Digit Numbers by One-Digit Numbers with the Multiplication Algorithm

- Roll and Multiply (Lesson 7.2)
- Snowball Fight (Lesson 7.3) (Use two-digit numbers on the snowballs to give your child practice with multiplying two-digit numbers times one-digit numbers.)

Unit 13
Written Multiplication, Part 2

Overview

In this unit, your child will learn how to multiply two-digit numbers by two-digit numbers. First, you'll teach her how to use the box method to multiply two-digit numbers. Then, you'll teach her how to use the traditional written algorithm. Just as with previous algorithms, you'll help her develop both conceptual understanding and procedural fluency as she learns this complex process.

What Your Child Will Learn

In this unit, your child will learn to:

- Multiply two-digit numbers by two-digit numbers with the box method
- Multiply two-digit numbers by two-digit numbers with the traditional written algorithm
- Multiply two-digit numbers to solve word problems

Lesson List

Lesson 13.1   Review the Box Method and Multiplication Algorithm

Lesson 13.2   Multiply Two-Digit Numbers with the Box Method

Lesson 13.3   Multiply Two-Digit Numbers by Multiples of 10

Lesson 13.4   Multiply Two-Digit Numbers in Steps

Lesson 13.5   Multiply Two-Digit Numbers with the Multiplication Algorithm

Lesson 13.6   Practice Multiplying Two-Digit Numbers with the Multiplication Algorithm

Lesson 13.7   Compare and Contrast the Box Method and Multiplication Algorithm

Lesson 13.8   Enrichment (Optional)

Extra Materials Needed for Unit 13

- 10 slips of paper
- For optional Enrichment Lesson:
    - *Great Estimations*, by Bruce Goldstone. Square Fish, 2010.
    - Tape measure

Teaching Math with Confidence:
Why Learn Two Methods to Multiply Two-Digit Numbers?

Earlier this year, your child learned how to use the box method and multiplication algorithm to multiply multi-digit numbers by one-digit numbers. In this unit, your child will learn how to use both methods to multiply two-digit numbers by two-digit numbers.

Both methods use the distributive property to split numbers into parts, multiply the parts separately, and then add the partial products to find the total product. The main advantage of the box method is its visual clarity. You can easily see the meaning of each partial product, and you can easily check for errors.

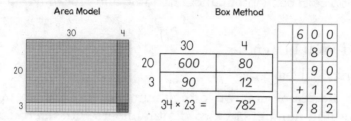

How to find 34 × 23 with the box method. The partial product in each box matches the area of part of the rectangle.

The main advantage of the traditional algorithm is its efficiency and compactness. When you use the traditional algorithm, you only have two partial products to record and add. However, the downside is that it's harder for children to understand the meaning of each step and fix any mistakes.

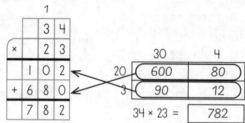

How to find 34 × 23 with the multiplication algorithm. Each partial product is the sum of two of the partial products from the box method. 90 + 12 = 102, and 600 + 80 = 680.

Both methods work well for finding the product of multi-digit numbers. In everyday life, though, most people use a calculator! While your child may not often need to multiply multi-digit numbers by hand, learning both methods helps her develop deep conceptual understanding of the distributive property. This property will show up throughout the next few years of your child's math education, especially when she learns to manipulate and solve algebraic equations. By teaching your child this fundamental principle now, you prepare her to use the distributive property with confidence when she later encounters it with x's and y's.

Lesson 13.1
Review the Box Method and Multiplication Algorithm

Purpose	Materials
• Practice mental multiplication • Use the box method and multiplication algorithm to multiply multi-digit numbers by one-digit numbers • Review the similarities and differences between the box method and multiplication algorithm	• None

Memory Work	
	• **What do we call a quadrilateral with 4 right angles?** *A rectangle.* • **What do we call a quadrilateral with 4 right angles and 4 equal sides?** *A square.* • **What do we call a quadrilateral with 4 equal sides?** *A rhombus.* • **What do we call a quadrilateral with 2 pairs of parallel sides?** *A parallelogram.* • **What do we call a quadrilateral with exactly 1 pair of parallel sides?** *A trapezoid.*

Warm-up: Practice Mental Multiplication

Ask your child the following oral multiplication problems.

- **20 times 30.** *600.*
- **40 times 2.** *80.*
- **30 times 70.** *2,100.*
- **20 times 50.** *1,000.*

- **40 times 3.** *120.*
- **6 times 500.** *3,000.*
- **7 times 2,000.** *14,000.*

If your child has trouble with any of the problems, write them on scrap paper. Remind her to underline the place-holder zeros, multiply the other digits, and tack on the place-holder zeros.

$$2\underline{0} \times 3\underline{0} = 600$$

Activity (A): Multiply Two-Digit Numbers by One-Digit Numbers with the Box Method and Multiplication Algorithm

We're beginning a new unit on multiplication today. In this unit, you'll learn how to use the box method and multiplication algorithm to multiply two-digit numbers by two-digit numbers. Today, we'll review both methods.

Let's pretend that we work at a sandwich shop. Our peanut butter and jelly sandwiches are big sellers! In the first problem, we want to find how much 93 jars of jelly cost. Each jar costs $6.

First, we'll use the box method to multiply 93 times 6.

- **First, we'll find how much 90 jars cost. What's 6 times 90?** *540.* **Write 540 as shown.**
- **Next, we'll find how much 3 jars cost. What's 6 times 3?** *18.* **Write 18 as shown.**
- **540 plus 18 equals 558, so 93 jars cost $558.** **Write 558 in the blank.**

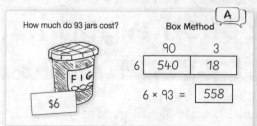

Remember, we call 540 and 18 the *partial products* in this problem. We call them partial products because each is part of the total product. We add the partial products to find the total product.

> Reviewing the term *partial product* will help your child distinguish between the different parts of multiplication problems later in the unit.

Now, let's use the multiplication algorithm to multiply 93 times 6.

- **First, we multiply 3 ones by 6. What's 3 times 6?** *18.* **18 ones equal 1 ten and 8 ones.** Write 1 above the tens-place and 8 in the answer's ones-place.
- **Next, we multiply the tens. We multiply 9 tens by 6, then add on the 1 extra traded ten. What's 9 times 6?** *54.* **Plus 1?** *55.* **There are a total of 55 tens.** Write 55 as shown. **93 times 6 equals 558.**

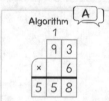

Have your child multiply 78 × 5 with both methods. **How much do 70 jars of peanut butter cost?** *$350.* **How much do 8 jars cost?** *$40.* **How much do 78 jars cost?** *$390.*

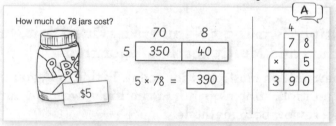

Activity (B): Multiply Three- or Four-Digit Numbers by One-Digit Numbers with the Box Method and Multiplication Algorithm

Now, we need to find out how much 325 loaves of bread cost. Each loaf costs $4, so we need to multiply 325 by 4.

325 has 3 digits, so we'll have 3 partial products for this problem. **What's the expanded form of 325?** *300 plus 20 plus 5.* We'll multiply the value of each digit by 4. Then, we'll add the partial products to find the total product.

- **First, we'll find how much 300 loaves cost. What's 4 times 300?** *1,200.* Write 1,200 as shown.
- **Next, we'll find how much 20 loaves cost. What's 4 times 20?** *80.* Write 80 as shown.
- **Next, we'll find how much 5 loaves cost. What's 4 times 5?** *20.* Write 20 as shown.

- **Now, we add the partial products to find the total cost. What's 1,200 plus 80 plus 20?** *1,300.* If your child isn't sure, allow her to write the numbers on paper and find their sum. Write 1,300 in the blank.

Then, have your child use the multiplication algorithm to find 325 × 4.

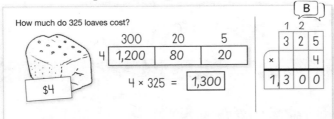

Read aloud the final word problem. **We need to multiply 1,245 times 7 to solve this problem. What's the expanded form of 1,245?** *1,000 plus 200 plus 40 plus 5.* Have your child write these numbers above the boxes. Write 7 to the left of the boxes. Have your child multiply to find the partial products. Then, have her add the partial products to find their total. **You may add up the partial products mentally or write a vertical addition problem in the grid to the right of the problem.**

Then, have your child use the multiplication algorithm to solve the problem.

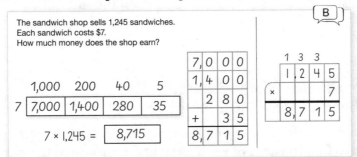

We found the products in this lesson with both the box method and multiplication algorithm. What do the two ways have in common? *Sample answers: You get the same answer. You multiply the numbers in parts and then add them.*

How are the two ways different from each other? *Sample answers: You have to add the partial products when you use the box method. You have to show trading when you use the algorithm.*

Both ways use the distributive property to split the numbers into parts, multiply the parts, and then add the parts. We just keep track of the parts differently and add them in a different order.

Independent Practice and Review

Have your child complete the Lesson 13.1 Practice and Review workbook pages.

Lesson 13.2
Multiply Two-Digit Numbers with the Box Method

Purpose	Materials
• Practice mental multiplication • Use the box method to multiply two-digit numbers	• 2 dice

Memory Work
- **What is a prime number?** *A number with exactly 2 factors.*
- **What is a composite number?** *A number with more than 2 factors.*

Warm-up: Practice Mental Multiplication

Ask your child the following oral multiplication problems.

- **6 times 4.** *24.*
- **60 times 4.** *240.*
- **60 times 40.** *2,400.*
- **7 times 8.** *56.*
- **70 times 8.** *560.*

- **70 times 80.** *5,600.*
- **9 times 9.** *81.*
- **90 times 9.** *810.*
- **90 times 90.** *8,100.*

Activity (A): Use the Box Method to Multiply Two-Digit Numbers by Two-Digit Numbers

In Unit 3, you learned how to use the area model to multiply. You split an array into smaller parts, multiplied to find the area of each part, and then added the partial products to find the total area. You also learned that the box method is a simpler way to keep track of the partial products.

Today, we'll use the area model and box method to multiply a two-digit number by a two-digit number.

This array has 23 rows and 34 columns. It's split into 4 parts to make the multiplying and adding easier. Point to the top left section of the array. **This rectangle is 20 by 30. What's 20 times 30?** *600.* **The section has 600 squares.** Write 600 in the corresponding box in the box diagram.

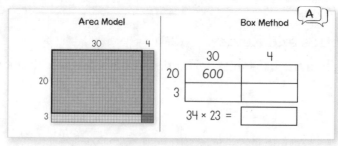

Repeat with the other sections of the array. Then, have your child add the partial products (either mentally or by writing a vertical addition problem in the grid). **What's the total area of the array?** *782 squares.* So, what's 34 times 23? *782.* Write 782 in the blank for the multiplication problem.

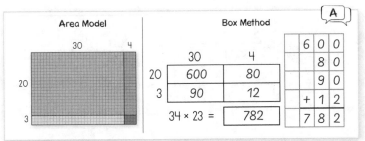

The next problem is 46 times 52. Have your child multiply to find the partial products. Then, have him add to find the total product, either mentally or with a vertical addition problem on the printed grid. **What's 46 times 52?** *2,392.*

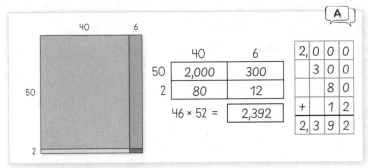

Activity (B): Play the Product Game

Play the Product Game. As you play, help your child split the factors into tens and ones and use the box method to find each product. Write the boxes on a separate piece of scrap paper.

The Product Game

Materials: 2 dice

Object of the Game: Score more points than the other player by creating greater products.

Roll 2 dice. Use the numbers on the dice to create a two-digit number and write it as the first missing factor on your game board. You may write the digits in either order. The best strategy is to use the larger digit in the tens-place and the smaller digit in the ones-place.

Then, roll the 2 dice again. Use the numbers to create another two-digit number. Write this number as the next missing factor on your game board. Then, set up the matching multiplication problem with the box method on a separate sheet of paper. Find the product of the two numbers. This product is your score.

Directions continued on next page.

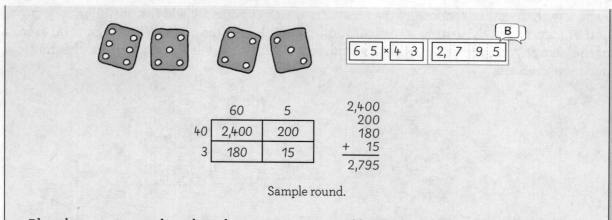

	60	5
40	2,400	200
3	180	15

$$
\begin{array}{r}
2,400 \\
200 \\
180 \\
+ \quad 15 \\
\hline
2,795
\end{array}
$$

Sample round.

Play then passes to the other player. Continue until both players have completed all 3 rounds. Add up all 3 scores for each player. The player with the higher total wins.

Independent Practice and Review

Have your child complete the Lesson 13.2 Practice and Review workbook pages.

Lesson 13.3
Multiply Two-Digit Numbers by Multiples of 10

Purpose	Materials
• Practice multiplying two-digit numbers by one-digit numbers with the multiplication algorithm • Use the multiplication algorithm to multiply two-digit numbers by multiples of 10	• Play money

Memory Work
- **Name 4 factors of 100.** *Possible answers: 1, 2, 4, 5, 10, 20, 25, 50, 100.*
- **Name 4 multiples of 100.** *Sample answers: 300, 600, 1,000, 2,600.*

Warm-up (A): Practice Multiplying with the Multiplication Algorithm

In Unit 7, you learned how to multiply two-digit numbers by one-digit numbers with the multiplication algorithm. Today, you'll learn how to multiply two-digit numbers by multiples of 10 with the multiplication algorithm.

Let's pretend you work as a referee for soccer games. You earn 3 ten-dollar bills per game. Place 3 ten-dollar bills on the table.

Let's see how many ten-dollar bills you earn after 14 games. Have your child use the multiplication algorithm to complete the vertical multiplication problem. **How many ten-dollar bills do you earn after 14 games?** *42.* **How many dollars is that?** *$420.*

Repeat with the other two problems.
- **How many ten-dollar bills do you earn after 18 games?** *54.* **How many dollars is that?** *$540.*
- **How many ten-dollar bills do you earn after 21 games?** *63.* **How many dollars is that?** *$630.*

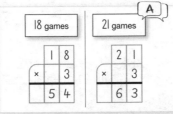

Activity (B): Use the Multiplication Algorithm to Multiply Two-Digit Numbers by Multiples of 10

In the warm-up, you used the multiplication algorithm to find the number of ten-dollar bills you earned. Then, you tacked on a zero to find the total number of dollars.

When you use the multiplication algorithm to multiply a two-digit number by a multiple of 10, you do these steps in the opposite order. First, you tack on a zero in the answer's ones-place. Then, you use the algorithm to multiply the other digits.

Let's find out how much money you earn if you referee 26 games. I'll show you how to use the multiplication algorithm to multiply 26 times 30.

- **First, I write a place-holder zero in the ones-place.** Write 0 in the answer's ones-place. **26 times 30 is the same as multiplying 26 times 3 tens. The final answer must be a multiple of 10, so we know there will be a zero in the ones-place.**

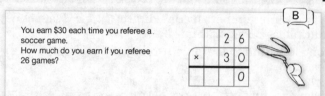

- **Next, we multiply the top number times the tens-place of the bottom number. We ignore the 0 in the bottom number while we do it.** Use your finger to cover the 0 in 30.

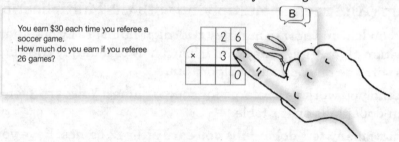

- Draw a ring around the 6 and 3. **6 times 3 equals 18.** Write 1 above the tens-place. Write 8 in the answer's tens-place.

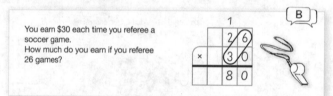

- Draw a ring around the 2 and 3. **2 times 3 equals 6. 6 plus 1 equals 7.** Write 7 in the answer's hundreds-place. **How much money would you earn if you refereed 26 games?** *$780.*

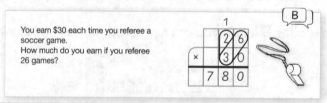

If your child is confused by this process, have her multiply 26 × 3 vertically on a piece of scrap paper. **If you refereed 26 games, you would get 78 ten-dollar bills. Each bill is worth $10, so 78 ten-dollar bills equal $780.**

$$\begin{array}{r} 26 \\ \times\ 3 \\ \hline 78 \end{array} \longrightarrow \begin{array}{r} 26 \\ \times\ 30 \\ \hline 780 \end{array}$$

Activity (C): Multiply to Find the Cost of Soccer Supplies

Let's pretend we're helping a youth soccer league order supplies for the spring season. Briefly discuss your child's experiences with youth sports or soccer. **We'll find the total cost for each item.**

The first item the soccer club needs is 32 sets of cones. How much does each set of cones cost? *$40.* So, we'll multiply 32 times 40 to find the total cost.

When you set up multiplication problems where one number is a multiple of 10, write the number with the place-holder zero on the bottom. That makes it easier to use the multiplication algorithm.

Write 32 × 40 in the first grid as shown. Have your child use the multiplication algorithm to solve the problem. **How much do the cones cost in all?** *$1,280.* Write $1,280 in the chart.

Repeat with the other items. Remind your child to write the place-holder zero before using the multiplication algorithm to multiply the other digits.

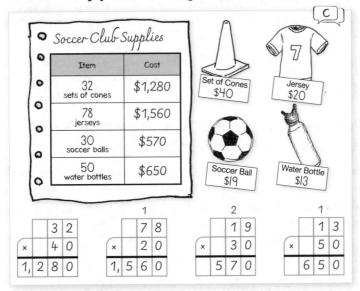

Independent Practice and Review

Have your child complete the Lesson 13.3 Practice and Review workbook pages.

The practice page includes a detailed example at the top for your child to refer to as he completes the page.

Lesson 13.4
Multiply Two-Digit Numbers in Steps

Purpose	Materials
• Practice multiplying two-digit numbers by multiples of 10 with the multiplication algorithm • Multiply the tens and ones separately to find the product of two-digit numbers	• None

Memory Work	• **What do we call an angle with a measure less than 90 degrees?** *Acute.* • **What do we call an angle with a measure equal to 90 degrees?** *Right.* • **What do we call an angle with a measure greater than 90 degrees and less than 180 degrees?** *Obtuse.* • **What do we call an angle with a measure equal to 180 degrees?** *Straight.*

In this lesson, your child will begin to use the multiplication algorithm to multiply two-digit numbers by two-digit numbers. For this lesson only, each problem will be broken into three separate written problems. In the next lesson, your child will learn how to combine the steps into one written problem.

Warm-up (A): Practice Multiplying Two-Digit Numbers by Multiples of 10 with the Multiplication Algorithm

In the last lesson, you learned how to multiply two-digit numbers by multiples of 10 with the multiplication algorithm. First, you write a place-holder zero. Then, you multiply the top number by the tens-place in the bottom number. Have your child complete the problems.

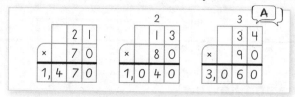

Activity (B): Multiply the Tens and Ones Separately at the Art Store

Today, you'll learn how to multiply two-digit numbers by two-digit numbers. We'll use the distributive property to solve these problems. We'll split each problem into tens and ones, multiply the tens and ones separately, and then add to find the final answer.

Let's pretend we're helping a teacher at an art studio order supplies for his art classes. Briefly discuss any experience your child has with art classes or other enrichment classes. **Each set of watercolor paints costs $24. The teacher needs 26 sets for a painting class, so we multiply 24 by 26 to find the total cost.**

First, we'll multiply 24 times 6 to find how much 6 sets cost. Then, we'll multiply 24 times 20 to find how much 20 sets cost. Last, we'll add to find the total cost.

- Have your child multiply 24 times 6 with the multiplication algorithm. **How much do 6 sets cost?** *$144.*
- Have your child multiply 24 times 20 with the multiplication algorithm. Remind him as needed to write a place-holder zero in the answer's ones-place. **How much do 20 sets cost?** *$480.*

- **Last, you add 144 plus 480 to find the total cost.** Write 144 and 480 as shown. Write a plus sign and draw a line below the numbers as shown. Have your child add to find the sum. **So, how much do 26 sets of paints cost?** *$624.*

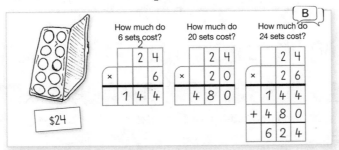

Make sure to write 144 on the first blank line and 480 on the next line, since this order matches the steps in the full multiplication algorithm.

The art teacher also needs 37 sketchbooks for a drawing class. Each sketchbook costs $15, so we'll multiply 15 by 37 to find the total cost.

The expanded form of 37 is 30 plus 7. First, we'll multiply 15 times 7 to find how much 7 sketchbooks cost. Then, we'll multiply 15 times 30 to find how much 30 sketchbooks cost. Last, we'll add to find the total cost. Have your child complete the problems to find the total cost.

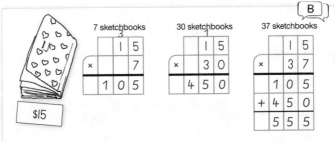

Last, the art teacher needs 34 blocks of clay for a pottery class. Each block of clay costs $18, so we'll multiply 18 by 34 to find the total cost. Have your child complete the problems to find the total cost.

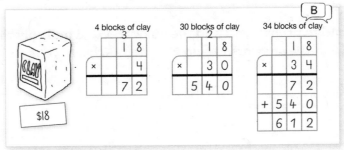

Independent Practice and Review

Have your child complete the Lesson 13.4 Practice and Review workbook pages.

Lesson 13.5
Multiply Two-Digit Numbers with the Multiplication Algorithm

Purpose	Materials
• Practice multiplying the tens and ones separately to multiply two-digit numbers • Use the multiplication algorithm to multiply two-digit numbers	• 2 dice

Memory Work • **How many milliliters equal 1 liter?** *1,000.*

In this lesson, you will teach your child how to combine the steps she learned in Lesson 13.4 to multiply two-digit numbers with the multiplication algorithm. Children often find this complex process challenging, and your child may need more guidance and coaching than usual as she learns the steps.

If this lesson takes longer than usual (or if your child tires more quickly than usual), split the lesson over two days:

• Day 1: Do the Warm-up, Activity A, and Activity B. Then, have your child complete the Review page only.

• Day 2: Review the steps in Activity B and play The Product Game (Activity C). Then, have your child complete the Practice page.

Keeping track of all the steps in multi-digit multiplication requires a lot of concentration and working memory. If you find your child struggling with the multiplication facts in this lesson, allow her to refer to the multiplication chart (Blackline Master 2).

Warm-up (A): Practice Multiplying the Tens and Ones Separately

In the last lesson, you learned how to multiply the tens and ones separately to multiply two-digit numbers. Read aloud the word problem: *Each set of oil paints costs $21. How much do 35 sets cost?*

We'll use the distributive property to find the answer. We'll multiply the tens and ones separately and then add the answers to find 21 times 35. Have your child complete the problems.

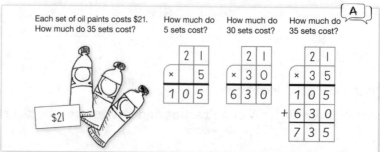

Activity (B): Use the Multiplication Algorithm to Multiply Two-Digit Numbers

In part A, you multiplied 21 times 35. You wrote out each step in a separate multiplication problem.

Point to the chart in part B. **This chart summarizes the steps you followed. Today, you'll learn how to use the multiplication algorithm to combine the steps. That way, you won't have to write out 3 separate problems!**

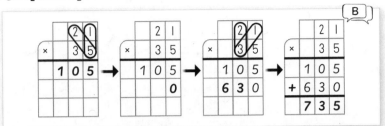

Now, I'll show you how to combine the steps to solve 32 times 54. First, I multiply the top number by the ones-place of the bottom number.

We ignore the 5 in the tens-place while we do it. Use your finger to cover the 5 in 54.

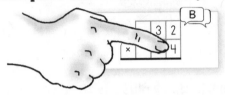

I'll write the partial product for 32 times 4 directly below the problem so that I don't have to recopy it later. Draw a ring around the 2 and 4. **2 times 4 is 8.** Write 8 as shown.

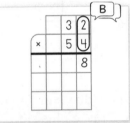

Draw a ring around 3 and 4. **3 times 4 is 12.** Write 12 as shown.

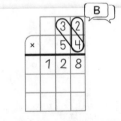

Next, I write a place-holder zero. I'm going to write the partial product for 32 times 50 directly below the first partial product. So, I write the place-holder zero on the next line. Write a place-holder zero.

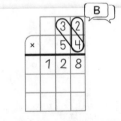

Then, I multiply the top number by the tens-place of the bottom number. The 5 in 54 is in the tens-place. So, we'll think of the 5 as 5 tens and ignore the 4 in the ones-place. Use your finger to cover the 4 in the ones-place.

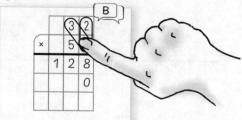

Draw a ring around the 2 and 5. **2 times 5 is 10.** Write 1 and 0 as shown.

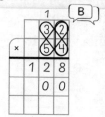

Draw a ring around 3 and 5. **3 times 5 is 15. 15 plus 1 is 16.** Write 16 as shown.

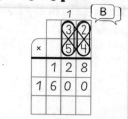

The fourth step is to add. The partial products are already written below the problem and lined up, so we're ready to add them. Draw a plus sign and line, and have your child add the partial products.

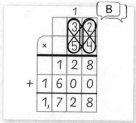

Have your child follow the steps to complete the 25 × 64 and 23 × 74 problems. If she has trouble remembering which pair of numbers to multiply, have her draw a ring around each pair of numbers before she multiplies them.

Children sometimes get confused when they need to trade multiple times in a problem and end up with multiple traded digits above the problem. If that's the case for your child, have her cross out each traded digit after she adds it.

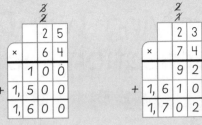

Activity (C): Play The Product Game

Play The Product Game.

The Product Game

Materials: 2 dice

Object of the Game: Score more points than the other player by creating greater products.

Roll 2 dice. Use the numbers on the dice to create a two-digit number and write it on the top line of your first blank multiplication problem. You may write the digits in either order. The best strategy is to use the larger digit in the tens-place and the smaller digit in the ones-place.

Then, roll the 2 dice again. Use the numbers to create another two-digit number. Write this number on the next line of the multiplication problem. Find the product of the two numbers. This product is your score.

Sample round.

Play then passes to the other player. Continue until both players have completed all 3 rounds. Add up all 3 scores for each player. The player with the higher total wins.

Independent Practice and Review

Have your child complete the Lesson 13.5 Practice and Review workbook pages.

Lesson 13.6
Practice Multiplying Two-Digit Numbers with the Multiplication Algorithm

Purpose	Materials
• Review multiplying multiples of 10 • Estimate answers for two-digit multiplication problems • Practice multiplying two-digit numbers with the multiplication algorithm	• 10 slips of paper

Memory Work	• **How many ounces equal 1 pound?** *16.* • **How many grams equal 1 kilogram?** *1,000.*

Your child will practice the multiplication algorithm in this lesson. As with long division, one minor error makes the entire problem wrong, so make sure to watch carefully as your child completes the problems. Stop him if he makes a mistake and correct any errors immediately, before he takes the next step in the problem. If you find that he needs lots of coaching and support, sit with him as he completes the Practice pages, too.

Warm-up: Review Multiplying Multiples of 10

Ask your child the following oral multiplication problems.

- **20 times 30.** *600.*
- **40 times 20.** *800.*
- **30 times 30.** *900.*

- **20 times 50.** *1,000.*
- **40 times 30.** *1,200.*
- **40 times 50.** *2,000.*

Activity (A): Estimate Products for Two-Digit Multiplication Problems

In the last lesson, you learned how to use the multiplication algorithm to multiply two-digit numbers. Today, we'll review the steps and practice some more.

Before we find the exact answer for 46 times 33, let's estimate the product. Estimating the product will help us know whether our answer is reasonable.

What's 46 rounded to the nearest ten? *50.* Write 50 as shown. **What's 33 rounded to the nearest ten?** *30.* Write 30 as shown. **What's 50 times 30?** *1,500.* Write 1,500 as shown.

Now, let's find the exact product. Guide your child as he completes the problem. If needed, have him draw a ring around each pair of numbers before he multiplies them.

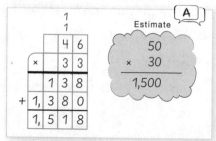

What's 46 times 33? *1,518.* **Our estimate was 1,500, so our answer seems reasonable.**

Activity (B): Play Snowball Fight

Play Snowball Fight. Have your child orally estimate the products before calculating them.

If you'd rather avoid throwing, put the paper wads in a bowl and draw 2 wads each turn instead. Replace the wads in the bowl after each turn.

Snowball Fight

Materials: 10 slips of paper

Object of the Game: Win the most points.

Write the numbers on the snowballs on separate slips of paper:

37   93   28   54   58   61   64   75   82   44

Crumple the slips of paper and place them on the table. Both players count down in unison from 10 while throwing the crumpled wads of paper at each other. When you reach 1, both players stop and pick up the 2 closest wads of paper.

Both players unfold their paper wads and write their numbers in the first blank grid on their scorecard. Both players multiply to find the product of the two numbers. Whoever has the greater product wins a point.

Crumple up your numbers and add them back to the pile of "snowballs." Repeat until you have filled in all the blank grids. Whoever wins more points wins the game.

Independent Practice and Review

Have your child complete the Lesson 13.6 Practice and Review workbook pages.

If your child is concerned that his estimates are too far away from the exact answer, explain that reasonable estimates for two-digit multiplication problems are often several hundreds away from the exact answer.

Lesson 13.7
Compare and Contrast the Box Method and Multiplication Algorithm

Purpose	Materials
• Practice multiplying two-digit numbers with the algorithm and box method • Compare and contrast partial products in the multiplication algorithm with the partial products in the box method • Use the multiplication algorithm and box method to solve word problems	• None

Memory Work	
	• **How many millimeters equal 1 centimeter?** *10.* • **How many centimeters equal 1 meter?** *100.* • **How many meters equal 1 kilometer?** *1,000.*

Warm-up (A): Practice Multiplying Two-Digit Numbers with the Multiplication Algorithm and the Box Method

In this unit, you've learned how to multiply two-digit numbers with the multiplication algorithm and with the box method. Today, you'll use both methods to solve word problems. We'll also talk about what the two methods have in common and how the two methods differ.

Read aloud the word problem: *Maggie earns $13 per hour as a babysitter. In May, she works for 18 hours. How much money does she earn?*

Have your child use the multiplication algorithm to complete the vertical problem. Then, have her use the box method to solve the problem as well. **How much does Maggie earn?** *$234.*

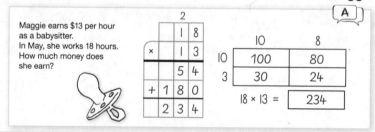

Have your child write the sum of the partial products on scrap paper if she has trouble adding them mentally.

Activity (A):
Compare and Contrast the Multiplication Algorithm and Box Method

You found the product of 18 times 13 in two different ways. What do the two ways have in common? *Sample answers: Both have the same total product. You multiply the numbers in parts and then add them.*

How are the two ways different from each other? *Sample answers: I had to add 4 numbers when I used the box method, but I only had to add 2 numbers when I used the multiplication algorithm.*

When you used the multiplication algorithm, you found two partial products and then added them. When you used the box method, you found four partial products and then added them.

- Point to 54 in the multiplication algorithm problem. **Which partial products in the box method add up to 54?** *30 and 24.*
- Point to 180 in the multiplication algorithm problem. **Which partial products in the box method add up to 180?** *100 and 80.*

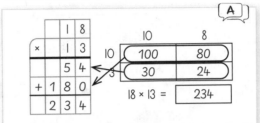

Both ways involve splitting the numbers into tens and ones, multiplying the parts, and then adding the parts. We just keep track of the parts differently.

See the Unit 13 **Teaching Math with Confidence** for more on the benefits of understanding both methods.

Activity (B): Use Multiplication to Answer "Would You Rather?" Questions

Now, we'll use both methods to answer "Would You Rather?" questions. These questions present two different scenarios, and you get to decide which scenario you prefer. There's no right answer to these questions as long as you have a good reason for your answer.

Read aloud the first question: *Would you rather work 28 hours and get paid $17 per hour or would you rather work 22 hours and get paid $19 per hour?*

Let's multiply to find how much you would make in each scenario. Have your child use the multiplication algorithm to multiply 28 × 17, and have her use the box method to multiply 22 × 19.

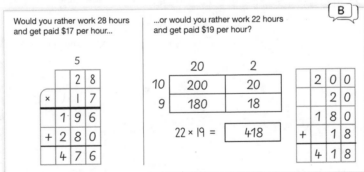

Your child may write the factors in the problems in a different order.

How much money would you make if you work 28 hours and get paid $17 per hour? *$476.*
How much money would you make if you work 22 hours and get paid $19 per hour? *$418.*
Which would you rather have? Why? *Sample answers: I'd rather work 28 hours, because I'd earn more money. I'd rather get paid $19 per hour, because I'd earn more money per hour.*

Accept any reasonable answer for this question and the following question.

Repeat with the other problem. **Would you rather pay \$35 per lesson for 16 tap dance lessons or \$42 per lesson for 12 tap dance lessons?** *Sample answers: I'd rather pay \$35 per lesson because I'd pay less per lesson. I'd rather pay \$42 per lesson for 12 lessons, because I'd pay less in all.*

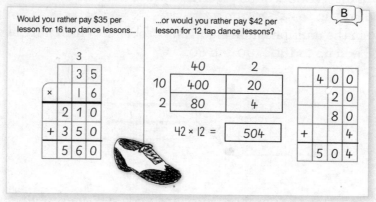

Independent Practice and Review

Have your child complete the Lesson 13.7 Practice and Review workbook pages.

Lesson 13.8
Enrichment (Optional)

Purpose	Materials
• Practice memory work • Use multiplication to estimate large quantities • Multiply two-digit numbers to compare area • Summarize what your child has learned and assess your child's progress	• *Great Estimations*, by Bruce Goldstone • Tape measure

Warm-up: Review Memory Work

Quiz your child on all memory work through Unit 13. See pages 536-537 for the full list.

Math Picture Book: *Great Estimations*

Read *Great Estimations*, by Bruce Goldstone. As you read, encourage your child to use his mental multiplication skills to find the estimates.

Enrichment Activity:
Multiply to Compare the Areas of Two Rooms or Two Pictures

Choose two rooms in your home that are roughly the same size. (Try to choose rooms whose lengths and widths are greater than 10 feet so that your child has a chance to use his two-digit multiplication skills.) Have your child predict which room has a larger area. Then, measure each room to the nearest foot and have your child multiply to find their exact areas.

If your family uses the metric system: Choose two posters or pictures that are roughly the same size. (Try to choose posters or pictures whose lengths and widths are greater than 10 cm and less than 100 cm so your child has a chance to use his two-digit multiplication skills.) Have your child predict which poster has a larger area. Then, measure each poster to the nearest centimeter and have your child multiply to find their exact areas.

Unit Wrap-Up

Have your child complete the Unit 13 Wrap-Up.

Unit 13 Answer Key

13.1 Practice

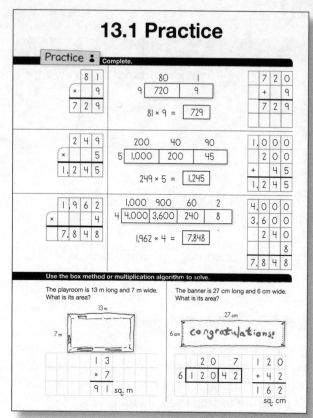

13.1 Review

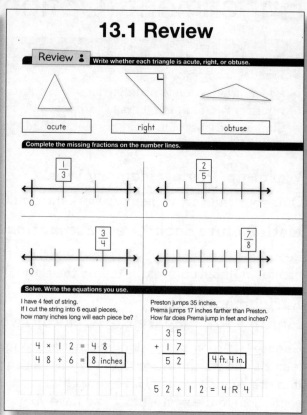

13.2 Practice

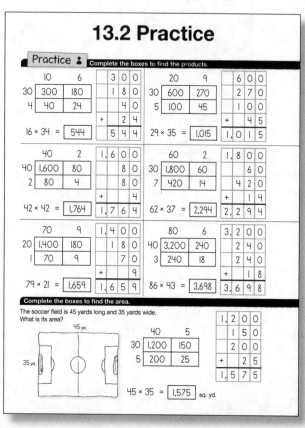

13.2 Review

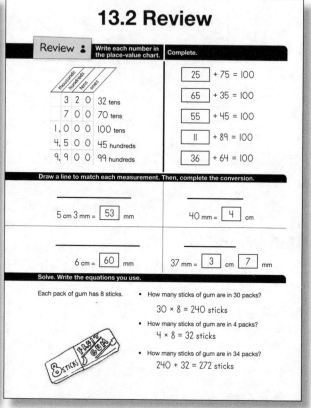

Unit 13 Answer Key

13.3 Practice

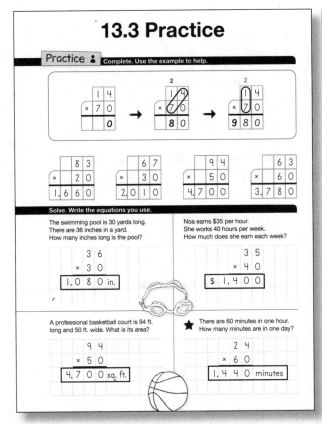

13.3 Review

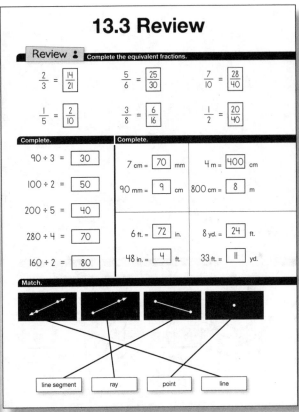

13.4 Practice

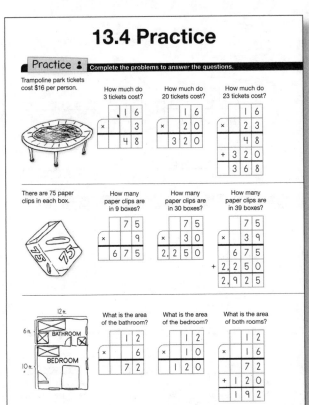

13.4 Review

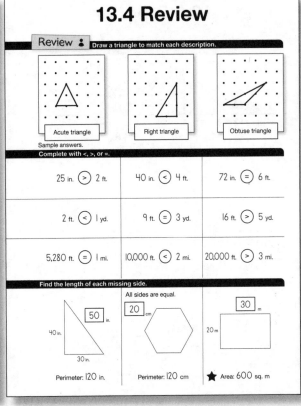

Unit 13 Answer Key

13.5 Practice

The Product Game

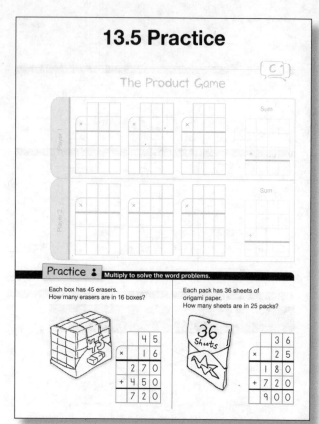

Practice — Multiply to solve the word problems.

Each box has 45 erasers.
How many erasers are in 16 boxes?

$$\begin{array}{r} 4\,5 \\ \times\ 1\,6 \\ \hline 2\,7\,0 \\ +\ 4\,5\,0 \\ \hline 7\,2\,0 \end{array}$$

Each pack has 36 sheets of origami paper.
How many sheets are in 25 packs?

$$\begin{array}{r} 3\,6 \\ \times\ 2\,5 \\ \hline 1\,8\,0 \\ +\ 7\,2\,0 \\ \hline 9\,0\,0 \end{array}$$

13.5 Review

Review — Use common denominators to compare the fractions.

$\dfrac{5}{9}$ $<$ $\dfrac{2}{3}$ → $\dfrac{5}{9}$ $<$ $\dfrac{6}{9}$

$\dfrac{1}{4}$ $=$ $\dfrac{3}{12}$ → $\dfrac{3}{12}$ $=$ $\dfrac{3}{12}$

$\dfrac{6}{10}$ $<$ $\dfrac{65}{100}$ → $\dfrac{60}{100}$ $<$ $\dfrac{65}{100}$

Use the diagram to tell whether each statement is true or false.

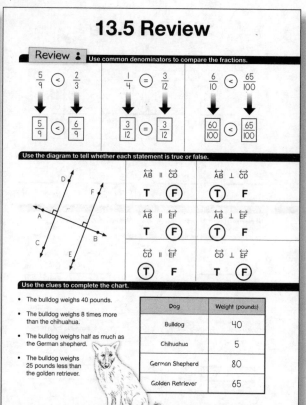

$\overleftrightarrow{AB} \parallel \overleftrightarrow{CD}$	$\overleftrightarrow{AB} \perp \overleftrightarrow{CD}$
T **(F)**	**(T)** F
$\overleftrightarrow{AB} \parallel \overleftrightarrow{EF}$	$\overleftrightarrow{AB} \perp \overleftrightarrow{EF}$
T **(F)**	**(T)** F
$\overleftrightarrow{CD} \parallel \overleftrightarrow{EF}$	$\overleftrightarrow{CD} \perp \overleftrightarrow{EF}$
(T) F	T **(F)**

Use the clues to complete the chart.

- The bulldog weighs 40 pounds.
- The bulldog weighs 8 times more than the chihuahua.
- The bulldog weighs half as much as the German shepherd.
- The bulldog weighs 25 pounds less than the golden retriever.

Dog	Weight (pounds)
Bulldog	40
Chihuahua	5
German Shepherd	80
Golden Retriever	65

13.6 Practice

Practice — Estimate the product for each problem. Then, find the exact answer. Use the sample problem to help.

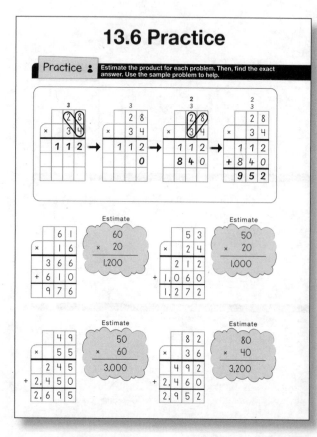

	Estimate
$\begin{array}{r} 6\,1 \\ \times\ 1\,6 \\ \hline 3\,6\,6 \\ +\ 6\,1\,0 \\ \hline 9\,7\,6 \end{array}$	$\begin{array}{r} 60 \\ \times\ 20 \\ \hline 1{,}200 \end{array}$

	Estimate
$\begin{array}{r} 5\,3 \\ \times\ 2\,4 \\ \hline 2\,1\,2 \\ +\ 1{,}0\,6\,0 \\ \hline 1{,}2\,7\,2 \end{array}$	$\begin{array}{r} 50 \\ \times\ 20 \\ \hline 1{,}000 \end{array}$

	Estimate
$\begin{array}{r} 4\,9 \\ \times\ 5\,5 \\ \hline 2\,4\,5 \\ +\ 2{,}4\,5\,0 \\ \hline 2{,}6\,9\,5 \end{array}$	$\begin{array}{r} 50 \\ \times\ 60 \\ \hline 3{,}000 \end{array}$

	Estimate
$\begin{array}{r} 8\,2 \\ \times\ 3\,6 \\ \hline 4\,9\,2 \\ +\ 2{,}4\,6\,0 \\ \hline 2{,}9\,5\,2 \end{array}$	$\begin{array}{r} 80 \\ \times\ 40 \\ \hline 3{,}200 \end{array}$

13.6 Review

Review — Complete the missing fractions on the number lines.

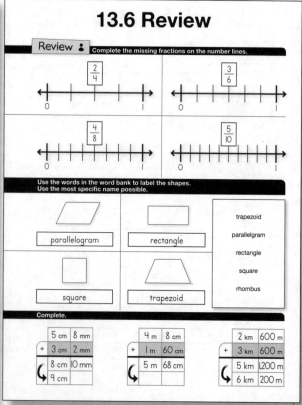

$\dfrac{2}{4}$

$\dfrac{3}{6}$

$\dfrac{4}{8}$

$\dfrac{5}{10}$

Use the words in the word bank to label the shapes. Use the most specific name possible.

parallelogram

rectangle

square

trapezoid

Word bank:
trapezoid
parallelgram
rectangle
square
rhombus

Complete.

	5 cm	8 mm
+	3 cm	2 mm
	8 cm	10 mm
↻	9 cm	

	4 m	8 cm
+	1 m	60 cm
	5 m	68 cm

	2 km	600 m
+	3 km	600 m
	5 km	1,200 m
↻	6 km	200 m

Unit 13 Answer Key

13.7 Practice

Practice 👤 Solve. You may use the multiplication algorithm or box method.

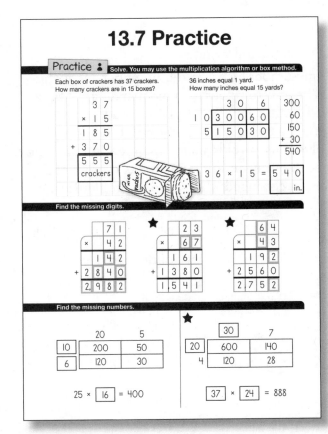

13.7 Review

Review 👤 Complete the equivalent fractions.

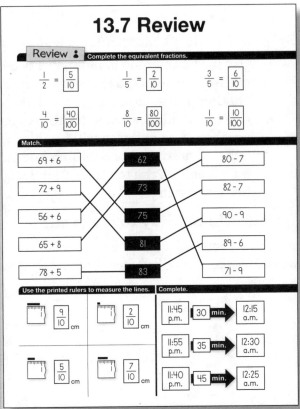

13.8 Unit Wrap-Up A

Unit Wrap-Up 👤 Complete.

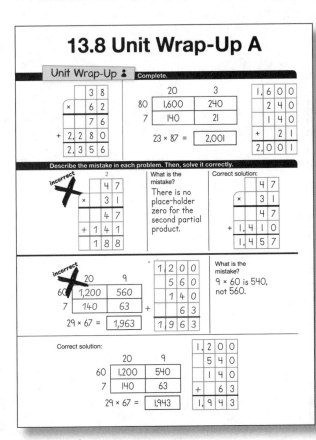

13.8 Unit Wrap-Up B

Unit Wrap-Up 👤 Use the chart to answer the questions. Write the equations you use. You may use the multiplication algorithm or the box method.

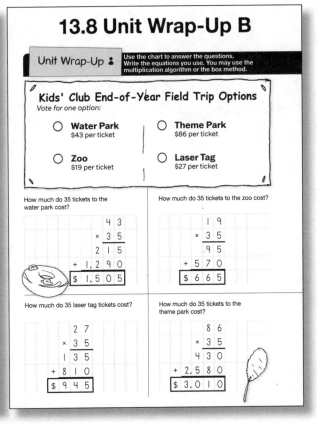

Unit 13 Checkpoint

What to Expect at the End of Unit 13

By the end of Unit 13, most children will be able to do the following:

- Use the box method to multiply a two-digit number by a two-digit number. Most children will understand these problems and be able to solve them independently. Many children will make occasional mistakes with the mental multiplying or adding.
- Use the multiplication algorithm to multiply a two-digit number by a two-digit number. Most children will be able to solve these problems independently, but some will still need a lot of coaching and support. Many children will make occasional mistakes with the multiplication facts or get confused when solving problems that involve trading.

Is Your Child Ready to Move on?

In Unit 14, you will introduce your child to decimals. Your child does not need to have mastered any specific skills before beginning Unit 14.

Unit 14
Decimals

Overview

Your child will extend his understanding of place value to read, write, and compare decimals to the hundredths-place. He'll learn how to write decimals as fractions or mixed numbers, and he'll also learn how to label decimal numbers on the number line. Throughout the unit, he'll explore decimals in many real-life situations, such as time, length, weight, and money.

What Your Child Will Learn

In this unit, your child will learn to:

- Read, write, and compare decimal numbers to the hundredths-place
- Understand place value in decimals and write decimals in expanded form
- Express decimals as fractions or mixed numbers
- Identify decimals on the number line and round decimals to the nearest whole number.
- Express money amounts and metric lengths with decimals
- Name decimal equivalents for common fractions

Lesson List

Lesson 14.1 Read and Write Decimals to the Tenths-Place

Lesson 14.2 Compare Decimals to the Tenths-Place

Lesson 14.3 Read and Write Decimals to the Hundredths-Place

Lesson 14.4 Compare Decimals to the Hundredths-Place

Lesson 14.5 Decimals on the Number Line

Lesson 14.6 Write Metric Lengths as Decimals

Lesson 14.7 Decimal Equivalents for Common Fractions

Lesson 14.8 Enrichment (Optional)

Extra Materials Needed for Unit 14

- Body temperature thermometer, either digital or analog
- Digital stopwatch or stopwatch app
- Paper clip
- For optional Enrichment Lesson:
    × *The Efficient, Inventive (Often Annoying) Melvil Dewey*, written by Alexis O'Neill and illustrated by Edwin Fotheringham. Calkins Creek, 2020.
    × Online access to your local library's catalog

Teaching Math with Confidence:
Understanding Decimal Place Value and Building Decimal Number Sense

In earlier grades, your child spent many lessons learning about place value in whole numbers. He learned that each place has 10 times the value of the next-smaller place, and that digits further to the left have a greater value than digits further to the right. He also learned that the value of each digit depends on what place it is in. (For example, a 4 in the tens-place has a value of 40, while a 4 in the thousands-place has a value of 4,000.)

In this unit, you'll introduce decimal numbers as an extension of the place-value system. The decimal point splits numbers into a whole number part and fractional part. To create places to the right of the decimal point, we divide each place by 10. So, each smaller place has one-tenth of the value of the previous place.

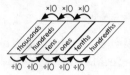

The value of each digit in a decimal number depends on its place, just as in whole numbers. A 4 in the tenths-place has a value of four-tenths, while a 4 in the hundredths-place has a value of four-hundredths.

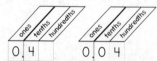

You'll use decimal squares to help your child develop number sense with decimals, just as you used base-ten blocks to develop number sense with whole numbers. Each decimal square stands for 1 whole. The squares can be split into tenths or hundredths and then shaded to represent various decimals. This visual representation makes decimal place value more concrete and gives meaning to the digits in decimal numbers. It also helps children see that decimals express parts of things, just like fractions.

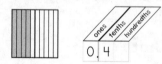

0.4 represented with a decimal square.

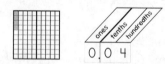

0.04 represented with a decimal square.

By connecting decimals to what your child already knows about place value and fractions, he'll develop deep conceptual understanding of decimals. In fifth grade, he'll build on his decimal number sense to add, subtract, multiply, and divide decimals.

Lesson 14.1
Read and Write Decimals to the Tenths-Place

Purpose	Materials
• Introduce tenths with degrees on a thermometer • Read and write decimals to the tenths-place • Express decimals to the tenths-place with fractions and mixed numbers • Model decimals to the tenths-place with decimal squares and the number line	• Body temperature thermometer, either digital or analog • Die

Memory Work	• **What do we call fractions that look different but have the same value?** *Equivalent fractions.* • **What do we call numbers that have a whole number and a fraction?** *Mixed numbers.*

Warm-up (A): Explore Tenths on a Thermometer

We're beginning a new unit on decimals today! Decimals are numbers with a decimal point. We often use decimals when we measure.

Point to 98.6. **The average normal body temperature is 98.6 degrees Fahrenheit. We can read this decimal as "98 point 6" or "98 and six-tenths."**

> If your family uses the metric system, explain that 98.6° Fahrenheit is the same as 37° Celsius.

The period in the middle of the number is the decimal point. In a decimal number, the digits to the left of the decimal point tell the whole number. The digits to the right of the decimal point tell the fractional part.

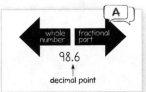

Point to the printed analog thermometer. **People used to use thermometers like this to measure body temperature. You would put the tip of the thermometer in your mouth, and then the red line would move based on your temperature.**

The space between each degree is split into 10 equal parts, so each space measures one-tenth of a degree. The red line in this thermometer is 6 spaces after 98 degrees, so this thermometer shows 98.6 degrees.

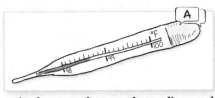

Use your family's thermometer (either analog or digital) to take your child's temperature. Read the thermometer and discuss how close your child's temperature is to 98.6°. Explain that people's average temperatures vary and that a temperature slightly above or below 98.6° Fahrenheit is perfectly normal.

Activity (B): Represent Decimals with Tenths in Multiple Ways

You already know that that each place in our number system has 10 times the value of the next-smaller place. Point to the arrows labeled "×10" above the place-value chart. **1 times 10 equals 10, 10 times 10 equals 100, 100 times 10 equals 1,000, and so on. We can continue that place-value pattern to make numbers as large as we need.**

Decimal numbers are just an extension of the usual place-value system. We can continue the pattern to make numbers as small as we need, too! Instead of multiplying by 10 to create places with a larger value, we can divide by 10 to create places with a smaller value. Point to the arrows labeled "÷10" below the place-value chart. **If you divide 1 whole into 10 equal parts, you get tenths. So, the next-smaller place after the ones-place is the tenths-place.**

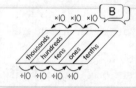

See the Unit 14 **Teaching Math with Confidence** for more on how decimals are an extension of the base-ten place-value system.

Point to 1.7. **What digit is in the ones-place?** *1.* **What digit is in the tenths-place?** *7.* **We read this number as "one point seven" or "one and seven-tenths."**

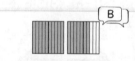

We can represent 1.7 many ways, just like we represent whole numbers and fractions many ways. One way is with decimal squares. Each square stands for 1 whole, and each square is split into 10 parts. 1 whole square plus seven-tenths of the other square equals 1 and seven-tenths.

The dark line in the middle of each decimal square makes it easier to see at a glance how many tenths are colored.

1.7 is a whole number plus a fractional part, so we can also write 1.7 as a mixed number.

$$1\frac{7}{10}$$

We can also label 1.7 on the number line, just like we label whole numbers and fractions. The spaces between whole numbers on this number line are split into tenths. 1 and seven-tenths is seven-tenths more than 1, so its dot is 7 spaces past 1 whole.

Point to 0.9. **What digit is in the ones-place?** *0.* **What digit is in the tenths-place?** *9.* **We read this number as "zero point nine" or "zero and nine-tenths."**

This decimal has a place-holder zero in the ones-place. Writing a place-holder zero in the ones-place makes it easier to see the decimal point. It also reminds us that there is no whole number part to the decimal and the number has a value less than 1.

Have your child shade the decimal square, write a fraction, and draw a point on the number line to show the position of 0.9.

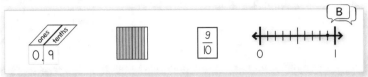

Developing the habit of writing a place-holder zero in the ones-place helps prevent mistakes in future grades, especially when your child learns to align decimal places to add and subtract decimal numbers.

Activity (C): Play Race to 3

Play Race to 3.

Race to 3

Materials: Die

Object of the Game: Be the first player to completely color all 3 decimal squares.

On your turn, roll the die. Color the matching number of tenths in one of your squares. You must complete the squares from left to right and completely color one square before beginning the next square. Then, write the total amount you have colored on your score card (as a decimal number).

For example, if you roll a 5 on your first turn, shade 5 tenths in your first square and write 0.5 on the top line of your score card.

Sample first play.

If needed, you may split your roll over 2 squares. For example, if you have 0.5 colored and roll a 6, color the final 5 tenths in your first square and then shade 1 more tenth in the next square (for a total of 1.1).

Sample second play.

For your final turn, you must roll the exact amount you need without going over. For example, if you have 2.9 squares filled, you must roll a 1 to complete your square. If you roll a different number, play passes to the other player.

Take turns until one person completes all 3 squares.

Independent Practice and Review

Have your child complete the Lesson 14.1 Practice and Review workbook pages.

Lesson 14.2
Compare Decimals to the Tenths-Place

Purpose	Materials
• Practice representing decimals with decimal squares • Compare decimals to the tenths-place • Put decimals in order from least to greatest	• 2 dice

Memory Work	• **What do we call the top number in a fraction?** *The numerator.* • **What does the numerator tell?** *The number of parts.* • **What do we call the bottom number in a fraction?** *The denominator.* • **What does the denominator tell?** *How many equal parts the whole was split into.*

Warm-up (A): Color Decimal Squares to Match Decimals

In the last lesson, you learned about decimal place value.

- Point to the 1 in 1.8. **What place is the 1 in?** *The ones-place.*
- Point to the 8 in 1.8. **What place is the 8 in?** *The tenths-place.*

Have your child color the decimal squares above 1.8 to match. Encourage him to first shade 1 whole square and then shade 8 tenths. Repeat with the rest of the decimals.

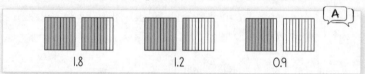

1.8   1.2   0.9

Activity (B): Compare Decimals with Tenths

Today, you'll learn how to compare decimals with tenths. We can compare decimal numbers just like we compare whole numbers, mixed numbers, and fractions.

Which is greater, 1.8 or 1.2? *1.8.* **How do you know?** *Sample answer: Both have one whole. 1.8 has more tenths than 1.2.* If your child isn't sure, suggest he look at the matching decimal squares for each number in part A. **When two decimal numbers have the same whole number part, we then compare the fractional part. Eight-tenths is greater than two-tenths, so 1.8 is greater than 1.2.** Write > in the blank.

1.8 (>) 1.2

Which is greater, 1.2 or 0.9? *1.2.* **How do you know?** *Sample answer: 1.2 is more than one whole, and 0.9 is less than one whole.* **When two decimal numbers have different digits in the whole number places, we can just compare the whole number places. 1 is greater than 0, so 1.2 is greater than 0.9.** Write > in the blank.

1.2 (>) 0.9

Which is greater, 1.8 or 2? *2.* **How do you know?** *Sample answer: 2 has two wholes, and 1.8 only has 1 whole.* **1 is less than 2, so 1.8 is less than 2.** Write < in the blank.

1.8 (<) 2

Have your child use similar reasoning to compare the other pairs of decimals. If he has trouble with any of the pairs, have him imagine the matching decimal squares.

$$0.3 \enspace ⓵ \enspace 3 \qquad 2 \enspace ⓵ \enspace 2.0 \qquad 2.5 \enspace ⓵ \enspace 1.9$$

If your child wonders why someone would write 2.0 instead of 2, explain that the .0 means that the measurement is accurate to the nearest tenth. **If you bought a pineapple at the grocery store that was labeled 2.0 kilograms, you'd know that its weight is within one-tenth of a kilogram of 2 kilograms.** Your child does not need to fully grasp this concept, and he'll learn more about the significance of decimal digits in future math and science classes.

Activity (C): Prepare to Play Decimal Least to Greatest

We're going to use this game board to play Decimal Least to Greatest. To play this game, you roll a die and then choose where to write the matching number on your game board. For example, if you roll a 5, you write 0.9 on your game board. What's the greatest number you can write? *2.* What's the least number you can write? *0.*

You win when you complete your game board with numbers that are in order from least to greatest. Be careful, though! Once you write a number, you can't move it. You can only use each number once.

Let's pretend you rolled a 5 on your first turn and got 0.9. Where do you think would be the best place to write 0.9? *Sample answers: In the middle of the game board. In the third blank from the left.* **Why?** *Sample answer: 0.9 is in the middle of the other numbers.*

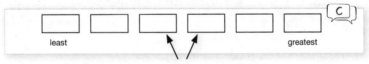

Writing 0.9 somewhere in the middle of the game board is a good first play.

0.9 is a little less than 1, so it's about halfway between 0 to 2. There's a good chance that about half of the numbers you roll after it will be greater than 0.9, and about half the numbers you roll after it will be less than 0.9.

Let's pretend I wrote 1.9 in the middle of the game board. Do you think that would be a good play? Why or why not? *Sample answer: That wouldn't be a good play, because there is only 1 number greater than it.* **If you write 1.9 in the middle of the game board, there aren't enough numbers greater than it to complete the game board.**

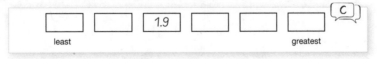

Writing 1.9 in the middle of the game board isn't a good play,
since there aren't enough numbers greater than 1.9 to fill the game board.

Activity (C): Play Decimal Least to Greatest

Play Decimal Least to Greatest.

Decimal Least to Greatest

Materials: 2 dice

Object of the Game: Be the first player to complete their game board with decimals in order from least to greatest.

On your turn, roll 2 dice. Find the matching decimal and write this decimal in one of the blanks on your game board. For example, if you roll a 5, the matching decimal is 0.9. You can write 0.9 in any blank on the game board.

Once you write a number, you may not change it. You must write the numbers in order from least to greatest. If you roll a number that you cannot write on your game board, play passes to the other player.

You may not write a number more than once on your game board. If you roll a number that you already have on your game board, play passes to the other player.

Take turns rolling the dice and writing the matching decimal on your game board. The first player to complete every blank on their game board (with the numbers in order from least to greatest) wins.

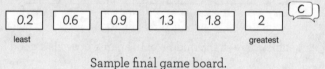

least   greatest

Sample final game board.

Independent Practice and Review

Have your child complete the Lesson 14.2 Practice and Review workbook pages.

Lesson 14.3
Read and Write Decimals to the Hundredths-Place

Purpose	Materials
• Explore hundredths with seconds on a stopwatch • Read and write decimals to the hundredths-place • Express decimals to the hundredths-place with fractions and mixed numbers • Write decimals to the hundredths-place in expanded form	• Digital stopwatch or stopwatch app

Memory Work	
	• **How do you know if a number is divisible by 2?** *It is even. It has a 0, 2, 4, 6, or 8 in the ones-place.* • **How do you know if a number is divisible by 5?** *It has a 0 or 5 in the ones-place.* • **How do you know if a number is divisible by 10?** *It has a 0 in the ones-place.*

Warm-up: Explore Hundredths of a Second on a Stopwatch

In the last two lessons, you learned about decimals with digits in the tenths-place. Today, you'll learn about decimals with digits in the hundredths-place.

At the Olympics, many of the events are timed. The swimmers, runners, and skiers try to be as fast as possible. If the officials measured the times with whole numbers of seconds, they might have lots of people with the same time. Instead, the officials measure the times with hundredths of a second to make the times more precise.

One second is a short amount of time, so one-hundredth of a second is very short! Set a stopwatch (or stopwatch app) to 0. Start the stopwatch and watch as the numbers increase. Point out the digits that count whole seconds and the digits that count hundredths of seconds. Stop the stopwatch after several seconds and explain what the numbers mean. For example: **4 whole seconds and 46 hundredths of a second have passed since I started the stopwatch.**

4.46

This conversation is meant to be an informal introduction to hundredths. Your child does not need to fully understand the hundredths-place at this point, and you will teach her more about the hundredths-place in the next activity.

Your stopwatch may look different than this one, since different stopwatches use different conventions for measuring hundredths of a second.

People often say the word Mississippi to help them count seconds. For example, to count 3 seconds, I could say, "One Mississippi, two Mississippi, three Mississippi." Have your child count three seconds in this way. Use the stopwatch to find exactly how long it takes her. For example: **You took 3.17 seconds. That's pretty close!**

If your family typically uses a different word to estimate seconds (such as "thousand" or "potato"), feel free to use that word instead.

Activity (A): Represent Decimals with Hundredths in Multiple Ways

In Lesson 14.1, you learned that decimal numbers are just an extension of the usual place-value system. We can divide by 10 to create places with a smaller value. Point to the arrows labeled "÷10" below the place-value chart. **If you divide 1 whole into 10 equal parts, you get tenths. If you divide each tenth into 10 equal parts, you get hundredths. So, the next-smaller place after the tenths-place is called the** *hundredths-place.*

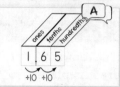

Can you guess what the place after the hundredths-place is called? *Thousandths.* **What about the place after that?** *Ten-thousandths.* **The decimal places follow the same pattern as the whole number places. Just like with whole numbers, we can continue this pattern forever to make numbers as small as we want! You'll learn about smaller places like the thousandths-place and ten-thousandths-place in future grades.**

Your child does not need to memorize or understand the places after the hundredths-place. This discussion simply previews the idea that the place-value system can be extended forever.

Today, you'll learn how to read and write decimals with digits in the tenths-place and hundredths-place. Point to 1.65. **What digit is in the ones-place?** *1.* **What digit is in the tenths-place?** *6.* **What digit is in the hundredths-place?** *5.* **We can read this number as "one point six five" or "one and sixty-five-hundredths."**

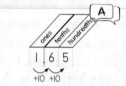

Point to the printed decimal squares. **In these decimal squares, each tenth is split into 10 equal parts, so each small square is one-hundredth of the whole square.**

- **Which part of the squares matches the 1 in 1.65?** *The whole square.*
- **Which part matches the 6?** *The 6 vertical columns.*
- **Which part matches the 5 hundredths?** *The 5 small squares.*

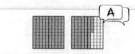

Point to the mixed number. **1.65 is a whole number plus a fractional part, so we can also write 1.65 as a mixed number.**

- Point to the fully-shaded decimal square. **1 is the whole number part.**
- Point to the partially-shaded decimal square. **How many hundredths of this decimal square are shaded?** *65.* **6 tenths equal 60 hundredths, so 65 hundredths are shaded. We represent the fractional part of 1.65 as sixty-five-hundredths.**

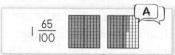

Point to the expanded form of 1.65. **We can also write 1.65 in expanded form. Just like with whole numbers, the expanded form is the sum of the value of each digit.**

- **We start with the digit in the place with the greatest value. The 1 is in the ones-place, so it has a value of 1.**

- The 6 is in the tenths-place, so it has a value of six-tenths.
- The 5 is in the hundredths-place, so it has a value of five-hundredths.

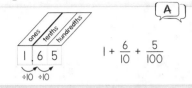

Have your child complete the chart to match the decimals.

Decimal	Decimal Squares	Fraction or Mixed Number	Expanded Form
0.49		$\frac{49}{100}$	$\frac{4}{10} + \frac{9}{100}$
1.37		$1\frac{37}{100}$	$1 + \frac{3}{10} + \frac{7}{100}$
0.25		$\frac{25}{100}$	$\frac{2}{10} + \frac{5}{100}$
0.07		$\frac{7}{100}$	$\frac{7}{100}$

After your child completes the chart, point to the last row. **0.07 has a place-holder zero in the tenths-place. This decimal would look like 0.7 if you didn't write the zero in the tenths-place, so it's important to include it!**

Activity (B): Write Decimals to Show Hundredths of a Second

Show your child the first time in part B. Set a stopwatch to 0. **I'm going to start the stopwatch. Watch the numbers and try to stop the stopwatch as close to 5 seconds as you can. You might want to count 5 "Mississippis" to help you stop the stopwatch at the right time.**

After your child stops the stopwatch, have her read the number of seconds showing on the display and write this number of seconds in the first blank below the printed time. Also have her tell whether the time is greater than, less than, or exactly equal to 5 seconds. For example: *The stopwatch shows 4 and 93-hundredths seconds. It's just a little less than 5 seconds.*

Repeat two more times. **Which time was closest to 5 seconds?** *Answers will vary.* Have your child circle the time that was closest to 5 seconds. Repeat with 3 seconds.

Sample answers.

Encourage your child to use mental math and the pairs that make 100 to find how close the times are to 3 seconds. For example: *93 and 7 equal 100, so 4.93 is 7 hundredths away from 5 seconds.*

Independent Practice and Review

Have your child complete the Lesson 14.3 Practice and Review workbook pages.

Lesson 14.4
Compare Decimals to the Hundredths-Place

Purpose	Materials
• Understand decimal place-value in money amounts • Use place-value thinking to compare decimals	• Counters of 2 colors • 2 dice

Memory Work	• **What do we call a quadrilateral with 4 right angles?** *A rectangle.* • **What do we call a quadrilateral with 4 right angles and 4 equal sides?** *A square.* • **What do we call a quadrilateral with 4 equal sides?** *A rhombus.* • **What do we call a quadrilateral with 2 pairs of parallel sides?** *A parallelogram.* • **What do we call a quadrilateral with exactly 1 pair of parallel sides?** *A trapezoid.*

Warm-up (A): Understand Decimal Place-Value in Money Amounts

In the last lesson, you learned how to read and write decimal numbers to the hundredths-place. We often use decimals to write money amounts. Have your child write each money amount with a dollar sign and decimal.

Point to the 1 in $0.01. **What place is the 1 in?** *The hundredths-place.* **How many pennies equal 1 dollar?** *100.* **Each cent is one-hundredth of a dollar. So, when we write 1 cent with a dollar sign, the 1 goes in the hundredths-place.**

Point to the 1 in $0.10. **What place is the 1 in?** *The tenths-place.* **How many dimes equal 1 dollar?** *10.* **Each dime is one-tenth of a dollar. So, when we write 10 cents with a dollar sign, the 1 goes in the tenths-place. The 0 in the hundredths-place is a place-holder zero.**

Point to the 1 in $1.23. **What place is the 1 in?** *The ones-place.* **When we write money amounts, each dollar is one whole. So, the number of dollars goes to the left of the decimal point. The number of cents is part of a dollar, so we write the number of cents to the right of the decimal point. 23 cents equals 2 tenths and 3 hundredths of a dollar, so we write a 2 in the tenths-place and 3 in the hundredths-place.**

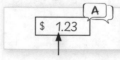

Activity (B): Use Place-Value Thinking to Compare Decimals

Today, you'll learn how to use place-value thinking to compare decimals to the hundredths-place.

Have your child color the decimal squares above 0.54 and 0.45 to match. Encourage him to first shade the tenths, and then shade the hundredths. **What fraction of each square is shaded?** *Fifty-four-hundredths and forty-five-hundredths.*

Which is greater, 0.54 or 0.45? *0.54.* **How do you know?** *Sample answer: 5 tenths is greater than 4 tenths.* **Both numbers both have 0 wholes, so we compare the tenths. Five-tenths is greater than four-tenths, so 0.54 is greater than 0.45.** Write > in the blank.

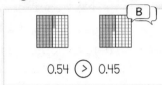

Have your child color the decimal squares above 0.29 and 0.3 to match. **What fraction of each square is shaded?** *Twenty-nine-hundredths and three-tenths (or thirty-hundredths).*

Which is greater, 0.29 or 0.3? *0.3.* **How do you know?** *Sample answers: 0.29 has 2 tenths and 0.3 has 3 tenths. Twenty-nine-hundredths is less than thirty-hundredths.* **When we compare whole numbers, numbers with more digits always have a greater value than numbers with fewer digits. But that's not always true for decimals!** Write < in the blank.

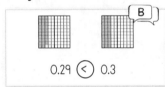

Have your child color the decimal squares above 0.40 and 0.04 to match. **What fraction of each square is shaded?** *Forty-hundredths (or four-tenths) and four-hundredths.*

Which is greater, 0.40 or 0.04? *0.40.* **How do you know?** *Sample answers: 0.40 has 40 hundredths, but 0.04 has only 4 hundredths. Four-tenths is greater than four-hundredths.* **These numbers have the same digits, but the digits are in different places. The 4 in the tenths-place is worth more than the 4 in the hundredths-place, so 0.40 is greater than 0.04.** Write > in the blank.

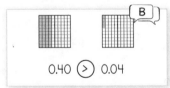

Have your child color the decimal squares above 0.40 and 0.4 to match. **What fraction of each square is shaded?** *Forty-hundredths (or four-tenths) and four-tenths.*

Which is greater, 0.40 or 0.4? *They're equal.* **How do you know?** *Sample answers: 40 hundredths is equivalent to 4 tenths.* **Both numbers have a 4 in the tenths-place. The place-holder zero in the hundredths-place doesn't add any value to 0.40. So, 0.40 equals 0.4.** Write = in the blank.

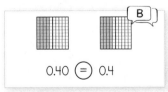

Activity (C): Play Decimal War

Play Decimal War. Encourage your child to use place-value reasoning to compare the decimals.

Decimal War

Materials: counters of 2 colors, 2 dice

Object of the Game: Win the most counters.

Give 7 counters of one color to Player 1. Give 7 counters of another color to Player 2.

To play, roll 2 dice. Add the numbers on the two dice and place a counter on the matching square on the game board. Then, the other player rolls, adds the numbers on the dice, and places a counter on the matching square. For example, if you roll a 6 and a 3, place your counter on the square labeled with a 9.

Have your child decide which player's counter is on a square with a greater decimal number. The player whose counter is on the square with the greater number wins both counters and places them in his "Won" pile. Counters in the "Won" pile are now out of the game and cannot be used again.

Decimal War	2	0.52	3	0.8	4	0.49
	5	0.06	6	0.35	7	0.28	8	0.4
	9	0.42	10	0.7	11	0.6	12	0.64

Sample play. The player whose counter is on 0.8 wins, since 0.8 is greater than 0.42.

Play until both players use up their original pile of counters. Whoever has more counters in their "Won" pile wins the game.

Independent Practice and Review

Have your child complete the Lesson 14.4 Practice and Review workbook pages.

Lesson 14.5
Decimals on the Number Line

Purpose	Materials
• Practice labeling decimals on a number line marked in tenths • Label decimals on a number line marked in hundredths • Round decimals to the nearest whole number	• None

Memory Work	• **What is an acute triangle?** *A triangle with 3 acute angles.* • **What is a right triangle?** *A triangle with a right angle.* • **What is an obtuse triangle?** *A triangle with an obtuse angle.*

Warm-up (A): Label Decimals with Tenths on the Number Line

Earlier in this unit, you learned how to find decimal numbers with tenths on the number line. This number line shows the distance from 0 to 1. The space between 0 and 1 is split into 10 equal parts, so each tick mark stands for one-tenth. Have your child draw lines to match each number to its tick mark on the number line.

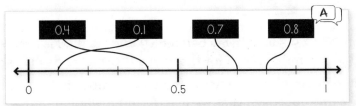

Activity (B): Label Decimals with Hundredths on the Number Line

Today, you'll learn how to label decimals on number lines marked in hundredths. You'll also learn how to round numbers to the nearest whole number.

This number line zooms in on the part of the number line from 0.5 to 0.7. Each tenth on this number line is split into 10 equal parts, or hundredths.

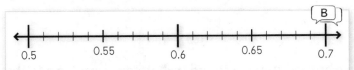

If your child is interested, point out that you can "zoom in" on the number line forever. No matter how small you make the interval between tick marks, you can always subdivide the interval further.

Point to 0.54. **What's the expanded form of 0.54?** *5 tenths plus 4 hundredths.* **0.54 equals 5 tenths plus 4 hundredths. On this number line, each tick mark stands for one-hundredth, so 0.54 is 4 is 4 tick marks after 0.5.** Count 4 tick marks past 0.5 and draw a line to connect the decimal to the tick mark.

Have your child use similar reasoning to connect the rest of the decimals to their locations on the number line. If your child has trouble, have her first tell the expanded form of the number before finding its matching tick mark.

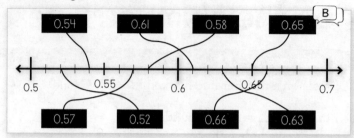

Activity (C): Round Decimals to the Nearest Whole Number

One way to round decimals to the nearest whole number is to use a number line.

The world record for the men's 100-meter dash is 9.58 seconds. About where would 9.58 go on this number line? *Child points to the space between 9.5 and the next tick mark.* If your child's not sure, say: **9.58 is a little more than 9.5. It's less than 9.6, so it goes between 9.5 and 9.6.** Draw a dot at the approximate location for 9.58 as shown.

WORLD RECORD for
men's 100-meter dash

9.58

Is 9.58 closer to 9 or 10? *10.* **9.5 is halfway between 9 and 10. 9.58 is greater than 9.5, so 9.58 is closer to 10 than 9. The world record for the men's 100-meter dash is about 10 seconds.**

Another way to round decimals to the nearest whole number is to use place-value thinking. We can use the same approach that we use to round whole numbers.

Here's how we do it. We want to round 9.58 to the nearest whole number, so I'll underline the digit in the ones-place. Underline the 9.

Now, I look at the digit in the tenths-place. If there are less than 5 tenths, I know that the number is closer to 9. If there are 5 tenths or more, I know the number rounds to 10. Point to the 5. **There are 5 tenths and some hundredths, so 9.58 is closer to 10 than 9.** Write 10 in the blank.

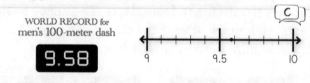

Mathematicians have agreed that we round in-between numbers to the higher number. If this number were exactly 9.5, I would still round it to 10.

Have your child use the same method to round the numbers in the chart to the nearest whole number. She should underline the digit in the ones-place and then look at the tenths-place to decide whether to round up or down.

World Record	Exact Time (Seconds)	Time Rounded to Nearest Second
Women's 100-meter dash	10.49	10
Men's 400-meter dash	43.03	43
Women's 400-meter dash	47.60	48

Sometimes, a rounded number is more helpful than the exact number, because it lets us focus on the big picture. For example, if you'd like to know the rough difference between the men's and women's 400-meter dash records, the rounded numbers are all you need. They make it easy to see that the men's record for the 400-meter dash is about 5 seconds faster than the women's record.

But if you'd like to know the rough difference between the men's and women's 100-meter dash records, the rounded numbers aren't much help. The men's and women's records are almost 1 whole second apart, but both records round to 10 seconds. If you only saw the rounded numbers, you might think the records were the same. When we round numbers in real life, we have to decide whether we want to focus on the big picture or know the exact numbers.

These world records are accurate as of 2023.

Independent Practice and Review

Have your child complete the Lesson 14.5 Practice and Review workbook pages.

Lesson 14.6
Write Metric Lengths as Decimals

Purpose	Materials
• Practice writing decimals • Write metric lengths with fractions, mixed numbers, and decimals • Draw lines with a given decimal length	• Paper clip • 30-centimeter (1 foot) ruler

Memory Work
- **How many millimeters equal 1 centimeter?** *10.*
- **How many centimeters equal 1 meter?** *100.*
- **How many meters equal 1 kilometer?** *1,000.*

Warm-up: Write Decimals

I'm going to read you some numbers. Write each number with a decimal point. Have your child write each number as a decimal on a piece of scrap paper.

- **One and nine-tenths.** *1.9.*
- **One and ninety-nine-hundredths.** *1.99.*
- **One and nine-hundredths.** *1.09.*
- **Nine-tenths.** *0.9.*
- **Nine and nine-tenths.** *9.9.*
- **Nine and ninety-nine-hundredths.** *9.99.*

Activity (A): Write Decimals for Lengths in Centimeters and Millimeters

In Unit 9, you learned how to write lengths as combinations of centimeters and millimeters. Today, you'll learn how to write these lengths with decimals.

Show your child part A. **The first line is 9 millimeters long. 9 millimeters is what fraction of a centimeter?** *Nine-tenths.* If your child's not sure, say: **10 millimeters equal 1 centimeter, so each millimeter equals one-tenth of a centimeter.** Write 9/10 in the first blank. **What decimal equals nine-tenths?** *0.9.* Write 0.9 in the second blank.

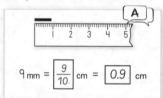

The next line is 3 centimeters and 7 millimeters long. 7 millimeters is what fraction of a centimeter? *Seven-tenths.* **So, 3 centimeters and 7 millimeters equals what mixed number?** *Three and seven-tenths.* Write 3 7/10 in the first blank. **What decimal equals three and seven-tenths?** *3.7.* Write 3.7 in the second blank.

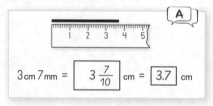

Activity (B): Play Decimal Race

Play Decimal Race.

Decimal Race

Materials: Paper clip; 30-centimeter (1-foot) ruler

Object of the Game: Draw a path that reaches the End square before your opponent.

Place one end of the paper clip in the middle of the spinner. Place the point of a pencil through the paper clip so that it touches the very middle of the circle.

On your turn, hold the pencil upright and spin the paper clip so that it spins freely around the circle and then stops on one of the lengths. Use the ruler to draw a straight line of that length, beginning at your starting dot. For example, if you spin 1.4 cm, draw a line that's 1.4 cm long. Draw a dot at the end of your line. You will start your next line at this dot. Then the other player takes a turn in the same way.

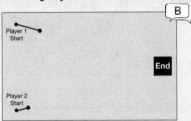

Sample first play by each player.

All lines must be straight and fit inside the game board. Lines may go in any direction, and they may cross any previously-drawn lines. The best strategy is to draw your line in the direction of the End square.

Take turns spinning and drawing lines. The game ends when one player's path touches the End square. The final line may cross the End square, and it does not have to end inside the End square.

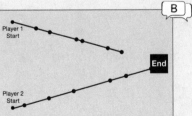

Sample final game board. Player 2 wins, because his path reached the End square first.

Activity (C): Write Decimals for Lengths in Meters and Centimeters

We can use the same kind of reasoning to write lengths in meters as decimals. 100 centimeters equal 1 meter, so 45 centimeters equal what fraction of a meter? *Forty-five-hundredths.* **Write 45/100 in the first blank. Forty-five-hundredths equal what decimal?** 0.45. **Write 0.45 in the second blank.**

$$45 \text{ cm} = \frac{45}{100} \text{ m} = \boxed{0.45} \text{ m}$$

If your child isn't sure, encourage him to imagine a decimal square: **Imagine shading 45 small squares in the decimal square. You'd shade 4 columns of 10, plus 5 more squares. So, you'd shade 4 tenths and 5 hundredths.**

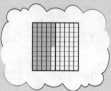

In Unit 9, you wrote these Olympic records as combinations of meters and centimeters. We can also write these distances with mixed numbers or decimals.

The Olympic record for men's high jump is 2 meters 39 centimeters. Each centimeter is one-hundredth of a meter, so we can also write the height as 2 and thirty-nine-hundredths. Write "2 39/100 m" in the chart. **What decimal equals 2 and thirty-nine-hundredths?** *2.39.* Write "2.39 m" in the chart. Repeat with the rest of the Olympic records.

Event	High Jump	Pole Vault	Long Jump	Triple Jump
Record (m and cm)	2 m 39 cm	6 m 3 cm	8 m 90 cm	18 m 9 cm
Mixed Number (m)	$2\frac{39}{100}$ m	$6\frac{3}{100}$ m	$8\frac{90}{100}$ m	$18\frac{9}{100}$ m
Decimal Number (m)	2.39 m	6.03 m	8.90 m	18.09 m

As in Unit 9, these records are rounded to the nearest centimeter and correct as of 2023.

Independent Practice and Review

Have your child complete the Lesson 14.6 Practice and Review workbook pages.

Lesson 14.7
Decimal Equivalents for Common Fractions

Purpose	Materials
• Write metric weights with decimals • Find decimal equivalents for 1/2, 1/4, and 3/4 • Tell whether decimals are greater than, less than, or equal to 1/2, 1/4 , and 3/4	• None

Memory Work	• **How many ounces equal 1 pound?** *16.* • **How many grams equal 1 kilogram?** *1,000.*

In this lesson, your child will learn to write decimal equivalents for common fractions. Knowing these fraction-decimal equivalents helps children develop better decimal number sense and prepares them to tackle percentages in future grades.

Warm-up (A): Write Weights as Decimals

In the last lesson, you wrote lengths as decimals. Today, you'll learn how to write weights as decimals. You'll also learn decimal equivalents for common fractions.

Point to the scale with the pineapple. **We often use decimals to make measurements more precise. For example, you could say that this pineapple weighs a little less than 2 kilograms. But, we can express its weight more accurately if we use a decimal. There are 10 spaces between the whole numbers of kilograms on this scale, so each tick mark stands for one-tenth of a kilogram. How much does the pineapple weigh?** *1.7 kilograms.* Write 1.7 in the blank. Have your child find the weight of the other items in the same way.

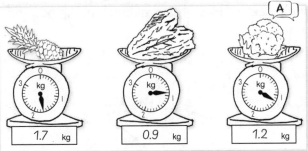

Activity (B): Find Decimal Equivalents for Common Fractions

Decimals and fractions are both ways to express parts of wholes. When we have part of a whole, we can express it with either a fraction or a decimal.

One-half of this decimal square is colored. How many tenths are colored? *5.* Write 5 in the fraction blank. **What decimal is equivalent to five-tenths?** *0.5.* Write 0.5 in the second blank.

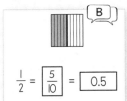

$$\frac{1}{2} = \boxed{\frac{5}{10}} = \boxed{0.5}$$

In future grades, your child will learn how to use equivalent fraction reasoning to convert fractions to decimals. For now, she may complete the fractions by simply counting the colored tenths or hundredths in the decimal squares.

One-fourth of the next decimal square is colored. How many hundredths are colored? *25.* **So, one-fourth equals twenty-five hundredths.** Write 25 in the fraction blank. **What decimal equals twenty-five-hundredths?** *0.25.* Write 0.25 in the second blank. Repeat with 3/4.

$$\frac{1}{4} = \boxed{\frac{25}{100}} = \boxed{0.25} \quad \frac{3}{4} = \boxed{\frac{75}{100}} = \boxed{0.75}$$

Your child may wonder why there aren't any whole columns of tenths colored to match the 2 in the tenths-place in 0.25. If so, explain that 20 hundredths equal 2 tenths no matter how they're colored on the decimal squares.

Activity (C): Use Decimal Equivalents to Compare Fractions and Decimals

Memorizing the decimals equal to 1/2, 1/4, and 3/4 helps you understand and compare fractions and decimals.

Cover part B with your hand or a piece of paper and quiz your child on the decimals equal to 1/2, 1/4, and 3/4. Allow your child to peek if she doesn't remember.

- **What decimal equals one-half?** *0.5.*
- **What decimal equals one-fourth?** *0.25.*
- **What decimal equals three-fourths?** *0.75.*

Read the first word problem aloud: *Victor needs at least one-half pound of tomatoes to make a salad. Which weights are more than one-half pound?*

What decimal equals one-half? *0.5.* **So, we need to find the packages with more than 0.5 pounds of tomatoes.** Have your child tell whether each weight is less than or greater than 0.5 pounds. Circle the packages with weights greater than 0.5 pounds. X the packages with weights less than 0.5 pounds.

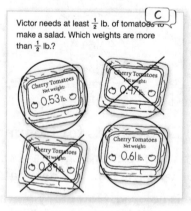

Read the next word problem aloud: ***Heidi needs about three-fourths of a kilogram of meat for a recipe. Which weight is closest to three-fourths of a kilogram?***

What is the decimal equivalent for three-fourths? *0.75.* **Which weight is closest to 0.75 kilograms?** *0.78 kilograms.* Circle 0.78 kg. If your child isn't sure, have her first tell how far each decimal is from 0.75. For example: *69 hundredths is 6 hundredths less than 75 hundredths, so it's 6 hundredths away.*

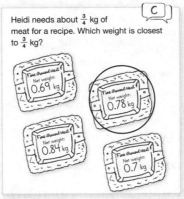

Independent Practice and Review

Have your child complete the Lesson 14.7 Practice and Review workbook pages.

Lesson 14.8
Enrichment (Optional)

Purpose	Materials
• Practice memory work • Understand how decimals help organize books at the library • Find the Dewey Decimal number for a favorite subject • Summarize what your child has learned and assess your child's progress	• *The Efficient, Inventive (Often Annoying) Melvil Dewey,* written by Alexis O'Neill and illustrated by Edwin Fotheringham • Online access to your local library's catalog

Warm-up: Review Memory Work

Quiz your child on all memory work through Unit 14. See pages 536-537 for the full list.

Math Picture Book: *The Efficient, Inventive (Often Annoying) Melvil Dewey*

Read *The Efficient, Inventive (Often Annoying) Melvil Dewey,* written by Alexis O'Neill and illustrated by Edwin Fotheringham. After you read, discuss your child's experiences finding books at the library and using the Dewey Decimal System.

Enrichment Activity: Find the Dewey Decimal Number for Favorite Subjects

Many libraries use a system called the Dewey Decimal System to organize non-fiction books. All non-fiction books are put into one of 10 classes. Show your child the following list and read it aloud.

<u>Dewey Decimal System</u>

000: *Computer Science, Information,*
& General Works
100: *Philosophy & Psychology*
200: *Religion*
300: *Social Sciences*
400: *Language*
500: *Science*
600: *Technology*
700: *Arts & Recreation*
800: *Literature*
900: *History & Geography*

Then, each class is divided further and further to make the categories more specific. For example, all books about owls are labeled 598.97. Each digit narrows down the category further. Show your child the following diagram. Have your child identify the new digit for each new subcategory.

500   **590**   **598**   **598.9**   **598.97**
Science   *Animals*   *Birds*   *Raptors,*   *Owls*
                                            birds of prey

The non-fiction books at many libraries are arranged in numerical order to match the Dewey Decimal System. That helps to find the book you want. You can go to any library that uses the Dewey Decimal System and know that the owl books will be at 598.97.

Have your child choose a non-fiction topic that he's interested in. Search for the topic in your local library's online catalog and find the Dewey Decimal number for the topic.

523.89
Constellations

Show your child how to use the Dewey Decimal number to find books on this topic the next time you go to the library. Discuss how knowing how to compare and order decimals helps you find the correct location.

Unit Wrap-Up

Have your child complete the Unit 14 Wrap-Up.

Unit 14 Answer Key

14.1 Practice

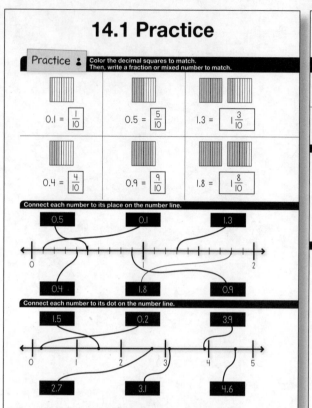

14.1 Review

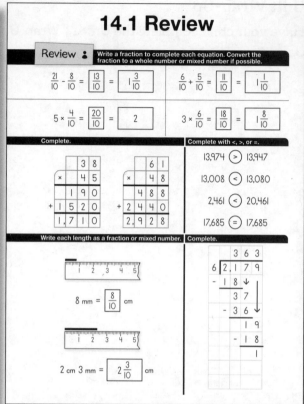

14.2 Practice

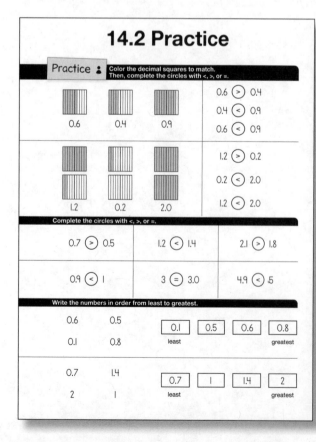

14.2 Review

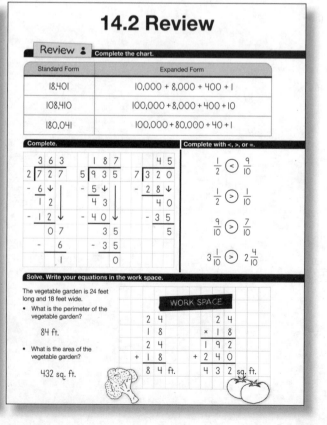

Unit 14 Answer Key

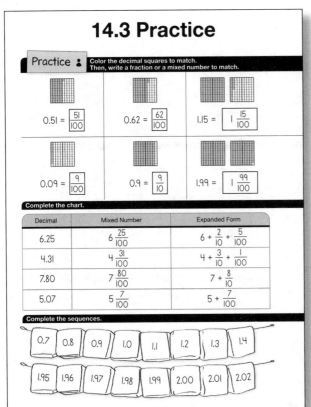

14.3 Practice

Practice Color the decimal squares to match.
Then, write a fraction or a mixed number to match.

$0.51 = \frac{51}{100}$ $0.62 = \frac{62}{100}$ $1.15 = 1\frac{15}{100}$

$0.09 = \frac{9}{100}$ $0.9 = \frac{9}{10}$ $1.99 = 1\frac{99}{100}$

Complete the chart.

Decimal	Mixed Number	Expanded Form
6.25	$6\frac{25}{100}$	$6 + \frac{2}{10} + \frac{5}{100}$
4.31	$4\frac{31}{100}$	$4 + \frac{3}{10} + \frac{1}{100}$
7.80	$7\frac{80}{100}$	$7 + \frac{8}{10}$
5.07	$5\frac{7}{100}$	$5 + \frac{7}{100}$

Complete the sequences.

| 0.7 | 0.8 | 0.9 | 1.0 | 1.1 | 1.2 | 1.3 | 1.4 |

| 1.95 | 1.96 | 1.97 | 1.98 | 1.99 | 2.00 | 2.01 | 2.02 |

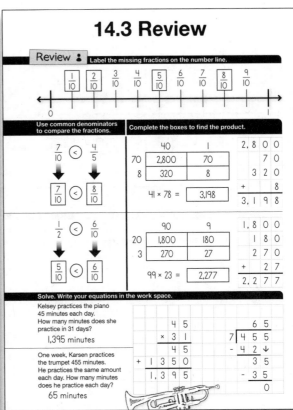

14.3 Review

Review Label the missing fractions on the number line.

$\frac{1}{10}$ $\frac{2}{10}$ $\frac{3}{10}$ $\frac{4}{10}$ $\frac{5}{10}$ $\frac{6}{10}$ $\frac{7}{10}$ $\frac{8}{10}$ $\frac{9}{10}$

Use common denominators to compare the fractions.

$\frac{7}{10}$ $<$ $\frac{4}{5}$

$\frac{7}{10}$ $<$ $\frac{8}{10}$

$\frac{1}{2}$ $<$ $\frac{6}{10}$

$\frac{5}{10}$ $<$ $\frac{6}{10}$

Complete the boxes to find the product.

	40	1
70	2,800	70
8	320	8

$41 \times 78 = 3,198$

```
  2,8 0 0
       7 0
      3 2 0
    +     8
  3,1 9 8
```

	90	9
20	1,800	180
3	270	27

$99 \times 23 = 2,277$

```
  1,8 0 0
      1 8 0
      2 7 0
    +   2 7
  2,2 7 7
```

Solve. Write your equations in the work space.

Kelsey practices the piano 45 minutes each day. How many minutes does she practice in 31 days?
1,395 minutes

One week, Karsen practices the trumpet 455 minutes. He practices the same amount each day. How many minutes does he practice each day?
65 minutes

```
      4 5
    × 3 1
      4 5
  + 1 3 5 0
  1,3 9 5
```

```
        6 5
    7 ) 4 5 5
      - 4 2 ↓
          3 5
        - 3 5
            0
```

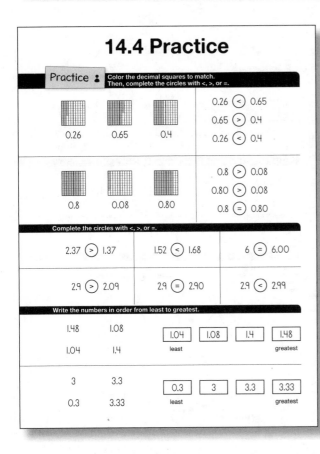

14.4 Practice

Practice Color the decimal squares to match.
Then, complete the circles with <, >, or =.

0.26   0.65   0.4

0.26 $<$ 0.65
0.65 $>$ 0.4
0.26 $<$ 0.4

0.8   0.08   0.80

0.8 $>$ 0.08
0.80 $>$ 0.08
0.8 $=$ 0.80

Complete the circles with <, >, or =.

2.37 $>$ 1.37 1.52 $<$ 1.68 6 $=$ 6.00

2.9 $>$ 2.09 2.9 $=$ 2.90 2.9 $<$ 2.99

Write the numbers in order from least to greatest.

1.48   1.08
1.04   1.4

| 1.04 | 1.08 | 1.4 | 1.48 |
| least | | | greatest |

3   3.3
0.3   3.33

| 0.3 | 3 | 3.3 | 3.33 |
| least | | | greatest |

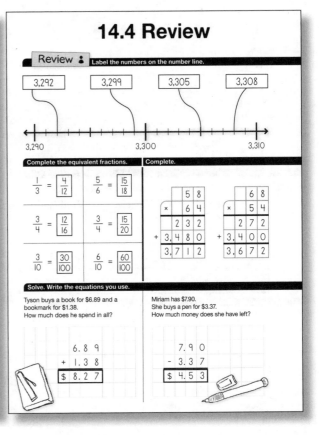

14.4 Review

Review Label the numbers on the number line.

3,292   3,299   3,305   3,308

3,290   3,300   3,310

Complete the equivalent fractions.

$\frac{1}{3} = \frac{4}{12}$ $\frac{5}{6} = \frac{15}{18}$

$\frac{3}{4} = \frac{12}{16}$ $\frac{3}{4} = \frac{15}{20}$

$\frac{3}{10} = \frac{30}{100}$ $\frac{6}{10} = \frac{60}{100}$

Complete.

```
      5 8
    ×  6 4
      2 3 2
  + 3,4 8 0
  3,7 1 2
```

```
      6 8
    ×  5 4
      2 7 2
  + 3,4 0 0
  3,6 7 2
```

Solve. Write the equations you use.

Tyson buys a book for $6.89 and a bookmark for $1.38. How much does he spend in all?

```
    6.8 9
  + 1.3 8
  $ 8.2 7
```

Miriam has $7.90. She buys a pen for $3.37. How much money does she have left?

```
    7.9 0
  - 3.3 7
  $ 4.5 3
```

Unit 14 Answer Key

14.5 Practice

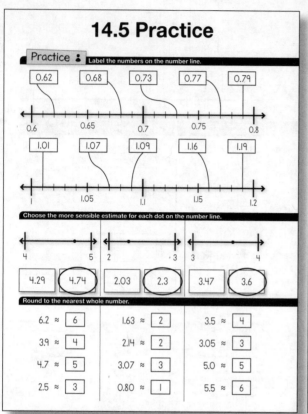

Practice — Label the numbers on the number line.

0.62 0.68 0.73 0.77 0.79

0.6   0.65   0.7   0.75   0.8

1.01 1.07 1.09 1.16 1.19

1   1.05   1.1   1.15   1.2

Choose the more sensible estimate for each dot on the number line.

4 — 5   2 — 3   3 — 4

4.29 **(4.74)**   2.03 **(2.3)**   3.47 **(3.6)**

Round to the nearest whole number.

6.2 ≈ **6**	1.63 ≈ **2**	3.5 ≈ **4**
3.9 ≈ **4**	2.14 ≈ **2**	3.05 ≈ **3**
4.7 ≈ **5**	3.07 ≈ **3**	5.0 ≈ **5**
2.5 ≈ **3**	0.80 ≈ **1**	5.5 ≈ **6**

14.5 Review

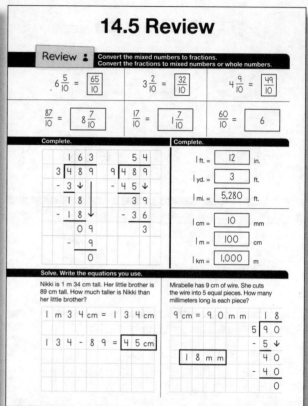

Review — Convert the mixed numbers to fractions.
Convert the fractions to mixed numbers or whole numbers.

$6\frac{5}{10} = \frac{65}{10}$ $3\frac{2}{10} = \frac{32}{10}$ $4\frac{9}{10} = \frac{49}{10}$

$\frac{87}{10} = 8\frac{7}{10}$ $\frac{17}{10} = 1\frac{7}{10}$ $\frac{60}{10} = 6$

Complete.

```
  1 6 3        5 4
3 4 8 9      9 4 8 9
- 3 ↓        - 4 5 ↓
  1 8          3 9
- 1 8 ↓      - 3 6
    0 9          3
  -   9
      0
```

Complete.

1 ft. = **12** in.		
1 yd. = **3** ft.		
1 mi. = **5,280** ft.		
1 cm = **10** mm		
1 m = **100** cm		
1 km = **1,000** m		

Solve. Write the equations you use.

Nikki is 1 m 34 cm tall. Her little brother is 89 cm tall. How much taller is Nikki than her little brother?

1 m 3 4 cm = 1 3 4 cm

1 3 4 − 8 9 = **4 5 cm**

Mirabelle has 9 cm of wire. She cuts the wire into 5 equal pieces. How many millimeters long is each piece?

9 cm = 9 0 m m

1 8 m m

```
    1 8
5 9 0
- 5 ↓
  4 0
- 4 0
    0
```

14.6 Practice

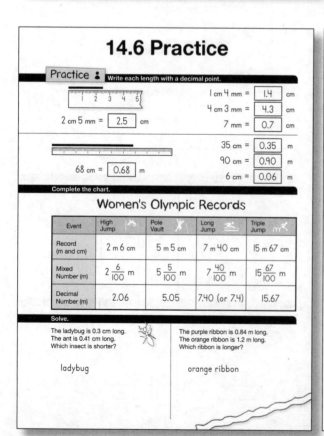

Practice — Write each length with a decimal point.

2 cm 5 mm = **2.5** cm	1 cm 4 mm = **1.4** cm
	4 cm 3 mm = **4.3** cm
	7 mm = **0.7** cm

68 cm = **0.68** m	35 cm = **0.35** m
	90 cm = **0.90** m
	6 cm = **0.06** m

Complete the chart.

Women's Olympic Records

Event	High Jump	Pole Vault	Long Jump	Triple Jump
Record (m and cm)	2 m 6 cm	5 m 5 cm	7 m 40 cm	15 m 67 cm
Mixed Number (m)	$2\frac{6}{100}$ m	$5\frac{5}{100}$ m	$7\frac{40}{100}$ m	$15\frac{67}{100}$ m
Decimal Number (m)	2.06	5.05	7.40 (or 7.4)	15.67

Solve.

The ladybug is 0.3 cm long. The ant is 0.41 cm long. Which insect is shorter?

ladybug

The purple ribbon is 0.84 m long. The orange ribbon is 1.2 m long. Which ribbon is longer?

orange ribbon

14.6 Review

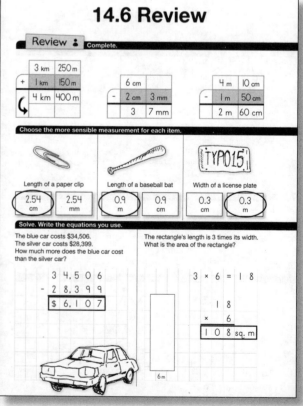

Review — Complete.

3 km	250 m
+ 1 km	150 m
4 km	400 m

6 cm	
− 2 cm	3 mm
3	7 mm

4 m	10 cm
− 1 m	50 cm
2 m	60 cm

Choose the more sensible measurement for each item.

Length of a paper clip
(2.54 cm)   2.54 mm

Length of a baseball bat
(0.9 m)   0.9 cm

Width of a license plate
0.3 cm   **(0.3 m)**

Solve. Write the equations you use.

The blue car costs $34,506. The silver car costs $28,399. How much more does the blue car cost than the silver car?

```
  3 4, 5 0 6
- 2 8, 3 9 9
$ 6, 1 0 7
```

The rectangle's length is 3 times its width. What is the area of the rectangle?

3 × 6 = 1 8

```
  1 8
×   6
1 0 8 sq. m
```

6 m

Unit 14 Answer Key

14.7 Practice

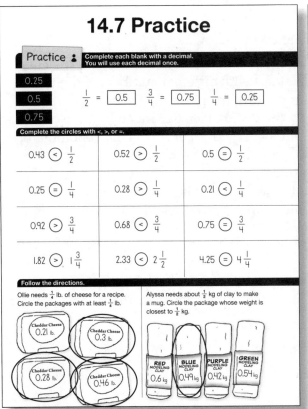

Practice — Complete each blank with a decimal. You will use each decimal once.

0.25
0.5
0.75

$\frac{1}{2}$ = 0.5 $\frac{3}{4}$ = 0.75 $\frac{1}{4}$ = 0.25

Complete the circles with <, >, or =.

0.43 < $\frac{1}{2}$	0.52 > $\frac{1}{2}$	0.5 = $\frac{1}{2}$
0.25 = $\frac{1}{4}$	0.28 > $\frac{1}{4}$	0.21 < $\frac{1}{4}$
0.92 > $\frac{3}{4}$	0.68 < $\frac{3}{4}$	0.75 = $\frac{3}{4}$
1.82 > $1\frac{3}{4}$	2.33 < $2\frac{1}{2}$	4.25 = $4\frac{1}{4}$

Follow the directions.

Ollie needs $\frac{1}{4}$ lb. of cheese for a recipe. Circle the packages with at least $\frac{1}{4}$ lb.

Cheddar Cheese 0.21 lb.
Cheddar Cheese 0.3 lb.
Cheddar Cheese 0.28 lb.
Cheddar Cheese 0.46 lb.

Alyssa needs about $\frac{1}{2}$ kg of clay to make a mug. Circle the package whose weight is closest to $\frac{1}{2}$ kg.

RED MODELING CLAY 0.6 kg
BLUE MODELING CLAY 0.49 kg
PURPLE MODELING CLAY 0.42 kg
GREEN MODELING CLAY 0.54 kg

14.7 Review

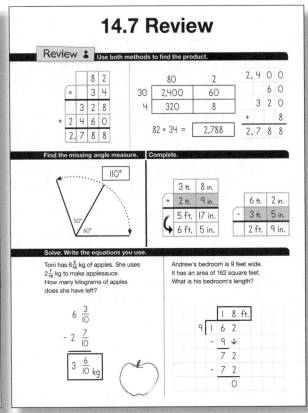

Review — Use both methods to find the product.

	8	2
×	3	4
	3	2	8
+	2	4	6	0
	2,	7	8	8

	80	2
30	2,400	60
4	320	8

82 × 34 = 2,788

2,400
60
320
+ 8
2,788

Find the missing angle measure.

110°
50°
60°

Complete.

   3 ft.   8 in.
+ 2 ft.   9 in.
   5 ft. 17 in.
↻ 6 ft.   5 in.

   6 ft.   2 in.
- 3 ft.   5 in.
   2 ft.   9 in.

Solve. Write the equations you use.

Toni has $6\frac{3}{10}$ kg of apples. She uses $2\frac{7}{10}$ kg to make applesauce. How many kilograms of apples does she have left?

$6\frac{3}{10}$
$- 2\frac{7}{10}$
$3\frac{6}{10}$ kg

Andrew's bedroom is 9 feet wide. It has an area of 162 square feet. What is his bedroom's length?

18 ft.

9) 1 6 2
  - 9 ↓
    7 2
  - 7 2
     0

14.8 Unit Wrap-Up A

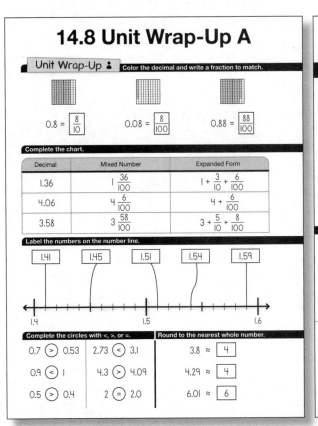

Unit Wrap-Up — Color the decimal and write a fraction to match.

0.8 = $\frac{8}{10}$ 0.08 = $\frac{8}{100}$ 0.88 = $\frac{88}{100}$

Complete the chart.

Decimal	Mixed Number	Expanded Form
1.36	$1\frac{36}{100}$	$1 + \frac{3}{10} + \frac{6}{100}$
4.06	$4\frac{6}{100}$	$4 + \frac{6}{100}$
3.58	$3\frac{58}{100}$	$3 + \frac{5}{10} + \frac{8}{100}$

Label the numbers on the number line.

1.41   1.45   1.51   1.54   1.59

1.4   1.5   1.6

Complete the circles with <, >, or =.

0.7 > 0.53	2.73 < 3.1
0.9 < 1	4.3 > 4.09
0.5 > 0.4	2 = 2.0

Round to the nearest whole number.

3.8 ≈ 4
4.29 ≈ 4
6.01 ≈ 6

14.8 Unit Wrap-Up B

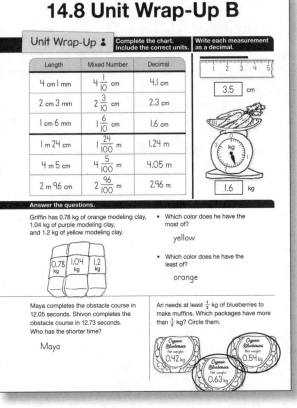

Unit Wrap-Up — Complete the chart. Include the correct units.

Write each measurement as a decimal.

Length	Mixed Number	Decimal
4 cm 1 mm	$4\frac{1}{10}$ cm	4.1 cm
2 cm 3 mm	$2\frac{3}{10}$ cm	2.3 cm
1 cm 6 mm	$1\frac{6}{10}$ cm	1.6 cm
1 m 24 cm	$1\frac{24}{100}$ m	1.24 m
4 m 5 cm	$4\frac{5}{100}$ m	4.05 m
2 m 96 cm	$2\frac{96}{100}$ m	2.96 m

3.5 cm

1.6 kg

Answer the questions.

Griffin has 0.78 kg of orange modeling clay, 1.04 kg of purple modeling clay, and 1.2 kg of yellow modeling clay.

0.78 kg   1.04 kg   1.2 kg

• Which color does he have the most of?

yellow

• Which color does he have the least of?

orange

Maya completes the obstacle course in 12.05 seconds. Shivon completes the obstacle course in 12.73 seconds. Who has the shorter time?

Maya

Ari needs at least $\frac{1}{2}$ kg of blueberries to make muffins. Which packages have more than $\frac{1}{2}$ kg? Circle them.

Organic Blueberries Net weight: 0.42 kg
Organic Blueberries Net weight: 0.54 kg
Organic Blueberries Net weight: 0.63 kg

Unit 14 Checkpoint

What to Expect at the End of Unit 14

By the end of Unit 14, most children will be able to do the following:

- Read, write, and compare decimal numbers with tenths and hundredths. Some children will still have trouble comparing decimals with different numbers of digits or decimals with zeros in the tenths-place or hundredths-place.
- Understand place value in decimals and write decimals in expanded form.
- Express decimals as fractions or mixed numbers (with 10 or 100 as the denominator).
- Label decimals with tenths and hundredths on the number line.
- Round decimals to the nearest whole number.
- Express money amounts and metric lengths with decimals.
- Name decimal equivalents for 1/4, 1/2, and 3/4, and use these equivalents to compare decimals to these fractions.

Is Your Child Ready to Move on?

In Unit 15, your child will learn how to convert time, weight, and capacity units and solve problems involving these measurement units. Your child does not need to have mastered any specific skills before moving on to Unit 15.

Unit 15
Time, Weight, and Capacity

Overview

Your child will learn how to convert units for time, weight, and capacity, within both the metric system and the U.S. customary system. She'll apply these skills to a variety of real-life situations and word problems.

What Your Child Will Learn

In this unit, your child will learn to:

- Convert units of time (days, hours, minutes, seconds)
- Convert weight and capacity measurements within the metric system (kilograms, grams, liters, milliliters)
- Convert weight and capacity measurements within the U.S. customary system (pounds, ounces, gallons, quarts, pints, cups, fluid ounces)
- Add and subtract compound units for time, weight, and capacity
- Solve two-step word problems that involve converting time, weight, and capacity units

Lesson List

Lesson 15.1   Days, Hours, Minutes, and Seconds
Lesson 15.2   Add and Subtract Units of Time
Lesson 15.3   Time Word Problems
Lesson 15.4   Kilograms and Grams

Lesson 15.5   Weight Word Problems
Lesson 15.6   Liters and Milliliters
Lesson 15.7   Pounds and Ounces
Lesson 15.8   Gallons, Quarts, Pints, and Cups
Lesson 15.9   Cups and Fluid Ounces
Lesson 15.10 Enrichment (Optional)

Extra Materials Needed for Unit 15

- Object that weighs about 1 kilogram, such as a pair of adult shoes, a pineapple, or this (printed) Instructor Guide, optional
- Object that weighs about 1 gram, such as a paper clip or thumbtack, optional
- 1-liter container (such as a large water bottle or measuring cup), optional
- Eyedropper, optional
- Object that weighs about 1 pound, such as a loaf of bread, can of vegetables, or box of pasta, optional
- Object that weighs about 1 ounce, such as a slice of bread, AA battery, or a stack of 5 quarters, optional
- 1-quart measuring cup, optional
- Container that holds 1 fluid ounce, such as a bottle of vanilla or other flavor extract, optional
- 1-cup measuring cup, optional
- For optional Enrichment Lesson:
  - × *How Heavy? Wacky Ways to Compare Weight,* written by Mark Andrew Weakland and illustrated by Bill Bolton. Picture Window Books, 2013.
  - × Your child's usual drinking glass
  - × Water
  - × *If you use U.S. customary units:* measuring cup marked in fluid ounces
  - × *If you use metric units:* measuring cup marked in milliliters

Note for Families that Use the Metric System

This unit is split into three parts:

- Time units (Lessons 15.1-15.3)
- Metric units for weight and capacity (Lessons 15.4-15.6)
- U.S. customary units for weight and capacity (Lessons 15.7-15.9)

If your family uses the metric system as your main measurement system, you may skip the lessons on U.S. customary units for weight and capacity.

Teaching Math with Confidence: Making Sense of Many Different Measurement Units

In this unit, your child will solve measurement problems with many different types of measurement units. She'll study both the metric system and U.S. customary system, and she'll solve problems that involve weight, capacity, and time. This adds up to 15 different measurement units!

days	*kilograms*	*milliliters*	*pounds*	*gallons*
hours	*grams*	*liters*	*ounces*	*quarts*
minutes				*pints*
seconds				*cups*
				fluid ounces

Children sometimes see the variety of units and feel overwhelmed, because they mistakenly think that they have to memorize a separate set of steps for each unit. However, these lessons actually focus on just three core skills.

- Multiplying or dividing to convert measurements
- Adding and subtracting compound units
- Using measurement conversions to solve multiplication and division word problems

Your child learned how to perform all of these calculations with length units in Unit 9, so these skills should be familiar to her. However, even though the skills are familiar, children sometimes find it challenging to transition from one type of unit to another. Use these tips to help your child tackle the many measurement problems in this unit with confidence:

- **Make sure to do the warm-ups.** The lesson warm-ups include concrete examples of the units discussed in the lesson to help your child make sense of the units and relate the printed numbers to real life. For example, when you introduce fluid ounces, you'll show your child a bottle of vanilla (either a real bottle or printed picture) so she can see what 1 fluid ounce looks like. Encourage your child to keep these examples in mind as she works. For example: **12 ounces is only 12 little bottles of vanilla, so it's not that much!**
- Your child may struggle to remember all the relationships between the different measurement units, even if she had them all memorized earlier in the year. It's perfectly normal for children to temporarily forget things when their brains are working hard to master and integrate new skills. If you find your child has trouble remembering equivalencies (like 1 kilogram equals 1,000 grams, or 1 pound equals 16 ounces), **help her to make a simple reference list on a separate piece of paper.** Allow her to refer to this list as she solves problems throughout the unit.
- Reassure your child that she can apply what she knows about length units to other types of units, too. **Point out similarities** between problems with different units and encourage your child to notice similarities, too. For example: **In this problem, you converted the liters to milliliters before dividing. It's just like when you converted meters to centimeters before dividing.**

Lesson 15.1
Days, Hours, Minutes, and Seconds

Purpose	Materials
• Create charts to convert time units • Convert between days, hours, minutes, or seconds	• Die • Counters

Memory Work
- **How many hours equal a day?** *24.*
- **How many minutes equal an hour?** *60.*
- **How many seconds equal a minute?** *60.*

Warm-up (A): Create Charts to Show Time Conversions

In Unit 9, you studied length. You learned how to convert lengths from one unit to another unit, add and subtract lengths, and solve word problems involving length.

In this unit, you'll apply those skills to time, weight, and capacity measurements. Today, we'll focus on time.

1 minute equals how many seconds? *60.* Write 60 on the top line of the first chart. **2 minutes equal how many seconds?** *120.* Write 120 on the next line. If your child's not sure, suggest she add 60 plus 60. Complete the first two charts in the same way.

Minutes	Seconds
1	60
2	120
3	180
4	240
5	300

Hours	Minutes
1	60
2	120
3	180
4	240
5	300

What do these two charts have in common? *The numbers are the same.* **Why are the numbers the same?** *Sample answer: 1 minute equals 60 seconds, and 1 hour equals 60 minutes. So, you multiply the number in the first column by 60 for both types of conversions.*

1 day equals how many hours? *24.* Write 24 on the top line of the last chart. **How many hours equal 2 days?** *48.* Write 48 on the next line. If your child's not sure, suggest she add 24 plus 24. Complete the remaining lines in the chart in the same way.

Days	Hours
1	24
2	48
3	72
4	96
5	120

Activity (B): Multiply or Divide to Convert Time Units

In Unit 9, you used a rhyme to help you remember whether to multiply or divide when you convert measurement units. It went: *Whole to parts? Multiply to start! Parts to whole? Division's in control!*

The same rhyme works to help you remember whether to multiply or divide when you convert other units.

Let's convert 3 minutes 1 second to seconds. First, we convert minutes to seconds. Do we multiply or divide by 60? *Multiply.* **When we convert minutes to seconds, we convert whole minutes to parts of minutes.** *Whole to parts? Multiply to start!*

What's 3 times 60? *180.* If your child isn't sure, have her look at the chart in part A. **Then, we add on the extra second. What's 180 plus 1?** *181.* Write 181 in the blank. **3 minutes and 1 second equal 181 seconds.** Repeat with the other exercises.

3 min. 1 sec. = | 181 | sec.

4 hr. 15 min. = | 255 | min.

2 days 3 hr. = | 51 | hr.

Write the multiplication and addition equations on scrap paper if your child has trouble keeping the numbers in her head.

Next, let's convert 125 seconds to minutes and seconds. Do we multiply or divide by 60? *Divide.* **When we convert seconds to minutes, we convert parts of minutes to whole minutes.** *Parts to whole? Division's in control!*

How many groups of 60 are in 125 seconds? *2.* If your child's not sure, encourage her to look at the matching chart in part A: **2 minutes equal 120 seconds, so that's as close as we can get to 125 without going over. How many seconds are left over?** *5.* **So, 125 seconds equal 2 minutes 5 seconds.** Write 2 and 5 in the blanks. Repeat with the other exercises.

125 sec. = | 2 | min. | 5 | sec.

200 min. = | 3 | hr. | 20 | min.

98 hr. = | 4 | days | 2 | hr.

Your child hasn't learned how to divide by two-digit numbers with mental or written division yet, so the chart provides an alternative way to divide.

Activity (C): Play Time Three in a Row

Play Time Three in a Row. Allow your child to use the charts in part A to help convert the times.

If you own transparent counters, use them for this game so you can see the printed times below the counters.

Time Three in a Row

Materials: Die, counters of two colors

Object of the Game: Be the first player to place 3 counters in a row (horizontally, vertically, or diagonally) in the squares in the center of the game board.

Have each player choose a different-colored counter to use as a game token and place it on one of the Start squares.

On your turn, roll the die and advance your token the corresponding number of squares clockwise around the path. If you land on a square with a compound unit, convert the measurement to the smaller unit. For example, if you land on 1 hr. 30 min., place a counter on 90 min.

Directions continued on next page.

If you land on a square with only one unit of time, convert the unit to a compound unit. For example, if you land on 49 hr., place a counter on 2 days 1 hr.

If your opponent already has a counter on the matching inner square, remove your opponent's counter and replace it with your counter. If you land on one of the Start squares, roll again.

Play until one player covers three inner squares in a row, either horizontally, vertically, or diagonally.

Answer Key:

315 sec. = 5 min. 15 sec.	195 min. = 3 hr. 15 min.	49 hrs. = 2 days 1 hr.
5 days 1 hr. = 121 hr.	1 hr. 30 min. = 90 min.	2 min. 45 sec. = 165 sec.
135 sec. = 2 min. 15 sec.	75 hr. = 3 days 3 hr.	295 min. = 4 hr. 55 min.
3 days 8 hr. = 80 hr.	4 min 25 sec. = 265 sec.	5 hr. 25 min. = 325 min.
75 min. = 1 hr. 15 min.	250 sec. = 4 min. 10 sec.	2 hr. 20 min. = 140 min.
	1 day 10 hr. = 34 hr.	

Independent Practice and Review

Have your child complete the Lesson 15.1 Practice and Review workbook pages.

Lesson 15.2
Add and Subtract Units of Time

Purpose	Materials
• Practice converting units of time • Add and subtract units of time	• Die

Memory Work	
	• **How many hours equal a day?** *24.* • **How many minutes equal an hour?** *60.* • **How many seconds equal a minute?** *60.*

Warm-up: Convert Time Units

Ask your child the following time conversion questions.

- **1 minute and 4 seconds equal how many seconds?** *64 seconds.*
- **1 hour and 4 minutes equal how many minutes?** *64 minutes.*
- **1 day and 4 hours equal how many hours?** *28 hours.*
- **72 seconds equal how many minutes and seconds?** *1 minute 12 seconds.*
- **72 minutes equal how many hours and minutes?** *1 hour 12 minutes.*
- **36 hours equal how many days and hours?** *1 day and 12 hours.*

If your child has trouble keeping the numbers and units in his head, write them as equations on a separate piece of paper. For example, to convert 1 min. 4 sec. to seconds:

$$1 \text{ min. } 4 \text{ sec.} = \underline{\qquad} \text{ sec.}$$

Activity (A): Add and Subtract Units of Time

In Unit 9, you learned how to add and subtract length units. We can add and subtract time units in the same way.

Show your child the first problem. **First, we add the smaller units. What's 15 minutes plus 30 minutes?** *45 minutes.* Write 45 min. as shown. **Next, we add the larger units. What's 3 hours plus 2 hours?** *5 hours.* Write "5 hr." as shown.

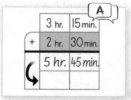

Then, we check whether we can trade any of the smaller units for larger units. **Do we have enough minutes to trade for hours?** *No.* We're done! The answer is 5 hours 45 minutes.

The second box below the problem is there in case you need to trade after you add. If you don't need to trade, leave it blank.

Have your child solve the second addition problem in the same way. When he reaches the trading step, say: **Do we have enough seconds to trade for minutes?** *Yes.* **70 seconds equal how many minutes and seconds?** *1 minute 10 seconds.* **So, we add 1 minute 10 seconds to 3 min. What's 3 minutes plus 1 minute 10 seconds?** *4 minutes 10 seconds.* Write "4 min. 10 sec." in the second box below the problem.

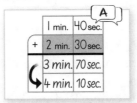

Subtracting time units is a lot like subtracting length units, too. First, we look at the smaller unit and check that we have enough of them to subtract. Point to the column for minutes. **Do we have enough minutes to subtract 40 minutes?** *No, we don't have any minutes.* **Before we subtract, we need to trade to get some minutes.**

We trade 1 hour for 60 minutes. Cross out 5 hr. and write "4 hr." above it. Write "60 min." as shown.

Now, we're ready to subtract! What's 60 minutes minus 40 minutes? *20 minutes.* Write "20 min." as shown. **What's 4 hours minus 2 hours?** *2 hours.* Write "2 hr." as shown.

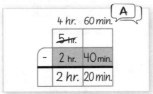

Point to the second subtraction problem. **Do we have enough seconds to subtract 35 seconds?** *No.* **We need to trade before we subtract.**

We trade 1 minute for 60 seconds. Cross out 6 min. and write "5 min." above it. **We add the 60 seconds to the 15 seconds we already have. What's 60 plus 15?** *75.* **Now, we have 75 seconds.** Cross out 15 sec. and write "75 sec." above it.

We're ready to subtract! Have your child subtract to complete the problem.

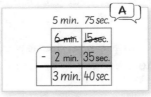

Activity (B): Play Race to 10 Hours

Play Race to 10 Hours.

Race to 10 Hours

Materials: Die

Object of the Game: Be the first player to reach 10 hours.

For your first turn only, roll the die twice. Write the matching numbers of hours and minutes on the top two rows of your score card and add them. Trade minutes for hours as needed. Write the final sum on the next line. (If you do not need to trade minutes for hours, simply recopy the sum on the next line.)

   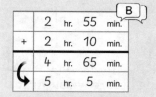

Sample first turn without trading. If you do not trade, recopy the sum onto the next line.
This sum becomes the first addend in the next problem.

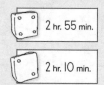

Sample first turn with trading. If you trade, write the final sum on the next line.
This sum becomes the first addend in the next problem.

On your subsequent turns, roll the die only once. Write the matching time on the next line of your score card. Add this time to your previous total. Again, trade minutes for hours as needed and write the final sum on the next line.

Take turns rolling the die and adding to find the new sum. If you run out of room, continue the score card on a separate piece of paper. Continue until one player reaches or goes past 10 hours.

Independent Practice and Review

Have your child complete the Lesson 15.2 Practice and Review workbook pages.

Lesson 15.3
Time Word Problems

Purpose	Materials
• Estimate times in hours, minutes, and seconds • Solve time word problems	• None

Memory Work	• **How many hours equal a day?** *24.* • **How many minutes equal an hour?** *60.* • **How many seconds equal a minute?** *60.*

Warm-up (A): Estimate Activity Lengths in Hours, Minutes, or Seconds

In the last two lessons, you've learned how to convert, add, and subtract times. Today, you'll use those skills to answer questions about how long you spend on activities like eating, sleeping, or brushing your teeth.

Help your child estimate how long she spends each day on each activity in part A. Use the printed units for each activity. If needed, round to the nearest whole number.

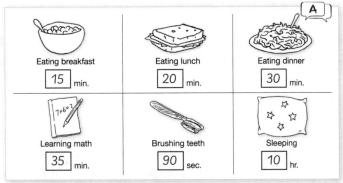

Activity (B): Solve Addition and Subtraction Time Word Problems

Read aloud the first question: ***How many minutes do you spend eating meals each day?*** **How can we find the answer?** *Add up the number of minutes I spend on meals.* Help your child set up and solve an addition problem to find the answer.

Then, read aloud the follow-up question: ***How many hours and minutes do you spend eating meals each day?*** Have your child convert the previous answer to hours and minutes. Write the answer below the question. If your child eats meals for less than 1 hour each day, simply write the number of minutes.

> **B**
> How many minutes do you spend eating meals each day?
>
> *15 + 20 + 30 = 65 min.*
> *1 hr. 5 min.*

Sample answers. Use your child's responses from part A for the addends in the problem.

Read aloud the next question: ***Do you spend more time eating or learning math each day?*** Help your child compare the two numbers of minutes and write the answer below the question.

Then, read aloud the follow-up question: *How many minutes longer?* Help your child set up and solve a subtraction problem to find the difference between the two lengths of time in minutes.

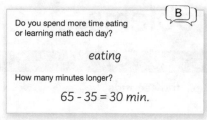

Do you spend more time eating
or learning math each day?

eating

How many minutes longer?

65 - 35 = 30 min.

Sample answers.

Activity (C): Use Multiplication to Solve Time Word Problems

Read aloud the first question in part C: *How many hours do you sleep in one week?* **How can we find the answer?** *Multiply the numbers of hours I sleep each day by 7.* Help your child write and solve a multiplication equation to find the answer.

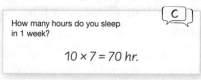

How many hours do you sleep
in 1 week?

10 × 7 = 70 hr.

Sample answer.

Read aloud the follow-up question: *How many days and hours do you sleep in one week?* Have your child convert the previous answer to days and hours. Write the answer below the question.

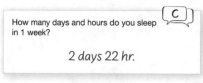

How many days and hours do you sleep
in 1 week?

2 days 22 hr.

Sample answer.

If your child has trouble converting the answer to days and hours, help her make a simple chart showing the relationship between days and hours (as in Lesson 15.1). Then, use the chart to help answer the question. For example: *I sleep about 70 hours per week. That's between 48 and 72, so I sleep 2 whole days. 70 minus 48 is 22 hours, so I sleep 2 days and 22 hours per week.*

Days	1	2	3	4
Hours	24	48	72	96

Have your child complete the final word problem in the same way.

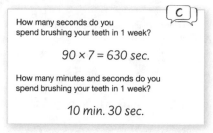

How many seconds do you
spend brushing your teeth in 1 week?

90 × 7 = 630 sec.

How many minutes and seconds do you
spend brushing your teeth in 1 week?

10 min. 30 sec.

Sample answers.

Independent Practice and Review

Have your child complete the Lesson 15.3 Practice and Review workbook pages.

Lesson 15.4
Kilograms and Grams

Purpose	Materials
• Review kilograms and grams • Convert kilograms and grams • Add and subtract kilograms and grams	• Object that weighs about 1 kilogram, such as a pair of adult shoes, a pineapple, or this (printed) Instructor Guide, optional • Object that weighs about 1 gram, such as a paper clip or thumbtack, optional

Memory Work · **How many grams equal 1 kilogram?** *1,000.*

The lessons in this unit move quickly from one type of measurement unit to another. See the Unit 15 **Teaching Math with Confidence** for tips on how to prevent your child from feeling overwhelmed by the variety of different measurement units.

Warm-up (A): Review Kilograms and Grams

In the last few lessons, you learned how to solve problems about time. In this lesson and the next lesson, we'll solve problems that involve grams and kilograms.

We use grams and kilograms to measure weight in the metric system. 1 gram weighs about the same as a paper clip. 1,000 grams equal 1 kilogram. A pair of adult shoes weighs about 1 kilogram. Show your child the printed images. Or, have him hold an object that weighs about 1 gram and an object that weighs about 1 kilogram.

Metric units like grams and kilograms are made from base units and prefixes. Grams are the base unit for measuring weight. The prefix kilo- means thousand. Underline "kilo" in kilogram. **So, kilogram means "one thousand grams."**

If your family uses the U.S. customary system, explain that 1 kilogram weighs a little more than 2 pounds.

Name each of the following items. Have your child tell whether each item weighs about 1 gram or 1 kilogram.

- **Thumbtack.** *1 gram.*
- **Pineapple.** *1 kilogram.*
- **Large paperback book.** *1 kilogram.*
- **1-dollar bill.** *1 gram.*

Technically, kilograms and grams measure mass, not weight. Mass is the amount of matter in an object, while weight measures how much force gravity exerts on the object. In everyday life, we use the two terms interchangeably, so *Math with Confidence* doesn't address this subtle distinction.

Activity (B): Convert Kilograms and Grams at the Candy Store

Some stores sell food in bulk. Instead of buying food that's already packaged, you measure out how much you want and pay for just that amount. **Have you ever been to a store that sells bulk food?** *Answers will vary.*

This sales chart shows how much candy the customers bought at a candy store. We'll complete the chart and then answer questions about it.

The first customer bought 2 kg of gummy bears. To convert kilograms to grams, do we multiply or divide? *Multiply.* **How do you know?** *Sample answers: Each kilogram equals 1,000 grams. We're going from a larger unit to a smaller unit.*

What's 2 times 1,000? *2,000.* **This customer bought 2,000 grams of gummy bears.** Write "2,000 g" in the chart.

Type of Candy	Weight (kg and g)	Weight (g)	B
Gummy bears	2 kg	2,000 g	

> Write the matching equation on scrap paper if your child has trouble keeping the numbers in his head.

The next customer bought 3 kg 175 g of gummy fish. First, we find the number of grams in 3 kilograms. What's 3 times 1,000? *3,000.* **Then, we add on the 175 extra grams. What's 3,000 plus 175?** *3,175.* Write "3,175 g" in the chart.

The next customer bought 1,600 grams of licorice. To convert grams to kilograms, do we multiply or divide? *Divide.* **How do you know?** *Sample answers: Each group of 1,000 grams becomes 1 kilogram. We're going from a smaller unit to a larger unit.*

What's 1,600 divided by 1,000? *1.* **How many extra grams are left over?** *600.* **So, 1,600 grams equal 1 kilogram 600 grams.** Write "1 kg 600 g" in the chart. Have your child complete the last line of the chart in the same way.

Type of Candy	Weight (kg and g)	Weight (g)	B
Gummy bears	2 kg	2,000 g	
Gummy fish	3 kg 175 g	3,175 g	
Licorice	1 kg 600 g	1,600 g	
Chocolate candies	2 kg 500 g	2,500 g	

Which customer bought the most candy? *The one who bought gummy fish.* **Which customer bought the least candy?** *The one who bought licorice.*

> If your child mostly uses the U.S. customary system, tell him the pound equivalents for each weight.
> - 2 kg weigh about 4 1/2 lb.
> - 3 kg 175 g weigh about 7 lb.
> - 1,600 g weigh about 3 1/2 lb.
> - 2,500 g weigh about 5 1/2 lb.

Activity (C): Add and Subtract Kilograms and Grams

Have your child read aloud the first word problem. **We need to find the sum of 1 kilogram 700 grams and 1 kilogram 400 grams. Adding kilograms and grams is just like adding other compound measurements. First, we add the smaller units. What's 700 grams plus 400 grams?** *1,100 grams.* Write "1,100 g" as shown.

Next, we add the larger units. What's 1 kilogram plus 1 kilogram? *2 kilograms.* Write "2 kg" as shown.

Then, we check whether we can trade any of the smaller units for larger units. Do we have enough grams to trade some for kilograms? *Yes.* **1,100 grams equal how many kilograms and grams?** *1 kilogram 100 grams.*

2 kilograms plus 1 kilogram 100 grams equals 3 kilograms 100 grams. Write "3 kg 100 g" in the final box below the problem.

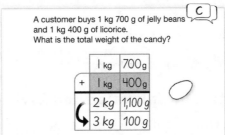

Have your child read aloud the next word problem. **Subtracting kilograms and grams is just like subtracting other compound units, too. First, we look at the smaller unit and check that we have enough of them to subtract.** Point to the column for grams. **Can we subtract 400 grams from 200 grams?** *No.* **Before we subtract, we need to trade to get more grams.**

We trade 1 kilogram for 1,000 grams. Cross out 2 kg and write "1 kg" above it. **We trade 1 kilogram for 1,000 grams and add the 1,000 grams to the 200 grams we already have. Now, we have 1,200 grams.** Cross out 200 g and write "1,200 g" above it.

Now, we're ready to subtract. What's 1,200 grams minus 400 grams? *800 grams.* Write "800 g" as shown." **What's 1 kilogram minus 0 kilograms?** *1 kilogram.* Write "1 kg" as shown. **So, what's 2 kilogram 200 grams minus 400 grams?** *1 kilogram 800 grams.*

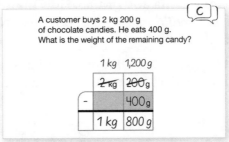

Have your child make up candy word problems to match the remaining problems in part C. For example: *One day, a customer bought 2 kg 800 g of black jelly beans and 1 kg 900 g of purple jelly beans. What was the total weight of the jelly beans?* Or: *A customer bought 3 kilograms of gummy fish and 1 kilogram 100 grams of gummy worms. How much more did the gummy fish weigh than the gummy worms?* Then, have your child solve the problems.

Independent Practice and Review

Have your child complete the Lesson 15.4 Practice and Review workbook pages.

Lesson 15.5
Weight Word Problems

Purpose	Materials
• Practice mental multiplication and division • Multiply grams and convert to kilograms • Solve word problems with kilograms and grams	• 2 dice

Memory Work · **How many grams equal 1 kilogram?** *1,000.*

Warm-up: Practice Mental Multiplication and Division

Have your child solve the following mental multiplication and division problems:

- 400 × 7 = 2,800
- 500 × 6 = 3,000
- 900 × 8 = 7,200

- 1,600 ÷ 2 = 800
- 2,700 ÷ 3 = 900
- 4,000 ÷ 8 = 500

Activity (A): Multiply Grams at the Candy Store

In the last lesson, you added and subtracted kilograms and grams. Today, you'll learn to multiply and divide weights in kilograms and grams.

You're a lucky customer, because you've won a candy shopping spree! You get to roll 2 dice to find how many bags of each type of candy you get.

Have your child roll 2 dice. Write the sum of the numbers she rolls in the first blank in the chart. **Each bag of gummy bears weighs 200 grams. How many grams of gummy bears do you get?** *Sample answer (if your child rolls a 7): 1,400 grams.* **How do you know?** *Sample answer: I multiplied 7 times 200.*

Then, have your child convert the weight to kilograms and grams. Write both weights in the chart. For example, if your child rolled a 7, write "1,400 g" and "1 kg 400 g." Repeat with the rest of the types of candy.

			Weight (g)	Weight (kg and g)
Gummy bears	7	× 200 g	1,400 g	1 kg 400 g
Gummy worms	5	× 500 g	2,500 g	2 kg 500 g
Chocolate candies	10	× 400 g	4,000 g	4 kg
Jelly beans	8	× 300 g	2,400 g	2 kg 400 g

Sample chart. Your child's answers will vary based on the numbers she rolls.

Activity (B): Solve Addition and Subtraction Word Problems

Now, we'll solve some word problems about the candy you won in the shopping spree.

Read aloud the first word problem: *What is the total weight of the candy in kilograms and grams?* **How can we find the answer?** *Add up the weight of all the candy.*

To solve this problem, you could add up the weights in grams, or you could add up the weights in kilograms and grams. What units are you supposed to use for the answer? *Kilograms and grams.* **So, let's add the weights in kilograms and grams so that the answer is already in the correct units.** Help your child write and solve an addition problem to solve the problem.

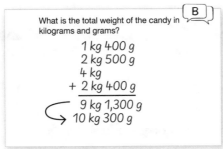

What is the total weight of the candy in kilograms and grams?

1 kg 400 g
2 kg 500 g
4 kg
+ 2 kg 400 g
_____
9 kg 1,300 g
10 kg 300 g

Sample problem. Use your child's answers from part A for the addends in the problem.

Read aloud the second problem: *You eat 350 g of the gummy worms. What is the weight of the remaining gummy worms in grams?* **How can we find the answer?** *Subtract 350 grams from the total weight of the gummy worms.* **What units are you supposed to use for the answer?** *Grams.* **So, let's subtract the weights in grams so that the answer is already in the correct units.** Help your child set up and solve a subtraction problem to find the answer.

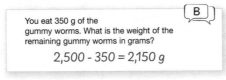

You eat 350 g of the gummy worms. What is the weight of the remaining gummy worms in grams?

2,500 - 350 = 2,150 g

Sample answer.

Activity (C): Use Division to Solve Weight Word Problems

Read aloud the first word problem in part C: *You split the jelly beans equally with a friend. How many grams of jelly beans do you each get?* **How can we find the answer?** *Divide the weight of the jelly beans by 2.* **What units are you supposed to use for the answer?** *Grams.* **So, let's divide the weight in grams by 2.** Help your child write and solve a division equation to find the answer. Your child may use mental math or long division.

You split the jelly beans equally with a friend. How many grams of jelly beans do you each get?

2,400 g ÷ 2 = 1,200 g

Sample answer.

Read aloud the last word problem: *You divide the chocolate candies equally into 8 bags. How many grams of chocolate candies are in each bag?* **How can we find the answer?** *Divide the weight of the chocolate candies by 8.* **What units are you supposed to use for the answer?** *Grams.* **So, let's divide the weight in grams by 8.** Help your child write and solve a division equation to find the answer. Your child may use mental math or long division.

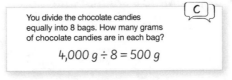

You divide the chocolate candies equally into 8 bags. How many grams of chocolate candies are in each bag?

4,000 g ÷ 8 = 500 g

Sample answer.

Independent Practice and Review

Have your child complete the Lesson 15.5 Practice and Review workbook pages.

Lesson 15.6
Liters and Milliliters

Purpose	Materials
• Review liters and milliliters • Convert liters and milliliters • Add and subtract liters and milliliters	• 1-liter container (such as a large water bottle or measuring cup), optional • Eyedropper, optional

Memory Work · **How many milliliters equal 1 liter?** *1,000.*

Warm-up (A): Review Liters and Milliliters

In the last two lessons, you learned about kilograms and grams. Today, you'll learn about liters and milliliters.

Liters are the base unit for measuring capacity in the metric system. When we measure something's capacity, we measure how much it can hold. A large water bottle holds about 1 liter. Show your child the printed water bottle or a real container that holds about 1 liter.

The prefix milli- means thousandth. Underline "milli" in milliliter. **Milliliter means "one-thousandth of a liter." So, 1,000 milliliters equal 1 liter. A small eyedropper can hold 1 milliliter of liquid.** Show your child the printed eyedropper or a real one.

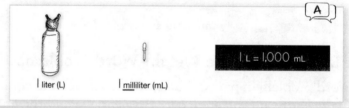

liter (L)   milliliter (mL)   1 L = 1,000 mL

If your family uses the U.S. customary system, explain that 1 liter is about the same amount as 1 quart. 1 milliliter is a little less than 1/4 teaspoon.

Name each of the following items. Have your child tell whether each item holds more than 1 liter or less than 1 liter.

- **Bathtub.** *More than 1 liter.*
- **Coffee mug.** *Less than 1 liter.*
- **Sippy cup.** *Less than 1 liter.*
- **Sink.** *More than 1 liter.*

Activity (B): Convert Liters and Milliliters

Show your child the pictures of drinks in part B. **Drink containers are often labeled in liters and milliliters. The lemon-lime soda bottle holds 2 liters. To convert liters to milliliters, do we multiply or divide?** *Multiply.* **How do you know?** *Sample answers: Each liter equals 1,000 milliliters. We're going from a larger unit to a smaller unit.*

What's 2 times 1,000? *2,000.* **2 liters equals 2,000 milliliters.** Write "2,000 mL" in the chart.

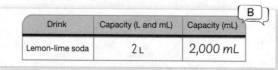

Drink	Capacity (L and mL)	Capacity (mL)
Lemon-lime soda	2 L	*2,000 mL*

Use your family's typical word for carbonated drinks (soda, pop, fizzy drink, etc.) as you complete the lesson.

The lemonade container holds 1 liter 550 milliliters. How many milliliters does 1 liter equal? *1,000 milliliters.* Then, we add on the extra 550 milliliters. What's 1,000 plus 550? *1,550.* Write "1,550 mL" in the chart.

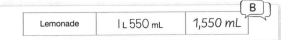

Lemonade	1 L 550 mL	1,550 mL

The orange juice container holds 1,750 milliliters. To convert milliliters to liters, do we multiply or divide? *Divide.* How do you know? *Sample answers: Each group of 1,000 milliliters becomes 1 liter. We're going from a smaller unit to a larger unit.*

What's 1,750 divided by 1,000? *1.* How many extra milliliters are left over? *750.* So, 1,750 milliliters equal 1 liter 750 milliliters. Write "1 L 750 mL" in the chart. Have your child complete the rest of the chart in the same way.

Orange juice	1 L 750 mL	1,750 mL
Pineapple juice	1 L 350 mL	1,350 mL
Cranberry juice	1 L 50 mL	1,050 mL
Ginger ale	1 L 200 mL	1,200 mL

Which container holds the most liquid? *The lemon-lime soda.* Which container holds the least liquid? *The cranberry juice.*

Activity (C): Add Liters and Milliliters in Punch Recipes

Have you ever had punch at a party? *Answers will vary.* Punch is usually made by mixing sodas and fruit juices. You can create different flavors depending on which sodas and juices you combine.

This Citrus Punch recipe calls for 3 different ingredients: 1 bottle of lemon-lime soda, 1 container of orange juice, and 1 container of lemonade. How can we find the total amount of punch that the recipe makes? *Add up the capacity of each drink container.*

To solve this problem, you could add up the capacities in milliliters, or you could add up the capacities in liters and milliliters. What units are you supposed to use for the answer? *Liters and milliliters.* So, let's add the capacities in liters and milliliters so that the answer is already in the correct units. With your child, look at the chart in part B to find the capacity of each drink container in the recipe. Then, help your child write and solve an addition problem to find how much punch the recipe makes.

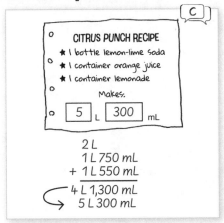

Now, you get to create your own punch recipe. Have your child choose 3 drinks to combine to create his punch recipe. Write each drink on the recipe card, as well as a name for the recipe.

Help your child use the capacities in the chart in part B to write a matching addition problem. Then, have him add to find how much punch his recipe makes.

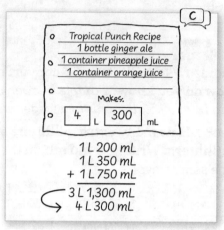

Sample recipe.

Which recipe makes more punch? *Answers will vary.*

Independent Practice and Review

Have your child complete the Lesson 15.6 Practice and Review workbook pages.

Lesson 15.7
Pounds and Ounces

Purpose	Materials
• Review pounds and ounces • Convert pounds and ounces • Multiply and divide to solve weight word problems	• Object that weighs about 1 pound, such as a loaf of bread, can of vegetables, or box of pasta, optional • Object that weighs about 1 ounce, such as a slice of bread, AA battery, or a stack of 5 quarters, optional

Memory Work · **How many ounces equal 1 pound?** *16.*

If you live outside the U.S. and do not use pounds and ounces, you can skip this lesson.

Warm-up (A): Review Pounds and Ounces

In the last few lessons, you learned about metric units for weight and capacity. **What metric units do we use to measure weight?** *Kilograms and grams.* **What metric units do we use to measure capacity?** *Liters and milliliters.*

For the next few lessons, you'll learn about the units used to measure weight and capacity in the U.S. customary system. Today, you'll learn about measuring weight with pounds and ounces.

A slice of bread weighs about an ounce. 16 ounces equal 1 pound. A small loaf of bread usually weighs about one pound. Show your child the printed pictures. Or, have her hold an object that weighs about 1 ounce and an object that weighs about 1 pound.

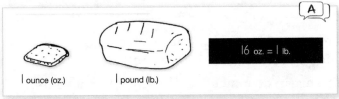

Name each of the following items. Have your child tell whether each item weighs about 1 ounce or 1 pound.

- **Can of vegetables.** *1 pound.*
- **Slice of cheese.** *1 ounce.*
- **One large strawberry.** *1 ounce.*
- **Box of pasta.** *1 pound.*

Activity (B): Multiply or Divide to Convert Pounds and Ounces

Let's complete this chart to show how many ounces equal each number of pounds. Then, we'll use the chart to convert some weights.

How many ounces equal 1 pound? *16.* Write 16 in the first column. **How many ounces equal 2 pounds?** *32.* Write 32 in the next column. If your child's not sure, suggest she add 16 plus 16, either mentally or on paper. Continue in the same way to complete the chart.

Pounds	1	2	3	4	5	6
Ounces	16	32	48	64	80	96

People who make pottery use pounds and ounces to weigh their clay. When they start a new project, they weigh out the correct amount so that their project will be the right size.

These weights may seem surprisingly heavy. Clay loses about one-fourth of its weight once it is fired, so finished pieces weigh much less than the original amount of clay used to make them.

It takes 1 pound 6 ounces of clay to make a small bowl. Let's convert 1 pound 6 ounces to ounces. First, we convert 1 pound to ounces. Do we multiply or divide by 16? *Multiply.* Write "(1 × 16)" to begin an equation.

Then, we add on the extra ounces. Continue the equation as shown. Have your child multiply and add to complete the equation. **1 pound 6 ounces equal how many ounces?** *22 ounces.* Write 22 in the blank.

$$(1 \times 16) + 6 = 22$$

1 lb. 6 oz. = $\boxed{22}$ oz.

Repeat with 3 lb. 5 oz. Encourage your child to look at the chart to find the product of 3 × 16. **3 pounds 5 ounces of clay equal how many ounces?** *53.*

$$(3 \times 16) + 5 = 53$$

3 lb. 5 oz. = $\boxed{53}$ oz.

It takes 40 ounces of clay to make a plate. Let's convert 40 ounces to pounds and ounces. Do we multiply or divide by 16? *Divide.* Write "40 ÷ 16 ="

How many groups of 16 are in 40 ounces? *2.* If your child's not sure, encourage her to look at the chart: **2 pounds equal 32 ounces, so that's as close as we can get to 40 without going over. How many ounces are left over?** *8.* Write "2 R8" as the answer to the division problem. **So, 40 ounces equal 2 pounds 8 ounces.** Write 2 and 8 in the blanks. Use the same process to complete the final exercise.

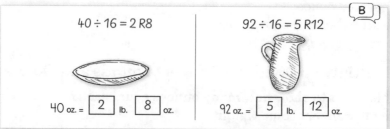

$$40 \div 16 = 2 \text{ R8}$$

40 oz. = $\boxed{2}$ lb. $\boxed{8}$ oz.

$$92 \div 16 = 5 \text{ R12}$$

92 oz. = $\boxed{5}$ lb. $\boxed{12}$ oz.

Activity (C): Multiply and Divide to Solve Word Problems

Read aloud the first word problem: *Keenan combines 7 balls of clay. Each ball of clay weighs 5 ounces. What is the total weight of the clay in ounces?* **How can we find the answer?** *Multiply 7 times 5.* Have your child write and solve the matching equation.

Read aloud the second part of the problem: ***What is the total weight of the clay in pounds and ounces?*** Have your child convert the previous answer to pounds and ounces. Write the answer below the question.

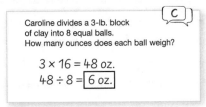

Read aloud the last word problem: ***Caroline divides a 3 pound block of clay into 8 equal balls. How many ounces does each ball weigh?*** **How can we find the answer?** *Divide the weight of the clay by 8.*

What units are you supposed to use for the answer? *Ounces.* **Let's find the weight in ounces before we divide. How many ounces equal 3 pounds?** *48.* Have your child look at the chart in part B if she's not sure.

Now, let's divide 48 ounces by 8. Have your child write and solve the matching equation.

Caroline divides a 3-lb. block
of clay into 8 equal balls.
How many ounces does each ball weigh?

$3 \times 16 = 48$ oz.
$48 \div 8 =$ 6 oz.

Independent Practice and Review

Have your child complete the Lesson 15.7 Practice and Review workbook pages.

Lesson 15.8
Gallons, Quarts, Pints, and Cups

Purpose	Materials
• Review cups, pints, quarts, and gallons • Perform simple conversions between cups, pints, quarts, and gallons • Informally add cups	• Pint, quart, or gallon-sized food items, optional • 1-quart measuring cup, optional • Die

Memory Work • **How many ounces equal 1 pound?** *16.*

Unless you do a lot of canning or cooking, you probably don't need to convert between cups, pints, quarts, and gallons very often in your daily life. This lesson focuses on helping your child understand the difference in magnitude between these units rather than performing calculations with them. If you live outside the U.S. and do not use cups, pints, quarts, and gallons, you can skip this lesson.

Warm-up (A): Review Gallons, Quarts, Pints, and Cups

In the last lesson, you learned about measuring weight with pounds and ounces. Today, you'll learn about measuring capacity with cups, pints, quarts, and gallons. These units are part of the U.S. customary system.

Show your child part A. Use the questions below to discuss your child's real-life experiences with cups, pints, quarts, and gallons.

- **We often use cups to measure ingredients for cooking. Have you ever measured ingredients in cups? What did you measure?** *Answers will vary.*
- **1 pint equals 2 cups.** Describe some real-life examples of pints. For example: **Cream sometimes comes in pints. We buy pints of blueberries at the farmer's market. When I make jam, I can it in pint jars.**
- **1 quart equals 2 pints.** Describe some real-life examples of quarts. For example: **Juice sometimes comes in quart containers. The large boxes of strawberries at the farmer's market are quart boxes. When Grandpa cans peaches, he puts them in quart jars.**
- **1 gallon equals 4 quarts.** Share several real-life examples where your family uses gallons: For example: **Milk comes in gallon containers. When I put gas in the car, I usually put in around 10 gallons. When we painted the living room, we used 1 gallon of paint.**

If you have any pint, quart, or gallon-sized food items in your kitchen or refrigerator, use them to concretely show your child the size of each unit. Dairy products (like milk and cream) often come in these units. Vinegar, sports drinks, and chicken stock are often packaged in pints or quarts.

1 pint equals how many cups? *2.* Write 2 on the top line of the first chart. **2 pints equal how many cups?** *4.* Write 4 on the next line. If your child's not sure, say: **Each pint holds 2 cups, so you can multiply the number of pints times 2 to find the matching number of cups.** Repeat with the other two charts.

Pints	Cups		Quarts	Pints		Gallons	Quarts
1	2		1	2		1	4
2	4		2	4		2	8
3	6		3	6		3	12
4	8		4	8		4	16
5	10		5	10		5	20

Activity (B): Play Race to 1 Gallon

In a minute, we'll use these printed measuring cups to play a game. Point to the 1-quart (4-cup) line on the first measuring cup in part B. If you own a similar 1-quart measuring cup, show it to your child. **If you poured 1 quart of water in this measuring cup, the liquid would come up to the top line.**

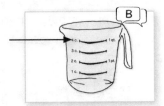

Ask your child the following questions about the measuring cup.

- **If you poured 1 cup of water into this measuring cup, what line would the liquid come up to?** *Child points to the 1-cup line.*
- **If you poured 2 cups of water into this measuring cup, what line would the liquid come up to?** *Child points to the 2-cup line.*
- **If you poured 3 cups of water into this measuring cup, what line would the liquid come up to?** *Child points to the 3-cup line.*
- **If you poured 4 cups of water into this measuring cup, what line would the liquid come up to?** *Child points to the 4-cup line.*
- **If you poured 1 pint of water into this measuring cup, what line would the liquid come up to?** *Child points to the 1-pint (2-cup) line.*
- **If you poured 2 pints of water into this measuring cup, what line would the liquid come up to?** *Child points to the 1-quart (4-cup) line.* **How do you know?** *Sample answer: 2 pints equal 1 quart.*
- **If you poured 1 quart of water into this measuring cup, what line would the liquid come up to?** *Child points to the 1-quart (4-cup) line.*

Each measuring cup holds 1 quart. How many quarts equal 1 gallon? *4.* **So, if you filled all 4 measuring cups, you would have 1 gallon of liquid.** Play Race to 1 Gallon.

Race to 1 Gallon

Materials: Die

Object of the Game: Be the first player to color in all 4 measuring cups.

On your turn, roll the die. Color in the matching number of cups in your measuring cups. Then, tell your total amount of liquid. Use the largest unit possible to describe the amount of liquid.

For example, if you roll a 3, color your first measuring cup to the 3-cup line. **I have 1 pint and 1 cup.**

Or, if you roll a 6, color your first measuring cup to the 4-cup line and the second measuring cup to the 2-cup line (for a total of 6 cups). **I have 1 quart and 1 pint.**

Take turns rolling the die and coloring the matching number of cups in your measuring cups. Always color your measuring cups from left to right and from bottom to top (to match how liquid would fill the measuring cups).

Continue until one player fills all 4 measuring cups and reaches or goes over 1 gallon.

Independent Practice and Review

Have your child complete the Lesson 15.8 Practice and Review workbook pages.

Lesson 15.9
Cups and Fluid Ounces

Purpose	Materials
• Introduce fluid ounces • Convert fluid ounces to cups • Solve capacity word problems	• Container that holds 1 fluid ounce, such as a bottle of vanilla or other flavor extract, optional • 1-cup measuring cup, optional

Memory Work   · **How many ounces equal 1 pound?** *16.*

If your family uses the metric system, you can skip this lesson.

Warm-up (A): Introduce Fluid Ounces

In the last lesson, you learned about cups, pints, quarts, and gallons. We use these units to measure capacity, or how much containers hold. Today, you'll learn about another unit we use to measure capacity in the U.S. customary system: fluid ounces.

A small bottle of vanilla holds about 1 fluid ounce. Show your child the printed container of vanilla or a real container that holds about 1 fluid ounce. **8 fluid ounces equal 1 cup.** Show your child the printed 1-cup measuring cup or a real cup.

1 fluid ounce (fl. oz.)   1 cup (c.)   8 fl. oz. = 1 c.

Fluid ounces are different from the ounces we use to measure weight. Fluid ounces measure capacity, and ounces measure weight.

One fluid ounce of water weighs one ounce, which is why the two units have such similar names. However, this holds true only for water! One fluid ounce of lead weighs much more than one ounce, and one fluid ounce of cotton balls weighs less than one ounce.

Name each of the following items. Have your child tell whether you would measure each attribute in fluid ounces or ounces.

- **How much a water bottle can hold.** *Fluid ounces.*
- **The weight of a water bottle.** *Ounces.*
- **The weight of a coffee mug.** *Ounces.*
- **How much a coffee mug can hold.** *Fluid ounces.*

Activity (B): Multiply or Divide to Convert Cups and Fluid Ounces

Let's complete this chart to show how many fluid ounces equal each number of cups. Then, we'll use the chart to convert some drink capacities.

How many fluid ounces equal 1 cup? *8.* Write 8 in the first column. **How many fluid ounces equal 2 cups?** *16.* Write 16 in the next column. If your child's not sure, suggest she multiply 2 times 8 (since each cup holds 8 fluid ounces). Continue in the same way to complete the chart.

Cups	1	2	3	4	5	6
Fluid Ounces	8	16	24	32	40	48

Drinks at coffee shops and convenience stores are often measured in fluid ounces. Let's find out how many cups are in each of these drinks.

The small coffee cup holds 12 fluid ounces. Let's convert 12 fluid ounces to cups and fluid ounces. Do we multiply or divide by 8? *Divide.*

What's 12 divided by 8? *1, with a remainder of 4.* **So, 12 fluid ounces equal 1 cup 4 fluid ounces.** Write 1 and 4 in the blanks. Repeat with the rest of the drinks.

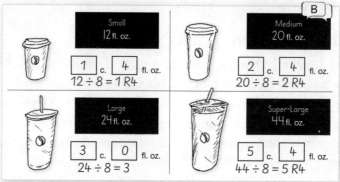

Activity (C): Solve Word Problems

Read aloud the first word problem: ***Cam's mom drank 2 small coffees. How many cups of coffee did she drink?*** **How can we find the answer?** *Sample answers: Add 1 cup 4 fluid ounces plus 1 cup 4 fluid ounces. Multiply 12 fluid ounces by 2 and then convert to cups.* Help your child write and solve an equation to answer the question.

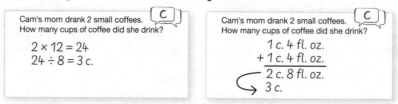

Two possible ways to find the answer.

Read aloud the next word problem: ***How many cups larger is a super-large drink than a small drink?*** **How can we find the answer?** *Sample answers: Subtract 1 cup 4 ounces from 5 cups 4 ounces. Subtract 12 ounces from 44 ounces and then convert to cups.* Help your child write and solve an equation to answer the question.

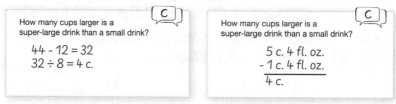

Two possible ways to find the answer.

Independent Practice and Review

Have your child complete the Lesson 15.9 Practice and Review workbook pages.

Lesson 15.10
Enrichment (Optional)

Purpose	Materials
• Practice memory work • Understand weight units in real-life contexts • Measure water in fluid ounces (or milliliters) to find how many glasses of water to drink each day • Summarize what your child has learned and assess your child's progress	• *How Heavy? Wacky Ways to Compare Weight,* written by Mark Andrew Weakland and illustrated by Bill Bolton • Your child's usual drinking glass • Water • *If you use U.S. customary units:* measuring cup marked in fluid ounces • *If you use metric units:* measuring cup marked in milliliters

The enrichment activity requires pouring water. You may want to teach the activity in the kitchen or near a sink.

Warm-up: Review Memory Work

Quiz your child on all memory work through Unit 15. See pages 536-537 for the full list.

Math Picture Book: *How Heavy? Wacky Ways to Compare Weight*

Read *How Heavy? Wacky Ways to Compare Weight,* written by Mark Andrew Weakland and illustrated by Bill Bolton. As you enjoy the book with your child, make sure to read the boxes that tell the weight of each item in standard units, too.

Enrichment Activity: How Many Glasses of Water Should I Drink?

Drinking water helps keep our bodies hydrated and healthy. Doctors say that people who are older than 8 years old generally need about 8 cups of water or other liquids each day.

This recommendation is from the American Academy of Pediatrics. Children's exact hydration needs vary depending on their activity level and weight, and hydrating foods also count towards this total.

8 fluid ounces equal one cup. 8 cups equal how many fluid ounces? *64.* If your child's not sure, suggest he multiply 8 times 8. **So, the recommendation is that you drink 64 fluid ounces of water each day.**

Let's find out how many glasses of water or other liquid you would need to drink to reach that goal. First, we'll find how much water your glass holds. Fill your child's usual drinking glass with water. Then, pour the water into a measuring cup labeled in fluid ounces. **How many fluid ounces of water are in 1 glass of water?** *Answers will vary.* If needed, round to the nearest fluid ounce.

If you do not have a measuring cup marked in fluid ounces, use a 1-cup measuring cup to estimate how many fluid ounces are in the glass of water. For example: **The glass of water fills 1 cup plus a little more, so it's about 10 fluid ounces.**

Have your child divide 64 by the number of fluid ounces in 1 glass of water. For example, if the glass holds 10 fluid ounces: *64 divided by 10 equals 6 with a remainder of 4.* Help him interpret the quotient and remainder in terms of glasses of water. For example: **To drink 64 fluid ounces of water, you would need to drink 6 glasses of water, plus 4 more fluid ounces.**

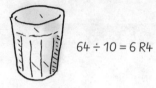

$64 \div 10 = 6 \, R4$

If your glass holds 10 fluid ounces of water, you'd need to drink
6 glasses plus 4 fluid ounces to reach the goal of 64 fluid ounces.

If your child is interested in exploring further, have him keep a record of how much water or other liquid he actually drinks in a day. Compare the final total to the 64-fluid-ounce recommendation.

Metric system option: If your family uses the metric system, use liters and milliliters to complete this activity. Make the following changes:

1. Explain to your child that doctors recommend children drink 1,800 mL of water per day.
2. Use a measuring cup marked in milliliters to measure the capacity of your child's usual drinking glass. Round the answer to the nearest 50 mL.
3. Make a chart like the following to find how many glasses of water he would need to drink to equal or exceed 1,800 milliliters. For example, if your child's usual drinking glass holds 200 mL: **You'd need to drink 9 glasses of liquid to reach 1,800 milliliters.**

Glasses	1	2	3	4	5	6	7	8	9
mL	200	400	600	800	1,000	1,200	1,400	1,600	1,800

Sample chart, based on a glass that holds 200 mL.
Your child should base his chart on the capacity of his glass.

Unit Wrap-Up

Have your child complete the Unit 15 Wrap-Up.

Unit 15 Answer Key

15.1 Practice

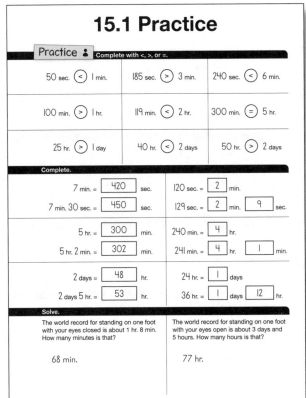

Practice 👤 Complete with <, >, or =.

50 sec. Ⓧ＜ 1 min.	185 sec. Ⓧ＞ 3 min.	240 sec. Ⓧ＜ 6 min.
100 min. Ⓧ＞ 1 hr.	119 min. Ⓧ＜ 2 hr.	300 min. Ⓧ＝ 5 hr.
25 hr. Ⓧ＞ 1 day	40 hr. Ⓧ＜ 2 days	50 hr. Ⓧ＞ 2 days

Complete.

7 min. = **420** sec.	120 sec. = **2** min.
7 min. 30 sec. = **450** sec.	129 sec. = **2** min. **9** sec.
5 hr. = **300** min.	240 min. = **4** hr.
5 hr. 2 min. = **302** min.	241 min. = **4** hr. **1** min.
2 days = **48** hr.	24 hr. = **1** days
2 days 5 hr. = **53** hr.	36 hr. = **1** days **12** hr.

Solve.

The world record for standing on one foot with your eyes closed is about 1 hr. 8 min. How many minutes is that?

68 min.

The world record for standing on one foot with your eyes open is about 3 days and 5 hours. How many hours is that?

77 hr.

15.1 Review

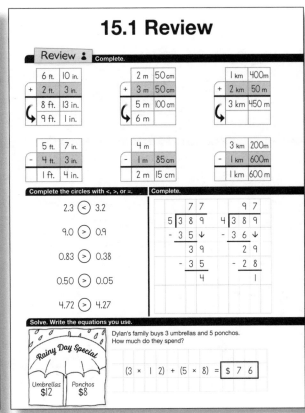

Review 👤 Complete.

Complete the circles with <, >, or =.

2.3 Ⓧ＜ 3.2
9.0 Ⓧ＞ 0.9
0.83 Ⓧ＞ 0.38
0.50 Ⓧ＞ 0.05
4.72 Ⓧ＞ 4.27

Solve. Write the equations you use.

Rainy Day Special
Umbrellas $12   Ponchos $8

Dylan's family buys 3 umbrellas and 5 ponchos. How much do they spend?

(3 × 1 2) + (5 × 8) = **$ 7 6**

15.2 Practice

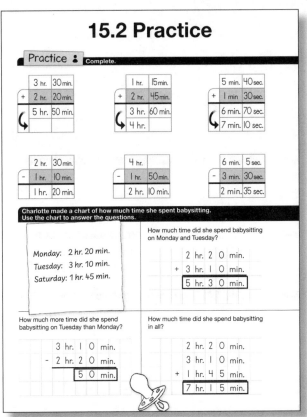

Practice 👤 Complete.

Charlotte made a chart of how much time she spent babysitting. Use the chart to answer the questions.

Monday: 2 hr. 20 min.
Tuesday: 3 hr. 10 min.
Saturday: 1 hr. 45 min.

How much time did she spend babysitting on Monday and Tuesday?

2 hr. 2 0 min.
+ 3 hr. 1 0 min.
5 hr. 3 0 min.

How much more time did she spend babysitting on Tuesday than Monday?

3 hr. 1 0 min.
- 2 hr. 2 0 min.
5 0 min.

How much time did she spend babysitting in all?

2 hr. 2 0 min.
3 hr. 1 0 min.
+ 1 hr. 4 5 min.
7 hr. 1 5 min.

15.2 Review

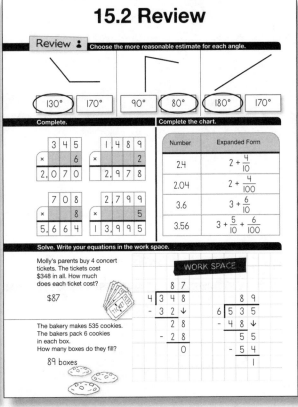

Review 👤 Choose the more reasonable estimate for each angle.

130° ⟨170°⟩   90° ⟨80°⟩   180° ⟨170°⟩

Complete the chart.

Number	Expanded Form
2.4	$2 + \frac{4}{10}$
2.04	$2 + \frac{4}{100}$
3.6	$3 + \frac{6}{10}$
3.56	$3 + \frac{5}{10} + \frac{6}{100}$

Solve. Write your equations in the work space.

Molly's parents buy 4 concert tickets. The tickets cost $348 in all. How much does each ticket cost?

$87

The bakery makes 535 cookies. The bakers pack 6 cookies in each box. How many boxes do they fill?

89 boxes

Unit 15 Answer Key

15.3 Practice

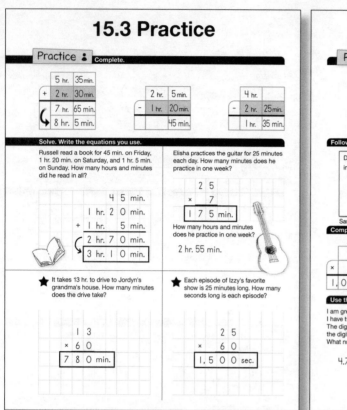

Practice 👤 Complete.

	5 hr.	35 min.
+	2 hr.	30 min.
	7 hr.	65 min.
↻	8 hr.	5 min.

	2 hr.	5 min.
−	1 hr.	20 min.
		45 min.

	4 hr.	
−	2 hr.	25 min.
	1 hr.	35 min.

Solve. Write the equations you use.

Russell read a book for 45 min. on Friday, 1 hr. 20 min. on Saturday, and 1 hr. 5 min. on Sunday. How many hours and minutes did he read in all?

		4	5 min.
	1 hr.	2	0 min.
+	1 hr.		5 min.
↻	2 hr.	7	0 min.
	3 hr.	1	0 min.

Elisha practices the guitar for 25 minutes each day. How many minutes does he practice in one week?

		2	5
×			7
	1	7	5 min.

How many hours and minutes does he practice in one week?

2 hr. 55 min.

★ It takes 13 hr. to drive to Jordyn's grandma's house. How many minutes does the drive take?

		1	3
×		6	0
	7	8	0 min.

★ Each episode of Izzy's favorite show is 25 minutes long. How many seconds long is each episode?

			2	5
×			6	0
	1	5	0	0 sec.

15.3 Review

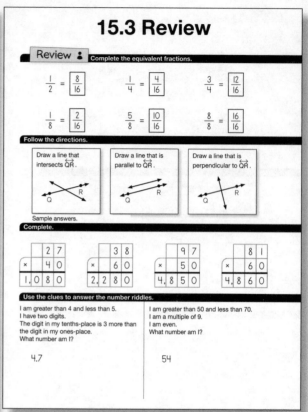

Review 👤 Complete the equivalent fractions.

$$\frac{1}{2} = \frac{8}{16} \qquad \frac{1}{4} = \frac{4}{16} \qquad \frac{3}{4} = \frac{12}{16}$$

$$\frac{1}{8} = \frac{2}{16} \qquad \frac{5}{8} = \frac{10}{16} \qquad \frac{8}{8} = \frac{16}{16}$$

Follow the directions.

Draw a line that intersects $\overleftrightarrow{QR}$.	Draw a line that is parallel to $\overleftrightarrow{QR}$.	Draw a line that is perpendicular to $\overleftrightarrow{QR}$.

Sample answers.

Complete.

		2	7
×		4	0
1,	0	8	0

		3	8
×		6	0
2,	2	8	0

		9	7
×		5	0
4,	8	5	0

		8	1
×		6	0
4,	8	6	0

Use the clues to answer the number riddles.

I am greater than 4 and less than 5.
I have two digits.
The digit in my tenths-place is 3 more than the digit in my ones-place.
What number am I?

4.7

I am greater than 50 and less than 70.
I am a multiple of 9.
I am even.
What number am I?

54

15.4 Practice

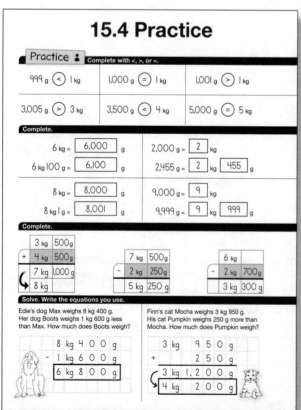

Practice 👤 Complete with <, >, or =.

$999\,g \;<\; 1\,kg \qquad 1,000\,g \;=\; 1\,kg \qquad 1,001\,g \;>\; 1\,kg$

$3,005\,g \;>\; 3\,kg \qquad 3,500\,g \;<\; 4\,kg \qquad 5,000\,g \;=\; 5\,kg$

Complete.

$6\,kg = \boxed{6,000}\ g \qquad 2,000\,g = \boxed{2}\ kg$

$6\,kg\,100\,g = \boxed{6,100}\ g \qquad 2,455\,g = \boxed{2}\ kg\ \boxed{455}\ g$

$8\,kg = \boxed{8,000}\ g \qquad 9,000\,g = \boxed{9}\ kg$

$8\,kg\,1\,g = \boxed{8,001}\ g \qquad 9,999\,g = \boxed{9}\ kg\ \boxed{999}\ g$

Complete.

	3 kg	500 g
+	4 kg	500 g
	7 kg	1,000 g
↻	8 kg	

	7 kg	500 g
−	2 kg	250 g
	5 kg	250 g

	6 kg	
−	2 kg	700 g
	3 kg	300 g

Solve. Write the equations you use.

Edie's dog Max weighs 8 kg 400 g. Her dog Boots weighs 1 kg 600 g less than Max. How much does Boots weigh?

	8 kg	4	0	0 g
−	1 kg	6	0	0 g
	6 kg	8	0	0 g

Finn's cat Mocha weighs 3 kg 950 g. His cat Pumpkin weighs 250 g more than Mocha. How much does Pumpkin weigh?

	3 kg		9	5	0 g
+			2	5	0 g
↻	3 kg	1,	2	0	0 g
	4 kg		2	0	0 g

15.4 Review

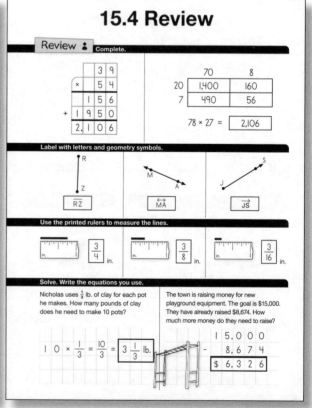

Review 👤 Complete.

		3	9
×		5	4
	1	5	6
+	1	9	5	0
	2,	1	0	6

	70	8
20	1,400	160
7	490	56

$78 \times 27 = \boxed{2,106}$

Label with letters and geometry symbols.

$\overline{RZ} \qquad \overleftrightarrow{MA} \qquad \overrightarrow{JS}$

Use the printed rulers to measure the lines.

$\frac{3}{4}$ in.　$\frac{3}{8}$ in.　$\frac{3}{16}$ in.

Solve. Write the equations you use.

Nicholas uses $\frac{1}{3}$ lb. of clay for each pot he makes. How many pounds of clay does he need to make 10 pots?

$10 \times \frac{1}{3} = \frac{10}{3} = 3\frac{1}{3}$ lb.

The town is raising money for new playground equipment. The goal is $15,000. They have already raised $8,674. How much more money do they need to raise?

	1	5,	0	0	0
−		8,	6	7	4
$		6,	3	2	6

Unit 15 Answer Key

15.5 Practice

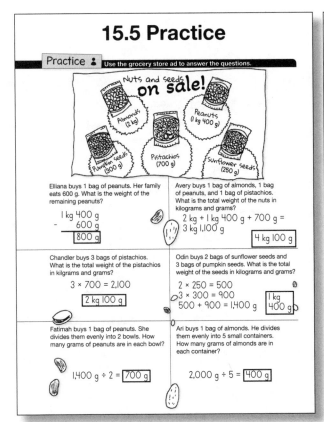

Practice 👤 Use the grocery store ad to answer the questions.

Nuts and seeds **on sale!**

Almonds (2 kg)

Peanuts (1 kg 400 g)

Pumpkin seeds (300 g)

Pistachios (700 g)

Sunflower seeds (250 g)

Elliana buys 1 bag of peanuts. Her family eats 600 g. What is the weight of the remaining peanuts?

1 kg 400 g
−   600 g
     800 g

Avery buys 1 bag of almonds, 1 bag of peanuts, and 1 bag of pistachios. What is the total weight of the nuts in kilograms and grams?

2 kg + 1 kg 400 g + 700 g =
3 kg 1,100 g   **4 kg 100 g**

Chandler buys 3 bags of pistachios. What is the total weight of the pistachios in kilgrams and grams?

3 × 700 = 2,100   **2 kg 100 g**

Odin buys 2 bags of sunflower seeds and 3 bags of pumpkin seeds. What is the total weight of the seeds in kilograms and grams?

2 × 250 = 500
3 × 300 = 900   **1 kg**
500 + 900 = 1,400 g **400 g**

Fatimah buys 1 bag of peanuts. She divides them evenly into 2 bowls. How many grams of peanuts are in each bowl?

1,400 g ÷ 2 = **700 g**

Ari buys 1 bag of almonds. He divides them evenly into 5 small containers. How many grams of almonds are in each container?

2,000 g ÷ 5 = **400 g**

15.5 Review

Review 👤 Label the numbers on the number line.

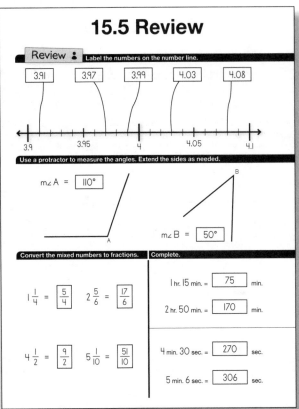

| 3.91 | 3.97 | 3.99 | 4.03 | 4.08 |

3.9   3.95   4   4.05   4.1

Use a protractor to measure the angles. Extend the sides as needed.

m∠ A = **110°**

m∠ B = **50°**

Convert the mixed numbers to fractions.   **Complete.**

$1\frac{1}{4} = \frac{5}{4}$ $2\frac{5}{6} = \frac{17}{6}$

$4\frac{1}{2} = \frac{9}{2}$ $5\frac{1}{10} = \frac{51}{10}$

1 hr. 15 min. = **75** min.

2 hr. 50 min. = **170** min.

4 min. 30 sec. = **270** sec.

5 min. 6 sec. = **306** sec.

15.6 Practice

Practice 👤 Complete.

3 L = **3,000** mL   4,000 mL = **4** L

3 L 250 mL = **3,250** mL   4,500 mL = **4** L **500** mL

9 L = **9,000** mL   8,000 mL = **8** L

9 L 990 mL = **9,990** mL   8,005 mL = **8** L **5** mL

Solve. Write the equations you use.

Mimi buys 1 L of apple juice and 850 mL of grape juice. How many milliliters of juice does she buy in all?

    1,000
 +   850
  1,850 mL

Zeke buys 1 L of grapefruit juice. He drinks 450 mL. How many milliliters of juice are left?

    1,000
 −   450
    550 mL

⭐ Fatimah buys 2 liters of cola. She pours the cola into 8 cups, and she pours the same amount into each cup. How many milliliters are in each cup?

       250
8) 2,000
  − 16 ↓
      40
    − 40 ↓
       00

    250 mL

⭐ William buys 6 cans of sparkling water. Each can holds 350 mL. How many milliliters of sparkling water does he buy?

      350
 ×   6
  2,100 mL

How many liters and milliliters does he buy?

2 L 100 mL

15.6 Review

Review 👤 Complete the equivalent fractions.

$\frac{2}{3} = \frac{4}{6}$ $\frac{2}{3} = \frac{6}{9}$ $\frac{2}{3} = \frac{8}{12}$

$\frac{1}{4} = \frac{2}{8}$ $\frac{1}{4} = \frac{5}{20}$ $\frac{1}{4} = \frac{10}{40}$

Connect each number to its dot on the number line.

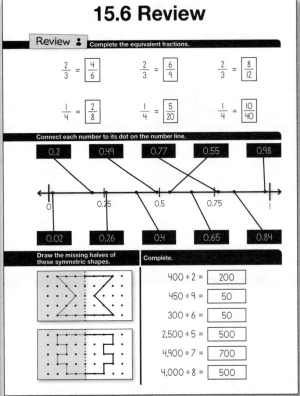

| 0.2 | 0.49 | 0.77 | 0.55 | 0.98 |

0   0.25   0.5   0.75   1

| 0.02 | 0.26 | 0.4 | 0.65 | 0.84 |

Draw the missing halves of these symmetric shapes.   **Complete.**

400 ÷ 2 = **200**

450 ÷ 9 = **50**

300 ÷ 6 = **50**

2,500 ÷ 5 = **500**

4,900 ÷ 7 = **700**

4,000 ÷ 8 = **500**

Unit 15 Answer Key

15.7 Practice

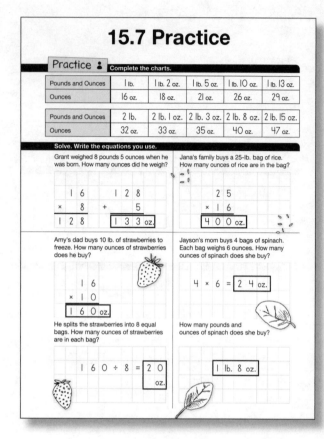

Practice — Complete the charts.

Pounds and Ounces	1 lb.	1 lb. 2 oz.	1 lb. 5 oz.	1 lb. 10 oz.	1 lb. 13 oz.
Ounces	16 oz.	18 oz.	21 oz.	26 oz.	29 oz.

Pounds and Ounces	2 lb.	2 lb. 1 oz.	2 lb. 3 oz.	2 lb. 8 oz.	2 lb. 15 oz.
Ounces	32 oz.	33 oz.	35 oz.	40 oz.	47 oz.

Solve. Write the equations you use.

Grant weighed 8 pounds 5 ounces when he was born. How many ounces did he weigh?

16 × 8 = 128   128 + 5 = 133 oz.

Jana's family buys a 25-lb. bag of rice. How many ounces of rice are in the bag?

25 × 16 = 400 oz.

Amy's dad buys 10 lb. of strawberries to freeze. How many ounces of strawberries does he buy?

16 × 10 = 160 oz.

Jayson's mom buys 4 bags of spinach. Each bag weighs 6 ounces. How many ounces of spinach does she buy?

4 × 6 = 24 oz.

He splits the strawberries into 8 equal bags. How many ounces of strawberries are in each bag?

160 ÷ 8 = 20 oz.

How many pounds and ounces of spinach does she buy?

1 lb. 8 oz.

15.7 Review

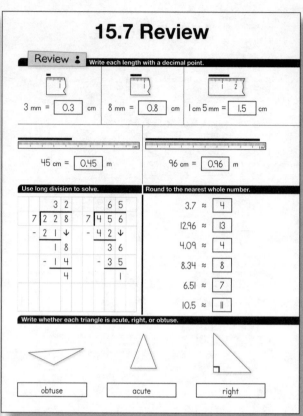

Review — Write each length with a decimal point.

3 mm = 0.3 cm   8 mm = 0.8 cm   1 cm 5 mm = 1.5 cm

45 cm = 0.45 m   96 cm = 0.96 m

Use long division to solve.

32
7)228
-21↓
  18
- 14
   4

65
7)456
-42↓
  36
- 35
   1

Round to the nearest whole number.

3.7 ≈ 4

12.96 ≈ 13

4.09 ≈ 4

8.34 ≈ 8

6.51 ≈ 7

10.5 ≈ 11

Write whether each triangle is acute, right, or obtuse.

obtuse   acute   right

15.8 Practice

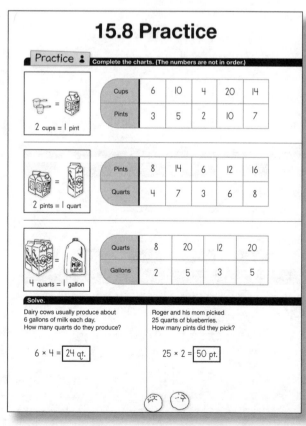

Practice — Complete the charts. (The numbers are not in order.)

2 cups = 1 pint

Cups	6	10	4	20	14
Pints	3	5	2	10	7

2 pints = 1 quart

Pints	8	14	6	12	16
Quarts	4	7	3	6	8

4 quarts = 1 gallon

Quarts	8	20	12	20
Gallons	2	5	3	5

Solve.

Dairy cows usually produce about 6 gallons of milk each day. How many quarts do they produce?

6 × 4 = 24 qt.

Roger and his mom picked 25 quarts of blueberries. How many pints did they pick?

25 × 2 = 50 pt.

15.8 Review

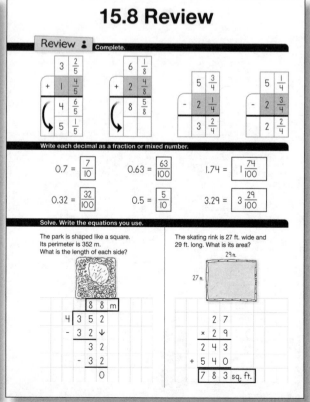

Review — Complete.

$3\frac{2}{5}$
$+ 1\frac{4}{5}$
$4\frac{6}{5}$
$5\frac{1}{5}$

$6\frac{1}{8}$
$+ 2\frac{4}{8}$
$8\frac{5}{8}$

$5\frac{3}{4}$
$- 2\frac{1}{4}$
$3\frac{2}{4}$

$5\frac{1}{4}$
$- 2\frac{3}{4}$
$2\frac{2}{4}$

Write each decimal as a fraction or mixed number.

$0.7 = \frac{7}{10}$ $0.63 = \frac{63}{100}$ $1.74 = 1\frac{74}{100}$

$0.32 = \frac{32}{100}$ $0.5 = \frac{5}{10}$ $3.29 = 3\frac{29}{100}$

Solve. Write the equations you use.

The park is shaped like a square. Its perimeter is 352 m. What is the length of each side?

88 m

88
4)352
-32↓
  32
- 32
   0

The skating rink is 27 ft. wide and 29 ft. long. What is its area?

29 ft.
27 ft.

27
× 29
243
+ 540
783 sq. ft.

Unit 15 Answer Key

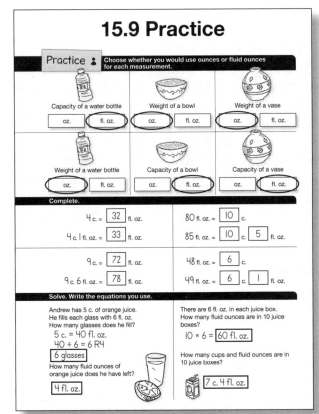

15.9 Practice

Practice 👤 Choose whether you would use ounces or fluid ounces for each measurement.

Capacity of a water bottle — oz. / **(fl. oz.)**
Weight of a bowl — **(oz.)** / fl. oz.
Weight of a vase — **(oz.)** / fl. oz.

Weight of a water bottle — **(oz.)** / fl. oz.
Capacity of a bowl — oz. / **(fl. oz.)**
Capacity of a vase — oz. / **(fl. oz.)**

Complete.

4 c. = **32** fl. oz.
4 c. 1 fl. oz. = **33** fl. oz.
9 c. = **72** fl. oz.
9 c. 6 fl. oz. = **78** fl. oz.

80 fl. oz. = **10** c.
85 fl. oz. = **10** c. **5** fl. oz.
48 fl. oz. = **6** c.
49 fl. oz. = **6** c. **1** fl. oz.

Solve. Write the equations you use.

Andrew has 5 c. of orange juice. He fills each glass with 6 fl. oz. How many glasses does he fill?
5 c. = **40 fl. oz.**
40 ÷ 6 = 6 R4
6 glasses
How many fluid ounces of orange juice does he have left?
4 fl. oz.

There are 6 fl. oz. in each juice box. How many fluid ounces are in 10 juice boxes?
10 × 6 = **60 fl. oz.**

How many cups and fluid ounces are in 10 juice boxes?
7 c. 4 fl. oz.

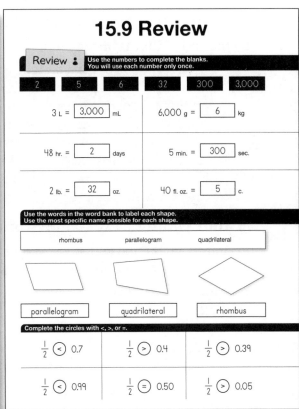

15.9 Review

Review 👤 Use the numbers to complete the blanks. You will use each number only once.

| 2 | 5 | 6 | 32 | 300 | 3,000 |

3 L = **3,000** mL   6,000 g = **6** kg

48 hr. = **2** days   5 min. = **300** sec.

2 lb. = **32** oz.   40 fl. oz. = **5** c.

Use the words in the word bank to label each shape. Use the most specific name possible for each shape.

| rhombus | parallelogram | quadrilateral |

parallelogram   **quadrilateral**   **rhombus**

Complete the circles with <, >, or =.

$\frac{1}{2}$ **(<)** 0.7 $\frac{1}{2}$ **(>)** 0.4 $\frac{1}{2}$ **(>)** 0.39

$\frac{1}{2}$ **(<)** 0.99 $\frac{1}{2}$ **(=)** 0.50 $\frac{1}{2}$ **(>)** 0.05

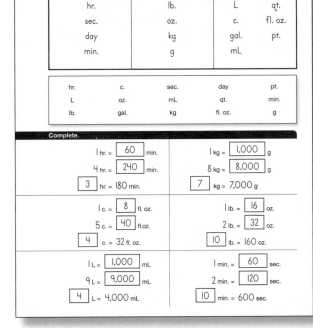

15.10 Unit Wrap-Up A

Unit Wrap-Up 👤 Write each unit in the correct part of the chart.

Units of Time	Units of Weight	Units of Capacity	
hr.	lb.	L	qt.
sec.	oz.	c.	fl. oz.
day	kg	gal.	pt.
min.	g	mL	

hr.	c.	sec.	day	pt.
L	oz.	mL	qt.	min.
lb.	gal.	kg	fl. oz.	g

Complete.

1 hr. = **60** min.
4 hr. = **240** min.
3 hr. = 180 min.

1 kg = **1,000** g
8 kg = **8,000** g
7 kg = 7,000 g

1 c. = **8** fl. oz.
5 c. = **40** fl.oz.
4 c. = 32 fl. oz.

1 lb. = **16** oz.
2 lb. = **32** oz.
10 lb. = 160 oz.

1 L = **1,000** mL
9 L = **9,000** mL
4 L = 4,000 mL

1 min. = **60** sec.
2 min. = **120** sec.
10 min. = 600 sec.

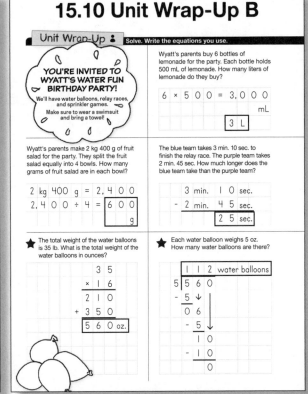

15.10 Unit Wrap-Up B

Unit Wrap-Up 👤 Solve. Write the equations you use.

YOU'RE INVITED TO WYATT'S WATER FUN BIRTHDAY PARTY!
We'll have water balloons, relay races, and sprinkler games. Make sure to wear a swimsuit and bring a towel!

Wyatt's parents buy 6 bottles of lemonade for the party. Each bottle holds 500 mL of lemonade. How many liters of lemonade do they buy?

6 × 500 = 3,000 mL
3 L

Wyatt's parents make 2 kg 400 g of fruit salad for the party. They split the fruit salad equally into 4 bowls. How many grams of fruit salad are in each bowl?

2 kg 400 g = 2,400
2,400 ÷ 4 = **600** g

The blue team takes 3 min. 10 sec. to finish the relay race. The purple team takes 2 min. 45 sec. How much longer does the blue team take than the purple team?

```
  3 min. 10 sec.
- 2 min. 45 sec.
      25 sec.
```

⭐ The total weight of the water balloons is 35 lb. What is the total weight of the water balloons in ounces?

```
    3 5
  × 1 6
  2 1 0
+ 3 5 0
  5 6 0 oz.
```

⭐ Each water balloon weighs 5 oz. How many water balloons are there?

```
      1 1 2 water balloons
5 | 5 6 0
  - 5 ↓
    0 6
    - 5
      1 0
    - 1 0
        0
```

Unit 15 Checkpoint

What to Expect at the End of Unit 15

By the end of Unit 15, most children will be able to do the following:

- Convert units of time, weight, and capacity, within both the metric system and the U.S. customary system. Some children will occasionally have trouble knowing whether to multiply or divide to perform the conversions.
- Add and subtract compound units for time, weight, and capacity. Some children will still need help, especially with subtraction problems that require trading.
- Solve two-step word problems that involve converting time, weight, and capacity units. Many children will still need help with these problems, especially ones that involve multiplication or division.

Is Your Child Ready to Move on?

In Unit 16, your child will study graphs and data. You will also review what your child has learned and celebrate completing the book!

Your child does not need to have fully mastered measurement conversions before moving on to Unit 16.

Unit 16
Line Plots and Averages

Overview

Your child will learn how to create and interpret line plots with both whole number and fractional increments. He'll also learn how to find the average for a small data set. Then, in the final lessons in this unit, you and your child will review the major concepts and skills he has learned and celebrate completing the book.

What Your Child Will Learn

In this unit, your child will learn to:

- Create line plots with whole number or fractional increments
- Interpret line plots
- Find the average for a small data set

Lesson List

Lesson 16.1	Line Plots	Lesson 16.6	Review Multiplication and Division
Lesson 16.2	Line Plots with Fractions		
Lesson 16.3	Find Averages, Part 1	Lesson 16.7	Review Fractions and Decimals
Lesson 16.4	Find Averages, Part 2	Lesson 16.8	Review Geometry, Measurement, and Data
Lesson 16.5	Enrichment (Optional)		

The optional enrichment lesson for this unit is in the middle of the unit so you can wrap up your study of line plots and averages before moving to the end-of-year review lessons.

Extra Materials Needed for Unit 16

- 12 slips of paper
- Paper clip
- Colored pencils or markers
- For optional Enrichment Lesson:
  - × *Show and Tell! Great Graphs and Smart Charts: An Introduction to Infographics,* written by Stuart J. Murphy and illustrated by Teresa Bellón. Charlesbridge, 2022.

**Teaching Math with Confidence:
How Are Line Plots Different From Bar Graphs?**

In earlier grades, your child learned how to draw and interpret bar graphs. Bar graphs display data using bars of different heights, and each bar represents the number of data points in that category. The categories are listed along the horizontal axis and the scale for measuring the bars is marked along the vertical axis (or sometimes vice versa).

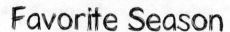

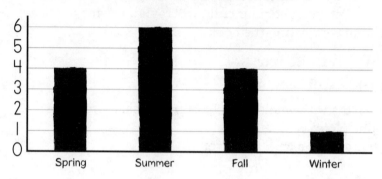

This bar graph has four categories along its horizontal axis (Spring, Summer, Fall, and Winter).
The tick marks along the vertical axis tell the number of people that chose each season as their favorite.

In this unit, your child will learn how to draw and interpret line plots. Line plots use part of the number line as their horizontal axis. Each data point is plotted with an X, and the number of Xs above each tick mark tells the number of data points corresponding to that number.

In this line plot, each X stands for one soccer player.
4 soccer players scored 0 goals, so there are 4 Xs above the tick mark for 0.

Both types of graphs allow you to compare the heights of the bars or Xs at a glance. For example, in the Favorite Season bar graph, you can immediately tell that more people chose summer than any other season, and that the fewest number of people chose winter. In the Goals Scored by Each Player line plot, you can immediately tell that the most children scored 0 goals, and that no children scored 5 goals.

Underneath these surface similarities, line plots are quite different from bar graphs. Line plots represent numerical data rather than categorical data, so they allow you to analyze the data beyond simple comparisons. In this unit, your child will learn to find the average (or mean) for data represented in line plots. In future grades, he'll learn how to calculate summary statistics (such as median, mode, and range) for data in line plots, and he'll learn how to draw conclusions based on the shape of the data in line plots.

Lesson 16.1
Line Plots

Purpose	Materials
• Practice mental math • Interpret and draw line plots	• None

Memory Work   · **How many fluid ounces equal 1 cup?** *8.*

Warm-up (A): Practice Mental Math

Have your child solve the following mental math problems.

- 300 × 2 = *600*
- 300 × 5 = *1,500*
- 300 × 8 = *2,400*
- 300 × 10 = *3,000*

- 300 ÷ 3 = *100*
- 300 ÷ 2 = *150*
- 300 ÷ 5 = *60*
- 300 ÷ 6 = *50*

If your child has trouble keeping the numbers in her head, write the problems horizontally on a piece of scrap paper.

Activity (A): Interpret a Line Plot

We're beginning a short unit on line plots and averages today. We use line plots to organize information and make it easier to understand, just like bar graphs.

You learned about bar graphs when you were younger. What are three things you remember about bar graphs? *Sample answer: They use bars to show information. They have a horizontal axis and a vertical axis. They can be horizontal or vertical.*

Today, you'll learn about line plots. Show your child the line plot in part A. **This line plot shows how many goals each player on the Falcons scored this year.**

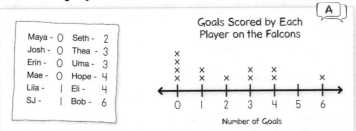

Each X on the line plot stands for one player. Four players scored 0 goals, so there are 4 Xs above 0. Go through each number from 1 to 6 and have your child identify how many children scored each number of goals.

How is this line plot similar to a bar graph? *Sample answer: Both have a title and horizontal axis. The height of the Xs tells you how many players scored each number of goals, just like the height of the bars in bar graphs tells you information.*

How is this line plot different from a bar graph? *Sample answer: It uses Xs instead of bars to show the amounts. It doesn't have a vertical axis. There are tick marks along the horizontal axis.*

Line plots use part of the number line as their horizontal axis. That's why there are tick marks on the line and arrows at either end of the line. Point to the arrows at either end of the line plot.

See the Unit 16 **Teaching Math with Confidence** for more on how line plots are different from bar graphs.

Cover the list of soccer players with your hand or a piece of scrap paper. **The line plot summarizes the information in the list, so we can answer these questions using just the line plot.** Read each question aloud. Help your child use the line plot to answer the questions. Allow her to peek at the list of players if needed.

What's the greatest number of goals scored by a player?	How many players scored fewer than 3 goals?	How many players are on the team?
6	7	12
What's the fewest number of goals scored by a player?	How many players scored 3 or more goals?	How many goals did the team score in all?
0	5	24

Activity (B): Make and Interpret a Line Plot

Show your child the list in part B. **This list shows how many goals each player on the Eagles scored this year. We call numbers like this** *data.*

Let's make a line plot to show how many goals each player on the Eagles scored. Jay scored 4 goals. I'll draw an X above the 4 to stand for Jay. Draw a small X above the 4 on the line plot. **I'll cross out Jay so I know I've already drawn the matching X for him.** Cross out Jay.

Have your child draw Xs on the line plot for the rest of the data. Encourage her to draw each X the same size.

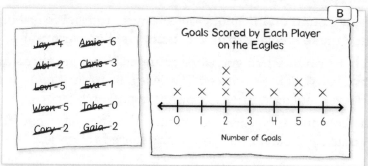

Cover the list of children with your hand or a piece of scrap paper. Then, have your child use the line plot to answer the questions.

What's the greatest number of goals scored by a player?	How many players scored fewer than 3 goals?	How many players are on the team?
6	5	10
What's the fewest number of goals scored by a player?	How many players scored 3 or more goals?	How many goals did the team score in all?
0	5	30

Look back at both line plots with your child. **If these two teams played each other, which team do you think would win?** *Sample answers: The Eagles have more players that scored 5 or 6 goals, so they might win. The Falcons have a lot of players who scored only 0 or 1 goals, so they might not score many goals.*

Independent Practice and Review

Have your child complete the Lesson 16.1 Practice and Review workbook pages.

Lesson 16.2
Line Plots with Fractions

Purpose	Materials
• Practice mental math • Interpret and draw line plots with fractional increments • Use line plots to draw conclusions about two data sets	• None

Memory Work
- **Name 4 factors of 6.** *1, 2, 3, 6.*
- **Name 4 multiples of 6.** *Sample answers: 12, 30, 36, 60.*

Warm-up: Practice Mental Math

Have your child solve the following mental math problems.

- 40 × 2 = *80*
- 40 × 20 = *800*
- 60 × 5 = *300*
- 60 × 50 = *3,000*

- 90 × 6 = *540*
- 90 × 60 = *5,400*
- 80 × 8 = *640*
- 80 × 80 = *6,400*

Activity (A): Interpret a Line Plot about Plant Heights

In the last lesson, you learned about line plots. All of the line plots had whole numbers on their number lines. In this lesson, you'll learn how to interpret and draw line plots with fractions or mixed numbers on their number lines.

Scientists often use line plots to help analyze data from experiments. We'll use line plots to investigate whether bean plants grow taller when they grow in the sun versus when they grow in the dark.

Do you predict the bean plants grew taller in the sun or the dark? *Sample answer: The sun.* **Why?** *Sample answer: Plants need sun to grow.*

First, we'll look at the line plot for the plants that grew in the sun. Each X stands for one plant. Point to the 3-inch-mark on the first line plot. **There are 2 Xs above 3 inches, so that means that 2 plants grew 3 inches high.** Go through each number on the line plot and have your child identify how many plants grew to that height.

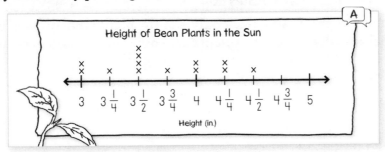

Activity (B): Make a Line Plot about Plant Heights

Point to the data in part B. **This chart tells the heights of the plants that grew in the dark. We'll use the data to make a line plot.**

The first number in the list is 4 and one-half. That means that one plant grew 4 and one-half inches tall. I'll draw an X on the line plot to stand for that plant. Draw a small X above 4 1/2 on the line plot. Cross out the 4 1/2 in the chart. Have your child draw Xs for the rest of the data on the line plot in the same way.

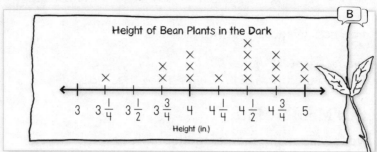

Then, go through each number on the line plot and have your child identify how many plants grew to that height.

Activity (C): Use Line Plots to Draw Conclusions about Plant Heights

Before we interpret the results, let's summarize the data for both sets of plants. Help your child use the line plots from part A and part B to complete the blanks in part C.

Plants in the Sun		Plants in the Dark	
Height of tallest plant	$4\frac{1}{2}$ in.	Height of tallest plant	5 in.
Height of shortest plant	3 in.	Height of shortest plant	$3\frac{1}{4}$ in.
Number of plants shorter than 4 in.	8	Number of plants shorter than 4 in.	3
Number of plants at least 4 in. tall	5	Number of plants at least 4 in. tall	13
Total number of plants	13	Total number of plants	16

Which plants seem to grow taller, the plants that grew in the sun or the plants that grew in the dark? *The plants that grew in the dark.* **How do you know?** *Sample answers: The plants that grew in the dark have more Xs from 4 to 5 inches than the plants that grew in the light. Most of the plants that grew in the dark were at least 4 inches tall, but only a few of the plants that grew in the sun were at least 4 inches tall.*

The summary charts in part C show that only 5 of the plants that grew in the sun grew to be at least 4 inches tall, but 13 of the plants that grew in the dark grew to be at least 4 inches tall.

We can see this information visually in the line plots, too. The Xs for the plants that grew in the dark are mostly to the right of the 4-inch mark, but the Xs for the plants that grew in the sun are mostly to the left of the 4-inch mark.

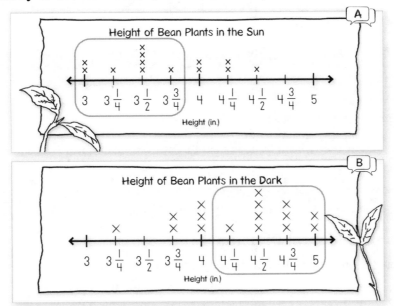

Are you surprised by the results? *Answers will vary.* When a plant grows, it uses the energy from its seed to grow until it reaches light. Then, it uses the energy from the light to make leaves and grow a strong stem.

A plant that grows in the dark never reaches light. Instead of making leaves and growing a strong stem, it puts all its energy into growing taller. Once it uses up the energy from the seed, the plant dies. Plants that grow in the dark are taller than plants that grow in the sun, but they're not as healthy.

Independent Practice and Review

Have your child complete the Lesson 16.2 Practice and Review workbook pages.

Lesson 16.3
Find Averages, Part 1

Purpose	Materials
• Practice mental math • Introduce averages • Find the average of a set of numbers	• None

Memory Work · **How many fluid ounces equal 1 cup?** *8.*

This lesson and the next provide a simple introduction to finding the average of the numbers in a small data set. In future grades, your child will learn more sophisticated ways to analyze data.

Warm-up: Practice Mental Division

Ask your child the following mental division problems.

- $36 \div 12 = 3$
- $36 \div 3 = 12$
- $36 \div 7 = 5\ R1$
- $36 \div 5 = 7\ R1$

- $36 \div 8 = 4\ R4$
- $36 \div 4 = 9$
- $36 \div 10 = 3\ R6$

Activity (A): Introduce Averages

Today, you'll learn how to find averages. We often use the word average in everyday life. For example, we might say that the average weight of a cat is 4 kilograms. Does that mean that every cat weighs exactly 4 kilograms? *No.* It just means that many cats weigh around 4 kilograms. Some cats weigh more, and some cats weigh less.

Or, we might say that the average high temperature for our area in May is 68 degrees Fahrenheit. Does that mean that the high temperature will be exactly 68 degrees each day? *No.* Some days may be much hotter, and some days may be much colder.

Show your child the line plots in part A. **In Lesson 16.1, you answered questions about the data shown in these line plots. One way to compare the two teams is to look at the line plots. We saw in Lesson 16.1 that the Eagles have more players that score a lot of goals than the Falcons.**

Another way to compare the teams is to find the average number of goals scored by the players on each team. Finding the average number of goals is like sharing the total number of goals equally with everyone on the team. To find the average, we first find the total number of goals the team scored. Then, we divide the total number of goals by the number of players on the team.

First, let's find the average number of goals for the players on the Falcons. The Falcons scored 24 goals in all, and they have 12 players on the team. Write "24 ÷ 12 =" below the chart. **What's 24 divided by 12?** *2.* Write 2 to complete the equation, and write 2 in the blank. The average number of goals per player is 2.

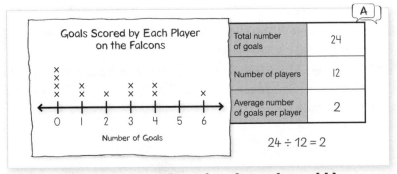

If every player had scored the same number of goals, each would have scored 2 goals.

Does that mean every player scored 2 goals? *No.* Some players scored more than 2 goals, and some players scored less than 2 goals. But the average number of goals that each player scored was 2.

Next, let's find the average number of goals for the players on the Eagles. The Eagles scored 30 goals in all, and they have 10 players on the team. Write "30 ÷ 10 =" below the chart. **What's 30 divided by 10?** *3.* Write 3 to complete the equation.

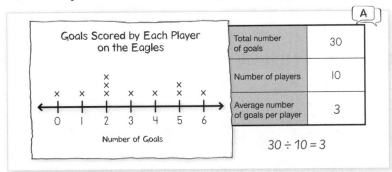

For the Eagles, the average number of goals that each player scored is 3. If every player had scored the same number of goals, each would have scored 3 goals.

Which team's players had a higher average number of goals? *The Eagles.* Over the course of the season, the Eagles scored an average of 3 goals per player. The Falcons scored an average of 2 goals per player.

Activity (B): Find the Average Number of Children Per Family

We can use the same approach to find the average for other data sets, too.

Show your child part B. **A fourth-grader did a survey of her friends. She asked each person how many children are in their family.**

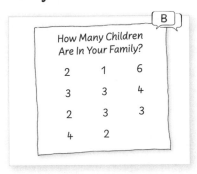

To find the average, we'll first find the total number of children. Then, we'll divide the total number of children by the number of families. **What is the total number of children?** *33.* If your child's not sure, suggest she add up the number of children in each family. Write 33 in the blank.

How many families are represented in the survey? *11.* If your child's not sure, say: **Each number stands for one family's response. So, count the number of numbers to see how many families there are.** Write 11 in the blank.

What equation tells the average number of children per family? *33 divided by 11.* Write "33 ÷ 11 =" and have your child complete the equation: 33 ÷ 11 = 3. **So, what's the average number of children per family?** *3.*

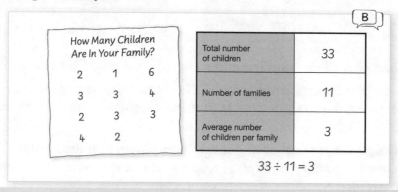

In the optional enrichment activity in Lesson 16.5, your child will have the chance to conduct her own survey and find the average of the results.

Independent Practice and Review

Have your child complete the Lesson 16.3 Practice and Review workbook pages.

Lesson 16.4
Find Averages, Part 2

Purpose	Materials
• Practice mental division • Find and compare averages	• Paper clip

Memory Work
- **What's zero times any number?** *Zero.*
- **What's zero divided by any other number?** *Zero.*
- **What's any number divided by zero?** *Undefined.*

The optional enrichment activity in Lesson 16.5 involves conducting a survey and making a line plot of the results. If you'd like to complete Lesson 16.5 in one day, have your child conduct the survey before you teach Lesson 16.5. See Lesson 16.5 for directions on how to help your child choose a survey question and conduct the survey.

Warm-up: Practice Mental Division with Small Numbers

Ask your child the following mental division problems.

- $8 \div 5 = 1\,R3$
- $5 \div 8 = 0\,R5$
- $9 \div 7 = 1\,R2$
- $7 \div 9 = 0\,R7$

- $10 \div 6 = 1\,R4$
- $6 \div 10 = 0\,R6$
- $0 \div 5 = 0$
- $5 \div 0 = Undefined$

Activity (A): Find the Average of Bowling Scores

In the last lesson, you learned how to find the average of a set of one-digit numbers. Today, you'll find averages with larger numbers.

Have you ever gone bowling? *Answers will vary.* **Bowlers often keep careful track of their scores and calculate their averages. This chart shows a bowler's scores for one week.**

What do you remember about finding an average? *Sample answer: You add up the numbers and then divide.* **To find the average for a set of numbers, we add up all the numbers and then divide the total by the number of numbers.**

"Divide by the number of numbers" is an awkward phrase, but children often find it very helpful for remembering how to find an average. Use it as needed to prompt your child.

Let's find the average of the bowler's Monday scores. First, we add the scores. Have your child add the scores, either mentally or with a vertical addition problem in the work space. **What's the total of the Monday scores?** *264.* **How many scores are there?** *3.*

What equation tells the bowler's average score for Monday? *264 divided by 3.* Have your child write the matching long division problem in the work space and solve. **So, what's the bowler's average score for Monday?** *88.* Write 88 in the blank.

Have your child find the average of the other days' bowling scores in the same way. For each day, have your child first find the total of the day's scores. Then, have him divide the total by the number of scores. If your child needs more space for the addition and division problems, have him write them on a separate piece of paper.

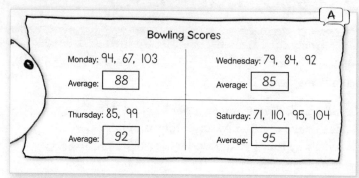

Bowling Scores

Monday: 94, 67, 103
Average: 88

Wednesday: 79, 84, 92
Average: 85

Thursday: 85, 99
Average: 92

Saturday: 71, 110, 95, 104
Average: 95

Which day did the bowler have the highest average? *Saturday.* **Which day did he have the lowest average?** *Wednesday.*

Activity (B): Play Spin to Win

Use the game board to play Spin to Win.

Spin to Win

Materials: Paper clip

Object of the Game: Have a greater average score than the other player.

Place one end of the paper clip in the middle of the top spinner. Place the point of a pencil through the paper clip so that it touches the very middle of the circle.

On your turn, hold the pencil upright and spin the paper clip so that it spins freely around the circle. Write the first number you spin in the first box on your score card. Then, have the other player take a turn in the same way.

Repeat 5 times (until both players have completed all 5 boxes on their score cards). Then, each player finds the average of their scores, either mentally or on a separate piece of paper. Whoever has the greater average of all 5 rounds wins.

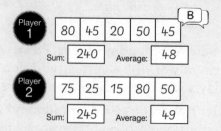

Player 1 | 80 | 45 | 20 | 50 | 45
Sum: 240   Average: 48

Player 2 | 75 | 25 | 15 | 80 | 50
Sum: 245   Average: 49

Sample final score card. Player 2 wins, since his average is higher than Player 1's average.

Independent Practice and Review

Have your child complete the Lesson 16.4 Practice and Review workbook pages.

Lesson 16.5
Enrichment (Optional)

Purpose	Materials
• Practice memory work • Interpret a variety of different charts and graphs • Make a line plot of survey results and find the average • Summarize what your child has learned and assess your child's progress	• *Show and Tell! Great Graphs and Smart Charts: An Introduction to Infographics,* written by Stuart J. Murphy and illustrated by Teresa Bellón

This optional enrichment lesson is in the middle of the unit so you can wrap up your study of line plots and averages before moving on to the end-of-the-year review and celebration lessons.

Warm-up: Review Memory Work

Quiz your child on all memory work through Unit 16. See pages 536-537 for the full list.

Math Picture Book: *Show and Tell! Great Graphs and Smart Charts: An Introduction to Infographics*

Read *Show and Tell! Great Graphs and Smart Charts: An Introduction to Infographics,* written by Stuart J. Murphy and illustrated by Teresa Bellón. As you read, discuss the information shown in each graph and chart.

Enrichment Activity: Make a Line Plot of Survey Results and Find the Average

In this activity, you get to conduct a survey. Then, you'll make a line plot of the results and find the average result. What would you like to survey people about? *Answers will vary.* Discuss possibilities with your child and help her choose a question with a well-defined, numerical answer. For example:

- How many pets do you have?
- How many pockets are in the outfit you're wearing right now?
- How many seconds can you balance on one foot with your eyes closed?

Help your child create a list of 8-10 people to survey, and plan how she will conduct her survey. Choose people who are easy to reach, such as family members or neighbors, and help your child contact them and record their answers.

If you don't have time to conduct a survey, choose one of the following options to quickly generate data:

1. Have your child count the number of pockets in one category of clothing (such as pants, shorts, or dresses).
2. Write down the number of children in 8-10 families you know.

After your child completes the survey, help her create a line plot of the results. Then, help her find the average of the responses.

If there's a remainder after you divide to find the average, simply ignore it. Your child will learn how to interpret remainders as fractions or decimals in future grades.

Unit Wrap-Up

Have your child complete the Unit 16 Wrap-Up.

Lesson 16.6
Review Multiplication and Division

Purpose	Materials
• Review memory work • Celebrate what your child has learned about multiplication and division • Practice multi-digit multiplication and long division	• Die • 12 slips of paper

Memory Work	See the warm-up activity for memory work review.

In the daily routine of lessons, it can be easy to forget how much progress your child has made since the start of the year. The final three lessons give both you and your child a chance to look back and celebrate how much he has learned.

Use green paper for Leaf Fight if you'd like the slips to look like spring leaves.

Warm-up: Review Memory Work

In this lesson and the next two lessons, we'll review and celebrate all that you've learned this year. Each day, we'll review some memory work. Today, we'll review memory work about multiplication and division.

- **What do we call the result when we multiply two numbers?** *The product.*
- **What do we call the numbers in a multiplication equation that we multiply together?** *Factors.*
- **What do we call the number to be divided?** *The dividend.*
- **What do we call the number we divide by?** *The divisor.*
- **What do we call the result when we divide two numbers?** *The quotient.*
- **What do we call an amount that is left over after division?** *The remainder.*
- **How do you know if a number is divisible by 2?** *It is even. It has 0, 2, 4, 6, or 8 in the ones-place.*
- **How do you know if a number is divisible by 5?** *It has a 0 or 5 in the ones-place.*
- **How do you know if a number is divisible by 10?** *It has a 0 in the ones-place.*
- **What is a prime number?** *A number with exactly 2 factors.*
- **What is a composite number?** *A number with more than 2 factors.*
- **What do parentheses mean in a math problem?** *Do this first.*
- **What's zero times any number?** *Zero.*
- **What's zero divided by any other number?** *Zero.*
- **What's any number divided by zero?** *Undefined.*

Activity:
Celebrate What Your Child Has Learned About Multiplication and Division

Today, we'll celebrate how much you've learned about multiplication and division. At the beginning of the year, you learned about factors and multiples. With your child, flip through the Unit 1 workbook pages.

If you no longer have the workbook pages, flip through the matching lessons in the Instructor Guide and have your child look at the workbook answer keys instead.

You learned lots of techniques for mental multiplication and division. Page through the Unit 3 and Unit 5 workbook pages.

Then, you learned how to multiply multi-digit numbers with the multiplication algorithm. You also learned how to use long division to divide large numbers. Page through the Unit 7, Unit 10, and Unit 13 workbook pages.

Next year, you'll learn how to multiply and divide even larger numbers. You'll also learn how to multiply and divide fractions and decimals!

Briefly discuss any concepts that were especially difficult for your child, and remind him how far he has come in his math learning. For example: **Remember how hard long division was at first? Now that you've practiced those problems so much, you know the steps well!**

Activity (A): Play Leaf Fight

Show your child part A. **We'll review multiplication and division with a special version of Leaf Fight today. In this version, you use the numbers from the leaves to fill in the two- and three-digit numbers on the game board. You roll a die to fill in the one-digit numbers. After we complete all the problems, we'll each add all of our answers to see who has the greater total.** Play Leaf Fight.

> If you'd rather avoid throwing, put the paper wads in a bowl and draw 2 wads each turn instead. Replace the wads in the bowl after each turn.

Leaf Fight

Materials: 12 slips of paper; die

Object of the Game: Have the greater total sum of products and quotients.

Write the numbers on the leaves on separate slips of paper:

35　47　82　90　51　28　63　74　381　256　194　407

Crumple the slips of paper and place them on the table. Both players count down in unison from 10 while throwing the crumpled wads of paper at each other. When you reach 1, both players stop and pick up the closest wad of paper.

Both players unfold their paper wads and write their number in one of the blank spaces on the score card. You may choose any blank with the same number of digits as the number on the crumpled paper. Throw the leaves as many times as needed until both players have filled in all of their two- and three-digit numbers.

Then, take turns rolling a die. Write the number on the die in one of the one-digit blanks on your score card. If you roll a 1, re-roll the die. Continue until both players have filled in all of their one-digit numbers.

After you complete all the missing digits, find the products for the resulting multiplication problems and the quotients for the resulting division problems.

Directions continued on next page.

On scrap paper, find the sum of the products of your multiplication problems and the quotients of your division problems. (Ignore any remainders.) Whoever has the greater final sum wins the game.

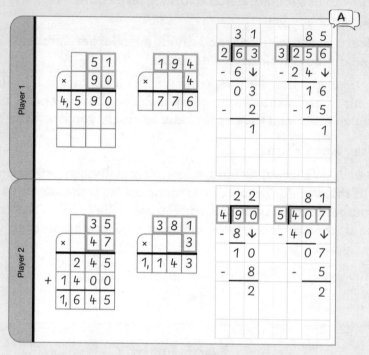

Player 1's final score is 5,482 (4,590 + 776 + 31 + 85). Player 2's final score is 2,891 (1,645 + 1,143 + 22 + 81). Player 1 wins.

Independent Practice and Review

Have your child complete the Lesson 16.6 Practice and Review workbook pages.

Lesson 16.7
Review Fractions and Decimals

Purpose	Materials
• Review memory work • Celebrate what your child has learned about fractions and decimals • Practice converting mixed numbers and fractions • Practice finding equivalent fractions • Practice writing decimals as fractions	• Counters

Memory Work See the warm-up activity for memory work review.

Warm-up: Review Memory Work

Today, we'll review memory work about fractions.

- **What do we call the top number in a fraction?** *The numerator.*
- **What does the numerator tell?** *The number of parts.*
- **What do we call the bottom number in a fraction?** *The denominator.*
- **What does the denominator tell?** *How many equal parts the whole was split into.*
- **What do we call fractions that look different but have the same value?** *Equivalent fractions.*
- **What do we call numbers that have a whole number and a fraction?** *Mixed numbers.*

Activity:
Celebrate What Your Child Has Learned About Fractions and Decimals

Today, we'll celebrate how much you've learned about fractions and decimals.

In Unit 4, you studied fractions and mixed numbers. You learned how to convert mixed numbers to fractions and fractions to mixed numbers. You also learned how to add and subtract fractions and mixed numbers. With your child, flip through the Unit 4 workbook pages.

In Unit 12, you learned how to find equivalent fractions. Then, in Unit 14, you learned about decimals. Page through the Unit 12 and Unit 14 workbook pages.

Activity (A): Practice Writing Fraction Equivalents for Mixed Numbers, Fractions, and Decimals

Show your child part A. **Throughout the year, you've learned many different ways to describe parts of wholes.**

You learned how to convert mixed numbers to improper fractions, and how to convert improper fractions to whole numbers or mixed numbers. Have your child complete the first column of problems.

You also learned how to multiply to create equivalent fractions. Have your child find the missing numbers in the equivalent fraction pairs in the middle column of problems.

You also learned that we can use decimals to describe parts of wholes. Have your child write fractions to match the decimals in the third column of problems.

$$1\frac{7}{8} = \boxed{\frac{15}{8}}$$ $\quad$ $$\frac{3}{4} = \boxed{\frac{6}{8}}$$ $\quad$ $$0.7 = \boxed{\frac{7}{10}}^{\text{A}}$$

$$2\frac{3}{5} = \boxed{\frac{13}{5}}$$ $\quad$ $$\frac{1}{3} = \boxed{\frac{5}{15}}$$ $\quad$ $$0.07 = \boxed{\frac{7}{100}}$$

$$\frac{9}{3} = \boxed{3}$$ $\quad$ $$\frac{5}{6} = \boxed{\frac{10}{12}}$$ $\quad$ $$1.49 = \boxed{1\frac{49}{100}}$$

$$\frac{13}{4} = \boxed{3\frac{1}{4}}$$ $\quad$ $$\frac{4}{5} = \boxed{\frac{20}{25}}$$ $\quad$ $$2.03 = \boxed{2\frac{3}{100}}$$

Activity (B): Play Four in a Row

The fractions, mixed numbers, and decimals from part A are printed on this Four in a Row game board. Use a piece of paper to cover part A. Then, use the gameboard in part B to play Four in a Row. If your child has trouble finding an equivalent decimal, fraction, or mixed number, allow her to peek at part A as needed.

Four in a Row

Materials: 12 counters per player, with a different color for each player

Object of the Game: Be the first player to place counters in 4 squares in a row, either horizontally, vertically, or diagonally.

On your turn, choose a box on the board. Find another box on the board with an equivalent decimal, fraction, or mixed number. Cover both boxes with a counter.

For example, if you choose the box with 7/100, cover the box with 7/100 and the box with 0.07.

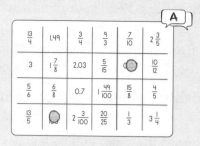

Sample play.

Play then passes to the other player. Continue until one player covers 4 boxes in a row, either horizontally, vertically, or diagonally.

Independent Practice and Review

Have your child complete the Lesson 16.7 Practice and Review workbook pages.

Lesson 16.8
Review Geometry, Measurement, and Data

Purpose	Materials
• Review memory work • Celebrate what your child has learned about geometry, measurement, and data • Practice measuring length with fractions and decimals • Reflect on the year and look ahead to fifth grade	• Paper clip • Ruler • Colored pencils or markers

Memory Work   See the warm-up activity for memory work review.

Warm-up: Review Memory Work

Today, we'll review the memory work about geometry, measurement, and data.

- **What does perimeter measure?** *The distance around the outside edge of a shape.*
- **What does area measure?** *The amount of space that a shape covers.*
- **How many inches equal 1 foot?** *12.*
- **How many feet equal 1 yard?** *3.*
- **How many inches equal 1 yard?** *36.*
- **How many feet equal 1 mile?** *5,280.*
- **How many millimeters equal 1 centimeter?** *10.*
- **How many centimeters equal 1 meter?** *100.*
- **How many meters equal 1 kilometer?** *1,000.*
- **How many grams equal 1 kilogram?** *1,000.*
- **How many milliliters equal 1 liter?** *1,000.*
- **How many ounces equal 1 pound?** *16.*
- **How many fluid ounces equal 1 cup?** *8.*
- **What do we call an angle with a measure less than 90 degrees?** *Acute.*
- **What do we call an angle with a measure equal to 90 degrees?** *Right.*
- **What do we call an angle with a measure greater than 90 degrees and less than 180 degrees?** *Obtuse.*
- **What do we call an angle with a measure equal to 180 degrees?** *Straight.*
- **What do we call a quadrilateral with 4 right angles?** *A rectangle.*
- **What do we call a quadrilateral with 4 right angles and 4 equal sides?** *A square.*
- **What do we call a quadrilateral with 4 equal sides?** *A rhombus.*
- **What do we call a quadrilateral with 2 pairs of parallel sides?** *A parallelogram.*
- **What do we call a quadrilateral with exactly 1 pair of parallel sides?** *A trapezoid.*
- **What is an acute triangle?** *A triangle with 3 acute angles.*
- **What is a right triangle?** *A triangle with a right angle.*
- **What is an obtuse triangle?** *A triangle with an obtuse angle.*

Activity: Celebrate What Your Child Has Learned About Geometry, Measurement, and Data

Today, we'll look back at how much you've learned about geometry, measurement, and data.

In Unit 6, we reviewed perimeter and area. With your child, flip through the Unit 6 workbook pages.

In Unit 8, you learned how to use a protractor to measure and draw angles. In Unit 11, you learned how to name and categorize quadrilaterals and triangles. Page through the Unit 8 and Unit 11 workbook pages.

In Unit 9, you learned how to convert, add, and subtract measurements for length. In Unit 15 you learned how to convert, add, and subtract measurements for time, weight, and capacity. You also solved lots of measurement word problems. Page through the Unit 9 and 15 workbook pages.

Finally, in this unit, you learned how to make line plots and find averages. Look over the Unit 16 workbook pages.

Activity (A): Play Measurement Tag

We played Measurement Tag in Unit 9 with centimeters and millimeters. Today, we'll play the game with lengths that involve fractions and decimals.

Remember, this game is like Tag, but on paper! One of us will be "it." The person who's "it" is the tagger and tries to catch the other person. Play Measurement Tag.

Measurement Tag

Materials: Paper clip; ruler; colored pencils or markers

Object of the Game: If you are the tagger (or "it"), your goal is to tag your opponent by landing within 1 cm of the end of their path. If you are not the tagger, your goal is to draw a path that avoids getting tagged for as long as possible.

Each player chooses a different color of colored pencil or marker to use to draw their line. Decide which player will be the tagger. The tagger is Player 1 and goes first.

On your turn, choose one of the spinners to spin. Place one end of the paper clip in the middle of the spinner. Place the point of a pencil through the paper clip. Hold the pencil upright and spin the paper clip so that it spins freely around the circle.

Use the ruler to draw a straight line with a length that matches the spinner. Begin your first line at your starting dot. For example, if you spin 2.6 cm, draw a 2.6 cm line that begins at your starting dot. (It may go in any direction.) Draw a dot at the end of the line. You will start your next line at this dot. Then the other player takes a turn in the same way.

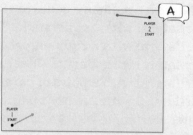

Sample first move by each player. Player 1 (the tagger) should try to draw a line towards the other player's position. Player 2 should try to draw a line that moves away from the tagger's position.

All lines must be straight and fit inside the game board. Lines may go in any direction, and they may cross any previously-drawn lines.

Directions continued on next page.

Take turns spinning the spinner and drawing lines. The game ends when the tagger's line comes within 1 centimeter of the other player's current end dot.

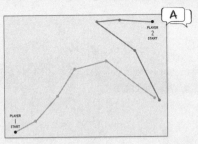

Sample final game board. Player 1 wins when his line comes within 1 centimeter of Player 2's current end dot.

Activity (B): Reflect on the Year

Read aloud the reflection questions in part B. Have your child answer each question, or scribe his answers for him.

	B
What was your favorite math activity this year? *I liked playing Leaf Fight and Four in a Row.*	What math topic was most interesting to you this year? *I liked learning about angles and using a protractor.*
What math skill did you work hardest to learn this year? *I worked hard to learn the steps in long division.*	What do you hope to learn in math next year? *I hope to learn how to add and subtract decimals.*

Sample responses.

Independent Practice and Review

Have your child complete the Lesson 16.8 Practice page. Then, complete the certificate on Workbook page 199 and present it to your child.

Unit 16 Answer Key

16.1 Practice

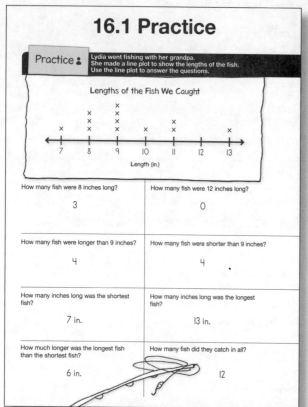

Practice — Lydia went fishing with her grandpa. She made a line plot to show the lengths of the fish. Use the line plot to answer the questions.

Lengths of the Fish We Caught

How many fish were 8 inches long?	How many fish were 12 inches long?
3	0
How many fish were longer than 9 inches?	How many fish were shorter than 9 inches?
4	4
How many inches long was the shortest fish?	How many inches long was the longest fish?
7 in.	13 in.
How much longer was the longest fish than the shortest fish?	How many fish did they catch in all?
6 in.	12

16.1 Review

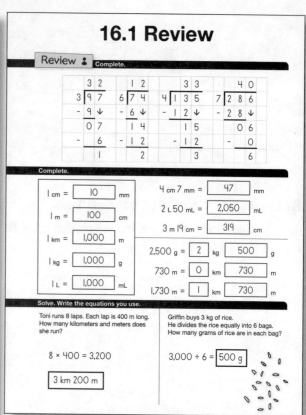

Review — Complete.

	3 2		1 2		3 3		4 0
3	9 7	6	7 4	4	1 3 5	7	2 8 6
−	9 ↓	−	6 ↓	−	1 2 ↓	−	2 8 ↓
	0 7		1 4		1 5		0 6
−	6	−	1 2	−	1 2	−	0
	1		2		3		6

Complete.

1 cm =	10	mm
1 m =	100	cm
1 km =	1,000	m
1 kg =	1,000	g
1 L =	1,000	mL

4 cm 7 mm = 47 mm

2 L 50 mL = 2,050 mL

3 m 19 cm = 319 cm

2,500 g = 2 kg 500 g

730 m = 0 km 730 m

1,730 m = 1 km 730 m

Solve. Write the equations you use.

Toni runs 8 laps. Each lap is 400 m long. How many kilometers and meters does she run?

8 × 400 = 3,200

3 km 200 m

Griffin buys 3 kg of rice. He divides the rice equally into 6 bags. How many grams of rice are in each bag?

3,000 ÷ 6 = 500 g

16.2 Practice

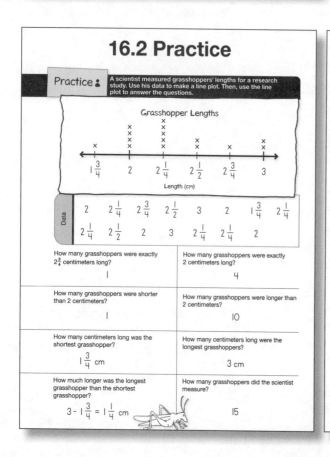

Practice — A scientist measured grasshoppers' lengths for a research study. Use his data to make a line plot. Then, use the line plot to answer the questions.

Grasshopper Lengths

Data	2	$2\frac{1}{4}$	$2\frac{3}{4}$	$2\frac{1}{2}$	3	2	$1\frac{3}{4}$	$2\frac{1}{4}$
	$2\frac{1}{4}$	$2\frac{1}{2}$	2	3	$2\frac{1}{4}$	$2\frac{1}{4}$	2	

How many grasshoppers were exactly $2\frac{3}{4}$ centimeters long?	How many grasshoppers were exactly 2 centimeters long?
1	4
How many grasshoppers were shorter than 2 centimeters?	How many grasshoppers were longer than 2 centimeters?
1	10
How many centimeters long was the shortest grasshopper?	How many centimeters long were the longest grasshoppers?
$1\frac{3}{4}$ cm	3 cm
How much longer was the longest grasshopper than the shortest grasshopper?	How many grasshoppers did the scientist measure?
$3 - 1\frac{3}{4} = 1\frac{1}{4}$ cm	15

16.2 Review

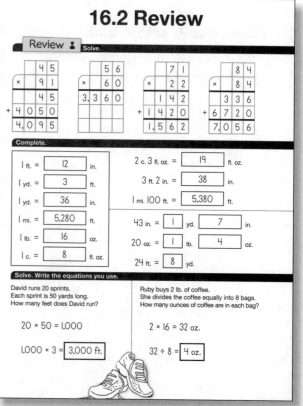

Review — Solve.

	4 5			5 6			7 1			8 4
×	9 1		×	6 0		×	2 2		×	8 4
	4 5		3,360			1 4 2			3 3 6	
+	4 0 5 0					+	1 4 2 0		+	6 7 2 0
	4,095						1,562			7,056

Complete.

1 ft. =	12	in.
1 yd. =	3	ft.
1 yd. =	36	in.
1 mi. =	5,280	ft.
1 lb. =	16	oz.
1 c. =	8	fl. oz.

2 c. 3 fl. oz. = 19 fl. oz.

3 ft. 2 in. = 38 in.

1 mi. 100 ft. = 5,380 ft.

43 in. = 1 yd. 7 in.

20 oz. = 1 lb. 4 oz.

24 ft. = 8 yd.

Solve. Write the equations you use.

David runs 20 sprints. Each sprint is 50 yards long. How many feet does David run?

20 × 50 = 1,000

1,000 × 3 = 3,000 ft.

Ruby buys 2 lb. of coffee. She divides the coffee equally into 8 bags. How many ounces of coffee are in each bag?

2 × 16 = 32 oz.

32 ÷ 8 = 4 oz.

Unit 16 Answer Key

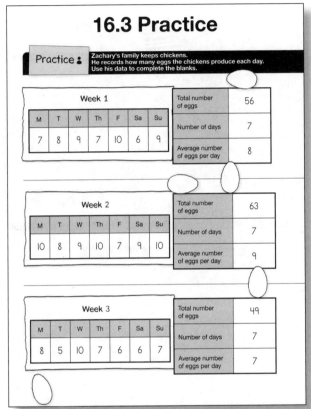

16.3 Practice

Practice : Zachary's family keeps chickens. He records how many eggs the chickens produce each day. Use his data to complete the blanks.

Week 1

M	T	W	Th	F	Sa	Su
7	8	9	7	10	6	9

Total number of eggs	56
Number of days	7
Average number of eggs per day	8

Week 2

M	T	W	Th	F	Sa	Su
10	8	9	10	7	9	10

Total number of eggs	63
Number of days	7
Average number of eggs per day	9

Week 3

M	T	W	Th	F	Sa	Su
8	5	10	7	6	6	7

Total number of eggs	49
Number of days	7
Average number of eggs per day	7

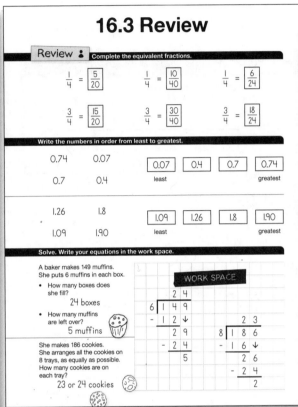

16.3 Review

Review : Complete the equivalent fractions.

$$\frac{1}{4} = \frac{5}{20} \qquad \frac{1}{4} = \frac{10}{40} \qquad \frac{1}{4} = \frac{6}{24}$$

$$\frac{3}{4} = \frac{15}{20} \qquad \frac{3}{4} = \frac{30}{40} \qquad \frac{3}{4} = \frac{18}{24}$$

Write the numbers in order from least to greatest.

0.74   0.07
0.7   0.4

0.07	0.4	0.7	0.74
least			greatest

1.26   1.8
1.09   1.90

1.09	1.26	1.8	1.90
least			greatest

Solve. Write your equations in the work space.

A baker makes 149 muffins. She puts 6 muffins in each box.

- How many boxes does she fill? **24 boxes**
- How many muffins are left over? **5 muffins**

She makes 186 cookies. She arranges all the cookies on 8 trays, as equally as possible. How many cookies are on each tray? **23 or 24 cookies**

```
WORK SPACE
        2 4
  6 | 1 4 9
    - 1 2 ↓
        2 9
      - 2 4
          5

          2 3
    8 | 1 8 6
      - 1 6 ↓
          2 6
        - 2 4
            2
```

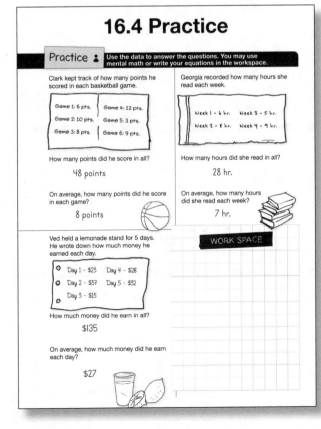

16.4 Practice

Practice : Use the data to answer the questions. You may use mental math or write your equations in the workspace.

Clark kept track of how many points he scored in each basketball game.

Game 1: 6 pts.   Game 4: 12 pts.
Game 2: 10 pts.   Game 5: 3 pts.
Game 3: 8 pts.   Game 6: 9 pts.

How many points did he score in all?

48 points

On average, how many points did he score in each game?

8 points

Ved held a lemonade stand for 5 days. He wrote down how much money he earned each day.

Day 1 - $23   Day 4 - $28
Day 2 - $37   Day 5 - $32
Day 3 - $15

How much money did he earn in all?

$135

On average, how much money did he earn each day?

$27

Georgia recorded how many hours she read each week.

Week 1 - 6 hr.   Week 3 - 5 hr.
Week 2 - 8 hr.   Week 4 - 9 hr.

How many hours did she read in all?

28 hr.

On average, how many hours did she read each week?

7 hr.

WORK SPACE

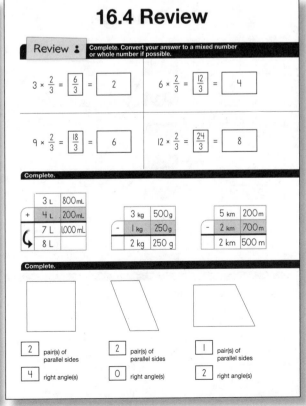

16.4 Review

Review : Complete. Convert your answer to a mixed number or whole number if possible.

$$3 \times \frac{2}{3} = \frac{6}{3} = 2 \qquad 6 \times \frac{2}{3} = \frac{12}{3} = 4$$

$$9 \times \frac{2}{3} = \frac{18}{3} = 6 \qquad 12 \times \frac{2}{3} = \frac{24}{3} = 8$$

Complete.

	3 L	800 mL
+	4 L	200 mL
	7 L	1,000 mL
	8 L	

	3 kg	500 g
-	1 kg	250 g
	2 kg	250 g

	5 km	200 m
-	2 km	700 m
	2 km	500 m

Complete.

2 pair(s) of parallel sides	2 pair(s) of parallel sides	1 pair(s) of parallel sides
4 right angle(s)	0 right angle(s)	2 right angle(s)

Unit 16 Answer Key

16.5 Unit Wrap-Up A

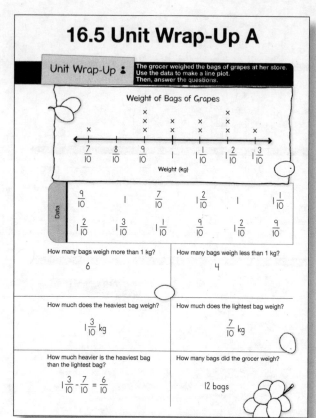

Unit Wrap-Up 👤 The grocer weighed the bags of grapes at her store. Use the data to make a line plot. Then, answer the questions.

Weight of Bags of Grapes

Weight (kg)

Data: $\frac{9}{10}$, 1, $\frac{7}{10}$, $1\frac{2}{10}$, 1, $1\frac{1}{10}$, $1\frac{2}{10}$, $1\frac{3}{10}$, $1\frac{1}{10}$, $\frac{9}{10}$, $1\frac{2}{10}$, $\frac{9}{10}$

How many bags weigh more than 1 kg?	How many bags weigh less than 1 kg?
6	4

How much does the heaviest bag weigh?	How much does the lightest bag weigh?
$1\frac{3}{10}$ kg	$\frac{7}{10}$ kg

How much heavier is the heaviest bag than the lightest bag?	How many bags did the grocer weigh?
$1\frac{3}{10} - \frac{7}{10} = \frac{6}{10}$	12 bags

16.5 Wrap-Up B

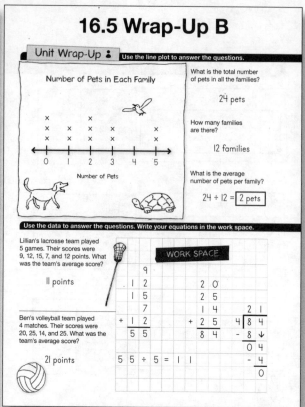

Unit Wrap-Up 👤 Use the line plot to answer the questions.

Number of Pets in Each Family

Number of Pets

What is the total number of pets in all the families?

24 pets

How many families are there?

12 families

What is the average number of pets per family?

$24 \div 12 = \boxed{2 \text{ pets}}$

Use the data to answer the questions. Write your equations in the work space.

Lillian's lacrosse team played 5 games. Their scores were 9, 12, 15, 7, and 12 points. What was the team's average score?

11 points

Ben's volleyball team played 4 matches. Their scores were 20, 25, 14, and 25. What was the team's average score?

21 points

WORK SPACE

$$9$$
$$12$$
$$15$$
$$7$$
$$+ 12$$
$$55$$

$$20$$
$$25$$
$$14$$
$$+ 25$$
$$84$$

$$55 \div 5 = 11$$

$$\begin{array}{r} 21 \\ 4\overline{)84} \\ -8\downarrow \\ \hline 04 \\ -4 \\ \hline 0 \end{array}$$

16.6 Practice

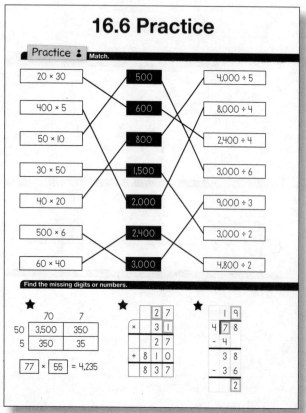

Practice 👤 Match.

20 × 30	500	4,000 ÷ 5
400 × 5	600	8,000 ÷ 4
50 × 10	800	2,400 ÷ 4
30 × 50	1,500	3,000 ÷ 6
40 × 20	2,000	9,000 ÷ 3
500 × 6	2,400	3,000 ÷ 2
60 × 40	3,000	4,800 ÷ 2

Find the missing digits or numbers.

⭐
×	70	7
50	3,500	350
5	350	35

$\boxed{77} \times \boxed{55} = 4,235$

⭐
$$\begin{array}{r} 2\,7 \\ \times\ 3\,1 \\ \hline 2\,7 \\ +\ 8\,1\,0 \\ \hline 8\,3\,7 \end{array}$$

⭐
$$\begin{array}{r} 1\,9 \\ 4\overline{)7\,8} \\ -\ 4 \\ \hline 3\,8 \\ -\ 3\,6 \\ \hline 2 \end{array}$$

16.6 Review

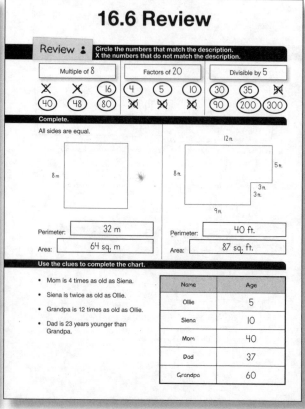

Review 👤 Circle the numbers that match the description. X the numbers that do not match the description.

Multiple of 8	Factors of 20	Divisible by 5
X̶ X̶ (16)	(4) (5) (10)	(30) (35) X̶
(40) (48) (80)	X̶ X̶ X̶	(90) (200) (300)

Complete.

All sides are equal.

8 m

Perimeter: 32 m
Area: 64 sq. m

12 ft.
8 ft.
5 ft.
3 ft.
3 ft.
9 ft.

Perimeter: 40 ft.
Area: 87 sq. ft.

Use the clues to complete the chart.

- Mom is 4 times as old as Siena.
- Siena is twice as old as Ollie.
- Grandpa is 12 times as old as Ollie.
- Dad is 23 years younger than Grandpa.

Name	Age
Ollie	5
Siena	10
Mom	40
Dad	37
Grandpa	60

Unit 16 Answer Key

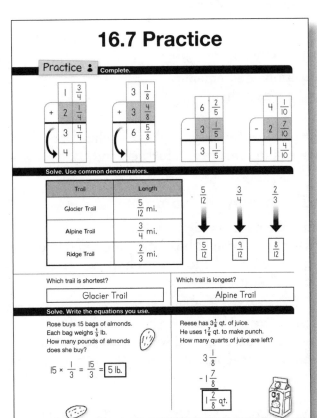

16.7 Practice

Practice Complete.

	$1\frac{3}{4}$
+	$2\frac{1}{4}$
	$3\frac{4}{4}$
	4

	$3\frac{1}{8}$
+	$3\frac{4}{8}$
	$6\frac{5}{8}$

	$6\frac{2}{5}$
−	$3\frac{1}{5}$
	$3\frac{1}{5}$

	$4\frac{1}{10}$
−	$2\frac{7}{10}$
	$1\frac{4}{10}$

Solve. Use common denominators.

Trail	Length
Glacier Trail	$\frac{5}{12}$ mi.
Alpine Trail	$\frac{3}{4}$ mi.
Ridge Trail	$\frac{2}{3}$ mi.

$\frac{5}{12}$ $\frac{3}{4}$ $\frac{2}{3}$

↓ ↓ ↓

$\frac{5}{12}$ $\frac{9}{12}$ $\frac{8}{12}$

Which trail is shortest? **Glacier Trail**

Which trail is longest? **Alpine Trail**

Solve. Write the equations you use.

Rose buys 15 bags of almonds. Each bag weighs $\frac{1}{3}$ lb. How many pounds of almonds does she buy?

$15 \times \frac{1}{3} = \frac{15}{3} = \boxed{5 \text{ lb.}}$

Reese has $3\frac{1}{8}$ qt. of juice. He uses $1\frac{7}{8}$ qt. to make punch. How many quarts of juice are left?

$3\frac{1}{8}$
$- 1\frac{7}{8}$
$\boxed{1\frac{2}{8} \text{ qt.}}$

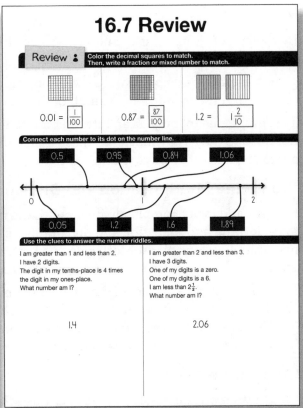

16.7 Review

Review Color the decimal squares to match. Then, write a fraction or mixed number to match.

$0.01 = \boxed{\frac{1}{100}}$ $0.87 = \boxed{\frac{87}{100}}$ $1.2 = \boxed{1\frac{2}{10}}$

Connect each number to its dot on the number line.

0.5   0.95   0.84   1.06

0.05   1.2   1.6   1.89

Use the clues to answer the number riddles.

I am greater than 1 and less than 2.
I have 2 digits.
The digit in my tenths-place is 4 times the digit in my ones-place.
What number am I?

1.4

I am greater than 2 and less than 3.
I have 3 digits.
One of my digits is a zero.
One of my digits is a 6.
I am less than $2\frac{1}{2}$.
What number am I?

2.06

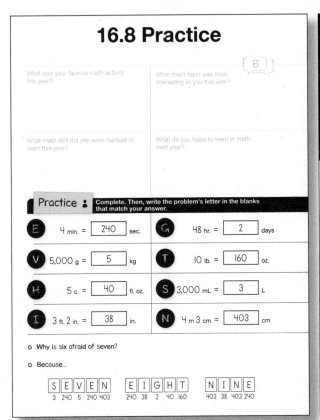

16.8 Practice

What was your favorite math activity this year?

What math topic was most interesting to you this year?

What math skill did you work hardest to learn this year?

What do you hope to learn in math next year?

Practice Complete. Then, write the problem's letter in the blanks that match your answer.

E   4 min. = $\boxed{240}$ sec.

G   48 hr. = $\boxed{2}$ days

V   5,000 g = $\boxed{5}$ kg

T   10 lb. = $\boxed{160}$ oz.

H   5 c. = $\boxed{40}$ fl. oz.

S   3,000 mL = $\boxed{3}$ L

I   3 ft. 2 in. = $\boxed{38}$ in.

N   4 m 3 cm = $\boxed{403}$ cm

▫ Why is six afraid of seven?

▫ Because...

S	E	V	E	N
3	240	5	240	403

E	I	G	H	T
240	38	2	40	160

N	I	N	E
403	38	403	240

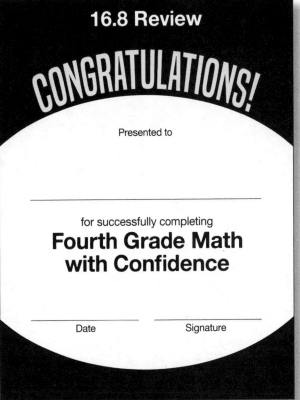

16.8 Review

CONGRATULATIONS!

Presented to

_____

for successfully completing

Fourth Grade Math with Confidence

Date   Signature

Unit 16 Checkpoint

What to Expect at the End of Unit 16

By the end of Unit 16, most children will be able to do the following:

- Create line plots with whole number or fractional increments.
- Interpret line plots and draw conclusions based on them.
- Find the average for a small data set.

This unit is meant only as an introduction to line plots and averages, and your child does not need to have fully mastered these skills. In future grades, he will further study line plots, averages, and other ways to analyze data.

Practicing Multiplication and Division Facts over the Summer

If your child is not completely fluent with the multiplication and division facts, you may want to review the multiplication and division facts over the summer. The better your child knows his multiplication and division facts, the better-prepared he'll be to tackle challenging topics like multiplying and dividing fractions and decimals in fifth grade.

If you'd like to do a methodical review of the multiplication or division facts over the summer, check out *Multiplication Facts That Stick* or *Division Facts That Stick*, also available from Well-Trained Mind Press. You'll find many games (some familiar and some new), as well as workbook pages to help your child further increase his speed and fluency with the math facts.

Congratulations!

Congratulations on finishing *Fourth Grade Math with Confidence*! Give yourself a pat on the back for all that you've taught your child this year.

Complete Picture Book List

Reading math picture books together is a delightful way to simply enjoy math. Most of these books relate to what your child will learn, but some expose your child to other interesting or fun math topics. **These picture books are not required.** You do not need to buy every book, and it's perfectly fine to use a book on a similar topic as a substitute.

Unit	Book
1	*I'm Trying to Love Math,* written and illustrated by Bethany Barton. Viking Books for Young Readers, 2019.
2	*A Million Dots,* written by Andrew Clements and illustrated by Mike Reed. Atheneum Books for Young Readers, 2006.
3	*Math Curse,* by Jon Scieszka and Lane Smith. Viking, 1995.
4	*The Wishing Club: A Story About Fractions,* written by Donna Jo Napoli and illustrated by Anna Currey. Henry Holt and Co., 2007.
5	*The Great Divide: A Mathematical Marathon,* written by Dayle Ann Dodds and illustrated by Tracy Mitchell. Candlewick, 2005.
6	*Spaghetti and Meatballs for All!,* written by Marilyn Burns and illustrated by Debbie Tilley. Scholastic, 2008.
7	*365 Penguins,* written by Jean-Luc Fromental and illustrated by Joëlle Jolivet. Harry N. Abrams, 2017.
8	*Sir Cumference and the Great Knight of Angleland,* written by Cindy Neuschwander and illustrated by Wayne Geehan. Charlesbridge, 2001.
9	*Millions to Measure,* written by David M. Schwartz and illustrated by Steven Kellogg. HarperCollins, 2006.
10	*The Multiplying Menace Divides,* by Pam Calvert and Wayne Geehan. Charlesbridge, 2011.
11	*Seeing Symmetry,* written and illustrated by Loreen Leedy. Holiday House, 2013.
12	*Fractions in Disguise: A Math Adventure,* written by Edward Einhorn and illustrated by David Clark. Charlesbridge, 2014.
13	*Great Estimations,* by Bruce Goldstone. Square Fish, 2010.
14	*The Efficient, Inventive (Often Annoying) Melvil Dewey,* written by Alexis O'Neill and illustrated by Edwin Fotheringham. Calkins Creek, 2020.
15	*How Heavy? Wacky Ways to Compare Weight,* written by Mark Andrew Weakland and illustrated by Bill Bolton. Picture Window Books, 2013.
16	*Show and Tell! Great Graphs and Smart Charts: An Introduction to Infographics,* written by Stuart J. Murphy and illustrated by Teresa Bellón. Charlesbridge, 2022.

Memory Work

Review Memory Work

In Unit 1, your child will review the memory work she learned in *Third Grade Math with Confidence*. If your child did not use *Third Grade Math with Confidence*, she will gradually memorize these items over the course of the year. She does not need to fully master every item by the end of Unit 1.

Topic	Memory Work
Numbers and Operations	• **What do we call the result when we add numbers together?** *The sum.* • **What do we call the result when we subtract a number from another number?** *The difference.* • **What do we call the result when we multiply two numbers?** *The product.* • **What do we call the numbers in a multiplication equation that we multiply together?** *Factors.* • **What do we call the number to be divided?** *The dividend.* • **What do we call the number we divide by?** *The divisor.* • **What do we call the result when we divide two numbers?** *The quotient.* • **What do we call an amount that is left over after division?** *The remainder.*
Measurement	• **How many inches equal 1 foot?** *12.* • **How many feet equal 1 yard?** *3.* • **How many inches equal 1 yard?** *36.* • **How many centimeters equal 1 meter?** *100.* • **How many meters equal 1 kilometer?** *1,000.* • **How many ounces equal 1 pound?** *16.* • **How many grams equal 1 kilogram?** *1,000.* • **How many cups equal 1 pint?** *2.* • **How many pints equal 1 quart?** *2.* • **How many quarts equal 1 gallon?** *4.* • **How many milliliters equal 1 liter?** *1,000.*
Fractions	• **What do we call the top number in a fraction?** *The numerator.* • **What does the numerator tell?** *The number of parts.* • **What do we call the bottom number in a fraction?** *The denominator.* • **What does the denominator tell?** *How many equal parts the whole was split into.* • **What do we call fractions that look different but have the same value?** *Equivalent fractions.* • **What do we call numbers that have a whole number and a fraction?** *Mixed numbers.*
Area and Perimeter	• **What does perimeter measure?** *The distance around the outside edge of a shape.* • **What does area measure?** *The amount of space that a shape covers.*
Geometry	• **What do we call an angle that looks like the corner of a piece of paper?** *A right angle.* • **What do we call a quadrilateral with 4 right angles?** *A rectangle.* • **What do we call a quadrilateral with 4 right angles and 4 equal sides?** *A square.* • **What do we call a quadrilateral with 4 equal sides?** *A rhombus.*

New Memory Work

Your child will gradually learn these memory work items over the course of the year. Not all units have new memory work.

Unit	Memory Work
1	• **Name 4 factors of X.** (Replace X with any number from 1 to 50.) *Answers will vary. Some numbers do not have 4 factors.* • **Name 4 multiples of X.** (Replace X with any number from 1 to 10.) *Answers will vary.* • **How do you know if a number is divisible by 2?** *It is even. It has 0, 2, 4, 6, or 8 in the ones-place.* • **How do you know if a number is divisible by 5?** *It has a 0 or 5 in the ones-place.* • **How do you know if a number is divisible by 10?** *It has a 0 in the ones-place.* • **What is a prime number?** *A number with exactly 2 factors.* • **What is a composite number?** *A number with more than 2 factors.*
3	• **What do parentheses mean in a math problem?** *Do this first.*
8	• **What do we call an angle with a measure less than 90 degrees?** *Acute.* • **What do we call an angle with a measure equal to 90 degrees?** *Right.* • **What do we call an angle with a measure greater than 90 degrees and less than 180 degrees?** *Obtuse.* • **What do we call an angle with a measure equal to 180 degrees?** *Straight.*
9	• **How many millimeters equal 1 centimeter?** *10.* • **How many feet equal 1 mile?** *5,280.*
10	• **What's zero times any number?** *Zero.* • **What's zero divided by any other number?** *Zero.* • **What's any number divided by zero?** *Undefined.*
11	• **What do we call a quadrilateral with 2 pairs of parallel sides?** *A parallelogram.* • **What do we call a quadrilateral with exactly 1 pair of parallel sides?** *A trapezoid.* • **What is an acute triangle?** *A triangle with 3 acute angles.* • **What is a right triangle?** *A triangle with a right angle.* • **What is an obtuse triangle?** *A triangle with an obtuse angle.*
15	• **How many fluid ounces equal 1 cup?** *8.*

Scope and Sequence

Unit	Objectives
Unit 1 Review	• Find answers for the multiplication and division facts (up to 10 × 10 and 100 ÷ 10) • Solve multiplication and division word problems • Use long division to solve simple division problems with a remainder • Find multiples of a given number • Tell whether numbers are divisible by 2, 5, or 10 • Find all factors of a given number • Tell whether a given number is prime or composite
Unit 2 Place Value and Large Numbers	• Read, write, and compare numbers to one million • Understand place value to the millions-place and write large numbers in expanded form • Round three- and four-digit numbers to any place • Round large numbers to the nearest thousand • Use place-value thinking to mentally add and subtract thousands • Use the addition and subtraction algorithms to add and subtract five- and six-digit numbers • Solve multi-step addition and subtraction word problems with large numbers
Unit 3 Mental Multiplication	• Mentally multiply one-digit numbers by a multiple of 10, 100, or 1,000 (e.g., 4 × 500 or 3,000 × 6) • Mentally multiply a multiple of 10 by a multiple of 10 (e.g., 40 × 80) • Write and solve expressions with parentheses • Understand the distributive property and use it to solve problems • Find answers for the ×11 and ×12 facts • Use the area model and box method to multiply two-digit numbers by one-digit numbers • Solve multiplication word problems, including multiplicative comparison problems and multi-step problems
Unit 4 Fractions and Mixed Numbers	• Identify and compare fractions and mixed numbers on the number line • Convert whole numbers and mixed numbers to fractions • Convert fractions to mixed numbers or whole numbers • Multiply fractions by whole numbers • Add and subtract fractions and mixed numbers with the same denominator
Unit 5 Mental Division	• Solve division word problems and interpret remainders depending on the context • Use multiplication (and addition) to check answers to division problems • Find answers for the ÷11 and ÷12 facts • Mentally divide multiples of 10, 100, or 1,000 (for example, 60 ÷ 3 or 3,000 ÷ 5)

Unit	Objectives
Unit 6 Area and Perimeter	• Use correct units to calculate perimeter and area • Find the perimeter of shapes with straight sides and understand how to use multiplication to add sides with equal lengths more efficiently • Understand how to split shapes composed of rectangles into parts and add or subtract to find total area • Write equations with parentheses to find perimeter or area • Solve multi-step perimeter and area word problems
Unit 7 Written Multiplication, Part 1	• Understand the steps in the written multiplication algorithm and model them with base-ten blocks or play money • Multiply a two-, three-, or four-digit number by a one-digit number • Use multi-digit multiplication to solve word problems • Use multi-digit multiplication to find area or perimeter
Unit 8 Angles	• Estimate angle measures in degrees • Identify acute, right, obtuse, and straight angles • Measure angles with a protractor • Draw angles with a given measure • Add or subtract to find the measure of an unknown angle
Unit 9 Length	• Convert length measurements within the U.S. customary system (inches, feet, yards, and miles) • Add and subtract feet and inches • Convert length measurements within the metric system (millimeters, centimeters, meters, and kilometers) • Measure with a ruler in centimeters and millimeters • Add and subtract compound units in the metric system • Solve two-step word problems that involve converting units
Unit 10 Long Division	• Use long division to solve division problems (up to four digits divided by one digit) • Use multiplication (and addition) to check answers to division problems • Use long division to solve word problems
Unit 11 Geometry	• Identify and label points, rays, lines, and line segments • Identify parallel, perpendicular, and intersecting lines • Identify, construct, and draw trapezoids, parallelograms, squares, rectangles, and rhombuses • Identify and draw right triangles, obtuse triangles, and acute triangles • Find lines of symmetry in triangles and quadrilaterals

Unit	Objectives
Unit 12 Equivalent Fractions	• Multiply the numerator and denominator of a fraction by the same number to create an equivalent fraction • Find missing numerators or denominators in pairs of equivalent fractions • Use equivalent fractions to identify and compare fractions of an inch or fractions of a meter • Use common denominators to compare fractions with different denominators
Unit 13 Written Multiplication, Part 2	• Multiply two-digit numbers by two-digit numbers with the box method • Multiply two-digit numbers by two-digit numbers with the traditional written algorithm • Multiply two-digit numbers to solve word problems
Unit 14 Decimals	• Read, write, and compare decimal numbers to the hundredths-place • Understand place value in decimals and write decimals in expanded form • Express decimals as fractions or mixed numbers • Identify decimals on the number line and round decimals to the nearest whole number • Express money amounts and metric lengths with decimals • Name decimal equivalents for common fractions
Unit 15 Time, Weight, and Capacity	• Convert units of time (days, hours, minutes, seconds) • Convert weight and capacity measurements within the metric system (kilograms, grams, liters, milliliters) • Convert weight and capacity measurements within the U.S. customary system (pounds, ounces, gallons, quarts, pints, cups, fluid ounces) • Add and subtract compound units for time, weight, and capacity • Solve two-step word problems that involve converting time, weight, and capacity units
Unit 16 Line Plots and Averages	• Create line plots with whole number or fractional increments • Interpret line plots • Find the average for a small data set

Materials List

What You'll Need in Your Math Kit

You'll use the following materials regularly in *Fourth Grade Math with Confidence*. Stash them in a box or basket and always keep them ready for your next lesson. (See pages 8-9 in the Introduction for more detailed descriptions of each item.)

- 40 small counters (20 each of 2 different colors)
- Play money (20 one-dollar bills, 20 ten-dollar bills, 10 hundred-dollar bills)
- Pattern blocks
- Base-ten blocks (20 unit blocks, 20 rods, and 10 flats)
- 1-foot (or 30-centimeter) ruler
- Protractor
- 2 packs of playing cards and 2 dice
- Blank paper
- Pencils

Other Supplies

Besides your Math Kit, you'll also need the following household items. You'll only need most of them once or twice, so you don't need to gather them ahead of time or store them separately. Check the unit overviews for the specific household items you'll need for each unit.

Items marked with an asterisk are needed for the optional enrichment lessons at the end of each unit.

- Colored pencils or markers
- Slips of paper (approximately 100 over the course of the year)
- Tape
- 2 paper clips
- Scissors
- *Pan of brownies or sheet cake, optional
- 6 dice
- *Almanac or internet access
- *Large piece of posterboard (or 9 sheets of paper and tape)
- *Recipe with mixed numbers and fractions
- *4 pieces of yarn of different colors, each 36 inches long
- *Wooden stick, about 1 foot long
- 8 toothpicks, craft sticks, or straws
- Large piece of paper (at least 12 inches by 12 inches)
- Yardstick, optional
- Meterstick, optional
- *2 pieces of centimeter graph paper
- *Calculator or calculator app
- Tape measure marked in feet and inches (at least 10 feet long)
- Tape measure marked in meters and centimeters, or knowledge of your child's height (in either meters and centimeters or feet and inches)
- *Cardboard strip, about 1 in. wide and 3 ft. long (or 3 cm wide and 1 m long)
- *Nutrition labels for several different types of cookies or crackers
- 4 craft sticks or narrow strips of paper
- *Paper square, approximately 6 inches by 6 inches
- *Pushpin
- *5 different colors of paper

- *Small bowl or cup (for tracing)
- *Glue, optional
- Body temperature thermometer, either digital or analog
- Digital stopwatch or stopwatch app
- *Online access to your local library's catalog
- Object that weighs about 1 kilogram, such as a pair of adult shoes, a pineapple, or this (printed) Instructor Guide, optional
- Object that weighs about 1 gram, such as a paper clip or thumbtack
- 1-liter container (such as a large water bottle or measuring cup), optional
- Eyedropper, optional
- Object that weighs about 1 pound, such as a loaf of bread, can of vegetables, or box of pasta, optional
- Object that weighs about 1 ounce, such as a slice of bread, AA battery, or a stack of 5 quarters, optional
- Container that holds 1 fluid ounce, such as a bottle of vanilla or other flavor extract, optional
- 1-cup measuring cup, optional
- *Your child's usual drinking glass
- *Water
- *If you use U.S. customary units: measuring cup marked in fluid ounces
- *If you use metric units: measuring cup marked in milliliters

Guide to the Blackline Masters

Digital Copies of Blackline Masters

Prefer to print the Blackline Masters rather than copy them from the book?
Download digital copies of all Math with Confidence Blackline Masters at welltrainedmind.com/mwc.

Reference Blackline Masters

Families often find it helpful to have the Memory Work pages and Multiplication Chart available for easy reference.

- Memory Work (Blackline Master 1)
- Multiplication Chart (Blackline Master 2)

For the Multiplication Chart, you'll find suggestions throughout the book on how to best use it. In general, encourage your child to recall the multiplication facts from memory as much as possible. But, if slow multiplication fact recall is causing frustration or making the lessons long and tedious, allow your child to use the Multiplication Chart as needed. For some children, using the chart for a few months makes a big difference in helping them solidify their multiplication fact fluency.

Short-Term-Use Blackline Masters

You will use these Blackline Masters for only a few lessons, and you do not need to save them after you finish the corresponding unit.

- Place-Value Chart (Blackline Master 4), used in Units 7 and 10 only
- Degree Wheel (Blackline Master 5), used in Unit 8 only
- Quadrilateral Cards (Blackline Master 6), used in Unit 11 only
- Geometry Reference Page (Blackline Master 7), used in Unit 11 only
- Shapes for Folding (Blackline Master 8), used in Unit 11 only

Optional Blackline Masters

The Multiplication Fact Assessment (Blackline Master 3) is optional for assessing your child's multiplication fact knowledge. See the Unit 2 Checkpoint (page 85) for details on whether or not you need it. If you have real pattern blocks, base-ten blocks, and play money, you do not need Blackline Masters 9, 10, or 11.

- Multiplication Fact Assessment (Blackline Master 3)
- Pattern Blocks (Blackline Master 9)
- Base-Ten Blocks (Blackline Master 10)
- Play Money (Blackline Master 11)

Memory Work (Blackline Master 1)

Addition, Subtraction, Multiplication, and Division Vocabulary

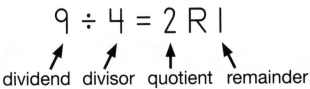

$$3 + 4 = 7$$

addends   sum

$$7 - 4 = 3$$

difference

$$3 \times 4 = 12$$

factors   product

$$9 \div 4 = 2\ R\ 1$$

dividend   divisor   quotient   remainder

Measurement

1 foot	=	12 inches
1 yard	=	3 feet
1 yard	=	36 inches
1 meter	=	100 centimeters
1 kilometer	=	1,000 meters
1 pound	=	16 ounces
1 kilogram	=	1,000 grams
1 pint	=	2 cups
1 quart	=	2 pints
1 gallon	=	4 quarts
1 liter	=	1,000 milliliters

Perimeter and Area

Perimeter measures the distance around the outside edge of a shape.

Area measures the amount of space that a shape covers.

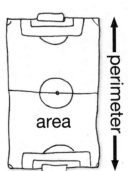

area   perimeter

Fractions

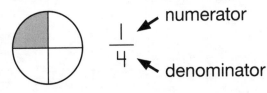

$$\frac{1}{4}$$

numerator

denominator

$$\frac{1}{2} = \frac{2}{4}$$

equivalent fractions

$$2\frac{1}{3}$$

mixed number

Geometry

Right Angle

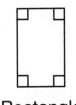

Rectangle
4 right angles

Square
4 right angles
4 equal sides

Rhombus
4 equal sides
2 pairs of parallel sides

Multiples and Factors

Multiples of 12:

12, 24, 36, 48, 60 ...

Factor Pairs of 12:

1 × 12, 2 × 6, 3 × 4

Prime and Composite

Prime numbers have exactly two factors.

Composite numbers have more than two factors.

3   4
prime   composite

Divisibility Rules

Numbers divisible by 2 have 0, 2, 4, 6, or 8 in the ones-place.

Numbers divisible by 5 have 0 or 5 in the ones-place.

Numbers divisible by 10 have 0 in the ones-place.

Multiplying and Dividing with Zero

Any number times zero equals zero.

Zero divided by any other number equals zero.

Dividing by zero is undefined.

Measurement

1 centimeter = 10 millimeters

1 mile = 5,280 feet

1 cup = 8 fluid ounces

Angles

Right angle
90°

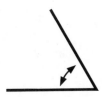

Acute angle
less than 90°

Obtuse angle
more than 90°

Straight angle
180°

Quadrilaterals

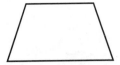

Trapezoid
1 pair of
parallel sides

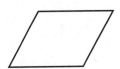

Parallelogram
2 pairs of
parallel sides

Triangles

Right triangle
1 right angle

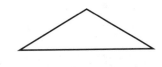

Obtuse triangle
1 obtuse angle

Acute triangle
3 acute angles

Multiplication Chart
(Blackline Master 2)

×	1	2	3	4	5	6	7	8	9	10
1	1	2	3	4	5	6	7	8	9	10
2	2	4	6	8	10	12	14	16	18	20
3	3	6	9	12	15	18	21	24	27	30
4	4	8	12	16	20	24	28	32	36	40
5	5	10	15	20	25	30	35	40	45	50
6	6	12	18	24	30	36	42	48	54	60
7	7	14	21	28	35	42	49	56	63	70
8	8	16	24	32	40	48	56	64	72	80
9	9	18	27	36	45	54	63	72	81	90
10	10	20	30	40	50	60	70	80	90	100

Multiplication Assessment (Blackline Master 3)

How to give the assessment: Use this multiplication assessment to assess how well your child knows the multiplication facts. Make sure to give the assessment at a time when your child is fresh and focused so that the results are as accurate as possible.

- Ask your child each math fact **orally**. Encourage her to respond with the answer as quickly as possible, without repeating the question. For example: **6 times 1?** *6*.
- Ask questions across the page *horizontally*, not vertically. Start by moving from left to right across the first row, then the second row, and so on.
- Mark the problem as correct (✓) if your child says the correct answer within 3 seconds. Mark the problem as incorrect (✗) if your child doesn't know the answer, takes longer than 3 seconds, or counts to find the answer.

Children who process information very quickly may be able to name the answers in less than 1 second, but children who are slower processors may always need a few seconds. As a general rule, aim for no more than **3 seconds** per fact, but adjust this guideline based in your individual child.

9 × 1 = 9 ☐	3 × 2 = 6 ☐	8 × 3 = 24 ☐	5 × 4 = 20 ☐	1 × 10 = 10 ☐
4 × 1 = 4 ☐	5 × 2 = 10 ☐	6 × 3 = 18 ☐	7 × 4 = 28 ☐	8 × 10 = 80 ☐
1 × 6 = 6 ☐	2 × 9 = 18 ☐	3 × 5 = 15 ☐	4 × 4 = 16 ☐	10 × 6 = 60 ☐
1 × 1 = 1 ☐	4 × 2 = 8 ☐	3 × 3 = 9 ☐	6 × 4 = 24 ☐	9 × 10 = 90 ☐
3 × 1 = 3 ☐	2 × 2 = 4 ☐	9 × 3 = 27 ☐	3 × 4 = 12 ☐	7 × 10 = 70 ☐
5 × 5 = 25 ☐	6 × 9 = 54 ☐	7 × 3 = 21 ☐	8 × 8 = 64 ☐	4 × 10 = 40 ☐
9 × 5 = 45 ☐	10 × 2 = 20 ☐	6 × 8 = 48 ☐	7 × 1 = 7 ☐	10 × 10 = 100 ☐
5 × 7 = 35 ☐	8 × 9 = 72 ☐	2 × 7 = 14 ☐	8 × 4 = 32 ☐	5 × 10 = 50 ☐
8 × 1 = 8 ☐	6 × 2 = 12 ☐	7 × 6 = 42 ☐	9 × 7 = 63 ☐	3 × 10 = 30 ☐
5 × 1 = 5 ☐	7 × 7 = 49 ☐	2 × 8 = 16 ☐	8 × 5 = 40 ☐	6 × 5 = 30 ☐
1 × 2 = 2 ☐	6 × 6 = 36 ☐	9 × 9 = 81 ☐	9 × 4 = 36 ☐	8 × 7 = 56 ☐

Place-Value Chart (Blackline Master 4)

tens	ones

thousands

hundreds

Degree Wheel
(Blackline Master 5)

Directions: Copy on sturdy paper and cut out on the dotted lines.
You will end up with two circles, each with a slit. See Lesson 8.2 for how to assemble.

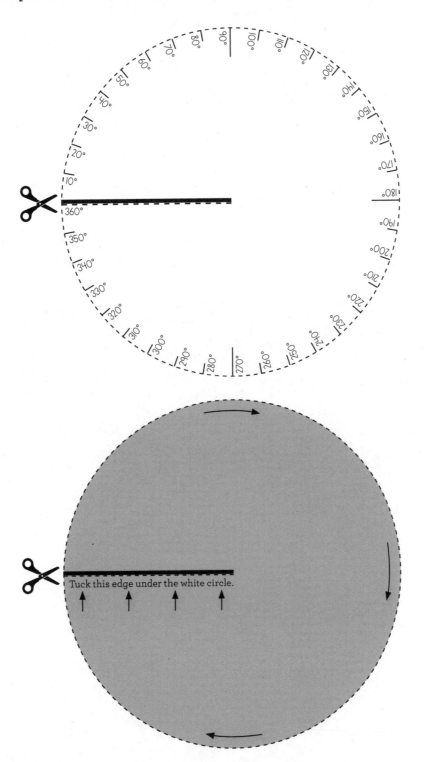

Quadrilateral Cards
(Blackline Master 6)

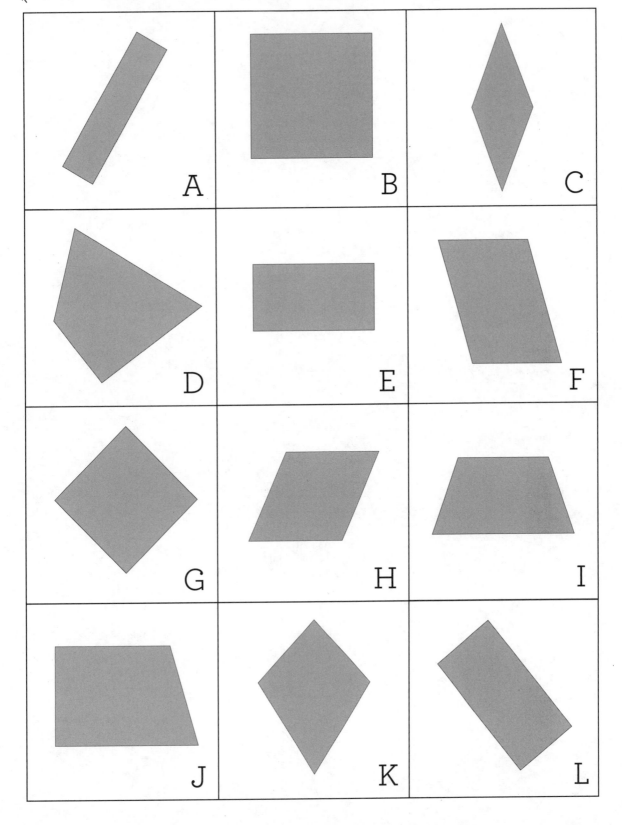

Geometry Reference Page (Blackline Master 7)

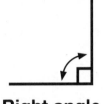

Right angle
90°

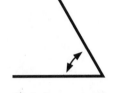

Acute angle
less than 90°

Obtuse angle
more than 90°

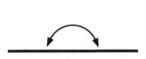

Straight angle
180°

Point

Line

Line segment

Ray

Parallel (∥)

Perpendicular (⊥)

Intersecting

Quadrilateral
4 sides

Square
4 right angles
4 equal sides

Rectangle
4 right angles

Trapezoid
1 pair of
parallel sides

Parallelogram
2 pairs of
parallel sides

Rhombus
4 equal sides
2 pairs of
parallel sides

Right triangle
1 right angle

Obtuse triangle
1 obtuse angle

Acute triangle
3 acute angles

Shapes for Folding (Blackline Master 8)

Directions: Cut out the shapes.

Pattern Block Templates (Blackline Master 9)

You do not need these if you already have pattern blocks. If you do not have access to wooden or plastic pattern blocks, you can use this paper version instead.

Directions: Make 3 copies on sturdy paper. Cut out the shapes and color them according to the following key:

- Hexagons: yellow
- Trapezoids: red
- Triangles: green
- Squares: orange
- Wider diamonds: blue
- Narrower diamonds: tan

Base-Ten Blocks
(Blackline Master 10)

You do not need these if you have real base-ten blocks.

Directions: Make 5 copies of this page on sturdy paper. Cut out the blocks on the dark lines.

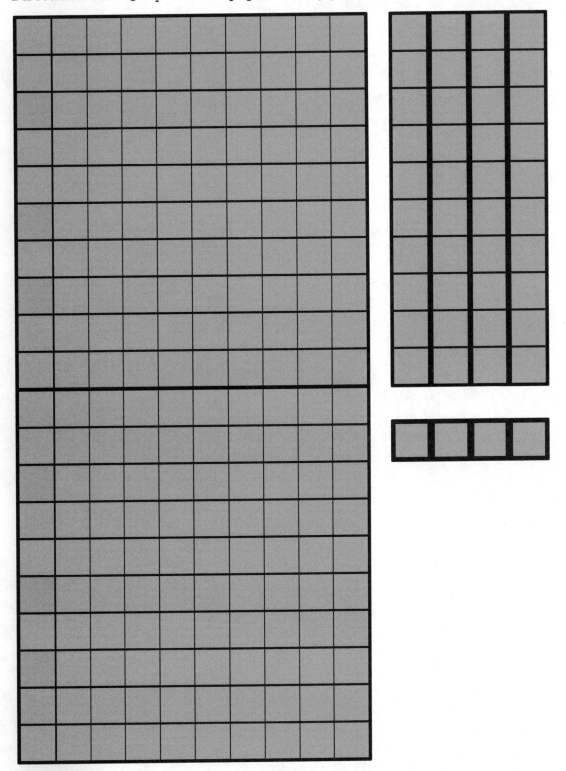

Play Money
(Blackline Master 11)

You do not need these if you have other play money, either from a toy cash register or board game.

Directions: Make 2 copies of this page on sturdy paper and cut out the paper bills.

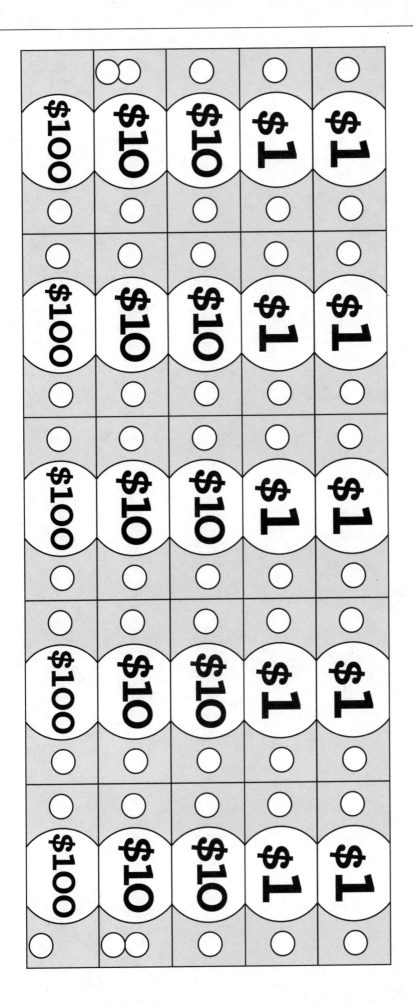

Acknowledgements

Thanks to Itamar Katz, whose design and illustration skills transform my Word document and messy sketches into this easy-to-use Instructor Guide and colorful, whimsical Student Book. These books wouldn't be the same without your thoughtful design suggestions and wonderful drawings, Itamar!

To my assistant Donna Hunter, for her indispensable help throughout the year, especially with the answer keys. To Melissa Moore, both for her expert project management and for her steadfast support and encouragement. To Justin Moore, for his thoughtful clarifying questions and indefatigable copy-editing. And to Susan Wise Bauer, for her guidance and advice as I honed the vision for the Math with Confidence series.

To Shane Klink, who designed the beautiful covers for the series. To Rachael Churchill, whose thorough editing improved the clarity of the Instructor Guide and cleaned up my typos and mistakes.

Finally, many thanks to the members of the *Fourth Grade Math with Confidence* pilot-test group. Thank you for finding the activities that didn't work, the workbook pages that were too long, and the lessons that needed a little more fun! This program is better because of you, and I appreciate all the time you spent giving me feedback, answering my questions, and helping me understand how your kids responded to the lessons. Beyond these practical matters, thank you for your generous encouragement and support. Your commitment to giving your kids an excellent math education motivates and inspires me, and it is an honor to be part of that journey with you.

Rebecca Agnew
Julie Barnett
Jacquelyn Beaumont
Krista Biggs
Kathryn Bitner
Nancy Bradford
Jade & Juniper Buchanan
Brennan & Emilia C.
Bridget Camp
Jolene Carpenter
Naomi Ching
Heidi Chou
Nicole Craig
Mandi Davidson
Kerri Enix
Lauren Funnell
Jill G.
Lindsay Gartner
Julie Gatewood
Bettina Gentry
Mary Ann Glenn
Kelly Gouss
Jessica Grime
Tara H.
Tiffany Hafner
Evelyn Hakimian

Bethany Haugen
Lisa Healy
Carrie & Forge Hickman
Donna Hunter
Rhebeka Hyland
Ashley & Samantha Jacobs
Elizabeth Jarmin
Evan Jarotkiewicz
Melissa Jones
Chialin K.
Katrina Kaucher
Meghan Kellner
Rachel King
Lindsey Klackle
Sabrina Koogler
Emily Kuhl
April Lee
Amy Lerner
Aleicia M.
Melissa Mackey
Angela Mackie
Amy Martello
The Martoncik Family
Nikki McCarthy

Christina McCarthy-Burger
Sarah McCormick
Danielle Gutowski Mello
Mageda Merbouh-Bangert
Holly Merryman
Sally Metcalfe
Kristi Mikkelsen
Elizabeth Millhouse
The Moffitt Family
Sarah Montgomery
Kate Nicolaus
Kim O'Connor
Tosin Olaiya
Lindsay Partridge
Angela Penk
Sheila Pollard
M. Preedin
Jennifer Price
The Pung Family
Rebekah Randolph
Jenna Rice
Crystal Rivera-Silva
Aleena S.
Laura Sandiford
Kathleen Joy Santos

Lacy Sanvictores
Brittany Schroeder
Katie Schulteis
Ashley Scofield
Meghan Shaffer
Karen Shiffler
Kirsten Shope
Mary & Will Shudy
Shannon Smith
Fran Snow
Rachel Sohn
Sandy Lorraine Tad-y
Tawheeda
Johanna Tomlinson
Amanda Troxell
Duski Van Fleet
Sietske Veenman
Sangeetha Vijay
Joanna Walters
Nikki Warsop-Lindo
Molly Wearly
Ashley Weaver
Stacy Whitaker
Anna White
Lily & Sophie Wise